From Post-War to
Post-Wall Generations

From Post-War to Post-Wall Generations

Changing Attitudes Toward the National Question and NATO in the Federal Republic of Germany

Joyce Marie Mushaben

WestviewPress

A Division of HarperCollins*Publishers*

Copyright © 1998 by Westview Press, A Division of HarperCollins, Inc.

Published in 1998 in the United States of America by Westview Press, 5500 Central Avenue, Boulder, Colorado 80301-2877, and in the United Kingdom by Westview Press, 12 Hid's Copse Road, Cumnor Hill, Oxford OX2 9JJ

Library of Congress Cataloging-in-Publication Data
Mushaben, Joyce Marie, 1952–
    From Post-War to Post-Wall generations : changing attitudes
toward the national question and NATO in the Federal Republic of
Germany / Joyce Marie Mushaben.
        p.   cm.
    Includes index.
    ISBN 0-8133-1152-7
    1. Political culture—Germany.   2. National characteristics,
German.   3. Germany—History—Unification, 1980.   4. National
security—Germany—Public opinion.   5. North Atlantic Treaty
Organization.   6. Germany—Military policy—Public opinion.
7. Public opinion—Germany.   8. Germany—Foreign relations—1990–
I. Title.
DD290.29.M87   1998
943.087—dc21
                                                        97-31491
                                                        CIP

The paper used in this publication meets the requirements of the American National Standard for Permanence of Paper for Printed Library Materials Z39.48-1984.

10   9   8   7   6   5   4   3   2   1

For Wally and Koko,
for Hanni, Eddi, Peter, and Susanne,
whose friendship and support have taught me over the years
that there really is ein anderes Deutschland.
For Josefine, Milena, Tim, Jan, and Michel,
who will reap the benefits of a new and peaceful German identity.

Contents

Domestic Dimensions of German National Identity, 362
Eulogies to the Nation Divided:
   Identities Lost and Found, 367
BRDDR: One Volk in Two Cultures, 373
External Dimensions of Identity and Security, 377
Identity and the Politics of Inclusion, 382
The New Germans: Thesis—Antithesis—Synthesis? 387
Notes, 393

Tables and Figures

Figures

Acknowledgments

Much of my FRG-fieldwork linking new social movements activists and their "long march through the institutions" to processes of political-cultural transformation was executed during my eighteen months as a visiting scholar, generously sponsored by the Alexander von Humboldt Foundation from August 1985 through December 1986. An earlier phase of this project, focusing on the born-again peace movement, was directly supported by the Center for International Studies and the Political Science Department at the University of Missouri-St. Louis, July 1983 to January 1984. The University of Missouri-St. Louis and the Lenz Peace Research Laboratory also helped to finance "updates" of my project during subsequent summer research leaves.

I am most grateful for the expert advice and moral support proffered by the countless "assistants" I encountered at a wide array of German research institutes and political foundations. While all merit my personal thanks, certain individuals deserve explicit mention here. They are: Dieter Roth of the *Forschungsgruppe Wahlen*; Karl-Heinz Reuband, then at the *Zentralarchiv für Empirische Sozialforschung*; Bertolt Meyer from the *Hessische Stiftung Friedens-und Konfliktforschung*; Dieter Dettke at the *Friedrich Ebert Stiftung*; and Hans Vorländer, formerly with the *Friedrich Naumann Stiftung*.

Nor can I forget the extraordinary displays of patience and the occasional outpouring of hospitality extended by the many members of the Bundestag (especially Peter Conradi), journalists (above all, Theo Sommer), peace-movement coordinators (in particular, Jo Leinen), local officials and "average citizens" who agreed to become part of my in-depth sample over a turbulent two-year period. I think quite fondly of my personal affinity-group, a now-dissolved *Wohngemeinschaft* in Stuttgart-Sonnenberg, whose members reacted at first with amusement and later with amazement at my ability to turn many a casual dinner party into a heated speak-out over the *deutsche Identität* no one had thought she or he possessed.

Formal words of thanks can hardly begin to repay the debt of gratitude I owe to another group of colleagues, not only for their comments on various portions of the manuscript but also for the professional insights they have shared across many years of personal friendship: Helga Welsh, Ann Phillips,

Jutta A. Helm, Lily Gardner Feldman, Art Gunlicks, John Bendix, and Elisabeth Strübel. Heartfelt thanks also go to those who provided critical "technical assistance" linked to earlier drafts, including Mary Hines and Jan Frantzen at the University of Missouri-St. Louis and staff members at the American Institute for Contemporary German Studies, especially Lindsay Thompson Gould who taught me everything I know about Word Perfect 5.1. Last but not least, I thank my mother for urging me on whenever the project seemed overwhelming.

My obsession with detail notwithstanding, I am no more immune to the problem of human error than scores of "identity" experts who have preceded me with books of their own. I accept full responsibility for whatever typos, misinterpretations, exaggerations, and oversights are still to be found in the finished product, despite thoughtful recommendations to the contrary extended by my colleagues. Many readers may interpret this work as too politically provocative; others may judge it too "personal" in orientation. My greatest hope is that some readers will feel that I have captured the essence of German identity somewhere in between.

Joyce Marie Mushaben

Introduction:
The Evolution of National-Security Consciousness in the Postwar German Federal Republic, 1949–1995

A generation is not a handful of outstanding men (sic), nor simply a mass of men; it resembles a new integration of the social body, with its select minority and its gross multitude, launched upon the orbit of existence with a pre-established vital trajectory. The generation is a dynamic compromise between mass and individual, and is the most important conception in history. It is so to speak, the pivot responsible for the movement of historical evolution.

—Ortega y Gasset (1974)

The Importance of Generationhood

The catalyst for this work was not the breath-taking process of German unification, made possible by way of the 1989 revolutions in Eastern Europe, but rather the "headline" response to one politician's assertion, five years earlier, that German division had become an accepted "fact of life."

Addressing a Communist Party forum in Rome in September 1984, Italian Foreign Minister Giulio Andreotti noted resolutely, "There are two German states, and two they shall remain."[1] Not surprisingly, Andreotti's comments triggered a wide range of official responses. Even moderate members of Helmut Kohl's CDU/CSU government felt it their "national" duty to feign shock and surprise: "The world knows the Preamble to the Basic Law," the Federal Chancellor's office responded. Unionists found quick reassurance in the rhetorical support offered by the trans-Atlantic foreign policy establishment, the reservations expressed by select *New York Times* savants notwithstanding.[2] Members of the Social Democratic opposition, cautiously seeking a new cause after their defeat over Pershing II and Cruise Missile deployments and mindful of the Right's traditional monopoly over the so-called national question, quickly affirmed their commitment to *Ostpolitik* as *Realpolitik*. The FDP, whose coalition shift had cleared the way for improved inter-German relations under Willy Brandt, tried to interpret Andreotti's remarks "in context." On the other side of the Berlin Wall, Erich Honecker's Socialist Unity government welcomed the declaration as a sign that its 30-year demand for de jure recognition was only fitting and just.

Like responses at the elite level which fell along conventional party lines, public reactions were somewhat divided. They seemed highly ambivalent for a citizenry long apprised of its constitutional obligation "to achieve the unity and freedom of Germany in free self-determination." Very few of my FRG friends and colleagues openly approved of Andreotti's assessment; most considered talk of reunification a gratuitous exercise. It was the latter group which piqued my interest. How could a relatively small, highly educated subset of West German citizens, well acquainted with the country's traumatic past and very opinionated with regard to contemporary nuclear missile deployments, find the subject of their own national division hardly worth discussing? Having spent six months as a participant-observer in the West German peace movement during 1983, I was more attuned at the time to changing perceptions of the Federal Republic's role in NATO than to questions of national identity per se. The link between the two issues began to emerge as I sought to explore the diffident reactions to Andreotti's remark among my FRG peers.

Reflecting on four decades of postwar German development, Federal President Richard von Weizsäcker had observed that "a question does not simply cease to exist because no one has an answer for it, especially when the state of affairs is such that it keeps raising the question anew."[3] Fueling the public's ambivalence was the sense that certain groups were raising the German Question again, for reasons that seemed quite divorced from any genuine search for answers. While the two German states had come to occupy a respected niche in the international community by the 1980s, neither side seemed to have found an acceptable home for its problematic national identity. Was it the Germans' historically overburdened and divided perception of themselves that continued to breed uncertainty about their future? Or was it outsiders' unwillingness to accept many political cultural changes which had redefined the concept of "German identity" since 1949 that kept *Angst* alive and well in Central Europe?

To many a foreign observer, the series of treaties ratified during the early 1970s under the rubric of *Ostpolitik* signaled an effort to close the book on a particularly ignominious chapter of German history. As read by the leaders of neighboring and allied states, the 1972 *Grundlagenvertrag* [Basis of Relations Treaty] posited an unspoken acceptance of the status quo by the two states most directly affected by the postwar division of Europe. The growing respect for *Realpolitik* displayed by the newly inaugurated Brandt and Honecker governments occasioned a collectively discrete sigh of relief among most inhabitants of the region. Opposing these efforts, to be sure, was a small but vociferous group of hardliners (including Soviet military officials and a few prominent American proponents of linkage), inclined to view any reconciliation effort as a form of capitulation to the other side. For the surrounding states, however, the onset of good neighborly relations between Bonn and East Berlin brought a welcome easing of tensions, after a long and troublesome phase of Cold War rivalry and arms proliferation.

The pace of normalization, as mandated by the 1972 Treaty, accelerated dramatically over the next ten years, bringing an extending web of cultural and trade relationships. Yet there had been little clarification at the highest levels as to whither such ongoing improvements in East-West German relations were ultimately supposed to lead. While FRG and GDR leaders were willing to agree on "process" [known as *Verhandlungspolitik* or the politics of negotiation], their mutually exclusive interpretations of German history undermined the prospects for establishing a common political end, i.e., unification. From the vantage point of the GDR, revisions in German historiography had officially closed the book on national unity and a belief in common identity, especially after 1974.[4] In the FRG, however, the 1980s unleashed a renewed debate among diverse political forces as to the "open" or "closed" nature of the German Question.

Although many scholars did touch upon the subject of historical identity during this period, western reconsideration of the German Question was defined largely in terms of specific issues. One was the growing demand for permanent recognition of the Oder-Neisse and Elbe River borders with Poland; a second focus grew out of a highly publicized debate among academics over the historical uniqueness of Holocaust atrocities. West German involvement in the construction of a chemical weapons plant in Libya, followed by the surprising 1989 electoral gains of a new ultra-Right party [*die Republikaner*] in the once Social Democratic bastion of West Berlin, called forth equally disconcerting specters of an unconquered past. As self-validating as both postwar states had become, the first official visit to the Federal Republic by an East German Premier in September 1987 did not serve to expunge the term reunification [*Wiedervereinigung*] from the speculative vocabulary of foreign journalists and political pundits. Uncertainty about the German future persisted, despite the fact that Honecker was received with military honors usually reserved for leaders of de jure sovereign states, an event described as "breathtaking in its normality."[5]

One camp, dominated by conservatives, insisted on the fundamentally "open" nature of the national identity question, as defined by historian Michael Stürmer (a participant in the *Historians' Controversy*, Chapter 2). In 1987, Stürmer described the German Question and its contemporary significance in the following terms:

How will the Germans see their country tomorrow, the West, or themselves? It is to be assumed that continuity will be overriding. But this is not a certainty. . . . Loss of orientation and search for identity are siblings. Whoever maintains, however, that this has no effect on politics and the future, ignores the fact that whoever fills the memory, forms the concepts and interprets the past wins the future in a land deprived of history.[6]

In short, the Germans themselves had both a right and a responsibility to determine the contents of their own identity. Possession of a "healthy national consciousness" was deemed essential to political consensus-building and, hence, to internal stability. The distortion of national identity which had occurred under the Third Reich, as well as across four decades of division, was seen as an aberration, at least against the broader background of a shared culture between the Germans of East and West.

Those who preferred a "closed" approach to the German Question, one shifting the burden of acceptance to outside observers, saw their anxieties laid to rest in 1975 by way of Gebhard Schweigler's path-breaking comparison of emergent national feeling in the two postwar states. *Ostpolitik*, as viewed by this more liberal school, marked the end of an all-German search for a common national consciousness and a shared role in global affairs; each side was instead presumed to have internalized the value imperatives of its respective Alliance community. Schweigler asserted that the German Question had found its "answer," the substance of which was unlikely to be threatened or challenged in future decades. In essence, a definitive settlement of the German Question would "make possible a state of peaceful relations in the heart of Europe which seemed unattainable as long as the German Problem kept everyone occupied." The aim of Schweigler's study "was to examine whether or not it has already been settled. Its firm conclusion is the German Answer: two Germanies, not one."[7] It was not a renewed search for unity but rather the acceptance of separate, postwar identities which would foster German stability and thus regional peace.

In view of the dramatic collapse of the East German regime in 1989, it is clear that Schweigler overestimated the extent of popular identification with the officially projected GDR-identity. But it is worth noting that his empirical assessment was grounded in developments of the early 1970s, a time in which Eastern citizens had experienced a measure of cultural liberalization, modest improvements in living standards, and a revived hope that international recognition would lead to contacts with peoples beyond the "socialist commonwealth." Attitudes would shift dramatically by the 1980s, once the East German economy encountered the full impact of the 1973 and 1979 oil crises.[8]

My switch from a study of security perceptions to an exploration of West German identity stemmed from a desire to grasp the broader impact of political cultural change since 1949, albeit in a manner that would allow me to pull together several disparate research interests.[9] Commencing a search for this highly amorphous national identity in 1984, it was my intention to advance a third interpretation, circumventing the teutonic debate as to whether the German Question was to be understood as forever "open" or eternally "closed." My fieldwork was structured around the proposition that "the" German Question had actually given birth to many new German Questions by the 1980s, hungering after real-political answers.

Other academics writing at the time pursued the German Question in conventional terms. One set of analysts sought to define Germany's national interests and strength relative to those of other international powers (grounded in Morgenthau's *Six Principles of Political Realism*); a second school emphasized the determinant influence of "domestic policy" on foreign policy decisions. Yet another group (mostly German) contended that the FRG enjoyed little room for maneuver, due to an inability to shake itself free of constraints imposed during the Occupation Era or because of the quasi-organic bonds that had evolved within the Atlantic Community.[10] Few of the dominant texts by International Relations experts (who tend to rely on a macro-political approach) posed the kind of questions I sought to raise as a Comparative Politics specialist, schooled in case-studies and political-cultural analysis.

More importantly, my earlier research had pointed to the increasing salience of generational differences with respect to questions of nationalism and peace. Other scholars' references to "the" successor generation did not capture the spectrum of orientations I had begun to discern among various anti-nuclear groups.[11] This moved me to explore one variable that was implicit in various security analyses but never highlighted as a significant determinant of national orientation in its own right: namely, the dynamics of generational change. By the spring of 1989 I had completed three chapters of this book and had already secured a fellowship to pursue a parallel study of GDR-identity, when my work—and that of all contemporary-Europe specialists—was overtaken by the events of history.

It is a rare event in the life of a social scientist to be able to test and retest a complete set of political speculations and empirical hypotheses against the backdrop of two "world orders." For many students of German politics, the period 1989 to 1993 nonetheless mirrored Charles Dickens's characterization of another revolution of '89: "It was the best of times, it was the worst of times." The generational approach adopted here seems to have withstood the test of transformation, insofar as the questions this study originally sought to raise not only persist; they have, in fact, acquired new significance since the re-establishment of a united Germany on October 3, 1990. The fundamental question then, as now, is whether the bonds of "common consciousness" between the Germans of East and West have transcended not only the horrors of war and the ignomy of defeat but also the imposition of diametrically opposed socio-economic systems since 1949; this raises the corresponding question, how have West German attitudes towards nationalism been altered by post-war and post-wall developments? This book argues that separate FRG and GDR identities had indeed emerged by 1989, and that both "national" identities can be further differentiated along generational lines. It moreover contends that there is a strong, albeit not always empirically testable link between the *national-identity* paradigms of three distinctive postwar generations, on the one hand, and their respective *national security* orientations, on the other. These linkages have already begun to surface in German responses to the Gulf War of 1991 and in reactions to war in the former Yugoslav Republic, for example.

One day after the Wall crumbled in November 1989, former Berlin Mayor and Ex-Chancellor Willy Brandt observed, "now that which belongs together can grow together." Too many observers inside and outside the Federal Republic mistakenly construed Brandt's remark as a self-fulfilling prophecy. United Germany now faces a broad assortment of growing pains, ranging from mass unemployment in the new states to a resurgence of rightwing extremism among East and West youth. Before one can begin to devise strategies for re-creating a shared sense of identity between the Germans of East and West, one must first comprehend how far and in what ways the peoples of the two states have grown apart over the past four decades.

Both identities have been rendered so complex by the experiences of division that it would violate the spirit of German *Gründlichkeit* [a "profound thoroughness"] to treat them simultaneously. This study concentrates primarily on the evolution of West German identity over the period 1949–1995, saving the story of East German identity for another time.[12] Its purpose is not to predict the future course of German foreign policy per se but rather to provide an overarching political-cultural framework, enabling readers to better understand the many contradictions typifying debates over the FRG's post-Wall national interests. As a rule, foreign policy discussions tend to be divorced from questions of personal identity, and vice versa. It is a key contention of this work that the relationship between the two is a reciprocal one in the Federal Republic: Personal feelings of political identity (or lack thereof) have conditioned citizens' perceptions of their national security needs and, correspondingly, the special imperatives of the FRG security paradigm have aided in the restructuring of their individual postwar political identities.

The Theoretical Focus: Generational Perspectives

This text revolves around a three-part thesis stemming from extensive field research conducted by this author since 1983. The parameters of this investigation read as follows:

- First, I contend that demographic polarization, a unique geostrategic location, the absence of a shared sense of national identity, and the accelerated pace of political-economic change in post-industrial society, played a key role in the rapid mobilization of protesters linked to the FRG peace movement of the 1980s. These experiences will provide a critical foundation for the national security orientations of Western Germans through the 1990s, especially in regard to "out-of-area" conflicts.

- Secondly, the diverse socialization experiences of three distinctive postwar generations have resulted in conflicting, generation-specific definitions of German national security needs, elements of which are directly at odds with security doctrines that have long prevailed within the Atlantic Alliance (which is also embarking on a difficult search for a new identity).

- Thirdly, insofar as certain generational differences hold ramifications for German participation in NATO, effective attempts to reconcile these differences will have to consider an evolving post-Wall German identity and its role in the development of an East-West "security partnership" system.

The search for a post-war turned post-wall identity is, in essence, the search for a broader consensus on key political qua national-security values that will render the perceived legitimacy of united Germany less dependent upon citizens' oft-cited satisfaction with economic miracles of the past.[13] It is no coincidence that a renewed debate as to the meaning of German identity took hold among intellectual forces of both the Left and the Right about the same time that the Federal Republic was beginning to grapple with the "limits to growth" besetting all advanced industrial states. Nor was it accidental that public interest in this debate increased with a heightening of tensions between the superpowers after 1979.

What follows is a study of four separate-but-related German Questions, as perceived, interpreted and answered by members of the postwar generations who constitute a majority of the citizens in the "old states" of the now united *Bundesrepublik*. It will focus on the identity trends manifested among members of three "successor" generations, labeled the "Economic Miracle Generation," the "Long March/Student Movement Generation" and the "No Future/Turn-Around Generation," respectively. I invented all three labels at the outset of my field investigation in 1985. The term "Turn-Around," as applied to the third generation, derived from a construct employed by youth researchers during the period: *Die Wendejugend*, as they were known, were those beginning to reaffiliate themselves with conservative values following the CDU/CSU's return to office in 1982. This realignment of political power after thirteen years of Social-Liberal rule was also referred to as *die Wende*. Who could have anticipated at the time that an even more dramatic, revolutionary *Wende* would overtake German history some five years later? Insofar as the youngest cohorts encompassed by this study will be the first to spend a major portion of their lives under a newly unified German state, my use of the label the "Turn-Around Generation" is now more fitting than ever.

Identity-building is a cumulative, multi-dimensional process, which I attempt to explore here in terms of four question-complexes. None of its dimensions is static in character, rendering any sort of comprehensive cohort analysis extremely difficult. In order to highlight the non-static character of national identity, I have identified particular cognitive "processes" that seem to capture the different socio-political dynamics involved in establishing its contours, summarized as follows.

The Process of Generational "Self-Socialization"

How do the three successor generations that attained political maturity during the 1950s, the late 1960s/early 1970s, and the 1980s, respectively, differ in the significance they ascribe to the peace movement and to the politics of détente, as both have evolved over the past four decades? What factors or developments account for those differences?

The Process of "Other-Identification"

How do the postwar generations differ in the degree of national identification they exhibited in relation to the Federal Republic prior to 1989? How do they differ in their sense of what it means to be German? How strong was their respective identification with "the other Germany" (GDR) or with "Europe" prior to unification in 1990? What accounts for those differences?

The Process of "Self-Definition" and "Image-Projection"

Is there such a thing as the new German nationalism? If so, what are its substantive dimensions? To what extent did it accept or reject traditional precepts of national sovereignty and the dream of reunification in favor of neutralism prior to 1989? Which cohorts would have preferred to maintain the divided status quo between the two German states? Who are the likely agents of this new nationalism, and what are the key issues that have given rise to it?

The Process of "Community Identification"

How do the postwar generations differ in their perceptions of the Atlantic Alliance as the most effective "keeper of the peace" in Central Europe? How have their attitudes changed regarding the formation of a "security partnership" with the states of Eastern Europe, and what implications do such changes harbor for the Federal Republic's future role in NATO?

Research Methodology: The Pandora's Box of Cohort Analysis

The research methods employed in this investigation have been quite eclectic. The search for empirical data turned into an incredible journey through the German past and present, best symbolized by the 21,540 kilometers I logged, with a little help from the German *Bundesbahn*, en route to archives and interview appointments in 1985–1986. Drawing on the works of Patton, Brown and Bailey, I opted for a mix of qualitative and quantitative data-collection methods and made deliberate use of multiple levels of analysis—individual, collective, elite, mass—in the hopes of capturing the inherently conflicted nature of postwar German identity.[14] My standard operating procedures included: content analysis of historical materials and daily media reports; continuous indirect observation (a.k.a. ethnomethodology, which means "living among the natives"); and frequent participant observation at peace demonstrations, government-sponsored forums and academic conferences. I also drew heavily on tomes of public opinion data housed in Mannheim (*Forschungsgruppe Wahlen*) and Cologne (*Zentralarchiv für empirische Sozialforschung*).

Last, but certainly not least, I subjected a multitude of unsuspecting public officials and personal acquaintances to a series of in-depth interviews. Officially scheduled interviews averaged ninety minutes each, ranging from one forty-minute session to two five-hour sessions; for my less fortunate friends, the interviews were never-ending in character. A translation of my questionnaire appears in Appendix A.

Interview appointments were solicited based on a loosely defined sample of individuals whom I could identify as members of the three generations, based largely on year of birth. My second sampling criterion was to include representatives from each of the four parties seated in the Bundestag at the time. My third rule for selection was to include equal numbers of women and men at each generational level and across party lines. This proved quite difficult among the older cohorts and among conservatives, owing to the conspicuous absence of women in positions of power, or due to the double burdens and heavy schedules shouldered by female politicians who had "made it."

The compelling nature of the topic itself moved 65 of some 90 targeted elected officials to respond positively to my request for a very lengthy interview during the final months of the 1986 national election campaign. Of those who agreed to participate, three sent their personal advisors as substitutes (including Willy Brandt, who later responded in writing to specific questions); seven were forced to cancel owing to last-minute campaign obligations (including then-Minister Rita Süssmuth). Given younger citizens' pervasive distrust of data-collection activities in general (due to the state's sometimes heavy-handed methods of searching out political "radicals"), I found it more effective to conduct this round of discussions informally, albeit using the same open-ended questionnaire. Discussions with younger citizens usually occurred within the context of university seminars, for example, in Essen, Frankfurt, Mainz, Mannheim and Kiel. Additional sessions took place at neighborhood *Kneipen* in Stuttgart and Berlin, or among groups of students who were swayed by promises of "coffee and cake" to convene at my rented quarters in Bonn.

I make no claims as to the representative nature of my interview sample, nor is it my intention to provide a statistically-unassailable coding of the responses I received. My primary aim throughout this project has been to concentrate on the proverbial Big Picture, that is, to address larger questions of political-cultural change often neglected by rigorously quantitative analyses. Flynn and Rattinger attest that there have been few political-psychological studies defining explicit links between the cognitive origins, factual components, and the internal/external dynamics of defense-related mass opinion.[15] A relatively streamlined, synchronic study of changing security perceptions in the FRG would have to start with an established set of models and theorems specifying exactly how attitudes towards foreign policy and national security are shaped, as well as their basic dimensions; such models would have to posit how stable these attitudes remain over time, as well as the influences to which they respond. The researcher would then have to classify the substantive aspects of national security attitudes, "such as overall goals, derived instruments and strategies; facts (past, present, and future), and actors," all of which would then have to be differentiated further "according to the familiar distinction of cognitive vs. affective vs. behavioral components." Last but not least, one would then have to go back and assess issues of "salience" or "personal importance" with regard to these three latter components.[16] An equally rigorous effort to distinguish life-cycle from cohort or period effects in relation to all of the above factors could easily become a life-long endeavor. I nonetheless take heart in the words of one cohort-analysis expert, Norval D. Glenn, who cautions: "The person who must have certitude, who cannot embrace conclusions tentatively, should not be engaged in social scientific research."[17]

This is *not* a work designed for specialists only, hence, it runs the risk of providing "too much background, not enough theory" for scholars already well acquainted with German politics. For readers less familiar with postwar developments, the opposite problem may emerge, "too much theory, not enough background." Each chapter incorporates the experiences of real people (as opposed to formal decision-makers), as well as many types of empirical data, in the hopes of satisfying an interdisciplinary audience. For the more theoretically inclined, the book begins with a treatment of key variables in the process of generational change, attempting to link the processes of identity-formation at the socio-psychological and national-systemic levels. The second chapter discusses character traits and historical images typically associated with the adjective *German*, with the aim of determining whether old stereotypes had lost their validity among members of the successor generations by 1989.

Admittedly dubious about the prospects for a re-constituted German *Staatsnation* at the start of this project, I set out to evaluate the "survivability" of a German *Kulturnation* in Chapter Three, by examining the national character traits ascribed to the other Germany prior to unification, especially among younger cohorts. The fourth chapter focuses on generational differences surfacing with respect to the FRG's role in NATO, while Chapter Five relates generational influences to particular attitudes towards deterrence, theater-nuclear deployments, bloc-disengagement and disarmanent strategies prior to the collapse of the Warsaw Pact. Chapter Six considers the security perceptions of an oft-neglected "silent majority," West German women, for whom the 1980s marked the commencement of a new Long March through the policy-making institutions. Chapter Seven takes up the disturbing topic of resurgent ultra-nationalism and violence among "unified" German youth. Chapter Eight concludes with reflections on generational change and "the blessings of late birth," arguing that both factors had contributed to the establishment of a non-provisional, post-national FRG-consciousness before the processess of unification turned the entire question of German identity on its head once again.

The task that I have set for myself, pulling together a number of ostensibly disparate themes whose overall impact on German political culture significantly exceeds the sum of the parts, has proved overwhelming at times. Though the project has occupied me for more than a decade, I have never doubted the critical need for such a work. While many scholars might prefer the intellectual satisfaction (read: methodological rigor) afforded by a narrowly defined public-and-defense study, it is the amorphous yet ever present spectre of German identity that seems to underlie such studies and yet is never included as a significant variable. Since 1971 I have spent more than eight years living and working in various parts of the Federal Republic and the former GDR; it is my own sense of having been affected by the day-to-day disturbances of low-altitude military aircraft, the repeated encounters with NATO tanks rolling past my West-Berlin bus stop on their way to maneuvers, and the surprising indifference displayed my FRG friends vis-à-vis the GDR, which has led me to challenge conventional presumptions regarding both West Germans' "desire" for reunification prior to 1989, and their more or less complacent acceptance of U.S.-preeminence in NATO. Through it all I have also been deeply moved by the many sincere efforts I have witnessed among German politicians, scholars, colleagues and friends attempting to come to terms with an unconquerable, violent national past, in the hopes of contributing to a secure and peaceful international future.

Routine teaching responsibilities, multiple conferences, countless speaking engagements related to the paradoxes of German identity, along with the complexities of a commuter-marriage and the birth of my son, have delayed the production of this book. At the same time, exchanges with a broader public have helped me to realize that Federal Republicans who seek to convey the same, albeit very complicated message to average U.S. citizens may not always be effective, for they speak, as they must, "in translation."

Drawing upon examples and analogies from everyday life in both countries,
I hope to render the German plight more "human" and therefore more
comprehensible to U.S. readers.

This study of changing attitudes towards the national question and
changing perceptions of NATO in postwar Germany is a composite of major
efforts and modest expectations. It will not reveal the existence of a singular
German identity taking hold in the Federal Republic through the process of
generational transformation. Rather, it unveils a spectrum of alternative socio-political identities which, individually and collectively, are giving rise to a
very different ideal of national consciousness than the one which prevailed
in Germany prior to 1945. This single text cannot do justice, in many respects, to the wealth of data, impressions and experiences its author has
gathered along the way. But it can provide a sense of direction for those
who would join me in an odyssey of generational change likely to continue
through the end of this century.

Notes

1. Theo Sommer, "Lieber zweimal Deutschland als einmal? Andreottis undiplo-
matische Wahrheiten," *Die Zeit,* September 28, 1984.

2. William Safire, "Revanche Is Sweet," *New York Times,* August 13, 1984; James
M. Markham, "For Both East and West, Two Germanys Is Better," *New York Times,*
September 23, 1984.

3. Richard von Weizsäcker, *Die deutsche Geschichte geht weiter* (München:
Deutscher Taschenbuch Verlag, 1985), p. 8.

4. See Joyce Marie Mushaben, *Identity Without a Hinterland? Continuity and
Change in National Consciousness in the German Democratic Republic, 1949–1989*
(Washington, D.C.: American Institute for Contemporary German Studies, 1993).

5. Elizabeth Pond, "Most Germans Applaud Honecker Visit," *The Christian Science Monitor,* September 11, 1987.

6. Michael Stürmer, "Geschichte in geschichtslosem Land," *Historikerstreit. Die
Dokumentation der Kontroverse um die Einzigartigkeit der nationalsozialistischen Judenvernichtung* (München: Serie Piper, 1987), p. 36.

7. Gebhard Ludwig Schweigler, *National Consciousness in Divided Germany*
(London/Beverly Hills: Sage, 1975), p. 281.

8. Striking differences between the levels of popular identification with the GDR
during the 1970s and 1980s are found in longitudinal surveys conducted by members of the former Central Institute for Youth Research in Leipzig. See Walter
Friedrich and Hartmut Griese, Hg., *Jugend und Jugendforschung in der DDR.
Gesellschaftspolitische Situationen, Sozialisation und Mentalitätsentwicklung in den
achtziger Jahren* (Opladen: Leske + Budrich, 1991).

9. For a sampling, see Joyce Marie Mushaben, "A Search for Identity: The German Question as an Independent Variable in Atlantic Alliance Relations," *World Politics,* Vol. XL, No. 3, April, 1988, pp. 395–417; "Grassroots and *Gewaltfreie Aktionen*: A Study of Mass Mobilization Strategies in the West German Peace
Movement," *The Journal of Peace Research,* Vol. 23, No. 2, 1986, pp. 141–154; "In-

nocence Lost: Environmental Images and Political Experiences Among the West German Greens," *New Political Science*, No. 14, 1986, pp. 39–66; "A Crisis of Culture: Social Isolation and Integration Among Turkish Guestworkers in the German Federal Republic," in *Turkish Workers in Europe: A Multi-Disciplinary Study*, Ilyan Basgöz and Norman Furniss, eds., Turkish Studies Series (Bloomington: Indiana University Press, 1985), pp. 125–150; and "Swords to Plowshares: The Church, the State and the East German Peace Movement," *Studies in Comparative Communism*, Vol. XVII, No. 2, Summer, 1984, pp. 123–135.

10. Hans Morgenthau, *Politics Among Nations: The Struggle for Power and Peace*, 5th edition (New York: Alfred Knopf, 1973); also, Karl W. Deutsch and Lewis J. Eddinger, *Germany Rejoins the Powers* (New York: Octogon, 1973). The second approach is reflected in Peter J. Katzenstein's work, *Policy and Politics in West Germany: The Growth of a Semi-Sovereign State* (Philadelphia: Temple University Press, 1987); also, Gebhard Schweigler, *Grundlagen der außenpolitischen Orientierung der Bundesrepublik Deutschland. Rahmenbedingungen, Motive, Einstellungen* (Baden-Baden: Nomos Verlag, 1985). For the third approach, try Hans-Peter Schwarz, *Die gezähmten Deutschen: Von der Machtbesessenheit zur Machtvergessenheit* (Stuttgart: Deutsche Verlags-Anstalt, 1985); Helga Haftendorn, *Sicherheit und Entspannung. Zur Außenpolitik der Bundesrepublik Deutschland 1955–1982* (Baden-Baden: Nomos Verlag, 1983).

11. An earlier work focusing on the foreign policy implications of "succession" was Stephen S. Szabo's *The Successor Generation: International Perspectives of Postwar Europeans* (London/Boston: Butterworths, 1983). My fieldwork led me to posit the existence of "three" groups, as opposed to "the" successor generation, in Joyce M. Mushaben, "Anti-Politics and Successor Generations: The Role of Youth in the West and East German Peace Movements," *Journal of Political and Military Sociology*, Vol. 12 (Spring 1984), pp. 171–190.

12. Joyce Marie Mushaben, *From Ossi to Wossi? The Persistence of East German Identity* (New York: St. Martin's Press, forthcoming).

13. See Kendall L. Baker, Russell J. Dalton and Kai Hildebrandt, *Germany Transformed–Political Culture and the New Politics* (Cambridge: Harvard University Press, 1981).

14. Michael Quinn Patton, *Qualitative Evaluation Methods* (Beverly Hills/London: Sage, 1980); Michael K. Brown, "Direct Observation: Research in a Natural Setting," in Jarol B. Manheim and Richard C. Rich, eds., *Empirical Political Analysis. Research Methods in Political Science* (Englewood Cliffs, NJ: Prentice-Hall, 1981); also, Kenneth D. Bailey, *Methods of Social Research* (New York/London: Free Press, 1978).

15. Gregory Flynn and Hans Rattinger, eds., *The Public and Atlantic Defense* (Totowa, NJ: Rowman & Allanheld, 1985), p. 5ff.

16. Ibid., p. 5. Further, Milton J. Rosenberg and Carl I. Hovland, "Cognitive, Affective, and Behavioral Components of Attitudes," in J. N. Rosenau *et al.*, eds., *Attitude Organization and Change: An Analysis of Consistency Among Attitude Components* (New Haven: Yale University Press, 1960), pp. 1–14.

17. Norval D. Glenn, *Cohort Analysis* (Beverly Hills: Sage, 1977), p. 17.

1

The Problem of Generations:
Identity-Formation and
the New "Unencumberedness"

Wenn Ihnen ein Deutscher sagt, die Nation spielt
keine Rolle mehr, dann seien Sie mißtrauisch.
Glauben Sie ihm nicht. Entweder ist er dumm, oder
er ist falsch, und beides ist gefährlich.

—Egon Bahr

The real success of Germany
Hamlet, German style, the key,
the question: to be and not to be.

—David Schonbaum (1985)

In January 1988 a man of impeccable German-patriotic credentials and a long-time critic of *Ostpolitik*, Franz Josef Strauss, flew to Moscow for a reconciliation meeting with a no less formidable proponent of national interests, Mikhail Gorbachev. Ascertaining that the new, charismatic General Secretary had indeed set in motion a process of fundamental socio-economic restructuring in the Soviet Union, the Bavarian Minister-President was persuaded that Germany's long-standing adversary would no longer be driven by its former "offensive, aggressive intentions." Summarizing his impressions after a Kremlin reception, the man widely perceived throughout Germany to represent the last of the Cold War Mohicans proclaimed: "The postwar period has come to an end."[1]

The death of Japanese Emperor Hirohito on January 7, 1989 marked the close of an imperial reign lasting more than six decades. Over 158 foreign emissaries travelled to Tokyo for funeral observances in late February; among their ranks were 55 heads of state, including many an enemy turned ally and trading partner. The dignitaries came to witness the passing of a man held singularly responsible for the commencement of war on the Eastern front—and credited with having secured the nation's peaceful reconstruction following Japan's unconditional surrender in August 1945.

Though mostly symbolic in nature, these two events marked the beginning of a new awareness among residents of the once vanquished nations of Germany and Japan that the postwar period was coming to an end, and that a new post-postwar era was about to begin. This is not to argue that the transition had been completed in relation to all policy spheres, at all levels of perception. The most substantial progress witnessed in both states up to that point lay in the realm of economic reconstruction. By 1989 countless advanced industrial and developing states looked to the German and Japanese technological "miracles" with a mixture of admiration, envy and, inevitably, trepidation. As to their respective political achievements, the new constitutions adopted by the Federal Republic (1949) and Japan (1947) had given birth to highly stable and widely accepted institutions of governance grounded in democratic principles. Both states had been re-accorded full membership in the international community, by virtue of their constitutionally-anchored renunciations of offensive weaponry and by way of their integration into the North Atlantic Treaty Organization.

Yet a forty-year record of economic achievement, political stability and peaceful coexistence does not automatically translate into universal international acceptance of the two as "normal" states. Whatever role they are called upon to play, German and Japanese leaders invariably sense that they are acting upon a haunted political stage. Though quite impressed by the quality of the overall performance, the global audience responds to the actors themselves with a measure of conscious ambivalence; it refuses to relinquish a suspicion that the German and Japanese peoples are still possessed by an unpredictably aberrant and latently aggressive national character.

At this point, however, the dilemmas of postwar transformation besetting the two countries begin to diverge. Under American tutelage, the Japanese moved to re-evaluate their national history, to purge their collective consciousness of its aggressive, militaristic components, and to instill the lessons derived from such efforts in future generations. As difficult and painful as the process has been, citizens of the new Japan were able to confront these tasks with a sense of national identity that remained more or less intact.

The Federal Republic, by contrast, has had a hard time defining what it means to be a postwar German without first disposing of the question, "Who are the real Germans?" after forty years of East/West division. Resurgent interest in the question of German identity [*deutsche Identität*] owes much of its intensity to the Federal Republic's geo-strategic location. The issues that have contributed to a rekindling of this historical debate— the Pershing II missile deployments, partisan feuding over the "open" or "closed" nature of the Oder-Neisse borders, and, of course, the dynamics of unification itself—have all impinged directly on the perceived security of neighboring states. Not all of these developments have been subject to German control.

European leaders throughout the 1980s welcomed improvements in FRG-GDR relations but reacted nervously to talk of nuclear disarmament or mutual disengagement from the existing military alliance system. "Too much" inter-German cooperation evoked a different set of fears world-wide than did ruminations about an expanded defense role for Japan. The international community is quite convinced that a democratic Japan will confine the last traces of its imperial tradition to the modern battlefields of semi-conductors and High Definition Television. Even the controversy surrounding its co-production of an FSX fighter system (a modified F-16) during the late 1980s appeared to hinge on fears of a possible "Japanese plot to take over the world aerospace market, driving America out of its last high-tech bastion."[2] A Germany seeking to develop new types of offensive weaponry independently of NATO would sooner be viewed as a *furor teutonicus*, a nation more likely to turn its irrepressible quest for power and *Lebensraum* against the weaker states of Europe than against U.S. defense industries.

This discrepancy in the "threat" associated with each country finds its roots in the Germans' historical propensity for alternating between "too much" and "too little" national identity.[3] Until 1871, the Germans were still a people in search of a unified nation-state. Consolidation under Bismarck laid the foundation for a new national consciousness that was soon undermined by the humiliating defeat of World War I. The period 1918 to 1933 saw Germans catapulted through a second cycle of "too little, then too much" nationalism. The capitulation of 1945 resulted in a state once again dismembered, and clearly deprived of any right to reassert its national consciousness and interests. Where the experiences of the 1940s obliged Japanese citizens to redefine the content of their national consciousness, division forced their German counterparts to wage an acrimonious debate as to whether they ought to claim one or two national identities, or possibly none at all.

By the 1980s, the balance of forces behind the identity-debate had already shifted dramatically, attributable in part to the processes of generational change. Two years after Strauss' visit to Moscow, the socialist regimes of Eastern Europe would collapse in domino-fashion, the Warsaw Pact would decree its own peaceful dissolution, and the Soviet Union would find itself careening along a quasi-democratic path of self-termination. Fundamental changes in the world-order created an extraordinary window of opportunity for those who had long desired German unification. The irony of history is that most of the citizens in the Western state had lost all interest in the topic by the time conditions were ripe. The strongest proponents of national restoration turned out to be their distant cousins in the East, who had always been taught officially that they were the better Germans.

This chapter looks to developments in the external environment as an important source of attitudinal change among West Germans with respect to questions of postwar national identity. It begins with a sketch of subtle yet significant changes in the European landscape which first alleviated and later revitalized nationalist tendencies among many post-industrial states. The next section defines key variables tied to identity-formation, based on theorems borrowed from the field of social psychology. The third part shifts the focus from the level of individual identity to collective identification, which ultimately serves as a framework for national consciousness-building. Next I attempt to transcend the conceptual limitations of my own discipline, political science, by developing a concentric model of identity. I then describe three distinctive sets of postwar-FRG cohorts, labeled the "Economic Miracle Generation," the "Long March Generation," and the "Turn-Around Generation," respectively. The chapter concludes with a spectrum of national-identity types which had evolved along generational lines in West Germany prior to the dramatic upheavals of 1989/90.

The Post-Postwar Environment

The first three decades following World War II saw many extraordinary changes in the European socio-economic environment at large. The social (welfare) state, anchored in the West German Basic Law, established a new foundation for social solidarity, personal security and self-determination, once the needs of material reconstruction had been met. Universal suffrage, expanded educational opportunity, the advent of mass communication, the socio-economic mobilization of women—these factors also contributed to a leveling of class differences and the consolidation of democracy in the FRG after 1945.

The postwar era moreover transformed many behaviors and role-expectations ascribed to youth. The first wave of postwar babies personified a rebirth of political idealism in Western Europe. Cohorts lucky enough to be "born late," after 1940, did not have political consciousness prematurely thrust upon them by the ravages of war, childhood memories of reconstruction and occupation notwithstanding. The adolescents of the late 1950s benefitted directly from the citizenship rights enshrined in new constitutions, from higher living standards brought by national "economic miracles" and a far-reaching scientific-technological revolution. Chastened by history, the first postwar generation was deliberately apolitical; as hard-working, soon-to-be-affluent consumers, members of this generation recognized that the Cold War was not theirs to fight.

Cohorts born during the 1950s abandoned the apoliticism of their elders, tending towards extreme politicization by the late 1960s. McLuhanesque transformations of the media and far-reaching (*Tel-Star*) advances in communication led pre-adults in most Western states to parallel discoveries of inequality at home and abroad. Many developed an awareness that national affluence brought neither a diffusion of economic power nor a redistribution of political power, e.g., between men and women. Paradoxically, an expansion of higher educational opportunities after 1965, under the slogan of *Chancengleichheit*, exacerbated the sense of relative deprivation among young protestors, fueled by unrealistic expectations over access to elite careers.[4]

Children conceived during the 1960s began to acquire political consciousness at an even earlier age. Expanded media access provided a daily diet of environmental catastrophes and conflicts world-wide throughout the 1970s, including Vietnam. By the time it learned of the Three Mile Island accident at the end of the decade, this generation's faith in the saving graces of a "technological fix" had already waned. Europe was perceived to enjoy a measure of ostensible peace resting upon a nuclear balance of terror, while the superpowers were seen to conduct their surrogate wars on the soil of underdeveloped countries.

Cohorts born throughout the 1970s experienced a rude political awakening in more personal terms. Coming of age in the 1980s, these adolescents faced multiple ecological hazards on the homefront, added to rapid increases in youth and academic unemployment.[5] Yet the limits to growth paradigm embraced by advanced industrial countries after the 1973 OPEC embargo only partially explains the socio-economic malaise of the late 1970s and early 1980s; the wisdom of hindsight allows us to argue that demography also played a role. Both the East and West German Baby-Booms had been delayed by the imperatives of reconstruction. As a consequence, the offspring of "the birth-strong years" stood poised to enter the paid labor market just as economic conditions worsened all around the two energy- and export-dependent states. Recession or stagflation impelled authorities to cutback heavily on social-spending at the very point when they should have expanded the network of higher educational and occupational opportunities for restive youth. Older generations were not immune to the perils of economic decline and environmental pollution, but adult and youth perceptions of these phenomena differed in at least one significant respect: the youngest generation encountered these developments without the psychological foundation of Reconstruction- or Economic-Miracle optimism to which the cohorts of earlier decades had been privy.

One byproduct of these developments was the curious resurgence of a romantic-idealist *Zivilisationskritik*, which manifested itself in the form of "alternative cultures." Those who flocked to join an array of protest movements apparently found nothing strange or discomforting about efforts to wed their preferences for small-is-beautiful and do-it-yourself politics to an older Germanic notion of *Heimat* [homeland].[6] The proliferation of their new social movements was itself the product of other dramatic changes that had (or had not) come to pass in the larger geo-strategic environment over the years.

First, the idea of Europe, coupled with a pride in their own economic achievements and a fixation with anti-communism, provided many West

Germans with an ersatz-identity through the 1950s and 1960s. By the 1970s, however, neither "the Six" nor "the Nine" had succeeded in bringing about the supranational integration of Europe foreseen by the Common Market's founders. With little direct knowledge of its institutional history and purposes, younger citizens came to perceive the European Community as a bureaucratic monolith in its own right. The EC's expanding web of highly technical regulations and artificially generated surpluses (mountains of butter and rivers of milk) offered little change of pace from the problems of state intervention, hierarchy and wasted resources witnessed within the national borders–rendering the idea of a United States of Europe no more lovable. The Great Leap Forward foreseen by the 1987 Single European Act did little to restore citizens' enthusiasm for integration.

Secondly, the euphoria of détente, commencing with the 1969 *Machtwechsel* [power-realignment] in Bonn, was disappointingly short-lived after decades of Cold War tension. Deterrence strategies and protracted arms control negotiations did little to eliminate antipathy and distrust between nations. Coinciding with the election of Ronald Reagan and the Soviet invasion of Afghanistan, the breakdown of détente in 1979 produced the most serious deterioration of East-West relations ever witnessed by those born after 1960. Successful efforts by peace movement activists to publicize the local-sites of regional nuclear missile deployments led Europeans to question the "advantages" of Flexible Response policy. By the mid-1980s, steadfast members of the tax-paying mainstream readily agreed with militant feminists, liberation theologists, granola-eating Greens and leather-toting Punks that the countries of Europe should not have to be destroyed in order to be defended.

The born-again interest in the German Question(s) surfacing at the end of that decade also owed to factors less geo-strategic in nature. As the European economies became more interdependent, citizens grew more savvy as to the spill-over character of many post-industrial problems, disturbingly symbolized by the accident at Chernobyl. The nation-state had lost many of its traditional functions, only to acquire new ones that leaders found even more difficult to manage.[7] Ironically, the problems of resource scarcity, economic decline and erratic fluctuations in superpower relations induced government officials everywhere to re-espouse the importance of national interests. No state wished to render its ability to survive, either economically or militarily, completely dependent upon the collective in the event of a major breakdown in superpower relations.

The late 1970s also brought mounting dissatisfaction with a perceived lack of symmetry between West Germany's real economic strength and the external limits placed on its exercise of power in global affairs. A rejection of the long-standing "economic giant, political dwarf image" ascribed to the FRG took hold in Bonn alongside a desire to wield greater influence outside the region. This new interest in sovereignty, registered prior to 1989, can best be interpreted as a step toward political normalization. Domestically, the Federal Republic had already come of age under a set of firmly established democratic institutions; the next stage of coming-out entailed questions of foreign policy autonomy, especially in regard to security issues.

The theme of normalization is likewise implicit in a third trend. Having demonstrated absolute fealty vis-à-vis their respective alliances over a period of forty years, Germans in both states believed by the mid-1980s that they had earned the right to a more sympathetic hearing regarding the dilemmas of division. They strove to elicit active support for mutual efforts to mitigate the human costs inherent in an on-going European division not entirely of their own making. Officials in Bonn and East Berlin pointed to material burden-sharing and the disproportionately heavy risks arising from the collective security requirements to which they voluntarily ascribed. Their willingness to shoulder such burdens, GDR and FRG leaders believed, entitled them to engage individually as well as collectively in the politics of damage limitation.

A fourth important development of the 1980s involves the processes of generationally-linked value change. Younger, better educated segments of the population were no longer disposed toward an uncritical acceptance of American dominance in European affairs. The United States' image in Europe had changed, owing partly to changing American attitudes towards the Continent, and partly to Europeans' altered perception of their own capacity for independent diplomatic action. Foreign policy adventurism under the Reagan Administration (e.g., displays of "Ramboism" vis-à-vis Lebanon, Grenada and Nicaragua) precipitated new tensions among Western allies. While differences of opinion were certainly not unknown among NATO partners, conflicts of the 1980s were exacerbated by military-technological developments (SDI), making a decoupling of American and German/European security interests possible, if not probable.[8] In contrast to ever-suspicious Americans, many West Europeans quickly succumbed to the spirit of "Gorbi-mania." Welcoming Soviet initiatives for conventional force reductions and nuclear disarmament, they challenged the USA to put forth peace proposals that were more constructive than reactive in nature.

Finally, the citizens of both German states had become irreversibly attached to the benefits of *Ostpolitik/Westpolitik*. Public support for an easing of inter-German tensions remained stable throughout the "good and bad weather" intervals in East-West relations over a period of two decades.[9] By the late 1980s, the politics of negotiation constituted an important plank in the platform of all parties seated in the Bundestag; in January 1989, the Alternative List (a wing of the allegedly anti-NATO Greens) was even elevated to the status of formal coalition partner in West Berlin's new government.[10] The East-West treaties, exchanges, and trade relations had acquired a dynamic of their own, the concrete gains of which were no longer to be traded lightly for abstract promises proffered by alliance partners.

As viewed by cohorts old enough to have experienced *Deutschland* before, during and after the war, the transformation of the postwar environment had been a dramatic one indeed. Yet an even larger group took the
changes born of national division as a given: by the onset of 1980, citizens
born after 1949 accounted for 62.4% and 63.8% of the FRG and GDR populations, respectively.[11] While many European states faced increases in the
proportion of residents under the age of 35, Germany's demographic losses
from two World Wars (the "missing generations") and a lack of "national"
continuity meant that the FRG was more likely than others to experience an
abrupt transfer of power from one generation to the next.[12]

Acceptance of the divided status quo was further enhanced by a reluctance
on the part of the oldest generation to confront the atrocities of the Third
Reich Era head on. The circumvention of history characteristic of the 1950s
contributed to the vehemence and intensity of conflicts staged between parents and their offspring at the end of the 1960s.[13] An unwillingness in many
quarters to confront the German past in its entirety has led to new problems in
the wake of unification: younger citizens are increasingly ill-informed regarding any but the most horrible events of the Third Reich era, as well as about
many developments pertaining to national division. The historical information-gap is certainly not restricted to West Germans under the age of 35; indeed, the rapid rise of self-proclaimed neo-Nazi groups in Eastern Germany
since 1989 suggests a need for intensified political reeducation on both sides.[14]

Enter the era of the New Unencumberedness and the renewed search for
national identity in the post-postwar environment. My first reaction to the
term *die neue Unbefangenheit* in the early 1980s was to see it as the product
of a typically-German dialectic. The "thesis" relates to the problem of *Befangenheit*, namely, the sense of implication, or co-responsibility ascribed to
older German cohorts as a function of their biographical proximity to the
events of 1933–1945. A sense of implication still runs through discussions
about the Nazi era with "average" West Germans, even among those
decades removed from it. Conflict between the generations over what co-responsibility "means" set the stakes for the *Historians' Controversy*, according to Charles Maier: "If 1968 was a revolt of sons against fathers (sic), the
Historikerstreit of 1986 was a more complicated generational interplay: on
one side, fathers, now grandfathers, striking back; on the other side, sons,
now grown fathers, no longer abjuring their elders' past, but insisting on
their own implication, *Befangenheit*, within it."[15] One camp construes implication as a matter of destiny, hence the desire to place the years 1933–1945
in a world historical context, leading to charges of relativization. On the
other side stand the proponents of political will, who claim that implication
stems from the Germans' general failure to organize a national resistance
movement after 1933. This orientation can lead to projections of collective
guilt, opposed by those who would "normalize" the Nazi era by embedding
it the broader flow of German/human history.[16]

Befangenheit finds its "antithesis" in a concept that has long captured the hearts and minds of participants in the new social movements, namely, *Betroffenheit*. Loosely translated, *Betroffenheit* falls somewhere between one's feeling of "being directly and personally affected by" and the sense of "being perplexed or confounded by" problems in the contemporary socio-political environment. The 1986 Chernobyl accident, for example, was frequently cited in interviews as having directly affected food supplies, children's sandboxes, and even mothers' milk. One's relation to these developments is far from casual: if one is "affected" at all, the feeling quickly escalates into a sense of existential *Angst* and peril, which then mobilizes the masses to join in organized protests against the perpetrators of modern-day atrocities. Perceptions of this sort can move many a Sunday-stroller to take a stand against the acid-rain damage in the Schwarzwald; they can motivate not only university students but also thousands of grandmothers to protest nuclear energy and weapons.

Die neue Unbefangenheit represents a not yet complete "synthesis" of historical cognition and personal-as-political involvement. A fundamental lack of encumberedness (meaning "an absence of prejudice and/or constraint") leads to a release from historical responsibility; it brings a psychological liberation from "the eternal yester-year," especially among those who have only recently acquired political consciousness. This new spirit of unencumberedness is characterized by a non-traditional openness to international developments and consumer trends; it moreover incorporates a distinctively casual acceptance of and identification with a new brand of do-it-yourself politics.

It is precisely this sort of psychological self-liberation from the events of Germany's tragic past which accounts for the process of generational change, according to classical theorist Karl Mannheim. Each society depends upon, indeed requires, the energy of a new generation to help shake itself free of obsolescent or obstructive values that have accumulated over time. The dynamic of generational succession ensures society a capacity for lifting "the moral blockade" imposed by its own history through "overall distancing."[17] Each generation's contribution to social progress and political development lies in its requisite ability "to forget" outdated behaviors and values. Mannheim observes: "That old people are more experienced than youth is in many respects an advantage, that youth for the most part lacks experience nonetheless means a reduction in the amount of historical ballast, which eases the prospects for future living."[18]

The challenge, therefore, is to assess the extent to which diverse segments of the West German citizenry had, to a greater or lesser degree, succeeded in "casting off"—in the sense of thoroughly working through—an extraordinary amount of historical ballast en route to a new, positive FRG-national identity prior to unification. I do not argue that it is merely the process of generational succession which accounts for societal change. Clearly, the ignomy of defeat, the political re-education efforts of the Occupying Powers, and the consolidation of new, democratic institutions have also played important roles in the restructuring of German national consciousness. The impact of structural variables on the political consciousness of individual citizens is nonetheless extremely difficult to establish. While the collective identities of the pre- and postwar German states may be intricately connected, the national consciousness to which various age or status groups aspire often divorces itself from the "ballast of the past" based on a strategy of selective memory. We are unlikely to discover a simple cause-and-effect relationship, no matter how systematic our efforts to link the processes of generational succession to patterns of socio-political change. First we need to establish a framework of analysis for classifying postwar cohorts, and it is to the complex task of generational delineation that we now turn.

Defining the Generations

This section explores the theoretical criteria used by experts from a variety of disciplines to draw the line between one generation and the next. Attempting to define such boundaries seventy years ago, Mannheim posited that the rate of change occurring within a given polity, as well as its nature, largely determines the speed with which new generations are granted access to the structures of political power; a society begins to institutionalize changes (in the form of new policies and laws) once leadership succession has taken place.[19] An acceleration in the rate of social change leads to a concomitant rise in the number of potential socializing events, along with an increase in the number of politically significant generational differences. Thus, political socialization plays a key role in efforts to differentiate among older and younger generational forces. This process, delineated by key events in a specific socio-historical context, gives rise to a "prevailing sense of self that becomes the motor for subsequent cultural change."[20]

Although Mannheim does not elaborate on this point, it is conceivable that the rate of social change has domestic as well as international antecedents. Generational influences on the course of political development may be reduced or intensified within a rapidly changing global environment. The historical discontinuities experienced by East and West German successor generations have been nothing short of extreme; thus a series of unique socializing experiences may have done more to widen the gap between citizens of the two Germanys than to provide a basis for a new, shared historical identity. The list includes but is not limited to: the Berlin blockade from 1948 to 1949; the Soviet crack-down in East Berlin on June 17, 1953; the 1961 erection of the Berlin Wall; and the protest-rife theater nuclear deployments of 1983–84. For the most part these socializing events coincided with critical shifts in East-West relations, that is, they derived from dramatic changes in the larger international environment. The picture is further complicated by the fact that developments in one state frequently triggered a reaction on the part of leaders and citizens in the other Germany. Hence, the cumulative influences of a unique geo-strategic location, externally supervised processes of reconstruction, and respective East/West commitments to mutually exclusive ideological systems, may have increased the number of significant socializing events experienced by young Germans, to a degree not seen among other European youth.

Studies conducted by many experts, ranging from historians Laqueur and Mommsen to sociologists Bettelheim and Braungart, attest to the fact that Germany is no stranger to the problem of generations.[21] Most scholars rely upon a common set of building-blocks which lead cohorts of a given era to forge a sense of generational consciousness; yet few reflect on the weight to be accorded each variable. Consciousness of one's membership in a particular generation is usually predicated upon:

- a common exposure and comparable reaction to events of historical proportion
- a comparable position within the socio-political opportunity structure, resulting in similar positive and negative "life chances"
- a rough equivalency between one's age and one's point in the life-cycle
- a shared identification with specific ("camp-dominant") ideological predispositions
- a simultaneous experience of a period of maximum receptivity to changes in the external environment
- a common internalization of epoch-specific "learning processes" which members will subsequently invoke throughout later stages of the life-cycle.

Dilthey defines a generation as "a restricted circle of individuals who are bound together into a homogeneous whole by their dependence on the same great events and transformations that appeared in their age of [maximum] receptivity, despite the variety of other subsequent factors."[22] Mannheim posits that generational identities "endow the individuals sharing in them with a common location in the social and historical process . . . , predisposing them for a certain characteristic mode of thought and experience, and a characteristic type of historically relevant action."[23]

Three frameworks regularly used to distinguish between patterns of intra- and inter-generational change are the maturational, experiential, and the interactional models, focusing our attention on the importance of life cycle, cohort and period effects.[24] The maturational or life-cycle model assumes that individual development pursues a relatively steady course within the context of a stable society.[25] Society allocates specific roles to successive co-horts largely as a function of age, whereby "each stage of each kind of aging consists of several changes which characteristically occur together."[26] It also presumes that as people grow older, they automatically temper their values in accordance with the new demands, duties and privileges incumbent to adult life.

While the life-cycle model concentrates on processes of individual change, the experiential or cohort model is oriented toward the process of collective change. A cohort is identified by its unique location in historical space and time which imparts a sense of "shared destiny" to each of its members. Col-lective exposure to a specific set of societal norms, political/economic op-portunity structures, technological breakthroughs or even cataclysmic events results in a configuration of group-values expected to remain more or less constant over time.

Last but not least, the interaction model leaves open the prospect for in-dividual, collective and cross-sectional changes during a given era. Hunting-ton stresses the importance of inter-generational conflict, which finds suc-cessive cohorts reacting against the values upheld by the ones preceding them; such "pendulum effects" imply that socio-political change is cyclical in nature, to the extent that conflicts "recur with each new generation to a fairly intense degree."[27] For Glenn, Jennings and Niemi, "period effects" are characterized by a lack of variation among members of different generations in response to key events at any single point in time.[28] A pure reliance on pe-riod effects would find generations equally affected by specific events or conditions, moving congruently over time. A less restrictive interaction model allows for the possibility of "spiral" rather than cyclical change.

It is extremely difficult to disaggregate the effects of age-cohort-period, insofar as any "two basic effects . . . are confounded with another."[29] While it might be possible to register overall changes in the composition of co-horts embedded in cross-sectional data, it is harder to isolate changes that may result from attrition, migration, new meanings accorded responses over time, et cetera. Complications of the methodological sort are compounded by conceptual problems inherent in these models. The correlation between age and social roles is never absolute; age is, at best, an expression of the ex-periences an individual *may* have accumulated by a particular point in per-sonal time.[30] By equating age with specific life-cycle effects, one "combines sociological and psychological as well as biological mechanisms into a single process."[31] In reality, changes in personality, behavior, status and roles at-tributed to aging may vary appreciably within a given cohort; experiences ascribed to one group can be thrown out of synch by a profusion of life-style changes. Expansion of the higher educational system, for instance, has pro-longed the schooling-phase for many West Germans: 22% of all FRG uni-versity students enrolled in 1989 were at least 30 years old, or had studied

15 semesters or more.[32] Emphasis on equalizing opportunity has also enabled many adults to "backtrack" in the life-cycle by means of continuing-
education programs. Modern forms of fertility control have made it possible
for women and men to postpone the parenting phase, or to skip this phase
altogether, while less rigid sexual mores may lead to higher rates of teen
pregnancy. Unlike members of previous generations who once ran the
gamut of time at approximately the same pace, new cohorts may find themselves running at different speeds, or undertaking stages of the life-cycle in a
different order. West German women once expected to marry and bear children before the age of 30 now tend to postpone such events until they have
established themselves in paid professions, a pattern *not* followed by East
German women.

The link between advancing age and political conservatism is also a spurious one. A once-liberal generation may retain its progressive values, albeit in
a social climate that has become more radical or reactionary over time.
Many children of former student-movement protesters have, in recent years,
embraced neo-conservatism. Several Red Army Faction terrorists over the
age of 20 abandoned their weapons and settled into GDR-family life prior
to 1989, while many FRG-women, thwarted in their efforts to combine career and family, radicalized their demands for equal opportunity as "thirty-
somethings."[33] The latter example points to a third flaw in the life-cycle
model: the scant attention paid to variables beyond age, especially sex and
class. Female socialization may exclude certain developmental stages and
roles altogether, and thus require different "consciousness" measures–rarely
a focus of empirical study.[34]

The experiential and interactional models share a further dilemma involving the issue of "succession." Originally defined in terms of a thirty-year
span, the boundaries of generational membership have become more fluid in
mass society. Prolonged adolescence, or post-adolescence, leads many youth
to remain economically dependent on older groups well beyond the point of
attaining an independent political consciousness.[35] Increasing longevity also
makes it difficult to predict the duration of any one generation's influence on
key institutions. Both models underestimate the extent to which older and
younger cohorts nowadays are often forced to coexist, communicate, compete and cooperate simultaneously. These dilemmas do not invalidate the importance of efforts to analyze generational influences per se; they do, however, require the researcher to look beyond cohort tables for evidence
affirming or refuting the existence of generationally based changes.

At a minimum, we can begin to identify generations in terms of their
"formative years." Rintala sees the boundaries of a political generation determined not so much by age as by unique historical events, which can produce "difficulty in intergenerational communication."[36] Dilthey lists three
more factors essential to generational consciousness: the simultaneity of ex-

perience shared by members of the same generation; their historical proximity to "great events" or select social changes; and their phase of maximal psychological receptivity to the messages of change. Mannheim emphasizes the rate of socio-cultural change, which can shorten or lengthen the span of years distinguishing one generation from another: the more accelerated the pace of change, the greater the chance that particular groups will react to new conditions "by producing their own entelechy."[37] Kriegel labels this the potential "shrinking space" of a generation.[38]

The phase of maximal receptivity to key social events, which I define as the take-off point in the formation of one's political consciousness, lies between the ages of 17 and 25; consolidation of changes in social status marking the passage from youth to adulthood usually occurs by age 30.[39] Adults are "less susceptible to change in at least some kinds of values, attitudes and behavior."[40] A tendency towards attitudinal rigidity may be linked to the aging process itself, e.g., neurological and hormonal changes. Mature adults are less likely to alter their social networks; they are further "shielded" against new *Weltanschauungen* by the cumulative forces of stimuli encountered throughout their lives. Older citizens in positions of power also display an increasing ego-involvement in their own views. This suggests that generational self-socialization, or value-reinforcement, is an ongoing process.

The combined influences of proximity, receptivity and rapid rates of change produce a stratification of experiences that is more or less unique to each generation. In other words, "the closer a generational group is in time to experiencing youthful or early adulthood socialization during years of crisis and tension, the greater is both the awareness and the salience of the problems involved."[41] The more precisely one can pinpoint phases of maximum receptivity and key historical epochs, the more one can begin to discern the influence of different "layers" of experience: consider, for example, the importance of reconstruction-optimism in defining the value-paradigm shared by FRG cohorts of the 1950s.

My own criteria for delineating Germany's successor generations draw upon age and key socializing events, respectively. The traumatizing effects of war, coupled with the "information boom" of later decades, leads me to specify the ages 15–30 as the phase of maximum receptivity. My purpose in expanding the age range is to account for the memorable exposure to war, and later the pervasive impact of mass media at the lower end, and to accommodate the developmental asymmetries of post-adolescence at the other. I draw upon key events in German history, summarized in Table 1.1, to identify three groups whose distinctive "layers of experience" have resulted in a separate generational consciousness. Inherent in this consciousness is a general acceptance of a particular pattern of political thought and action, a widespread consensus as to the critical issues of its time, and a shared level of intensity relative to the goals each generation has opted to pursue.

TABLE 1.1   Historical Epochs Influencing the Formation of Political
Consciousness Among German Cohorts

Epoch Characterization	*Duration*	*Cohorts Coming of Age*
Kaiserreich	pre-1915	pre-1900
World War I	1915–1918	1895–1913
Revolution and Reconstruction	1917–1924	1899–1909
Weimar Republic and Consolidation	1924–1929	1904–1914
Great Depression and Regime Crisis	1929–1933	1908–1918
Entrenchment of National Socialism	1933–1939	1914–1924
World War II	1939–1945	1920–1930
Occupation and Reconstruction	1945–1955	1928–1940
Adenauer and the Economic Miracle	1955–1965	1940–1950
Student Movement and Political Realignment	1966–1972	1947–1957
Détente I and the New Politics	1972–1980	1955–1965
Cold War II and the New Peace Movement	1981–1984	1959–1969
Conservative Turn-Around *(Wende I)*	1983–1987	1962–1972
Détente II and *Glasnost/Perestroika*	1987–1989	1973–1983
GDR-Collapse *(Wende II)* and Unification	1989–1994	post-1983

The *Wirtschaftswunder* or "Economic Miracle Generation" encompasses
the citizens who acquired their political consciousness during a period extending from the pre-war days through the formal close of Occupation in
1955. This group, consisting of cohorts born by the end of 1940, includes
the FRG's founding fathers and mothers, whose lives focused on the imperatives of material construction. The members of this generation did, for a
time, actively uphold the dream of political reunification. Somewhat paradoxically, the group most inclined to support German unity was the one
most reluctant to re-establish the parameters of national identity, wrangle
though they might with their GDR-counterparts over the right to issue
"German" passports or to house Prussian art treasures. It was only a few
years prior to the GDR's collapse that the "Economic Miracle Generation"
began to shed its collective belief that national identity was best left undis-
cussed, out of a reluctance "to open old wounds."[42]

The *Langer Marsch* or "Student Movement Generation" embraces FRG
citizens whose critical socialization phase, from the early 1960s through the
mid-1970s, corresponded with a wave of political and educational "explo-
sions," with dramatic turning-points in East-West relations, as well as with
the end of the Economic Miracle itself. Born between 1941 and 1960, these
cohorts are allegedly post-materialist in their values and also highly politicized, in contrast to their predecessors. Intellectual-activists of this generation associate the complexities of the national question with the need to
process the past and also with the hope of casting off a postwar hostage con-

sciousness. Their emphasis throughout the 1980s fell on the necessity of re-defining FRG-GDR national interests in terms of peaceful coexistence, not in terms of reunification per se.

Die Wendejugend or the "Turn-Around Generation" (including a rowdy "No-Future" segment) consists of the Western cohorts born after 1961—the year the Berlin Wall was erected. This generational span includes the peak of the Baby Boom as well as the low point of the *Pillenknick* (a drop-off in births due to contraception): 1964 witnessed the highest number of live births in Bavaria, while 1978 saw the lowest number of newborns to date in the largely Catholic state. Prior to unity, analysts had predicted that these cohorts would comprise a "post-materialist majority" by the year 2015.[43] The cost of rebuilding the GDR, however, has imposed an extraor-dinary economic burden upon the FRG; the combination of rising unem-ployment and higher taxes will have a considerably different impact on the material expectations of younger cohorts for several years to come.

This generation began to cross the threshold of political maturity in an en-vironment witnessing many dramatic ups and downs in East-West relations, *de facto* international recognition of the two Germanys, multiple challenges to German competitiveness, as well as a series of ecological disasters. Subsets comprising this group range from pre-materialist *Aussteiger* [drop-outs] to pro-materialist *Anpasser* [conformists]. One segment was easily mobilized around the issues of peace and ecology, yet a majority remained intentionally apolitical prior to unification. Finding few grounds for identification with their GDR-counterparts, members of this generation were largely inclined to consider the national question moot, or at least superfluous.

Each generation has developed its own postwar political identity of sorts. Their outlooks vary with respect to their sense of obligation toward the other Germans and their definition of primary national interests, as well as in relation to their national security preferences. They also differ noticeably in their willingness to engage in conventional or unconventional politics. Whether the sum of those identities amounts to an FRG-national conscious-ness remains to be seen in later chapters. Let us first consider how that po-tential collective identity comes about.

In Search of Individual, Collective, and National Consciousness

This section explores the ways in which identity is formed, and why the ex-perts believe it is important to have one! Not all scholars agree as to the shape of identity; some see it evolving in a linear fashion, others view it as a dynamic configuration based on relationships, while a few believe that it ex-ists in some absolute fashion, e.g., as a never-changing national character. My own model, favoring the dynamic approach, envisions identity as a set of concentric circles (defined below). In any case, identity seems to find its deepest roots in the attitudes and behaviors of individuals.

While we should not expect to find a perfect correspondence between identity-theories derived at the level of human psychology and those applied at the political-systemic level, we cannot discount important linkages between the two. Scholars often lose sight of these ties, owing to a lack of interdisciplinary research in this area. The links between individual and collective identity formation are more than coincidental, as difficult as it may be to establish a direct causal nexus.

Experts from diverse fields agree that identities develop along four different axes, whether the focus is on the creation of self-identity or the construction of national identity. Identity, in either case, represents a composite of cognitive, affective, contextual and interactional elements; it is both subjective and objective in nature. The acquisition of cognitive and affective orientations towards the self has long occupied the attentions of psychologists and psychiatrists, ranging from Piaget to Freud. Theories regarding the contextual and interactive components of self-identity are less well developed but all the more interesting because of their inherently dynamic character. A broader, interdisciplinary perspective helps us to bridge the gap between individual and collective identification processes.

Richard Logan argues that an "individual's sense of self inevitably and necessarily reflects the general world views prevailing in a given era"; at the same time, "the prevailing sense of self [found in that era] . . . may be a 'cause' of subsequent cultural change."[44] Gergen's emphasis on the contextual dimensions of self-identity recognizes that "what have traditionally been viewed as both mental and behavioral events are now held to be historically situated constructions emerging from social process."[45] Mildred Schwarz also stresses the interdependent nature of identity formation processes:

> Out of the interaction of historical events, actions of government, activities, personalities, and ideologies of leaders, and conflicts and accommodations between interests, a nation emerges, and in so doing, acquires a distinctive character. This image of a nation then provides the focus for the personal identities of its members, sometimes lying dormant and other times becoming mobilized in the self-definitions of citizens.[46]

Historically and psychologically intertwined, self-identity and national consciousness become mutually reinforcing.

While the construction of any given identity requires some differentiation between self and other, context yields a unique configuration of particulars which establishes the parameters of identity at a specific point in time. Stryker emphasizes "the degree to which an individual's relationships to particular others depend[s] upon his or her being a given kind of person, i.e., occupying a particular position in a network of relationships, playing a particular role, and having a particular identity."[47] McCall suggests that identity-formation is a cyclical process, moving through the stages of acquisition, development, transformation and eventual phasing out.[48] The important point is not that identities per se change—as one advances through the life cycle, for example—but that the functions of and the relationships between identities also change. Representing a collective effort to assess the meaning of past, present and future states of being, identities "must be negotiated" as well as "validated."[49]

Individuals who have experienced deep-seated identity problems in the past will be more inclined to persist in a problemistic search for "self" than those persons for whom identity implies a steady state.[50] The more difficult that search has been in the past, the higher the degree of salience accorded one's present identity, and the more sensitive its bearer will remain to external evidence confirming or repudiating that identity. Clearly, there is a distinction to be made "between normal self-awareness, embarrassed self-consciousness (as an act of shame), and hypochondriacal preoccupation with self."[51] Nonetheless, previous crises linked to identity force individuals, or communities, to visualize "a particular situation as an opportunity to perform [in terms appropriate to their new identity] by increasing sensitivity to cues calling for the performance of roles attached to highly salient identities."[52] Perhaps this dynamic helps to explain why the "Bonn is/is not Weimar" syndrome is so endemic to the discourse on postwar German politics.

An individual's search for identity raises complex questions involving personal and political motivation. Abraham Maslow's scale of needs builds upon a series of relationships that gives identity its dynamic character. Drawing on motivational theory, Maslow defines five categories of hierarchically ordered needs; his model presumes that as each need is satisfied, new and still higher needs will emerge that come to dominate the individual organism.[53] This hierarchy consists of: (1) physiological or sustenance needs; (2) safety or security needs; (3) "belonging" and love needs; (4) esteem, status and independence needs; and finally, (5) the need for self-actualization. Having fulfilled the basic "biological" or survival needs specified in the first two categories, an individual strives to discover her place within the larger community, a step leading to collective qua national identity-building. Self-actualization implies that identity cannot be limited to a process of other-identification or demarcation; it extends beyond a definition of "what one is not." In Maslow's words, "what a man (sic) *can* be, he *must* be," in order "to be ultimately at peace with himself," and presumably with the rest of the world.[54]

Baker, Dalton and Hildebrandt were among the first to posit the existence of a Maslowian-type scale of national needs and political interests surfacing in *Germany Transformed*.[55] Inglehart carried the analogy one step further, drawing upon the scale of needs as a framework for his post-materialist analysis. According to the latter, "given individuals pursue various goals in hierarchical order—giving maximum attention to the things they sense to be the most important unsatisfied needs at a given time."[56] The Economic Miracle of the 1950s and 1960s, he argued, made it possible for citizens of the 1970s and 1980s to pursue political goals and causes which "no longer have a direct relationship to the imperatives of economic security."[57] The internal logic of this needs-scale, applied to Germany as a whole in 1981, led Baker and company to predict that "the approaching resolution of material and security issues will result in the addition of new issues to the political agenda. Increasingly, politics will be concerned with the questions of life styles and the quality of life, rather than the quantity of economic rewards."[58]

Identity extends well beyond a continuity of action implicit in role; it seeks to consolidate interlocking symbols, as well as to enhance its own sense of acceptance and integration.[59] These processes may give rise to generational asymmetries, especially in a country where "it has been a component of the political culture that younger people should define themselves at a distance from the nation."[60] Asymmetries become especially problematic when younger cohorts begin to reject not only the concept of national identity, but also the form and substance of specific roles which have entrenched themselves as identity's substitute: consider the so-called post-materialists, unwilling to derive their self-worth from the FRG's "miraculous" economic achievements. A concentration on the performance of certain roles may deflect questions of identity, but only temporarily; ultimately, "it does not follow . . . that there is some peculiar and unique way in which Germans can define their identity by not having one."[61]

The manner in which an individual relates to her country can be studied at the socio-psychological level, as well as at the political-systemic level. The personal and political dimensions of identity become effectively intertwined through the process of community-identification. Searching for links between these two levels of analysis, Kelman holds that a nation goes beyond the conception of "this is the way we do things" to a conception of "there is something unique, special and valuable about our way of doing things." It is ideologizing of this sort that makes it possible to develop allegiance to and invest one's identity in a collectivity that goes beyond in both space and time one's primary-group, face-to-face contacts.[62]

The German concept of *Heimat* clearly illustrates how one's personal identity begins to interface with an explicitly political or national consciousness. Divorced from an older notion of "love of fatherland" by virtue of historical necessity, the Federal Republic witnessed a new emphasis on homeland as a potential source of security and community after 1982, introduced by no less a figure than Rhinelander Helmut Kohl. Steeped in tradition, the term *Heimat* evokes a sense of personal security mixed with comfortable familiarity [*Gemütlichkeit*] in an otherwise alienating, de-personalized mass society. The sudden popularity of a TV-series bearing that name, a revived interest in the preservation of local dialects, the instant best-seller status of biographies involving regional heroes of yesteryear (e.g., the Swabian Duke, Karl Eugen) are but a few developments testifying to the rehabilitation of *Heimat* as a component of German-identity during the early 1980s. It also resurfaced as a basis for grassroots mobilization and protest, stimulated by the small-is-beautiful emphasis of anti-nuclear eco-think.

Heimat is a concept that has been largely purged of nationalistic overtones in the parlance of younger generations. When questioned about their respective "feelings" of identity in 1985, students at the Universities of Frankfurt and Mannheim labeled themselves *schwäbish*, *norddeutsch*, or *bayerisch*; one discussant in Frankfurt referred to me as "the only German-nationalist in the room!" Cohorts socialized during the 1960s and 1970s have an insufficient grasp of what it means to be a nation; historically distant from its military manifestations, they displayed little interest in the topic prior to 1989. Yet they may be reluctant to abandon nationalism as a component of their own identities, as long as they are uncertain as to what they might be giving up. In this they differ significantly from the first postwar generation for whom "the avoidance of any approach to our real identity as Germans, the virtual tabooing of the subject and its absence from public discussion and personal conversation no doubt give a certain feeling of relief and release."[63] The price to be paid for that relief may have been the incapacity to mourn detected by psychologists Alexander and Margarete Mitscherlich in the late 1960s.[64] The price to be paid for disinterest may be an incapacity to accord intrinsic value to one's membership in a national community, rendering it devoid of organic solidarity.

Nationalist sentiments are but one aspect of an individual's relationship to the nation-state. Even if nationalism is rejected or discounted at the affective level, it is imperative that citizens develop alternative modes of personal involvement with the political system in order to satisfy other material and integrational needs.[65] Ironically, the rejection of nationalism evinced by postwar generations once again renders the Germans exceptional or aberrant, pitting them against neighboring populations who enjoy "normal" national identities. This is not to argue that conventional feelings of nationalism are inherently "rational" in the post-modern era. As Isaacs observes, "nationalism has remained the most powerful of all political drives even though it has long since become the most sterile of all political solutions in human affairs . . . in a globalizing world of power, resources, technology and communication."[66] The rhetoric of national interests nevertheless prevails, especially when times appear to be getting tougher.

Citizen involvement with the national system can be grounded in symbolic, normative, or functional types of commitment.[67] Kelman highlights six patterns of personal involvement with the nation-state, promoting a sense of attachment to the system also known as loyalty. Sentimentally motivated individuals recognize the state's rights to allocate roles and impose duties based on shared cultural ideals or value preferences. Alternatively, citizens may commit themselves to a national system viewed as an extension or enhancement of their personal identities. Thirdly, they may identify out of a commitment to the "sacredness" of the state, reifying a like-minded community of the whole. By comparison, instrumental attachment emerges as a function of one's commitment to a particular set of socio-economic institutions. Secondly, it may stem from a commitment to the effective, institutionalized performance of specific social roles. Finally, instrumental attachment can derive from a commitment to law and order as desirable ends per se.[68] The stability of the modern nation-state rests upon a balanced mixture of commitment types, more or less randomly distributed throughout the population. Personal attachment becomes a source of political legitimacy to the extent that it stimulates further involvement with the system. Participation, in turn, generates a greater sense of collective consciousness, opening the door to an identification with the state in which it is housed.

The bonds of collective qua national consciousness are woven from the fibers of common language, ethnicity, religion and customs, usually within the framework of a shared history. For Karl Deutsch, the essence of nationhood rests in shared systems of social communication and economic interchange, linked to a center which has the power to compel cohesiveness among citizen-members.[69] Schafer's ten-fold criteria are more rigorous, and thus harder to apply in the case of newly created states. They include: territorial unity; shared cultural characteristics; common socio-economic institutions; a common sovereign government; belief in a common history and heritage; a shared community of values; commitment to a whole array of historical, cultural and political factors; common pride in achievements, as well as common regret over failures; demarcation and recognition of enemies, including a devaluation of others; and, finally, belief in a "golden future" in which all members will share.[70]

The nation-state functions as the institutional embodiment of a common national consciousness. National identity, however, is short-hand for many types of collective consciousness prevailing within a given territory. Correspondingly, the identity projected onto a given state by external actors, allies and adversaries may be largely at odds with that state's conception of itself. The German language is replete with terms that seek, on the one hand, to draw a number of fine but significant lines between various modes of collective consciousness and, on the other, to blur any ultimate distinctions among those types. Most citizens of the postwar Republic had embraced a new *Staatsbewußtsein* [state-consciousness] by 1989 but evinced little enthusiasm for the image of an older *Bewußtseinsnation* [nation of consciousness]; by the onset of unification they had yet to satisfy an abstract craving for a single *Staatsnation* [nation-state], though their need was hardly a pressing one.

The internal debate over semantics may obscure a more significant political dialectic, however. Kühnl insists that the meanings assigned to nation, national identity, nationalism and the national question are determined by those who debate these constructs with the aim of advancing a specific political agenda.[71] At issue here is the larger process of self-definition and image-projection. This confusion over fine distinctions and major consequences derives, at least in part, from a phenomenon I have labeled the FRG's Nation vs. State Identity Paradox.

Prior to November 9, 1989, the parameters of the Nation vs. State Identity Paradox were preordained by the preamble to the West German *Grundgesetz*. Promulgated on May 23, 1949, the Basic Law was intentionally "provisional" in nature, functioning until that day when it might be replaced by a new constitution adopted in free self-determination by the entire German People—a populace not limited to residents of the former western occupation zones but presumably excluding Austrians, the Swiss and the Volga-Germans. The reunification imperative contained in the Preamble was addressed to *das deutsche Volk*, not to the FRG government itself.[72] Nor did the Preamble dictate the total fusion of all political, economic and military institutions operating within the two states. The constitutional emphasis fell not on unity per se but on unity and freedom.

Intent on preserving the link between the nation past and future, the FRG was not free to cultivate an identification with itself in the form of a self-contained, deeply rooted state-consciousness; consolidating its own identity would have undermined the prospects for the re-establishing national consciousness. Official insistence on the continuity of the nation, reinforced by a 1973 Constitutional Court ruling, was rather ironic, given the fact that throughout the 1950s and 1960s, "the primary objective of historical and political education in both parts of Germany [appeared] to be the vilification of the other side in order to stimulate systemic supports for their [own] side."[73] Willy Brandt's formula stressing the existence of two states in one nation offered some legitimacy to those who wished to present the Federal Republic as an independent actor on the global stage, as host-nation to the 1972 Olympics, for example. Still, the Two-States thesis suggested that FRG citizens would first have to forge an identification with their own state, before they could develop an identity shared with the other German state and, eventually, with the nation reunified.

Disassociating itself from the fascist past, the German Democratic Republic avoided the pitfalls of the Nation/State Paradox by projecting a positive commitment to its own nationhood. Hoping to legitimize its own existence, the GDR dropped all references to a future-oriented, united German nation-state by 1968, characterizing itself as "the socialist state of the German nation." Articles 1 and 8 of the 1968 Constitution (calling for step-by-step rapprochement) found no mention in a revision undertaken in October

1974; the GDR would henceforth be known as the socialist German nation (as opposed to the capitalist nation, the FRG). Shortly thereafter, Premier Honecker opted to confront the identity-problem head on with his dialectical formula, "Citizenship—GDR, Nationality—German."

Over the next decade, the SED leadership deliberately moved to de-Germanize its share of the former Reich, replacing the term *German* with the label *GDR-national* in the names of major publications and organizations.[74] Its own demarcation policies notwithstanding, the Eastern government "rediscovered" a common history in the early 1980s, as illustrated by its rehabilitations of Luther, Bismarck, and even Frederick the Great. But the return to a common historical framework, attesting to the ongoing existence of a German *Kulturnation*, offers no guarantee that a people divided will interpret its history in the same light, or derive the same lessons for the future. A search for collective consciousness predicated on the cultural-nation alone results in "commonality without identity."[75]

The Federal Republic was thus left to its own devices in the search for German identity. This raised the intriguing question at the outset of my investigation: what becomes of the two-states-in-one-nation minus one-state-turned-nation? Is the inevitable result two nations in the longer run? Weidenfeld, like Schweigler, predicted in 1983 that the Germans would learn to live with an identity of many layers, with separate versions of FRG- and GDR-state consciousness moving into the foreground. West Germany's desire for sovereignty and self-determination would supercede the diffuse, psychological support for reunification mandated by the Basic Law. The Preamble would retain its function as a "profession of faith" but would not become a "call to action."[76] Developments since 1989 prove that divergent approaches to the Identity Paradox adopted during the 1970s did give rise to two-cultures-in-one-*Volk*, one of which (the East) is perceptibly more "pro-national" than the other.

A nation seeking to establish itself within the formal boundaries of statehood must do more than simply reflect the ethno-cultural identity of its constituents. This was especially true for the old FRG and the former GDR: the loss of connections to family and friends by the late 1970s made it difficult to sustain the sentimental bonds of earlier decades, necessitating their replacement with instrumental ties. Though the FRG-GDR case is somewhat unique in having carved two identities out of one, "the push from state to nation . . . is not at all inconsistent with historical precedents. Whether such a push will succeed . . . depends on the extent to which the state contains a well-functioning society with members who are interdependent and whose needs and interests are adequately met."[77] This leaves unresolved the question as to whether or not the Germans at home in either state might have benefited from a separate identity that was national in the conventional sense.

Despite the unnatural creation of two separate German states after 1945, both postwar governments worked (albeit to different degrees, using divergent strategies) to become more effective representatives of citizen interests. By the 1960s both countries had opted for a pride-in-state vested in their respective economic miracles, a non-antagonistic surrogate for historical identity-lost. The "national" thrust exhibited by the Eastern state after 1974 derived primarily from a need to sever old ties to the West in order to secure its own legitimacy. Deep-seated emotional attachments were neither encouraged nor pursued too actively in the Western state, for fear of raising suspicions among victorious powers and vanquished neighbors, or out of fears that such pursuits would compromise an abstract hope that reunification could "someday" be achieved. The political stability evinced by West German political institutions through the economic disruptions of the 1970s and 1980s testified to a diffuse, if not active support for a system whose legitimation was no longer solely dependent on economic performance. This lends credence to Kelman's argument that "the perception of the state as representative of national unity can compensate for failures to meet the peoples' needs and interests. On the other hand, the perception of the state as meeting the people's needs and interests can compensate for a lacking sense of national identity, and can in fact help to create such an identity."[78]

While the experts may not agree on a single set of variables determining national consciousness world-wide, most do share an understanding that identity is grounded in a complicated pattern of relationships developed over many years, under very diverse circumstances. Unfortunately, too many identity-seekers view the forces permeating each set of relationships as the province of a particular social science discipline. To grasp the phenomenon of national identity in its entirety, we must conceive of it as an interdisciplinary product, that is, as one that is essentially concentric in nature (see Figure 1.1).

Identity begins with the individual, adding "layers" as it moves into the larger communities of family, neighborhood, state, nation and even continent. Under my concentric model, the inner circle equates identity with the psychology of the individual; the second circle expands the boundaries of identity on the basis of specific patterns of communal or societal interaction; the outer circle sees identity moving beyond the informal, collective entity to an historically and legally significant configuration known as the nation-state.

In concrete terms, the core of individual identity among postwar Germans would encompass feelings of self-worth, a sense of personal competence and security, recognition of one's own rights and responsibilities, and a perceived need for involvement with other members of society. The next ring would entail an individualized, affective attachment to *Heimat*, that is, to those people and places making up one's day-to-day world beyond the nuclear family. In this context, an individual would acquire a sense of social belonging in relation to her neighborhood, her workplace, the physical landscape, aspects of local culture or dialect (*Kölsch, Schwäbisch*, etc.). The next circle incorporates a regional or subaltern identification (e.g., *west-, nord-* or *süddeutsch*), embedded in a more abstract value community, that is, within the framework of

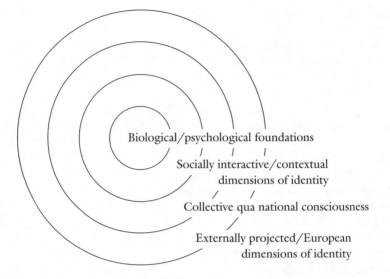

FIGURE 1.1   Concentric Model of Identity

"constitutional patriotism." The third ring signifies a conscious, cognitive affiliation with the nation-united, namely, with the Federal Republic or *Deutschland*, perhaps culminating in a broader European consciousness represented
by the outermost circle. This is not to argue that the Germans of East and
West, over the next ten years, will exhibit the same type of attachment to their
immediate environs, the nation-state, or to the European Union, respectively.
Nor does it assume that citizens in the old and new *Länder* will necessarily
identify with each "circle" to an equal degree.

Since 1945 many components of a once-shared *German* identity have
been fundamentally redefined, or even deliberately expunged from citizen
consciousness. Many people in united Germany will find it difficult to seek a
new identity at the "national" level; such a move might even prove counterproductive, as waves of rightwing violence among youth suggest. As of this
writing, the Eastern Germans evince a much stronger affinity for *Heimat*,
the ecologically degraded nature of their immediate environs notwithstanding. The resurgence of homeland-feeling witnessed since 1989 is likely to be
more psycho-social than nationalist at its core, the rhetoric of extremists
notwithstanding. A renewed emphasis on the homeland assists East-Ger-
mans in refuting the charge that they once embraced the official GDR-identity now so disparaged by the "victors." At the same time, it entails a backlash response to *Besserwessis* [know-it-all Westerners], ostensibly intent on
imposing their own political values, legal standards and administrative practices without any concessions to Eastern experiences of the last four
decades. By contrast, West Germans intent on evading an officially defined

FRG-identity (with its stress on historical continuity) were more likely to cultivate a partial identification with Europe prior to 1989. Whatever New German identity might emerge over the next decade, one can be quite grateful that its future character will be far from monolithic.

The Generational Spectrum: Identities Classified

As anticipated by Schweigler two decades ago, the rise of a West German or FRG-national consciousness has been grounded in a "passionless" yet stable acceptance of democratic values and institutions. And yet, both post-war and post-Wall identities must evince a strong historical imprint, as an anti-dote to younger cohorts' lack of "perspective" regarding the age-old problem of German nationalism. The overbearing, imbalanced or otherwise deficient treatments of the Nazi era in West German secondary schools have resulted in visibly alienated [*ich hab' die Schnauze voll . . .*] reactions tending in two extreme directions, as affirmed by my experiences with young citizens. One faction feels the burden of history weighing too heavily upon its shoulders, and consequently holds that "no national identity is a good identity." A second group rejects any suggestion that "guilt" is transferable, which leads these youth to claim their national identity "as a right," or even finds them denying that the Nazis could have been all that bad.[79]

A core segment of the Economic Miracle and Student Movement Generations would be satisfied with the development of a constitutional identity, an ideal espoused by Habermas.[80] This "identity of the new type" would represent their internalization of the democratic values enshrined in the Basic Law, including but not limited to free development of the personality; equality between the sexes; freedom of religion, speech, assembly, art, teaching and research; social justice or solidarity; the right to asylum; and a ban on preparations for offensive war (see Figure 1.2). An extended period of great social turbulence (such as that witnessed since 1989) can compel FRG leaders to draw upon a sense of legitimacy which supersedes mere material satisfaction. They must call upon loyalties which transcend popular attachments to specific institutions—the embodiments of constitutionally prescribed values—until such time as confidence in those institutions and the normal power equilibrium can be restored.

My discussion partners were asked point blank whether they "felt" themselves to be Germans, Federal Republicans, Europeans or *sonst was* [other] in 1985/86, and how they would rank-order those identities. Limited though the sample was, they evinced a wide array of identity-orientations prior to unification. Those categorized as members of the Economic Miracle Generation might best be labeled the "historical Germans" [*die Gesamtdeutschen*]. The "national" inclinations articulated by this group can be further delineated into three sub-classes. Among this contingent were:

Preamble to the Basic Law (1949–1990)

The German People
in the Länder of Baden, Bavaria, Bremen, Hamburg, Hesse,
Lower Saxony, North Rhine-Westphalia, Rhineland-Palatinate,
Schleswig-Holstein, Württemberg-Baden and Württemberg-
Hohenzollern
Conscious of their responsibility before God and men (sic)
Animated by the resolve to preserve their national and political
*   unity and to serve the peace of the world as an equal partner*
*   in a united Europe,*
Desiring to give a new order to political life for a transitional
*   period,*
Have enacted, by virtue of their constituent power, this Basic
*   Law for the Federal Republic of Germany.*
They have also acted on behalf of those Germans to whom partici-
*   pation was denied.*
The entire German people are called upon to achieve in free self-
*   determination the unity and freedom of Germany.*

FIGURE 1.2

(1) the sentimental-wistful Germans who regretted the loss of an affective sense of national consensus, though not on a day-to-day basis; (2) the so-cialized-but-distant Germans who had grown up under one nation but had come to recognize the benefits of a democratized rump-state; and (3) the forcefully expelled, more actively pro-reunification Germans.

The second generation, consisting of Long Marchers in both the literal and figurative sense, seemed to have the most trouble balancing the past–ver-sus–the future components of its own identity. The subdivisions within this group were, consequently, more radically defined. Their ranks included: (1) the internationalists, who subscribed to the belief that "no national identity is a good identity"; (2) the Europeanists, a group further subdivided into "enthusiastic" and "resigned" categories vis-à-vis institutionalized integra-tion; (3) the rapprochement Germans, who usually had some connection to Berlin and had first discovered their Germanness through interaction with other European peace groups; and (4) the pragmatic frequent-flyer Ger-mans, or those who view their nationality as a matter of "administrative-tech-nical necessity" for securing passports, pensions, etc.

Among the 60 plus individuals comprising my Bundestag sample (all from the EM and LM cohorts), I discovered only one member of parliament will-ing to label herself a Federal Republican, first and foremost. No one ven-tured a response to my follow-up question, posed only half in jest, "if you don't feel like a Federal Republican, then why sit here [in the Bundestag] representing *that* specific constituency?" A majority of my MdB repondents admitted that their children would identify more closely with the postwar state than they did. That presumption was largely confirmed by the reactions of younger discussion partners.

Members of the Turn-Around Generation, the alleged beneficiaries of "the blessing of late birth," fell into two categories at the time of my interviews. The smaller of the two groups, whom I call the Germans of conviction [*Gesinnungsdeutsche*] consisted of neo-conservatives who often had refugee parents and/or sustained contacts with relatives in the GDR. Among the second group, designated the no-big-deal Federal Republicans, citizenship and nationality were construed as an accident of birth to be taken for granted, not an existential quality requiring cultivation. As diverse as the identity-orientations of the three generations sound, they seemed to have settled into a state of "peaceful coexistence" prior to 1989. Whether the cohorts will continue to manifest different degrees of national feeling beyond unification is a question reserved for later chapters.

The dilemma of German identity rests with the need, so eloquently described by Schonbaum, "to be *and* not to be."[81] It is the vague, improvised nature of postwar national consciousness that sometimes renders it vulnerable to old conceptualizations, especially among outside observers. FRG-cohorts have distanced themselves from many character traits historically attributed to the Germans—and not only by virtue of the fact that two-thirds were born after 1945. Most citizens reject a simplistic attachment to duty, diligence, law and order (though self-proclaimed neo-Nazis constitute an obvious exception to this rule).

Whatever negative trade-offs might ensue from a postwar focus on self-actualization, the New Unencumberedness vis-à-vis the national past and the loosening of older, personal ties to the other Germany during the 1970s and 1980s has resulted in a greater independence of thought and action among younger cohorts. The proof shall lie in the future construction of a positive, self-affirming German identity, the specific generational components of which we shall now explore.

Notes

1. Cited by Theo Sommer, "Kein Maß, Kein Mittelmaß," *Die Zeit*, October 14, 1988.

2. Daniel Sneider, "Ire over Fighter Jet Deal—Japan Blasts U.S. for Backtracking," *Christian Science Monitor*, April 4, 1989; also, Clyde H. Farnsworth, "Basic Issues Still Face Bush on Japan Jet Deal," *New York Times*, March 17, 1989.

3. Rudolf von Thadden, "Das Schwierige Vaterland," in Werner Weidenfeld, Hg., *Die Identität der Deutschen* (München/Wien: Hanser, 1983), p. 54.

4. For details, see Joyce Marie Mushaben, *The State v. the University: Juridicalization and the Politics of Higher Education at the Free University of Berlin*, Dissertation, Indiana University, 1981, especially pp. 368–387.

5. Youth unemployment rates doubled in the OECD nations between 1965 and 1975; see Arnold J. Heidenheimer, Hugh Heclo and Carolyn Teich Adams, *Comparative Public Policy: The Politics of Social Choice in Europe and America* (New York: St. Martin's Press, 1983), p. 153.

6. Harro Honolka, *Schwarzrotgrün—Die Bundesrepublik auf der Suche nach ihrer Identität* (München: Beck, 1987), p. 16.

7. Peter Alter, *Nationalismus* (Frankfurt/M: Suhrkamp, 1985); Reinhard Kühnl, *Nation, Nationalismus, Nationale Frage* (Köln: Pahl-Rugenstein, 1986); Jürgen Habermas, Hg., *Stichworte zur 'Geistigen Situation der Zeit,'* Bd. 1, *Nation und Republik* (Frankfurt/M: Suhrkamp, 1982); Robert O. Keohane and Joseph S. Nye, Jr., *Power and Interdependence* (Boston: Little, Brown, 1977).

8. For a discussion of tensions relating to Emerging Technologies, see Catherine Kelleher and Gale A. Mattox, eds., *Evolving European Defense Policies* (Lexington: Lexington Books, 1987).

9. Nearly four-fifths (64% of the men, 52% of the women) polled in January 1972 supported the treaties signed with the Soviet Union, Poland and the GDR. By January 1980, 78% of the male and 74% of the female respondents favored a continuation of *Entspannungspolitik*. See Berthold Meyer, *Der Bürger und seine Sicherheit—Zum Verhältnis von Sicherheitsstreben und Sicherheitspolitik* (Frankfurt/M: Campus, 1983), pp. 247–254. Also, Richard Löwenthal, "The German Question Transformed," *Foreign Affairs*, Winter 1984–85, p. 313.

10. Joachim Nawrocki, "Ringen um Papiere, Posten und Personen," *Die Zeit*, March 31, 1989.

11. Data stem from the West German *Statistisches Bundesamt* (Wiesbaden: 1982) p. 59, and the GDR's *Staatliche Zentralverwaltung für Statistik* (Berlin: 1982), p. 346.

12. Robert D. Putnam examines the *missing generation* problem among West German elites in "The Political Attitudes of Senior Civil Servants in Britain, Germany, and Italy" in Mattei Dogan, ed., *The Mandarins of Western Europe—The Political Role of Top Civil Servants* (New York: Sage/Halstead, 1975), pp. 115–116. The term has taken on new meaning since 1990, implying a "lost generation" in the Eastern states. Many professionals over the age of 40 will miss out on positions of influence based on their assumed complicity with the old regime.

13. The *Kuby Affair*, which unleashed the free-speech movement at Berlin's Freie Universität, grew out of Karl Jaspers's cancelled appearance commemorating the 20th anniversary of liberation from the Nazis. The debate over democratization of university governance structures triggered protests over the "shrouded continuity of transmissions from the Nazi period," as did demonstrations against the re-release of Veit Harlan films. See Jürgen Habermas, *Protestbewegung und Hochschulreform* (Frankfurt/M: Suhrkamp, 1969), pp. 156–172. Further, Tilman Fichter and Siegward Lönnendonker, *Kleine Geschichte des SDS. Der Sozialistische Deutsche Studentenbund von 1946 bis zur Selbstauflösung* (Berlin: Rotbuch Verlag, 1977); F. Duve, Hrsg., *Die Restauration entlässt ihre Kinder oder der Erfolg der Rechten in der Bundesrepublik* (Reinbek: Rowohlt, 1968); and Peter H. Merkl, "Conclusion: Were the Angry Old Men Wrong?" in Merkl, ed., *The Federal Republic of Germany at Forty* (New York: New York University Press, 1989), pp. 464–497.

14. For more on youth's information-deficit regarding the Hitler era, see Dieter Bossmann, Hg. *Schüler über die Einheit der Nation. Ergebnisse einer Umfrage* (Frankfurt/M: Fischer, 1978). A July 1986 FGW-poll for the TV-program *Kennzeichen D* found that more than three-fourths of its sample did not know the correct answer to the question, In which year was the Berlin Wall built?

Year	*18–24*	*25–29*	*30–39*	*40–49*	*50–59*	*60+*
Pre-1956	12.9	8.8	4.8	10.0	4.6	7.6
1956–1960	8.8	13.9	15.4	12.2	11.5	10.3
1961	20.8	21.2	23.9	28.0	26.0	25.0
1962–1966	23.0	24.1	23.2	27.7	25.7	9.7
After 1966	1.3	1.4	1.7	3.0	1.8	2.5
Don't Know	33.0	30.7	31.1	19.1	30.4	34.9

Concerned that lack of knowledge about the terms of German division would undermine support for reunification, the State Educational Ministers incorporated a module on the German Question into the public school curriculum in 1978.

15. Charles S. Maier, "*Jenseits des Historikerstreits*: The Significance of the Historikerstreit," *German Politics and Society*, Nr. 13 (February 1988), p. 4.

16. Saul Friedlander, "Some Reflections on the Historicization of National Socialism," *German Politics and Society*, ibid, pp. 9–21. Also, Dan Diner, Hrsg., *Ist der Nationalsozialismus Geschichte? Zu Historisierung und Historikerstreit* (Frankfurt/M: Fischer, 1988), pp. 34–50.

17. Friedlander, op. cit., p. 11ff.

18. Karl Mannheim, "Das Problem der Generationen" (1928), reprinted in Ludwig von Friedeburg, Hg., *Jugend in der Modernen Gesellschaft* (Köln: Kiepenheuer & Witsch, 1985), p. 39.

19. Richard J. Samuels, ed., *Political Generations and Political Development* (Lexington, MA: Heath, 1977), p. 6.

20. Richard D. Logan, "Historical Change in Prevailing Sense of Self," in Krysia Yardley and Terry Honess, eds., *Self and Identity. Psychosocial Perspectives* (Chichester, NY: John Wiley & Sons, 1987), p. 13.

21. Walter Laqueur, *Young Germany: A History of the German Youth Movement* (New York: Basic Books, 1962); Wolfgang J. Mommsen, "Wandlungen der nationalen Identität," in Weidenfeld, *Die Identität der Deutschen*, op. cit., pp. 170–192; Bruno Bettelheim, "The Problem of Generations," in Erik H. Erikson, ed., *The Challenge of Youth* (Garden City, NJ: Anchor Books, 1965); Richard G. Braungart, "Historical generations and youth movements: A theoretical perspective," presented at the World Congress of Sociology, Mexico City, August 16–21, 1982.

22. Wilhelm Dilthey's original 1875 essay, "Über das Studium der Geschichte der Wissenschaften vom Menschen, der Gesellschaft und dem Staat," is cited by Carl E. Schorske, "Generational Tension and Cultural Change: Reflections on the Case of Vienna," *Daedalus*, 107 (1978), p. 121.

23. Karl Mannheim, *Essays on the Sociology of Knowledge* (London: Routledge and Kegan Paul, 1952), p. 291.

24. This classification stems from Samuel P. Huntington, "Generations, Cycles, and their Role in American Development," in Samuels, op. cit., pp. 9–27.

25. S. N. Eisenstadt, *From Generation to Generation: Age Groups and Social Structure* (Glencoe, IL: Free Press, 1956).

44   *The Problem of Generations*

26. Norval D. Glenn, *Cohort Analysis* (Beverly Hills, CA: Sage, 1977), p. 19.

27. Huntington, op. cit., p. 11.

28. Glenn, op. cit.; also, M. K. Jennings and R. G. Niemi, *Generations and Politics: A panel study of young adults and their parents* (Princeton, NJ: Princeton University Press, 1981), Chapter 5.

29. Glenn, op. cit., p. 13.

30. William Claggett, "Partisan Acquisition versus Partisan Intensity: Life-Cycle, Generation, and Period Effects, 1952–1976," *American Journal of Political Science*, Vol. 25, May 1981, p. 197.

31. Neal E. Cutler, "Generational Succession as a Source of Foreign Policy Attitudes: A cohort analysis of American opinion, 1946–1966," *Journal of Peace Research*, Vol. 7, No. 1, 1970, p. 33.

32. "Almost One Student in Five Over 30," *The Week in Germany*, published by the German Information Center, March 31, 1989.

33. For reports on the GDR's practice of granting "safe haven" to former RAF members, and their later prosecution under a unified German government, see "Strafjustiz," *Der Spiegel*, April 29, 1991, pp. 111–117; ". . . die Lotterie geht weiter," and "Terrorismus: Jetzt ein Plotz, *Der Spiegel*, May 27, 1991, pp. 103–109, pp. 112–113; "Dein Vater ist ein Mörder, *Der Spiegel*, June 23, 1991, pp. 43–50.

34. Exceptions include J. Francis and G. Deele, "Reflections on Generational Analysis: Is there a shared political perspective between men and women?" *Political Studies*, Vol. XXVI, No. 3 (September 1978), pp. 363–374; Lucy Friedman, Alice R. Gold and Richard Christie, "Dissecting the Generation Gap: Intergenerational and Intrafamilial Similarities and Differences," *Public Opinion Quarterly*, Vol. 36 (Fall 1972), pp. 334–346; Jennings and Niemi, op. cit., Chapter 9.

35. *Post-adolescence* refers to an extended transitional period, a life-stage between youth and adulthood, "characterized by the fact that its members have attained full independence in regard to intellectual, political and sexual matters but nonetheless remain economically dependent," as coined by Klaus Dörre and Paul Schäfer, *In den Strassen steigt das Fieber. Jugend in der Bundesrepublik* (Köln: Pahl-Rugenstein, 1982), p. 25ff.

36. Cited in Richard G. Braungart and Margaret M. Braungart, "Generational Politics," in Samuel Long, ed., *Political Behavior Annual* (Boulder, CO: Westview, 1984).

37. Mannheim, *Essays in Sociology*, op. cit., p. 310.

38. Annie Kriegel, "Generational Difference: The History of an Idea," *Daedalus*, Vol. 107, No. 4 (Fall 1978), p. 23.

39. These are parameters set by Helmut Fogt, *Politische Generationen: Empirische Bedeutung und theoretisches Modell* (Opladen: Westdeutscher Verlag, 1982), pp. 56–58; also, Ole R. Holsti and James N. Rosenau, "Does Where You Stand Depend on When you Were Born? The Impact of Generation on Post-Vietnam Foreign Policy Beliefs," *Public Opinion Quarterly*, Vol. 44, No. 1, (Spring 1980); Sigmund Neumann, *Permanent Revolution: The Total State in a World at War* (New York: Harper, 1942), pp. 235–36; and James David Barber, *The Presidential Character* (Englewood Cliffs, NJ: Prentice Hall, 1972).

40. Glenn, op. cit., p. 23, p. 59.

41. Cutler, op. cit., p. 41.

42. Adam Krzeminski, "Preussen, Preussen und was weiter?" *Die Zeit*, November 13, 1981.

43. Fogt, op. cit., p. 174.

44. Logan, cited in Yardley and Honess, op. cit., p. 13.

45. Kenneth J. Gergen, "Toward Self as Relationship," in Yardley and Honess, op. cit., p. 53.

46. Mildred A. Schwarz, *Public Opinion and Canadian Identity* (Berkeley: University of California Press, 1967), p. 9.

47. Sheldon Stryker, "Identity Theory: Developments and Extensions," in Yardley and Honess, op. cit., p. 97.

48. George J. McCall, "The Structure, Content and Dynamics of Self: Continuities in the Study of Role Identities," in Yardley and Honess, op. cit., p. 137.

49. Ibid., p. 135; Stryker, op. cit., p. 95.

50. *Problemistic search* involves a decision-maker's incremental tendency to search for solutions in the area closest to the problem, based on a limited range of variables. See Richard Cyert and James G. March, *A Behavioral Theory of the Firm* (Englewood Cliffs, NJ; Prentice Hall, 1963), pp. 114–127.

51. Susan M. Andersen, "The Role of Cultural Assumptions in Self-Concept Development," in Yardley and Honess, op. cit., p. 273.

52. Stryker, op. cit., p. 95.

53. Abraham Maslow, *Motivation and Personality* (New York: Harper, 1954), p. 854.

54. Ibid., p. 91.

55. Kendall L. Baker, Russell J. Dalton and Kai Hildebrandt, *Germany Transformed—Political Culture and the New Politics* (Cambridge: Harvard University Press, 1981).

56. Ronald Inglehart, "The Silent Revolution in Europe: Intergenerational Change in Post-Industrial Societies," *American Political Science Review*, Vol. 65 (1971), p. 991.

57. Ibid., p. 991.

58. Baker, Dalton and Hildebrandt, op. cit., p. 2.

59. Peter du Preez, *The Politics of Identity—Ideology and the Human Image* (New York: St. Martin's, 1980).

60. Erwin K. Scheuch, "Die Deutsche Nation im Bewußtsein der Bevölkerung der Bundesrepublik," in Klaus Weigelt, Hg., *Heimat und Nation. Zur Geschichte und Identität der Deutschen* (Mainz: Hase & Koehler Verlag, 1984), p. 161.

61. Ralf Dahrendorf, cited in Wolfgang Pollak, ed., *German Identity—Forty Years After Zero* (Sankt Augustin: Friedrich Naumann Stiftung, 1987), p. 47.

62. Herbert C. Kelman, "Patterns of Personal Involvement in the National System: A Social-Psychological Analysis of Political Legitimacy," in James N. Rosenau, ed., *International Politics and Foreign Policy* (New York: Free Press, 1969), p. 284.

63. Cornelia Schmalz-Jacobsen, cited in Pollak, op. cit., p. 110.

64. Alexander and Margarete Mitscherlich, *Die Unfähigkeit zu trauern. Grundlagen kollektiven Verhaltens* (München: Piper, 1967).

65. John Delamater, Daniel Katz and Herbert C. Kelman, "On the nature of involvement: a preliminary study," *Journal of Conflict Resolution*, Vol. XIII, No. 3, (September 1969), p. 320.

66. Harold R. Isaacs, "Fathers and Sons and Daughters and National Development," in Samuels, op. cit., p. 49.

67. Symbolic commitment entails "a strong emotional investment in the nation and its values, and a positive affective orientation to its symbols." Normative commitment reflects "an orientation toward the sanctions attached to the national role expectations as the individual perceives them." Functional integration entails "an instrumental relationship to the ongoing system" commensurate with the perceived rewards of participation. Alienation from the system usually results in non-involvement. Delameter *et al.,* op. cit., pp. 322–323.

68. Kelman, op. cit., pp. 280–283.

69. Karl W. Deutsch, *Nationalism and Social Communication: An Inquiry into the Foundations of Nationality* (Cambridge, MA: MIT Press, 1966 ed.).

70. Boyd C. Shafer, as summarized by Jörg-Dieter Gauger, "Nation, Nationalbewußtsein und Nationwerdung in der deutschen Geschichte," in Weigelt, op. cit., p. 27.

71. On this point, leftist Kühnl overlaps with conservative Michael Stürmer. Kühnl, op. cit., p. 52ff.

72. Eberhard Schulz, *Die deutsche Nation in Europa. Internationale und historische Dimensionen* (Bonn: Europa Verlag, 1982), p. 166ff.

73. Gebhard Schweigler, *National Consciousness in a Divided Germany* (Beverly Hills: Sage, 1975), p. 41.

74. A curious exception to this rule was the SED itself, the Socialist Unity Party of Germany. Hartmut Zimmermann, with Horst Ulrich and Michael Fehlauer, "Nation und Nationale Frage," *DDR Handbuch,* Bd. 2 (Köln: Verlag Wissenschaft und Politik, 1985), pp. 924–926.

75. Rudolf von Thadden, op. cit., p. 84.

76. Weidenfeld, op. cit., pp. 38–43.

77. Kelman, op. cit., p. 285.

78. Ibid., p. 285.

79. For illustrations, see Peter Sichrovsky in *Schuldig geboren. Kinder aus Nazifamilien* (Köln: Kiepenheuer & Witsch, 1987).

80. Jürgen Habermas, "Der DM-Nationalismus," *Die Zeit,* April 6, 1990.

81. Schonbaum is cited in Pollak, op. cit., p. 159.

2

What Does It Mean to Be *German?* From Beethoven to Bitburg, From Demagogues to Democrats

Keep the country German, it's the only thing that works.
Keep the country German, it's the only thing that works.
Wonder what would happen if we lost the Turks.
I got those Gastarbeiter, open-border, unemployment,
social service, national state and falling birthrate,
Einigkeit und Recht und Freiheit, I got those terrorist
and German Question, von Trotta film, Soldaten-Zeitung,
I got those red and green, those black and blue
I got those Weltschmerz blues.

—David Schonbaum,
Pacific Workshop on German Affairs,
CSU-Long Beach, April 1987

The treatment of national consciousness and German identity in the FRG, Erwin Scheuch wrote in 1984, evinces many of the qualities associated with the traditionally loved/feared Loch Ness monster. Their first common feature is that the phenomenon in question always looks different, depending on the side from which it is observed, yet it never takes on a clearly delineated shape. Secondly, devoid of concrete referents, the apparition welcomes the kind of media treatment that leaves much to personal imagination and prejudice. Last but not least, any attempt to capture the creature's essence in a systematic or objective manner, the dream of many a clever investigator, invariably results in its dissolution into the fog.[1] The mythical qualities of German identity, like those of Nessie, are usually accorded greater significance than its empirical contours. Political myths can be used as strategic resources in the service of state power; they are often invoked "in order to win a broad basis of adherents in a situation of perceived dissolution of the social, economic and political order."[2]

This chapter centers on the process of self-definition and image-projection, exploring the extent to which old myths about German national character have or have not lost their meaning for members of the postwar generations. The author assesses the importance of the national question at a

47

variety of levels, arguing that the socially cohesive ultra-nationalism of old has given way to more fragmented, individualized and often contradictory notions of "what it means to be a (West) German." She contends further that all three postwar generations have come to embrace an identity of many layers, one that is fundamentally democratic and "open to the world" in nature, despite certain limits imposed by a "blood-based" concept of FRG-citizenship.

The chapter begins with a review of the dilemmas inherent in the Germans' search for "too much" or "too little" identity over the last century. Next, we compare elite attitudes (gleaned from personal interviews) and mass orientations (derived from public opinion data) across three generations, both of which focus on the dynamics of *Vergangenheitsbewältigung*, that is, on efforts to come to terms with the National-Socialist past. This is followed by an exploration of individual perceptions regarding "the need for" and "the functions of" German identity, questions which appear to produce little inter-generational consensus. We then survey generational perspectives regarding the positive and negative features of postwar identity, before closing the chapter with an assessment of their respective attitudes towards the existing institutions, constitutional values, and new modes of political participation. A further, albeit analytically distinct question as to whether or not age-old notions of what is typically German persist among the FRG's allies and rivals is reserved for a later chapter.

Conflicting Images: What Is *Typisch Deutsch?*

As of May 1945, unconditional surrender and "provisional" division reduced the former Reich to two German states deprived of the right to a clearly defined national consciousness; their promulgation of separate constitutions in 1949 erected new barriers to its reemergence. Discussions of postwar identity formation were restricted in the Federal Republic by virtue of a self-imposed "muzzling" contained within the Preamble and by way of an externally imposed (but only partly internalized) commitment to proletarian internationalism in the GDR. In the western state, select groups such as the refugee associations [*Vertriebenenverbände*] sought to keep the dream of reunification high on the political agenda, despite Adenauer's ostensible rejection of this goal in favor of FRG integration into the Western Alliance. The East German government was neither inclined nor permitted to pursue an independent reunification course, the Stalin Note of 1952 notwithstanding.[3] In either case, effective moves towards the reestablishment of a united Germany were clearly out of the question during the first decade of formal Occupation.

What little truly national consciousness or love of Fatherland remained had to anchor itself to the realities of two diametrically opposed systems stripped, for a time, of formal sovereignty and historical legitimacy. More deep-seated emotional attachments were neither encouraged nor pursued throughout the Occupation years, based on the abstract hope that reunification could "someday" be achieved. By the late 1960s both Germanys had opted for a pride-in-state vested in the material benefits of their respective economic miracles. The blossoming of détente through the 1970s brought new opportunities for peaceful cooperation between the two states, grounded in a de facto recognition of their separateness. Just as the instrumental value of national consciousness began to pale in the face of increasing global interdependence, the early 1980s witnessed a surprising shift in orientations. Born of the hefty debate over the deployment of Pershing II and cruise missiles, critics from diverse ideological camps suddenly joined forces to protest their lack of sovereignty and to reclaim their right to a bona fide German national identity vis-à-vis the superpowers.

Despite the flood of publications generated by coalescing schools of old and new identity-patriots over the last decade, the contents of this born-again national consciousness had yet to be clearly defined by 1989, based on so simple a measuring process as a survey of titles among the books piled up in my own study. After forty years of division, it was still difficult to delineate what *Germany as a Whole* ought to include, or to ascertain what *German Identity Today* was supposed to mean. There were at least *Three Questions Regarding Germany,* beginning with the query, *Are We Really One Nation?* Anyone seeking to predict *What Will Become of the Germans?* or, alternatively, *Can We Still Be Saved?* had first to determine *Where Germany Lies*—whether in the West, in the East, or somewhere in the middle of Europe.[4]

For many participant observers in this debate, including *The Wall-Jumper* and other beneficiaries of *The Blessing of Late Birth,* this *Attempt to Explain the Federal Republic to Ourselves and Others,* based on countless hours of *Meditating over Germany* tended to find its denouement in a *Perplexed Normality.* For patriots who wished to promote *Germany as Our Mission* more actively, there existed the openly optimistic perspective, *German Unity Will Surely Come!* or the more reserved but nonetheless hopeful appeal, *Without Germany, Nothing Goes.* Despite the querulous persistence of *The German Neurosis* and *The Fear of Germans* in what was *Germany as a Provisional State,* it has indeed been the case that *German History Moves On.* However, in raising the question, *Is National-Socialism Just History?* or otherwise challenging the uniqueness of Third Reich extermination policies, one can only hope that *The Germans*—whoever they may be—are not marching to the beat of "two steps forward, one step backwards."[5]

The question "what is German?" possesses an unfortunately negative tradition, both in an ideological and a methodological sense. Determining who was German, historically speaking, rested on the technique of negative integration: namely, "the differentiation between friends of the Reich and enemies of the Reich, good Germans and apprentices without a Fatherland,

[and] consequently the practice of rendering those who thought differently despisable as un-German."[6] The consolidation of democratic institutions after 1950 meant that *Deutsch-sein* [being German] was no longer equivalent to an assertion of imperial self-superiority. At the same time, postwar efforts to define the meaning of "German" bore witness to a subtle territorial shift of emphasis, namely, from a focus on the non-Germans of the Occupational era to the presumption that one was essentially interested in *West* Germans by the 1970s.[7]

Prior to 1945, the designation "typically German" was understood to mean "the bonding of the valuation of order, discipline and obedience with the belief in the state as the realization of the moral idea, that frequently rejected the idea of human rights, of citizen maturity, of the independent capacity for good judgment."[8] Nowadays the phrase *typisch deutsch* is often saddled with overtones of frustration, anger or resignation, as anyone who has heard it enunciated by native speakers can testify. Younger cohorts use the term not to laud Rhineland-style *Gemütlichkeit* but to express their impatience with the older generation's love of "order." Liberals employ it to decry a lack of political tolerance, and almost everyone resorts to the term following a bad experience with "the bureaucracy."

It is often the case that what is perceived as one's national identity abroad bears little resemblance to the self-image accepted by the citizens of a particular state. Germans are more likely to be critical of themselves and their history when dealing with each other than they are when talking to people from other countries. They tend to fight vehemently among themselves, with that typical, pain-staking thoroughness known as *Gründlichkeit*.

Media efforts to convey the significance of FRG-domestic conflicts into the homes of average Americans are sporadic, and slanted, at best. Most U.S.-voters are woefully uninformed as to the many political cultural changes that have taken hold within the two parts of Germany since 1949. To the extent that TV has become the sole source of news for most of the U.S. population, life inside Germany does not appear to have changed much. Indeed, a 1983 survey of thirteen private and public universities conducted by researchers from the USA and Tübingen found that when students were asked to name a famous German politician, almost 100% responded with Hitler; (then Chancellor) Helmut Schmidt was the only postwar politician to rate some measure of recognition, while 37.6% listed Konrad Adenauer as the one person who had *not* been an FRG-Chancellor.[9]

Coming from the heartlands, I noticed in the early 1980s that the FRG had fallen prey to a serious image problem among average U.S.-citizens, one regularly fed by a long-standing practice of airing old Nazi and great-escape-from-Berlin movies on midwestern television (especially on PBS!). I conducted a spontaneous, albeit not strictly representative survey of the print-media landscape in order to discern the nature of the German image presented to the U.S. public at large. Relying on the 1984 *Reader's Guide to Periodical Literature* and the *New York Times Index,* I uncovered such journalistic tidbits as: "Those troubled Germans" (*New York Times*); "Which way will the Germans go?" (*New York Review of Books*); "Germany's new era—The problems fester" (*U.S. News and World Report*); "After the West German spy scandal—Are Star Wars secrets safe?" (*Business Week*); "Feeling the stigma" (*Time*); and, of course, there was Bitburg, Bitburg, Bitburg. Negative German images prevailing in the public domain are, on occasion, counterbalanced by positive experiences with German exchange students and personal good-times-had-by-all at the local summer *Straßenfest*. Still, one is often left to wonder what the United States stands to gain by maintaining a special relationship with a country from which we continue to expect little more than *Weltschmerz, Sturm und Drang!*

The fundamental problem remains U.S.-citizens' lack of knowledge about the real-life conditions which have shaped security policy orientations in Germany over the last forty years. Most West Germans subscribe to "a completely unheroic ideal of society" grounded in bourgeois values revolving around family, security, and health.[10] Having substituted pride in the FRG's economic achievements for national feelings during the first two decades, citizens internalized a functional commitment to constitutional principles and democratic institutions over the next two decades of their state's existence. By the mid-1980s younger cohorts had more or less come to equate their instrumental acceptance of these two factors with national identity per se, having had no experience with its sentimental variant. U.S.-Americans, ethnic-Russians, Poles, Italians, and the French, by contrast, project their own highly emotional love-of-country into the West German heart each time the phrase national interest resounds. Residents of those countries find it very hard to comprehend the words of former FRG-President Gustav Heinemann: "I do not love the state, I love my wife." Absolute love of Fatherland is an anomaly in the West German pyramid of affections. Many contributors to Janssen-Jurreit's book on "national feeling" admitted that they had to undergo a catharsis before they could even begin to address the question: "Do you love Germany?"[11]

One's willingness to reiterate the phrase, "I am proud to be a German," is a poor measure of the ties that really bind in weighing citizens' loyalty to postwar institutions and commitment to democratic values. Expressions of pride in America seem to run a mile wide and an inch deep, evoking few, if any, associations with the extermination of Native Americans, slavery, colonial and McCarthy-era witch hunts, Vietnam or other dark periods of U.S.-national history. German pride, by comparison, is narrow but concentrated in scope, invariably overshadowed by grim historical associations. Our search for German national identity must therefore begin with an assessment of historical consciousness among average citizens in the postwar Republic.

Historical Consciousness: Can the Past Be Conquered?

Relativization as a Tool for "Mastery of the Past"

The Federal Republic's first genuinely "postwar" Chancellor, Helmut Kohl (born in 1930), has repeatedly characterized his own lack of personal connection to the events of 1933–1945 as "the blessing of having been born late." If, however, "the secret of redemption lies in remembrance," then not one of the postwar cohorts can exonerate itself from "history's inescapable impact on the present."[12]

One outspoken representative of the Long March Generation, Peter Schneider, finds little grounds for exculpating the members of Kohl's generation. He calculates that the very individuals who seem bent on "normalizing" their own histories, for example, Kohl himself, Alfred Dregger and Ernst Nolte, fell between the ages of 15 and 25 by the war's end. They are, in short, the direct products of an educational system dominated by the Nazis through 1945, leading Schneider to conclude:

> If it is true that a human being is emotionally and intellectually molded by childhood experiences, then no generation was more completely offered up to National Socialist indoctrination than the one for which Helmut Kohl claims the blessing of having been born too late. His generation was born too late only in the sense that it didn't have to pay for its enthusiasms as did those who were a generation older.[13]

Schneider finds evidence of a fundamental tension between the ruling generation's desire for wholeness and its use of selective memory to achieve a measure of group solidarity. Elite efforts to "normalize" Germany's present status too often result in a campaign to relativize its past. Consider, for example, the case of Ronald Reagan's visit to Bitburg in 1985.

Situated in Rheinland-Pfalz, Bitburg is a small town of 12,200 adult residents, known largely for its beer (*Bitte, ein Bit*) and its proximity to a U.S. Air Force Base where Nike-Hercules missiles were formerly deployed. The controversy began with reports that Chancellor Kohl had been barred from attending services in June 1984, memorializing the Allies' D-Day landing at Normandy.[14] He nonetheless invited U.S.-President Reagan to visit a German military cemetery during his next European trip (scheduled for the summer of 1985), in hopes of achieving peace and reconciliation with another of Germany's former adversaries "across the graves." Reagan refused to visit the Dachau concentration camp; he stressed his desire to focus on the future, declaring "I want to put history behind me."[15]

Drawing broad public criticism, Reagan cancelled his plans to commemorate V-E Day in the FRG, but American and West German advance teams agreed to schedule a presidential trip to the Kolmeshöhe cemetery at Bitburg. In Kohl's words, it was "only natural to consider the military cemetery two miles away from a U.S. air base." Still refusing to pay his respects at a concentration camp, Reagan stated on March 21 that "none of [the German people] who were adults and participating in any way" in the second World War would still be alive, adding that "very few . . . even remember the war. . . . They have a guilt feeling that's been imposed upon them, and I just think it's unnecessary"—although Reagan himself was a member of that generation who obviously did remember some, if not the most significant aspects of WWII.

April 15 brought the first media reports that the Bitburg cemetery contained the remains of 30 (later, 49) members of the *Waffen SS*, labeled a matter "of secondary importance" by an FRG-spokesperson. After reviewing the burial records, Kohl stressed that 30 of those laid to rest at Kolmeshöhe "had not had a chance to evade conscription"; the cemetery visit would provide "a sign for young people serving in the Bundeswehr, indicating that we have learned the lesson of history."

Over the next few weeks, representatives of the U.S. Holocaust Memorial Council, joined by fifty-three members of the U.S. Senate, petitioned Reagan to cancel the Kolmeshöhe excursion. The latter responded: "there is nothing wrong with visiting that cemetery where those young men are victims of Nazism also. . . . They were victims as surely as the victims in the concentration camps." The President's effort to relativize the role of *Waffen SS* troops triggered new cries of outrage, resulting in a White House declaration that Reagan would also pay homage at the Bergen-Belsen concentration camp. On April 20th, Bundestag-Member Alfred Dregger (floor leader of the CDU) wrote to Senator Howard Metzenbaum (co-initiator of the U.S. petition) that efforts to force a cancellation amounted to an "insult to my brother and his fallen comrades." Dregger himself had served from 1939–1945, rising to the level of batallion commander in the *Wehrmacht*. Five days later, 257 members of U.S. House of Representatives sent a letter urging the Chancellor to release Reagan from his promise to visit Bitburg; their action paralleled a motion submitted to a Bundestag vote by the Greens (rejected 398 to 24). On April 26th, the U.S. Senate accepted a resolution with 85 co-sponsors exhorting Reagan to reconsider. Two days later the *New York Times* revealed that the SS-soldiers buried at Bitburg had been members of *Das Reich*, the Second SS Tank division responsible for one of the worst civilian massacres of WWII: the slaying of 642 French villagers in Oradour-sur-Glane in 1942. By a vote of 390 to 26, the House passed a second resolution urging Reagan to alter his cemetery plans.

On May 5, 1985, the 40th anniversary of the war's end, both Reagan and Kohl placed wreaths and offered a short address at Bergen-Belsen, followed by a stop at the Kolmeshöhe site and a presidential speech at the nearby Air Force Base. The day was marked by protest demonstrations at the camp and graveyard sites. Reagan's remarks at Bergen-Belsen bore witness to his own selective remembrance of history: "Here lie the people—Jews—whose death was inflicted for no reason other than their very existence"; he failed to mention the 50,000 Soviet prisoners of war who had been among the first to perish in the camp. Both leaders sought to personalize the suffering at the site with references to Anne Frank, who died there shortly before the camp's liberation. On June 13, 1985, the Bundestag approved the *Law against Auschwitz Lies*, rendering it a criminal offense for anyone to deny the authenticity of atrocities committed under the Nazi regime. One day later Helmut Kohl became the first Chancellor since Adenauer to attend a reunion of ethnic Germans expelled from Silesia after unconditional surrender, suggesting support for their demands for a return of the Eastern territories.

This incident illustrates the paradoxical nature of assertions by Kohl and other officials that postwar Germans have mastered the lessons of history and thus deserve to be treated as a "normal" state in the community of nations. Neighbors and allies would like to believe that Germans are now capable of engaging in peaceful pursuit of their national interests, and that they have indeed become "better" or "tamed," to cite Schwarz.[16] As ambivalent foreign reactions to the events of 1989/90 testified, however, the "house-broken" Germans are still suspected of wanting something greater than mere self-determination. Honolka has argued that

> either our neighbors cannot imagine that the Germans have, in fact, thrown all feelings of national pride overboard, based on their own thoughts and feelings; or they must believe that the nationalism-deficit of FRG-citizens will one day lead to a great compensatory need that, because of its fatal tendency towards "all-or-nothing" thinking, will be something to fear. . . . When Polish children play war they still set themselves up as Poles against the Germans, and no one wants to belong to the German side.[17]

Hence, the paradoxical lesson of history, the acceptance of which might augur a "return to normalcy" among the postwar generations, is that the Germans have never been normal. The existence of a single, stable, peace-loving German nation-state has constituted the exception rather than the rule in European historical experience; one of my discussion partners even insisted that the pattern of the last two centuries mirrors a "national" affliction reaching as far back as the era of Walther von der Vogelweide (1170–1230)! The starting point of all efforts to strengthen Federal Republican identity, without posing a threat to the security of its neighbors,

> has to be a working-through of the German past in the sense of an affective as well as a cognitive exposition. . . . This does not mean [we need] to run around in sackcloth and ashes but rather to preserve the memory of the truth about the Holocaust, no search for alternative exits out of the national identity as in Bitburg or through the claim that one was born late.[18]

In other words, West Germany's commitment to rehabilitation and reconciliation vis-à-vis its European neighbors cannot be reduced to a question of birthdate or the mere replacement of one generation of leaders by another.

Knowledge is but one prerequisite linked to an effective, persuasive processing of the past. The facts at one's disposal must further be subjected to critical interpretation, an activity that still raises the hackles of many German analysts, even among scholars too young to have accumulated their data first-hand. The so-called *Historians' Controversy* of 1986–1987 signified much more than a bonfire of the social scientific vanities in the FRG. It all began with an effort by historians Ernst Nolte, Andreas Hillgruber and Michael Stürmer, inter alia, to place the Third Reich experience in a "world-historical" context dominated by centuries of wars and massacres. At the height of the controversy, critical theorist Jürgen Habermas accused the protagonists of relating to the past in a manner analogous to an atomic energy plant "for whose radioactive wastes one has found no permanent method or disposal site, risking dangerous complications based on temporary dumping and storage."[19] At its best, the *Historikerstreit* amounted to a serious if misguided effort to assess the import of the Nazi period on the evolution of the historical sciences in postwar Germany. At its worst, it sought to relativize the atrocities of the fascist era in a way that seemed to sanction a "moral decommissioning" of national responsibility. A resurgence of neo-Nazi orientations among younger cohorts since 1990 raises the question as to whether some of the most important historical memories have actually been "stored" at all; further processing has yet to occur.

Personal Attitudes Towards Vergangenheitsbewältigung

A number of surveys conducted prior to unity indicated that young West-Germans' knowledge of the Holocaust era was very uneven in quality—or lacking altogether in some quarters. There was also evidence of a growing information-gap regarding critical turning points in the FRG's own short-lived history. In order to determine what role historical consciousness plays in the structuring of postwar FRG-identity, we must look for answers to three important questions: First, what fundamental changes in attitude towards past personalities and events had taken root in the Western Republic between 1949 and 1989? Secondly, how substantial was the perceived need for additional knowledge about the Nazi period prior to unification? Thirdly, what are the most salient lessons conveyed by the past, as perceived by average citizens?

The desire to be considered a good German is linked to a broad spectrum of instrumental needs and relationships. My treatment of historical consciousness can only highlight questions of greatest relevance and focus on the direction of attitudinal change among average citizens.[20] The most dramatic shift in orientations rests with the more or less consistent break with Hitler across all age groups. Between 1953 and 1967, citizens of the new Republic were asked at regular intervals whether or not they might be willing "to vote for or against a man like Hitler." The number of persons opposed rose from 67% in

1953 to a high of 86% in 1961; four-fifths of all age groups, women and men, rejected such a figure between 1958 and 1961, leveling out at 83% in 1967. The creation of the Berlin Wall does not appear to have affected basic orientations; the 1960s did see a curious rise in those claiming to have "no opinion," however [for reasons considered below].

Survey data such as these provide little insight as to respondents' actual knowledge about the Third Reich era. One can understand, at least in part, why average citizens might desire to repress all thoughts of the war and get on with their lives immediately after 1945. The death of loved ones, material scarcities, the loss of one's job through denazification, all seemed "punishment enough" for the common people; most preferred to see themselves as the victims, not as the accomplices of fascism. Blaming Hitler and maintaining collective silence were two easily adopted methods of "coping with the past," at least in the short run. As comprehensible as this avoidance-strategy may seem at the level of individual consciousness, it provides no substitute for collective atonement, nor does it ensure a fundamental change in those attitudes or beliefs which laid the foundation for Nazi attrocities. The latter required a long term response along preventative, institutional lines. The Occupational Powers ordered an infusion of democratic principles via the school system, known as political re-education, though the hierarchical, stratified educational structures of the pre-war era remained more or less intact.[21] It was the exceptional family, the real school of the nation, which confronted its past head-on and imparted a sense of personal responsibility, at a time when former Nazi-party members were reestablishing themselves as political leaders and architects of an Economic Miracle to come. Among the "rehabilitated" figures were Federal-President Karl Carstens (NSDAP, with SS ties), jurist Hans Globke (one of the authors of the Nuremburg Race Laws), and Baden-Württemburg's Minister-President Hans Filbinger (Nazi Marine judge).

The traditional tendency to reject manners and peoples classified as non-German found its most abominable expression in the mass extermination of the Jews, which is not to forget the Poles, Slavs, Communists, homosexuals, and other so-called *Untermenschen* [subhumans] who perished under the Nazi reign of terror. Collective qua public anti-semitism has clearly become a thing of the past, even if this has not precluded occasional, scandalous outbursts on the part on individuals and right-wing minority groups.[22] Occupation-era polls executed in August 1949 and December 1952 found no steady pattern (in contast to the rejection of Hitler) regarding individuals' "general attitude towards the Jews." Some 41% expressed tolerance for Jews at the time of the FRG's founding, falling to 23% in 1952; 23% supported anti-semitic views in 1949, a figure which rose to 34% in 1952; 15%–18% said they had "reservations." Asked whether anti-semitism had increased or decreased in Germany as a whole since 1945, 32% of those polled perceived an overall reduction in 1949, a view held by only 24% in 1952.[23]

The picture improved dramatically by 1960, when EMNID reported that 79% rejected and denounced anti-semitic expressions in general.[24] Minimal voter affinity for the right-wing NPD (4.3 % in 1969), triggered by the first postwar recession of 1966/67, proved quite short-lived. Asked in 1981 whether one would consider a joke involving the extermination of the Jews "very bad," "rather bad" or "not worth mentioning," a total of 78% opted for the first two responses. Younger cohorts were more inclined to judge such utterances "very bad:" 56% among 14–19 year olds, and 52% among those aged 20–29, versus 45% among respondents between 50 and 64. Women exceeded men by 10% in rejecting such disparaging references.[25]

Somewhat paradoxically, generational proximity to or distance from key historical personalities and events may heighten sensitivity to causal factors while also eroding the very sense of collective responsibility necessary to persuade the FRG's neighbors that Germans have changed forever. The real question for postwar citizens should not be "how much is enough?" but rather which specific displays of sensitivity and responsibility will best serve to assuage outsiders' resurgent fears.

The tension between West Germany's sensitivity to and responsibility for the past was reflected, for example, in the debate concerning the statute of limitations for the prosecution of Nazi criminals. In one poll conducted at the close of 1978, only 34% favored the ongoing pursuit and prosecution of all crimes committed under the Third Reich; 64% held that it was time "to draw a line under the past" by allowing the statute to expire. Respondents under 30 were more inclined to advocate continuing prosecution; higher levels of education also contributed modestly to this trend. Repeated in 1979, the same questions produced a noticeable shift in support: 50% favored a lifting of statutory limits to permit further prosecutions, 46% preferred a break with the past (see Table 2.1).

How can we explain this shift? One answer rests with the first airing of the American made-for-TV-film, *Holocaust*, in 1979. The question whether or not to broadcast this program in West Germany led to vociferous debates and even to assaults on transmitting facilities, especially in Bavaria. As witnessed by this author, the public's response—in the form of thousands of telephone calls to panels of psychologists, historians and politicians immediately following each segment—was highly emotional, compounded with widespread disbelief. Its impact was tremendous if temporary, despite attempts by far-left critics to disqualify the program as a typical example of American *schmalz*, and despite right-wing efforts to deny the film's veracity based on its inaccurate presentation of military insignia and other minutiae. Among those who had actually watched *Holocaust*, 60% favored a continuation of prosecution, 39% opposed the extension; only 34% of the non-viewers polled saw the need for further legal activity, with 63% arguing against.[26]

Knowledge about Nazi atrocities, conveyed in terms of their human consequences is clearly a critical factor in heightening public sensitivity to the

TABLE 2.1   Statute of Limitations for Prosecution of Nazi Crimes

1978[a]	Total %	M %	F %	Age					Educational Level			
				14–19	20–29	30–49	50–64	65+	Grade School	Elementary with Vocational Training	Middle School	Abi, University
"NS crimes should be pursued further"	34	38	30	38	39	32	34	28	30	34	37	38
"One should now draw a line under the past"	64	60	68	57	61	65	64	69	69	64	60	61
No answer	2	3	1	4	1	2	2	3	2	2	3	1

1979[b]	Total	M	F	14–19	20–29	30–49	50–64	65+	Grade Sch.	Ele. Voc. Trg.	Mid. Sch.	Abi, Univ.
"Pursue further"	50	51	49	42	53	55	44	47	45	52	52	50
"Line under the past"	46	43	49	49	45	41	52	52	50	46	44	45
No answer	4	5	2	8	2	5	3	1	5	3	4	5

[a] Emnid-Information, Nr. 11/12, 1978, 30. Jg
[b] Emnid-Information, Nr. 1, 1979, 31. Jg.

lessons of history. A February 1983 survey found higher rates of support for further prosecution among the younger and more highly educated respondents.[27] Unfortunately, much of the information available to adolescents has been packaged in abstract, quantified terms (millions of deaths) for the historical record, which does little to foster the sense of personal reponsibility or civic courage needed to preclude a recurrence.

Public officials will naturally be called upon more often than average citizens to prove that the Germans have done their historical homework. That it is possible to achieve an effective balance between sensitivity and responsibility was best demonstrated by Federal-President Richard von Weizsäcker (born in 1920), in an eloquent Bundestag address commemorating the fortieth anniversary of the war's end. Distributed in manuscript and record-album form, the speech he delivered on May 8, 1985 (the same day as Kohl's Bitburg visit) was most compelling in its efforts to embrace *all* of fascism's victims. In the President's own words,

> We commemorate especially the six million Jews, who were murdered in German concentrations camps . . . all people who have suffered in war, above all the unspeakable numbers of citizens in the Soviet Union and in Poland, who lost their lives . . . the murdered Sinti and Roma, the homosexuals killed, the mentally ill put to death, the people who had to die for their religious or political convictions . . . the resisters among the labor force, in the unions, the resistance of Communists. . . . Perhaps the largest burden, loaded upon humankind was borne by the women: world history forgets their suffering, their self-sacrifice and their quiet strength.[28]

Von Weizsäcker bore witness to the historical uniqueness of Holocaust atrocities, stressing the need for collective remembrance. More importantly, his reflections coupled a recognition of public responsibility with a sense of personal remorse, the very quality many of the FRG's neighbors have found lacking in its otherwise acceptable efforts to portray itself as a normal postwar state. By contrast, the first resolution issued by the democratically elected East German parliament on April 12, 1990 expressed feelings of "sadness and shame"; it also asked forgiveness of many peoples, ranging from the Israelis, to the Soviets (WWI and WWII), to the Czechs (1968).

The overwhelmingly positive response to von Weizsäcker's cathartic "sermon" at home and abroad was echoed in the interview responses collected by this author in 1985/86. Questioned first about their general familiarity with the May 8th speech, interview partners were asked whether they "felt personally addressed or affected" by its contents. They were then urged to comment on what they found to be particularly positive or negative about the speech.

Individuals classified as members of the Turn-Around Generation were clearly less personally moved, more "matter of fact" about the speech and its message than older respondents. For younger respondents, its importance rested with the idea that this was a "value-conservative" head of state giving public voice to "what should be the basic consensus," and "should have been said in 1970." Some expressed disappointment that the President did not go far enough in exposing the root causes of fascism, citing the need for a recognition of guilt, but not an obsession with it.

Representatives of the middle or Long March Generation tended to respond immediately to the second question, signaling, perhaps, a degree of emotional distance from the talk which did not detract from praise for its "positive, balanced synthesis," as well as for its differentiated treatment of guilt and responsibility. Most noted the deeper respect conveyed towards *all* of Hitler's victims and inferred the need to undertake a more active processing of the past, as one pillar of a public consensus "that ought to be taken for granted." While von Weizsäcker was seen to contribute to a "new standard for political discussion in the FRG," many were skeptical about a "moral breakthrough" among hardline CDU/CSU officials. Poignantly summarizing the impact of the speech, one peace activist declared: "Richard von Weizsäcker makes it easier for me to feel like a German" (Eva Quistorp).

The degree of "personal affectedness" was unquestionably highest among Economic Miracle Generation respondents, a number of whom used the phrase "spoke out of my own heart." Others identified von Weizsäcker's position with their own religious convictions. Cited among the most positive elements were its attempt to embrace all victims, the President's moral tone and his "peace-orientation" towards the future. Critical voices from identifiable conservatives stressed dissatisfaction with the speech's "narrow" or "German" content; one observed that "1933 is not comprehensible without 1919," another faulted the talk for not sufficiently implicating "the other dictatorship" [the GDR]. For the rest, however, von Weizsäcker's eulogy thus far stands "as the best speech delivered in Germany since the war's end" (Marion Gräfin von Dönhoff).

Just how quickly the fragile balance between personal sensitivity and collective responsibility can be destroyed (albeit unintentionally) is illustrated by the outcome of a comparable address to the Bundestag, delivered on November 10, 1988. In a speech marking the fiftieth anniversary of the 1938 anti-Jewish progroms known as *Kristallnacht* [Night of the Broken Glass], parliamentary President Philipp Jenninger (born in 1932) attempted to create an understanding for the conditions and times which had generated mass support for Hitler's regime. His remarks conveyed the unfortunate impression that the Germans themselves had been the hapless victims of the era, to the righteous indignation of many (SPD/Green) MdBs who walked out of the assembly prior to its conclusion. The difference between the two addresses rested not so much with their substantive emphases but rather with the second speaker's alleged effort to relativize the sufferings of fascism's countless targets by declaring that Germans, too, had been victimized. Negative domestic and foreign reactions to the speech compelled Jen-niger to resign his post as Bundestag-President the next day.[29]

Sensitivity to the darker side of German history among the younger gener-ations is a function of two factors, namely, the amount of information individ-uals have at their disposal, and the manner in which it has been transmitted. The general consensus, reflected in both surveys and interviews, is that there is still much educating to be done among Germans now decades removed from the war experience. Asked in 1960 whether FRG-children were learning enough about developments under Hitler and after the war, 44% of 1,000 parents with school-aged children responded "too little," 28% "enough" and 3% "too much," while 25% (!) had "no opinion." Responses among parents whose children were destined for schools beyond the elementary or voca-tional level were 50%, 39%, 2% and 9%, respectively. Questioned as to whether children were receiving "the right picture" with regard to those years, 62% replied no proper picture was being conveyed, 15% saw the picture as correct, 2% thought it only partially correct, and 21% voiced no opinion.[30]

A 1975 poll (pre-*Holocaust* airing) put the question in broader terms: participants were asked whether they agreed with the idea "that it is not necessary [today] to familiarize young people in school with the historical past of the Germans." A majority among all age groups (53% total) claimed instruction was still necessary, 10% said it was not, and 37% gave no answer; 38% judged the need for "historical consciousness among youth" more im-portant than the need "to learn from the past" (29%) or the belief that Ger-mans "had nothing to hide" (6%).[31]

Among my own 1985 sample, representatives of the three generations did agree, for the most part, on the need for further "processing of the past," al-though opinions varied with respect to questions of "what" and "how." Very striking was the polarization among the youngest cohorts, stemming from a German tendency to place "too much" or "too little" emphasis on the topic. For some, history as taught at school had ended in 1933—al-though their teachers commonly claimed that they simply ran out of time in light of other curricular obligations. More adventurous students had pur-sued developments related to Weimar and the Third Reich as their final ex-amination [*Abitur*] topics, while others insisted they had heard about the Nazi period "to the bursting point." In one case, the "end of history" and "saturation" experiences were recounted by students in Bonn who had actu-ally attended the same secondary school.

As to "what could be done," younger citizens overwhelmingly disap-proved of the decision that had allowed former Nazis to return to promi-nent positions after 1949. The majority expressed an interest in learning more about the psychological dimensions of fascism ("How could they have done that?"). Many held that the use of oral history, e.g., school visits by former concentration-camp internees or resistance fighters, would prove much more effective than anonymous photos or emotionally overpowering trips to the camps themselves. They saw the media as problematic, citing the sensationalistic quality of most WWII-movies which failed to elaborate on the human as well as the geo-political consequences of war. About half subsequently admitted that they did not know the text to the national anthem, with its infamous *Deutschland, Deutschland über alles* verse.[32]

Respondents born between 1941 and 1959 were conscious of their anomalous position between the fathers and mothers who had been directly involved in the war, and grandchildren far removed from the experience. They looked to the broader context, referring to the deflective character of postwar anti-communism, or to the need to highlight democratic traditions, such as the labor movement, without "picking all of the raisins out of history." Given the social-sciences boom of the Student Movement era, it is not surprising that members of the second generation called for new textbooks, better pedagogical methods, progressive educational policies, intensified scientific pursuit of Holocaust themes, and differentiated media coverage. "Ending national broadcasting every night with the national hymn as a sleeping pill is a step backwards," Quistorp declared [a practice introduced in 1985]. Institutional treatment of the topic was rated as largely inadequate; many Long Marchers stressed a need for youth exchanges, and class-trips to concentration camps— albeit with extensive preparation, coupled with parental involvement in the discussion. Positions varied regarding the appropriate age of exposure, some suggesting 10, but most allowing for intensified study at 15–16 years of age. Left-of-center respondents mentioned the need to compensate all war victims (e.g., forced laborers) as well as to cultivate positive role models (such as resistance fighters). They advocated discussions comparing developments of the Nazi era with resurgent hostility towards foreigners in the 1980s.

The reactions of those more directly connected to the travesty of the past, namely, cohorts born prior to 1941, were more "partisan" in character, especially in reference to how much responsibility ought to be attributed to Germans alone. Self-identified conservatives desired a wider historical context, stressing that the GDR needed to assume "its share" of the guilt burden. The same group pointed to "the other twelve" countries, including Poland, who had not digested their own past, and urged me to consider the price that had been "paid" in relation to German refugees and borders. Social-liberal members of this generation openly rejected policies requiring memorization of all three verses of the national anthem in the schools, a "ludicrous," "painfully embarrassing," and "regressive" strategy for instilling historical consciousness among youth. They linked a processing of the past to the (East and West) Germans' future responsibility for disarmament and common security. Consciousness-raising, they recognized, had to be linked to social behavior, admittedly something that could only be achieved "milimeter by milimeter."

One empirical analysis of secondary school curricula, executed by Long Marchers Hopf, Nevermann and Schmidt, confirms the perception of many

TABLE 2.2   Time Devoted to the Study of the Weimar and National Socialist Eras, Grades 11–13 [Sekundarstufe II] in Northrhein-Westphalia and Schleswig-Holstein

I. Number of Months Devoted to Basic Courses *[Grundkurs]*

Time Spent:	Up to 3 months	Up to 4 months	Up to 5 months	Up to 6 months	More than 6 months	Total
Location:						
NRW urban area	0	0	1	1	4	6
NRW rural region	0	1	1	0	2	4
SH urban area	4	0	1	2	1	8
SH rural region	4	1	1	0	0	6
Total Schools	8	2	4	3	7	24

II. Number of Months Devoted to Advanced Courses *[Leistungskurs]*

Time Spent:	Up to 3 months	Up to 4 months	Up to 5 months	Up to 6 months	More than 6 months	Total
Location:						
NRW urban areas	0	0	3	0	1	4
NRW rural region	0	1	2	1	0	4
SH urban area	1	1	2	0	0	4
SH rural region	4	0	1	2	0	7
Total Schools	5	2	8	3	1	19

Source: Christel Hopf, Knut Nevermann, Ingrid Schmidt, *Wie kamen die National-sozialisten an die Macht? Eine empirische Analyse von Deutungen im Unterricht* (Frankfurt/New York: Campus Verlag), pp. 28–29.

discussion partners that the formal transmission of information about the Third Reich is fraught with inadequacies.[33] Based on a 1980–81 survey of history teachers and school directors in Northrhine-Westphalia and Schleswig-Holstein, their project set out to compare the interpretation(s) of Nazi-era developments presented in state-sanctioned textbooks and curricular plans. Key themes included the emergence of totalitarianism, the role of specific institutions (industry, church, military), the treatment of resistance, and anti-semitism. One noteworthy finding of the study was the limited amount of time officially devoted to the Weimar and National Socialist eras at the senior high-school level, shown in Table 2.2. Each Land is free to set its own curricular requirements, though the general standard is fourteen mandatory hours and seven optional hours on "National Socialism and World War II," out of one hundred total hours of historical instruction.

The researchers discovered a high degree of polarization between the critics of right-versus-left totalitarianism, a reluctance to dwell on the role of industry and the church (aside from "resistance" efforts), and a narrow focus on Holocaust atrocities (rather than on the deeper cultural roots of anti-semitism). One factor contributing to the tunnel-vision perspectives found at the secondary level was the degree of state-ministerial control over textbook selection and lesson-planning, highly partisan processes in and of themselves.

The social-psychological impact of revelations about the Nazi period is far from uniform, suggesting that *how* one has been exposed to it is as important as *what* one knows. Two works compiled by Peter Sichrovsky link family specifics to general orientations about the past, one dealing with the children of Hitler's Jewish victims, the other depicting children "born guilty" by virtue of their Nazi parents.[34] The second study, in particular, offers a wide range of emotional reactions among persons between the ages of 19 and 43. Two strains prevail throughout the interviews: first, either parents refused to talk about their experiences in detail, or they talked about them constantly; secondly, the successors perceived themselves (and usually their parents) as "victims" rather than as evil-doers. A central dilemma for the offspring in talking with or about Jews was that it denied them their own "victim" status, that is, as individuals who had lost a parent or faced other recriminations after the Nuremburg trials.

Sichrovsky's profiles highlight the psychological double-bind afflicting many born after the war. Affective bonds to parents had been forged prior to a cognitive recognition of their past political involvements: "The first shock came when I learned about what had happened . . . the second when I learned that my father had participated in it," according to *Anna, the Proper One*, born in 1947.[35] Families maintained much of their authoritarian character for those born through the 1940s and 1950s (who would later instigate the "anti-authoritarian education" campaign in the 1960s). For many, the only escape was to leave home; such escapes were physical at best.

Three citations cover the spectrum of emotions, from conscious denial, to cautious acceptance, to active responsibility, reflected in interviews with Nazi offspring. Completely disassociating herself from the past is *Stefanie, the Proud One*, born in 1967:

> I've had enough, enough that it is only we the Germans who were the evil ones. That we always have to be reminded. What does it mean—we started the war, gassed the Jews, destroyed Russia. I wasn't the one, damn it. And no one out of my class, and none of my friends and certainly not even my father. . . . What do they still want from me? No one can convince me it is shameful to be German. That time is past. . . . I don't like the Greens. With them there can't be any new pride.[36]

Anxious to move beyond the past is *Jonathan, the Innocent One*, born in 1948:

> It is no longer a question as to whether the past can be overcome or lives on. . . . Who wants to orient oneself permanently to the past? We Germans have many more important tasks today. Let us visit the yester-year in museums

here and there, a part of historical instruction. It should not be allowed to take away our strength for the present and for the future, for we will need all of our energies to protect Germany from a new demise.[37]

Relying heavily on the past to secure a peaceful future is *Werner, the Transmitter,* born in 1946:

> A son of the guilty, a father of the innocent. It is my task to give the innocent ones a chance. The guilty ones had theirs. My generation is the one with the guilty conscience. . . . The different destinies in my family are also typical for Germany of the 20th century. One grandfather who fell in the first world war, a second who became a Communist, a father who makes his career with the SS and denounces his own stepfather. The son sees his own role model in the Communist and becomes a leftist by conviction. These leaps are most improbable, however . . . a symbol that there has always been "another" Germany.[38]

Two autobiographical books by Niklas Frank and Renate Finchk, respectively, provide even more detailed insight into the complex dynamics of parent-children ties after 1933. Frank presents a very embittered, rather abusive exposition of his father, Hans Frank, former Reich-Minister for the Uniformity of Justice and also Governor-General of occupied Poland. The purpose of Frank's anti-memoire is to record the countless times his father might have sided with the "good" Germans in denouncing Nazi atrocities. Instead, Frank the elder adheres to a rather shallow vision of "what it means to be German," resulting in a remorseless death by hanging after his 1946 conviction at Nuremberg.[39] Finchk, on the other hand, reconstructs her experiences as a leader in Hitler's *Bund Deutsche Mädel*, in the hopes of explaining her situational motives, her late awakening, and her sense of contrite responsibility towards her own eight childen. Unlike Frank's testimony which ends in self-destructive isolation, Finchk looks for self-comprehension as a first step towards German re-identification and reconciliation.[40]

West Germans who have made no effort to come to terms with the ignominious past are, fortunately, the exception to the rule, especially among politically active citizens of the first and second generations. Fundamental changes in attitudes towards the past shared by postwar cohorts do not, however, automatically result in common conclusions about the future significance of the German nation.

Symbols, Nationhood, and Nationality

The 1970s found the Federal Republic in active pursuit of political rehabilitation vis-à-vis its once victimized European neighbors by way of the Eastern Treaties. The 1980s, by contrast, stand out as a decade of sometimes overly ambitious reconciliation with its own national-historical symbols. The wisdom of ages suggests that "no state can function without national symbols. Symbols are needed in order to bear witness to the presence or power of the state: On the borders through a delineation of sovereignty, in public agencies relying on the use of seals, or on celebratory occasions, through [use of] the anthem and the flag."[41] Intended to evoke an affective or "sentimental" attachment to the state, the reappearance of such symbols on the German political stage does not in and of itself signify a rebirth of nationalism of the old type—nor a genuine "conquering of the past."

The resurgent interest in national symbols coincided with and was indeed propelled by the Conservatives' return to political power in 1982. The search for positive sources of emotional identification with the nation might also be viewed as a partial response to the 1979 TV-broadcast of *Holocaust*. Dissatisfied with the American portrayal of the Nazi years (but hardly in a position to refute it), the West German media countered with several docu-drama series of their own, including *Heimat* (ARD), *Deutsche Geschichte*, a seven-part portrayal of *Rekonstruktionen* (ZDF), and last but not least, the schmalzier *Schwarzwald-Klinik* (a German version of *St. Elsewhere* with *Dallas* undertones). The printed media followed suit, initiating the published speaker series *Talking about One's own Country* and commissioning two multi-volume studies on pre- and postwar German history.[42]

The "questions addressed to German history" were not limited to the years 1933–45 but also looked to the nineteenth century legacy of militarism which had laid the foundation for ultra-nationalism after 1918.[43] Proposed by SPD-Mayor Dietrich Stobbe in 1977, the Gropius Building in Berlin housed an exhibition (sensational at the time) from August to November 1981 under the title *Prussia—In Search of a Balance*. Not to be outdone by Social Democrats (long considered *vaterlandslose Gesellen*) in efforts to appropriate the national cause, the new Kohl Government announced its own plan to establish two permanent sites promoting national consciousness in 1983, namely, the German Historical Museum in Berlin and the House of History in Bonn. Questions regarding their location and content quickly triggered a highly intellectualized, revisionist debate, affording, in retrospect, a prototype of the Historians' Controversy of 1987.[44]

Despite the strident, partisan character of these debates, the FRG public began to open itself to a kind of "creeping patriotism" with regard to national symbols. As early as 1965, citizens enjoying the first fruits of the Economic Miracle were asked about their preferences concerning the most appropriate symbol for their country. Of the total sample, 45% chose "the eagle," 26% favored the black-red-gold flag, and 2% opted for the national anthem; 14% of the men and 29% of the women gave no answer.[45] A further move towards self-recognition was inherent in the name they accorded to the homeland. When asked in 1974 which label ought to be used by radio, TV and newspapers, 57% (total) chose *Bundesrepublik Deutschland*, as opposed to 22% for "Germany" and 9% for "the FRG." There were discernible age differences: 63% of the respondents aged 16–29 preferred the Federal Republic, 13% selected Germany; for citizens 60 and older, the figures were 53% and 32% respectively.[46]

It is ironic, yet also "typically German," that a country that had become so politically stable and economically successful had yet to identify with a holiday commemorating its positive postwar experience by the late 1980s. With the exception of significant anniversary years (e.g., its 40th "Founders' Day" in 1989), the date marking the promulgation of the postwar constitution has been little noted by average citizens. Both May 8th (the surrender of 1945) and June 17th (the East German uprising of 1953) seemed to figure more prominently than May 23rd (1949) in public memory, though the interpretations of those dates were also subject to dispute. Old versus new patriots debating such issues were divided as to whether the date of German capitulation ought to be viewed as a day of *Befreiung* [liberation] or *Besetzung* [occupation]. Citizens were polled in 1985 as to whether they observed the 8th of May as "a day of joy" or as "a day of mourning." The sample was evenly split between the first two options (16% and 16%), while an astounding 66% felt that one should take no special note of the occasion.[47] Conservatives refused to let the debate die as late as 1995; they organized a manifesto in time for the 50th anniversary of the war's end, emphasizing May 8th as a day of *Vertreibung* [forced expulsion from the East] as well.

June 17th, the so-called Day of German Unity, memorialized the workers' rebellion in the GDR which led to a direct intervention by Soviet troops in 1953. Asked in 1964 as to how this day might best be recollected, 38% of the respondents favored a "work-free" day devoted to commemorative programs (40–46% for age groups under 30, 34–36% for those over 30). Another 35% preferred a work-free day left open to "self-determined" activities; only 16% supported commemorative services at school or one's place of employment.[48] The suspicion that "not going to work" might have been the key selling point (West Germans already enjoy the world's most generous vacation benefits) was laid to rest by a 1982 survey, however: when asked whether June 17th should be abandoned as a special holiday in favor of an extra vacation day, 67% favored its retention.[49]

In a curious twist of fate, the soon-to-be-united Germans were unable to discover a positively shared national holiday—at long last—in the night the Wall came tumbling down in 1989. November 9th marks the abdication of the Prussian Kaiser Wilhelm II and Karl Liebknecht's proclamation of the new (socialist) Republic, thus terminating the first World War in 1918; in this respect it could have been developed to reinforce the collective desire for a New European Peace Order. Unfortunately, November 9th is also entrenched in historical memory as the date of Hitler's unsuccessful *Bierhaus-Putsch* in 1923 and the infamous *Kristallnacht* of 1938. Promulgation of a new, all-German constitution is unlikely, leaving only the anti-climactic day when formal political unity was achieved, October 3, 1990.

Another indicator of creeping patriotism is reflected in changing attitudes towards the national hymn, *das Deutschlandlied,* penned by Hoffmann von Fallersleben to the tune of Joseph Hayden's *God save Franz the Kaiser* in 1841. While less than a third of the citizens polled in 1976 thought the hymn ought to be played at the close of each radio programming day, 55% approved its daily airing on television, initiated in 1985.[50] Support for broadcasting is not to be equated with knowledge of its current text, however. The official version is limited to the third verse, stressing *Einigkeit und Recht und Freiheit* [Unity and Justice and Freedom]; it specifically excludes the stanza *Deutschland, Deutschland über alles,* reminiscent of Third Reich abuses. A 1962 survey revealed that only 32% of those questioned knew the correct first line, in contrast to 46% who began with *Deutschland, Deutschland. . . .* The share of right answers rose to 42% in 1977, with 24% unable to offer any cue-line at all.[51] In 1985, the Federal Center for Political Education began to distribute recordings of the anthem free of charge to schools. Educational Minister Mayer-Vorfeld (CDU) provoked a hefty debate across state and party lines by requiring the children of Baden-Württemberg to memorize all three verses prior to graduation from secondary school. Meanwhile, the proportion of citizens who expressed a sense of "happiness" in viewing the black-red-gold of the federal flag rose from 23% in 1951, to 40% in 1972, to 47% by 1981.[52]

The reintroduction of national symbols has met with more indifference than active enthusiasm in the FRG. Older residents express concern about foreign reactions to the symbolic entrappings of the past; younger citizens taking part in international exchanges admit they still "feel funny" about intoning national folksongs as casually as their U.S.-American or French counterparts.[53] Flag-waving remains the province of conservative or right-wing groups, despite an exceptional display of national harmony on November 9, 1989—the day *all* members of the Bundestag rose to sing the national anthem (third verse only) when the opening of the Berlin Wall was announced to the plenum. Ironically, Kohl's own attempt to lead the crowd in singing the Western anthem in front of the Brandenburg Gate the next day resulted in a massive chorus of boos, owing to thousands of GDR citizens among the crowd who had not begun to consider the possibility of rapid unification.

Prior to the momentous events of 1989, FRG-citizens might well have been classified as post-national in orientation.[54] They continued to count Goethe (25%), Bismarck (30%) and Schiller (13%) among the "great Germans," although Adenauer (42%) had moved into the lead by 1983.[55] Toni Schumacher, Steffi Graf and Boris Becker, sports idols who would have undoubtedly attracted a larger share of the youth vote, were not included among the standardized survey options. Postwar citizens are now less reserved about expressing pride in many things German: their classical writers (71%); the beautiful landscape (71%); Beethoven and other composers (63%); the technical achievements of German industry and science (59%); the social security system (55%), and even the German work ethic (52%).[56] Most are satisfied with their own living conditions and, prior to 1989, they anticipated positive, personal futures.[57] Yet all things considered, a majority of FRG citizens still find it hard to admit that they are, unequivocally, proud to be German.

The average FRG-citizen associates *Heimat* not with the historical nation-lost but rather with birthplace, family and friends. The belief that "the word Fatherland . . . has a nice sound" correlates negatively with age; the younger the respondent, the less the term "fits into" the current political landscape.[58] By the mid-1980s, a growing segment of the population nonetheless accepted the idea that national feeling and national consciousness "are something one should have nowadays," including a majority of those under the age of 30.[59]

This trend naturally raises the question, why does one need a national consciousness, in general? Among members of the Economic Miracle Generation, there was a stronger proclivity among female respondents to question the need for any national feelings at all. The women in my sample held that the concept was historically tainted [*stark angeknackst*], though intricately connected with language and culture. They found it typical, albeit unnatural, that little such consciousness seemed to exist in the FRG; two out of eight noted, however, that they could just as easily live in England. The men of the war/reconstruction era (ten out of twelve), seemed to confirm Gilligan's findings on socialized gender-differences; they emphasized "national interests" and the right to identity as a matter of principle, that is, as an "ordering factor" as well as an instrument of politics.[60]

Orientations among interviewees from the Long March Generation were less divided along gender lines yet generally more negative. Few would view their national roots as a framework for the future; more important, in their judgment, was the need to emphasize the "human" dimension and constitutional values. One could "live anywhere in the world," albeit with a measure of "international consciousness" (views voiced by SPD and Green sympathizers, especially). CDU-affiliates linked national consciousness with a "willingness to sacrifice" or to become otherwise actively engaged in establishing the rule of law [*Rechtsstaat*].

My youngest interview partners in 1985 were decisively negative regarding the need for an explicitly national consciousness. They associated the term with "a subordination to power," "something sick without content," and viewed it as a trait "that was distant . . . which Germans cannot exhibit." A majority found it most strange that this consciousness, which evolves at "the emotional, irrational level" (as they saw it), is supposed to make collective-cultural sense and provide a concrete basis for self-definition.

The next question I posed, "why does one need a German identity, in particular?" led many first-generation respondents to focus on dimensions of state consciousness. Constitutional consciousness alone could not fill a perceived emotional vacuum, nor stimulate democratic involvement in "institutions one had not struggled for oneself." The German component implied an "inter-connectedness" to the GDR, albeit under "many different skins." One person remarked that with national consciousness reduced to a minimum, it might be necessary to forge state-consciousness with ethnic-consciousness [*Volksbewußtsein*]—a prescient observation in light of post—1991 developments-in order to arrive at an FRG consciousness per se. The fine lines drawn between these various forms of consciousness are difficult to comprehend for those of us who have been spared the fate of a divided homeland. For Germans, however, they remain critical distinctions.

Distance and discomfiture were the prevailing reactions to this particular question among the middle cohorts. Their "late births" notwithstanding, some members of this group reported that they had encountered serious "problems" in foreign countries by virtue of their being German, e.g., in England, Denmark and the Netherlands. Others recognized they could not deny their being German, despite gaps in their own political education or despite a deliberate tendency to rely on "Western identity . . . as a crutch."

My discussions with members of the Turn-Around Generation yielded similarly vague definitions of identity and even fewer clear statements as to why they might "need" to cultivate one that was specifically German. One peace activist noted that her sole concession to German identity "was to fly only with Lufthansa because it does not crash" (Mechthild Jansen). Prescriptions regarding its future contents revolved around the acceptance of constitutional values, renunciation of the use of force, greater tolerance and support for "grass roots" democracy.

The opening of the Berlin Wall produced real emotional confusion on the part of many postwar citizens who had already concluded that "provisional" division was permanent. Neither the tears, the champagne toasts, nor even the sudden realization that one is different yet somehow the same can automatically give birth to a shared national consciousness. The effects of forty years of estrangement and demarcation will manifest themselves in "the little things"—"the devil is in the details," as they say. In the long run, commonality is a necessary but not a sufficient condition for the (re)creation of national identity. Even if West Germans had not abandoned all hopes for re-securing the unified nation-state, they were quite surprised to find themselves realizing that vision in 1990 [we examine their views on re-unification in Chapter 3].

It is highly unlikely that the newly united Germans will now pursue nationalism as it is conventionally understood. Postwar citizenship is rooted in a commitment to democratic values, first, and nationality, second: that is, to unity in freedom, not at its expense. The inability to forge an inter-generational consensus on what it means to be "German" persists, the consequences of which are not always positive. If postwar citizens are ostensibly reluctant to pursue new forms of national consciousness and identity, then what has become of the stereotypical virtues once ascribed to them? Do West Germans still characterize themselves as disciplined, orderly, punctual and duty-conscious? Are they still perceived as such? Let us probe more deeply into the personality-structure of Federal Republicans.

Character Traits and the West German *Weltanschauung*

I recall my first trip to Dresden in August 1986 with my friend Koko (born in 1952), who picked me up at the West Berlin border on her way from Hamburg. We were both a little nervous as we approached the first checkpoint, and the guards were indeed suspicious of the DM 200 (about $140) worth of "exotic" foods we had loaded in the trunk, ranging from fresh artichokes to Swabian *Maultaschen*. They poked every item thoroughly, having gleaned from our visas that we "were not cooks by profession." Even more unsettling was the stern admonition my friend received for having neglected to sign the back-side of her entry paper. "What an undisciplined state-citizen [*Staatsbürgerin*] you are," the guard observed gruffly, before waving us through the final Zarrentin barrier. Usually a very talkative person, Koko shifted gears and remained silent for fifteen minutes, finally bursting out, "but I don't *want* to be a disciplined state-citizen!" That line became the leitmotif of our eight-day trip through the "other" Germany.

Koko is admittedly a little more free-spirited than most West Germans I have met since 1971; she spent two years in Australia and rejected civil-service tenure for many years, afraid it might make her "dependent"—yet her *Weltanschauung* is typical of her peers. She spends as many vacation days as possible out of the country, as does Wally in Stuttgart and Eddi in Berlin, looking for "a place in the sun." She has a moderate interest in politics but strong political opinions. She is self-confident and can communicate well in one or more foreign languages; she alternates between peppered criticisms of my country and her own, depending on the latest news developments. She does not find it easy to be a German, even though she usually fits my image of a trendy, post-postwar, grassroots-feminist Federal Republican to a "T." She reads profiles collected by Sichrovsky with great interest and would undoubtedly find it difficult to answer Janssen-Jurreit's point-blank question, "Do you love Germany?"

Asked about their personal attachment to the nation in the early 1980s, a wide variety of public figures found it almost impossible to provide a straight answer to Janssen-Jurreit's query:

> No/ Do you think I'm a necrophiliac?/ I only love a relationship/ . . . as I love my destiny/ . . . perhaps, somehow . . . / Love? Which Germany? /I love Karstadt. Something to fear . . . / I have no country./ What else can I do?/ Hate-love/ . . . Germany as duty/ . . . repulsed by national borders/ . . . a little

/Yes, I love this land, although I'm never certain about my own feelings./ Explain love . . . / Whales are cosmopolitan.

As the spectrum of reactions suggests, countless FRG citizens have yet to overcome their ambivalent "feelings" towards the homeland. Unequivocal professions of love-for-country are the exception, not the rule; many would prefer to avoid the question altogether. More typical are the cautious sentiments expressed by two publicists. One is Marlies Menge, born in 1934, who has served as the East-Germany correspondent for *Die Zeit* since 1978:

> First the problem, can I really love a whole country? . . . I can love a man, my children, friends, maybe my dog—but a whole country at once? . . . Perhaps [love of country] is something a human needs in order to live somehow: one's home, one's language, one's poets, maybe even, but here I am hesitating again, one's national role models. If I really love this land, then I love it above all for its weaknesses. Its internal strife, its wounds touch me, they affect me personally. And perhaps that is not the worst reason to love a country.[61]

The second is Dieter Wellershoff, a free-lance journalist, author and editor for a major publishing house, who was born in 1925:

> I was born and raised as a German. Now I am a citizen of the Federal Republic of Germany, that is how my passport identifies me. This labelling makes me feel strange. It has about the same emotional propulsion-power as the General German Automobile Club, an association in which the word "German" appears like burnt-out cinder, already cold and without further energy. I am a member of the General German Automobile Club and a citizen of the Federal Republic of Germany. . . . To me it sounds like I am talking about my membership in an association to which I belong without passion or deeper involvement. I support the organization's statute, I pay my dues, I quickly peruse its newsletters to orient myself to club-life, I participate regularly in the election of its executive and other organs, I occasionally voice my opinion about controversial questions, I know to appreciate the advantages I enjoy as a member, and I am therefore prepared to give the club my critical loyalty and support. I think that's a lot, because one can live with it. It is nevertheless an association of interests, not an association based on feelings, as the French have for France, the English for England. . . . For trips abroad I stick a "D" for *Deutschland* on my auto-body. But these self-gluing stickers adhere poorly and keep falling off.[62]

Neither of these two respondents would question the need for an instrumental attachment to the system. Yet the lack of *emotional* attachment provides a source of relief for some and evokes a sense of nostalgic (albeit passive) longing among others.

Viewed historically, there is something typically German about this asymmetrical attachment to the national ideal. In 1810, Madame de Stael portrayed the Germans in the following terms:

There is no great love of fatherland in a Reich that has been divided for several centuries, where Germans have gone to the battlefield against Germans, usually in response to forces from outside; the desire for fame lacks vitality where a center, a national capital and comraderie are lacking. . . . The political and societal possessions of the people: the same government, the same religious services, the same laws, the same interests, a classical literature, a prevailing opinion; the Germans find they have none of these. As a result, every state is certainly more independent, every science better developed; but the nation as a whole disintegrates into such subcomponents that no one knows to which part of the Reich one should affix the name Nation.[63]

Perhaps the residual, instrumental attachment has historically outweighed one's longing for that which is missing. Their passion for exotic travel notwithstanding, fewer than 10% of the West Germans desire to emigrate in search of a more encompassing national feeling.[64]

Many of the personality traits stereotypically ascribed to Germans are no longer a part of the self-image projected by citizens of the old FRG, beginning with "punctuality." The university convention of beginning classes fifteen minutes after the hour (*cum tempore*) has permeated the consciousness of all too many of my generational counterparts. They are usually delayed well beyond the point of fashionableness by their search for a parking place which, in turn, results in the creative vehicular occupation of inner-city sidewalk space, whether in Berlin, Hamburg or Stuttgart. Most Bundesbahn trains continue to operate with reassuring temporal efficiency, however. The pervasiveness of up-to-the-minute fashions, especially among younger citizens, indicates that consumerism has replaced "thriftiness"—even among the Swabians, whose *Ländle* generated over DM 29 billion in domestic Mercedes and Porsche sales in 1988. Their rejection of "fast food" (except for *Würste* and *pommes frites*, consumed at unsheltered street-stands) has been replaced by runs on McDonalds, Pizza Hut, and *döner kabob* carry-out windows–thanks to the presence of enterprising guestworkers; it often seems that the internationalization of FRG cuisine has done more to open the German mind to foreign cultures than many a canned speech on "tolerance."

Survey data attest to a shift away from the orderly, hierarchical mentality of earlier decades. Citizens of all ages classify the virtues of yester-year [*deutsche Tugende*] among the more annoying, negative traits still evinced by Germans; few seek to instill such qualities in their children. Less than one-fifth emphasized obedience by 1975, while more than half valued independence and freewill among their offspring. Affluence has also allowed West Germans to place less emphasis on their own "industriousness," though they do preach the need for such vis-à-vis the newly enfranchised Easterners. The proportion of those assessing themselves as diligent or *arbeitsam* fell from 72% in 1952, to 66% in 1970 to 46% in 1979, rising again to 68% in 1981. Military valor is definitely "out," having plummeted from 7% in 1952 to 1% by 1970.[65]

Fading notions of order, discipline, duty and hierarchy notwithstanding, adults continue to transmit a sense of cultural pessimism to their generational successors. The widely cited Shell studies published in 1981 and 1985 portrayed the Turn-Around Generation as having internalized a global-catastrophe-is-pending mindset even more dire than that manifested by adults. By the mid-1980s, 74% thought that technology and chemistry would destroy the world, 70% held that unemployment would continue to grow, and 39% believed that the world would end in an atomic war; girls were more pessimistic than boys.[66] Who could blame these younger cohorts for failing to project an optimistic outlook in a land where major sociological studies have branded them the Superfluous Generation, the Fractured Generation, the Insecure Generation, the Narcissist Generation, the No Future- and Don't-give-a-damn Generation?[67]

Germans believe that their negative character traits still render them "unloved in the world," even if "the hard currency they bring in" has opened many doors abroad.[68] When pushed to reveal which typically-German character traits they consider especially positive or negative, most of my interview partners reacted with embarrassed laughter. Positive traits cited by older discussants included: reliability, their romantic or enlightenment leanings, persistence of debates "of a higher order," and a new openness to foreign culture, especially to France; some noted their critical orientations towards the state. Negatively valued were bureaucratic "over-efficiency," cultural pessimism, traces of political irrationalism/emotionalism, a pervasive sense of arrogance, superiority, and egocentrism. One noted sardonically that her fellow-citizens had actually become so "terribly American."

The Long March discussants were more reluctant to admit the collective existence of typical traits, although it was noted that one "speaks about them constantly" or sees them reflected in one's own behavior. Viewed positively was the Germans' historical sensitivity, and their increased consciousness involving a special responsibility for peace. Most replied in negative terms, stressing dogmatic or absolutist proclivities: conformism, factionalism, an unwillingness to compromise, petty-bourgeois tastes [*spiessig!*], and authority hang-ups of various types [*Untertanengeist, Obrigkeitstick*]. Members of the Turn-Around Generation also focused heavily on negative qualities: extremism, lack of pragmatism, hostility towards experimentation, absolutist thinking, over-emotionalism, coldness, unfriendliness. On the positive side of the ledger stood their respect for nature and their *Bierseligkeit* [beer-drinking bliss, a term that augurs new problems with the rise of right-extremism].

In short, the self-image of Federal Republicans has largely divorced itself from historical stereotypes. For Krippendorf, "the Germans are no longer that which they once and allegedly always were: hard-working, duty-conscious, true to authority, obedient, disciplined and, also no longer nationally conscious, militaristic and culturally overbearing." Even their language, he notes, has become "more flexible, creative, full of fantasy, unruly"–although the recognition that *Tschörman is' aut* meets with less enthusiasm in other quarters.[69] Roth describes the new German as "self-confident, modest, obliging him/herself faithfully to ethically motivated tasks"; he insists the number of "good Germans" would be even greater "if only there existed better communication among the Germans themselves."[70]

While many West Germans are still attuned, collectively speaking, to a world-view grounded in *Weltschmerz* and skepticism, most are anxious to cast their individual destinies in an ever more positive light. As Peisl and Mohler write, "the Federal Republic is a country in a bad mood, but its residents are happy and satisfied."[71] Noelle-Neumann and Köcher claim that the contradiction between individually optimistic and collectively pessimistic assessments of the future has rendered the FRG more open to social change than all of its European neighbors.[72] While the asymmetry seems quite normal to Germans, it is precisely this contradiction that confuses outside observers, reinforcing fears that an unpredictable outburst of collective ill-will might occur at some future date. There is little West Germans can do to lay these fears to rest, to the extent that these gloom-and-doom notions are the very instruments upon which they rely in order to monitor their own behavior and to hold their own self-righteousness in check. A better empirical measure of profound changes in the German character rests with the citizenry's stable attachment to democratic institutions and constitutional freedoms.

Political Interests and Institutional Loyalty

By the early 1960s more than two-thirds of the public agreed that the present offered the best situation ever experienced by Germans in the twentieth century. Very few evinced a willingness to trade living standards or high wages for a chance to count among the nations of "world importance in 30 years." "Good health" was their pre-eminent New Year's wish, consistently registered from 1961 to 1984, while peace and freedom ranked second [pollsters have an annoying habit of treating such items as mutually exclusive].

State, administration and society are no longer perceived to comprise an organic whole among citizens of the postwar Republic. The principle of the *Rechtsstaat* [state of law] has been reinterpreted since 1949, the new emphasis falling on the preeminence of law as an expression of citizens' rights over the reification of state interests. As is true of all democracies, the German government must appeal to a pyramid of citizen groups; in addition to a broad base of non-active, "silent majority" types, it faces alternating strata of moderately interested conformists, participatory reformists, full-time activists, added to a small but sharply critical bloc of radical protesters and even terrorists. The Western distinction between the state, on the one hand,

and civil society, on the other, owes to sweeping political re-education measures initiated after 1945, as well as to increasing levels of citizen participation in diverse "extra-parliamentary" campaigns since the 1960s. The evolution of civil society (at the expense of unquestioning loyalty to the state) has resulted in a new emphasis on self-actualization, especially among the post-materialist cohorts. Ironically, Western Germans have come to expect many things from their state, yet they tend to believe they owe it very little (see Chapter 5 on military conscription). These distinctions have yet to be understood, much less internalized, by newly incorporated Eastern Germans.

The segment of West Germans expressing an interest in politics rose from 27% in 1952, to 45% in 1969, to 56% in 1979.[73] Political interest among younger citizens has been stimulated by higher levels of education and veritable "living room" exposure to many sensational political developments of the past decade (TV reports on terrorist acts, massive peace demonstrations, the breaching of the Wall, etc.). In the early 1980s, the antics of the Green Party brought a "breath of fresh air" to what had become a staid but passionless parliamentary system; they also served to enfranchise groups which might have otherwise "dropped out" or gone underground.

Some 74% of those under 19 and 58% of the 20–29 year olds welcomed the Greens' entry into the Bundestag in 1983, a move opposed by 67% aged 50–64, and 79% among those over 65.[74] In addition to placing new and increasingly popular issues on the political agenda, the Greens often raised the quality of debate within the Bundestag itself, through their impressive command of environmental and military data as well as through their active assault on political scams such as the Flick Affair. In contrast to complaints of the early 1960s that West Germany remained a "subject culture," many critics of the 1980s inferred that younger cohorts had become too radically democratic in their participatory orientations!

In terms of succession politics, Bonn's coalitions have proved to be more durable and long-lived than is true of most West European states since 1945. FRG citizens witnessed only one genuine constructive vote of confidence (against Brandt in 1971), one staged vote (against Schmidt in 1982), and six complete changes of government in forty years; Kohl's tenure in office has already surpassed that of *every* European-democratic leader since WWII. The most pressing tasks ascribed to elected officials since 1950 have consistently revolved around the themes of full employment, price stability, expanding pensions and social services, and securing the peace. Environmental protection was added to the list after 1979. Asked to choose which form of government they "judge best for the Germans"—democracy, monarchy, or a return to an authoritarian regime—an overwhelming majority has regularly voiced its support for the liberal-democratic order since 1953.

The Federal Republic also evinces a high degree of consensus regarding the characteristics deemed most fundamental in securing effective democ-

racy. Citizens accord highest priority to freedom, followed by popular sovereignty, justice and tolerance of political opposition. Prior to unity, most
were self-confident about their ability to induce the state to change its
course when necessary, by using national elections to compel an improvement in relations with the East after 1969, for example. A 1984 survey
found 82.1% "very" or "sooner satisfied" with democracy as then manifested within FRG borders; approval rates ranged from 61–67% among the
youngest respondents, to 70–76% among those over 30.[75]

Trust in their own democratic institutions had risen commensurately. The
institution enjoying the highest measure of respect and approval during the
1980s was the Federal Constitutional Court, seen as the ultimate preserver
of individual rights and freedoms. Expressions of trust registered in the 80+
percentile across all age groups (an assessment tarnished by the Court's May
1993 ruling on abortion reform). The 1984 rankings provided one curious
exception: those 60 and older rated the police slightly higher than the
Court. The elderly were also the only group to place more faith in the
Church than in other juridical and parliamentary organs. The *Bundeswehr*
enjoys considerably less confidence among citizens under 40, while the media appear to inspire very limited trust, irrespective of age.[76]

The mid-1970s gave rise to concerns over mounting political alienation
or disinterest among FRG youth, ironically following complaints of the
1960s regarding the politicization of schools and universities. In reality, the
period 1979–1984 marks a particularly colorful and creative, though admittedly chaotic phase of political development in the postwar republic, largely
owing to youth activism. Among the young participants in the punk-, squatters'-, anarcho-, ecology-, peace- and autonomous-feminist movements, the
radical soon became the routine. "Happenings," demos and citizen-initia-
tives took precedence over ballot-box politics, in part because many of the
political newcomers had been exposed to unconventional forms of participation through TV or siblings years before they were old enough to vote. No
longer considered newsworthy by 1989, the "alternative cultures" which as-
sorbed many would-be rowdies and dropouts continue to flourish in major
cities and university towns.[77] Younger citizens' affiliation with the Greens is
often more philosophical than active-political in character, according to the
motto "Eat green, vote red, and work on the black market!" For all their ostensible rowdiness, the causes around which youth rallied during the 1960s,
1970s and 1980s were very much in the spirit of deepening and widening
the democratic process—in stark contrast to adolescent mobilizations of the
1990s (see Chapter 7).

Anxious public officials commissioned a variety of studies on youth
protest, including a major parliamentary inquiry whose findings were widely
publicized in 1983. To the consternation of the new Kohl Government, the
Enquette Commission attributed the phenomenon of *Politikverdrossenheit*

[political vexation] not to "the kids" themselves but to the system's failure to provide effective remedies for problems these cohorts judged to be most pressing, ranging from overcrowded universities, youth unemployment, acid-rain and environmental destruction, to nuclear proliferation and a shortage of low-cost housing. The report concluded: "a political order which, because of a lack of opportunities for identification with it, is not seen as being worth defending, finds itself in a crisis of legitimacy."[78] Government-commissioned studies painted a more "normal" profile of young citizens in the 1980s, testifying to the inherently political character of sampling techniques and question formulation.

West German youth prior to 1989 were more politically conscious than their USA-counterparts, and thus more easily mobilized. Young Germans often attack "the state" as the source of their discontent because they recognize it as a key provider of goods and services in the social-market economy. This particular feature of FRG political culture contrasts starkly with American notions of rugged individualism and that government-is-best-which-governs-least. Like youth everywhere, however, German adolescents were primarily interested in rock music, intimate relationships, travel, sports and "self-actualization" during the last decade. Post-1960s cohorts usually offset their global "gloom and doom" proclivities with a personal sense of humor ["We have no chance, but we'll use it"], a rare trait among "beer-earnest" older cohorts. Prior to 1989 they seemed much more tolerant of *Andersdenkende* ["those who think differently"], even if their only exposure to Rosa Luxemburg came through the cinema. Even more striking evidence of value-change among German youth is reflected in their attitudes towards rights and protests, considered next.

Fundamental Freedoms and Legitimate Protest

Beyond their generalized acceptance of the free-democratic basic order, post-war generations west of the Wall have developed a strong consensus regarding the specific freedoms needed to sustain that order. The campaigns against rearmament and nuclear deployment (1950s), against executive national-emergency powers (1968), and the opposition to career-bans against radicals (1972), in retrospect, were attempts to test the limits of popular sovereignty and freedom of association in the FRG. The Constitutional Court has thus far proscribed the use of plebiscites over questions of military deployment, and it still allows public agencies to deny jobs to citizens whose posture vis-à-vis the state is "disinterested, cool, internally distant." Neither protest activity nor membership in constitutionally-suspect organizations are sufficient conditions for a so-called *Berufsverbot* or career-ban, however.[79]

Citizen support for freedom has emerged as the preeminent characteristic of West German democracy since 1949. An earlier emphasis on freedom from need (26% in 1949) was overtaken by the public's growing stress on freedom of political expression (44%–58%) between 1958 and 1977.[80] War experiences, along with limited incomes resulting from retirement, contribute to older citizens' support for freedom from need, but even the youngest cohorts expect their government to provide a modicum of economic security by way of the social-market economy. Significantly less emphasis on government by the people through the 1970s lends itself to three possible interpretations: either postwar Germans have learned to define democracy primarily in terms of individual rights; or they remain skeptical regarding the ability of "public servants" to act in the best interests of all citizens; or they embody both tendencies. Since the 1970s their "understanding of democracy" has broadened to incorporate the principles of gender equality and human rights, with some 40% even open to the idea of a separate Women's Party as of 1979.

Public tolerance of radical factions prior to 1989 was subject to a measure of Right-Left differentiation, invoking different degrees of sensitivity among the three generations and suggesting that each has derived different lessons from its familiarity with national history. By 1977, the post-1950s cohorts were almost twice as willing to allow communist party members to hold public service jobs as were respondents born prior to 1930.[81] Younger citizens, most likely to be affected by the Radical Ordinance against leftists, were quick to point to the state's "blindness in the right eye," owing to its toleration of far-right teachers in public schools. Their suspicion found some confirmation in a major "social-empirical investigation of extremism" commissioned by the Interior Ministry and published by Infratest in 1980. Drawing upon a random sample of 4,008 participants (aged 16–50) spread across eight Länder, the researchers focused exclusively on left-extremism, except for their two-page discussion of "the Left-Right continuum."[82]

Compared to older cohorts who were particularly troubled by disturbances of the social order, younger residents seemed more concerned about the terroristic orientations of neo-Nazi groups. Yet a clear majority at both ends of the age spectrum expressed anxiety over a growing penchant for violence during the early 1980s. In a survey of 1,019 conducted March 11–25, 1981, respondents under 30 were almost evenly split among those who considered right- or left-wing radicalism more dangerous (11% vs 10% for those under 19, 12% versus 13% for the ages 20–29). When the same question was put to another group of 1,011 in November/December, 25% of those under 19 strongly opposed the Right, while only 2% indicated greater fear of the Left; 20–29 year olds remained evenly divided.[83] The intervening period was in fact marked by a wave of neo-Nazi incidents; membership in right-extremist organizations rose from 17,300 in 1979 to 20,300 by 1981.[84] A number of sensationalized trials against members of the leftist Red Army Faction during the same interval also contributed to mixed sympathy among younger groups. While the two studies showed that citizens over 30 were more fearful of the Left, a majority of all survey participants perceived "both as dangerous to the democratic order." One can conclude that younger as well as older West German citizens are aware of differences between the two brands of extremism. Most would prefer to see no groups active at the extreme ends of the political spectrum but are loathe to eradicate them at the cost of restricting the right to free political expression.

One very striking aspect of postwar political development has been the dramatic change in attitudes towards the legitimacy and effectiveness of unconventional forms of participation, including protest. The 1950s campaigns against rearmament and NATO nuclear deployments derived their support largely from intellectuals, church activists and militant trade unionists, as did the Anti-Emergency Law protests of 1968; all three mobilizations failed to achieve their objectives. The aims of the student movement, by contrast, were too diffuse—and usually too esoteric—to secure widespread public support, particularly once violence penetrated its fringes after June 2, 1967 (the German "Kent State"). The mobilizations of the 1970s assumed an altogether different quality, having been initiated largely at the grassroots level. The physical proximity of many a pending ecological crisis allowed these campaigns to attract a motley crew of supporters, ranging from pastors to housewives to punks. Joined by university-linked *Sponti* (spontaneous) elements, these activists eschewed the influences of major organizations like unions, in favor of do-it-yourself strategies and an emphasis on personal networks.

Issue "proximity," inherent in the concept *Betroffenheit* [personal affectedness], became a particularly critical variable in securing popular acceptance of the later movements. Given the nation's role in World War II, questions pertaining to military deployment were considered "taboo" by most of the population through the 1960s. A clear majority (59%) sympathized with a few student protests, e.g., against increases in ticket prices for public transportation in 1967, no doubt because they felt more affected by "low politics" of this sort than by the "high politics" of NATO. Only one-fourth believed that student protests involving more elitist issues, such as radical free-speech, the anti-Vietnam crusade and overcrowded university conditions, were justified between 1966–68.[85] Another decade would pass before the links between nuclear deployments, nuclear-energy waste and the quality of one's own environment became obvious to the population at large as a matter of "local politics."

The pervasive influence of the media was not the only factor that awakened members of the silent majority to conditions in their own backyards. The expansion of the educational system after 1965 coincided, for better or worse, with the West German Baby Boom, infusing the political landscape with a numerically significant, better informed, and critically energetic bloc of new voters. Many took literally Willy Brandt's inaugural challenge to "Dare more democracy!" following the Social Democrats' first electoral victory and consolidation, 1969–1972. Once they jettisoned the highly factionalized ideological baggage of the Student Movement days, second and third generation activists succeeded in forging an overarching issue-consensus among disparate groups, becoming more self-confident, pragmatic and efficacious in the process.

Between 1976 and 1978 the proportion of the population recognizing the political effectiveness—"very often," or "now and then"—of the newly established *Bürgerinitiativen* [Citizen Initiatives or BIs] rose from roughly one-half to two-thirds. By 1981, a clear majority of young adults polled by EMNID admitted their general willingness to participate in such a group; in fact, almost twice as many said they would sooner work with a *BI* than with a "sympathetic" political party. The segment of those over 50 who declared that they were personally prepared to join an initiative grew from 19% to 31% between 1981 and 1983.[86]

According to peace movement activists I have interviewed, the public's willingness to engage in unconventional protest behavior—missile-site occupations, human chains, unofficial "people's referenda"—has tended to rise and fall with the perceived imminence of the "threat" to the home environment. Data from Mannheim affirm this trend, reflecting a slight decrease in public support for a variety of protest activities from 1984 (after the Pershing II/GLCM deployments) to 1986 (onset of Gorbachev's *New Thinking*). As Table 2.3 shows, Long-March and Turn-Around cohorts are those most willing to engage in all forms of direct political action; higher levels of education also correlate positively with an openness to more radical tactics. The activist orientations of well-educated youth may be doubly reinforced, through feelings of "affectedness" as well as through enhanced self-confidence and "know-how." Individuals who are 35 and older, on the other hand, encounter certain life-cycle effects; the need to protect and provide for one's family is likely to inhibit adult participation in activities leading to arrest, loss of job or potential physical injury.

The "bottom line" for most would-be protestors continues to rest with the possible application of physical force. From 1978 to 1981, less than 10% of the West German population accepted the use of force against people and property as a means of achieving important political objectives. Fewer than 20% were open to violence against objects (e.g., state property), compared to two-thirds who opposed the application of any type of force; differences between age groups at the time were minimal.[87] Other persuasive evidence of the Germans' postwar desire to renounce force as a political instrument rests with a more mundane example: close to 80% of the persons polled in 1980 said they would welcome a ban on the sale of war-related toys for children, as already legislated in Sweden.[88]

TABLE 2.3   Willingness to Engage in Types of Direct Action, 1984

	Total	Age						Education Level				Men	Women
		-24	-29	-39	-49	-59	60+	Elementary, No Apprenticeship	Elementary Apprenticed	Middle & HigherSchool	Abitur and University		
Collecting Petition Signatures													
Certainly	41.1	62.8	58.0	48.1	38.9	37.4	24.9	27.7	38.5	47.6	62.8	43.5	39.5
Maybe	39.5	31.0	32.6	36.6	39.6	44.3	44.7	40.6	43.2	37.7	25.5	40.3	38.8
Definitely not	19.1	5.9	9.4	14.4	21.0	18.3	30.3	31.8	18.1	14.1	10.8	16.3	21.5
Political Demonstrations													
Certainly	13.7	33.0	22.3	15.3	11.1	6.2	5.1	6.2	11.0	16.0	30.4	15.7	11.2
Maybe	24.7	37.2	35.3	33.9	24.8	20.3	12.3	13.5	25.4	29.2	33.0	27.5	22.4
Definitely not	61.8	29.5	42.1	50.3	64.1	73.1	82.6	80.3	63.6	54.3	36.3	56.6	66.3
Boycott													
Certainly	6.9	14.4	9.8	8.7	6.4	5.4	2.4	2.9	6.6	6.7	16.9	7.8	6.1
Maybe	21.0	35.6	30.7	24.1	18.6	18.3	12.2	12.1	18.0	27.8	33.9	22.7	19.6
Definitely not	71.9	49.7	59.5	66.6	74.7	76.2	85.3	85.0	75.1	65.3	48.9	69.4	74.0
Demonstration with Force													
Certainly	0.9	2.0	2.7	1.1	0.4	0.6	0.1	0.0	0.7	0.9	3.2	1.0	0.8
Maybe	5.8	21.1	10.9	5.9	2.4	1.3	1.6	3.9	3.6	5.9	18.9	7.2	4.6
Definitely not	93.1	76.6	86.4	92.5	97.1	98.1	98.1	96.1	95.5	92.8	77.5	91.8	96.3
Damage Military Property													
Certainly	0.3	0.6	1.4	0.5	0.2	0.0	0.0	0.0	0.3	0.3	0.9	0.4	0.2
Maybe	1.8	5.0	4.5	1.0	1.1	0.9	0.8	0.4	1.5	2.4	4.3	2.1	1.6
Definitely not	97.6	94.1	94.1	97.7	98.5	99.1	99.1	99.5	97.9	97.1	94.5	97.3	98.0
Damage Public Property													
Certainly	0.2	0.4	1.4	0.0	0.0	0.0	0.2	0.0	0.2	0.2	0.9	0.3	0.2
Maybe	1.3	4.2	1.9	1.3	0.5	0.5	0.7	0.2	1.4	1.7	1.9	1.7	0.9
Definitely not	98.2	94.6	96.7	97.8	99.4	99.3	99.1	99.5	98.1	97.7	96.9	97.9	98.4

Withhold Taxes

Certainly	2.9	8.2	4.5	3.6	1.9	0.5	1.5	1.6	3.4	2.0	6.1	3.9	2.0
Maybe	17.7	28.0	26.1	25.3	17.3	16.3	6.7	9.8	16.8	22.6	24.8	19.0	16.6
Definitely not	79.2	63.6	69.4	70.6	80.9	83.3	91.7	88.6	79.8	75.1	68.8	76.9	81.2

Blockade

Certainly	2.5	9.3	4.2	2.3	1.4	1.4	0.1	0.0	2.1	2.6	8.8	3.3	1.7
Maybe	10.2	23.6	14.9	13.0	9.4	5.5	3.6	7.4	8.5	12.0	18.1	10.7	9.7
Definitely not	87.1	66.8	80.9	84.2	89.3	92.6	96.2	92.5	89.2	85.5	72.7	85.8	88.3

Citizen Initiative

Certainly	24.5	47.3	35.8	31.1	20.9	19.6	11.2	11.5	22.8	31.4	40.0	27.4	22.0
Maybe	38.0	31.0	43.6	42.8	42.2	40.3	32.5	31.6	41.1	37.3	39.5	39.6	36.6
Definitely not	37.3	21.4	20.6	25.6	36.9	39.4	56.2	56.7	35.9	30.9	20.2	32.7	41.2

Source: IPOS, Mannheim, Einstellungen zu aktuellen Fragen der Innenpolitik, Question #25.

The generalized acceptance and local successes of alternative parties and Citizen Initiatives show that West Germans have not only mastered the lessons of democracy in textbook form. Millions have embraced the values of social justice, environmental consciousness, grassroots participation and non-violence. They have pushed the meaning of democracy one step further by involving themselves in policy debates to a degree unknown among their European neighbors. Paradoxically, the far-right nationalist parties (the Reps, DVU) that have emerged since unification owe much of their existence, and some of their mobilizational success, to new "spaces" in the political opportunity structure carved out by the Greens. Ecology activists were the first to convert frustration with the larger system-parties into extra-parliamentary vehicles for chipping away at tenuous electoral majorities, forcing the latter to court the fringes as much as the center (a nearly impossible task).

The problem is not that the major parties' approaches to the new national question are too diverse but that they all suffer from the same policy-paralysis. Entrenched in the bureaucratic, back-scratching practices of the past, the CDU/CSU, the SPD and the FDP have lost many of their core supporters under the rehoisted banner of *Parteiverdrossenheit;* they have been criticized by no less an insider than Richard von Weizsäcker. Some observers find a disconcerting parallel between party developments of the 1990s and the political circumstances described by Otto Spengler in 1924. The enormous pressures of unification have fed the perception that the all-German Republic is "not a form of state but a corporation. Its statute speaks not about the people but about parties. We have no more fatherland but rather parties; no rights but parties; no goal, no more future, rather the interests of parties."[89] Does the rise of new far-right parties actively promoting an older vision of *das Vaterland* mean that the Germans have come full circle?

Fears aroused by the re-emergence of radical-right groups in the now-united Germany will always be greater than anxiety generated by comparable trends in France or Britain; yet prior to 1989, no other European state reacted so allergically to the presence of extremist groups within its own borders. Nor could the FRG's neighbors boast of as many grassroots democratic initiatives actively combatting their proliferation. Even the more suspect acts initiated by the *Bundesregierung,* such as the 1972 Radical Ordinance and the 1983 plan for a less-than-anonymous public census, were intended "in theory" to reinforce the rule of law; each policy of this sort met with formidable resistance when "the practice" threatened a reduction of civil liberties. The bottom line is that outsiders' perceptions of the Germans have failed to change as fundamentally as the Federal Republicans' image of themselves.

Conclusion: The New Germans as Constitutional Patriots

Pundits, foreign and domestic, routinely question Germany's stability; thus it is not surprising that the turmoil born of unification has rekindled the perennial debate as to whether Bonn is/is not Weimar.[90] (Ironically, discomfiture over the Bundestag's decision to relocate the capital to Berlin, inviting direct comparisons with Prussia or the Third Reich, was quite subdued). Though many would-be Cassandras call upon history to legitimate their "concerns," their use of the Weimar analogy seems to be highly inappropriate, if not outright ahistorical.

The conditions responsible for the collapse of the Weimar Republic in 1933 are the antithesis of those warranting the success of the Western Republic from 1949 to 1989. The destruction of civilian life and property experienced during the second World War far exceeded the devastation of the first; it thus resulted in an immediate, more pervasive leveling of antagonistic class differences after 1945. Secondly, the uniqueness of Nazi atrocities did more to thoroughly discredit German nationalism than did the horrors of the trenches inflicted in equal measure by all nationalistic parties to WWI. Nor could any post-WWII leader have dared to refire the nationalist spirit by using the kind of "stab in the back" arguments propagated by the German Right after 1929, given the complicity of the masses under the Third Reich. Thirdly, the excessive reparations required of Germany at Versailles in 1918, coupled with the impact of the Great Depression after 1929, provided Weimar citizens with no grounds for positive identification with the fledgling democracy during the first ten years of its existence. Extreme material need and party-political chaos reinforced a search for centralized, absolutist remedies. Contrast these developments with the 1947 infusion of Marshall Fund aid, the entrepreneurial impulses unleashed by the 1948 currency reform, the CDU's extended "reign," and the rapid take-off of an Economic Miracle sustained across two decades. Material security provided substantial "positive reinforcement" for the new democratic institutions which, in turn, helped to make the economic miracle possible, as average Westerners soon realized.

Last but not least, one must consider the geo-strategic factors which contributed to Weimar's failure and conditioned the Federal Republic's success through 1989. The integrating forces of NATO and the European Community ensconced the FRG in a "family" of values and markets that has all but eliminated the search for a German *Sonderweg*, in contrast to its post-WWI isolation. Given the globally interdependent nature of its economy, the internationalized tastes and travel preferences of its citizens, and its status as a well-respected partner in regional affairs, the all-German leadership now has little to gain and much to lose by attempting to go-it alone in the name of "national interests." The post-1989 push for German unity was born of "dialectical materialism," rooted in a rapidly eroding GDR economy, a genuine democratic awakening, and long-cultivated hopes for a demilitarized European "peace" order. West German responses to unification did not derive from *nationalism* as it is conventionally and historically understood.

It is extremely difficult to assess the national identity of real people based on their responses to "representative" surveys, even though these are often the only indicators social scientists have at their disposal. Consider the question raised earlier in this chapter, as to whether Germans feel "happy" when they sight the black-red-gold of their national flag. "Happiness" is something most people associate with the way their personal or professional lives seem to be going on any given day. Aren't personal feelings of identification with one's country sooner conveyed through one's behavior as a responsible tax-paying, law-abiding, regularly-voting citizen?

In an effort to determine the importance of national feeling at the level of individual perception, I asked my interview partners point-blank: "How do things stand with your own national consciousness, with your German or Federal Republican identity? Do you *feel*, above all, like a Federal Republican, like a German, or like a European?" Many automatically chose to rank-order their identities. Three-fourths of my pre-1940 respondents identified themselves, first and foremost, as Germans, who then divided fairly evenly into the qualifying categories "in the Federal Republic" or "in Europe." The remainder characterized themselves as "European," as a *Mensch* [human being] or, in one case, as a "socialist." Members of the Long March Generation provided the most ambivalent reaction to the identity question. Some grudgingly resorted to the classification "German," owing to an inability to identify outright with either the FRG or Europe, while a second group sought refuge in regional categories, as North-Germans, Berliners or Swabians. A third set accepted citizenship in the Federal Republic as a primary reference point; still others admitted they had acquired a new awareness of their "Germanness" by virtue of personal contacts with GDR residents or through their involvement in the peace movement. Aptly summarizing the ambivalence of this generation, Wilhelm Bruns (recently deceased) labeled himself "a European as a matter of duty . . . a diffident German . . . and a citizen of the Federal Republic as an administrative-technical necessity, for passport purposes."

Responses among the post-1960 cohorts focused on "the place I was born/where I live." These individuals referred to Western Europe or saw themselves as West German citizens—a clever way of evading the deeper distinctions inherent in the original question. Because these answers were generally compiled in a group setting, there was less opportunity for younger discussants to sit back and soul-search for very long. Though the answers were diverse in and of themselves, the impression conveyed during these conversations was that it was "no big deal" to choose a self-label and move on to the next question. This impression was reinforced by seminar encounters at the universities of Frankfurt and Mannheim, where students stressed their local-patriotic affinities for Bavaria, Baden, Württemberg (same Land but very different regions, as any devoted wine-drinker knows), or Northern-Germany. The topic of German identity evoked a much livelier discussion among students in Mainz, which continued well beyond midnight at a neighborhood *Stammtisch*; the sustained interest witnessed there no doubt owes to the fact that I was the guest of Professor Werner Weidenfeld, who began focusing on the identity question in 1975.

The students' perception that I was much more passionately engaged in searching for a positive national consciousness than most Germans themselves reinforces my belief that the latter have internalized many important lessons of history. It is not yet clear whether this will also hold true for the first Post-Wall Generation. The citizens socialized in the Federal Republic prior to 1989 are not Germans who merely changed with the times: They are literally, or demographically speaking, different Germans. The majority consists of anti-authoritarian, westward-oriented individualists, consciously committed to the values of constitutional democracy; there are, however, exceptions to this rule, as demonstrated in Mölln and Solingen.

Western Germans exhibit a sense of pride in their peaceful socio-economic and technological achievements, a pride not to be equated with a sense of racial superiority derived from merely having been born "German." They have cultivated an identity of many layers to help them cope with the most painful aspects of that accident of birth. Compelled by the deep-seated, more emotional national identities of their neighbors (think of Poland and France), as well as by the anomolous existence of a second German state until 1989, they have gradually come to accept the need for some form of collective identity. They continue, however, to define their personal identification with "their" state as loosely as possible.

My own appeal to the post-postwar citizens I encountered through the 1980s echoed the sentiments of Reinhard Kühnl:

> I do not plead for lighting the fire of an ideological campaign for new Federal-Republican nationalist feelings. I am pleading, however, that the feelings described above be regarded as normal, as feelings that democrats and socialists can also possess with a clear conscience, without right away fomenting suspicions about a return of the old nationalism or even of fascist master-race conceits.[91]

Most citizens of the Federal Republic have distanced themselves from the symbols, self-perceptions and absolutist-state orientations that fueled the ultranationalism of the Nazi era. Master-race conceits are a mask worn only by those who have, regrettably, come to perceive themselves as the dispossessed in the face of so much West German affluence.

Attempts to "get on with democracy" by short-changing a confrontation with the fascist past incite as much criticism within the Federal Republic as without. Long before Westerners dared to engage in new displays of their national colors, Hans Magnus Enzensberger warned that an existential lie [*Lebenslüge*] of the first order would return to haunt the Republic: namely, the assertion of the Adenauer era that "we are all democrats." The protesters of the 1960s challenged that premise head on, leading Schweigler to report a decade later that "all criticism in (sic) our form of the state culminates in the call for *more* democracy."[92] While this tendency persisted throughout the 1980s, Habermas insists that Post-Wall developments have given rise to a second, equally worrisome existential lie. In particular, he questions the solidity of a constitutional consensus which rests on the self-serving premise that "we are 'normal' once again."[93] Though skeptical that another '68 Generation will eventually emerge in the newly enlarged Republic to dispell the second lie, the Frankfurt philosopher admits that it is "the Left and the liberal masses," not the political elites, who have taken a stand against new signs of anti-semitism and antipathy towards foreigners.

The political-cultural disruptions of the last few years are hard to digest for a citizenry now quite accustomed to governmental stability and material well-being. Who among us can define what our own reaction might be, were such a fundamental transformation of the national setting to occur on this side of the Atlantic? Unification processes have given all Germans many new grounds for criticizing "the state," but they have also brought to light another special dilemma for Western citizens. In contrast to the fledgling Weimar Republic whose collapse stemmed from the fact that it was supported by too few democrats, the Federal Republic now appears to suffer from too many democrats who have come to take certain constitutional values for granted, and hence may be hard to rally when there is no personal loss at stake. Having successfully broadened the institutional foundations of democracy, postwar citizens have engaged in sincere efforts to define what it does *not* mean to be a German. The opening of the Wall has nevertheless led to the unwitting discovery of another "democratic deficit" in their crusade to overcome the past: they have yet to master the formidable challenge of redefining citizenship as it applies to non-Germans living within their borders. Before we can wrestle with that dilemma, we must first examine the relations that used to exist between FRG-citizens and "the other Germans," at home in the GDR prior to 1989.

Notes

1. Erwin Scheuch, "Die deutsche Nation im Bewußtsein der Bevölkerung der Bundesrepublik," in Klaus Weigelt, Hg., *Heimat und Nation—Zur Geschichte und Identität der Deutschen* (Mainz: Hase & Koehler Verlag, 1984), p. 161.

2. Detlef Grieswelle, "Mangelnde Integration und extremer Nationalismus—Der politische Mythos des Nationalsozialismus als Identitätsangebot," in Weigelt, ibid., p. 97.

3. Rolf Steiniger challenges mainstream historians who discount Stalin's sincerity in offering to permit German reunification in exchange for neutralization in *Eine vertane Chance: Die Stalin-Note vom 10. März 1952 und die Wiedervereinigung* (Berlin: J. H. W. Dietz, 1985).

4. Gottfried Zieger, Boris Meissner and Dieter Blumenwitz, Hg., *Deutschland als Ganzes. Rechtliche und historische Überlegungen* (Köln: Wissenschaft und Politik, 1985); Peter von Berglar, Hans Filbinger, et al., *Deutsche Identität heute* (Weikersheim: Hase & Koehler, 1983); Josef v. Häussling, Klaus Held, et al., *Drei Fragen zu Deutschland—58 Antworten* (München: Albrecht Knaus Verlag, 1985); Karl Moersch, *Sind wir denn eine Nation? Die Deutschen und ihr Vaterland* (Bonn: Bonn Aktuell, 1982); Egon Bahr, *Was wird aus den Deutschen? Fragen und Antworten* (Reinbek: Rowohlt, 1982); Peter Petersen, *Sind wir denn noch zu retten? Der Bundestagsabgeordnete schreibt an seinen 19jährigen Sohn, der sich Sorgen um die Zukunft macht* (Stuttgart: Burg Verlag, 1984); and Günter Gaus, *Wo Deutschland liegt—Eine Ortsbestimmung* (Hamburg: Hoffmann und Campe, 1983).

5. Peter Schneider, *Der Mauerspringer* (Darmstadt: Luchterhand, 1982); Gert Heidenreich, *Die Gnade der späten Geburt* (München: Piper, 1986); Peter Brücker, *Versuch, uns und anderen die Bundesrepublik zu erklären* (Berlin: Verlag Klaus Wagenbach, 1984); Werner Weidenfeld, Hg., *Nachdenken über Deutschland* (Köln: Wissenschaft und Politik, 1985); ibid., *Ratlose Normalität—Die Deutschen auf der Suche nach sich selbst* (Osnabrück: Interfrom, 1984); J. B. Gradl, *Deutschland als Aufgabe* (Köln: Wissenschaft und Politik, 1986). Further, Wolfgang Venohr, Hg., *Die deutsche Einheit kommt bestimmt!* (Bergisch Gladbach: Gustav Lübbe Verlag, 1982); ibid., *Ohne Deutschland geht es nicht—7 Autoren zur Lage der Nation* (Drefeld: SINUS, 1985); Anton Peisl and Armin Mohler, Hg., *Die deutsche Neurose. Über die beschädigte Identität der Deutschen* (Frankfurt/M.: Ullstein, 1980); Jürgen Leinemann, *Die Angst der Deutschen. Beobachtungen zur Bewußtseinslage der Nation* (Reinbek: Rowohlt, 1982); Wilfried von Bredow, *Deutschland—Ein Provisorium?* (Berlin: W. J. Siedler Verlag, 1985); Richard von Weizsäcker, *Die deutsche Geschichte geht weiter* (München: Deutscher Taschenbuch Verlag, 1985); Dan Diner, Hg., *Ist der National-sozialismus Geschichte? Zu Historisierung und Historikerstreit* (Frankfurt/M: Fischer, 1987); and Gordon A. Craig, *The Germans* (New York: Putnam Publishing Group, 1982).

6. Helge Pross, *Was ist heute deutsch? Wertorientierung in der Bundesrepublik* (Reinbek: Rowohlt, 1982), p. 64.

7. Gebhard Schweigler, *National Consciousness in a Divided Germany* (Beverly Hills: Sage, 1975), p. 59ff, p. 183.

8. Pross, op. cit., p. 56.

9. Kurt Stapf, Wolfgang Stroebe and Klaus Jonas, *Amerikaner über Deutschland und die Deutschen—Urteile und Vorurteile* (Opladen: Westdeutscher Verlag, 1986), p. 124ff.

10. Pross, op. cit., p. 74.

11. Heinemann was cited by several contributors to Marie Louise Janssen-Jurreit's anthology, *Lieben Sie Deutschland? Gefühle zur Lage der Nation* (München: Piper, 1985), p. 9ff.

12. See Kohl's address marking the 40th anniversary of the liberation of the Bergen-Belsen camp (April 21, 1985), "The Secret of Redemption Lies in Remembrance" (Bonn: Federal Press and Information Office, translation issued 1988).

13. Peter Schneider, "Hitler's Shadow. On being a self-conscious German," *Harper's Magazine*, September 1987, p. 51.

14. In a statement published after the Bitburg visit, Kohl claimed he had notified the hosts earlier that he was "not interested in being invited." Unless otherwise indi-

cated, all Kohl citations regarding the chain of events leading up to the cemetery visit derive from a publication titled, *Remembrance. Sorrow and Reconciliation. Speeches and Declarations in Connection with the 40th Anniversary of the End of the Second World War in Europe* (Bonn: Press and Information Office of the Government of the Federal Republic of Germany, 1985).

15. This and subsequent Reagan citations stem from the chronology compiled by Geoffrey H. Hartman, *Bitburg in Moral and Political Perspective* (Bloomington: Indiana University Press, 1986).

16. Hans-Peter Schwarz, *Die gezähmten Deutschen. Von der Machtbesessenheit zur Machtvergessenheit* (Stuttgart: Deutsche Verlags-Anstalt, 1985).

17. Honolka, op. cit., p. 130, p. 149.

18. Ibid., p. 96–97.

19. Ibid., p. 47. Not a single female historian was featured among the twenty-seven participants in this debate. See *Historikerstreit. Die Dokumentation der Kontroverse um die Einzigartigkeit der national-sozialistischen Judenvernichtung* (München/Zürich: Piper, 1987). Further, Hans-Ulrich Wehler, *Entsorgung der deutschen Vergangheit? Ein polemischer Essay zum "Historikerstreit"* (München: Verlag C. H. Beck, 1988). For an American assessment, see Charles S. Maier, *The Unmasterable Past. History, Holocaust, and German National Identity* (Cambridge: Harvard University Press, 1988).

20. For a more comprehensive treatment, try Alphons Silbermann, *Sind wir Anti-Semiten? Ausmaß und Wirkung eines sozialen Vorurteils in der Bundesrepublik Deutschland* (Köln: Verlag Wissenschaft und Politik, 1982).

21. Joyce Marie Mushaben, *The State vs. the University. Juridicalization and the Politics of Higher Education at the Free University of Berlin, 1969–1979*, Dissertation, Indiana University, 1981.

22. One such case centered on the posthumous premier of Rainer Werner Fassbinder's play, *Der Müll, die Stadt und der Tod* in Frankfurt, as reported in *Der Spiegel*, Nr. 27, June 30, 1986.

23. Elisabeth Noelle and Erich Peter Neumann, *Jahrbuch der Öffentlichen Meinung, 1947–1955* (Allensbach: Verlag für Demoskopie, 1956), pp. 128–129.

24. *Emnid-Informationen*, 12. Jg., Nr. 9, March 5, 1960.

25. Ibid., 33. Jg., Nr. 11, March 1981.

26. Ibid., 31. Jg., Nr. 2, January 1979.

27. *Allensbacher Berichte*, IfO-Umfrage 4024, Nr. 10, February 11–20, 1983. Age and educational levels are related insofar as younger citizens will have benefitted from the mid-1960s campaign promoting equal educational opportunity, which is also likely to level out differences in male and female responses over time.

28. Von Weizsäcker's speech was reprinted in the May 25, 1985 edition of *Europa-Archiv*, Folge 10, D 265–272. Helmut Kohl challenged von Weizsäcker's best-selling record with a market entry of his own: under the title "What This Historic Hour Has Made Possible," the Chancellor released the album/cassette featuring his speeches on the occasions of November 28, 1989 (the "10-Point Program"), December 19, 1989 (visit to Dresden), and December 22, 1989 (opening of the Brandenburg Gate). The soundprint, "already a historical document" according to Federal Press and Information Officer Wolfgang Bergsdorf, was offered free of charge to 100,000 GDR citizens—at the cost of $90,000 to the West German taxpayers!

29. For the text of Jenninger's address, along with reactions to his resignation, see *Das Parlament*, Nr. 48, November 25, 1988.

30. *Allensbach Pressedienst*, Nr. 31, December 1960, Tables 1 and 2; *Emnid-Informationen*, 27. Jg., Nr. 6, February 1975.

31. *Emnid*, ibid.

32. As part of an alleged crackdown on terrorists in the 1970s, candidates for state teaching certification were randomly tested on their ability to recite the hymn's complete text, e.g., in Berlin and Baden-Württemburg.

33. Christel Hopf, Knut Nevermann and Ingrid Schmidt, *Wie kamen die National-Sozialisten an die Macht? Eine empirische Analyse von Deutungen im Unterricht* (Frankfurt/New York: Campus, 1985). Nevermann was a prominent student leader at the Free University in the late 1960s. For a partisan assessment, see Manfred Hättich, Hg., *Die politische Grundordnung der Bundesrepublik Deutschland in Politik—und Geschichtsbüchern* (Sankt Augustin: Konrad Adenauer Stiftung, 1985).

34. Peter Sichrovsky, *Wir wissen nicht was morgen wird, wir wissen wohl was gestern war* (Köln: Kiepenheuer & Witsch, 1985); ibid., *Schuldig geboren. Kinder aus Nazifamilien* (Köln: Kiepenheuer & Witsch, 1987).

35. *Schuldig geboren*, ibid., p. 33.

36. The characterizations *proper, proud*, etc., are Sichrovsky's. Ibid., p. 43, p. 46, p. 49.

37. Ibid., p. 59.

38. Ibid., p. 161, p. 172.

39. Niklas Frank, *Der Vater. Eine Abrechnung* (München: C. H. Bertelsmann, 1987).

40. She emphasized these points in a November 1985 interview with this author; Renate Finckh, *Mit uns zieht die neue Zeit* (Baden-Baden: Signal Verlag, 1978).

41. This is the rationale for a long-playing album on the history of the national anthem; see *Einigkeit, Recht und Freiheit. Nationale Symbole und nationale Identität* (Bonn: Bundeszentrale für politische Bildung, 1985).

42. Diether Groh, Hg., *Die Geschichte Deutschlands* (Berlin: Propyläen, 1982 and forthcoming, eight volumes in all); also, Karl-Dietrich Bracher, Theodor Eschenburg, Hg., *Die Geschichte der Bundesrepublik Deutschland 1945–1982* (Stuttgart/Wiesbaden: DVA, in cooperation with F. A. Brockhaus, 1983). Further, Hellmut Diwald, *Geschichte der Deutschen* (Ullstein: Ullstein Verlag, 1987).

43. *Fragen an die deutsche Geschichte—Ideen, Kräfte, Entscheidungen von 1800 bis zur Gegenwart. Historische Ausstellung im Reichstagsgebäude in Berlin* (Katalog), Deutscher Bundestag, Hg., Bonn: 10. Aufl., 1984. Also, *Preussen. Versuch einer Bilanz*, 15 August–15 November 1981, Gropius Bau Berlin (Reinbek: Rowohlt, 1981).

44. Geschichtswerkstatt Berlin, Hg., *Die Nation als Ausstellungsstück, Planungen, Kritik und Utopien zu den Museumsgründungen in Bonn und Berlin* (Hamburg: VSA-Verlag, 1987)

45. *Allensbacher-Berichte*, 22. Jg., Nr. 31, October 1965.

46. *Allensbacher-Berichte*, Nr. 2., August 1974.

47. Some 30% under the age of 30 could not identify the historical event associated with May 8th, as reported in *Emnid-Informationen*, 37. Jg., Nr. 5, February 1985.

48. Ibid., 16. Jg., Nr. 24, 8. June 1964.

49. Ibid., 34. Jg., Nr. 4, March/April 1982.

50. Honolka, op. cit., p. 103.

51. *Allensbacher-Berichte*, 33. Jg., August 14–19, 1976; *Allensbach Pressedienst*, Nr. 7, May 1962; and *Emnid*, 29. Jg. Nr. 2, January 1977.

52. *Allensbacher-Berichte*, 38. Jg., Nr. 23, 1981, IfD-Umfragen 040, 050, 061, 1059, 2123, 3047, 3098.

53. This was the collective sentiment of Germans I encountered during a "debriefing" session at Georgetown University on July 12, 1989 for high-school students participating in the Congress/Bundestag year-abroad exchange program.

54. Freimut Duve defines *post-national* in terms of a growing sensitivity to international problems and dependencies among postwar Germans, deriving from the fears they associate with a return to a monolithic nation-state. See "200 Jahre danach, sind wir postnational?" *Politik und Kultur*, Nr. 4, 1989, pp. 35–43.

55. *Emnid*, Nr. 5/6, May 1983; cf. *Allensbacher Berichte*, Nr. 22, 1964.

56. *Allensbach Archiv*, IfD-Umfrage 4049, September/October 1984.

57. Elisabeth Noelle-Neumann, *Die verletzte Nation. Über den Versuch der Deutschen, ihren Charakter zu ändern* (Stuttgart: Deutsche Verlags-Anstalt, 1987), pp. 31–34.

58. In 1975, only 41% of those aged 16–29 thought *Vaterland* had a nice ring to it, compared to 82% among those 60 and older; by 1981 the figures stood at 59% and 81%, respectively. *Allensbacher-Berichte*, Nr. 5, 9–21 February 1981.

59. Noelle-Neumann, op. cit., p. 36–37.

60. Female socialization purportedly leads women to emphasize "human relationships," while men are taught to stress "abstract principles" in matters of morality and justice. Carol Gilligan, *In a Different Voice: Psychological Theory and Women's Development* (Cambridge: Harvard University Press, 1982).

61. Cited in Janssen-Jurreit, op. cit, p. 281, p. 286.

62. Dieter Wellershoff, "Deutschland—Ein Schwebezustand," in Habermas, *Stichworte*, op. cit., pp. 77–79.

63. Madam Germaine de Stael, *Über Deutschland* (Frankfurt/M: Insel Verlag, 1985 ed.), pp. 34–35.

64. See Emnid and Allensbach data regarding the emigration question, 1950–1974. The number who would not leave ranged from 73% in 1950 to 90% in 1966, and 84% in 1974, as reported by Roth, op. cit., p. 69.

65. Ibid., p. 158; *Emnid-Informationen*, 31. Jg., Nr. 8, 1979, Table 9, and 33. Jg., Nr. 4, 1981, Table 9.

66. Jugendwerk der Deutschen Shell, Hg., *Jugend '81. Lebensentwürfe, Alltagskulturen, Zukunftsbilder* (Hamburg: JDS, 1981) and *Jugendliche + Erwachsene '85. Generationen im Vergleich*, Bde. 1–5 (Opladen: Leske +Budrich, 1985), pp. 116–120. Encompassing 1,472 adolescents, aged 15–24, the 1985 study reported that 47% viewed their personal futures as "sooner secure," 9% as "sooner dismal," and 44% as "mixed," p. 106ff. A federally commissioned study of 2,012 "youth" aged 15–30 preferred the glass-half-full approach: it found 50.1% optimistic about their own futures, and 57.3% satisfied with politics and societal conditions. Bundesministerium für Jugend, Familie und Gesundheit, Hg., *Die verunsicherte Generation. Jugend und Wertewandel*, Materialienband 200/1+2 zur SINUS Studie (Stuttgart/Berlin: W. Kohlhammer, 1985), Tables 81, 180, 52, 564.

67. Half of the *Jugend '85* sample characterized themselves as "the uncertain generation," 43% chose the "no future" label; 48% of the adults interviewed designated themselves "the spoiled generation," 41% used "the protest generation." Shell, ibid., Bd. 1, p. 82. Further, Claus Richter, Hg., *Die überflüssige Generation. Jugend zwischen Apathie und Aggression* (Königstein TS: Athenäum, 1979); Walter Hollstein, *Die Gegengesellschaft—Alternative Lebensformen* (Reinbek: Rowohlt, 1981); and *Die gespaltene Generation—Jugendliche zwischen Aufbruch und Anpassung* (Berlin/Bonn: J. H. W. Dietz Verlag, 1983). Also, Thomas Ziehe, *Pubertät und Narzissmus* (Frankfurt/ Köln: Athenäum, 1984); Margrit Frackmann, Hinrich Kuhls and Klaus-Dieter Luhn, *Null Bock, oder Mut zur Zukunft? Jugendliche in der Bundesrepublik* (Hamburg: VSA-Verlag, 1981).

68. Some 30% ascribed their unloved status to arrogance and ostentatiousness, 32% to recollections of the Nazi period. *Emnid-Informationen*, 34 Jg., Nr. 7, September/October 1982.

69. Cited in Roth, op., cit., p. 112. One columnist bemoaned an FRG-landscape dominated by non-German movie titles, as well as the many Americanisms which pervade domestic discourse, in "Unser Sprache. Tschörman is' aut," *Die Zeit*, Nr. 31, July 29, 1988.

70. Roth, op. cit., p. 124.

71. Peisl and Mohler, op. cit. (Ftn. 4), p. 7.

72. Noelle-Neumann and Köcher, op. cit.

73. Allensbach data, in Martin and Silvia Greifenhagen, *Ein schwieriges Vaterland. Zur politischen Kultur Deutschlands* (Frankfurt/M: Fischer Verlag, 1979), p. 340; and *Emnid*, 31. Jg., Nr. 7, 1979.

74. Reported in *Emnid, Aktueller politischer Dienst*, March 1983.

75. Compiled by the Institut für Praxisorientierte Sozialforschung (IPOS) Mannheim, "Einstellungen zu aktuellen Fragen der Innenpolitik 1984," Question #1.

76. IPOS, Question #5, repeated in 1986, Question #8. Compare the Emnid results, 34. Jg., Nr. 3, 1982, and 35. Jg., Nr. 4, 1983.

77. *Die Zeit* published a series on the up-and-coming "alternative economies" under the heading "Die Firma ohne Chef" from May through November 1982; a decade later the editors were ready to eulogize the '*68 Generation*. See Knut Nevermann, "Staatstragend—doch kritisch geblieben, *Die Zeit*, Nr. 11, 19. March 1993; and Hartmut Zwahr, "Den Maulkorb festgezurrt," *Die Zeit*, Nr. 24, 18. Juni 1993.

78. Enquete Kommission (Deutscher Bundestag), Hg., *Jugendprotest im Demokratischen Staat. Bericht und Arbeitsmaterialien* (Bonn: Bundeszentrale für politische Bildung, 1983), p. 12. Also, Joyce Marie Mushaben, "Youth Protest and the Democratic State: Reflections on the Rise of Anti-Political Culture in Prewar-Germany and The German Federal Republic," *Research in Political Sociology*, Vol. 2. (Greenwood: JAI Press, 1986), pp. 171–197; and Peter Roos, *Kaputte Gespräche. Wem nützt der Jugend-Dialog?* (Weinheim und Basel: Beltz Verlag, 1982).

79. For a look at the *Radikalenerlaß* and its impact, see Mushaben, *The State vs. The University*, op. cit., Chapter Six; Peter Frisch, *Extremistenbeschluss* (Leverkusen: Heggen Verlag, 1977); and Gerard Braunthal, *Political Loyalty and Public Service in West Germany* (Amherst: University of Massachusetts Press, 1990). In 1989/90

Bavarian officials tried to extend the 1972 ban to all former members of the Socialist Unity Party who had relocated to the FRG after the GDR's collapse.

80. *Emnid-Informationen*, 16. Jg., No. 30, 1964; ibid., 29. Jg., No. 3, 1977.

81. This poll, executed in 1977, preceded the formal creation of the Greens in 1980; *Emnid*, 29. Jg., Nr. 9, 1977; *Emnid*, 31. Jg., Nr. 11/12, 1979.

82. Infratest Wirtschaftsforschung Gmbh., Hrsg., *Politischer Protest in der Bundesrepublik Deutschland. Beiträge zur sozialempirischen Untersuchung des Extremismus* (Stuttgart/Berlin: Kohlhammer, 1980). Given the age range, it is hard to imagine that *all* participants evincing "extremist" tendencies would have been leftists. Federal officials routinely use different categories of activities in registering right-extremist and left-extremist crimes (see Chapter 7).

83. Reported in *Emnid*, Nr. 6, 1980, ibid., 33. Jg., Nr. 2/3, 1981; ibid., 34. Jg., Nr. 1/2, 1982.

84. Bundesminister des Innern, Hg., *Verfassungsschutzbericht 1984* (Bonn: Clausen & Bosse, 1985), p. 131.

85. Compare *Emnid*, 19. Jg., Nr. 2, 1967; *Emnid*, 20. Jg., Nr. 3/4, April 1968, and 21. Jg., Nr. 3., March 1969.

86. Contrast data from *Emnid*, 28. Jg., Nr. 3, 1976; ibid., 30. Jg., Nr. 7, 1978; ibid., 35. Jg., Nr. 10, 1983.

87. This survey relied on 2,100 respondents, interviewed between December 1–12, 1981, as reported in *Allensbacher Berichte*, Nr. 2, 1982.

88. *Emnid*, 32. Jg., Nr. 9/10, 1980.

89. Quoted by Volker Ulrich, "Das Weimar-Syndrom," *Die Zeit*, Nr. 28, July 16, 1993.

90. For contrasting views, see Marion Gräfin Dönhoff, "Von Weimar kann keine Rede sein," *Die Zeit*, Nr. 48, November 27, 1992; and Völker Ullrich, "Das Weimar-Syndrom," *Die Zeit*, Nr. 28, July 16, 1993.

91. Reinhard Kühnl, *Nation, Nationalismus, nationale Frage. Was ist das und was soll das?* (Köln: Pahl-Rugenstein, 1986), pp. 111–112.

92. Schweigler, op. cit., p. 193.

93. Jürgen Habermas, "Die zweite Lebenslüge der Bundesrepublik: Wir sind wieder 'normal' geworden," *Die Zeit*, Nr. 51, December 18, 1992.

3

Perceptions of the Other Germany: "Reunification Maybe, But I'd Hate to Take My Vacation There"

Ich will die Einheit nicht anders als mit Freiheit und will lieber Freiheit ohne Einheit als Einheit ohne Freiheit.

—Karl von Rottecks
Vormärz

For the citizens of the Federal Republic, November 9, 1989 stands out not only as a day of chaotic yet joyful reunion with Eastern brothers, sisters and cousins but also as one that rattled the very foundations of their own postwar identities. The events of 1989/90 caused millions of FRG residents to reflect consciously—many for the first time—on the blessings derived not only from the happy accident of *when* they were born but also *where*. Suddenly, German history as transcribed during the 20th century was no longer perceived "as a chain of stations along the wrong road, terminating in a [national-cultural] cul-de-sac."[1] Since that fateful November night, former *Bundis* and *Zonies* no longer meet in the dreary youth club sessions that were a regular feature of officially subsidized class-trips to East Berlin but rather elbow-to-elbow in discos, supermarkets and subway trains. Now that these encounters are taking place on one's home turf, normally self-confident Westerners seem a little perplexed: the Easterners they meet are strange yet familiar, not as politically savvy yet somehow more national, even more German than citizens of the old Länder themselves.

At the level of mass perception, German unification had become a non-topic by the mid-1970s, in Schweigler's view:

> most West Germans themselves never considered re-unification worthy of substantial personal sacrifices. They were not willing, for instance, to be reunified under a Communist regime, nor were they prepared to forego "security from the Russians.". . . Neither were they ready to make significant financial sacrifices in the hypothetical form of a tax-surcharge . . . the promises of national unification never appeared attractive enough.[2]

Granted, older citizens could still identify with Gräfin Dönhoff's nostalgic image of the Germans biding their time "in the waiting room of history."[3] In the meantime, even the prewar cohorts had learned to travel with cars, planes, and Neckermann, only occasionally glancing over their shoulders to check whether the unity-train might yet pull into the station. For most of the population, the medium became the message, and movement(s), not the belief in a final destination, served as the basis for political engagement. There had been little perceptible movement on the other side of the Wall since 1953, not even during the heady days of the 1968 cultural revolution in West Berlin—and Prague. Hence, one's perceptions of relatives to the East were hazy, grey, contradictory, and largely irrelevant to the pursuit of one's own life, liberty and happiness. By January 1989, Dönhoff herself had concluded that the idea of reunification "had been long overtaken by history."[4]

Germany is not alone in the class of divided nations: consider the 20th century plights of China, Ireland, Korea, Vietnam and Yemen. Populations whose sense of national community has been torn asunder by war or revolution socialize themselves into acknowledging their differences as well as their similarities. Differences become more pronounced over time and are eventually taken for granted by subsequent generations who have only known "national life" as it stands. By the mid-1980s I had already concluded, along with millions of citizens in both Germanys, that the restoration of a German *Staatsnation* would not come to pass during my lifetime. Thus the aim of my work was to determine whether the German *Kulturnation* still existed, and if so, to predict whether or not it might survive the millennium. Having been turned on its head by the forces of history, this chapter now aims to show that the process so many deemed impossible, namely, the reestablishment of a single nation-state, may prove to have been the easier task after all. The fabric of the cultural-nation has become so discolored and tattered that it will take years of painstaking labor to reweave the ties that bind its people.

A nation seeking to recreate itself within the legal boundaries of statehood must avail itself of two essential sources of political legitimacy. First, the system must be perceived to reflect and respect the ethnic *qua* cultural identity of its subjects, the definition of which has already proved quite controversial in united Germany. While ethnic identity has clear empirical referents, cultural identity entails a mixture of objective and subjective factors. The German language, for example, provides a vague sense of cultural linkage among the peoples of Switzerland, Austria and the FRG; yet no one would argue that the ability to share literary masters or reflect on common historical turning points would suffice to reforge a shared national identity among these states.

Secondly, the system must prove capable of responding effectively to the material needs and security interests of its constituents. For many Germans the "basic necessities of life" are now defined to include food, clothing and shelter, as well as automobiles, guaranteed pension plans, stereo equipment and vacations. Still, eliminating material want is a rather straight-forward process; finding ways to assuage a people's need for security is not. My introductory proposition, that the relationship between a citizen's national consciousness and her orientations toward national security is a reciprocal one in the FRG, puts a new spin on the question of societal merger in unified Germany: not one, but two sets of identity perceptions are likely to clash, the first pertaining to self-images (with ramifications for domestic policy), the second relating to images of the other (with implications for foreign policy). Since 1989, many German security perceptions have been thrown out of kilter by the so-called New World Order. Germans-united are now subject to the same security needs vis-à-vis the outside world, but their material needs diverge in terms of internal, everyday culture. Germany's security dilemma is now more intricately connected to questions of national identity than seemed to be the case prior to unification.

Focusing on the process of "other" identification, this chapter examines important cultural differences between East and West Germans which had evolved prior to unity. It argues that by the mid-1980s a broad majority of FRG citizens had come to accept national division as a normal state of affairs, and therefore viewed the unity mandate embedded in the "provisional" constitution as an historical relic, not as an active agenda item. Although most welcomed the "liberation" of East Germany in 1989, few citizens were ready or willing to assume the burdens of national unity placed upon them by way of power-politics.

The analysis begins with an overview of the sources FRG-citizens might have used to inform themselves about "life in the GDR" prior to 1989. I then compare mass perceptions of the sisters and brothers over there with impressions reported by my interview partners. My aim is to show that the influences of Father-Time were more effective in diminishing their interest in the other Germans than were Father-State's efforts to sustain the myth of a single national identity. The third section pinpoints differences between the "mentalities" of FRG and GDR Germans by describing typical problems of adjustment experienced by Easterners who had fled to the West prior to the Wall's demolition. The concluding section examines the clash of cultures which has surfaced since unification, in an effort to grasp its long-term significance for a united-German identity.

Die da drüben: Images of "the Other Germans"

The degree of interest in East German developments displayed by average FRG citizens has long been a function of "current events" and levels of international tension. Particularly dramatic occurrences, such as the workers' uprising of June 1953, the erection of the Berlin Wall in August 1961, and ratification of the controversial Eastern Treaties in 1971–72, stimulated general curiosity about the afflictions of life on the other side, only to have the GDR fade from mass consciousness during periods of relative stability.

The self-righteous, anti-authoritarian stance of the Student Movement notwithstanding, few New Leftists or subsequent Greens established personal contacts with the alleged beneficiaries of real-existing socialism. The GDR assumed a model-character for forces of the Left and the Right, epitomizing all that was theoretically "bad" or "good" about life in the *Bundesrepublik*. Characterizations on both sides sooner derived from ideology and sensational cases than from ongoing empirical analysis, regular encounters or daily experiences vis-à-vis the other state.

The Socialist Unity Party embarked on a rigid course of demarcation [*Abgrenzung*] shortly after the GDR's founding. Professionals were denied the right to fraternize with their Western peers, average citizens lost the right to travel, and all were expected to avoid the "sabotaging" influences of the FRG media, especially after 1961, rendering the other Germany a closed society throughout the 1950s and 1960s. Formal as well as informal sources of information about life beyond the Wall were thus limited in scope and biased in nature. In the eyes of many Westerners, official statistics and legal documents issued by the Pankow government were not to be trusted— when they were made available at all.

Like classical anthropologists, GDR researchers had to scan the fields of literature, economics, history and political theory in search of key fragments to be glued together by virtue of the dialectical imagination. For those with access to GDR documents, content analysis was an exercise in reading between the lines; one often determined the significance of events and personalities by virtue of the fact that they were not, or no longer, mentioned in the Party's central publications, *Neues Deutschland* and *Einheit*. The more critical the analysis or the more sensitive a topic, the greater the likelihood that the researcher would be barred from entering the GDR itself.

Despite the occupational hazards, a small circle of researchers generated a steady flow of detailed studies regarding the evolution of the second German state. Many FRG scholars struggled to present a balanced or even positive picture of policy ebbs and flows in the East, while a second school sought distance in more historical treatments; others concentrated almost exclusively on the repressive elements of GDR existence.[5] A separate realm existed for those more attuned to Eastern literary or artistic developments. Most of these portrayals were conceived as scholarly works, and hence evoked little mass interest in system dynamics and policy specifics.

In 1973 the Social-Liberal government published its first extensive comparison of conditions in the two Germanys. It was complemented by four documentary/statistical volumes on *The State of the Nation in Divided Ger-*

many undertaken in 1971, 1972, and 1974, but not reissued under the Conservatives until 1987.[6] Government publications provided free of charge to schools focused primarily on the political-historical dimensions of German division, generating as much enthusiasm as would a normal textbook among younger readers. Bossmann's study of 2,200 school children, appearing in 1978, affirmed a common complaint that one learned "really only negative things about the GDR." State-issued educational materials, one professor admonished, upheld a national ideal that had become "politically stereotyped and pedagogically sterile."[7]

A fourth source of information regarding life in the other Germany was rooted in personal accounts and memoirs published by Western journalists and diplomats following their tours of duty in the East. More anecdotal in nature, profiles presented by Gaus, Bölling and others shared an undertone of self-discovery, i.e., delineating one's self through the "other."[8] The clientele for these books consisted, predictably, of other journalists, officials and social scientists. In 1964 Marion Dönhoff, Rudolf Leonhardt and Theo Sommer, three editors from *Die Zeit*, toured the GDR for ten days; an account of their experiences, published under the title *Trip to a Distant Land*, put them on the best-seller list for several weeks. Joined by five more staff members, the three undertook a second expedition during the spring of 1986. The serialized account of their encounters, *Trip to the Other Germany*, again drew a very favorable response, coinciding with a new high point of public interest in the GDR after an extended theater-nuclear deployment debate. Reaffirming his belief in the permanently-provisional nature of the two states, Sommer concluded after his second "tour of duty":

> The unified central state is not the only vessel in which the German destiny will be able to fulfill itself. . . . In any case, the mandate for unity must subordinate itself to the mandate for freedom. It must be more important to us to render the GDR more humane and free than to see it unified with us. . . . Germany—for a long time it will be not half and not whole but rather something doubled.[9]

The 1979 NATO Double Decision enhanced awareness among East and West Germans that they occupied the same geo-strategic boat, and hence faced the same dismal chances for survival in the event of nuclear attack, no matter how limited. In a joint declaration issued at the end of their 1981 summit meeting, FRG Chancellor Helmut Schmidt and GDR Premier Erich Honecker emphasized that war should "never again emanate from German soil." The official posture articulated that year at Schorfheide began to merge with the public's own premonition, "the shorter the missile range, the deader the Germans." The discovery of an atomic "community of destiny" [*Schicksalsgemeinschaft*] gave rise to a new genre of GDR studies. A profusion of how-to-and-why texts published by peace activists in the

FRG was paralleled by the appearance of detailed profiles of underground *eco-pax* [ecology + peace] movements in the GDR.[10] Anti-nuclearism moreover stimulated new modes of interaction between the intellectuals of East and West, beginning with the December 1981 meeting of prominent authors for peace in East Berlin.[11]

The pool of average citizens with an incipient curiosity about the other Germany expanded to include many church, peace, environmental, feminist and human rights sympathizers between 1981 and 1984. Infratest found that even among otherwise apolitical young adults (ages 14–29), the proportions following GDR developments "with great attention" rose from 23% to 35% between the Hot Autumn of 1983 and May 1984.[12] The spread of *Gorbi-mania* [enthusiasm for Gorbachev] after 1985, news regarding spontaneous East-youth unrest in 1987, and a 1988 crackdown on marchers commemorating the deaths of Rosa Luxemburg and Karl Liebknecht also fostered public interest in life *drüben* at the end of the decade.

Reaching a broader audience still were intermittent newspaper accounts of GDR politics and society; some sources were more balanced than others, the partisan spectrum ranging from FAZ to "taz."[13] Yet like all industrial societies, the FRG saw ever more citizens shifting to television for their daily dose of world affairs. Ironically, weekly programs such as *Kennzeichen D* (named after the car-sticker used for trips abroad), *Kontraste* and *Panorama* also became popular sources of information about conditions in the GDR for Easterners, thanks to the accessibility of FRG-airwaves. While only 30% of the GDR-Germans had telephones, over 90% owned televisions (40% color-TVs) by 1987.

Unsuccessful in their efforts to prevent citizens from viewing *West-TV* through career sanctions or arrest, Honecker and his minions resorted to the strategy, "if you can't beat 'em join 'em." The Party ordered a fundamental restructuring of its TV and radio formats in 1982, with the result that its own national-news broadcast, *Aktuelle Kamera*, was eventually sandwiched between the FRG's programs, *Heute* (7 p.m.) and *Tagesschau* (8 p.m.)—a kind of *glasnost* à la GDR.[14] East Germans interviewed by this author claimed to be among "the best informed in the world" as a result of their exposure to "both sides of the news."

While an estimated 90% of all GDR-dwellers had been tuning in to West-channels since the late 1970s, there are no studies reporting how many FRG-viewers regularly turned their antennas eastward; West Berliners and border-town dwellers could, in theory, access two GDR stations. A July 1986 poll inferred some public dissatisfaction with the lack of GDR coverage offered by the FRG media. Among 1,047 respondents, only 5.3% thought that their own newspapers and networks provided "too many" reports about the GDR, while 47.5% complained there were "too few." More than half of the respondents younger than 30 complained that there was "too little" coverage; a clear majority of viewers over the age of 50 found the existing levels of information "just right."[15]

The same survey confirmed youth's "need" for more information about conditions next door: less than 30% realized that some private grocery stores existed in the GDR, while a mere 2.4% correctly estimated the percentage of GDR adults who were Communist Party members (about one-fifth); 37% had "no idea."[16] Only 24.6% could identify the year during which the Wall had been built; 30.1% "didn't know"; the results among individuals aged 40 and over were not much better, with 25–28% offering the correct answer.[17] Not until November 1989 did West-communities outside the border region pressure local authorities to install satellite-dish antennas, as GDR programming became interesting and even sensational.

A more easily digestible source of knowledge about life "over there" consists of numerous literary works penned by East German writers but published in the West. These texts lost some of their appeal as "forbidden fruit," once the SED's desire to amass hard currency reserves led it to cease prosecution of these literary Wall-jumpers as traitorous currency-smugglers. Unification has generated a regrettable backlash against formerly "privileged" GDR-literati; figures such as Christa Wolf, Stefan Heym, Hermann Kant and dramatist Heiner Müller have seen their lifetime achievements suddenly discredited by virtue of their alleged complicity with the regime.[18] A further category of western-published works included the occasionally embittered autobiographies and exposés written by permanent resettlers from the East.[19]

A less sensationalized, thus often overlooked source centers on the garden-variety writings of GDR authors who had *not* incurred the wrath of the SED-state. Novels by women writers, especially, afforded more detailed insights into the short-falls of socialist policy than many social science analyses combined. The problems of health care, juvenile delinquency, alcoholism and the double-burdens of working women, deemed non-existent in the newspeak of official publications, were regularly featured by Maxie Wander and Sibylle Muthesius, inter alia.[20] The fact that such problems were addressed in women's literature rendered them less subject to charges of "treason against the state" but also contributed to their general invisibility and neglect.

Last but not least, Westerners' personal contacts with relatives and acquaintances, sustained through long years of division, provided a less clinical (albeit non-generalizable) foundation for ongoing identification with Eastern counterparts. Private contacts gradually declined in number prior to the 1980s, as nuclear family members (parents, siblings) died, and interest in extended-family ties faded among the successor generations. The decline is not directly related to SED efforts to seal off the East by way of the Wall in 1961, as Table 3.1 shows. Rather, the break occurred during the mid-1970s, at the very time when the political, cultural, economic and technical exchanges born of détente were enhancing the possibilities for more direct communica-

TABLE 3.1   Private Contacts with the East German Population

	1953	1958	1963 (March)	1965 (Jan.)	1979
Friends or Relatives	41	35	34	36	25%
Sent packages	26	26	34	31	63%*
Visited the GDR	–	3	2	5	5%**

Source: Emnid Informationen, 17. Jg., Nr. 11, 15. März 1965; ibid., 31. Jg., Nr. 4, 1979 (Table 6).

* Christmas packages specifically mentioned.

** Visits during the last 12 months preceding interview.

tion. The segment of FRG-dwellers who claimed to have friends and relatives in the East fell from 41% to 36% between 1953 and 1965; that figure was nearly halved by 1979, dropping to a mere 13.6% in 1985.

Another poll from 1984 revealed that roughly 80% of those under 30 had neither relatives nor friends in the GDR, compared to 77% of those aged 30 to 39, 65–66% of those 40 to 59, and 61.5% of the respondents over 60. Over three-fourths of those 20 or older who had visited the GDR did so because of ties to relatives; less than one-fifth, on average, had traveled to the East for touristic purposes.[21]

Adolescents in these later studies comprise a special category, owing to their participation in obligatory class trips sponsored by state educational offices. A 1981 study sponsored by the Ministry for Inter-German Affairs discovered that a one-time-only trip actually reinforced schoolchildren's pre-existing prejudices about Easterners. Only repeated visits, resulting in personal relationships, led to revised assessments and a general dispelling of negative attitudes.[22] Implicit in this prejudice was a recognition that the citizens of East and West had already become very different species, each well adapted to its particular postwar habitat. "Silke" (born in 1961) insisted in the late 1970s that "the GDR should not be allowed to call itself German, because it's a state that's more like Russia than Germany." Another pupil, "Peter" (born in 1962) declared "it would take years until the Germans could find the way back to each other again, because the Eastern Germans have become too inhibited."[23]

The gradual decline in direct, family-based contacts was halted, if not reversed, by the dramatic increase in GDR citizens allowed to resettle permanently to the West beginning in 1984. The first emigration wave of 40,000 came after the SED liberalized directives on the right to travel (especially for those with Western family ties) in February 1982. A signatory to the 1975 Helsinki Accords, the GDR leadership was motivated less by human rights concerns than by a desire for international recognition of its sovereignty and by its insatiable need for the hard currency and Western goods with which

TABLE 3.2   Family and Friendship Ties to GDR Residents (%)

	1989 (Nov.)	1985 (Aug.)	1984 (Jan.)	1980 (Nov.)	1979 (Sept.)
Ties in East Berlin or GDR:					
Only Relatives	21.9	14.7	13.8	16.0	17.2
Friends and Acquaintances	13.9	6.9	7.1	9.5	7.7
Relatives and Acquaintances	7.7	6.7	9.3	8.7	8.2
None	56.4	71.5	69.7	65.6	66.6
DDR Relatives, Acquaintances					
Yes	43.6	28.3	30.3	34.4	33.4
No	56.4	71.5	69.7	65.6	66.6
n =	1,017	1,050	1,009	1,072	

Source: Representative sample for special broadcast on *ZDF-Magazin,* compiled by the Forschungsgruppe Wahlen e. V., Mannheim, 17–23 August 19.

visitors were likely to return. The old guard's refusal to grant unlimited travel-rights to *all* citizens triggered a steady stream of applications for permanent emigration, which met with paradoxical approval over the next five years.[24] Vagaries of the socialist postal and telephone systems aside, the nearly 200,000 GDR-citizens who headed West between spring 1984 and June 1989 undoubtedly would have re-activated "contacts with relatives and friends" left behind (though not without some risk of harassment for the latter), had the breaching of the Wall itself not ordained the reestablishment of "one people."

Though not "representative" in statistical terms, my own sample clearly shows a generational differentiation had taken hold by the 1980s, both with regard to the intensity of personal contacts and in relation to expressions of interest in the GDR as a neighbor-state. Almost all of my Economic Miracle Generation discussants mentioned close or distant relatives, and some had spent part of their own lives on what had become GDR territory. A majority of those who visited the East through the 1980s did so for professional reasons—not surprising, given my focus on Bundestag-Members. Of the four who referred to their children, two recounted their offspring's reluctance or refusal to accompany them on these eastward excursions. A majority of the EM-discussants expressed a growing interest in the other state, linked to new political developments in Eastern Europe or as a result of their direct professional involvement with inter-German questions.

Closer personal ties, in some cases to real brothers and sisters in the East, did not suffice to mask an estrangement or awkwardness my interview partners felt in their dealings with GDR citizens. SPD security-expert Egon Bahr (born in the Eastern city of Treffurt) claimed that it had been much harder to evoke a smile from Erich Honecker (born in the Saarland) than from Soviet hard-liner Andrei Gromyko during countless *Ostpolitik* negotiations prior to 1981. One Green MdB, Dirk Schneider, voiced embarrassment over the fact that he knew very little about GDR-internal affairs, even though one of his brothers remained in the East after the 1960s, and despite his active involvement with issues regarding the status of Berlin. A publicist of East-Prussian descent admitted that she paid only irregular visits to East Berlin, although she recognized that the GDR "had to bear the total burden of division." At least five persons interviewed expressed a "theoretical" interest in a future visit to the GDR but claimed they had "no time." None raised the possibility of using their generous allotment of paid vacation days (about six full weeks per year!) in order to undertake such a trip.[25]

Only one of fifteen interviewees from the second generation had living relatives in the GDR; three (Antje Vollmer, Peter Brandt and Wilhelm Bruns) had established friendships over the years based on political or professional interactions. Another female peace activist characterized East Germans as "people who are alien to me," and "rather narrow-minded." Long-March respondents who had lived or studied in Berlin saw some increase in their own interest, but as Torsten Lange (MdB-Greens) pointed out, the Student Movement of the 1960s in which many of these discussants had participated could actually be construed as "the highpoint of non-identity" between New Leftists and citizens of the real-existing socialist state. Infrequent visits on the part of this group did not signify disinterest per se, since peace activists and Green politicians were routinely barred from entering the GDR through the 1980s. European Parliament member Eva Quistorp noted with pride in 1990 that she was among the last to be stricken from the border patrol's *Entry-Forbidden* list *after* the Wall's opening in 1989, due to her human rights agitation vis-à-vis the Eastern state.

As was true of older cohorts, those whose contacts were not explicitly political in nature had often developed their first acquaintanceships through church channels instead. A second orientation shared with members of the EM-Generation was their admission that a trip to the "other" Germany would be undertaken out of a sense of duty, political curiosity, or for purposes of information-gathering, not as an enjoyable opportunity for sight-seeing or relaxation.

"Curiosity" best characterizes the attitudes of citizens born after 1960. A few had undertaken class-trips to Berlin, the assessments of students in Bonn overlapping with those voiced by four women then living in the divided-city: it was "not disinterest but a lack of connection" that resulted in little motivation to visit the East. All conceded that they might like to see more of the other state but that getting there was "unpleasant . . . too complicated . . . too expensive" and "disgustingly German." Besides, "there were many more fascinating places" one could visit free of such hassles. All members of the Bonn/Berlin groups had already vacationed or resided for a longer period in some other "foreign" country.

Limited though my sample was, the responses presented here follow the lines of representative surveys conducted by the *Forschungsgruppe Wahlen*. While 81.8% of the FGW sample realized it was legally possible to spend one's vacation in the GDR, only 9.3% had already done so by 1986; 81.3% had never thought about taking such a trip. Persons with higher levels of schooling were more willing to consider the possibility (40% for those under 34, 32.6% aged 35 and over).[26] After specifying that visa and obligatory exchange requirements would be eliminated in January 1990, pollsters found 62% intent on visiting the GDR sometime during that year.[27] The dramatic increase in potential travelers no doubt owes to the opening of the Wall, which turned the GDR into a "happening" and also eliminated the fear-factor of earlier times.

While the politics of negotiation significantly increased the flow of visitors between the FRG and the GDR after 1971, personal contacts were still limited to specific segments of the population, above all, diplomats, academics, entrepreneurs, or those with direct family ties. In 1987, there were 5.5 million visits (not to be equated with the number of visitors) registered from West to East. GDR pensioners undertook 3.8 million visits to the FRG and Berlin-West, with another 1.2 million visits registered among citizens under the age of 65 for men, 60 for women.[28] Some political officials, journalists and academics traveled repeatedly to the other state, meaning that less than 5–10% of the FRG population (approximately 61 million) could confirm or correct their impressions of life-in-the-GDR through first-hand observations between 1961 and 1989. This raises some question as to the "representativeness" of one sample reported by Infratest in 1983, according to which 32% of the total claimed to have personal knowledge of the GDR based on visits to/from there.[29]

The opportunities for personal exchange were noticeably enhanced by the initiation of the first inter-German Sister City program between Saarlouis and Eisenstadt in 1985. In return for the recognition afforded Honecker by way of his first FRG-summit meeting in 1987, the GDR leadership approved the formation of nearly 50 city-to-city partnerships through 1989.[30] Participation in these and other exchanges remained rather lopsided, particularly with regard to youth. Some 70,000 to 80,000 FRG adolescents crossed the border in 1987–1988, to take part in a multitude of GDR-sponsored cultural, touristic and sporting events. During the same period, a mere 3,800 to 5,000 East-youth were permitted to head West to engage in musical, educational, athletic and Sister-City activities.[31]

Given a growing communication gap at the mass level, images of the other society impersonally transmitted through highly politicized channels served as the critical determinants of how much shared identity actually existed prior to 1989. The imbalanced nature of face-to-face exchanges occurring over a twenty-year period did not alleviate critical asymmetries in each Germany's perception of the other. The stereotypical nature of information bits regularly absorbed by average Federal Republicans had all the makings of a classical "double bind." The political identities of the East and West Germans were nurtured by way of a steady diet of ideological "enemy-images," coupled with mutually reinforcing denunciations of the other system's right-to-exist, especially through the 1950s and 1960s. In terms of their socio-cultural identities, citizens of the two states were expected to distinguish between the "good Germans" who were their friends and relatives, and the "bad Germans" atop each power structure responsible for their personal separation and suffering.

The ambivalence this generated on both sides is reflected in the Germans' inability to find an appropriate name for each other prior to 1989, viz., one that would convey both commonality and separateness. Depending on the occasion, FRG-dwellers were known to refer to their Eastern neighbors as *DDR-Deutsche, Ostdeutsche, Ostler, DDR'ler, DDR-BürgerInnen*, as *DDR-BewohnerInnen, Ossis, Zonis, Deutsche-Russen* and *Rote-Preussen*. GDR-residents made alternate use of the labels *Bundesdeutsche, West-Deutsche, Westler, BRD'ler, BundesbürgerInnen, BundesrepublikanerInnen, Wessis, Bundis* and *West-Goten*. The Germans of East and West occupy a territory characterized by Herbert Wehner as *inneres Ausland*, an internally-foreign country.

No matter how much one regretted or pitied their plight, the ultimate FRG-perception has been and remains that East Germans "are not like us." Although some distinction was made between the "people" and "the country," neither was imagined in a particularly positive light: 46% of a 1983 Allensbach sample labeled the country "unsympathetic," and only 26% considered the people "likeable." Asked to rank them among other European populations, Westerners judged East Germans less amiable than Austrians, the Swiss, French and Dutch citizens but better than Italians, the British, Greeks, Czechs, and Russians.[32]

Surveys are inaccurate devices for capturing the "feelings" one harbors towards people one has never met. But how can we expect two German identities to merge into one after forty years of division, if individuals find it difficult to project commonalities even in abstract, cost-free terms? Paying homage to the West German obsession with vacations, Noelle-Neumann has repeatedly posed the question as to how one would react to a GDR-citizen encountered on "a holiday along the Black Sea." The number of Westerners who would consider the latter no more a fellow country-wo/man than an Austrian rose from 20% in 1970 to 32% in 1983; the "undecideds" rose from 10% to 13%. While 18% of the respondents 60-and-over equated the two in 1983, 37% of the 30–44 year olds, and 43% of those under 29 saw East Germans as "unrelated" as the Austrians. Yet 79% of the younger cohorts said they might pursue a discussion; 49% of the latter would have proposed "having a drink to-gether," in contrast to 39% of the oldest group.[33] Of the two populations, GDR-citizens were seen to exhibit more "love of fatherland."

As the crumbling of the Wall made clear, East Germans have more to gain, materially speaking, from a re-identification with the Nation. Having de-pended for years on care packages and hard currency channeled through "rich aunts and uncles" in the West, some now admit that they resented the "eco-nomic miracle arrogance" with which those goods—soap, coffee, second-hand clothing—were often delivered.[34] The treatment Western callers received when visiting families "over there" was also subject to misinterpretation, as re-counted by GDR acquaintances. Not wishing to appear as poor cousins, the host family would set the table with the best provisions East-Marks could buy. The West-guest would respond with the typical compliment, *nicht schlecht* [not bad], subconsciously concluding that life in the GDR wasn't so deprived after all—but failing to realize that the hostess had probably spent several days mobilizing contacts in order to procure a real beef-roast and a few "locally-ex-otic" condiments like parsley. By offering "material support" to poor relations in the struggle against the new authoritarian-state, West-guests could over-look the ways in which their own behavior helped to sustain postwar division. Indeed, 69% of the West Germans polled in 1979 saw political freedom as the most significant advantage one would enjoy in the FRG vis-à-vis the GDR; 20% stressed material well-being.[35]

By the mid-1970s, wealthier FRG-souls began to encounter a revolution of rising expectations among *les misérables* of the GDR, also rooted in cultural misunderstanding. Exposed to the capitalist way of life via television, the ben-eficiaries of *West-visits* started clamoring for pocket calculators, cassette recorders and designer jeans, in lieu of chocolates, alarm clocks and hand-me-downs. As one adolescent with relatives "in the East-zone" complained,

[they think] that our basement is full of money, so that we can easily give them a wheelbarrow of it . . . they take notes on the items they see in our television commercials . . . then they come shopping with a long list—although A+P [*At-traktive + Preiswert*, generic brand] noodles are much cheaper than Schüle-Gold-Dot-Fresh-Egg noodles, everything will be bought that they've written down. A pleated skirt for 39 DM is a loser, no, it has to be one for 80 DM.[36]

Having very few brands to choose from at home, East-residents miscon-strued the high-gloss, hard-sell character of West-advertising, presuming that FRG-consumers bought nothing but the best for themselves. GDR-cit-izens who "resettled" during the 1980s found themselves quickly promoted to the status of "West" uncles and aunts, long before they had overcome their feelings of "actually being an emigrant in one's own country."[37]

Mutual misperception was and remains one of the occupational hazards of national division. Former East-citizen Irene Böhme characterized pre-unity exchanges between FRG and GDR acquaintances in the following manner:

> The West German will not be able to forget the kind of broken person into whose soul he has peered, how abruptly this oppressed creature defended the state. The East German will not be able to forget that he has revealed himself to an ignoramus, looking for a discussion over the meaning of life with someone who doesn't even want to think about it. Both suppress their discomfiture. . . . The one does not know how strongly Slavic a part of him has already become. The other does not know how American he thinks and feels in certain areas. . . . Each considers his behavior normal, has no idea that he could be different because he has led a different daily life in some other Germany for over 35 years. One's own being and that strange being, [such a gap] simply cannot exist.
>
> After a few astonishing observations the West German heads for home, satisfied with his good deed. He did not reveal that the smell of the streets was indeed odious, he overlooked the disorder and the dirt. . . . He was a good guest, which cost him nerves and money. He resolves to travel again to the GDR, because he has comprehended how important his visit is for his fellow countryman. . . . Now he knows for certain that he prefers his worries and needs, that he not only lives better but also more correctly. . . .
>
> The East German waves goodbye to the departing guest with the satisfied feeling that he has been a good host, having offered something that cannot be found in other places. That has cost him nerves and money. He has set aside a few prejudices, yet affirmed his judgment about these Westerners, that you just can't talk freely and openly with them. After this visit he knows more exactly that he may live more poorly but also more correctly.[38]

In summary, the average West-perception of country-women and men to the East, grounded in little first-hand knowledge, was fraught with discomfiting ambiguities. One experienced a dialectical tension between the closeness one was supposed to feel toward the other Germans (as dictated by the constitution) and one's cognitive identification with "German" history, language and culture, on the one hand, and a psychological desire not to overburden one's own good fortune, on the other. Younger people attribute their indifference towards the GDR to the fact that post-industrial society in general has become quite me-centered: "nothing personal," they argue, just "no time," or "too much stress." Most apartment dwellers hardly know their neighbors, they rationalize, and even lots of nuclear families have been estranged through physical distance or divorce.

Because many citizens born after 1945 were conscious of their diffidence towards questions of German identity, they were very confused by their own emotional reactions the night the Wall came tumbling down. The sentiments of one control group, my WG-Round Table from Stuttgart, help to illustrate this "non-identity identification" dilemma. As my friend Wally (born in 1954) wrote in February 1990:

Political events have become like somersaults here . . . I am perpetually discussing the latest developments with Ulla, Lothar, Claudia, and with Peter
Conradi. . . . I am trying my best to view it all pragmatically. I was quite moved
by what Monika Maron wrote recently in *Der Spiegel*. What will remain of socialism, for example, the day care facilities? The daily revelations of corruption
within the system forcibly drive [GDR citizens] into the Western arms. . . .
There are no more places for the resettlers here, the announcement that more
school gymnasiums will be used as provisional camps has led to massive protests
among those who want to continue their sports activities. In Berlin parents,
teachers, and trainers have "occupied" a gym to guarantee that their children
get physical education. You ask about "free self-determination." I'm afraid that
this exactly what is happening. The people from the GDR . . . want their piece
of the Western cake now. When I see the pictures on television of people all
shouting "Germany, united Fatherland," I have to stop myself from judging
them negatively. They see their only "salvation" in unity . . . I simply don't
want to believe it . . . I would have wished for a GDR that could preserve her
own identity, but I fear that the Western economy and the people won't go
along with it. And when "the people" want to share in Western affluence, we
simply have to accept that.[39]

FRG-citizens willing to accept their destiny vis-à-vis the GDR-Germans
do so in the realization that both sides now possess an identity of their own.
Still, the bonds of national identity are multi-dimensional, and continuously
subject to environmental influences. What has grown apart over four
decades may conceivably grow back together, under the classical formula of
thesis-antithesis-synthesis. The first dimension essential to the prospective
fusion of German identities centers on the formal ties of citizenship, the
construct to which we now turn.

Citizenship and Assimilation: (Un)Settling Experiences

As we saw in Chapter 2, West Germans have, for the most part, abandoned
the nationalistic, my-country-do-or-die orientations that rendered them the
scourge of Europe through two world wars. The FRG's new role in the interdependent postwar environment has resulted in an instrumental, pragmatic conceptualization of its national interests. The official understanding
of membership in the national community, by contrast, remains quasi-meta-
physical and rigidly legalistic in nature (see Chapter 7). The GDR's former
distinction between *nation* and *nationality* might help us to grasp the most
important elements of the West German "citizenship" construct.

As late as 1968, the GDR identified itself as the socialist state of the German nation, a label which lost favor among Communists once Willy Brandt
endorsed the idea of "two states in one nation." In 1971, it re-named itself
the socialist German nation (versus the capitalist German nation), followed

by a 1974 revision which deleted the term nation from the constitution, re-placing it with "the state of workers and farmers"; the aim was to dispel pub-lic confusion over Premier Honecker's new distinction between "Citizen-ship: GDR" and "Nationality: German." Official historians Alfred Kosing and Manfred Schmidt refined the GDR's self-concept still further by drawing a line between the objective and subjective components of national identity. Nation was defined as an "historical community of human beings which de-rives from the formation of community based on its economic relations, its territory, its language, the specifics of culture, its character."[40] This concept emphasized the primacy of socio-ecomomic structures, the nature of the so-cietal order, relations between classes, and relations of production; its devel-opment was seen to follow the "immutable, objective laws" of history.

Nationality, by contrast, referred to the subjective dimensions of identity, grounded in a shared past. The bonding potential inherent in certain ethnic features and a common language were important, but theorists held that these factors did not embody the essence of what it meant to be a nation. Nationality accounted for a limited degree of "continuity" in the identity of divided Germans, insofar as affective-psychological ties to ethnicity were likely to persist for several generations. The German Democratic Republic insisted that it was a new nation, albeit one "still stamped with birthmarks of the old society from whose womb it emerges," since the national identity of its citizens was grounded in a new paradigm of socio-political and eco-nomic-class relations.[41] A common national past in no way dictated a shared national future; indeed, the spectres of twentieth century German history rendered the re-establishment of a single nation-state not only undesirable but impossible.

Rather than divorce itself from the legacy of the Third Reich, the Federal Republic understood itself as the legitimate successor-nation from the time of its founding in May 1949 until unity was attained in 1990. This included recognition of its national responsibility to offer financial compensation to many of Hitler's victims and to pursue active political reconciliation vis-à-vis countries it had once attacked. Even the weather maps used on FRG-TV were used to uphold the ideal of a single German nation, by never display-ing a line between the two states through 40 years of broadcasting (in stark contrast to GDR weather maps). Nevertheless, the West German definition of citizenship and nationality entailed even finer constitutional distinctions than the ones espoused by GDR ideologues.

Prior to unification, the parameters of citizenship were defined in two separate paragraphs of the Basic Law, Article 16 (see Chapter 7) and Article 116. Article 116 decrees, in circular fashion, that a German enjoying the ba-sic freedoms and protections of the constitution is "a person who possesses German citizenship." It reinstates the membership status of those forced to abandon or renounce their citizenship during the Nazi era, and also defines as German anyone "admitted to the territory of the German Reich within the frontiers of 31 December 1937 as a refugee or expellee of German stock or as the spouse of such a person." Grounded in the Roman tradition of *jus sanguinis* (which renders citizenship a matter of "bloodline"), the Basic Law posits the existence of two categories of Germans beyond those born of native parents and raised on FRG soil. The term *ÜbersiedlerIn* referred to persons who "settled over" (legally or illegally) from the GDR, whose "separate citizenship" the FRG refused to recognize. Prior to 1990, these migrants automatically received West German passports, as well as special social-service benefits to expedite their assimilation. The *AussiedlerInnen* [persons "settling out"] were ethnic-Germans (and their offspring) who relocated from Eastern territories that fell within the borders of the Reich prior to 1937. The latter were likewise entitled to multiple "re-integration" benefits. Foreigners who did not fit these two categories or who had not applied for asylum fell largely outside the realm of constitutional protection (see Chapter 7). Of the various groups, one would expect former "East-Zone" residents to prove most capable of rapid assimulation into FRG-society. Thus, the *ÜbersiedlerInnen* might offer a potential "test for reunification," both in terms of Western reactions to Easterners' return to the fold and with regard to differences in the two German identities that have evolved under diametrically opposed systems since 1949.[42] Clearly, the absorption of 16 million GDR-Germans into an FRG population of 61 million poses qualitatively different challenges than the integration of 400,000 since 1984—or 3 million since 1949. At issue here is not the problem of economic disruption, however, but rather questions of socio-cultural differentiation.[43] As one "resettler" described the dilemma of divergent identities in the 1980s, "it is virtually impossible to live in a state for three decades without accepting it more or less for itself."[44]

The general practice in the FRG prior to 1989 was to welcome prominent exiles and defectors—like musician Wolfgang Biermann, philosopher Rudolf Bahro and economist Hermann von Berg—with great fanfare, in testimony to the ideological superiority of capitalism. It was then hoped (a hope shared by GDR officials!) that the new arrivals would fade into oblivion before they "complicated" dealings with the East, or before they grew too critical of conditions in the West, as many indeed did.

Consider the fate of "Rudi the Red" Dutschke, born in Schönefeld/Luckenwalde, who fled from the East in 1961 shortly before the Wall went up. Rejecting all forms of authoritarianism, Dutschke became the quintessential philosopher and a key mobilizer of the New Left/Student Movement, until he was seriously wounded in West Berlin by a rightwing assassin in April 1968. At the time of his premature death in 1979, this critic of monopoly capitalism *and* state socialism was actively engaged in efforts to create the Green Party. Jena peace-activist Roland Jahn, author Jürgen Fuchs and Professor Rudolf Bahro followed a similarly critical course. Rather than retire from politics once they had made it to the West, these ingrate-dissidents continued to advocate visions of a demilitarized socialism-with-a-human-face, while also agitating against NATO.[45] A querulous personality from the start, Wolf Biermann has been known to criticize not only old-guard Communists and young Stasi-informers but also the Western Right and Left; the latter became his target during the 1991 Gulf War.

Published interviews with individual Wall-Jumpers reveal deep-seated differences in the identity-perceptions of the Germans divided, reinforced by broader empirical studies of their integration problems over time. Theater-critic Irene Böhme (born in 1933 in Bernburg/Saale) made the leap from East to West Berlin in 1980. She described her former compatriots as curious, hungry for details and genuinely interested in culture, in contrast to West-visitors who only stayed at the best hotels, took away places at the best GDR restaurants, and spent too much time talking about their jobs, even if theirs was not "the state of workers and farmers."[46]

GDR-Germans developed an inferiority complex vis-à-vis wealthier Westerners well before 1989, resulting in a schizophrenic self-identity. Those who remained trapped in the wrong part of Germany—"the unblessing of late birth," as one noted—regularly characterized their FRG counterparts as cold and materialistic; but many also hoped for a chance to become more like them. Easterners who did succeed in crossing over before 1989 issued even more unflattering assessments of the West Germans they encountered at close range. Nine emigrés ranging from 28–59 in age, interviewed by transplanted journalist Martin Ahrends, offered the following impressions:

- *The people here have it too good. . . . There is too much of everything here, including culture and art* (Martin, theologian, age 40).
- *Even the possibilities for travel lose their glow because they no longer signify an exception. A saturation-melancholy takes over. . . . The one thing I never want to get used to is: having no time. Having no time here serves as a status symbol, idle fussing* (Ludwig, linguistics specialist, age 44).
- *Everything one learned over there seems to have been in vain. . . . The question regarding the meaning of life . . . it's like going through puberty a second time. . . . They speak differently about women here. One talks more about body parts, [as if they were talking] about consumable items. Most women here have problems with a man as an institution. But I'm no institution* (Günter, lighting technician, age 45).
- *The western men I have met are afraid of closeness. Maybe they are also afraid of the women's movement: [women] should not be strong but they aren't allowed to be weak either. . . . Sex as a high achievement sport as (sic) the main thing of value in a love relationship* (Angelika, medical-technical assistant, age 28).

- *Sitting in the West, the East only looks half as bad. . . . I am conscious that I will never have the same relationship as I did to my friends in the GDR. And I suddenly have the feeling that I have traded my home away for this super-affluence* (Werner, church musician, age 31).[47]

Even re-settlers who seemed to master the transition in the short run, outfitted with new jobs, new apartments and new loves, continued to feel that "somehow we are all a little GDR-damaged and cannot escape this so quickly."[48]

Different reasons for leaving the "homeland" may well ease or complicate one's adaptation to FRG-life. GDR citizens who emigrated under the more restrictive provisions in the early 1980s faced very different conditions, and offered other motives than those who crossed the Austro-Hungarian border en masse in August 1989. For the pre-1989 emigrés, "the decision to flee [was] first and foremost a "no" to the GDR or a "no" to Poland or to Czechoslovakia, and not a "yes" to America, not a "yes" to England, or to limit it to Germany, not a "yes" to the Federal Republic of Germany. I went away in order to document my "no" to the GDR," declared Stefan R., born in 1945.[49] The countless Easterners who headed West after the Wall opened said "yes" to the other Germany, as did millions who stayed behind to vote for rapid unification.

Volker Ronge's panel study of new arrivals since 1984 affords a valuable socio-demographic profile of the first major wave of legal GDR-emigrants. He cautions readers as to the self-selective character of his sample, noting that successful integrators would have been more inclined than maladjusted individuals to discuss their condition with outsiders before the GDR's collapse. Of the 32,000 *Ostler* who relocated during the first half of 1984 (60% men, 40% women), an estimated two-thirds were paid laborers. Nearly 68% were between the ages of 18 and 39, signifying that they had been exposed to the full range of socialization processes in the GDR, including exposure to West-TV after 1971. Questioned as to their first impressions of the real Federal Republic, 39% "felt like they were entering a foreign country," while 57% perceived the new land "as home."[50]

As to their motives for departure, phase one of the interval study revealed a combination of factors at work. Over two-thirds stressed the lack of free speech and subjection to "political pressure," followed by limitations on the right to travel (56%), and unsatisfactory living conditions (46% of the total, 59% of the Dresden sample).[51] Many found their initial enthusiasm for the West quickly curbed by the realities of the free-market system: 57% had expected to find employment within the first week, yet only 18% had been placed in jobs after three weeks of searching. A later investigation determined that 30% of the women, in contrast to 10% of the men, were still looking for work three months after resettlement; females landed in jobs well beneath their level of formal qualification more frequently than males— an augur of things to come after unification.[52]

More important for the purposes of this work than the fate of the migrants themselves is the shift in West German views towards their integration that surfaced in the early 1980s. The attitudes in question center on, first, the general willingness to welcome and absorb additional waves of so-called *brothers and sisters* from the East; and secondly, an acceptance of the duty to provide material support towards their assimilation. Ronge's sampling of 2,000 West-reactions in April/May 1984 generated five classes of respondents: (1) persons hostile to resettlers and opposing further assistance (22%); (2) citizens friendly towards the new arrivals who also recognized a personal responsibility for rendering assistance (26%); (3) people who tolerated the settlers' presence but rejected the provision of public aid (26%); (4) insecure residents who were prepared to help in theory yet feared economic competition or "trouble-making" (25%); and (5) persons completely disinterested in the phenomenon (1%).[53] Only 18% of the sample concurred that GDR emigration was "good without reservation," 46% saw a mix of "good and bad" elements, and 22% judged the exodus in primarily negative terms. Four-fifths of the participants expected the new arrivals to experience "integration problems," and 47% voiced fears regarding an influx of East German spies![54]

Less than half (43%) of the 1984 survey-participants justified benefit-programs for recent arrivals in terms of "a special historically rooted right to support," implying that GDR-migrants were to be aided for humanitarian reasons, not because they qualified as Germans.[55] Nearly three-fourths deemed the Germans of East and West "ONE people" (58% of those under 30 agreed), despite the fact that 83% (86% among 14–29 year olds) saw the FRG and the GDR as "TWO states." While 22% characterized the other Germany as "a foreign country" in 1973, one-third espoused this view by 1984 (49% among persons under 30).[56] The perception of East Germans as very distant cousins was moreover reflected in a greater willingness to accord formal recognition to GDR-citizenship. Overall figures rose from 13% in June 1958 to 59% in October 1961 (Emnid poll); by 1980 FGW data showed a strong correlation between age and support for de jure recognition. By 1988, 45% of the younger cohorts viewed all other German-stock immigrants [*AussiedlerInnen*] as "foreigners" as well.[57]

At the time of the first mass immigration (1984), the international scene was dominated by major tensions between the superpowers over new European nuclear deployments and the conflagration in Afghanistan. Leaders of the two German states sought to "limit the damage" to their own tenaciously negotiated relations, as evidenced by frequent referrals to their "coalition of reason" and their "community of responsibility."[58] The brief reigns of Soviet Premiers Andropov and Chernenko provided a new source of insecurity for the Honecker regime in the foreign policy arena, where the GDR premier had actually begun to garner a measure of grudging respect among his own populace.

While the FRG and GDR leaders moved closer together on formerly taboo topics, their populations grew farther apart at the level of peer identification. Westerners distanced themselves from the concept of "family ties" more quickly than did their (materially dependent) GDR-counterparts. If reactions to the 1984 *Übersiedler* wave can be construed as an indirect test of their openness to reunification, the *Wessis* clearly failed to pass it. Ronge concluded in 1985 that

> a materialist, egoistic attitude is widespread among the federal population, and it strikes at the relationship to the "brothers and sisters" from "over there" whenever things get serious over the "social costs of reunification.". . . Especially among postwar youth lacking the foundation of an all-German experience, the relation to the other Germans in the GDR is increasingly mixed with a humanitarian perspective which suppresses the national orientation . . . but which, surprisingly perhaps, is much more behaviorally effective when put to the test than the latter.[59]

In summary, the Germans of East and West were more conscious of their differences than of their similarities by the mid-1980s, though their perceptions were rarely grounded in concrete knowledge of the other's life conditions. Common traits and beliefs rooted in language, culture and history had clearly receded into the background. Nevertheless, attitudes derived from a limited number of face-to-face exchanges under the far from normal circumstances of mass emigration cannot be construed as a direct test of popular interest in national unity. It is necessary to confront the issue of unification head-on, that is, as it *consciously* figured in the hearts and minds of Federal Republicans across four decades of division.

Reunification: Bidding Adieu to Illusions, 1949–1988

As of December 1989, officials in Bonn and East Berlin dropped the familiar reference to reunification [*Wiedervereinigung*], in favor of the less common term unification [*Vereinigung*]. One partial explanation for the shift in terminology rests with the dynamics of the Autumn 1989 "revolution." The intellectuals, artisans, religious, peace and ecology activists who led the first anti-regime demonstrations from October through November hoped to transform the GDR into a democratic system based on socialism with a human face. They rejected the idea of a rapid fusion, preferring interim-Premier Hans Modrow's call for a *Community of Treaties* and an eventual federation between the two states.[60] Once workers and farmers joined the protests in December, both the objectives and the time-frame of their "reassociation" were radically redefined. Rear-guard protesters moved into the foreground, waving imported FRG flags and chanting a line taken, ironically, from their own national anthem: "Germany, united Fatherland!"[61] Insofar as the real catalyst for a national merger came from the streets of Leipzig, Dresden and East Berlin, it was fitting that East German phraseology should prevail.

Secondly, the breath-taking pace of developments in Eastern Europe threatened to unhinge the major security structures credited with maintaining the stability of the region since 1949. Rather than awaken memories of a *furor teutonicus*, it was in the best interest of both Germanys to embed their move towards unity in the process of accelerated European integration. By describing the processes coterminously as German unification and European unification, FRG officials could alleviate fears that the Germans might once again embark upon a "special path." Rejection of the term re-unification also implied that German-united would not extend beyond the forty-year Oder-Neisse border.

A third reason for the shift to "unification" goes directly to the heart of the identity question: One cannot *re*unify what did not exist prior to 1949, namely, one predominantly capitalist-democratic-federal state with one socialist-authoritarian-centrally planned state of Germany. It was during the negotiations on the first State Treaty of June 23, 1990 that the leaders of the two polities began to comprehend how far they had grown apart over the years, as they looked for ways to merge their respective social, legal and economic systems. While Federal Republican values, regulations and institutions have dominated, indeed dictated procedures from the start, the Germany which awaits us ten years hence will have been dramatically transformed by the unification experience per se.

Had national division not extended across four decades—covering three full generations by my count—a hefty dose of legal tinkering and economic stretching might have sufficed to weld the two parts back together again. Re-unification could have been rapidly achieved in 1952, and perhaps even as late as 1959. At the end of the first decade both populations still bore the markings of a "subject culture," displaying little sense of citizen efficacy.[62] Both had learned, albeit in different ways, to accept systemic transformations imposed by their respective Occupational Powers. They subscribed to but had not yet internalized the new values signified by their new constitutions, and could rely upon each other as reference points, based on continuing family and friendship ties. All that changed with the cementing of the Berlin Wall in 1961.

The Wall sealed off concrete hopes for a quick attainment of the unity-in-freedom mandated by the Basic Law, shifting the emphasis from "unity, eventually" to "freedom first." For West Germans of the 1970s, the re-establishment of national unity remained a vaguely desirable, collective aim, but daring more democracy and advancing the quality of life in one's own state assumed priority at the individual level. Most embraced the idea that *Ostpolitik* and the politics of small steps afforded the least destabilizing means towards larger, national ends. Most citizens of the 1980s were not the same

Germans who had personally hoped for a unified nation-state until August 13, 1961; they were, in fact, Federal Republicans, since two-thirds of them had been born after World War II. They faced too many pressing global problems (e.g., nuclear proliferation) to worry about an unknown quantity like the GDR in any special way, although they recognized that East Germans deserved the same access to political freedom, quality consumption and foreign travel that they themselves enjoyed. Securing the peace between East and West took precedence over FRG-GDR unification, however. By 1987, an overwhelming majority had "bid adieu to the illusion of reunification."[63] FRG citizens could distinguish once and for all (or so they thought) between the desirability and probability of national unity. They were ill-prepared for the revolutionary surprises that would overtake them in 1989/90. Yet their astonished reactions, even disbelief, regarding all that has come to pass since November 1989, may prove to be their saving grace.

Pre-1989 attitudes towards reunification must be assessed along three distinct lines, the first involving the question of desirablilty, the second pertaining to West Germans' realistic expectations, and the third relating to sacrifices and conditions deemed acceptable in pursuit of this goal. Having "reprocessed" some thirty-five years' worth of German public opinion data, I can argue that many "empirical analyses" of popular attitudes towards reunification prior to 1989 were simplistic at best or consciously partisan at worst. As a survey item, the idea of *Wiedervereinigung* has usually been presented as an all-or-nothing proposition: either one is for it, against it, or one "doesn't know." The idea of a German confederation (as a gradual approach), for example, was rarely if ever presented as an option. Any specification of the "conditions" under which national unity might have been achieved implied a worst-case-scenario, e.g., through neutralization or a proposed dismantling of the free-market economy. Moreover, to ask citizens whether they might oppose reunification was to encourage an act of verbal treason against the Basic Law—in a country where the Chief Justices had decreed that anyone certifiably "cool and internally distant" towards the state could be banned from all forms of public employment.[64]

In short, few survey accounts have done either historical or psychological justice to the systemic dimensions of unity, to its global prerequisites and its likely domestic consequences.[65] Until 1989, working towards reunification was portrayed as one's patriotic duty, entailing no concrete costs for the individual FRG citizen: easy to "desire" under those conditions, one would think. One factor contributing to faulty assessments of the public's desire for unification was a propensity among FRG officials to report select responses "for" or "against" unity out of context. Many such findings prior to 1989 lose their compelling character when we view surveys in their entirety, that is, by comparing the number of FRG-dwellers who desired unity with those who actually expected it to come about. Yet on more than one occa-

TABLE 3.3   Reunification as "the Most Important Question Facing the Federal Republic"[a] (%)

Date		Total	Key Events of the Period
October	1951	18%	Stalin Note
July	1952	23%	Korean War
January	1953	17%	
August	1953	38%	
January	1955	34%	FRG—full member in Nato
January	1956	38%	Hallstein Doctrine,
			Berlin Crisis,
January	1957	43%	Khruschchev ultimatum
January	1959	45%	
January	1960	38%	
February	1961	35%	Mass GDR exodux,
February	1962	30%	Berlin Wall
January	1963	31%	
January	1964	41%	
January	1965	45%	
January	1966	29%	
January	1967	18%	Grand Coalition, CDU-SPD
January	1968	23%	
January	1969	22%	New left/Student Movement
Jan./Feb.	1970	12%	
January	1971	3%	Beginning of *Ostpolitik*
May	1972	2%	ratification of the *Ostvertraege*
February	1975	under 0.5%	and the *Grundlagenvertrag*
January	1976	1%	Both Germanys admitted to UN
February	1977	1%	
January	1978	1%	
January	1979	1%	
January	1980	under 0.5%	Nato Double-Track Decision
January	1981	1	
January	1983	under 0.5%	Peace Movement, mass demonstrations

[a] Early questionnaires referred to "West Germany."
Source: Allensbacher Archiv, cited by Elisabeth Noelle-Neumann, "Im Wartesaal der Geschichte. Bleibt das Bewusstsein der deutschen Einheit lebendig?" in Weidenfeld, Hg., *Nachdenken über Deutschland,* op cit., p. 134.

sion I was denied permission to examine specific questionnaires or raw data; the reason given was usually "copy-right law" [*Urheberprinzip*].

The first point to be made regarding popular commitment to reunification pertains to the salience of the issue. Clearly the plight of some twelve million refugees, missing relatives and prisoners of war rendered the desire for national unity a very personal concern for many Germans through the end of Occupation in 1955. Yet as Table 3.3 illustrates, the surveyed-majority (as opposed to its silent counterpart) never specified re-unification as its top priority when polled as to "the most important question with which the Federal Republic should generally concern itself." Respondents were regularly expected to choose from a list of seven or more alternatives, ranging from the situation in Berlin, European integration and atomic-weapons proliferation, to price stability and social policy; in the minds of many Germans these are not mutually exclusive but intricately connected items.

A second distinction worth noting is whether or not reunification is perceived as a pressing problem or as a desirable albeit idealistic policy goal. It is hard to assess the impact of question wording, but experiences in other issue areas prove that semantics can and do make a difference.[66] Through the mid-1960s, unification was mentioned more often as a "wish" or a "question" than as a "problem" requiring immediate attention, based on countless Emnid and Allensbach polls I reviewed at the Institute for Empirical Social Research (Köln).

We also need to differentiate between a human capacity for hope [*Prinzip Hoffnung*], on the one hand, and expectations grounded in the FRG-citizenry's grasp of global realities, on the other. In one of the first surveys run by Noelle and Neumann, a scant majority (58% among men, 45% among women) favored the creation of a West German federal-state in March 1949; this figure implied a desire among survivors to distance themselves from a centralized Germany held responsible for the travesty of war, not a wish for sustained division.[67] As late as May 1955, 51% (34% of the men, 66% of the women) admitted that they "were not familiar with the constitution" promulgated in 1949, and therefore could not judge it "good" or "bad."[68] Traditional gender roles aside, apoliticism was the order of the day, given the traumas of National Socialism, Occupation and the extraordinary demands of reconstruction preceding the survey. Many refrained from having any attitudes at all about the "state of the nation," or at least refused to express them.

Consolidation of the FRG's democratic institutions brought relatively stable expressions of support for (re)unification, albeit as an abstract hope. One indicator was the public's consistently positive reaction to the "unity mandate" anchored in the Basic Law. Questions concerning a possible deletion of key lines in the Preamble—"The entire German people are called upon to achieve in free self-determination the unity and freedom of Germany"—drew the responses between 1973 and 1982 shown in Table 3.4.

The higher levels of support displayed in the Allensbach survey or, conversely, the greater degree of skepticism reflected in the Emnid poll may owe to wording. Allensbach respondents could draw upon a wider range of personal motives for wishing to retain the passage ["should this sentence be left . . . ?"], for example, "as a piece of constitutional history" (interview

120

TABLE 3.4 Attitudes Toward the "Unity Mandate," According to Age

Allensbach Surveys	1973					1982				
	20–29	30–39	40–49	50–59	60–69	30–39	40–49	50–59	60–69	70+
Keep in Basic Law	61%	75%	72%	85%	82%	74%	76%	82%	83%	82%
Strike it	24%	9%	10%	5%	5%	14%	9%	10%	5%	2%
Undecided	15%	16%	18%	10%	13%	12%	15%	8%	12%	16%
	100%	100%	100%	100%	100%	100%	100%	100%	100%	100%

Emnid Surveys	1980					1985				
	<19	20–39	30–49	50–64	65+	<19	20–29	30–49	50–64	65+
Work towards, keep in	70%	49%	69%	71%	72%	61%	49%	64%	74%	77%
Give up goal, strike text	25%	42%	27%	25%	22%	27%	49%	33%	24%	19%
No answer	5%	9%	3%	4%	6%	12%	2%	3%	2%	3%

with Stuttgart Mayor, Manfred Rommel). Emnid's subjects, by contrast, were asked whether the Federal Government ought to continue to work towards reunification, or to surrender its mandate by striking the key clause. In 1973, 1980 and 1985, respondents in the 20–29 or 20–39 year-old bracket were more inclined to abandon the provision than any other age group. In 1973 those cohorts were most closely identified with the New Left Movement, and hence most inclined to criticize the nationalistic behavior of the preceding generation. By 1980 and 1985, these cohorts were actively associated with the eco-peace movements, and thus even more sensitive to the border-transcending nature of these issues.

Majority support for the abstract goal of *Wiedervereinigung* persisted, despite the fact that reportedly 75% (!) claimed familiarity with a 1974 revision of the GDR constitution, expunging all references to an eventual unification of the two states.[69] Indirect measures of identification with the belief in one German nation presented a fuzzier picture, however. Only 21% were "disturbed" by the use of the GDR flag and the GDR anthem at the time of the 1972 Munich Olympics, implying that most accepted its self-proclaimed sovereignty.[70] By the end of the decade, 57.2% associated the word Germany with the Federal Republic, in contrast to 27.4% who interpreted it to mean both states. Even the number of (ostensibly pro-unity) CDU/CSU voters equating *Deutschland* with the *Bundesrepublik* rose to 64.1% in 1985, exceeding the figures for all other partisan groups, with the exception of Green sympathizers (70.5%).[71]

Given their general embrace of the Basic Law, it is only logical that millions of duty-conscious citizens would respond positively when asked, "Do you strongly desire reunification, or is that not so important to you?" More interesting than the 60% who concurred in a 1976 Allensbach study, followed by 61% in 1981, are the 40% who spoke out against such a desire, including a majority of those aged 16–29 in both polls.[72] Surveys compiled by the *Forschungsgruppe Wahlen* recorded even higher levels of personal support in 1980 and 1984, as detailed in Table 3.5. Their findings nonetheless merit a closer look.

Most studies cited in this book claim to draw upon "representative" samples. The Allensbach data reviewed by this author include neither the actual sample size, nor the proportion of respondents in each age group. Concentrating on the FGW figures, it appears that the "totals" favoring reunification are skewed by the age distribution of the sample itself. Respondents most desirous of national unity are found in the 60-and-older category. The elderly comprised nearly 25% of the November 1980 FGW-pool, while they made up 28% of the January 1984 base; these cohorts accounted for 19.4% and 20.3% of the actual FRG population during those years. If the category is expanded to include all individuals who could be classified as members of the Economic Miracle Generation, their sample share rises to 42% (452 in 1980,

TABLE 3.5 Personal Support for Reunification, According to Age

November 1980 (in percentages)

	Total	M	F	18–24	25–29	30–39	40–49	50–59	60 and over
Personally									
For reunification	76.9%	77.1%	76.6%	62.1%	63.5%	75.9%	77.5%	81.0%	85.4%
Against reunification	7.0%	8.1%	6.2%	20.0%	11.3%	5.9%	7.1%	2.2%	3.7%
Indifferent	15.2%	13.6%	16.5%	17.9%	23.2%	16.3%	13.8%	16.8%	10.6%
n = 1,072	1,072	489	583	125	88	193	215	181	271

January 1985

	Total	M	F	18–24	25–29	30–39	40–49	50–59	60 and over
Personally									
For reunification	79.6%	80.5%	78.8%	61.0%	67.6%	76.8%	82.1%	88.0%	88.2%
Against reunification	3.9%	3.5%	4.2%	7.8%	7.2%	2.8%	3.7%	2.0%	2.5%
Indifferent	16.2%	15.8%	16.4%	31.2%	25.2%	18.6%	13.7%	10.0%	9.3%
n = 1,009	1,009	466	542	113	100	159	191	144	282

Sources: "Representative Population Survey for ZDF Barometer," conducted by Forschungsgruppe Wahlen, E. V., Mannheim, November 1980 and January 1984.

446 in 1984); these cohorts comprised less than 32% of all Federal Republicans for the periods in question.[73] Thus older groups evincing a sentimental attachment to the ideal of national unity were overrepresented in these samples; younger cohorts (many of whom refuse to participate in surveys) were seriously underrepresented in pre-1989 studies, though their lives have been more deeply affected by the merger processes of the last five years.

It was mounting indifference, rather than outright rejection, which began to undermine the dream of unity by the time of the FRG's thirtieth anniversary in 1979. Indifference was partly a function of age, afflicting most directly citizens whose "national experience" had been exclusively limited to the Western state. Diffidence among younger cohorts was also linked to skepticism over the political feasibility of unification. According to Emnid, the proportion of FRG-dwellers who *expected* German division to end in the establishment of a common state dropped from 10% in 1951, to 5% in 1959, and to 2% in 1973; the number convinced that unity would *not* come about rose from 28% in 1951 to 53% in 1973.[74] Infratest confirmed this trend in later studies: in 1972, 78% of all persons interviewed said they wished for reunification, but only 13% said they expected it to occur; figures for those aged 14–29 were 65% and 12%, respectively. By 1984, 78% of the total still wished for unity, but only 5% expected to see it happen; among participants under 30 the respective rates were 65% and 3%.[75]

Table 3.6 likewise shows that most Federal Republicans never anticipated a return to a unified nation-state during their lifetimes. Though the sample is weighted with residents "strongly desiring" unity, an overwhelming majority considered it an unattainable goal. By 1985, 67.6% of the population had been born after WW II or had been younger than 10 at war's end.[76] The rest more or less joined the post-postwar cohorts in embracing the benefits of *Entspannungspolitik*, the tension-reducing policies granting de facto if not de jure recognition to the GDR.

My own discussion partners were directly subjected to the expectations-test in 1985/86 via the question, "Do you believe in reunification, and if so, in what form?" With four exceptions (all self-avowed hardline-conservatives), the answers were uniformly negative across the generations. Typical responses included such remarks as: "That train left the station long ago" or *tote Hose;* "I don't even want it"; "not for the next 500 years"; "our neighbors would not agree to it"; "not under these conditions in Europe;" "I believe in God but not in reunification"; and "miracles happen in the church, not in politics." About half favored retaining the Preamble to the Basic Law, "as no particular barrier" to the improvement of East-West relations or simply "as a piece of constitutional history."

To ask whether a declining interest in reunification had lowered expectations regarding its probable occurrence, or, conversely, whether reduced expectations had led to a decreased interest in unity, is like raising the question

TABLE 3.6   Expected Time-Frame for Reunification (%)

FGW: "Do you believe that the merging *(Zusammenschluß)* of the two German
states into a single state within the next 30 years will certainly occur, possibly
occur *(eventuell)*, is not very probable, or that it is completely impossible?"

	September 1979	November 1980	January 1984	August 1985**
Is certain to occur	3.5	2.4	1.7	2.9
Possibly, "eventually"	18.4	15.0	17.2	14.6
Not very probable	50.5	51.1	51.7	51.7
	} =77.9%	}=82.3%	}=80.7%	}=82.1%
Impossible	27.4	31.2	29.0	30.4
n =	984	1,072	1,009	1,050

Emnid: "What do you believe, will the reunification of Germany become possible in
the foreseeable future? If yes, within the next 10 years, within the next 20
years, or even later?"

	June 1965	April 1966	March 1980	May/June 1985
Yes, within the next 10 years	20	25	4	4
Yes, within the next 20 years	15	25	8	5
Yes, but still later	15	13	18	13
No, not at all in the foreseeable future	39	28	52	59
No answer	11	9	18	18
	100%	100%	100%	100%

Sources: Emnid Informationen, 32. Jg., Nr. 4, 1980. Ibid., 37. Jg., Nr. 5, June
1985.
** The question posed in 1985 offered the time-frame "within the next 20–30
years."

as to the historical precedence of the chicken versus the egg. The same
dilemma applies to efforts to establish whether interest in unity, expectations
that it will occur, and one's willingness to pursue single-statehood actively are
dependent or independent variables. As Emnid reported in 1961, 49% of the
West Germans believed "much patience was needed" in order to achieve
unity over a period of two to three decades, a view shared by 55% in 1964;
23% of those polled in 1961, and 26% in 1964, thought it necessary to "press
quickly ahead," even if certain perils were involved.[77] Allensbach surveys
(summarized in Table 3.7) signal a clear break with the past by 1983, the
point at which a majority clearly favored leaving German unity up to "fate."
    We also need to consider external barriers to reunification, real or imag-
ined, which may have eroded interest and expectations over time. The Cold

TABLE 3.7   Reunification: How Actively Should It Be Pursued?

Allensbacher Surveys: "How do you see the situation at this time? Does it have any purpose (make any sense) to keep demanding that Germany should be reunited, or should we simply leave that up to time?"

	September 1956 %	February 1958 %	April/May 1959 %	April 1964 %	November 1983 %
Keep demanding	65	64	65	69	33
Leave up to time	25	24	25	21	55
Undecided	10	12	10	10	12

Source: Cited by Elisabeth Noelle-Neumann, "Im Wartesaal der Geschichte. Bleibt das Bewußtsein der deutschen Einheit lebendig?" in Weidenfeld, Hg., *Nachdenken über Deutschland,* op. cit., p. 134 (Allensbacher Archiv, IFD-Umfragen 098, 1016, 1030, 1088, 4035).

War features most prominently throughout the 1950s, when the blame for division was attributed primarily to the Eastern bloc. As early as 1952, only 5% believed it possible to bring about unity within a year under the auspices of the United Nations; 43% saw no prospect for attaining this end, due to an intensification of the Cold War. The share of absolute-pessimists reached 51% in 1955, rising to 74% by 1958.[78]

Nearly three-fifths (58%) agreed that overcoming division was completely dependent upon the designs of the Occupying Powers.[79] While 49% specified the behavior of Moscow and East German officials as the main hindrance in 1954, only 28% blamed the socialist camp in 1958. Nearly one-third (29%) had come to see the antagonistic contradictions between East and West as the real barrier to unity.[80] Pollsters found in 1952 that a clear majority (55%) was "in no case" prepared to renounce all claims to territories beyond the Oder-Neisse border as a prerequisite for unity. The next year 43% declared that they would not accept a Soviet demand for a bloc-free Germany; 67% held that free elections in both parts of Germany would have to precede a consultative assembly (with an equal number of delegates) as a framework for unification. At the same time 69% rejected the possible participation of Communists in a government thus unified, and 84% would have required the complete de-nationalization of agricultural and industrial properties.[81]

Cold War impediments receded into the background during the early stages of détente, leading West Germans to redefine the conditions under which they might welcome reunification. Over the next decade certain attitudinal changes began to take on a life of their own, including one very important orientation not reflected in Table 3.8: by the end of the 1970s the public had come to view concession of the Eastern territories as a given. Among my own interview

TABLE 3.8 Acceptance of Conditions for Reunification

Question: "Imagine that the GDR also displays a very strong interest in reunification. Which of the following conditions would you be willing to accept if that would make it possible?"

	Leaving NATO, Becoming Neutral			Soviet Troops in the FRG, Western Troops in GDR Until Treaty is Final			Free Elections Delayed as a Prerequisite			Communist Participation in Government			Restrictions on the Current Economic System (e.g., Freedom of Competition)		
	Total	M	F	Total	M	F	Total	M	F	Total	M	F	Total	M	F
Prepared	35	34	36	13	13	13	11	12	10	19	21	17	17	16	18
Not prepared	46	51	41	69	72	66	70	72	68	63	61	65	61	66	55
Don't know	16	10	21	16	11	20	16	11	20	13	11	15	19	13	24
No answer	3	4	2	3	4	2	4	5	3	5	7	3	3	5	2

N = 1,004
Male = 402
Female = 532

Source: Emnid Informationen, 30. Jg., Nr. 6 - 1978.

partners only three individuals with personal ties to the Refugee Associations called for a return to the pre-1937 borders by way of a peace treaty. Most of my respondents believed that a dramatically transformed global environment had rendered the idea of a "peace treaty" more or less irrelevant by 1985.

Attitudes towards the question of unity at the cost of neutrality are a little more complex than the data imply. Allensbach registered a positive trend among those who would have "welcome[d] a reunification of Germany" under this condition, climbing from 38% in 1978, to 47% in 1980, to a high of 53% in 1981.[82] The most plausible explanation for this increase is not the changing of the generational guard per se, but rather the adoption of the NATO Double Track Decision in December 1979, sparking the mobilization of a country-wide peace movement. The Soviet Union alone was no longer faulted for holding the Germans hostage to a potentially nasty fate; ever more citizens reached the conclusion that it was the proliferation of nuclear weapons in their own backyards that would sustain division "until death do us unify."[83] Hence, deliberate efforts to reestablish a common Father-State took a backseat to the more pressing problems of nuclear-weapons and nuclear-energy proliferation.

Although most West Germans no longer viewed re-unification as a serious agenda item by 1980, two issues continued to enjoy special status in recognition of old national bonds. The first centered on the extension of special credits to the GDR, such as a DM 1.2 billion appropriation for the Hamburg-Berlin *Autobahn*, to secure the transit route. Approval of this and similar credits was nevertheless qualified. Two-thirds deemed financial assistance acceptable only if the GDR delivered human rights concessions in exchange; nearly three-fourths expressed dissatisfaction with the paltry liberalization measures that the GDR had undertaken to date.[84] This author was unable to locate data on attitudes towards Bonn's practice of "buying out" imprisoned or persecuted GDR citizens dating back to the mid-1960s. According to recently declassified documents, the amount of hard currency poured into this "exchange" was substantial, totaling over DM 50 billion across 22 years.[85]

The second centered on the status of Berlin, which retained its Front-City status more than twenty-five years after its physical division. Roughly four-fifths of the inhabitants of "Rest"-Germany (as Berliners referred to the other ten *Länder*) consistently supported efforts to keep West-Berlin free between 1953 and 1978, ranging from 78–88%.[86] Berlin was associated with the term *Hauptstadt* [capital-city] between 1953–1958, following a 1957 Bundestag's resolution re-affirming its "future" role; references to the Four-Sector City, a carry-over from Occupation, declined from 29% to 11% during the same period.[87]

The equation Berlin = *Mauer* moved into the foreground of FRG consciousness after August 13, 1961; "the Wall" accounted for 36% of the Berlin-associations in 1962, rising to 55% in 1968, and 58% (evenly spread across all age groups) in 1979.[88] Despite the Wall's prominence, only 12% believed that a military confrontation was "likely" to ensue over its creation, 47% thought it "possible," and 33% judged it "improbable"—in a poll conducted on August 28, 1961! Only 21% identified Berlin as the problem necessitating Bonn's "most urgent response," though less than two-thirds believed that Allied Powers would come to the city's defense in the event of a Soviet incursion.[89] Berlin-divided very quickly shifted from serving as a "symbol of confrontation to [a] keystone of stability."[90]

The 1980s gave rise to a few disturbing trends from the vantage point of the Berliners. The Half-City's reputation as a gathering place for Leftist radicals, militant feminists, housing-squatters, anarcho-punks, asylum-seekers, gay-rights activists and alternative cultures began to chip away at the traditional support among the Rest-Germans. Once transit routes had been secured under the *1971 Quadripartite Treaty* and the *1972 Basis of Relations Treaty*, related problems facing the "island city" faded from public consciousness. "Mainlanders" underestimated the incredible financial and infrastructural burdens imposed by West-Berlin's status as a city-without-a-hinterland, ranging from its need to retain emergency-reserves (DM 100 million worth of food and supplies per year) as a hedge against future blockades, to its formidable problems of waste disposal.[91] An August 1985 survey indicated that 50.9% of the non-Berliners found Bonn's annual subsidies-payment of nearly DM 12 billion to the city "just about right"; 42% favored a reduction. Yet 73% agreed that Berlin should again serve as the Republic's capital city at some unspecified future date.[92]

In 1987 Berlin commemorated its 750th anniversary, with celebratory events clearly divided along the East-West fault line. In a 1986 survey of 1,018 Berlin residents, 27.3% cited unemployment as the most serious problem facing the city, and 17.2% referred to "foreigners"; a mere 7.8% mentioned the Wall (or shoot-to-kill orders among GDR border guards). Citizens under 30 were most anxious about unemployment and environmental issues; "the foreigner problem" was mentioned most often by older cohorts.[93] Over two-thirds felt they could rely further upon West-German support, in contrast to 28% who characterized their countrywo/men as *berlinmüde* [tired of Berlin]. Curiously, more Berliners (48.3%) were bothered by the "hardship" that the city's island-status posed for their ability to undertake weekend-trips than by the fact that they could not vote in direct elections to the Bundestag (28.7%)! Local residents deviated significantly from the "party lines" drawn by the city's reigning CDU and SED governments over preparations for the 750th anniversary celebration. More than three-fourths asserted that the mayors of East and West Berlin should have participated in each other's respective commemorative events.[94]

In short, an overwhelming majority of West Germans had reconciled themselves to the idea that "provisional" national division had become permanent by the 1980s. Political-economic asymmetries generated by the FRG's "rump-state" status were accepted as facts of life. The German cultural-nation had lost most of its relevance for the post-1960s cohorts who knew or cared little about the achievements of the classical *Dichter und Denker*. Cultural ties between the young Germans of East and West were more likely to find their roots in the music of *Pink Floyd* than in the compositions of Beethoven and Mozart, in the latest episodes of *Dallas* and *Dynasty* rather than in the dramas of Schiller and Lessing. Just as younger citizens had come to view the radical as the routine, many older cohorts joined in the perception that the abnormal had become the norm. The deprivation of liberty experienced by their Eastern neighbors was a matter of humanitarian, not "national" concern. Thus, it was relatively easy for West Germans of all ages to join in the euphoric celebrations that commenced on the night of November 9, 1989—but all the more difficult to digest the turn of events that followed.

Conclusion: November the 9th and the National Paradigm Shift

Mikhail Gorbachev's ascension to power in 1985, coupled with signs of real political change in Poland and Hungary, provided a new backdrop for inter-German relations. Twice cancelled under Soviet hard-liners Brezhnev and Chernenko, Erich Honecker's first visit to Bonn as the GDR head-of-state in September 1987 gave birth to modest hopes for reform-from-within among the Eastern citizenry and even among the ranks of the SED itself.[95] Honecker's bold advances on the foreign policy front, in response to the first Soviet nuclear deployments on GDR soil in 1983–84, were not matched by an affinity for *glasnost* and *perestroika* on the domestic front.

On the contrary: the SED argued that it had already successfully restructured its economy in the early 1960s by decentralizing many of its industrial enterprises. It was thus able to interpret Gorbachev's thesis that countries could rightfully pursue nationally-specific paths to socialism as an affirmation of its own course. The GDR-gerontocracy refused to budge, hoping that Gorbachev's New Political Thinking would soon be nipped in the bud by Moscow hard-liners.[96] East Berlin therefore initiated a crackdown against its own peace and ecology activists, going so far as to prevent the distribution of *glasnost* and *perestroika* publications imported from the Soviet Union, such as the magazine *Sputnik*.

GDR party-bosses meanwhile sought to appease the silent majority by increasing the opportunities for family visits and legal migration to the West, although securing the proper papers for both purposes remained a nerve-wracking and demeaning process. Liberalized travel provisions had the unfortunate effect of dividing East German society all the more clearly into haves and have-nots: it delineated households with FRG-relatives who could take advantage of the travel code, receive packages, or buy scarce goods with Western currency, from residents who had no such contacts and thus had to make-do with the deficiencies of the system.

The rapid deterioration of living standards outside the "Capital City of the GDR" after 1985 transformed modest hopes for reform into mass resignation, intensified by the 1987–88 crackdowns. Scarce construction materials and skilled laborers were siphoned off to Berlin for vanity projects such as the Nikolai Quarter, while cities like Leipzig and Dresden literally fell apart.[97] Bombastic SED plans for the 750th anniversary celebration provoked tremendous resentment beyond the city limits, though discontent was often shrouded in black humor, to avoid problems with the secret police. Angered by the *750 Years—Berlin* bumper-stickers issued at state expense, for example, provincial residents crafted signs reading "861 Years—Leipzig" and "350 million Years—*Erzgebirge*." Refusing to heed the warnings of district party officers, the leadership added insult to injury in 1989 with its fraudulent conduct of the May communal elections, added to its pomp-and-circumstance plans for the country's 40th anniversary observance in October.

In May 1989 Hungary agreed to uphold the free-passage provision of the Geneva Convention on Refugees, leading it to dismantle its own barbed-wire borders. The ramifications of this decision did not become clear until August, when a tidal-wave of would-be-Westerners suddenly headed for the "green frontier" from their vacation spots along Lake Balaton outside of Budapest. Nearly 100,000 not-so-happy-GDR-campers poured into Austria, virtually overnight, on their way to a new life in the Federal Republic— to the utter shock and amazement of the natives. The initial Western reaction was one of warm welcome, accompanied by a clear willingness to assist newcomers in their search for housing and jobs. Overtaken by a chain of events utterly at odds with its penchant for order and predictability, the Federal Republic suddenly saw itself as a chaotic country in a good mood, culminating in the euphoric night of November 9–10, 1989.

The flood of refugees and visitors recounting their tales of "day-to-day misery" made West Germans acutely aware of their own good fortune; some even felt a little guilty. During Phase One of the *Wende* (August through November), the hosts displayed a strong willingness to take in ever more kindred spirits from the other Germany. Significant numbers were prepared to open their arms, if not their wallets, to the new arrivals (see Table 3.9). While less than one-half welcomed the influx at the outset, over two-thirds viewed immigration positively by October. The critical turning-point came in late November, after both Honecker and his heir-apparent, Egon Krenz, had resigned, and after the Wall itself had miraculously opened.

The first calls for a "Germany, united Fatherland" were heard in Plauen on November 25 but did not reverberate throughout the East until *after* the November 28th proclamation of Kohl's Ten-Point Program.[98] Millions

TABLE 3.9   Reactions to the GDR Übersiedler and Refugees, 1989–1990

Question: "Right now many resettlers and refugees from the GDR are moving over here. Do you welcome or do you not welcome this development?"

GDR – Immigrants	August 1989 %	September 1989 %	October 1989 %	November 1989 %
Welcome the influx	48.9	66.1	64.1	69.3
Do not welcome the influx	46.0	27.7	28.1	26.1
Don't know	5.1	6.2	7.8	4.6
n =	1,002	1,003	1,011	1,017

Question: "When citizens from the GDR now still desire to move over to the Federal Republic, can you fully understand that, is it only partially comprehensible or do you not understand [this desire]?"

	December 1989 %	January 1990 %	February 1990 %
Understand completely	26.3	22.0	22.8
Have some understanding	49.4	52.6	41.0
Can't understand it	24.0	24.9	35.4
n =	978	1,016	1,006

of GDR-dwellers had taken the opportunity to "test the West" during the three weeks following the breaching of the Wall. But rather than stem the flow, the freedom to travel brought a new outpouring of resettlers who felt they had waited long enough for their share of the national pie. Intellectuals and church activists who had boldly instigated the first mass-demonstrations in Dresden, Leipzig and Berlin were soon displaced by rowdier proletarians, once the threat of a forceful governmental response was eliminated.[99] The no-longer silent majority displayed little interest in the efforts of New Forum and other opposition groups to establish Round Tables and to plan for a democratic transformation. The reconstruction of their own society would have required too much time, effort and additional hardship, as they understood the realities of dialectical materialism. By relocating to the FRG thousands expected the chance to live the good life immediately, largely at the expense of Western taxpayers.

Transitional camps had to accommodate 2,500–3,000 new arrivals per day from November through January, aggravating problems of housing, unemployment and budget deficits for city administrators in Giessen, Hannover, Berlin, and Bremen, inter alia. Having preached unification-gospel for decades, reigning conservatives in Bonn were unwilling to supplement

TABLE 3.10   Potential Disadvantages of Unification, 1989–1990

Question: When you think about jobs, are you afraid that you might personally face
disadvantages because of the refugees and GDR resettlers coming here?
Question: And how about the housing situation, do you think that you might be
personally disadvantaged by the refugees and resettlers from the GDR?

	Sept. '89 %	Oct. '89 %	Nov. '89 %	Dec. '89 %	Jan. '90 %
Disadvantages regarding jobs					
Yes	14.3	14.9	16.4	18.7	21.4
No	83.9	83.8	82.0	80.9	77.9
Not applicable, don't know	1.8	1.2	1.6	—	—
n =	1,003	1,011	1,017	978	1,106
Disadvantages regarding apartments					
Yes	25.6	30.4	29.0	32.8	30.5
No	73.3	69.0	70.2	66.7	69.0
Not applicable, don't know	1.2	0.6	0.8	—	—
n =	1,003	1,011	1,017	978	1,016

the coffers of overburdened (and largely SPD-ruled) city governments once the process was underway. Overcrowded shopping areas, massive traffic jams, increasing pollution, and no apparent end to the flood of refugees eventually impelled the FRG and GDR leaders to move towards unification sooner rather than later.[100]

While the Kohl Government continued to present unification as a relatively low-cost operation—despite hefty criticism from SPD Chancellor-candidate Lafontaine—the public began to realize that national unity would not come cheaply. Perceived disadvantages likely to befall average citizens caused public opinion to shift in a less generous direction, as Tables 3.10 and 3.11 show. The percent of West Germans who feared increasing competition in the labor market rose from 14.3% in September to 21.4% by January. Their anxiety stemmed from early reports that most of the resettlers were young, "highly skilled" workers; the latter soon discovered that the technologies for which they had been trained lagged fifteen years behind those used in FRG-manufacturing. Worries over new pressures on an already tight housing market were even more pronounced, rising from 25.6% to 30% over a five-month period. Least comfortable with the turn of events

TABLE 3.11 Perceived Disadvantages Regarding Housing and Jobs, According to Age and Education Levels

September 1989

	Total	M	F	-24	-29	-39	-49	-59	60 and older
	1,003	463	540	130	89	177	166	164	276
Disadvantages, Job									
Yes	14.3	9.3	18.7	22.0	19.6	15.7	14.5	12.8	9.0
No	83.9	89.7	78.9	78.0	79.3	83.5	84.1	85.5	87.4
Not applicable	1.8	1.0	2.4	0.0	1.2	0.9	1.4	1.7	3.6
Disadvantages, Housing									
Yes	25.6	19.4	30.8	41.4	34.9	27.0	20.2	24.5	18.0
No	73.3	79.2	68.2	57.1	65.1	71.2	79.8	74.1	80.5
Not applicable	1.2	1.4	1.0	1.5	0.0	1.8	0.0	1.4	1.5

Age and Education	Total	-34 Volks-schule	-34 Mittel-schule	-34 Abitur	35+ Volks. o. Lehre	35+ Volks. m. Lehre	35+ Mittel-schule	35+ Abitur
	1,003	104	104	108	126	279	17	112
Disadvantages, Jobs								
Yes	14.3	33.0	16.0	11.4	18.3	14.7	8.7	1.6
No	83.9	65.5	84.0	88.6	78.6	82.5	90.7	95.4
Not applicable	1.8	1.5	0.0	0.0	3.1	2.8	0.6	3.0
Disadvantages, Housing								
Yes	25.6	46.4	34.6	27.2	23.9	24.8	20.2	8.0
No	73.3	51.6	62.9	72.8	73.4	75.2	78.4	90.6
Not applicable	1.2	2.0	2.5	0.0	2.7	0.0	1.3	1.4

January 1990

	Total	M	F	-24	-29	-39	-49	-59	60 and older
	1,016	474	542	139	94	178	162	160	283
Disadvantages, Job									
Yes	21.4	16.7	25.5	26.3	33.2	20.0	16.7	25.4	16.4
No	77.9	83.1	73.3	73.7	66.8	80.0	82.2	74.6	81.6
Disadvantages, Housing									
Yes	30.5	25.4	35.1	60.6	36.3	27.8	19.4	24.8	25.2
No	69.0	74.3	64.3	39.4	62.7	71.9	79.5	75.2	74.3

	Total	-34 Volks-schule	-34 Mittel-schule	-34 Abitur	35+ Volks. o. Lehre	35+ Volks. m. Lehre	35+ Mittel-schule	35+ Abitur
	1,016	100	120	105	143	259	174	114
Disadvantages, Jobs								
Yes	21.4	39.8	28.4	11.3	30.8	19.8	13.6	11.1
No	77.9	60.2	71.6	88.7	68.2	79.0	84.6	88.9
Disadvantages, Housing								
Yes	30.5	40.3	45.9	45.7	27.2	26.5	22.3	18.9
No	69.0	59.1	53.3	54.3	71.8	72.8	77.7	81.9

were the younger or less well-educated FRG-groups, which was understand-able insofar as these strata faced the greatest competition for new jobs and affordable housing under normal circumstances.

One series of polls conducted between August 1989 and February 1990 effectively captures the rapid pace of East German developments, along with their impact on Western attitudes towards unity during those months. Ta-bles 3.12 and 3.13 indicate that roughly three-fourths of the respondents (more than half of the December sample) favored unification as a general principle; question-wording did not specify a probable time-frame nor sug-gest any particular costs. Very little was known about the abysmal condition of the Eastern industrial landscape until the final negotiations for "acces-sion" were well under way. While age, educational level and party affiliation explain some of the variation in support levels, they unfortunately provide little insight as to citizens' motives for favoring or opposing a merger of the two states. One interesting feature of these data (Table 3.13) is the ostensi-ble break in support found between persons younger than 39 and respon-dents over 40, especially compared to those aged 50 and older (December data drew upon different question-wording).

Responses to other questions convey the difficulty many West Germans had shifting their attitudinal gears in an effort to keep pace with the trans-formational impulses in the East. In August 1989, 33.9% felt that the CDU Government was "doing too little" to promote *Wiedervereinigung* (term used by pollsters), 8.3% argued "too much," and 50.2% found the level of activity "just about right"; in fact, unity was not even on its agenda at the time.[101] When asked in October whether a reunification of the two German states would "come within the next ten years," 27.7% of the Westerners said yes, 63.5% thought it impossible. Over 58% of the people principally op-posed to unity nonetheless supported the idea of financial assistance to to secure reforms East of the border; the day after Honecker's abdication (Oc-tober 18), 53% doubted that fundamental changes would ensue.[102]

Among the individuals who favored unification in November, 53.4% were willing to accept neutrality as its pre-condition. Only 48.1% of this sample expected unity to become a reality over a ten-year period; 95% thought that the flow of refugees would cease with the execution of Western-style elec-tions in the GDR. Roughly 81% of the anti-unity respondents favored the provision of extensive financial aid on the condition of free elections.[103] As of December 1989, 33.8% expected to witness the creation of a single state, compared to 41.7% who imagined a confederation being formed over a ten-year period; 78% labeled the Kohl Plan "good," yet 32% felt that govern-mental aid to the GDR "went too far" (little had been paid out by then, be-yond "welcome money" for first-time visitors). A majority held that leading FRG politicians were "interfering too much" in GDR reforms; another 42% claimed that incoming migrants were receiving too many benefits.[104]

TABLE 3.12 Attitudes Toward Unification Before and After the Opening of the Wall, 1989–1990

Question: Are you personally for reunification of the two German states, are you against reunification, or are you really indifferent regarding reunification?

Reunification	August, 1989			October, 1989			November, 1989			December, 1989*			February, 1990		
	Total	M	F	Total	M	F	Total	M	F	Total	M	F	Total	M	F
For	78.8	78.6	79.1	75.0	75.0	75.1	69.8	64.9	74.0	55.6	56.4	54.9	78.2	81.6	75.1
Against	8.4	7.5	9.1	10.8	12.1	9.6	14.9	17.7	12.5	41.3	40.4	42.1	11.8	10.8	12.8
Indifferent	11.5	13.3	10.0	11.7	10.4	12.8	12.1	14.6	10.0	—	—	—	7.7	6.4	8.9
Don't know	1.3	0.7	1.8	2.4	2.3	2.5	3.2	2.8	3.5	3.1	3.2	3.0	2.3	1.2	3.2
n =	1,002	467	536	1,011	470	541	1,017	474	543	978	457	521	1,006	470	536

* Question rephrased: When you think of the future of the Federal Republic and the GDR, should the Federal Republic and the GDR form one common state, or should they remain two independent German states?

Source: Forschungsgruppe Wahlen. Representative surveys for ZDF Politbarometer (courtesy of Dieter Roth).

TABLE 3.13 Attitudes Toward Reunification, 1989–1990, According to Age

For Reunification:	Total	Age					
		Under 24	25–29	30–39	40–49	50–59	60/older
August '89	78.8	66.7	66.3	65.4	79.0	93.2	88.8
October '89	75.0	66.2	65.4	66.2	72.9	77.6	87.4
November '89	69.8	57.2	57.2	68.5	65.2	84.7	75.7
December '89	55.6	51.4	44.7	37.4	59.0	66.5	65.4
February '90	78.2	61.8	55.3	63.6	84.9	89.9	93.1

Sources: Forschungsgruppe Wahlen E. V., Mannheim, representative surveys for ZDF Politbarometer, August, September, October, November, December 1989, January, February 1990.

When asked to consider the reform dynamic in the GDR, 32.8% of respondents felt that the process was moving "too quickly," 26% said "too slowly," and 36.4% found it "exactly right" as of January 1990. The majority no longer objected to intervention by West-politicians, but 52% now complained about "too many" benefits for resettlers.[105] With the first free election campaign in full swing by February, 52.3% had come to expect that unification would occur within a year, although 54.7% believed that the merger would bring more disadvantages than benefits in the short run. Two-thirds welcomed the decision to introduce the Western D-Mark as soon as possible; a majority associated unification with a feeling of "joy," but 18.6% looked to its occurrence with a sense of *Angst*.[106] The Western mood as of this writing (1995) seems to be one of "grimace and bear it." Long partial to the notion that they embody an historical community of destiny, the new Germans fortunately have at their disposal a much more positive, peaceful set of ideals and institutions than ever accorded them by destiny in the past.[107]

Shortly before the Turn-around of 1989, Antonia Grunenberg rejected the idea that identity could simply be transferred from a self-contained, individual level to an enduring, collective level. Common political behaviors do not automatically flow from from an abstract reference system based on history and language. Efforts to apply a standard measure of identity to the two Germanys is an approach doomed to fail:

> The projection of [such an] identity-concept onto societies or peoples has as its prerequisites a societal consensus, a commonality of experience and an intellectual processing which does not exist [in the German case]. . . . If need be, one can nowadays call forth a patriotism among segments of the population using pure demagogy, but the [essence] of what it was once considered to be in its historical tradition, namely, as the consciousness of belonging to one's own country, as pride in its traditions and historical achievements, that is something that cannot be produced *ex cathedra*. . . . Identity emerges out of the problems of life. . . . It is the ability to come to an understanding, not the unification of the two Germanys with different foundations, and their "nuance-rich" communication with European neighbors in the East and West which could in this sense serve as a beginning, set free a new European identity.[108]

De jure unification may be a necessary condition for restoring understanding between the citizens of the former postwar states, but problems emerging over the last five years prove that it is not a sufficient condition for re-establishing a truly national identity. The evidence presented above affirms my thesis that by the 1980s a substantial segment of West German society no longer believed unification was particulary desirable, few thought it was likely to occur during their watch, and almost no one expected to pay a great deal in order to make the nation whole again.

Since the two states officially became one on October 3, 1990—old and new, Eastern and Western—countless polling organizations have sought to determine whether the unified Germans are "different" or "alike." The short-term nature of most post-Wall comparisons is rather problematic; the categories used mirror a Western bias, and findings often reinforce negative stereotypes. In an effort to come full circle, let us briefly consider two such studies which point to a number of substantial differences, and curious similarities, between the peoples of the former postwar states. *The Profile of the Germans* compiled by *Der Spiegel* reflects the opinions of some 3,400 East and West residents, sampled between mid-September and early October 1990.[109] The second study, published by the *Süddeutsche Zeitung*, involved 2,000 people interviewed between early October and mid-November 1990.[110] Both covered a wide variety of political, life-style and value orientations, though the *Spiegel* analysis offered a more detailed picture of particular subgroups, for example, women and youth.

Most striking are the equivalent levels of support accorded major political parties in conjunction with the first all-German elections to the Bundestag (December 2, 1990). The victorious CDU/CSU secured 44.3% of the Western vote, 41.8% of the Eastern vote. In the old Länder, 35.7% cast their ballot for the SPD, matched by a figure of 24.3% in the new Länder; 10.6% in the West and 12.9% in the East opted for the FDP. The predominance of the Western parties, their aggressive campaign styles and their "household-name" candidates, account for much of this congruence, following a pattern set during the first free *Volkskammer* elections (March 18, 1990). Slightly lower levels of support for the two main contenders owe largely to the "vote of gratitude" (6%) Easterners cast for the Alliance '90/Greens, as well as to the 11% garnered by the SED-turned-PDS among ex-communist functionaries. While Kohl's Western supporters included many industrialists and financiers ("capitalists"), his Alliance for Germany voters in the East drew largely from the working class, hoping for a quick end to the socialist malaise; these two constituencies may prove irreconcilable in the long run, however. By 1994, the SPD and even the ex-communist PDS witnessed a comeback at the state level, in reaction to the "the tax lie" propagated by Kohl in the West and in response to efforts by these parties to promote "native-born" candidates in the East.

Citizens in the old and new Bundesländer manifested different degrees of self-confidence in 1990, affecting their feelings of political efficacy. The so-called *Ossis* [Easterners] described themselves as more modest, more considerate of others, less money-oriented and friendlier towards children; they also saw themselves as more insecure and dependent, more provincial and less entrepreneurial. Three-fourths expected to retain the staus of second-class citizens many years after unification. Almost twice as many *Wessis* [Westerners] rated their personal economic situations as very good; they were also twice as willing to "close the book on history" after 40 years (40% West: 23% East), while the newly enfranchised stressed a need to investigate the past and prosecute the culpable.[111] Easterners are stronger proponents of work-force opportunities for women, state subsidies for child-care, and liberalized abortion regulations. Westerners are more averse to nuclear energy and more insistent on designating environmental protection the government's top priority (74% West: 59% East).[112]

It is not only the past four decades of authoritarian education but also the rising crime rates, youth violence and mass unemployment that have reinforced a desire among Eastern residents for more discipline, a stronger police presence and respect for state authority over the last five years. Many speak of an ever-thicker Wall-in-the-head, reflected in a proliferation of often bitter *Ossi* and *Wessi* jokes, as well as in a growing spirit of *Ostalgie* [East-nostalgia].[113]

One pundit attending a 1990 Harvard conference on East-West "differences" compared German unification to the plight of a couple once engaged but separated over a long period of time. After 40 years, the fiancée suddenly reappears and utters those fateful words, "Take me, I'm yours!" While both have aged considerably, the prospective bride now strikes the groom as rather fat and ugly, the commentator mused [given the "triple burden" faced by real GDR women, she would probably look underfed and overworked]. Yet the groom has no alternative but to honor his word.

As millions of Baby-Boomers realize, the processes of dating, cohabitating, and being married are fundamentally different. No matter how prolonged the first two stages, the final, presumably permanent stage always brings countless surprises and many unanticipated conflicts: Marriage can make many things that are molehills suddenly turn into mountains. Differences that may have seemed inconsequential in relation to the identity-orientations of Germans living apart take on a whole new meaning, now that their union has been witnessed and blessed by the international community. Officials in the old and new states cannot simply wait for a common national consciousness to emerge; like any marriage, the Germans will have to strive continuously to "make this one work." The partners are quite mismatched in terms of their ability to build or control the relationship, a setting very familiar to the nation's women. The dominant partner, as of this writing, is reluctant to give up his identity as a swinging-single, though he realizes that being a "couple" brings new obligations. When GDR-demonstrators began to chant "We are one People," Westerners responded—only half in jest—"So are we!"

Many difficult times lie ahead. The need to promote rapid economic growth in the new states is sharply at odds with the necessity of reviving its poisoned environment, at least in the eyes of many investors. Women face an acute crisis of adjustment as regards their access to new employment opportunities, child-care facilities, and legal abortion (see Chapter 6). The search for common ground between the two peoples should not begin with a requirement that both identify with a German *Kulturnation* of ages past but with efforts to secure their mutual commitment to a new European Peace Order in the years ahead. It is to the national security orientations of the old and new Federal Republicans that we now turn.

Notes

1. Peter Brandt and Herbert Ammon, Hg., *Die Linke und die nationale Frage. Dokumente zur deutschen Einheit seit 1945* (Reinbek: Rowohlt, 1981), p. 17.

2. Gebhard Schweigler, *National Consciousness in a Divided Germany* (London/Beverly Hills: Sage, 1975), p. 168.

3. Dr. Marion Gräfin Dönhoff, in *Die deutsche Frage neugestreut* (Hamburg: Körber-Stiftung, 1983), p. 19.

4. Dönhoff, "Von der Geschichte längst überholt. Wiedervereinigung oder Europäische Union—keine Alternative mehr," *Die Zeit*, Nr. 4, 27. January 1989.

5. A standard reference work commissioned by the Bundesminister für innerdeutsche Beziehungen is Hartmut Zimmermann's *DDR Handbuch*, Vol. 1 and 2 (Köln: Verlag Wissenschaft und Politik, most recent edition 1985). Gisela Helwig, editor of *Deutschland Archiv*, wrote frequently on social policy; see *Frau und Familie in beiden deutschen Staaten* (Köln: Wissenschaft und Politik, 1982). Gert-Joachim Glaeßner produced a very insightful anthology, *Die DDR in der Ära Honecker. Politik—Kultur—Gesellschaft* (Opladen: Westdeutscher Verlag, 1989), shortly before *die Wende*, as did Antonia Grunenberg, *Aufbruch der inneren Mauer. Politik und Kultur in der DDR 1971–1990* (Bremen: Edition Temmen, 1990). Historical "classics" include Peter C. Ludz, *Die DDR zwischen Ost und West. Politische Analysen von 1961 bis 1976* (München: C.H. Beck, 1980); and Dietrich Staritz, *Geschichte der DDR, 1949–1985* (Frankfurt/M: Suhrkamp, 1985). Representing the last camp is Karl W. Fricke, *Politik und Justiz in der DDR. Zur Geschichte der politischen Verfolgung, 1945–1968*. Berichte und Dokumentation (Köln: Wissenschaft und Politik, 1979). GDR-research per se became a focus of heated political debate, as explained by Glaeßner in "Die Mühe der Ebene. DDR-Forschung in der Bundesrepublik," in *Die Ära Honecker*, loc.cit., pp. 111–119.

6. Bundesministerium für innerdeutsche Beziehungen, Hg., *Zehn Jahre Deutschlandpolitik, Die Entwicklung der Beziehungen zwischen der Bundesrepublik Deutschland und der Deutschen Demokratischen Republik 1969–1979* (Bonn: 1980); further, BMIB, *Materialien zum Bericht zur Lage der Nation im geteilten Deutschland*, issued in Bonn, 1971, 1972, 1974 and 1987.

7. Dieter Bossmann, Hg., *Schüler über die Einheit der Nation: Ergebnisse einer Umfrage* (Frankfurt/M: Fischer Verlag, 1978). Bossmann and Münster historian Erich Kosthorst are cited in "Wiedervereinigung—'gefährliches Lernziel'?" *Der Spiegel*, Nr. 15, April 1978, p. 97ff.

8. Examples include Günter Gaus, *Wo Deutschland liegt—Eine Ortsbestimmung* (Hamburg: Hoffmann und Campe, 1983); and Klaus Bölling, *Die fernen Nachbarn. Erfahrungen in der DDR* (Hamburg: Gruner + Jahr, 1983).

9. Impressions gleaned from the second trip were first reported in *Die Zeit* (June 13–August 15, 1986), then under the auspices of Theo Sommer, Hg., *Reise ins andere Deutschland* (Hamburg: Rowohlt, 1986).

10. See, inter alia, Wolfgang Büscher, Peter Wensierski and Klaus Wolschner, Hg., *Friedensbewegung in der DDR, Texte, 1978–1982* (Hattingen: Scandica Verlag, 1982); Wensierski and Büscher, *Beton ist Beton, Zivilisationskritik aus der DDR* (Hattingen: Edition Transit, 1981); Büscher and Wensierski, *Null Bock auf DDR. Aussteigerjugend im anderen Deutschland* (Reinbek: Rowohlt, 1984); Wensierski, *Von oben nach unten wächst gar nichts. Umweltzerstörung und Protest in der DDR* (Frankfurt/M: Fischer, 1987). Also, Klaus Ehring and Martin Dallwitz, *Schwerter zu Pflugscharen—Friedensbewegung in der DDR* (Reinbek: Rowohlt, 1982).

11. "Berliner-Begegnung zur Friedensförderung," *Deutschland Archiv*, 15, Nr. 3, March 1982, pp. 313–36.

12. Figures cited in Anne Köhler, "Wiedervereinigung—Wunsch und Wirklichkeit. Empirische Beiträge zur Frage der nationalen Orientierung unter innerdeutschen Aspekten," in Werner Weidenfeld, Hg., *Nachdenken über Deutschland. Materialien zur politischen Kultur der Deutschen Frage* (Köln: Wissenschaft und Politik, 1985), p. 148.

13. The two papers cited are the conservative *Frankfurter Allgemeine Zeitung* and the alternative-left daily, *die tageszeitung*.

14. Gunter Holzweißig, *Massenmedien in der DDR* (Berlin: Verlag Gebr. Holzapfel, 1989), p. 45, p. 128 ff.

15. Forschungsgruppe Wahlen e. V. (Mannheim), "Repräsentative Bevölkerungsumfrage" from July 1986, Question #22. A government-commissioned study found 40% of the respondents interested in learning more about the sister-state in 1974, reporting a high of 63% among those under 25 in *Materialien zum Bericht zur Lage der Nation* (1974), op. cit., p. 119.

16. Ibid., Questions #24 and #25.

17. Ibid., Question #26. Participants in earlier surveys did a better job when given the specific date and asked to indicate its significance; 45% correctly identified August 13, 1961 in June 1976, compared to 52% in July 1981. *Allensbacher Berichte*, Nr. 15, July 1981; also, Paul Schwarz, "Ich weiß nichts über die DDR. Unkenntnis über das andere Deutschland," in *Die Zeit*, Nr. 25, June 17, 1983.

18. Stemming largely from the pens of West German journalists, the attacks completely overlooked the extent to which Christa Wolf, in particular, had been viewed as the conscience of the nation by many East Germans, despite her privileged status. Western publicists leading the charge against Wolf's "opportunitistic" post-unity account of her own *Stasi*-experience [*Was bleibt?*] had no record of supporting GDR-opposition forces, in contrast to Günter Grass and others who came to Wolf's defense. See "Nötige Kritik oder Hinrichtung? Spiegel-Gespräch mit Günter Grass über die Debatte um Christa Wolf und die DDR Literatur," *Der Spiegel*, Nr. 29, 16. July 1990; also, "Ich war ein Aktivist der DDR: Der ostdeutsche Schriftsteller Hermann Kant über seine Rolle und den Stellenwert der Literatur im SED-Regime," *Der Spiegel*, Nr. 32, 6. August 1990.

19. Examples include Ulrich Pietzsch, *Verdammte Heimat. Du entstehst erst, wenn Du nicht mehr bist* (Berlin: 1984); Karl Winkler, *Made in GDR. Jugendszenen aus Ostberlin* (Berlin: Oberbaum Verlag, 1983); also, Horst-Günter Kessler and Jürgen Miermeister, *Vom großen Knast ins Paradies? DDR-Bürger in der Bundesrepublik, Lebensgeschichten* (Reinbek: Rowohlt, 1983).

20. Dorothy Rosenberg, "Reflection or Interaction: Literature and Social Policy in the GDR," paper presented at a Regional Symposium on Germany sponsored by the DAAD at the University of Oregon, April 22–24, 1988. Further, Maxie Wander, *Guten Morgen, du Schöne* (Berlin: Buchverlag der Morgen, 1977); Sibylle Muthesius, *Flucht in die Wolken* (Berlin: Buchverlag der Morgen, 1981); and Ingrid Johannis, *Das siebente Brennesselhemd* (Berlin: Neues Leben, 1986).

21. Forschungsgruppe Wahlen [hereafter, FGW], survey conducted for *ZDF-Politbarometer* in January 1984, Question #21.

22. Cited by Gerd-Joachim Glaeßner, "Offene deutsche Fragen—Von Schwierigkeiten, einander anzuerkennen," in *Die DDR in der Ära Honecker*," op.cit., p. 32.

23. "Wiedervereinigung—'gefährliches Lernziel'?" op. cit., p. 97 ff.

24. Its final 1989 revision continued to privilege persons with family ties; "DDR-Verordnung über Reisen und Ausreisen," reprinted in *Deutschland Archiv*, 22. Jg., Nr. 1, January 1989.

25. The average amount of leisure-time enjoyed by Federal Republicans rose 9.2%, from 2,617 hours in 1985 to 2,858 hours in 1989, follwing a 30% increase between 1975 and 1985. The amount of money spent on leisure-activities climbed 430% between 1965 and 1985, reaching DM 7,200 per year for an average working household. Among those who used paid vacation time for travel (40.2 million out of 61 million), 31.3% toured the FRG in 1988 and 67.6% visited foreign countries (excluding the GDR). See "Freizeitmarkt: Sport oder Spaghetti," *Wirtschaftswoche*, Nr. 27, June 30, 1989, pp. 44–57.

26. FGW survey executed for *ZDF-Politbarometer*, July 19–25, 1986, Questions #28, #29, and #30.

27. FGW survey for *ZDF-Politbarometer* conducted in December 1989, Question #19.

28. The SED allowed retirement-age persons to visit the West, having little to lose if they remained there at FRG expense. Data appear in Bundesministerium für innerdeutsche Beziehungen, Hg., *Texte zur Deutschlandpolitik*, Reihe III, Bd. 5, 1987, p. 379.

29. Anne Köhler, "Wiedervereinigung. . . ," in Weidenfeld, *Nachdenken über Deutschland*, op. cit., p. 148.

30. Jan Hoesch, "Drei Jahre kommunale Partnerschaften mit der DDR," *Deutschland Archiv*, 22. Jg., Nr. 1, January 1989, pp. 37–51.

31. Reported in *Der Tagesspiegel* on August 4, 1989, p. 1.

32. Elisabeth Noelle-Neumann, "Im Wartesaal der Geschichte. Bleibt das Bewußtsein der deutschen Einheit lebendig?" in Weidenfeld, *Nachdenken über Deutschland*, op. cit., pp. 145–146.

33. Bordering on the "socialist fraternal countries" of Bulgaria, Romania and the Soviet Union, the Black Sea was one location where West and East Germans could randomly meet under the old travel restrictions. Ibid., pp. 140–142.

34. The term stems from Hendrick Bussiek, *Die real existierende DDR. Neue Notizen aus der unbekannten deutschen Republik* (Frankfurt/M: Fischer, 1984), p. 11.

35. As cited in *Emnid-Informationen*, Nr. 4, 1979.

36. Cited by Gerd-Joachim Glaeßner, "Offene deutsche Fragen—Von den Schwierigkeiten, einander anzuerkennen," in *Die DDR in der Ära Honecker*, op. cit., p. 31.

37. Martin Ahrends, Hg., *Mein Leben, Teil Zwei* (Köln: Kiepenheuer & Witsch, 1989), p. 131, p. 134.

38. Irene Böhme, *Die da drüben. Sieben Kapitel DDR* (Berlin: Rotbuch Verlag, 1983), pp. 16–17.

39. See Monika Maron's essay, "Warum bin ich selbst gegangen?" *Der Spiegel*, Nr. 33, 14. August 1989.

40. Alfred Kosing and Manfred Schmidt, "Zur Herausbildung der sozialistischen Nation in der DDR," *Einheit*, 29. Jg., Heft 2 (1974), pp. 179–188; further, Hermann Axen, *Zur Entwicklung der sozialistischen Nation in der DDR* (Berlin: Dietz Verlag, 1973).

41. Karl Marx, "Critique of the Gotha Program," in Robert Tucker, ed., *The Marx-Engels Reader* (New York: W. W. Norton, 1978), p. 386.

42. Anne Köhler and Volker Ronge, "Ein Test auf Wiedervereinigung? Die Reaktion der Bundesdeutschen auf die Übersiedlerwelle aus der DDR vom Frühjahr 1984," *Deutschland Archiv*, 18. Jg., Nr. 1, p. 54.

43. Kristina Pratsch and Volker Ronge, "Arbeit finden sie leichter als Freunde. DDR-Übersiedler der 84-Welle nach einem Jahr im Westen," *Deutschland Archiv*, 18. Jg., July 1985, pp. 716–725.

44. Bussiek, op. cit., p. 13.

45. See Fuchs' dialogue with Rolf Henrich in *40 Jahre DDR ... und die Bürger melden sich zu Wort*, Ralf Hirsch, Hg. (Frankfurt/M: Büchergilde Gutenberg Hanser, 1989). A top SED-functionnary, Rudolf Bahro openly criticized bureaucratic centralism, hoping to provide a reform-framework from *within* the existing system; sentenced to eight years in prison in 1978, he was released and resettled to the West in 1979. See *Die Alternative—Zur Kritik des real existierenden Sozialismus* (Köln: Europäische Verlagsanstalt, 1977).

46. Böhme, op. cit.

47. Ahrends, p. 40, pp. 75–79, p. 84, p. 99, p. 128.

48. Ibid., op. cit., p. 157.

49. Kessler and Miermeister, *Vom 'Großen Knast' ins Paradies?* op. cit., p. 37.

50. Volker Ronge, *Von drüben nach hüben. DDR-Bürger im Westen* (Wuppertal: Verlag 84 Hartmann + Petit, 1985), p. 15, pp. 24–25.

51. Prior to the mid-1980s, Dresden was the one major GDR city with no access to West-TV, owing to its geographic location; it was also a city whose problems of scarce-goods exceeded those in other urban areas. It consequently became the city with the highest per capita rate of emigration-applications. To assuage discontent, the Party eventually installed a satellite dish, enabling itself to benefit from negative reports about unemployment, drugs, and homelessness aired on West-TV. Figures appear in Ronge, ibid., p. 18, p. 22.

52. Anne Köhler, "Ist die Übersiedlerwelle noch zu stoppen? Ursachen—Erfahrungen—Perspektiven," *Deutschland Archiv*, 23. Jg. Nr. 3, March 1990, p. 428.

53. Ronge, *Von drüben nach hüben . . .* , op.cit., p. 42 ff.

54. Köhler, "Wiedervereinigung—Wunsch und Wirklichkeit. Empirische Beiträge zur Frage der nationalen Orientierung unter innerdeutschen Aspekten," in *Nachdenken über Deutschland*, op. cit., p. 160.

55. Ronge, *Von drüben nach hüben . . .* , op. cit., p. 34, p. 38.

56. Köhler, op. cit., pp. 151–153.

57. *Emnid-Informationen*, 10 Jg., 21. June 1958 and 14. Jg., 2. April 1962; FGW, Question #14, November 1980. Further, Gerhard Herdegen, "Aussiedler in der Bundesrepublik—Einstellungen und Problemsicht der Bundesbürger," *Deutschland Archiv*, 22. Jg., Nr. 8, August 1989, p. 920.

58. Joyce Marie Mushaben, "Peace and the National Question: A Study of the Development of an 'Association of Responsibility' between the two Germanys," in *Coexistence: A Review of East-West and Development Issues*, Vol. 24 (1987), pp. 245–270.

59. Ronge, *Von drüben nach hüben...*, op. cit., p. 46.

60. Modrow proposed the creation of a *Vertragsgemeinschaft* the day he formed his provisional coalition government, on November 17, 1989—eleven days prior to the proclamation of Kohl's "10 Point Program." Christoph Links and Hannes Bahrmann, *Wir sind das Volk—Die DDR im Aufbruch. Eine Chronik* (Berlin/ Weimar: Aufbau Verlag, 1990).

61. Not coincidentally, this was the title Modrow gave his own Seven-Point Plan for unification, announced on February 1, 1990; see *Deutschland Archiv*, 23. Jg., Nr. 3, March 1990, pp. 471–472.

62. Gabriel Almond and Sidney Verba, *The Civic Culture* (Princeton: Princeton University Press, 1963).

63. Gerd-Joachim Glaeßner, *Die andere Deutsche Republik. Gesellschaft und Politik in der DDR* (Opladen: Westdeutscher Verlag, 1989), p. 81.

64. See the verdict on the Radical Ordinance of 1972, *BVerfGE 39, Beschluss vom 22. Mai 1975.*

65. One example of this tendency is Gerd Langguth, "Wie steht die junge Generation zur deutschen Teilung?" *Politische Studien*, Nr. 289, September/October 1986, pp. 524–542.

66. Gregory Flynn and Hans Rattinger address this problem in *The Public and Atlantic Defense* (Totowa, NJ: Rowman & Allanheld, 1985). See the response variations that emerged in reference to the Pershing II deployments in "Question Wording Makes a Difference: German Public Attitudes toward Deployment," *Public Opinion* (December/January 1984), pp. 38–39.

67. Elisabeth Noelle and Erich Peter Neumann, *Jahrbuch der öffentlichen Meinung 1947–1955*, IfD (Allensbach: Verlag für Demoskopie, 1956), p. 157 ff.

68. Ibid.

69. *Emnid-Informationen*, 26. Jg., Nr. 10/11, 1974, Table 2.

70. They were presumably disturbed for political reasons, not because Easterners demonstrated greater athletic prowess. *Allensbacher Berichte*, Nr. 21, April 1972.

71. FGW, "Überblick über die Ergebnisse einer Sondererhebung für das ZDF-Magazin," Nr. 14, August 17–23, 1985, Question #11.

72. Noelle-Neumann, "Im Wartesaal der Geschichte. Bleibt das Bewußtsein der deutschen Einheit lebendig?" in *Nachdenken über Deutschland*, op. cit., p. 144.

73. Calculations derive from the *Statistisches Jahrbuch für die Bundesrepublik Deutschland* (Stuttgart/Wiesbaden: Metzler-Poeschel Verlag, 1989).

74. *Emnid-Informationen*, Nr. 8/9, August 1983.

75. Köhler, "Wiedervereinigung . . . ," op. cit., p. 154.

76. *Statistisches Jahrbuch* for 1989, op. cit.

77. *Emnid-Informationen*, 16. Jg., Nr. 25, June 15, 1964.

78. Elisabeth Noelle and Erich Peter Neumann, *Jahrbuch der öffentlichen Meinung 1947–1955*, op. cit., p. 315; *Emnid-Informationen*, 10. Jg., Nr. 38, September 1958.

79. Noelle and Neumann, ibid., p. 316.

80. Ibid., p. 321.

81. Ibid., p. 320, p. 321.

82. *Allensbacher Berichte*, Nr. 13, 1982, Table 2, IfD-Umfragen 3060, 3070, 3183, 4103, 4002.

83. Alternative Liste Berlin, *Paktfreiheit für beide deutsche Staaten oder bis daß der Tod uns eint?* (Berlin: AL, 1982).

84. *Emnid-Informationen*, Nr. 7, July/August 1983; FGW, Sonderauswertung für ZDF-Magazin, January 1984, Question #20.

85. The average price per person was DM 40,000 until 1977, and DM 95,847 thereafter. See "Freikäufe: Beim Menschenhandel kassierte die Stasi mit," *Der Spiegel*, 45. Jg., Nr. 14, April 1, 1991, pp. 65ff.

86. *Allensbacher Berichte*, Nr. 31, April 1978, Table 1.

87. *Emnid-Informationen*, 10. Jg., Nr. 35, August 30, 1958.

88. *Emnid-Informationen*, 15. Jg., Nr. 30, July 22, 1963; ibid., 31. Jg., Nr. 10, 1979. The *Wall*, ironically, was one of the most frequently cited "German tourist attractions" among American university students; Kurt Stapf, Wolfgang Stroebe and Klaus Jonas, *Amerikaner über Deutschland und die Deutschen, Urteile und Vorurteile* (Opladen: Westdeutscher Verlag, 1986), p. 124–125.

89. *Emnid-Informationen*, 13. Jg., Nr. 34, August 28, 1961; ibid., Nr. 49, November 11, 1961.

90. James S. Sutterlin and David Klein, *Berlin–From Symbol of Confrontation to Keystone of Stability* (New York: Praeger, 1989). Many analysts posit that the "stability" afforded by the Wall made *Ostpolitik* possible under ex-Berlin Mayor Brandt. Also, Richard L. Merritt and Anna J. Merritt, eds., *Living with the Wall: West Berlin, 1961–1985* (Durham: Duke University Press, 1985); and Peter Wyden, *Wall. The Inside Story of Divided Berlin* (New York/London: Simon and Schuster, 1989).

91. See "Berlin—Zucker von Thälmann," *Der Spiegel*, 44. Jg., Nr. 34, August 20, 1990.

92. FGW, *Sonderauswertung für ZDF-Magazin*, August 1985, op. cit., Question #23. DM 12 billion was the amount rechanneled to Berlin *after* it had contributed DM 4.9 billion to the federal tax pool; this made up 52% of the city's budget in 1987. Activities deemed worthy of subsidization were quite diverse, ranging from direct credits for business investment, to special low interest "marriage loans," to subsidized airfares, and payments under the European Recovery Program fund.

93. Percentages are based on first-mention responses; unemployment and foreigners also ranked highest in the second- and third-named categories, according to FGW, *"Berlin vor der 750 Jahresfeier." Repräsentative Bevölkerungsumfrage*, December 1986, Question #11.

94. FGW, ibid., Questions #16, #17, #20, # 22 and 23.

95. Honecker actually took his first trip to the post-war zone in November 1947, as head of the communist youth organization, seeking to stimulate a unification dialogue among youth in the two parts of Germany.

96. Ilse Spittmann, "Wie lange noch auf alte Weise?" in *Deutschland Archiv*, Nr. 5, May 1988, pp. 470–473; "Weichenstellungen für die neunziger Jahre, *Deutschland Archiv*, Nr. 12, December 1988, pp. 1249–1253.

97. Many Leipzigers were forced to erect wooden scaffolds in front of their main entrances, to avoid being hit by chunks of stone breaking off the facade.

98. See Links and Bahrmann, *Wir sind das Volk, op. cit.; also, Deutschland Archiv*'s "Chronik der Ereignisse in der DDR" (Köln: Verlag Wissenschaft und Politik, 1989).

99. Peter Förster and Günter Roski, *DDR zwischen Wende und Wahl. Meinungsforscher analysieren den Umbruch* (Berlin: LinksDruck, 1990), pp. 159–170.

100. "Die Welt als Flohzirkus," *Der Spiegel*, Nr. 31, 30. July 1990, pp. 72–133.

101. FGW, op. cit., August 1989, Questions #17, #24.

102. FGW, op. cit., October 1989, Questions #14, #15+a, #61.

103. FGW, November 1989, Questions # 15ab, #16, #17, #18+a.

104. FGW, December 1989, Questions #12, #13, #14, #15, #18.

105. FGW, January 1990, Questions # 18, #19, #15.

106. FGW, February 1990, Questions #12+a, #14, #17, #13.

107. Otto Bauer introduced the idea of a *community of destiny* in his analysis of national movements prior to the collapse of the Austro-Hungarian empire. See Brandt and Ammon, *Die Linke und die nationale Frage*, op. cit., p. 15ff.

108. Antonia Grunenberg, "Zwei Deutschlands—Zwei Identitäten? Über deutsche Identität in der Bundesrepublik und der DDR," in Glaeßner, *Die DDR in der Ära Honecker*, op. cit., pp. 105–107.

109. Data were collected by Emnid Institute and the now "dissolved" Central Institute for Youth Research. See *Das Profil der Deutschen. Was sie vereint, was sie trennt*, Spiegel Spezial, Nr. 1, January 1991.

110. Peter Meroth assesses this Infratest study in "Deutschland 2000—Der Staat, den wir uns wünschen," *Süddeutsche Zeitung Magazin*, Nr. 1, 4. January 1991.

111. *Das Profil der Deutschen*, op.cit., p. 12, p. 16.

112. Meroth, op cit., p. 10.

113. "Asphalt des Ostens: Haß-Witze über Wessis," *Der Spiegel*, Nr. 28, 8. July 1991, p. 84–85; further, Ingolf Serwuschok and Christine Dölle, *Der Besser Wessi* (Leipzig: Forum Verlag, 1991).

4

Partnership and Its Discontents: Assessing the Federal Republic's Role in NATO

And he shall judge among many people, and rebuke strong nations afar off; and they shall beat their swords into plowshares, and their spears into spades; nation shall not take sword against nation; neither shall they learn war anymore.

—Micha, Michaes
Chapter 4, Verse 3

Man muß den status quo akzeptieren, um ihn zu verändern.

—Willy Brandt

The lessons of war do not come easily. The nights in air-raid shelters, loss of loved ones, forceful expulsion from one's homeland, the national humiliation of conditionless surrender—these are but the immediate costs of war. As two World Wars attest, there is no guarantee that those who learn from history shall be spared its repetition, for its participants may derive very different lessons from their experiences. One can only hope that the forces of time will lead to an understanding of war's causes, enabling its many victims to embrace new values and new political structures more attuned to the preservation of peace.

Earlier chapters advanced the thesis that West Germans who have come of political age since 1949 are truly "different," that is, more self-consciously democratic than the generations preceding them. Drawing on qualitative and quantitative sources, I showed that one's sense of "belonging" to the German nation, rooted in personal experience and selective memory, is indeed multi-dimensional in character, and more subject to change over time than generally apparent to outsiders. As to the negative side of German national character, I provided evidence that postwar citizens consciously reject the old foundation of such a character, to the extent that it still exists. A persistent willingness to embrace freedom at the expense of unity, at least prior to 1989, not only "proved" that West Germans desired to divorce themselves from the trappings of ultra-nationalism; it also provided a stable foundation for a positive identification with their new state.

This chapter explores that new identification by assessing public attitudes towards select dimensions of West German security policy, which might be construed as a projection of national identity vis-à-vis the world outside. It argues that the new Republic's commitment to a foreign policy course of regional integration and East-West cooperation, especially after 1969, afforded postwar Germans a second, equally significant source of positive identification with their own state beyond that of material well-being. In short, deep-seated changes in German attitudes towards representative democracy were accompanied by increasing public acceptance of the politics of détente. Our task is to establish a more direct link between two levels of analysis—between the changing definition of the Federal Republic's official national interests and the evolving security-policy preferences of average citizens.

Grounded in the process of community identification, the FRG's incorporation into the Western system of values was never really open to question. Yet its willingness to sever ties with the other German state, paradoxically, opened the door to a convergence of their respective "national" security interests. This chapter considers the options and limits inherent in the FRG's unique position within the Western collective security system. It reviews competing definitions of the German Question pursued by the main political parties prior to 1989, coupled with a survey of major turning-points in West German security policy development. This is followed by an examination of public attitudes regarding the re-creation of a German army, the costs and benefits of FRG membership in NATO, changing threat-perceptions vis-à-vis the Soviet Union, and assessments of West European integration. I then turn to improvements in inter-German relations and the manner in which they altered the FRG's approach to broader questions of global conflict. The argument here is that the implementation of détente depended upon—and found—widespread public acceptance for the politics of negotiation. Viewed as a successful mechanism for addressing the FRG's complex security needs, *Ostpolitik* effectively linked national interests at the macro-political level with a positive notion of what it meant to be German at the individual level. It did so by servicing both sets of needs: by expanding trade, extending visitation rights, encouraging disarmament, and by opening the door to public debate over formerly taboo security questions. The centrality of *Ostpolitik* in postwar German security thinking, I contend, not only laid the foundation for a process of peaceful national unification but also for a creeping "democratization" of foreign policymaking in the *Bundesrepublik*.

West German foreign policy has evinced a significant degree of internal consistency and bipartisan consensus over the last two decades. Citizens shared with their rulers a commitment to FRG membership in NATO as "the lesser of two evils" in the face of possible Warsaw Pact encroachments. Yet this did not preclude their assuming a vanguard role in the search for alternative approaches to European security. In order to comprehend the exceptional conceptual shifts that have come to dominate all-German security thinking, we must first consider the nature of the geo-strategic environment from the perspective of average citizens in the decade preceding the opening of the Berlin Wall. Let us begin by "translating" German conditions of the 1980s into an American-heartland equivalent.

Understanding West German and American Security Dilemmas

Lack of knowledge as to the true nature of the German security predicament constitutes one source of misunderstanding between citizens of the FRG and the USA. Students enrolled in my introductory comparative politics course at the University of Missouri-St. Louis were often quite surprised to learn that both the Western and Eastern sectors of Berlin lay deeply embedded within the Zone, for example. Being "pragmatic" Americans, many presumed that the former capital of the Third Reich must have been divided because it rested on the border between "our" Germany and "theirs." In an effort to convey the uniqueness of the FRG security dilemma, I regularly exhorted my classes during the 1980s to imagine how they would feel:

- If, instead of 5 million people, Missouri (not quite as big as the FRG) encompassed 61 million residents;
- If, in place of one nuclear energy plant (Callaway) and no chemical/bacteriological arsenals, the state housed some twenty-five atomic energy plants already on line, and planned to add two nuclear-waste reprocessing plants (Wackersdorf, Gorleben);
- If, instead of storing no bacteriological or chemical weapons within state lines, Missourians already tolerated the world's highest concentration of "ABC" weapons (atomic, bacterial, chemical), and
- If, in lieu of the 300 Minutemen II missiles deployed in Missouri at the time, its borders contained over 6,000–7,000 nuclear weapons, some with a range of only 20–75 miles—in other words, atomic devices programmed to detonate within state lines.[1]

Suppose the Germans came to us in the 1990s as a reemergent superpower, I postulated, and insisted that we deploy 108 first-strike-capable Pershing IIs aimed at the capital of Mexico, dominating a Central American bloc overtaken by socialist revolutions (a scenario projected by the Reagan Administration at the time). The military strategy of the Germans, intent on "defending" our freedom, would focus on weapons whose use could neither be vetoed by the U.S. President, by Missouri officials, nor by popular referendum. By this point in the exercise, it seemed superfluous to ask how students might feel about having two-thirds of their state subject to 5,000 annual troop maneuvers causing over $40 million (1984 figure) in damage to agricultural lands, the repair costs of which would naturally be born by Missouri taxpayers. Nor did students wait to factor in the irritation produced by low altitude test-flights permitted twenty-four hours a day over two-thirds of the entire state. The consensus emerging from this scenario was that Missourians would openly rebel against such conditions within their own borders.

A failure to distinguish between the theory versus the practice of partnership was another source of conflict between the two allied parties during the 1970s and 1980s, as two examples show. West Germans were quite aggravated by the Reagan Administration's penchant for invading first and "consulting" later, as in the 1983 assault on Grenada and the 1986 bombing of Libya. They were likewise shocked when the U.S. President, suddenly converting to "peace-keeping" by means other than the MX missile, nearly agreed at Reykjavik in 1986 to eliminate all land-based nuclear weapons in Europe–without any joint-deliberation by the NATO powers. A real security partnership would engage NATO's member-states in strategic deliberations, on an equal basis, instead of largely expecting them to co-finance diverse U.S. invasions after the fact.

Many security debates of the late 1970s moreover neglected a number of historically rooted cultural differences leading to friction between the U.S. and the FRG. Reagan's 1980 victory over Jimmy Carter reflected an American desire to reclaim the sense of "national mission" and national pride lost in the wake of Vietnam, Watergate and the Iranian hostage crisis. For younger West Germans, any display of military assertiveness or use of messianic rhetoric, e.g., against "the Evil Empire," resurrects the spectres of ultra-nationalism and war-mongering. Acts of perceived "Rambo-ism" against Grenada, Lebanon, Panama, and Iraq can trigger fears of global imperialism among German cohorts too young to have experienced uniformed Americans as WWII liberators. Neither Germans or Americans are well-versed in the language used by the other side to rally public support, as distinct from that employed in behind-the-scenes negotiations.

FRG-citizens, on the other hand, show little sympathy for the complicated interplay of economic security and the fortunes of the military-industrial complex in the United States. Most German companies involved in defense production through the mid-1980s devoted less than 15% of their industrial capacity to military contracts, allowing them to absorb cutbacks in defense procurement without major disruptions in their core planning and finance operations.[2] Perceived in the U.S. as an unfair advantage, West Germany's ability to take cover under the American/NATO nuclear umbrella not only "freed" state resources for other investment purposes after 1949, it also impelled FRG defense contractors to pursue military research and development under very different competitive standards.

This stands in stark contrast to the evolution of military procurement processes in the USA, where entire industries and cities have become dependent upon specific weapons contracts. As the citizens of Seattle, St. Louis and Long Beach can attest, national security = jobs = economic security, validated by their experiences with Boeing in the 1970s and McDonnell Douglas in the 1980s. It is not that the American people are more war-mongering by nature; after all, the volunteer army relies heavily upon the job-seeking sons and daughters of middle and lower-class families to fill its ranks. Rather, the lack of a welfare-state cushion, taken for granted in Europe, renders those employed in U.S. defense industries economically vulnerable, and thus somewhat ambivalent toward sweeping arms control agreements.[3] Production workers in Marshall, Texas were easily reconciled to the 1987 Treaty on Intermediate Nuclear Forces, since it required them to complete production of 108 Pershing II missiles prior to their "peaceful" destruction in the presence of U.S.-Soviet verification teams.[4] The 1991 cancellation of the A-12 *Stealth*-bomber proved less fortuitous for 8,000 employees at McDonnell Douglas facilities in St. Louis and Long Beach, shortly after a 1990 lay-off of 4,000 workers at "Mac."[5]

A fifth factor accounting for German-American tensions over defense issues is the concept of security itself. Germans display a much stronger historical attachment to security as an underlying social value, as opposed to the American emphasis on freedom. The term security serves as a "crystalization point" for a multitude of associations in the discourse of politicians as well as in the day-to-day consciousness of citizens.[6] It was not a Bolshevik revolutionary but an anti-socialist Chancellor, Otto von Bismarck, who laid the foundation for the German welfare state back in 1881. It was the unfortunate confluence of excessive war-reparation demands, high inflation, and mass unemployment brought on by the Great Depression, not national character per se, which precipitated the rise of National Socialism in the 1930s. This is why the FRG's postwar constitution upholds the model of a social market economy, warranting a minimum of socio-economic security for its citizens. While West Germans have internalized the values of freedom and democracy since 1949, their acceptance of the state's obligation to provide social security has stood for more than a century. By contrast, Americans whose forebearers abandoned Europe in the hopes of escaping the strong state were not compelled to rethink the government's role in securing citizens' livelihood until the 1930s. The appeals of U.S. politicians, urging German leaders to cut welfare spending in order to increase their contributions to NATO, fall on deaf ears even among conservatives. They also reinforce negative sentiments among younger cohorts concerned with the "moral bankruptcy" of the United States, given its problems of homelessness, drug addiction and infant mortality.

Last but not least, the security perceptions of Germans and Americans differ as a function of geography and the geo-strategic experiences that implies. The people of the United States take for granted the blessings of continental separation and size; bound by oceans to the East and West, they share their frontiers with friendly trading partners to the North and South. Between 1949 and 1989, the Federal Republic shared its frontiers with nine other states, two of which were members of a hostile alliance (accounting for 35% of the border). Equivalent in size to New York and Pennsylvania combined, its population of 61 million was subject to a density ten times greater than that of the United States. Nearly 30% of its residents and 25% of its industries were concentrated in the 60-mile strip bordering on the GDR and Czechoslovakia; Warsaw Pact fighter planes were situated but ten minutes away from any designated target on FRG territory.[7] Whereas Americans measure burden sharing and defense costs in dollar figures itemized in the federal budget, postwar Germans look to the unquantifiable asymmetries of risk sharing—their homeland having been saturated by nuclear weapons possessing many times the "kill-power" of the Hiroshima bomb.

The last war fought on the U.S. mainland was one Americans bloodily imposed upon themselves, using 19th century implements of destruction. Because its subsequent battles have all been fought in distant places, a relatively small segment of the U.S. population has suffered direct exposure to war's physical deprivations. For a third of the FRG's population, war was not an experience confined to the silver screen, at least prior to 1989; some could recall the atrocities of not one but two world wars. The presence of ruins in most major cities—the Kaiser Wilhelm Memorial Church along Berlin's most traveled thoroughfare, the *Ku'damm*, for example—stands as a daily reminder of war's consequences to all casual passers-by.

It is only by turning back the pages of postwar history that one can appreciate the many bold albeit small steps towards peace undertaken by West German leaders over the last four decades. The overarching goals of peace and security, freedom and national unity have often stood in dialectical relationship to one another (thesis—antithesis—synthesis). It was the occasional, antagonistic contradiction surfacing among these four values, rather than any logically constructed "grand design," which provided the impetus for each successive phase of *West-* and *Ostpolitik*, eventually culminating in the country's 1990 unification. Before we can assess *Ostpolitik's* beneficial impact on German national identity per se, we need to examine the ways in which competing political elites sought to reconcile the sometimes conflicting values of peace, unity and freedom, changing their own understanding of security in the process.

Partisan Perspectives on Identity Questions, 1949–1989

Outsider's confusion over the nature or scope of German nationalism is often compounded by the fine lines drawn by postwar parties in their efforts to woo diverse segments of the voting public. The Federal Republic, Dahrendorf observed, "is a terribly explicit society in which everything has to be set down in the most exact of terms, and that always has negative consequences. The more explicitly a society attempts to define the boundaries of social consensus, the greater the probability that people will by virtue of this determination be defined out of the system."[8] Postwar party organizations have yet to abandon an older German tradition manifested by both the Right and the Left, namely, "the propensity to seek out absolutes."[9]

In 1979 Horst Ehmke cautioned his fellow politicians not "to endanger and inhibit the identification of citizens of the Federal Republic with their [own] democratic state by artificially maintaining the openness/closure of the German Question" in absolute terms.[10] Prior to 1989, West German leaders often did just that; parties routinely employed the German Question as a club for opposition-bashing, in the hopes of garnering an eventual electoral majority (a standing attained only once, by the CDU in 1957). Yet party stances on the German Question had shifted and blurred considerably in practice prior to the GDR's demise. By the late 1980s one was able to find just as much consensus between various wings of competing parties as serious conflict within each of the key parties.

The conservative or Christian-Democratic camp has most consistently and adamantly ascribed to the fundamentally open nature of the German Question. But in retrospect, the CDU/CSU policies of the 1950s and 1960s contributed most to the establishment of separate identities within the two postwar states by impelling the GDR towards ultimate demarcation. Under Adenauer the party upheld the official prescription for unity in freedom, while accepting complete *Westintegration* as a prerequisite for eventual reunification. Through the adoption of the Hallstein Doctrine in 1955, the CDU-CSU government sought to induce official denial of the other Germany's legitimacy among its allies and trade partners. Its campaign was subliminally reinforced by the media's routine use of quotation marks in each reference to "the so-called GDR," a practice continued by the Springer Press until August 1989. Adenauer's dicta of "no experiments" and "negotiation through strength" were sooner attuned to the consolidation of the new order and the re-attainment of sovereignty than to the potentially disruptive restoration of unity.

The CDU/CSU's vehement denunciation of reconciliation efforts initiated by the Brandt government in 1969 continued well beyond 1972, despite clear signals from the press and the electorate that the time had come for a new mode of *Ostpolitik*. Conservatives sought—and found—ultimate justification for their politics of the open question in the Constitutional Court ruling of July 1973, circumscribing the 1972 Basis of Relations Treaty between the two Germanys. The Court decreed that the Federal Republic comprised not a new German state but rather the partial reorganization of the still-existent Reich; it expressly prohibited all constitutional organs from abandoning the pursuit of unity as a key political objective. The justices left it open to those organs, however, to determine "which paths to bring about reunification they [saw] as politically correct and purposive."[11]

The mainstream conservative view as to what was politically correct and purposive was dramatically redefined between the mid-1970s and the early 1980s. Allied with the Adenauer tradition, Helmut Kohl stressed the theme of continuity following the Union's return to power in 1982, albeit with a number of contradictory themes and tactical twists. Continuity, as articulated in the Union's 1987 electoral slogan, *Weiter so, Deutschland* [Carry on, Germany], meant stressing the Preamble's theme of unity in freedom and asserting that German nationhood remained a legitimately open question.

More disorienting, until 1990, was the party's stance on the openness of the Oder-Neisse borders, although one scholar claims that Adenauer had accepted the northeastern boundaries as permanent back in 1955, leaving Brandt with the arduous task of rendering them publically acceptable.[12] CDU/CSU hardliners and lobbyists for the postwar refugee associations, like Herbert Hupka and Herbert Czaja, continued to insist on the validity of the pre-1937 borders based on the motto, "Silesia remains ours." Moderate conservatives had come to see Four-Power references to the pre-1937 frontiers as an administrative framework linked to the Occupation of the former Reich, not as an endorsement for border revision.[13] As of 1982, the second element of continuity espoused by the Union actually amounted to a break with its own past policies: its operational politics featured an internalized acceptance of the territorial status quo and the cultivation of "good neighborly relations with the GDR"—the pillars of *Ostpolitik* for which it had vehemently denounced the Brandt Government ten years earlier.

This does not mean that the CDU/CSU had totally abandoned the politics of the Open Question. It made regular use of the dates June 17, 1953 and August 13, 1961 for public exhortations concerning *Wiedervereinigung*, even though the dream's defenders failed to provide a concrete image of a Germany-someday-united for forty years running. The Open-Question approach stood in direct contradiction to the Union's hopes of rekindling a sense of national patriotism within the bosoms of younger citizens. Its strategy precluded the systematic cultivation of an FRG-identity, at the same time officials actively sought to promote its separate symbols, e.g., by displaying the flag and distributing free recordings of the "national hymn" to public schools. More than any other partisan group, the Christian Union held itself captive to the Nation vs. State Identity Paradox, despite its eventual embrace of Brandt's formula, "two states in one nation." Exceptions to the rule were Bernhard Friedemann and Alfred Dregger, who demanded as late as 1987 that NATO make German reunification a precondition for Geneva negotiations regarding strategic arms reductions.[14]

The hardline position acquired new tactical significance in early 1989, given the CDU/CSU's need to thwart the electoral challenge embodied by the new far-right *Republikaner* Party. Its back-to-the-nation tactic was not particularly successful, as illustrated by subsequent elections in West Berlin, Hesse and the European Parliament; recycled rhetorical appeals for unity backfired at the Länder level to the benefit of the Social Democrats, the Greens and the Reps themselves. Pro-unity forces within the party saw themselves vindicated less than six months later, however, as dramatic events unfolded in the GDR.

East Germany's decision to abolish most travel restrictions, accidentally opening the Berlin Wall on November 9, 1989, gave new life to the rhetoric, as well as to the eventual reality of reunification. International reactions to Kohl's Ten Point Plan on *Deutschlandpolitik* were initially characterized by the same ambivalence that had dominated all moves towards closer German-German reassociation over the last four decades. During the first six months after the autumn "revolution," diverse heads of state expressed their sympathy, in theory, for the Germans' desire to reestablish the historically elusive unity of the nation. At the time, however, most seemed to prefer the Belgian Prime Minister's dictum, "it is urgent to wait"; they would have done so, in practice, had their hopes for a slow fusion of the two states within the context of accelerated European integration not been completely overtaken by the politics of mass action.[15]

The Kohl Plan, first made public on November 28, 1989, aimed to promote unity as a three-stage process, moving from the establishment of joint consultative commissions, to the formation of transitional "confederative structures," to the eventual fusion of political, economic and security institutions. The Chancellor provided no concrete time-frame for completing each stage; all three were to have as preconditions the implementation of fundamental domestic reforms in the GDR, the intensification of European Community integration and the Helsinki process, as well as major progress in arms control and disarmament.[16] In its original form, the proposal amounted to a summation of *Ostpolitik* objectives long espoused by the SPD—except for its curious failure to mention the need for de jure recognition of the Oder-Neisse border with Poland. The sensational nature of "the plan" had more to do with factors surrounding its issuance than with any specific point in the document itself: namely, Kohl's timing, his use of the reunification label, his failure to consult with the Allies prior to its proclamation, and the euphoric-turbulent mood pervading Europe during that period.

The New Right, personified by Franz Schönhuber, unabashedly asserted in the late 1980s that the time had come to return "Germany to the Germans."¹⁷ Whether the appeal applied in equal measure to ethnic repatriates from Silesia, the Volga region, and Romania, as well as to increasingly mobile GDR citizens remained unclear. The new national populists seemed largely intent on purging the postwar territory of guest-workers, asylum-seekers and other ethnically indiscrete groups who had settled into the *Wirtschaftswunderland* over the years. It was not a commitment to the openness of the inter-German Question alone which moved this group after 1987; equally compelling was the theme of renewed national sovereignty, freed from the bonds of superpower domination. Appealing initially to less well-educated, economically disgruntled males, the Reps were preempted by the CDU/CSU's pro-unity forces during the 1990 elections. Unification altered the playing field for the radical right by adding 16 million Eastern voters to the rolls, a minority of whom also began to exhibit anti-foreigner proclivities.

Occupying the political center, the Free Democratic Party deserves more credit than it usually receives for its consistent support of improvements in inter-German relations. Liberal utterances prior to 1952 were not especially "national" in tone; though less enthusiastic about Western-integration policy, party members largely concurred with the Union's anti-communist stance. Early FDP reservations regarding CDU/CSU foreign policy were grounded in Adenauer's willingness to tie a reunited Germany almost unconditionally to the western alliance.¹⁸ Bonn's refusal to consider the 1952 Stalin proposal contributed to the emergence of a distinctive Liberal position, searching for balance between the pulls of East and West. The FDP's push for normalized inter-German relations led to a coalition shift, and hence to the major political realignment [*Machtwechsel*] which gave birth to *Ostpolitik* under Brandt in 1969. The party's stance on the German Question bears the strong imprint of its long-standing Foreign Minister, Hans-Dietrich Genscher, whose stress on the European framework grew stronger after 1982 and continued until his retirement in 1992. Its Friedrich Naumann Foundation sponsored major conferences on *Culture and Nation* and *German Identity* through the 1980s, while Wilfried von Bredow and Christian von Krockow published treatises on the "permanently provisional" nature of the two states, coupled with a new German "openness to the world."¹⁹

Better known for its later ties to the politics of rapprochement, the Social Democratic Party experienced its first abrupt policy shift in 1959–60. Throughout the reconstruction era, party-chief Kurt Schumacher vehemently denounced Adenauer's "sell-out" to Western integration at the expense of unity. The party's early refusal to embrace NATO, rooted in strong rank-and-file opposition to rearmament, rested on the fear that FRG membership would institutionalize division, making it permanent. The SPD's last programmatic effort to uphold the prospect of unification centered on Herbert Wehner's *Deutschlandplan*, jettisoned by way of the Godesberg Program in 1959/60.

Like the CDU, the SPD often had to contend with a number of radical-versus-moderate elements vying for influence over its *Deutschlandpolitik* platform. Conflicts among the ranks, dating back to the 1960s, were exacerbated by a changing of the generational guard. While all essentially ascribed to Brandt's Two-States thesis, the twenty-year search for "commonalities in division" and "change through rapprochment" did not preclude new debates over context as of 1979. Born of dissension surrounding the NATO Double Track Decision, disparate voices within the party joined in criticism of Kohl's Ten-Point Plan at the time of its pronouncement; factions were divided in part by their Atlanticist versus Germany-first leanings. The older, more conservative wing (Richard Löwenthal, Kurt Sontheimer, Arno Klönne and Hans Mommsen) warned against a German *Sonderweg*, favoring tighter Western integration. The group evoking the sympathies of younger party members (Erhard Eppler, Oskar Lafontaine, Günter Gaus and, sporadically, Egon Bahr) stressed the theme of common security wedded to an evolving community of responsibility with the other German state. Had the November '89 revolution not intervened, the SPD would have no doubt continued its politics of small steps, which had already produced a dense network of treaties and face-to-face contacts with the Socialist Unity Party. More controversial moves at the end of the decade included the promulgation of the August 1988 *SPD/SED Common Paper*, along with individualized calls for the de facto recognition of a separate GDR citizenship.[20]

A marginal group of Neo-Right intellectuals (Hellmut Diwald, Wolfgang Venohr, Bernard Willms, Arnim Mohler and Michael Stürmer) found their mirror images in an independent National-Left represented by Peter Brandt (son of Willy), Herbert Ammon and Peter Bender.[21] Both sides of the New-Patriotism school issued a mid-1980s call for the de-Americanization of German defense and culture, but they differed in their proposals for a European security alternative. The "academic" tone of works by these authors supports a belief among most of my interview partners that the "search for German identity" throughout the 1980s was largely an intellectuals' exercise. Most citizens were oblivious to efforts by Right and Left fringe-elements to create a common security agenda. Brandt and Ammon did attract some attention among peace activists; they were the first to resurrect the idea of an inter-German confederation, which included plans for restructuring relations between the two Berlins.[22]

Routinely if inaccurately labeled the far-left-anti-NATO-party, the Greens have harbored their own breed of internal dissensus regarding the future of the German Question. Established in 1980, the party draws its members primarily from the post 1940s cohorts. Their lack of direct experience with the once-existent nation helps to explain, in part, why the party was initially plagued by seven different schools of thought regarding the German Question. Many of those positions began to crystalize in 1986, due to a special congress staged in Cologne under the rubric "For a Different Europe." Briefly, they included: (1) those who viewed the national question as an ideological "paper tiger," a reflex reaction born of Old Politics which overlooked the realities of global interdependence; (2) those who hoped to bury "pan-German" illusions through self-recognition, emphasizing the FRG's own status as a nation-state (Probst, Schnappertz); (3) those who preferred to cultivate a "pan-German" peace order (Becker, Stolz); (4) those who aimed to discover a new collective identity anchored in Central Europe; this group rejected unification but did foresee a special German mediator role (earlier, Schily and Mechtersheimer); (5) those who ascribed to (4) in substance but with a heavier dose of historical consciousness, requiring a full processing of the German past from within, rather than mere external disengagement from the bloc system; this wing also called for de jure recognition of the GDR (Vollmer, Fischer); and (6) those who advocated "the patriotism of the province," rooted in the small-is-beautiful thinking which attracts many ecological fundamentalists. Last but not least came the affiliates of the former K-Groups (Student-Movement communists) who persisted in holding monopoly capitalism responsible for East-West division and the arms race. This group had the most difficult time digesting *perestroika* and all that followed; some, like Trampert and Ditfurth, eventually quit the party.[23] As disparate as their positions seem, the Greens are significant insofar as their ranks include some of the most politically active members of the Baby Boom, cohorts who stand to inherit the reins of power by the year 2000.

The 1989 opening of the Wall, Kohl's Ten-Point Program, and GDR-demonstrators' calls for a "Germany, united Fatherland" failed to forge a non-partisan consensus on the ramifications of unity. On the contrary, old theoretical distinctions quickly gave way to new rifts, as parties began to calculate the costs and benefits of an accelerated merger between the two states.[24] Hoping to take all of the credit, the CDU/CSU wound up taking lots of blame for the heavy financial burden of unification. The party which had done the most to reinstitute contacts between the two peoples (and also came closest to predicting the real price of unity), the SPD was the one left out in the cold by voters following the first all-German elections of 1990. The FDP fared even worse in subsequent elections, failing to secure the 5% necessary to assume seats in a number of state parliaments. Although their platform goals (ecological preservation, women's rights, social justice, grassroots participation and non-violence) corresponded most closely with the needs of the newly enfranchised Germans, the Greens opted for a course of (temporary) self-destruction over coalition-building with their eastern counterparts; they lost all seats in the first enlarged Bundestag. Regardless of their positions on the GQ prior to 1989, all of these parties have been forced to reconsider their programmatic identities, owing to the diverse if not irreconcilable nature of their Eastern and Western constituents. The next section traces turning points in the evolution of West German foreign policy which eventually compelled a fundamental realignment of their respective national paradigms.

Restoration, Rearmament, and West-Integration, 1949–1963

It is ironic that the German nation, divided for the purpose of securing its de-nazification, demilitarization and democratization, would eventually achieve the third goal by quickly abandoning the first two. Members of the German and Allied High Commands signed the document of unconditional surrender on May 8, 1945, but the victors' goals had already been spelled out at the Yalta Conference of February 1945 and the Potsdam Conference of August 1945. Besides mandating complete disarmament and control of all industries linked to military production, the Control Council sought "[T]o convince the German people that they have suffered a total military defeat and that they cannot escape responsibility for what they have brought upon themselves" through their ruthless warfare and fanatic nationalism. Their second aim was "to dissolve all Nazi institutions . . . , and to prevent all Nazi and militarist activity or propaganda." Their third priority was to pave the way for the "reconstruction of German political life on a democratic basis and for eventual peaceful cooperation in international life by Germany."[25] While its immediate demands left the Germans little room for maneuver, the Potsdam agreement did not challenge the "provisional" character of the Eastern borders. Mutually exclusive reconstruction plans advanced by the Western and Soviet Allies soon gave rise to decades of "cold war and hot peace."[26]

Both the Federal Republic and the German Democratic Republic were the progeny of the Cold War, hence their primary security dilemma is rooted in the East-West struggle which gave them life in 1949. A redistribution of global power grounded in bipolarism, added to a battle of antagonistic ideologies waged in a geo-strategically significant space, reinforced a German proclivity towards all-or-nothing thinking in security matters.[27] The one position the two states would share for the next forty years was their precarious location along the East-West frontline; as a result, domestic policy quickly became intertwined with foreign policy on both sides of the German border. Soviet control of the East led de-nazification to become interwoven with anti-communism in the West, laying the foundation for its foreign policy correlate, containment doctrine. U.S. policy regarding Germany came to embody a three-fold objective: "to keep the Germans down, the Americans in, and the Russians out."

Containment doctrine (and its short-lived corollary, *roll-back*) augured more than a strictly defensive role for whatever German forces might be reconstituted. The Three-Power decision to create a western state subsequent to the Berlin Blockade (June 1948 to May 1949) meant a further loosening of the Occupational reigns.[28] The newly installed government assumed the job of orchestrating Germany's political-economic transformation in the fall of 1949, after the founding fathers and mothers adopted a number of constitutional mechanisms designed to secure the new democracy against future dismantlement.[29] The Basic Law moreover established unprecedented limits on the defense capabilities of the fledgling state outside of a newly created NATO framework (see Chapter 5).

Several competing foreign policy orientations were already in evidence prior to the formation of the new state, two more significant than the others. The first was embodied by the new Chancellor, Konrad Adenauer, who devised a subtle but masterful strategy to secure a gradual roll-back of the Occupational statutes. A Catholic Rhinelander, the elderly CDU-statesman defined the contours of national policy for more than a quarter of the Republic's divided existence (1949–1963). In the spirit of "rather half of Germany completely than the whole with half-control," his consolidation strategy centered on economic reconstruction and the cultivation of unshakable ties to the West in communion against the Soviet Union.[30]

Representing the second school was the Chancellor's vehement albeit highly respected SPD-rival, Kurt Schumacher, who agitated for the establishment of socialist democracy in a re-united Germany. This former Reichstag deputy and concentration-camp survivor insisted that American Occupational policy hindered the establishment of a "new order" and would thus lead to permanent division.[31] He envisioned the new Germany joining a bloc of Western and Central European socialist states, maintaining its independence vis-à-vis a capitalist United States and against a dictatorial Soviet Union. Schumacher struggled to have the SPD recognized as an equal partner in democratic reconstruction; it was "the sole political force which had engaged in principled resistance against national socialism from the beginning and therefore embodied 'the better part' of Germany." His moral claims for equal standing were ignored by Allied officials, however, "since they saw in the Social Democrats first Germans and then anti-fascists."[32] Though he opposed the forced merger of the German Communist Party (KPD) and the Eastern Social Democratic Party (SPD) in 1946 and denounced the Stalinist leadership as hegemonic and "national-Russian," the SPD chief violated Allied sensitivities by his strong insistence on a German right to national restoration. He continued to clash directly with the Chancellor of the Allies until his death in 1952, refusing to accept any measures deigned to alter the "provisional" status of the new state. Adenauer embraced the status quo and pursued an active course of West-integration as a necessary if not a sufficient condition for the restoration of German sovereignty.[33]

Divisions over the future defense role of the western state were reflected in the lack of consensus over terminology. Those intent on downplaying the

historical import of German rearmament less than five years after unconditional surrender employed the term *Wiederbewaffnung*, suggesting a "re-
supplying" of weapons for defensive purposes. The use of *Wiederaufrüstung*
as rearmament, by contrast, implied the reintroduction of armed forces (albeit under an integrated NATO command), coupled with regular national-
economic investment. The word *Remilitarisierung* provoked the most controversy among the public at large; its critics railed against reestablishment
of the military as an inherently nationalistic state institution.[34] For Baring,
"the so-called *re*-arming was in reality . . . the second and most important
establishment phase, as a *new*-arming of a state first planned and erected as
one without weapons."[35] Rudolf Augstein attacked the largely anti-communist thrust of both re-armament and state-formation: "The new army was
not created in order to protect the Bonn state, but rather the new state was
created, in order to position a new army in the field against the Soviets–even
if this rationale had not completely entered the consciousness of sponsors at
home and abroad."[36]

Philosopher Karl Jaspers later criticized the anti-democratic nature of rearmament decisions through the 1950s: "Back then [the plan] came into being
almost in total silence. . . . The people were never informed regarding the significance of the matter."[37] Popular opinion at the time was overwhelmingly
opposed to the vision of a rearmed Germany. Between June 1949 and November 1950, the segment of West Germans who objected to themselves or
family members becoming soldiers rose from 60% to 73%. Three-fourths of
those polled opposed the reintroduction of universal conscription; 40% said
they would make use of their right to conscientious objection (Art. 4GG).[38]
Open debates over military security remained taboo long beyond the termination of formal Occupation, based on the "retained rights" of the Allies codified in the 1954 Paris Treaties.[39] Though restricted, internal debates over rearmament were more vehement than those concerning the framework for a new
socio-economic order; yet the two were intricately connected:

> To the extent that every group within society took a position on the military
> question, the debate signifie[d] a political anatomy of society in the Federal Re-
> public which was without precedent and which would remain a determinant for
> the future capacities of the state for a long time to come. . . . Advocacy and op-
> position were not firmly grounded in any sociological typology, but rather cut-
> across and through all segments of Federal-German society.[40]

Each faction posited the existence of different linkages between rearmament, the institutionalization of division, and the impact of Alliance membership on prospects for reunification.

Domestic controversies were superceded, however, by a wave of crises
well beyond Bonn's control. They included the "forced merger" of the

Communist and Social Democratic Parties, producing the East German Socialist Unity Party in 1946; intensification of the Cold War in 1947; the 1948 currency reform and the Berlin Blockade, leading to the formation of separate German states in 1949. These events were followed by the 1950 outbreak of the Korean war; the Allies' rejection of a 1952 proposal for reunification cum neutrality; the East German workers' uprising of June 17, 1953; and the failure of the Four-Power Moscow Conference of 1954. The larger picture suggests that external, centrifugal forces played a more important role than domestic factors in promoting the consolidation of German division. While historians differ in their assessment of when the Federal Republic's projected NATO role assumed definitive form, there is evidence that U.S. deliberations commenced soon after the war. In 1947 the Joint War Plans Branch of the U.S. Army began to deliberate on the future role of Germany and Japan in conjunction with the strategic balance of powers. It was resolved at a 1948 State Department meeting involving Secretary Dulles that Germany should be turned into "a bulwark against Russia."[41]

Four-Power limits on the foreign policy prerogatives of the new state offered the Chancellor a surprising amount of room for maneuver. Served by an "agency" rather than a Foreign Ministry, Adenauer ordained the creation of an "Office Blank" (named after Theodor Blank who would become the first Defense Minister) in 1950 to deal with brewing questions of de/remilitarization; this channel enabled Adenauer to keep responsibility for defense and external affairs in his own hands until 1955. His attempt to roll back the strictures of Occupational control met with notable success during his first two months in office. The Petersberg Agreements, concluded by the Allied Powers on November 22, 1949, called a halt to industrial dismantling in exchange for a German pledge of demilitarization.[42] De-industrialization would no longer take place in line with reparation demands but in response to Allied security concerns. Control of heavy industry permitted a measure of FRG involvement, e.g., through the functional integration of German coal and steel production (Schuman Plan) in May 1950. The Pleven Plan raised the idea of an integrated European army, with German participation, only a few weeks after the Washington Conference had declared an end to the state of war and decreed the territory of West Germany and Berlin part of the western defense zone.

Adenauer likewise recognized the political opportunity afforded by the commencement of the Korean war, which opened the possibility of a partnership role based on "equal treatment." The Chancellor proposed a strengthening of the Occupational troop presence, as well as a German contribution towards the establishment of a West European army. The result was a highly charged process of remilitarization within five years of surrender, as the price to be paid for limited sovereignty. January 1951 saw the beginning of German-Allied negotiations as to the nature of this FRG contribution; deliberations intensified between September 1951 and May 1952, setting the terms for the General Treaty that would end its occupied status.

The idea of a future European Defense Community provided a central focus for Bonn's foreign policy agenda through the mid-1950s. Intent on blocking an accord solidifying FRG membership, Stalin appealed to the West in his Note of March 10, 1952, offering to pursue a peace treaty with Germany (with provisions for a national defense force) in exchange for neutralization. Adenauer's response, articulated in his Siegen Talk of March 16, 1952, set the tone for nearly two decades of inter-German relations; his insistence on "politics from a position of strength" translated into the politics of non-recognition, no negotiations, and "no experiments." Stalin blamed the West for perpetuating German division, leaving the Soviet Union free to pursue the consolidation of a separate East German state.

The signing of the European Defense Community Treaty, as well as the formal acceptance of the *Deutschlandvertrag* [General Treaty over the Relations of the Federal Republic and the Three Powers] in May 1952, closed the window of opportunity on short-term prospects for German unification. Stalin's death in March 1953 activated hopes for a change in the international climate, but Soviet intervention in the GDR's June 17th uprising led to a final delineation of the East-West spheres of influence. In a curious twist of fate, France's rejection of the EDC treaty on August 30, 1954 effected the FRG's permanent incorporation into the Western Alliance.

Western Powers signed the Paris Treaties on October 23, 1954, terminating the Occupational regime and embracing "their" Germany as a full NATO member. They moreover agreed to support reunification, recognized the FRG's claims to exclusive representation [*Alleinvertretungsanspruch*] of all Germans, left the Oder-Neisse border question open to eventual peace-treaty regulation, and promised to preserve the freedom and security of Berlin. As the GDR saw it, the 1955 implementation of "the Paris war-treaties, the integration of West Germany into NATO and the execution of the armed forces law . . . created a completely new situation in Europe and Germany . . . the remilitarization of West Germany deepened and carved the German division into stone."[43]

Following the watershed of 1954/55, the Federal Republic adhered to a static, hard-line confrontation course against the East through 1963. The Soviet Union proposed a normalization of relations with Bonn in June 1955; Khrushchev made a July stop-over in East Berlin, long enough to proclaim that the *Two-State-Theory* would henceforth shape Soviet-German relations. The Chancellor neither demanded nor secured concessions on the German Question during his surprising September 1955 visit to Moscow. The Twentieth Party Congress of the CPSU in February 1956 briefly heralded a "thaw" in Cold War relations; all hopes for eliminating Euorpean division were dashed, however, by the October 1956 rebellion in Budapest, quelled by Soviet troops. Khrushchev's Berlin ultimatum of November 27, 1958 reactivated a sense of ultimate dependency on the U.S.-German partnership.[44] Mounting superpower tensions compelled the SPD to withdraw its *Deutschlandplan* after the failed 1959 Geneva meeting. The party severed its ideological ties to Marx and accepted the necessity of NATO membership, as ordained by its Godesberg Program.

The January 1961 inauguration of President Kennedy soon led to a redefinition of NATO defense strategy: the doctrine of Mutually Assured Destruction (MAD) made way for Flexible Response. In early August, the NATO Council outlined three "essentials" regarding the status of Berlin which "made the Wall possible."[45] Adenauer's refusal to travel to Berlin in response to the August 13th crisis undermined his electoral support, provoked the displeasure of the FDP, and enhanced the popularity of the city's reigning SPD mayor, Willy Brandt. The non-response evinced by West Germany's "best friend" was equally troubling—the United States assumed a wait-and-see posture, necessitated by the limitations of its own MAD strategy.

Adenauer's success in ensconsing the new republic in the NATO alliance, despite widespread public aversion to rearmament, owes to "the lesser of two evils" logic prevalent throughout the Cold War. Although 74.6% (Emnid) of the West Germans rejected a return call-to-arms in 1950, the outbreak of hostilities in Korea led an estimated 35% to fear that third world war would "probably" occur; 48% thought it possible.[46] Allensbach found 53% "worried" that a new world war would erupt.[47] The perceived imminence of an East-West military confrontation, reinforced by personal memories of World War II, conditioned a reluctant acceptance of rearmament under the integrated command of the new North Atlantic Treaty Organization.

Because *Angst* is an abstract quality, it is impossible to assign specific psychological weights to security perceptions collected at the individual level but analyzed at the macro-political level. Longitudinal trends provide a more accurate reflection of shifts in public opinion than do individual polls. With this caveat in mind, the public's "fear of war" evinces a number of inconsistent ebbs and flows in conjunction with specific East-West crises.[48] The Korean War and the Soviet intervention in Hungary led to a heightening of collective anxiety, while the creation of the Berlin Wall appears to have paved the way for a tendential lessening of fears sustained throughout the next two decades.[49] Emnid data compiled between 1950 and 1980 show a steady decrease in future-war projections, especially after the FRG's full integration into NATO; the number who thought world war might ensue fell from 35% to 5% between July 1950 and May 1956, rising to 13% after the Soviet intervention in Hungary. A majority also deemed war unlikely in September 1961, perhaps because the Berlin Wall solidified the status quo, dampening fears of further territorial encroachment by the Soviets. The Cuban Missile Crisis—which almost triggered a *real* nuclear exchange between the superpowers—did not induce a pessimistic response. Because the conflict site lay far from the heart of Europe, 55% of those polled in September 1962 felt that a new world war was unlikely.[50]

Anxieties over the probability of war are linked to the perceived proximity of the threat and to the nature of the peril at hand. Variations in the threat perceptions of men and women mirror their different experiences during war and occupation. Through the 1950s and 1960s, women were more anti-communist yet favored unification over Alliance membership; they responded in more America-friendly tones but voiced less approval for U.S. troop deployments on German soil. It is not that women of the first generation were more nationalistic or neutralist than their men; they fixated instead on matters of personal security, in view of the traumas of war and Occupation. Men believed that "the Russians" would not initiate a war in Europe (61% to 41% in 1960), a perception that reversed direction in 1977: 72% for men, 76% among women. The majority feared that the Soviet goal of world revolution necessarily meant rendering all of Germany communist. Faced with an either/or proposition, more than half consistently opted for security against the Russians over German unification from 1952 to 1959.[51] Both sexes discounted the idea that things "weren't so bad for honest workers" in the Soviet Zone in 1951, although a majority felt in 1962 that reunification should take precedence over securing free elections in East Germany based on a renunciation of unity aims.[52]

One's ability to tolerate a perceived external threat is naturally a function of the relative strength accorded one's allies and adversaries. Prior to 1954, the United States was the only power capable of playing the nuclear-card (which did not hinder Soviet incursions into the GDR and Hungary). The *Sputnik* shock of 1957 gave the Soviets an ostensible technological edge, but NATO powers were seen to have a slight advantage over WPO forces through the late 1960s. It is difficult to determine what motivates individuals in their perception of one side or the other. Was it the personal war experience, the geographical proximity of the adversary, the actual behavior of the Soviets, or was it the USSR's penchant for a larger conventional force which magnified its strength in the eyes of the Germans? The evidence is contradictory at best: While 40% of the Emnid respondents deemed the West the stronger of the two sides in 1954 and 1957, only 24% and 17%, respectively, held NATO capable of turning back a Soviet attack on Germany.[53] The Germans' lack of confidence in pre-1961 Western defense capabilities is puzzling in light of the U.S. nuclear monopoly (the USSR's first atomic explosion in 1949 should not be equated with a strategic-delivery capability).

The creation of a quasi-national defense force in 1956 gave rise to a number of "security paradoxes" for the FRG. West Germany's complete integration into the political framework of NATO demonstrated "how the entanglements of interdependence can be used to enhance sovereignty," at the same time it "tempered nationalism and militarism and provided an effective additional means of civilian control of the military."[54] Despite its stabilizing impact, postwar Germans were more inclined to view the physical presence of NATO as a necessary evil, rather than as a positive force for the promotion of peace, while the Occupying Powers saw the restoration of the German military as absolutely essential for the survival of the fledgling democracy.[55]

One priority reflected in the plans for a country-based defense force was "to find an enduring equilibrium in civil-military relations within the new democratic German state."[56] With Western blessing, Adenauer initiated the search for an organizational mode that would not only guarantee military security against external threats, but also provide international security (fostering the eventual acceptance of Germany in the region) and civic security (preventing the reemergence of a militarized "state within the state"). The Bundeswehr's structural requirements were inherent in the statutes of the North Atlantic Treaty Organization; its institutional parameters were implicit in the Himmerode Memorandum, a planning document secretly commissioned by Adenauer in October 1950. Each phase of the negotiations, Kelleher notes, was characterized by the preeminence of never-again thinking: "Never again meant never again a dominant military or political leadership wielding military authority without constraint."[57] The new security forces would adopt three fail-safe mechanisms to preserve their democratic character: submission to an integrated NATO command, adherence to the concept of *Innere Führung* [internal leadership] and, last but not least, a reliance on the "citizen-soldier."

The new military code [*Principles on Leadership and Civic Education*] required members of the Bundeswehr to engage actively in the democratic process as well as in its physical defense, that is, to balance "the citizen's demands for freedom in a liberal democracy with the soldier's duties in an organization devoted to the highest degree of military efficiency."[58] Military amendments to the Basic Law (1955–57) specified the means by which these aims were to be achieved.[59] The primacy of political over military control obliged the government to appoint a civilian Minister of Defense and to screen all high-ranking military personnel. Next, universal conscription would be used to ensure societal penetration of the Bundeswehr to hinder the resurgence of a special "warrior caste"; recruits would be drawn from all segments of society, subject to parliamentary legislation and oversight. A third measure, politicization of the military, would preclude domination by a single partisan group or ideological faction. No group could be excluded as an "illegitimate" partner from debates over national security, provided it remained loyal to the precepts of the free-democratic basic order. Finally, the state bore direct reponsibility for upholding the civil rights of each conscript, including the right to conscientious objection. The public remained skeptical: 66% of the men, and 46% of the women polled in 1956 doubted that *Innere Führung* would prevent a return to military-business-as-usual.[60]

The idea of a German army, independent or not, failed to elicit majority support between 1950 and 1956.[61] Citizens were less inclined to reject the Bundeswehr once formal induction of the first voluntary force had taken place; more than half of the people surveyed between 1956 and 1961 wanted to maintain the new army, with the exception of 1960 (48%).[62] The idea of career military enjoyed a slight edge from 1954 to 1956, but opinion began to shift in favor of universal conscription by 1957.[63] A surprising 55% of the men and 63% of the women polled in 1956 agreed that youth needed the military in order to acquire the virtues of "order and propriety," that the Bundeswehr would serve, in Kiesinger's words, "as the school of the nation"—though less than 10% were enthusiastic about enlisting themselves. Roughly half continued to back a recruit's right to conscientious objection, especially among those who had relatives in the East-Zone (54% in 1956).[64]

In summary, the personal trust Adenauer enjoyed among the Allies allowed the Federal Republic to acquire enough "national" sovereignty to warrant room for maneuver in the conduct of foreign affairs—at the expense of unification. The first Chancellor secured the right to recreate a German army, albeit one "irreversibly" integrated into the Western Alliance; by 1955 the Federal Republic had become "the most important *Vorpost* of western bloc in the cold war."[65] Adenauer's fall from grace in 1963 owed not to his overstepping the boundaries of authority vis-à-vis the conquerors-turned-partners but rather to his misreading of domestic concerns. His attempt to downplay the Berlin Wall crisis, his efforts to discredit follow-on candidate Ludwig Ehrhard, and his Cabinet's direct links to the *Spiegel Affair* signaled that the time was ripe for succession.[66] The *Spiegel Affair* produced its own happy ending, however: in the first major show-down between the imperatives of external security versus internal democracy, the principles of free press and due process won. By 1963, the division of Germany which held the two states hostage to a "provisional" condition of insecurity had itself become the most stable, "permanent" element in a destabilizing global confrontation between the Eastern and Western blocs.

The Rise of Anti-Nuclearism

Early protests against remilitarization were not so much a manifestation of anti-militarism pure and simple as they were a reflection of conflicting German motivations and expectations. The Federal Republic would prove the most steady of all the larger European states, when evaluated on the basis of such objective measures as price stability, unemployment rates and electoral succession. But its persistent dilemma, characterized by this author as the Stability versus Security Paradox, was that the West Germans could not believe it; objective stability was not matched by a sense of subjective security.[67]

Prior to the Korean crisis, the mood of the German public was aptly reflected in the slogan "Never again War," yet for many "pacifism" still bore the stab-in-the-back connotations used to explain Germany's humiliating defeat in World War I. Genuine pacifist sentiment was strongest among clerics and intellectuals; among proletarian activists, anti-militarism was closely linked to hopes for a new socio-economic order. Capitalism had been discredited not by virtue of its exploitation of the working class but by way of the historical records of Flick, Krupp, IG-Farben, Siemens, AEG, Thyssen, Klöckner, the Commerzbank, the Deutsche and Dresdener Banks, private companies that had functioned as the pillars of the Nazi war economy.[68]

Adenauer himself provided the catalyst for a rapidly growing anti-war movement with his August 28, 1950 proposal for rearming Germany. Revealed only to the Cabinet, the memorandum triggered the resignation of Interior Minister Gustav Heinemann three days later. Explaining his dramatic gesture in a "think piece" dated October 13, 1950, Heinemann supplied a philosphical foundation for three decades of anti-militarist protest to follow:

> Especially important is the question whether a West German military participation would be taken as a provocation by Russia. . . . A European war with our participation would not only entail a national war for us as it might affect all other peoples, but it would moreover be a war of Germans against Germans. And it would, in view of the way things lie, take place on German soil. We legitimize the idea of Germany itself as a battlefield if we allow ourselves to be pulled into rearmament.[69]

Heinemann's mobilization efforts culminated in the creation of the pro-peace All-German People's Party (GDVP) in November 1952, which joined in the 1955 *Paulskirche* Movement.

NATO resolved on September 26, 1950 to utilize "the German human-potential and the sources of German assistance" to strengthen the Alliance foundation.[70] Anti-militarist groups reacted by publicizing restrictions outlined in the Basic Law, though attempts to block government action through the courts were quickly dismissed. Youth groups actively planned *Anti-War Day* events (September 1st) in 1947, 1948, and 1949. Public opinion stood on the side of the protestors: one southern German newspaper, polling 16,000 readers in October 1950, found 73% opposed to rearmament; over 90% of the students at universities in Stuttgart, Munich and Erlangen rejected remilitarization.[71]

Rearmament's most fervent supporters were found among members of the ruling parties (CDU/CSU, FDP). Mindful of profit and job opportunities inherent in revived military production, industrial managers and trade union officials assumed a posture of silent advocacy, countered by the outspoken anti-militarism of production workers. Chairing the largest Bundestag caucus, SPD-delegate Erich Ollenhauer (at odds with Schumacher) declared his party's refusal to consider remilitarization in December 1949.

Hesitant at first, the Catholic Church eventually placed itself squarely in the government camp. The Evangelical-Lutheran Church opposed the policy, given its historical roots in Central Germany and its fears of undermining reunification. Pacifists found a courageous spokesperson in Martin Niemöller, once the "personal prisoner" of Hitler in the camps of Sachsenhausen and Dachau. Acting on behalf of the fraternal council of the *Confessing Church*, Niemöller personally appealed to Adenauer to recognize German guilt vis-à-vis Poland and the Soviet Union; he cautioned against the demonization of communism as an excuse for remilitarization.[72] The anti-militarist orientation of the Left was, in fact, pitted against the infusion of anti-communist sentiments from the Right. A partial surrogate for national identity lost, "anti-communism was elevated to the status of the sustaining philosophy of the state."[73]

Anti-militarist candidates registered gains during the 1950 elections conducted in Hesse, Württemberg-Baden, and Bavaria. A loose coalition emerged among representatives of the Communist Party (KPD), the leftist Catholic German Center Party, the German People's Party (DVP), the German Peace Society, the International Fellowship for Reconciliation, the German branch of War Resisters International, and the Democratic Women's League. More than 600 peace committees were registered in the western zones; a Peace Congress scheduled for January 1951 drew 1,700 activists to Essen. Youth groups occupied the island of Helgoland to stop Allied Powers from using its unique landscape as a practice site for bombing maneuvers; despite arrests, adolescent protestors repeated the occupation in April 1951, when maneuvers were finally halted.

Attention shifted to plans for a national referendum, posing the question: "Are you opposed to remilitarization and in favor of conclusion of a peace treaty with Germany in the year 1951?" Activists in Rheinland-Pfalz accrued 32,000 signatures within three days. Adenauer declared the plebiscite unconstitutional on April 24th. Eastern officials scheduled the referendum for June 3–5, 1951; endorsed by the Volkskammer, the idea was reportedly affirmed by 96% of the GDR voters.[74] Thwarted on the referendum front, countless activists took to the streets in Bonn, Düsseldorf and Hannover or distributed leaflets at the Krupp factory gates; protests resulted in 7,321 arrests and over 1,000 trials. The German Trade Union Federation (DGB) resolved to oppose an independent FRG army, and convened an Extraordinary Federal Congress in June 1951. 1952 saw the creation of the West German Women's Peace Union (WFFB), as well as the staging of a youth "peace caravan" which drew 30,000 to Essen. All measures proved ineffective. By the time the General Treaty was ripe for signing, it was no longer a question of whether remilitarization would occur but only under what modus.

The next wave of protest centered on the FRG's full integration into NATO. *Amt Blank* was revealed to have engaged in a war-simulation under

the code-name of *Carte Blanche*, resulting in a fictive death toll of 1.7 million, and 3.5 million wounded on BRD soil.[75] Cradle of the 1848 revolution, the Paul's Church in Frankfurt provided a familiar forum for opponents to the Paris Treaties. Prominent figures such as Heinemann (GVP),
Georg Reuter (DGB), Ollenhauer (SPD), scientist Alfred Weber, Evangelical theologian Helmut Gollwitzer, and Catholic theologian Johann Hessen
organized a January 29, 1955 convocation under the slogan, "Save Unity,
Peace and Freedom! Against Communism and Nationalism!" They issued a
German Manifesto, warning that rearmament would end all prospects for reunification. Organizers gathered 100,000 signatures in Northrhine-Westphalia and collected 250,000 more in Bavaria within three weeks.[76] Support
for rearmament was strongest among ruling-party voters (61%) and West
Berliners (60%).[77] The Federal Republic became a full-fledged member of
NATO on May 5, 1955; the Warsaw Pact Treaty Organization was called
into existence on May 14th.

A shift in U.S. strategic doctrine, under the Radford Plan, replaced conventional deterrence with an emphasis on nuclear deterrence. Adenauer's
objection to the policy change, characterized on August 21, 1956 "as the
greatest danger for humanity," came as a surprise to peace groups.[78] Many
believed that once the Bundeswehr commenced operations, the next item
on Adenauer's agenda would be to lobby for atomic weapons on FRG territory so as to place it on equal footing with Britain and France. Franz Josef
Strauss (CSU) had voiced support for a nuclear-arming of West German
forces five months earlier, a "necessity" he addressed even more pointedly
on January 13, 1957. The U.S. government confirmed on March 14th that
atomic weapons had already been deployed on West German soil; two days
later, the Peace Committee of the FRG (formed in 1949) issued a formal
appeal, titled *Out with the Nuclear Weapons in West Germany*.

The last six months of 1957 saw a rash of anti-nuclear initiatives and campaigns. Eighteen of Germany's most prominent atomic scientists, including
three Nobel Prize winners, signed on to the Göttinger Declaration of April
12, 1957. The Government tried to discredit the scientists (though many had
ties to the CDU), charging them with providing "unintentional service to
communism."[79] A major demonstration on May 1st was followed by an
"Open Letter to the Federal Chancellor" circulated by ninety-nine scientists,
authors and artists. The *Paulskirche* once again served as a forum for the
Women's Peace Conference in July. The Franconian Circle against Atomic
Weapons for the Bundeswehr collected 6,000 signatures, reinforced by the
collective support of a Conference of West German Writers in September.

Adenauer nevertheless prevailed with his 1957 campaign slogan, "Prevent
the Destruction of Germany," securing the CDU's one and only parliamentary majority to date. The new government dismissed the Rapacki Plan of
October 1957, namely, the call for an atomic weapons-free zone for Central

Europe presented by the Polish Foreign Minister at the United Nations.[80] The Chancellor delivered his ex-post-facto acceptance of nuclearization to the NATO Council on December 18, 1957.

Opposition Social Democrats resolved in January 1958 (the 25th anniversary of the 1933 Nazi Empowerment Law) to initiate a country-wide "enlightenment campaign," inviting forty delegates from unions, churches, research institutes and literary circles to plan a major march for May 23, 1958. Their Godesberg meeting resulted in the formation of the Action Society Against Nuclear Armament. In March they unleashed an extra-parliamentary protest campaign under the rubric of "Struggle against Atomic Death" [*Kampf dem Atomtod*]. The Bundestag debated the merits of the Rapacki Plan, the Kennan proposal for nuclear disengagement, and the NATO Document MC 70 for one week; the majority approved NATO's nuclear arming of the Bundeswehr on March 25th, a decision rejected by two-thirds of the citizenry (see Table 4.1).[81]

The vote triggered a wave of spontaneous silent marches, protest assemblies and short strikes, tactics borrowed from the British Campaign for Nuclear Disarmament. According to Emnid, 52% would have supported a general strike to prevent atomic weapons being used by indigenous forces.[82] Professional organizations circulated manifestoes, while younger citizens staged a Berlin Student Congress against Nuclear Armament in January 1959. Local action committees organized 1,500 May-Day "demos"; the Republic was rocked by demonstrations "with mass character" in every city of 200,000 or more residents.[83]

SPD leaders felt that ongoing opposition to NATO and nuclear weapons clashed with the party's hope of becoming a coalition partner at the federal level, leading to a rift with the masses. The national plebiscite over nuclearization was thwarted by a Constitutional Court injunction, then a formal ruling on July 30. An October 1958 poll showed that the government would have lost, had the issue been put to a popular vote (42% opposed, 16% in favor; 17% would have abstained).[84] Khrushchev's Berlin ultimatum signaled the final, painful defeat for the anti-nuclear campaign.

The SPD-internal split over the nuclear issue would intensify through the 1960s, reinforced by a growing generation gap between the party's moderate and radical wings. The post-Godesberg era nonetheless saw the consolidation of a foreign policy "formula" that had begun to take shape in the years after Schumacher's death. Building on the 1967 Harmel Report, Social Democrats developed a two-step approach to national security: they stressed the need to explore the political opportunities afforded by negotiations, but they moved to support Alliance plans for deployment in the case that negotiations failed.

The first cycle of anti-nuclear protest produced a number of "learning experiences" critical to the democratization of German political culture. First,

TABLE 4.1 Nuclear Weapons for the Bundeswehr, 1956–1960

Question: "Consultations are now taking place over the future arming of the Bundeswehr. Are you for or against the arming of German troops with atomic weapons?"

	March 1956			April 1957	Dec. 1957	March 1958	April 1958	June 1958	Sept. 1960
Response (in percent)	Total	M	F						
Against	49	44	54	64	64	69	65	63	49
For	32	44	20	17	19	15	17	21	23
Undecided	19	12	26	19	17	16	18	16	28

Source: IFD Allensbach data, *Jahrbuch 1957, Jahrbuch 1958–1964;* reprinted as Table 11.3.1 in Faiss and Meyer, p. 237.

the late 1950s gave birth to a fundamental opposition movement which, despite its quick shift from extra-party to extra-parliamentary tactics, kept one foot firmly planted in the legislative system (through its ties to the SPD). Secondly, the anti-rearmament campaign drew much of its strength from the involvement of traditionally non-political actors, e.g., the clergy, writers, scientists and women; historical awareness of the high price paid for their earlier failure to resist rendered these groups capable of coalition-formation to an unprecedented degree. A third lesson woven into the fabric of the new democracy was that dissent could no longer be repudiated by branding protestors as "traitors to the fatherland." Many fundamental conflicts impinging on national security would henceforth be channeled through the courts, invoking "the constitutional powers to decide" over international as well as domestic security issues. Fourth, the government's disregard of public fears conditioned thousands to engage in new and predominantly non-violent forms of self-organization and interest articulation. Finally, the campaigns of the 1950s led FRG activists to associate nuclear technology with the perception of "imminent danger" in the early stages of its development–in stark contrast to the technology-friendly, more-is-better approach that would dominate the strategic thinking of NATO's preeminent member, the USA, through the 1980s.[85]

Instrumentalization of the European Idea

Foreign policy-makers in the FRG faced a double mandate anchored in the Basic Law: Responsible for the "preservation of national and state unity," they were also required to advance world peace by way of their equal partnership "in a united Europe." Germany's role in the western security community rested on four policy "pillars." *Atlantikpolitik* centered on the FRG's "special relationship" with the United States. Next came *Europapolitik*, promoting the cause of supranational integration; the third involved *Entspannungspolitik* [détente], processes geared toward a mitigation of East-West tensions. Last but not least, there was *Deutschland-* and *Ostpolitik*, seeking to cultivate cooperative relations with the East, especially with the GDR.[86]

French rejection of the EDC Treaty in 1954 put a temporary brake on the German pursuit of the European idea, moving Adenauer to introduce an early form of *Ostpolitik*: Taking advantage of the short-lived spirit of Geneva, the Chancellor established diplomatic relations with the Soviet Union in 1955. Yet new tensions arose between Bonn and Moscow, stemming from the FRG's claim that it remained the sole representative of Germany-as-a-whole. The Adenauer government had to devise a means for inhibiting the formal recognition of the GDR by other countries without jeopardizing its own tenuous links with the Soviet Union. The result was the promulgation of the Hallstein Doctrine: the *Bundesrepublik* would construe the establishment of diplomatic relations between any third state and "the so-called GDR" as a hostile act intended to deepen the division of Germany.

Given its self-imposed isolation vis-à-vis the Eastern states, Bonn's membership in the European Community served as "a lifeline for gaining equal status among the family of nations, for pursuing economic recovery, and for establishing internal and external stability."[87] Waxing and waning interest in the plans for economic integration and implementation of the 1957 Treaty of Rome mirrored ebbs and flows in East-West developments. In addition to reigning in the Germans, the institutionalization of the Common Market, the Coal and Steel Community (ECSC), and the European Council fostered Western Europe's emergence as a balancing force between the USSR and the United States.

The Federal Republic emerged as one of most emphatic supporters of the supranationality principle, rooted in Article 24 of the Basic Law. Its willingness to subordinate its nation-state designs to the welfare of the larger community ensured a dramatic change in status, from that of former "whipping boy" to "model child." When asked to choose between independent statehood and European integration, FRG citizens consistently opted for the latter (42%–62%) between 1950 and 1966.[88] Neither the highpoint of *Ostpolitik* nor the era of European malaise saw a decline in their preferences for Community integration *over* German unification; EC support outweighed unity by a ratio of 2:1 in 1973 and 1983. The majority's belief that EC-membership was "a good thing" for Germans persisted through 1980, although two-thirds were content to limit the Community's decision-making powers to the economic sphere.[89] In the final analysis, Bonn's "locomotive" role in the European integration process proved "crucially important for the rehabilitation, confidence, and security of the Federal Republic."[90]

West German expectations as to the benefits of integration were higher than those of other partner states, compensating perhaps for the FRG's lack of "national" status. Between 1951 and 1959 the proportion of citizens who viewed the FRG as a full member in the community of western peoples (rather than as the enemy of yesteryear) had risen from less than 10% to over 45%. By July 1958, an overwhelming majority moreover recognized that national defense could not be achieved without new forms of international cooperation: 92% favored the creation of a world-wide monitoring organization to ensure that no country would engage in the proliferation of nuclear bombs. Some 73% were willing to report the production of forbidden weapons, should they observe such activity in their own country.[91] While 65% had heard about the "peaceful uses of atomic energy," the term atomic energy continued to evoke associations with bombs, atomic war, destruction, devastation, *Angst* and danger for over three-fourths of those polled in 1960.[92]

The German Question is, was and remains a European Question. The four pillars of FRG foreign policy engendered yet another set of dialectical relations, which I label the National Unification versus European Integration Paradox. Adenauer had promoted integration as the pre-condition for eventual reunification, as did the Basic Law itself. The higher the tension level between the superpowers, the more closely and irreversibly the Federal Republic integrated itself into the western value community. The more actively the West Germans appeared to accept the necessity of a significant defense contribution of their own, "the sooner the Western powers could tolerate their claimed right to reunification."[93] It would have been impossible for Germany to reunify without the acquiescence of both its European neighbors *and* the Soviet Union. Yet for three decades, the more institutionalized the FRG's commitment to the West became, the more unacceptable her efforts to merge with the GDR seemed to the Soviet Union, Poland and to the East Berlin leadership itself—until Gorbachev's New Political Thinking embraced the idea of a security partnership in the mid-1980s.

The Paradigm Shift: Deterrence plus Détente, 1964–1979

West German hopes for reunification based on a strategy of "No negotiation" were laid to rest on August 13, 1961. The GDR's decision to seal off the Eastern sectors of Berlin terminated "the politics of the long breath" espoused by Adenauer; the Hallstein Doctrine had done nothing to prevent this ultimate affront to the ideal of national unity. The need for a more pragmatic approach had already penetrated public consciousness: 70% had heard of the non-recognition policy by 1965, but only 48% approved of its use vis-à-vis Cuba and Yugoslavia.[94] The desire for greater foreign policy flexibility helped to pave the way for the "politics of the small steps" under a new Social-Liberal coalition commencing in the late 1960s.

Political Realignment and Generational Change

The Social Democrats had moved closer to the Government's position by committing to NATO and withdrawing their final *Deutschlandplan* in June 1960, but some party members began to search for a more flexible strategy regarding relations with the other Germany. The new approach was articulated by MdB Egon Bahr in his Tutzinger address of July 15, 1963. Under the formula "change through rapprochement" [*Wandel durch Annäherung*], Bahr maintained "that reunification is not a single act that can be put into practice on the basis of an historical resolution on an historical day at an historical conference but is rather a process with many steps and many stations."[95] Chancellor Ludwig Erhard, the much-lauded architect of the Economic Miracle, seemed incapable of managing the uncertainties of a globalized East-West conflict. Berlin Mayor Willy Brandt moved into the foreground by proposing that the Christian Union and the SPD join in a governmental partnership of limited duration, the foundations of which had been laid behind the scenes by Herbert Wehner.

Characterized as "a marriage of elephants," the Grand Coalition of Kiesinger and Brandt (1966–69) was unpopular from the start, especially among restive post-adolescents (since it eliminated a formal Opposition). At the time of its inception, the Social Democrats faced a vociferous "internal-parliamentary opposition" dating back to the anti-Atomic Death campaign. The police-induced death of Free University student Benno Ohnesorge on June 2, 1967, followed by the April 1968 assassination attempt against SDS-leader Rudi Dutschke, unleashed the furies of another major "Extra-Parliamentary Opposition" [*APO*] Movement. The first wave attracted hundreds of thousands to demonstrations in twenty-seven cities, involving 21,000 police, 400 injuries and two deaths.[96] The anti-atomic Easter Marches, the anti-Springer Press campaign, protests against the Emergency Laws, and mounting opposition to American assaults on Vietnam merged into a cultural revolution, which only Brandt and Heinemann dared to address. Recognizing the Student Movement as herald to a new era in FRG-history, the would-be Chancellor and the future Federal-President expressed a willingness to explore the root causes of unrest, provided the violence ceased.[97]

The FDP had begun to reconsider its position on rapprochement with the East a decade earlier under the influence of Erich Mende and Karl-Georg Pfleiderer. The threat of political extinction augured by the Grand Coalition compelled a more intense search for a new FDP profile between 1966 and 1969. Walter Scheel replaced Mende as party chief at the Freiburg Convention of January 1968, joined by Hans-Dietrich Genscher and Hermann Müller as the new vice-chairpersons. Though few saw this changing of the guard as a shift towards the Left, the team of Brandt and Scheel would effect a dramatic realignment of the country's party-political landscape over the next four years.[98]

The international system also witnessed a critical realignment through the mid-1960s, grounded in major arms control treaties, Third World decolonization movements, and the definitive rupture of Sino-Soviet relations. NATO responded by commissioning a self-study regarding its future tasks, the Harmel Report of December 1967. Stressing the need for a dual strategy (soon to develop a life of its own under *Ostpolitik*), the Report ascribed two primary functions to the Alliance:

> The first consists of the maintainance of military strength and political solidarity that is sufficient to deter acts of aggression and other forms of applied pressure, and to protect the territory of the member states in the event that aggression takes place. . . . It is within this climate [of stability, security and trust among its members] that the Alliance can fulfill its second function: the further search for progress in the direction of lasting relationships, with whose help the fundamental political questions can be resolved. Military security and the poli-

tics of tension-reduction present themselves not as a contradiction but rather as a mutual complement [to each other].[99]

Entspannungspolitik or détente, as understood by the signatories, was not an end in itself but rather one component of a long-term process, fostering a militarily secured European "peace order."

Public sentiments regarding reunification were noticeably ambivalent by the mid-1960s, many characterizing the policy as a "dead-end." A leak of Wehner's 1966 proposal for the step-by-step creation of an "economic community" between the two parts of Germany provoked a stir inside and outside ministerial offices, motivating Bielefeld pollsters to incorporate a new response option into their perennial query over *Wiedervereinigung*. In contrast to earlier surveys in which a majority had felt the need for "lots of patience," 40% held in 1966 that "reunification could come more quickly than we think" on the basis of a systematically pursued *Ostpolitik*.[100] Executed before the Grand Coalition was formed, this poll implies that the public had moved more quickly towards a new East-orientation than policy-makers themselves.

Berlin's emergence as the hotbed of protest after 1966 owed to several special conditions that had become the hallmark of everyday life in a divided city. First, its Four-Power status and the presence of NATO forces were a constant reminder of limited sovereignty, to a degree not experienced by any other German metropolis. Secondly, the Wall gave a special salience to Berlin's frontline status, physical proximity to the other Germany and, hence, to the human consequences of war. Third, due to its Four-Power status the city was officially designated a conscription-free zone for all male residents of draftable age; those of anti-militaristic bent were more likely to move there before being called up for uniformed service. A fourth factor was the higher absorptive "capacity" of Berlin's universities, owing to a 1972 Constitutional Court ruling on the *Numerus clausus* [limitations on admissions in each discipline]. The combined effect of a constitutional right to education (Art. 12 GG) and the 1968 call for "equal opportunity" was an enrollment explosion of unprecedented proportions. The number of students registered at the Free University alone would rise from 14,994 in 1968, to 20,859 in 1972, to 30,687 in 1975—a staggering growth rate accompanied by a major fiscal crisis.[101]

Quantitatively better prospects for university admission, coupled with participatory academic-governance rules (until the High Court threw out the Group University in 1973), rendered the city especially attractive to ambitious, reform-oriented youth. The Student Movement had its roots in demands by prominent officials for a democratic restructuring of the higher educational system, dating back to 1964; modelled after the Berkeley Free-Speech campaign, its sit-in tactics were "borrowed" from the U.S. civil rights movement. The student protests of the 1960s consolidated an institutional turnabout to the Left in a state system that had been dominated by the Right for more than one hundred years. Last but not least, generous constitutional guarantees of political asylum brought a dramatic increase in Third World migrants seeking refuge within the city's western boundaries; their presence nourished a variety of liberation-based solidarity campaigns among students and church activists. All of these conditions contributed to a higher level of consciousness regarding the links between foreign policy decisions and domestic consequences among Berlin's residents.

Particularly unsettling in this regard was a federal proposal first advanced in 1958, known as *die Notstandsgesetze* [State of Emergency Laws], which sought to limit the exercise of free speech, suspend postal privacy, restrict trade union activities, and extend the powers of the executive branch in the case of a "national emergency." Earlier initiatives to this effect had provoked waves of protest in 1963, 1965 and 1966. Students, intellectuals, the clergy, and trade unionists joined forces again, opposing Bonn's support for an American "defense of democracy" in Vietnam while it pushed to curtail freedoms at home. For many, the Grand Coalition's efforts to render these emergency provisions the law of the land implied that Bonn was secretly preparing to engage the Bundeswehr in the intensified Southeast Asian conflict.[102]

Their timing hardly coincidental, the Allied Powers proclaimed their intention to lift Occupational rights reserved under the 1954 Germany Treaty. Article 5 required the FRG to "undertake effective measures to protect the security of the armed services, including the ability to counter a serious disturbance of the public security and order."[103] On May 30, 1968, the Bundestag approved the Emergency Laws, thanks to the yes-votes cast by a majority of the SPD members. The vote reflected a new approach to security on the part of the Social Democratic Party: over the next decade it would assume a tougher stance against fundamental leftist opposition from within, in exchange for the right to negotiate with established communist leaderships outside the country's borders. It was a strategy affirmed by the SPD's Radical Ordinance of 1972 and subsequent acceptance of a judicial crackdown on domestic terrorism.

The impulses released by generational change and Brandt's 1969 exhortation to "dare more democracy" eventually found new institutional channels. Internal factionalization portended the collapse of the APO movement, paralleled by new opportunities for parliamentary influence following the Bundestag's decision to lower the voting age from 21 to 18 in July 1970. The SPD's success in garnering the youth vote was grounded in reasons well beyond the charismatic, pro-reform style of Willy Brandt. Viewed historically as the organized embodiment of the Left, the SPD suddenly stood out as a viable opposition party capable of clearing the 5% electoral hurdle. No other party was willing to recast its platform in terms of untested issues amidst turbulent times (prior to the 1980 formation of the Greens).[104] Social Democrats moreover exhibited a good deal of openness towards the

other Germany, in contrast to the CDU/CSU, having responded positively
to new GDR overtures (an exchange of letters); Eastern leaders would
change their mind about the value of direct contacts after the SED's Sev-
enth Party Congress of 1967.[105] Curiously, the SPD was reluctant to ban the
reconstituted DKP (Communist Party); at the same time it supported a
1969 move by CDU-Interior Minister Benda to outlaw the Students for
Democratic Socialism [SDS] as inimical to the constitution.

More than any other party, the SPD had benefited from, and was plagued
by, the demographic sea-change besetting the FRG as the 1960s drew to a
close. The enfranchisement of new voters was a key factor in the 1972 elections, securing the no longer Marxian *Sozis* their highest tally ever, 45.8%.
As reported at its 1973 Hannover convention, biology accounted in large
measure for the loss of 350,000 among the 650,000 citizens registered as
members back in 1964. By 1973 only 300,000 of its one million dues-pay-
ing members could claim ten-year standing or more; of the 160,000 who
joined the party in 1972, two-thirds were under the age of 35. The newcomers redefined the social composition of the party: comprising over 55%
of the membership in 1962, workers accounted for only 28% of the party's
core in 1972.[106]

The share of Federal Republicans expecting to witness reunification had
fallen from 29% in July 1966 to 15% by the summer of 1972, while the
number of skeptics had increased from 47% to 69%. Three months into the
Grand Coalition, nearly two-thirds still supported FRG claims to be the sole
representative of all of Germany; 32% stressed the freely elected character of
the western state and 13% cited historical reasons ("belongs to us").[107] The
public meanwhile opened itself to de facto recognition; between 1955 and
1970, the number willing to deem "the so-called GDR" a sovereign state
rose from 9% to 47%.[108]

The Politics of Small Steps

Brandt's address to the Bundestag on January 14, 1970 was no garden-variety
state-of-the-union message; like John F. Kennedy's 1960 proclamation of the
New Frontier, it appealed especially to the idealism of politicized youth. Together with his inaugural address of October 28, 1969, Brandt's remarks signaled a change in foreign policy philosophy as well as a redirection of the domestic policy agenda. The thesis of Two States in One Nation was accepted as
the framework for external relations, while structural reform and citizen participation were declared the mainstays of policy from within.[109]

The January address outlined the five-fold aims of the new Social-Liberal
coalition. They included a focus on measures to secure a European peace order; promotion of the Germans' right to self-determination; the initiation of
new steps to prevent a further "growing apart" of the Germans divided; cul-

tivation of a "special relationship" between the two parts of Germany as non-foreign states; and a renunciation of a possible use of force against the GDR itself.[110] Breaking with the CDU tenet of *Gegeneinander* [working "against each other"], the new government would pursue an active course of *Nebeneinander* [living "next to each other"] in order to lay the foundations for an eventual *Miteinander* [cooperation "with one another"].

The optimism implicit in the 1969 *Machtwechsel* soon paid off by way of a proliferation of Eastern Treaties. Despite the initial consternation of its Allies, Bonn expeditiously negotiated and ratified the Moscow Treaty of August 12, 1970, incorporating a general renunciation of force. There followed in quick succession—though not without painstaking wrangling on both sides—the Warsaw Treaty of December 7, 1970 and the Quadripartite Agreement on Berlin, signed September 3, 1971. The crowning achievement of this era was the 1972 Basis of Relations Treaty [*Grundlagenvertrag*] between the two German states per se which led to the opening of permanent diplomatic missions in Bonn and East Berlin. This was supplemented by accords regarding questions of commercial transit, the regulation of postal and telephone services, health service provisions, and rules concerning the waiver of automobile fees and taxes for visitors. Separate agreements between the Berlin Senate and the GDR Government brought improvements in travel and visitation traffic, and established passage rights for territorial enclaves. By December 1973 Bonn had established full diplomatic relations with Czechoslovakia, Bulgaria and Hungary (renegade Romania having been recognized in 1967), and both German states had been accorded full membership in the United Nations. Seeking to avoid the perils imputed to "singularity," the Federal Republic became an active sponsor of the Conference on Security and Cooperation in Europe (CSCE), leading to the 1975 Helsinki Accords.

The positive gains of détente were by no means limited to the economic and domestic arenas. *Ostpolitik* brought a measure of global prestige for West German state, culminating in a Nobel Peace Prize for Brandt in 1971. In 1974 a member of the Chancellor's personal staff, Gunter Guillaume, was charged with espionage in the service of the GDR government. Though his personal popularity remained intact, Brandt submitted his resignation in May. His departure marked the end of Phase One of *Ostpolitik*, the aims of which had been to normalize relations with Eastern Europe and to establish "good neighborly relations" with the GDR. Phase Two, under Chancellor Helmut Schmidt, would look to the continuation, consolidation and broader cultivation of ties with the other German state, despite superpower pressures to the contrary.[111] The late 1970s brought the cross-fires of Afghanistan, the imposition of martial law in Poland, the mushrooming of human rights groups in Warsaw Pact states, and the hotly contested NATO plans for theater-nuclear modernization (TNF) to counter Soviet SS-20 de-

ployments. Instead of braking further steps towards inter-German reconciliation, these developments moved the leaders of both states to embrace an
older justification for intensifying their non-military contacts: they sought
to "limit the damage" based on a mutual belief that "war should never again
emanate from German soil."

On the surface, the politics of negotiation merely seemed to take advantage of a sudden "thaw" in East-West relations after a decade of Cold War
demarcation; but the search for mutually beneficial mechanisms undertaken
by Bonn's own shuttle-diplomats grew out of a much more complicated
balancing act. At issue were the newly emergent "sovereignty" needs of the
Germans, on the one hand, and the well-entrenched interests of the superpowers, on the other. The Brandt Government faced many critical challenges from within, not the least of which was a CDU/CSU effort to have
the *Grundlagenvertrag* declared unconstitutional in 1973. The politics of
many, many small steps, undertaken by the two states created new opportunities for cooperation between the Eastern and Western blocs. *Ostpolitik*
provided a complex, dynamic framework for superpower relations, even
amidst the ebbs and flows of the 1970s and 1980s. The next "great debate"
over the modernization of theater nuclear missiles in Western Europe would
testify to *Ostpolitik's* deep roots in the security consciousness of FRG citizens. The politics of détente moreover fostered a sense of political sovereignty among the West German citizenry directly at odds with the semi-sovereign character of the country's Alliance status. The effects of generational
change were nowhere more pronounced than in the desire to untangle the
FRG from the web of ongoing superpower tensions.

The questions used by this author to assess attitudinal changes towards
Germany's semi-sovereign status relied upon the intentionally provocative
language of the times (1985–86). My interview partners were asked, first,
whether or not they perceived themselves to be living in an "occupied state"
[*Besatzungsstaat*]; and, secondly, whether or not they would favor a withdrawal of NATO/U.S.-American troops from their home territory. They
were also urged to take a stand on various elements of NATO strategy.
Without exception, men of the Economic Miracle Generation answered
"no" to the first question, with many sharing Egon Bahr's belief that "the
FRG has more competencies than she utilizes." The reserved rights of the
Allies did not determine day-to-day consciousness, even if West Germans
had grown tired of an intermittent U.S. threat to withdraw troops, used as a
"pressure instrument" whenever NATO-internal disputes arose. Others, like
Gaus and Koppe, distinguished between a functional-military occupation
and the political-juridical powers of the FRG. No one supported an increase
in Bundeswehr capabilities in the event of a U.S. withdrawal under radically
altered international conditions (a situation which miraculously ensued less
than five years later); the West German military "had enough to do."

Women of the first generation were more cautious in voicing perceptions of their country's occupied status, converging around the assessment "normally not [but] tendentially, yes." The issue of troop withdrawal was viewed by all as a question of global conditions. Yet one self-professed Atlanticist, who found the label *Besatzungsstaat* "shameful," admitted that she "would not cry out loud if 50% [of the troops] were suddenly removed." The women, too, rejected any strengthening of the Bundeswehr.

The members of the Long March Generation, male as well as female, were visibly divided over their "occupied" status. Members of this group emphasized *de jure* aspects of the question and the extent to which the 1983 deployments had brought them to light. Views on NATO troop withdrawal were more polarized, despite an overwhelming rejection of additional powers for the West German military. As Green-parliamentarian Antje Vollmer observed, "the whole point of greater sovereignty is not to promote the remilitarization of the FRG." Prospective withdrawals were frequently linked not to improvements in superpower relations but to the need for greater European cooperation and the search for common disarmament interests. Not even the Leftists among them favored a sudden, unilateral reduction in NATO troop strength.

Group discussants representing the Turn-Around Generation agreed that they had never actually perceived their state as subject to Occupation, until they traveled abroad and observed that no one else faced the array of uniforms that they had internalized as "normal." Reactions among the Berliners were more negative regarding the troops, no doubt because of the latter's salient presence in that city. While some preferred more consultation and codetermination rights for the FRG within NATO, no one favored an increase in Bundeswehr capabilities.

Thus, the desire to restrict the role of indigenous military forces was shared by all three generations. Representative samples polled during the 1980s testify to an even broader generational consensus with respect to preferred defense modes. As Table 4.2 shows, an overwhelming majority favored a reduction of all forms of weaponry by 1983, not only for the FRG but for NATO as a whole—an orientation that transcended party lines. General opposition to an expansion of the Bundeswehr's role would come home to roost five years later, in conjunction with Allied participation in the Gulf War against Iraq.

Opinions concerning the utility of a peace treaty forty years after the war reflected a political divide between the oldest cohorts and their successors. Younger cohorts viewed the conclusion of a formal peace treaty as largely irrelevant, repeatedly invoking the phrase "that train has already left the station." There was more consensus with respect to the border question; with the exception of those linked to the Refugee Associations, discussion partners across all three generations accepted the territorial status quo. Most

182

TABLE 4.2 Preferred Tactics and Mechanisms for the Defense of the Federal Republic, 1983

Appropriate [geeignet] for ensuring peace, freedom and the security of the Federal Republic in the long term are . . . .

	TOTAL	CDU/CSU	SPD	FDP	Greens
Renunciation of the storage and use of chemical and bacteriological weapons in Europe	84%	81%	89%	89%	88%
Convocation in the near future of a European conference for disarmament and tension-reduction with American and Soviet participation	83%	80%	88%	79%	87%
A treaty between NATO and the Warsaw Pact based on a renunciation of force.	83%	81%	88%	86%	88%
A treaty renouncing the development of new weapons systems by the USA and the Soviet Union.	81%	78%	87%	80%	84%
Creation of a nuclear weapons-free zone in Europe on both sides of the border between East and West	60%	49%	67%	63%	84%
The West should take its own first steps toward disarmament in Europe, even if the Soviet Union and Warsaw Pact do not immediately follow suit	35%	23%	47%	21%	74%
Strengthening the armaments of the Bundeswehr within the framework of NATO	26%	40%	17%	26%	7%
Deployment of more and new nuclear weapons by the Americans in the Federal Republic and Western Europe.	14%	23%	7%	10%	4%
Creation of a space-based defense system (SDI) by the Americans.	16%	24%	12%	16%	1%

Source: Hg. Friedrich Ebert Stiftung, "Sicherheitspolitik, Bündnispolitik, Friedensbewegung. Eine Untersuchung zur aktuellen politishen Stimmungslage im Spätherbst 1983" (Munich: SINUS, October 1983), p. 38.

saw younger citizens as more willing to question NATO strategies pushed by the USA.

A deep-seated commitment to *Ostpolitik* was echoed in their approval of efforts by FRG and GDR leaders to "limit the damage" in relation to the Pershing II and Cruise Missile deployments. While von Bülow's proposal for "structurally non-offensive defense capabilities" initially provoked quite a stir among those intent on eschewing conflict within the Atlantic Alliance, its basic premises were inherent in the rhetorical appeals of both Kohl and Honecker.[112] The exhortation that "war should never again emanate from German soil" was often coupled with references to a community of responsibility [*Verantwortungsgemeinschaft*], coupled with a stress on the need for a coalition of reason [*Koalition der Vernunft*] between the FRG and the GDR. Parallel to my interview phase, the SPD had already began to promote a framework for a future Security Partnership, under the influence of Egon Bahr. Both the idea of common security (misinterpreted in U.S. circles) and that of a German confederation had also made their way into daily political discourse.

The frequency with which these constructs were employed by government officials bore little relation to the public's familiarity with their content, however. Though my own sample drew largely from circles actively interested in security issues, few discussants could specify differences in meaning beyond the level of "it would be nice, but . . . "; "it's useless . . . I'm against it"; most felt "they are all about the same." More discerning respondents ascribed both past and future dimensions to the community of responsibility, noting that the GDR would have difficulty accepting historical responsibility for German breaches of the peace (viz., Bender, Schmude, Menge, Rupprecht and Bruns). Persons greatly concerned about Germany's ongoing need to confront its past were most supportive of the term's "heuristic value," to quote Wensierski. Positive or negative reactions to a security partnership and common security followed partisan lines, although a majority deemed them largely interchangeable.[113] Interviewees left of center thought the terms called for a bridge between the two blocs, based on the nuclear-age reality that common survival could only be ensured to the degree that each side respected the security needs of the other. They found justification for this form of "partnership" in Article 5 of the *Grundlagenvertrag*; its *modus operandi* would parallel proposals of the Palme Commission (see Chapter 5). Those whose orientations lay right of center would only accept the idea of a "shared" security system among members of their own Alliance. A few sought to extend the idea of co-responsibility to cooperation regarding environmental issues.

Attitudes regarding the prospects for a German confederation are all the more interesting when pitted against post-1989 developments. The overwhelming majority characterized the very idea in 1985/86 as "irrelevant," "garbage," "improbable," "problematic," or "unrealistic." At best, it held a wistful "model" appeal for over-30 repondents with direct ties to Berlin or the GDR, somehow "tempted [by a confederation] as a loophole for those who can't conceive of unification" (Schneider). For several discussants born after 1960, the idea evoked "only goose bumps." Indeed, third-generation reactions to all of the terms cited above were more negative than those among the other two. In defense of its purveyors, however, one individual noted that "politics/policies can also be advanced on the basis of speech"; the framework of "change through rapprochement," Gunter Gaus stressed, generated tremendous, concrete political consequences.

Public opinion was not immune to the global disruptions of the 1980s, yet the general climate stabilized by 1987. Leaders of the two Germanys succeeded in "limiting the damage" of the INF deployments, and the superpowers themselves were moving towards an astounding disarmament agreement. Nearly three-fourths of the FRG citizens supported a withdrawal of superpower troops from both German states, rising to four-fifths among those under 30 years of age.[114]

The post-TNF deployment period found the German heads of state continuing their mutual homage to a coalition of reason. Chancellor Kohl reissued a summit invitation to GDR Premier Honecker, resulting in their historic meeting of September 7–11, 1987. The first "working visit" by an East German Premier on Western territory entailed twelve hours of face-to-face discussions, leading to three new treaties in the areas of science/technology, environmental cooperation, and nuclear radiation protection. Honecker's visit included a meeting with 300 representatives of West German trade and industry, a side-trip to the General Secretary's birthplace at Wiebelskirchen, as well as discussions with reigning Minister-Presidents of the Saarland (Oskar Lafontaine, SPD), Rheinland-Pfalz (Bernhard Vogel, CDU), and Bavaria (Franz-Josef Strauss, CSU).

The final communiqué assessing the inter-German summit was less than dramatic in its tone and its impact; indeed, the entire meeting was characterized by Elizabeth Pond as "breath-taking in its normality."[115] Following the excursion to his former hometown, Honecker asserted that it was "all too understandable that the borders are not what they should be" owing to fundamental differences between the two systems. He continued, rather dialectically:

> when we act in accordance with the provisions of the communiqué which we have negotiated in Bonn and [when on this basis we] achieve peaceful cooperation, then the day will also come when the border will no longer separate us but unite us, just as the border between the German Democratic Republic and the People's Republic of Poland unifies us.[116]

FRG officials deemed the visit "neither a conclusion nor a new beginning" but one representing a stabilization of existing relations. The meetings permitted "a comprehensive exchange of opinions over the further development of relations" conducted in an open atmosphere. They were expected to serve as a "stabilizing factor for constructive East-West relations" and as a "positive impulse for peaceful cooperation and dialogue in Europe" grounded in a special German responsibility. The two sides agreed to "respect the independence and sovereignty of the other in its internal and external affairs."[117] Both leaders placed great value on environmental preservation; they expressed satisfaction that the development of economic ties had been largely positive, and that difficult negotiations over war-time expropriation of artworks were nearing completion. The two heads of state embraced the Helsinki Final Act and the Stockholm Conference as important standard-setters for the resolution of security problems, while expressing "their frank opinions" regarding the realization "of all human rights." Both advocated a 50% reduction with respect to offensive weaponry, urged the elimination of chemical weapons, and called for verifiable non-proliferation of nuclear weapons. The GDR Premier invited Chancellor Kohl to visit the other Germany, the date of which would be established later.

Highlighting attititudinal differences between older and younger cohorts, reactions to the historic visit also reinforced public perceptions of major systemic differences between the two states. A January 1988 poll asking citizens to identify "the most important event of 1987" found them placing little emphasis on the Honecker visit (named by a mere 5%); those displaying the greatest interest in the summit fell between the ages of 50 and 64 (roughly 11%). The public accorded much more significance to the INF disarmament negotiations and the Reagan-Gorbachev summit meeting. Age differentials were clearly at work: while 46% of the total emphasized the superpower summit, only 29% of those younger than 19 did so; the importance of that event was noted by a near majority among those 30 and older, ranging from 47–53%. Some 26% of the respondents under 30 ascribed greater importance to the *Barschel Affair* (involving the bath-tub suicide of a CDU gubernatorial candidate from Schleswig-Holstein).[118]

Expectations as to the long-term consequences of the visit were quite subdued. According to FGW figures, 63.2% "welcomed the visit," an increase over the 55.5% who would have welcomed Honecker's trip at the time it was first scheduled in 1984; 9.1% opposed the visit altogether. Over 52% anticipated improved relations between the two states, a clear majority among all but those 60 and older, while 45% foresaw no change. The public was skeptical about the visit's ability to induce political reforms within the GDR, even if the SED regime did appear to benefit most from the meeting. Questioned as to what Honecker was able to achieve for the GDR through his visit, 49% of an Allensbach sample said "more money." Some 51% stressed the increased recognition for the GDR as a sovereign state; 53% thought the summit would enhance Honecker's image, while 33% saw it as a distraction from his troubles at home. More citizens expected the trip to

TABLE 4.3   Reactions to the Honecker Visit, September 1987

Response (in percent)	Total	Male	Female	Age Groups						
				18–24	25–29	30–39	40–49	50–59	60+
Welcome the visit	63.2	63.1	63.2	54.3	60.4	69.4	64.6	63.6	63.7
Oppose the visit	9.1	9.4	8.8	12.1	10.6	5.8	9.5	10.4	7.7
Indifferent	27.4	26.9	27.8	32.1	29.0	24.4	25.8	25.1	28.5
Expect improved relations	52.4	57.4	48.0	57.8	63.2	52.6	50.0	54.5	46.3
Expect worse relations	2.1	2.3	1.9	2.7	0.3	2.3	2.3	2.2	2.3
Expect no change	45.1	40.0	49.6	38.2	36.5	45.1	47.7	43.0	50.8
Peace will be more secure									
Yes	31.8	30.5	31.9	28.8	31.2	33.8	33.3	32.1	29.2
No	68.2	69.2	67.4	71.2	68.0	66.2	66.7	66.9	69.6
Liberalization will occur in the GDR									
Yes	47.8	49.3	46.5	45.9	48.2	54.9	50.4	42.9	45.9
No	51.3	50.0	52.4	54.1	51.0	44.0	49.6	54.3	53.4
Shoot-to-kill orders at the GDR border									
Will cease	14.0	11.7	15.9	15.4	9.7	13.4	15.8	12.4	14.7
Won't cease	84.6	87.4	82.2	84.6	87.7	85.5	84.2	84.1	83.7

n = 1,034, conducted August 21–28, 1987
Source: Forschungsgruppe Wahlen, representative sample for ZDF Politbarometer, August 1987, Questions #9, #10, #12.

serve the improvement of German-German relations (57%) than to enhance East-West rapprochement (48%).[119]

It is striking that more than one-fourth of the FGW respondents expressed indifference towards the one event which might have been construed either as the culmination of *Ostpolitik* or as the penultimate gesture of acceptance of Germany's permanent division![120] In the minds of average citizens, relations between the two states had already been "normalized" with the ratification of the 1972 Basis of Relations Treaty; thus the "historic" summit merited no more attention than a protocol visit by the head of any other sovereign state. The Federal Republicans' general willingness to accept the GDR as a "normal state" conditioned their readiness for a third, albeit short-lived phase of *Ostpolitik*.

The next stage in the unfolding of *Ostpolitik* would not be orchestrated by Brandt's successor, Helmut Schmidt, but by his newly appointed FDP-Foreign Minister, Hans-Dietrich Genscher. Described in some quarters as "the best Chancellor the CDU ever had," Schmidt adopted a hardline approach in matters of international economics. It was his hang-tough stance on questions of nuclear modernization, however, that fractured the SPD and compelled his departure from office in 1982.[121] Genscher stayed on, ensuring continuity in the wake of a sudden change in leadership [*die Wende*] under CDU Chancellor Helmut Kohl. More importantly, Genscher's personal brand of shuttle-diplomacy would set the parameters for the extraordinary Four-Power negotiations over German unification in 1990.

Ostpolitik, Phase III, emerged out of the new global interdependence triggered by the energy crises of the 1970s, on the one hand, and the "environmental turbulence" engendered by a serious deterioration of U.S.-Soviet relations during the 1980s, on the other. Side-lined by the election results of 1983, the SPD pursued a course of extra-parliamentary negotiations with the East German SED, resulting in "shadow treaties" over the future elimination of chemical weapons and the establishment of a nuclear-free zone. Its agreement-to-disagree on fundamental values, according to terms outlined in their 1987 *Common Paper*, did, in fact, create new opportunities for dissent among "those who thought differently" within the GDR—although the SPD came to view its participation in that process as an embarrassment rather than as a source of pride during the immediate post-Wall period. Had it resumed control of government prior to 1989, the SPD would have shifted "from *Deutschlandpolitik* to *DDR-politik*," starting with a de jure recognition of GDR citizenship.[122]

Instead it fell to a former "resettler" from Halle to stage-manage the dramatic transition from two-states-in-one-nation to one nation, albeit in two cultures. Foreign Minister Genscher did not fit the image of a deferential ally, nor was he very warmly received by successive U.S. Administrations prior to the outbreak of democratic revolutions in Eastern Europe. The flaws in

Genscher's thinking—as judged from "inside the Beltway"—were two-fold. First, his approach was "too European" for a United States intent on preserving its *primus inter pares* status within the Alliance. Secondly, it focused too heavily on the peace-keeping potential of non-military institutions at a time when the U.S. was losing faith in its ability to compete in the global economic arena.

Genscherism stressed the FRG's continuing adherence to NATO and a clear rejection of neutralism. At the same time it placed greater emphasis on nuclear and chemical arms reductions, to be complemented by a shift to structural non-offensive defense. It foresaw an increasing reliance on the CSCE process as a vehicle for confidence-building vis-à-vis Eastern Europe, as well as a new focus on building security partnerships. Last but not least, Genscher urged national policy-makers to recognize their special "German" responsibility for the establishment of a positive European peace order—a framework through which the FRG would eventually come to occupy but one room (albeit a large one with an impressive view) in the European common house. The Foreign Minister frequently summarized his philosophy with a 1953 citation from exiled-writer Thomas Mann: "We want not a German Europe but a European Germany," that is, a reconfiguration of alliance interests enabling the Federal Republic to seek "unity in national solidarity."[123]

Genscherism overlapped with new streams in SPD security thinking in all but one respect: when the winds of change began to sweep through Eastern Europe in 1989, the Foreign Minister of nearly two decades would not hesitate to push for direct unification. The SPD, which had in fact planted the seeds of *Annäherung*, would revisit the age-old crisis of "the Left versus the Nation"—and thus miss out on the historical opportunity it had helped to create. The Opposition's failure to embrace rapid unification allowed a long recalcitrant CDU/CSU government to reap the ultimate benefits of détente under the politics of the seven-league boots. In contrast to Kohl, however, unity-architect Genscher refused to challenge the permanence of the Oder-Neisse border, nor was he prepared to tolerate claims over the Eastern Territories stretching from Silesia to Königsberg.

The pace of formal unification was simply breathtaking. The opening of the Wall on November 9, 1989, was followed by the first free elections on East German soil on March 18, 1990. The new CDU Premier, Lothar de Maizière, set out immediately to negotiate the dissolution of his own state, the preliminary terms of which were specified in a State Treaty ratified by both parliaments on June 22, 1990. Hoping to stem the massive flow of GDR emigrants, Bonn opted for the pre-emptive creation of a German Economic, Monetary and Social Union on July 1, 1990. To everyone's amazement, the Kohl-Gorbachev meeting of July 15–16 in Stavropol secured the Soviet acceptance of unification *and* permitted Germany's ongoing membership in NATO. After four rounds of the "Two Plus Four" talks [two Germanys, four WW II victors], the Allied Powers terminated their own rights and restored full German sovereignty in a Treaty signed on September 12th.[124] The Treaty on German Unity was formally ratified by the legislatures of the two postwar states on September 20, 1990. The grand fireworks display and the hoisting of a single flag on October 3, 1990 proclaimed the demise of the GDR and the inception of a new all-German national holiday. In a dialectical, round-about, that is, *Wende* fashion, *Ostpolitik* had achieved its ultimate—though never consciously posited—aim.

Germans to the Front? Redefining National Security Roles

Might the cause of world peace be better served by a confinement of Germany's security rights and responsibilities to the European arena, or should the Federal Republic be pressured into assuming a more global role? Debates over national security policy since 1989 imply that a "special German path" is unlikely to garner public acceptance beyond marginal right-wing groups. One alternative might be to minimize its risk of entanglement in global confrontations through an intensification of Germany's regional security role (the "Europeanization of Europe" proposed by Bender over decade ago), through a renewed emphasis on the CSCE framework and the West European Union, for instance.[125] A third possibility would be to "go global," taking literally ex-President Bush's notion of partnership-in-leadership through an extension of Germany's opportunities for military intervention world-wide. These broad categories naturally allow for many variations in practice.

The 1991 Gulf War (see Chapter 5) precipitated a highly charged partisan debate over the limits of Articles 24 and 26 in the Basic Law. Dissolution of the Warsaw Pact Organization in 1991 blurred the already fuzzy lines between the so-called *Bündnisfall* [case of Alliance obligation] and *Verteidigungsfall* [state of defense].[126] While the two would have overlapped in the event of an aggressive onslaught from the East prior to 1989, the boundaries are not so clear in cases where a member-state itself engages in provocative behavior—as many interpreted the launching of U.S. missiles against Iraq from NATO bases in Turkey.

A further collective-security dilemma arises in conjunction with Article 25 of the United Nations Charter which requires sovereign members to "carry out" the resolutions of the Security Council. Prior to unification, German participation in UN military actions was restricted by special conditions set forth in Article 43. The FDP took its coalition partner to Court in 1991 to clarify the constitutionality of German engagement in NATO's Gulf operation "Deny Flight" (upheld by Karlsruhe). Social Democrats filed suit against the Chancellor in 1993 over a commitment of UN-supervised German NATO troops to Yugoslavia and Somalia.[127] On July 12, 1994, the High Court declared that FRG participation in collective military operations outside of NATO territory does not violate the Basic Law, provided such interventions are approved by a simple Bundestag majority. On June 26, 1995 the Bundestag voted to send 1,500 German soldiers, along with combat-ready *Tornado* fighter planes, to assist UN forces in Bosnia.

Having crossed a critical internal threshold with regard to armed engagement, Germany's ability to expand its security commitments world-wide still faces certain external limits. The 1990 Treaty on Final Settlement "circumscribes a good deal of the foreign policy agenda of a united Germany" and declares the Oder-Neisse border issue "permanently" resolved.[128] Denuclearization of the new states and, for that matter, of the old Länder (removal of Lance missiles) has already become a reality under terms set by the 1987 INF Treaty. Germany-united has reaffirmed its renunciation of NBC weapons and tightened existing export controls on dual-use technologies.[129] Despite these formal limits, the New Germany faces the ultimate "predicament of power"—it will be damned if it does and damned if it doesn't become actively engaged in the rehabilitation of Central Europe and the post-Soviet Republics.[130]

As underscored earlier, the collapse of the East German regime in 1989 occurred by accident, not by West German design. The Germans-divided were not the only ones taken by surprise, however; the United States was likewise confronted with a foreign policy vacuum vis-à-vis Eastern Europe's Velvet Revolutions. American policy towards the region had essentially been one of "non-relations" with the hard-liner states and minimal interaction with those who occasionally tested the limits of Soviet control (e.g., Poland and Romania). When the Wall finally crumbled, the United States found it necessary to defer to the one Alliance partner most ready and able to help put the Eastern economies back together again.

Germany not only manages the most powerful economy in the region; it also possesses the most consistent track record of relations with the Eastern nations, extending well beyond the usual exchange of diplomats, museum exhibits, and rhetorical commitment to the free-market system. The FRG's experience in granting credits to Hungary, Poland and the Czech Republic under *Ostpolitik* has positioned it to assume the role of trade-and-investment-partner extraordinaire. Physical proximity, a sense of historical responsibility and, until recently, its own constitution have moreover impelled Germany to take in largest number of refugees since the opening of the Iron Curtain.

Bonn's efforts to secure a "dignified withdrawal" of former Soviet forces by way of substantial assistance payments is only the tip of the (aid)iceberg; the fears of a *Stavrapallo* were highly overrated. Channeled through bilateral and multilateral institutions, other states' contributions to the USSR's successor-Republics between September 1990 and January 1992 seem stingy by comparison. During this period the FRG committed DM 73.6 billion in aid, only DM 14 billion of which was directly linked to troop withdrawal (this excludes funds for the relocation of ethnic-Germans). The combined payments of the remaining EU-members ran a not-so-close second, amounting to DM 24.6 billion; the United States was a distant third, extending DM 8.4 billion, with Japan as an "also-ran" at DM 4.1 billion.[131] The Federal Republic was quick to sign Treaties of Good Neighborliness and Cooperation with Poland, the now "divorced" Czech/Slovak Republics and Hungary. Central European exports to Germany increased by 14.3% in 1989–90, and FRG trade accounted for 30–35% of all commercial exchanges with these countries by 1995—a figure matching the Soviet share during the best years of the Council for Mutual Economic Assistance.[132]

The idea of an East-West security partnership lies at the heart of the Partnership for Peace strategy supported by CDU-Chancellor Kohl and adopted by NATO in January 1994. United Germany has fostered Association Agreements between the newly democratizing states and the European Union, promoted their inclusion in the North Atlantic Cooperation Council, and lobbied actively for NATO's November 1991 Declaration on Peace and Cooperation. The bottom line of German policy toward the region is that security must henceforth be defined in terms of economic stability and development.

These developments suggest a great deal of continuity between Germany's pre- and post-unity conception of its proper foreign policy role. The perceived effectiveness of the Eastern Treaties and the 1975 Helsinki Accords led average West Germans to internalize a two-pronged security strategy. Their preferred formula for peace, according equal weight to each element, reads: SECURITY = DEFENSE + DETENTE. Just as importantly, Bonn's commitment to advancing European peace and cooperation prior to 1989 helped to establish a new, positive source of national identity for millions of post-postwar Germans—not only in the West but also in the East. Through *Ostpolitik*, the Left-Right polarization of security themes assumed a new quality, linked to emerging technologies and reinforced by new generational cleavages. The rise of a critically self-informed opposition rooted in church and labor during the 1950s gave way to a core of academic "counter-experts" in the 1970s, who deliberately transcended the alleged knowledge-gap which had long impelled the public to defer to federal officials over all national security matters. Having internalized both the values of grassroots democracy and the spirit of détente, members of the post-postwar generations were less inclined to view domestic affairs and foreign policy as "worlds apart," one reserved for citizens, the other for governmental elites. Their efforts to institutionalize linkages between the two are the focus of our next chapter.

Notes

1. Gary L. Siegel and L. Anthony Loman, *Missouri at Ground Zero: What Nuclear War Would Do To One State* (St. Louis, MO: Institute of Applied Research, 1982).

2. My thanks to Herbert Wulf who shared this insight in 1984. Wulf later helped to compile a list of the top 100 arms-producing companies in Western Europe: the FRG firms of Daimler-Benz, MBB, AEG/Daimler Benz, Siemens and Krupp, were ranked fourth, tenth, thirteenth, twenty-fourth and twenty-sixth, respectively. A shift occurred with Daimler's purchase of Messerschmitt-Bölkow-Blohm's military-industrial complex in 1987. Ian Anthony, Agnès Courades Alleback and Herbert Wulf, *West European Arms Production—Structural Changes in the New Political Environment.* SIPRI Research Report (Stockholm, October 1990), pp. 64–65.

3. Germans began to sympathize with U.S. communities in 1990 as a result of NATO/WPO troop withdrawals. Unification forced major cuts in the FRG defense budget, including elimination of the *Supergun G 11* ("the most precise killing machine in the world"), which had brought one town DM 84.1 million from the defense coffers; termination of the project meant a loss of 2,000 jobs among the 14,000 residents of Oberndorf. It also affected two-thirds of the labor force in neighboring Black Forest towns, where the munitions firms of Mauser and Junghans are housed. See, "Rüstung: Weg ist weg," *Der Spiegel,* Nr. 3, January 21, 1991, pp. 68–72.

4. The December 8, 1987 Treaty on the Elimination of Intermediate-Range and Shorter-Range Missiles, and the *Protocol on Procedures Governing the Elimination of the Missile Systems Subject to the Treaty Between the United States of America and the Union of the Soviet Socialist Republics,* appear in *Arms Control and Disarmament Agreements* (Washington, D.C.: United States Arms Control and Disarmament Agency, 1990), p. 350ff.

5. Molly Moore, "Stealth Jet For Navy Is Cancelled;" and Stuart Auerbach, "A-12's End Points to Tough Future for Defense Firms," both in *The Washington Post,* January 9, 1991. The fact that less than 6% of all defense contracts were awarded on the basis of competitive bidding in the 1980s, coupled with the practice of guaranteed "cost-plus" profits, renders the military industrial complex a curious anomaly: its ultimate reason for being is to protect the free-market system. See Joshua Cohen and Joel Rogers, *On Democracy: Toward a Transformation of American Society* (New York: Penguin Books, 1984); also, Tim Weiner, *Blank Check. The Pentagon's Black Budget* (New York: Warner Books, 1990).

6. Daniel Frei, *Sicherheit. Grundfragen der Weltpolitik* (Stuttgart: Kohlhammer, 1977), p. 13ff.

7. Press and Information Office of the Federal Ministry of Defense, *The German Contribution to the Common Defense* (Bonn: Druck Carl Weyler KG, 1986), p. 8.

8. Ralf Dahrendorf, cited by Pross (Chapter 2), p. 123.

9. Heiner Kipphardt, cited by Iring Fetscher, "Die Suche nach der nationalen Identität," in Jürgen Habermas, Hg., *Stichworte zur 'Geistigen Situation der Zeit,'* Bd. 1. (Frankfurt/M: Suhrkamp, 1979), p. 119.

10. Horst Ehmke, "Was ist des Deutschen Vaterland?" in Habermas, ibid., p. 65.

11. *Decision of the Federal Constitutional Court re the treaty regarding the Basis of Relations between the Federal Republic of Germany and the German Democratic Republic of 31. July 1973,* 2 BVerfG 1/73, B/III/1 and 2.

12. Karl Kaiser, "Die Bundesregierung stellt keine Ansprüche . . . Konrad Adenauer und die Oder-Neisse-Linie," *Die Zeit,* September 29, 1989.

13. This was the official position of the GDR; see Jürgen Hofmann in *Ein neues Deutschland soll es sein. Zur Frage nach der Nation in der Geschichte der DDR und der Politik der SED* (Berlin: Dietz Verlag, 1989), p. 25.

14. Harro Honolka, *Schwarzrotgrün—Die Bundesrepublik auf der Suche nach ihrer Identität* (München: C. H. Beck, 1987), p. 48.

15. Martens was cited by Edward Cody, "Allies open talks on German Unity," in the *Washington Post*, December 5, 1989. Alfred Grosser had declared a decade earlier that "the Western allies [and everyone else in Europe, for that matter] only want reunification as long as it is impossible," cited by von Weizsäcker in *Die Deutsche Geschichte geht weiter*. The political groups who made the GDR's peaceful revolution possible in 1989 *opposed* unification, a fact quickly overlooked by CDU politicians preaching the gospel of self-determination for *all* Germans since 1949. See the reformers' November 1989 appeal, "For our country," reprinted in the *New York Times*, December 8, 1989.

16. The Ten-Point Program appeared in the *Frankfurter Rundschau* on November 29, 1989, p. 6; for a translation, see M. Donald Hancock and Helga A. Welsh, *German Unification. Process & Outcomes* (Boulder, CO: Westview Press, 1994), pp. 329–337.

17. "Schönhuber hat die Brücke gebaut," *Der Spiegel*, Nr. 22, May 29, 1989; "Die Leute haben uns satt," *Der Spiegel*, Nr. 26, June 26, 1989. For an analysis of the born-again Right, see Hans-Georg Betz, *The Politics of Resentment: Postmodern Politics in Germany* (New York: St. Martin's Press, 1990).

18. Rolf Zundel, *Die Erben des Liberalismus* (Freudenstadt: Eurobuch-Verlag, 1971), p. 54ff.

19. W. v. Bredow, op. cit.; Christian Graf von Krockow, "Auf der Suche nach der verlorenen Identität," *Revue d'Allemagne et des pays de langue allemande*, Vol. XVII, (Janvier 1985), pp. 62–70.

20. Horst Ehmke, Karlheinz Koppe, Herbert Wehner, Hg., *Zwanzig Jahre Ostpolitik—Bilanz und Perspektiven* (Bonn: Verlag Neue Gesellschaft, 1986); Wolfgang Brinkel and Jo Rodejohann, Hg., *Das SPD-SED Papier. Der Streit der Ideologien und die gemeinsame Sicherheit* (Freiburg: Dreisam Verlag, 1988); Ann L. Phillips, *Seeds of Change in the German Democratic Republic: The SED-SPD Dialogue* (Washington, D.C.: American Institute for Contemporary German Studies, 1989).

21. See Bernard Willms, *Die Deutsche Nation* (Köln-Lövenich: Edition Maschke "Hohenheim," 1982); Venohr, *Die deutsche Einheit kommt bestimmt* (Chapter 2), and *Ohne Deutschland geht es nicht*, (Chapter 2); Peter Brandt and Herbert Ammon, Hg., *Die Linke und die nationale Frage* (Reinbek: Rowohlt, 1981).

22. Peter Brandt, et al., *Paktfreiheit für beide deutsche Staaten oder Bis daß der Tod uns eint?* (Berlin: Arbeitsgruppe Berlin und Deutschlandpolitik der AL, 1982).

23. See the Green's "reader," *Kongress: Für ein anderes Europa*, Köln: 28–30 November 1986, Berufsbildungszentrum (Perlengraben-Südstadt); further, die Grünen (Baden-Württemberg), Reader: *Friedensvertrag, Blockfreiheit, Neutralität. Deutschlandpolitischer Kongress*, Karlsruhe, 9–11 März 1984.

24. A 1990 study predicted that the cost of restructuring East German industry would run over DM 918 billion; the social services bill exceeded DM 130 billion as of 1993. Finance Minister Theo Waigl (a CDU free-marketeer!) urged the OECD to pick up part of the cost, leading Maggie Thatcher to scold the Germans for trying to reduce their contribution to accelerated European integration. See "900 Milliarden—und es brummt," *Der Stern*, Nr. 7, 8. February 1990; "Milliarden auf Jahre hinaus," *Der Spiegel*, Nr. 7, February 12, 1990, p. 24ff; cf. "Einheit ohne Steuer-Opfer," *Der Spiegel*, Nr. 4, April 2, 1990.

25. See Article 12 (a) of the Surrender Terms, in *Documents on Germany, 1944–1961*, published by the U.S. Department of State, Washington, D.C.: GSPO.

26. Walter Goerlitz, cited by Catherine Kelleher in "Fundamentals of German Security: Creation of the Bundeswehr—Continuity and Change," in Stephen Szabo, ed., *The Bundeswehr and Western Security* (New York: St. Martin's Press, 1990), p. 16.

27. Anselm Doering-Manteuffel, *Die Bundesrepublik in der Ära Adenauer, Außenpolitik und innere Entwicklung 1949–1963* (Darmstadt: Wissenschaftliche Buchgesellschaft, 1983), p. 7.

28. Conditions were outlined in the *Genehmigungsschreiben der Militärgouverneure zum Grundgesetz vom 12. Mai 1949*.

29. Specific mechanisms included a *constructive* vote of non-confidence, a ban on any party inimical to the constitutional order, and the "five-percent clause" designed to inhibit extreme partisan fragmentation. Manteuffel refers to the "anti-totalitarian fixation of the Basic Law," op. cit., p. 23.

30. This was the charge leveled by GDR historians; see Jürgen Hofmann, op. cit., p. 57.

31. William D. Graf, *The German Left since 1945. Socialism and Social Democracy in the German Federal Republic* (Cambridge, UK: Oleander Press, 1976), p. 67ff.

32. Manteuffel, op. cit., p. 40.

33. Graf, op. cit., p. 68; Manteuffel, op. cit., p. 40. A third school, personified by Jakob Kaiser, looked to a middle course of "swing politics" first propounded by Gustav Heinemann in the 1920s; it envisioned Germany as a "bridge power" between the western-democracies and Eastern socialist systems. Fearing self-isolation, Kaiser stressed the fledgling state's need for a positive *modus vivendi* vis-à-vis the USSR, a proposal little attuned to the conditions of the times.

34. Ulrich Albrecht, *Die Wiederaufrüstung der Bundesrepublik. Analyse und Dokumentation* (Köln: Pahl-Rugenstein, 1980), pp. 9–10. As late as 1978, a school director barred an examination topic proposed by a would-be teacher at the Free University of Berlin. Pursuing a theme suggested by a Professor at the Otto Suhr Institute, the student analyzed the evolution of the SPD's stance on rearmament between 1945 and 1960; the term *Remilitarisierung*, used in the title, was rejected by the outside examiner as "too tendentious," implying a leftist-critical stance.

35. Arnulf Baring, "Gründungsstufen, Gründungsväter–Der lange Weg der Bundesrepublik zu sich selbst," p. 20, in Walter Scheel, Hg., *Nach dreißig Jahren. Die Bundesrepublik Deutschland–Vergangenheit, Gegenwart, Zukunft* (Stuttgart: Klett-Cotta, 1979).

36. Augstein, cited by Albrecht, op. cit., p. 14. Craig claims that the protracted debate over German rearmament commenced in 1950 as Americans began to counteract a "growing threat" from the East. Gordon A. Craig, "Germany and NATO: The Rearmament Debate, 1950–1958," in Klaus Knorr, ed., *NATO and American Security* (Princeton: Princeton University Press, 1959).

37. Karl Jaspers, *Wohin treibt die Bundesrepublik* (München: Piper, 1966 ed.), p. 91.

38. Figures are cited by Albrecht, op. cit., p. 35.

39. Specifically, the Western Agreement on the Exercise of Retained Rights in Germany [*Aufenthaltsvertrag*] of October 23, 1954, the Paris Protocols Amending the Brussels Treaty and Establishing the Western European Union of October 23, 1954, and the North Atlantic Treaty on the Accession of the Federal Republic of Germany, October 23, 1954 [*Deutschlandvertrag*].

40. Manteuffel, op. cit., p. 74.

41. See Albrecht, op. cit., pp. 11–12. The same evidence, U.S.-Document A 2170, from the Record of the 79th Congress in 1945 is cited by Lorenz Knorr, *Geschichte der Friedensbewegung in der Bundesrepublik* (Köln: Pahl-Rugenstein, 1983), p. 22.

42. The FRG declared "its strong determination to preserve the de-militarization of the Ruhr region and to prevent the reformation of any armed forces with all the means at her disposal," in Albrecht, op. cit., p. 25.

43. Hofmann, op. cit., p. 145.

44. The Chancellor's success in rendering the FRG a self-sufficient state lent him increasing room for maneuver within the international system, but its status as a "penetrated state" (J.N. Rosenau), via retained Allied rights, made a genuinely independent German foreign policy impossible. See Wolfgang Däubler, "Souveränes oder besetztes Land? Grundgesetz und westliches Bündnissystem," pp. 118–122, in Rolf Stolz, Hg., *Ein anderes Deutschland—Grün-alternative Bewegung und neue Antworten auf die Deutsche Frage* (Berlin: Edition Ahrens, 1985).

45. W. Stützle, *Kennedy und Adenauer*, as restated by Manteuffel, op. cit., p. 112. Only violations of these precepts were to be considered grounds for à defensive response: (1) the presence of Western powers in West Berlin had to be guaranteed; (2) unimpeded access to Berlin had to be secured; (3) warranties had to be upheld regarding the economic viability of West Berlin through its ties to the Federal Republic. Because the Wall did not directly violate these principles, the Western Allies were restricted to acts of verbal protest.

46. Graf, op. cit., p. 110.

47. Jürgen Harmut Faiss and Berthold Meyer, *Sicherheitspolitik und Öffentliche Meinung—Eine Umfragedokumentation* (Tübingen, 1981), p. 2, 4.

48. Early studies on defense/security orientations followed the interest of the parties commissioning them; not all samples met the requirements of "representativeness," and questions were posed with different degrees of "objectivity." By simply raising key defense issues, pollsters may have induced special attention or provided information among heretofore undecided respondents, presented with "either/or" choices which may have voided their more complicated feelings on the subject. See Berthold Meyer, *Der Bürger und seine Sicherheit. Zum Verhältnis von Sicherheitsstreben und Sicherheitspolitik* (Frankfurt/M: Campus Verlag, 1983), pp. 30–50.

49. Institut für Demoskopie Allensbach, *Jahrbuch 1947–1955*, p. 354 and *Jahrbuch 1957*, p. 361; also, Allensbacher Archiv, IFD Umfragen 1057, 1073, 1085, 1098, 2029, 3022 and 3097.

50. The original Emnid data are reported in Faiss and Meyer, p. 2; there is a one-percent discrepancy in the figure reported by Emnid and in the source-book, op. cit., p. 197. See *Emnid-Informationen*, Nr. 44, October 29, 1962, p. 2.

51. Ibid., p. 31, p. 37.

52. Wording may be a factor here; many no doubt presumed that unification would quickly lead to free and democratic elections in the East. See Faiss and Meyer, p. 37, pp. 45–46.

53. Emnid and Allensbach data are found in Faiss and Meyer, op. cit., p. 92 and p. 204, respectively.

54. Stephen F. Szabo, ed., *The Bundeswehr and Western Security* (New York: St. Martin's Press, 1990), pp. 2–3.

55. The number who saw it as a "welcome protection" rose from 14% to 23%, as an "unavoidable necessity" from 33% to 54% between 1952 and 1960. *Emnid-Informationen*, 12. Jg., Nr. 38, September 24, 1960, p. 4.

56. Catherine M. Kelleher, "Fundamentals of German Security: Creation of the Bundeswehr—Continuity and Change," in Szabo, ibid., p. 15ff.

57. Ibid., p. 25.

58. Donald Abenheim, "The Citizen in Uniform. Reform and its Critics in the Bundeswehr," in Szabo, op. cit., p. 32ff. The *citizen-soldier* is reminiscent of Cincinnatus, who takes up the burdens of state (in this case, national defense), and then returns to "normal life" in civil society.

59. The Basic Law was first amended on March 26, 1954 to allow the formation of a German army; the law regulating military service on a volunteer basis passed on July 23, 1955; a second change took effect on March 19, 1956, followed by the law introducing universal conscription on July 7, 1956.

60. IfD Allensbach, *Jahrbuch 1957*, op. cit., p. 310. By 1970, only 5% feared that Bundeswehr officers might support a new dictator, 4% saw the danger of such officers seizing control themselves; 64% affirmed their commitment to a defense of the constitution, as reported in *Emnid-Informationen*, 22. Jg., Nr. 8/9, August/September 1970.

61. Surveys cited by Faiss and Meyer found 46% opting for an "independent" army in 1952, op. cit., p. 214. For a broader range of attitudes towards rearmament, see the Allensbach *Jahrbuch der öffentlichen Meinung, 1947–1955*, op. cit., especially pp. 350–359, pp. 374–379.

62. IFD Allensbach, *Jahrbuch 1958–1964*, p. 470.

63. Faiss and Meyer cite a DIVO study which noted a rise in those favoring conscription from 39% to 45% between 1954 and 1957, op. cit., p. 222; according to Allensbach, 44% favored conscription, 37% supported a professional military in April 1956. Ibid., p. 223.

64. IfD, *Jahrbuch 1957*, op. cit., p. 308. Further, Faiss and Meyer, op. cit., Tables 13.1.1 and 13.2, p. 263.

65. Manteuffel, op. cit., p. 53.

66. The *Spiegel* offices were raided in Hamburg and Bonn, based on its publication of allegedly classified information over FRG participation in the NATO maneuver *Fallex 62*. The October 26/27th break-in and the arrest of its prominent editor, Augstein, was approved by then-Defense Minister Franz Josef Strauss; David Schoenbaum, *Ein Abgrund von Landesverrat. Die Affäre um den Spiegel* (Wien/München/Zürich, 1968).

67. Richard Löwenthal, "Stabilität ohne Sicherheit—Vom Selbstverständnis der Bundesrepublik Deutschland," *Der Monat*, (1978), p. 75.

68. Michael Schneider, *Kleine Geschichte der Gewerkschaften. Ihre Entwicklung in Deutschland von den Anfängen bis heute* (Berlin: Dietz Verlag, 1989).

69. Cited by Lorenz Knorr, op. cit., pp. 35–36.

70. Ibid., pp. 38–39.

71. Ibid., p. 41.

72. The peace activism of the Confessing Church was rooted in the *Stuttgarter Schuldbekenntnis* of 1945 which accepted official responsibility for the Church's failure as an institution to resist Hitler. The Essen Church Synod of 1950 unequivocally opposed rearmament.

73. Knorr, op. cit., p. 72. Golo Mann notes, "Anti-communism spared the Germans any reflections about their own past, as would have been their area of concern after 1945. Right away one had to suffer through justice and injustice; right away one found oneself positioned on the nearest front against an absolutely evil enemy." Cited by Albrecht, op. cit., p. 16.

74. By March 1952, organizers had polled 6,267,312 West Germans, of whom 5,917,683 rejected re-militarization. Hans Karl Rupp, *Außerparlamentarische Opposition in der Ära Adenauer* (Köln: Pahl-Rugenstein, 1980), pp. 52–53.

75. Alfred Grosser, *The Western Alliance. European-American Relations Since 1945* (New York: Continuum, 1980), p. 167.

76. Rupp, op. cit., p. 68; Lorenz, op. cit., p. 81.

77. Allensbach data, in Faiss and Meyer, op. cit., p. 217a.

78. Knorr, op. cit., p. 92.

79. Involved in the action were Max Born, Otto Hahn, Werner Heisenberg, Max von der Laue, Fritz Strassmann, and Carl-Friedrich von Weizsäcker, inter alia. Lorenz, p. 94.

80. Marian Dobrosielski, "Der Rapacki-Plan—noch immer aktuell," in Horst Ehmke, Karlheinz Koppe and Herbert Wehner, Hg., *Zwanzig Jahre Ostpolitik. Bilanz und Perspektiven* (Bonn: Verlag Neue Gesellschaft, 1986), pp. 103–108.

81. *Emnid-Informationen*, Nr. 16, April 19, 1958.

82. Rupp, op. cit., p. 167; Knorr, op. cit., p. 107.

83. The Hamburg demonstration of April 17, 1958 drew 150,000 protesters; 630,000 Dortmund residents turned out to protest on February 4, 1959. See, Rupp, p. 182ff; Knorr, p. 112.

84. Reprinted in Faiss and Meyer, op. cit., p. 239.

85. Joachim Radkau, *Aufstieg und Krise der deutschen Atomwirtschaft 1945–1975. Verdrängte Alternativen in der Kerntechnik und der Ursprung der nuklearen Kontroverse* (Hamburg: Rowohlt, 1983).

86. Schwarz prefers a metaphor of "layers." See Hans-Peter Schwarz, "Die außenpolitischen Grundlagen des westdeutschen Staates," in Richard Löwenthal and Hans-Peter Schwarz, Hg., *Die zweite Republik. 25 Jahre Bundesrepublik Deutschland—Eine Bilanz* (Stuttgart: Seewald Verlag, 1974), pp. 27–63.

87. Emil J. Kirchner, "The Federal Republic of Germany in the European Community," in Peter Merkl, ed., *The Federal Republic of Germany at Forty* (New York: New York University Press, 1989), p. 425. The SPD initially rejected European integration under the *4-K formula*, saying no to all "conservative, clerical, capitalist and cartellistic [and by inference, anti-democratic] efforts to create a Europe." It also opposed the Schuman Plan and the EDC treaty, until the Messina Conference brought a shift in SPD policy, allowing for a common position between the ruling and opposition parties after 1955. Walter Lipgens, "Europäische Integration," in *Die zweite Republik*, op. cit., p. 532ff.

88. *Emnid-Informationen*, 18. Jg., Nr. 29, July 18, 1966, p. 2.

89. Faiss and Meyer, Table 12.1.1, p. 245. *Emnid-Informationen*, 32. Jg., Nr. 7/8, 1980. In 1970 69% supported the EC's aim of a unified, *political* community, according to *Allensbacher Berichte* Nr. 4, January/February 1970. New financial burdens brought on by EC expansion produced a sense that the FRG had become a net contributor rather than a net beneficiary of the Community, a condition that further integrative steps intensified.

90. Kirchner, op. cit., p. 426.

91. *Emnid-Informationen*, 11. Jg., Nr. 8, February 21, 1959; ibid., 10. Jg., Nr. 30, July 26, 1958.

92. Ibid., 12. Jg., Nr. 17, April 30, 1960; ibid., Nr. 18, May 7, 1960.

93. Eberhard Schulz, *Die deutsche Nation in Europa. Internationale und historische Dimensionen* (Bonn: Europa Union Verlag, 1982), p. 159.

94. *Allensbacher-Berichte*, Nr. 9, 1965, p. 5.

95. Cited by Helga Haftendorn, in "Wurzeln der Ost- und Entspannungspolitik der Sozial-liberalen Koalition," in Ehmke et al., *Zwanzig Jahre Ostpolitik*, op. cit., p. 19.

96. Arnulf Baring, *Machtwechsel: Die Ära Brandt-Scheel* (München: Deutscher Taschenbuch Verlag, 1984 ed.), p. 71. Non-violent Easter March demonstrations had already increased in frequency as well as in size between 1963 and 1967; the number of participants rose from 1,000 in 1960 to 50,000 in 1963 to 150,000 by 1967; the number of events rose from 130 to 800 per year, according to Karl A. Otto, *Vom Ostermarsch zur APO. Geschichte der außerparlamentarischen Opposition in der Bundesrepublik 1960–1970* (Frankfurt/M: Campus, 1982), p. 147.

97. On the *APO*-era, see Gerhard Bauss, *Die Studentenbewegung der sechziger Jahre in der Bundesrepublik und Westberlin* (Köln: Pahl-Rugenstein, 1977); Tilman Fichter and Siegward Lönnendonker, *Kleine Geschichte des SDS. Der Sozialistische Studentenbund von 1946 bis zur Selbstauflösung* (Berlin: Rotbuch Verlag, 1977); Peter Mosler, *Was wir wollten, was wir wurden. Studentenrevolte—zehn Jahre danach* (Reinbek: Rowohlt, 1977).

98. Baring, op. cit., p. 97.

99. NATO-Informationsdienst, Hg., *Das atlantische Bündnis. Tatsachen und Dokumente*, 6th ed. (Brussels: 1982), pp. 325–327.

100. *Emnid-Informationen*, 19. Jg., Nr. 1, January 31, 1967.

101. Joyce Marie Mushaben, *The State versus the University: Juridicalization and the Politics of Higher Education at the Free University of Berlin, 1969–1979*, Dissertation (Indiana University: Bloomington, 1981), pp. 215–242.

102. Bauss, op. cit., especially pp. 134–166.

103. *Erklärung der Drei Mächte vom 27. Mai 1968 zur Ablösung der alliierten Vorbehaltsrechte gemäß Artikel 5 Abs. 2 des Deutschlandvertrages*. Further, Rolf Stolz, "Souveränität—Truppenabzug—Abkopplung," in *Ein anderes Deutschland soll es sein. Grün-alternative Bewegung und neue Antworten auf die Deutsche Frage* (Berlin: Edition Ahrens, 1985), p. 103 ff.

104. Joyce Marie Mushaben, "The Changing Structure and Function of Party: The Case of the West German Left," *Polity*, Vol. XVIII, No. 3, Spring 1986, pp. 432–456.

105. In a February 1966 letter to the SPD, Ulbricht admitted "that the SED can not resolve the German question on its own" but insisted that "the two major parties of Germany [SED + SPD] could together bring about the decisive contribution to the solution of the German question." Brandt and Ammon, op. cit., pp. 264–5.

106. Reported by Baring, op. cit., pp. 91–92.

107. Data compiled by Faiss and Meyer, op. cit., Table 5.1.1.7 (Allensbach data), p. 112, and Table 5.4.2.1, p. 137.

108. Allensbach data stem from the yearbooks 1957, 1958–64, and 1968–73, cited in Faiss and Meyer, op. cit., pp. 150–151.

109. On domestic reforms that never came to pass, see Joyce Marie Mushaben, "Planning as a Vocation: The Changing Role of the West German Bureaucrat," Master's Thesis (Bloomington: Indiana University, 1977).

110. Bundesminister für innerdeutsche Beziehungen, Hg., *Materialien zum Bericht zur Lage der Nation 1974* (Bonn/Berlin: Elsnerdruck, 1974), p. 4 ff.

111. Ann L. Phillips, "The West German Social Democrats' Second Phase of Ostpolitik in Historical Perspective," in Peter Merkl, ed., *The Federal Republic of Germany at Forty* (New York: New York University Press, 1989), pp. 408–424.

112. Andreas von Bülow, *Das Bülow Papier. Strategie vertrauensschaffender Sicherheits-Strukturen in Europa, Wege zur Sicherheits-Partnerschaft* (Frankfurt/M: Eichborn Verlag, 1985).

113. Egon Bahr and Dieter S. Lutz, Hg., *Gemeinsame Sicherheit. Idee und Konzept,* Bd. I: Zu den Ausgangsüberlegungen, Grundlagen und Strukturmerkmalen Gemeinsamer Sicherheit; and *Gemeinsame Sicherheit. Dimensionen und Disziplinen,* Bd. II: Zu rechtlichen, ökonomischen, psychologischen und militärischen Aspekten Gemeinsamer Sicherheit (Baden-Baden: Nomos Verlag, 1986, 1987). For more radical "restructuring" models, see Studiengruppe Alternative Sicherheitspolitik, Hg., *Strukturwandel der Verteidigung. Entwürfe für eine konsequente Defensive* (Opladen: Westdeutscher Verlag, 1984); Peter Barth, Alfred Mechtersheimer and Ines Reich-Hilweg, *Europa—Atomwaffenfrei!,* Forschungsinstitut für Friedenspolitik e.V, Starnberg (Munich: ibf Verlag, 1983); J. Löser and U. Schilling, *Neutralität für Mitteleuropa. Das Ende der Blöcke* (Munich: C. Bertelsmann, 1984). Also, Oskar Lafontaine, *Angst vor den Freunden. Die Atomwaffen-Strategie der Supermächte zerstört die Bündnisse* (Hamburg: Rowohlt, 1983).

114. Given a hypothetical Soviet offer of unification, tied to neutralization, 72.6 % of a May 1987 sample opted for neutrality, 13.9 for troop withdrawal only. Neutrality support was stronger among SPD and Green sympathizers (80–85%) than among CDU/FDP voters (65%); persons aged 25–39 evinced a stronger preference for troop withdrawal. FGW, ibid., Question #17.

115. Elizabeth Pond, "Most Germans Applaud Honecker Visit," *Christian Science Monitor,* September 11, 1987, p. 7.

116. Bundesministerium für innerdeutsche Beziehungen, Hg., *Der Besuch von Generalsekretär Honecker in der Bundesrepublik Deutschland,* Bonn: 1988, p. 7.

117. Ibid., pp. 37–42.

118. *Emnid-Informationen,* 40. Jg., Nr. 1/1988, Table 5.

119. Gerhard Herdegen, "Perspektiven und Begrenzungen. Eine Bestandsaufnahme der öffentlichen Meinung zur deutschen Frage," *Deutschland Archiv,* 21. Jg., April 1988, pp. 391–403.

120. FGW, *ZDF-Politbarometer,* August 1987, Question #9. The ultimate gesture would have been for the FRG to accord de jure recognition to the East German state.

121. On Schmidt's role in the Double Decision, see Hans Günter Brauch, *Die Raketen kommen! Vom NATO-Doppelbeschluß bis zur Stationierung* (Köln: Bund Verlag, 1983); also *Hart am Wind. Helmut Schmidts politische Laufbahn* (Hamburg: Albrecht Knaus Verlag, 1978).

122. The justifications for such a move were spelled out by Wilhelm Bruns, *Von der Deutschland-Politik zur DDR-Politik?* (Opladen: Leske + Budrich, 1989).

123. Hans Dietrich Genscher, "German Unity within the European Framework," speech at the Tutzing Protestant Academy, January 31, 1990, provided by the German Information Center, *Statements and Speeches*, Vol. XIII, No. 2, February 6, 1990. And, Robert Leicht, "Vom Berufspolitiker zum Politiker aus Berufung," *Die Zeit*, Nr. 20, May 12, 1989.

124. See M. Donald Hancock and Helga A. Welsh, eds., *German Unification. Process and Outcomes* (Boulder, CO: Westview Press, 1994). For views on the regional impact of unification, see Paul B. Stares, ed., *The New Germany and the New Europe* (Washington, D.C.: Brookings Institution, 1992).

125. Peter Bender, *Das Ende des ideologischen Zeitalters. Die Europäisierung Europas* (Siedler: VVA, 1981).

126. Prior to 1990, establishing the existence of a "state of defense" on FRG territory required the backing of two-thirds of the Bundestag (Article 115a GG). Previous BVerfG verdicts held that parliamentary "co-determination rights" did not apply to chemical weapons or nuclear armament, already regulated by the NATO Treaty. See the interview with Albrecht Randelshofer, "Verteidigt uns mal schön," *Der Spiegel*, Nr. 8, February 18, 1991, pp. 41–47.

127. Genscher insisted that the Gulf deployment was not a NATO deployment in "'Ich habe Kurs gehalten.' Außenminister Hans-Dietrich Genscher über die Deutschen und den Krieg am Golf," *Der Spiegel*, Nr. 6, February 4, 1991, pp. 22–25. 139. Unwilling to bow to U.S. pressure shortly before his death, Brandt asked: "Where, after all, is it being decided how the burden will be distributed and how whatever we contribute will be used? . . . The NATO Treaty foresees that every state determines for itself, what consequences it draws from the Iraqi attack." See "Warum sollen wir nicht dabeisein?" *Der Spiegel*, Nr. 7, February 11, 1991, pp. 27–30. For far-left positions, see "Bundeswehr—Tolerant, charakterfest," *Der Spiegel*, Nr. 23, June 3, 1991, pp. 20–23.

128. Karl Kaiser, "Germany in Central and Eastern Europe," in Dick Clark, ed., *United States Relations with Central and Eastern Europe* (Queenstown, MD: Aspen Institute, 1992), p. 27.

129. Regarding lax enforcement of technology-export laws, see Müller, op. cit, p. 142–146; and Wolfgang Hoffmann, "Deutschland an vorderster Front," *Die Zeit*, Nr. 11, March 19, 1993.

130. "The Predicament of Power" was the title of a special edition of *German Politics and Society*, Issue 26 (Summer 1992).

131. Kaiser, op. cit., p. 32.

132. Andres Inotai, "Economic Implications of German Unification for Central and Eastern Europe," in Stares, op. cit., pp. 279–304.

5

Successor Generations and Security Doctrine: "Deterrence, Yes, But Not in My Backyard"

Das grosse Cathargo führte drei Kriege.
Es war noch mächtig nach dem ersten,
noch bewohnbar nach dem zweiten.
Es war nicht mehr auffindbar nach dem dritten.
—Berthold Brecht, *Cathargo*

The Western security dilemma of the 1980s was in many respects an American dilemma. Initial U.S. support for moves towards the postwar creation of a United States of Europe had been grounded in two contradictory beliefs: the first posited that a Germany thoroughly integrated into the Western community would become a nation democratized and demilitarized; the second was that a recovered Europe would quickly assume responsibility for its own defense *and* offer a growing market for the disposition of American exports. What the United States acquired instead was a Europe that remained militarily dependent at the same time it managed to become the USA's most formidable competitor in the global economic arena. Another surprise, after three decades of outspoken appreciation and emulation, was that the successor generations would become increasingly resentful of a creeping Americanization of their economy and culture, no longer viewed as conducive to "German" national interests. Their objections to military developments inside and outside NATO's official sphere of operations would eventually lead them to challenge the very foundations of the Western security paradigm.

It took the NATO Double Decision of December 12, 1979 to break a twenty-year taboo on public debate over the meaning of mutually assured destruction and flexible response. The push for détente from below was nonetheless rooted in the demographic changes and democratic processes that had already begun to transform West German political culture by the early 1960s. New channels of mass communication contributed to higher levels of information, leading more citizens to take a stand on foreign policy and defense issues. The stronger their reactions to specific Cold War developments, the more average citizens would seek to influence security policy through new forms of do-it-yourself mobilization.

The previous chapter traced the evolution of German defense policy through the FRG's formative years, highlighting the extent to which both the leadership and the public had begun to embrace a new concept of security after the 1970s. In the process, Federal Republicans discovered another source of positive identification with their new state, rooted in a commitment to East-West rapprochement. This new dimension of identity would assume even greater importance among younger citizens during the the 1980s, as post-materialist values began to displace an ersatz-identity rooted in the reconstruction "miracle."

This chapter explores moves by successor generations to establish a more direct link between their domestic identity as Germans, that is, as constitutional-patriots living under a Western-style democracy, and the identity attributed to Germany beyond its own borders. Their efforts begin with a successful campaign to break the "taboo" on public debate over defense strategy and nuclear deployment, limits imposed by the Victorious Powers but instrumentalized by FRG leaders to subvert challenges to existing policies. The activists of the 1970s and 1980s not only lobbied to secure greater foreign policy autonomy for their own government as a member of NATO; they also struggled to apply grassroots-democratic principles to a wide range of security concerns traditionally reserved for political elites. Their new emphasis on unconventional forms of participation, developed in conjunction with a plethora of new social movements at home, would lead to a revaluation of violent "means" used to secure peaceful "ends" at the level of international relations. The organizational and strategic links cultivated between and among those movements affords several important insights into the processes of generational "self-socialization" and "self-definition."

The chapter begins with an overview of "peace-protest cycles" since the 1970s, coupled with an analysis of changing attitudes towards nuclear arms sparked by the NATO Double-Track Decision. Next it addresses the relationship between political activism among younger cohorts and alleged anti-Americanism during the 1980s; this is followed by a profile of the peace movement itself, including an assessment of its "wins and losses" in the wake of the Pershing II deployments. The argument here is that the overall effectiveness of the peace movement left the Kohl Government little choice but to become an ardent supporter of the INF Treaty and to push more recalcitrant Alliance partners to accept Gorbachev's "New Thinking." I contend further that a resegmentation of the peace movement after 1985 cannot be equated with an abandonment of an anti-militarist, anti-nuclear consciousness among the public at large.

To substantiate this point I offer a preliminary analysis of the most recent cycle of peace mobilization, linked to the Gulf War of 1991. My aim here is to show that the use of military force against Iraq has led to a new division among peace movement activists tied to a core component of postwar German identity–namely, the reluctance of Long March cohorts to assume the mantle of national responsibility for "coming to terms with the past." The final section considers the broader impact of unification on the national qua security consciousness of Federal Republicans, as reflected in public reactions to war in the former Yugoslav Republic.

"Time-Bomb NATO" and the Rise of Nuclear Pacifism, 1979–1985

Increasing political interest and improved citizen access to foreign-policy information should be seen as positive developments in any democratic society. Still, the technologically complex nature of "the data," added to every state's desire for secrecy in matters of national security, usually renders the public dependent on "expert interpretation." Government supporters naturally rely on assessments which legitimize the policies leaders have already chosen to implement relative to national defense. Those opposed to military involvement may sooner feel "that defense experts look to the 'voice of the people' not to determine what they really want but in order to establish in what direction 'public opinion' will have to be processed and steered, so that voters will continue to accept governmental policy."[1]

While peace and disarmament are easily counted among a country's "most pressing problems" in times of international crisis, they tend to be latent concerns during periods of stability. In 1977 (détente era), only 9% of the FRG's residents claimed to know the location of the nearest air-raid shelter; though 91% had no idea where to look, 53% maintained that government should have been "doing more" for civil-defense.[2] By 1983 (heightened superpower tensions), an incredible array of doctors, nurses, pastors, laiety, athletes, feminists, environmentalists, lawyers, and grandmothers would not only come to know where the missiles themselves stood; they would also prove capable of debating the weaknesses of Flexible Response, Forward-Defense, Air-Land-Battle and Strategic-Triad doctrines with the sophistication of many a defense planner.

The proposal to deploy 108 Pershing II and 464 ground-launch Cruise Missiles (GLCMs) initiated a sea-change in German perceptions of key national security issues in two important respects. Constituting the third cycle of peace protest in the FRG, the anti-Pershing mobilizations of the 1980s attained a "penetration of the personal" not witnessed during the first two rounds.[3] Grassroots-networks sharing information over the location of deployments past and pending turned latent fears into manifest anxieties among millions of citizens. The public came to view NATO's doctrinal shift from Mutually Assured Destruction to Nuclear Utilization Theory (in other words, from MAD to NUT) as an increasingly insane approach to conflicts between the superpowers. Secondly, debate over the Double-Track Decision not only induced changes in the security thinking of "average" citizens; it also impelled a change of heart among defense experts across party lines, leading them to counter U.S. arguments of insufficient "burden-sharing" with a new emphasis on German "risk-bearing."

The first signs of nuclear-deployment discomfiture among the European public surfaced in the late 1970s, when the U.S. Congress refused to ratify the second Strategic Arms Limitation Treaty (SALT II). Then Commander-in-Chief Jimmy Carter announced a shift in U.S. strategy from counter-value to counter-force under Presidential Directive 59; by promising to attack military installations rather than civilian centers, PD 59 rendered the prospect of nuclear war a little less heinous and therefore a little more conceivable. Carter's further decision to pursue deployment of the "neutron bomb" raised the anxiety-level another notch across the Atlantic: the alleged advantage of the Enhanced Radiation Warhead (ERW) lay in its ability to terminate enemy lives without destroying physical facilities and targeted urban areas. The potential for trans-Atlantic conflict was not diminished when Carter reversed his neutron-bomb decision without Allied consultation in 1978, to the particular chagrin of Chancellor Helmut Schmidt who had already lobbied for a NATO response to the Soviet SS-20 build-up. In March 1981, 62% of an Emnid sample claimed familiarity with the U.S. neutron-bomb proposal, with 57% opposing its deployment in the Federal Republic. By August, 83% maintained that the ERW question needed to be jointly resolved by all NATO members; only 15% thought that the U.S. should exercise a right to decide.[4]

NATO's Nuclear Planning Group had officially outlined its plan for theater-nuclear modernization at a Brussels meeting of the North Atlantic Council in December 1979. There was a striking consistency between the Double-Track Decision of 1979 and the Harmel Report of 1967. Both documents affirmed a commitment to the European security based on a strategy of nuclear deterrence while professing the ultimate importance of steps aiming to ease tensions and promote arms control. The United States continued to focus on the military "balance of terror" vis-à-vis the Soviet Union. A decade of détente, along with dramatic changes in the domestic political landscape, had conditioned West Germans to assign highest priority to the tension-reduction cum arms-control track, however. A clash between American and German interests over the TNF issue was more or less inevitable.

By August 1981, 89% of the men and 76% of the women polled had already heard about the decision to deploy new medium-range nuclear weapons on West German soil (99% among the higher educated). While 34% felt the move would enhance FRG security, 26% saw it posing a greater danger, a figure rising to 49% among those under 19. Some 32% maintained that a recently introduced peace slogan, *Frieden schaffen ohne Waffen* [Create Peace Without Weapons] was "realistic and implementable"; 66% disagreed.[5] By autumn the topic had become so "hot" that the Emnid Institute undertook a detailed study of attitudes towards armaments and pacifism among 2,148 voting-age citizens.

The Bielefeld team uncovered very limited protest potential among its initial sample, despite broad familiarity with the NATO resolution. As of late September/early October 1981, 53% said they would not partake in actions for or against the missiles, and 16% would have urged friends and colleagues *not* to participate in protests. On the other side, 23% were willing to sign petitions, 6% claimed they would attend demonstrations, and 4% considered joining a "Citizen Initiative" to oppose the new deployments; respondents under 25 were those most open to active protest.[6] The public would soon change its mind about the need for direct involvement in the missile debate.

The June 1981 Congress of the Evangelical-Lutheran Church in Hamburg marked the onset of a politically hot summer, leading to the rebirth of the peace movement (PM). The synod's formal theme *Fear Not* attracted thousands of unexpected youth participants under the counter-slogan of "Fear Indeed—Atomic Death Threatens Us All," in view of the spiraling arms race.[7] Militant environmentalists engaged in protracted site-occupations against proposed nuclear-energy plants in Brokdorf and Gorleben, while even more radical elements sought to halt construction of the *Startbahn West* runway at the Frankfurt airport (which they claimed was needed for U.S. deployments to the Middle East).[8] These protests overlapped with a new wave of terrorist assaults against NATO facilities in Heidelberg and Ramstein initiated by the Red Army Faction.[9] A number of (unrelated) forceful house evictions directed against the "squatter's scene" through the summer led to the death of 18-year-old Klaus Jürgen Rattay in Berlin-Kreuzberg. This incident fostered the spread of a highly volatile Punk qua anarchist youth movement, later to prove the bane of the peace movement's existence.[10] The "Autonomous Ones" would test the tolerance of all anti-nuclear organizations committed to non-violent means for the attainment of peaceful ends.

Re-initiation of the peace campaign mirrored the turbulence of the times. In mid-September 1981, some 50,000 people gathered in Berlin to protest a visit by U.S. Secretary of State Alexander Haig, the largest demonstration witnessed in the divided city in more than a decade. Most participants fell between 15 and 30 years of age; they quickly encountered 7,000 police charged with securing the Secretary's route. Citing Voltaire, Haig disagreed with protesters' demands but claimed he would "defend to the death" their right to articulate them. The demonstrators' ranks included 300 masked youth chanting "Germany must die so that we can live"; 105 protestors were arrested, and 151 police were injured amidst the flying stones, shots of tear gas, the burning autos and garbage containers.[11]

The tenor of the movement was rapidly transformed under the adroit leadership of several protest "veterans" who later served as core members of an ad hoc national Coordinating Committee. Attendance at the first anti-Pershing demonstration in Bonn on October 10, 1981 surpassed even the most optimistic projections of its organizers, an estimated 300,000 protesters. Representatives from 600+ West German Initiatives were joined by a variety of anti-neutron bomb groups under the direction of the Dutch Interchurch Peace Council (IKV). The IKV had commenced its staging of an annual Peace Week in 1967 under the motto, "Let us rid the world of nuclear arms, beginning with the Netherlands." The movement also took significant cues from the German Evangelical Church Synod that had attracted so many young participants in June.

The next round in late October was more subdued. A Peace Congress held at the Free University of Berlin drew 3,000–4,000 participants, many of whom booed invited SPD-discussants Hans-Jochen Vogel and (former New Leftist) Karsten Voigt off the stage. Jo Leinen, an executive of the Federal Association of Citizen Initiatives for Environmental Protection [BBU], summarized the mood of the gathering with the words, "Unrest [over the nukes] must overtake and reign this country."[12] The framework for future protests would focus on the three G's: the movement would be *gewaltfrei, gesamteuropäisch,* and *gesamtdeutsch* [non-violent, all-European, and inter-German].

The sudden upsurge in protest during the fall of 1981 found the major political parties deeply divided as to an appropriate response. While CDU Mayor Richard von Weizsäcker attempted to "dialogue" with autonomous protesters in Berlin, his counterparts allowed the use of "CS" and "CN" nerve-gas against crowds near Bielefeld and Frankfurt.[13] The SPD engaged in another vehement internal debate over whether "to integrate, or not to integrate" youth protesters in general and the nascent peace movement in particular.[14] As a newly constituted party (December 1980), the Greens were not yet sufficiently equipped to capture the youth vote as a way of compensating for the "failure of integration" among the system parties.

Anti-nuclear momentum increased dramatically over the space of a few weeks, fueled by a Reagan comment professing the conceivable "winnability" of a limited nuclear war.[15] From October through December, anti-nuclear demonstrators took to the streets in Berlin, Brussels, Paris, Amsterdam, London, Stockholm, Athens, Rome, Madrid, Helsinki, Oslo, Copenhagen and even Bucharest, attracting an estimated two to three million participants.[16] By the time Reagan appeared before the National Press Club in Washington, D.C., on November 18th, the Administration had decided to shift its focus, rendering the Zero Option the central focus of the President's speech.[17] His proposal envisioned a *moratorium* on all Pershing II and

Cruise Missile deployments to begin in 1983, in exchange for a Soviet withdrawal of all SS-20, SS-4 and SS-5 missiles installed west of the Urals since 1976. The pronouncement was judged so important that it was broadcast live via satellite transmission to Europe at American expense.[18] Formal talks focusing on a reduction of theater nuclear forces (TNF) commenced in November 1981, the Reagan Administration having been "pushed to the bargaining table by political forces" ranging from the U.S. Nuclear-Freeze movement, to European peace mobilizations, to the importunings of leaders from other NATO states.[19]

Most West Germans continued to express confidence in the U.S. at this point, as underscored by the 1981 Emnid study, in which two-thirds had voiced their support for NATO membership. Their acceptance of the collective security system was not always matched by personal commitment to the common defense, however: only 23% of the males indicated a willingness to volunteer for military duty, though 60% would have allowed themselves to be drafted (figures were 22% and 61% for women, despite their non-draftable status). Nearly 30% of the men younger than 30 would have refused conscription or opted for alternative service.[20]

The reluctance to serve the difficult Fatherland by donning uniform and weapon did not signify that a majority had converted to pacifism at the outset of the TNF debate. Less than 8% labeled themselves pacifists in 1981 (8–13% among respondents of draftable age), but more than 40% "tolerated" the right of others to assume this posture. A liberalized conscription law had already contributed to a dramatic increase in the number of men performing alternative service as of 1977. The number of applications for conscientious-objector status rose from 3,000 annually during the 1960s, to nearly 57,000 by the end of 1981. The trend continued despite the fact that civilian-service was extended from sixteen to twenty-four months shortly thereafter.[21]

Both the reluctance to volunteer and the willingness to respect the pacifist position were linked to negative perceptions regarding one's prospects for surviving a nuclear war. Although most citizens were unaware of the ranges of weapons deployed on FRG soil prior to 1981, 80% expected to perish in the wake of a nuclear exchange; 17% gave themselves a "50/50" chance. Though shared by all age groups, atomic-pessimism did not seem to influence one's stance regarding the incipient peace movement; more than three-fourths rejected it irrespective of their survival assessments.[22] Bear in mind that pollsters found high levels of familiarity with the existence of the 1979 Double-Track Decision during this period but not necessarily with its *contents*. That education would ensue over the next three years.

It is not that Federal Republicans had become more trusting of the Soviets. On the contrary, they hoped to prevent the direct provocation that new weapons might embody for a geriatric Moscow leadership still reveling in its own tales of the Great Patriotic War.[23] Another factor which undoubtedly pushed West Germans towards the idea of equidistance was the 1981 inauguration of Ronald Reagan. The presidential election increased confidence in the United States' ability "to cope with major world problems" among 27% of the people surveyed but triggered a decline in confidence among 31%. Reagan's promise to pump-up the U.S. defense budget led 45% to perceive a heightened danger of war. Public unease derived not from any particular improvement in the Soviet image—only 12% would have welcomed a withdrawal of U.S./NATO troops in the wake of unrest in Poland and the 1979 invasion of Afghanistan. Instead it was grounded in the feeling that both superpowers were now to blame for a "lack of interest in" disarmament negotiations (see Table 5.1). Over the next two years the long-standing Cold War question, "What will we do if the Russians come?" would be superseded by the question, "What will we do if the Americans stay?"

Members of the political establishment, on the surface, displayed a stronger attachment to prevailing Alliance doctrines and strategies. A survey of elite orientations conducted by Weede, Schlösser and Jung in the early 1980s assessed views towards deterrence and détente among 620 persons defined as "experts" on the basis of security-related jobs.[24] Their findings seem open to reinterpretation, however, in light of security-policy developments between 1983 and 1987. The authors found stable support for nuclear deterrence, but closer examination of that "support" suggests that the MAD doctrine was construed as the lesser of two evils, not as a brilliant strategy per se. The spectrum of opinions they uncovered points to a symbiotic relationship between the experts' understanding of deterrence *and* détente–implying an unwillingness to sacrifice the latter on the altar of the former. Among this sample, 12% believed that deterrence could not be replaced by détente as a guarantee of European peace; 26% understood détente as a complement to military deterrence; 41% advocated military deterrence "to ensure strategic stability," which was deemed a prerequisite for détente; and 20% attributed détente with the promotion of the political conditions necessary for overcoming military deterrence; only 1% considered deterrence an absolute danger to peace in Europe. The authors stressed that "neither détente nor economic cooperation between East and West" could be considered "acceptable substitutes for deterrence." Equally important, albeit downplayed by the authors, was the orientation espoused by 53% (94% among SPD sympathizers) that "despite all reversals and problems, even today there is no alternative to a policy of détente."[25]

West German conservatives assumed office in late 1982 quite conscious of the divisive nature of the TNF issue which had, in fact, triggered Schmidt's resignation. By the time the Bundestag ratified the decision to commence deployments in November 1983, Kohl had few doubts as to the price he might pay for an acceptance of future modernizations—hence, his

TABLE 5.1 General Attitudes Toward the Superpowers, the Use of Force, and the Arms Race, 1981

Response (in percent)	Total	M	F	Age Group							Party Preference			
				18–21	22–25	26–29	30–39	40–49	50–64	65+	CDU/CSU	SPD	FDP	Greens
The Russians' invasion of Afghanistan has shown that Moscow has not abandoned its goal of expanding its power.														
Correct	74	75	74	74	76	81	72	76	74	73	80	72	78	62
False	12	14	10	13	9	10	19	9	10	10	9	13	16	12
Can't say	14	10	16	12	15	9	9	14	15	17	10	14	6	26
No answer	*	1	*	*	1	—	*	2	—	*	1	*	—	—
Force can only be prevented through the use of counterforce.														
Correct	31	34	28	28	27	29	31	36	30	30	38	27	30	5
False	53	53	54	57	51	61	60	46	54	52	49	58	61	79
Can't say	15	12	18	14	21	10	9	17	16	18	12	15	9	16
No answer	*	1	*	*	1	—	*	2	—	*	1	*	—	—
Without the Americans we would already be lost.														
Correct	55	58	54	47	32	52	51	57	63	61	65	48	70	13
False	26	29	23	36	37	30	36	26	19	15	18	34	19	66
Can't say	18	13	23	17	30	18	13	15	18	23	16	18	12	21
No answer	1	1	1	*	1	—	1	2	*	*	1	*	—	—
We must put an end to the arms race. If necessary, the West must begin with disarmament.														
Correct	52	53	54	54	61	56	51	49	52	53	44	59	55	87
False	27	31	23	24	23	30	26	30	27	24	31	21	32	9
Can't say	21	16	24	21	15	14	23	19	21	22	24	19	13	4
No answer	*	1	*	*	1	—	*	2	—	*	1	*	—	—

(continued)

TABLE 5.1 (continued)

Response (in percent)	Total	M	F	Age Group							Party Preference			
				18–21	22–25	26–29	30–39	40–49	50–64	65+	CDU/CSU	SPD	FDP	Greens
The soldier who fulfills his duty in the Bundeswehr contributes more to the preservation of peace than the peace movement.														
Correct	51	53	50	34	43	45	48	53	56	58	62	47	50	9
False	26	30	24	44	37	35	34	23	20	19	19	29	29	76
Can't say	22	17	26	21	18	20	18	24	24	23	19	23	21	15
No answer	*	*	1	*	2	—	1	—	*	*	*	*	—	—
Already a portion of the nuclear weapons at the disposal of the superpowers would suffice to annihilate the human race. It has become senseless to strive for military balance.														
Correct	58	58	58	65	54	67	59	58	56	57	53	65	64	75
False	23	28	20	23	21	13	24	26	27	19	27	20	22	18
Can't say	18	14	21	11	22	20	17	16	17	24	19	15	14	7
No answer	*	*	1	*	2	—	1	—	*	*	*	*	—	—

n = 2,148

Source: EMNID, "Aufrüstung and Pazifismus," op. cit., Table 55.

subsequent reluctance to consider an upgrading of the Lance Missiles. Correspondingly, had the U.S. been governed by an Administration less intent on eradicating "the evil empire," peace protest in the FRG might not have congealed to the point where it became not only salient but also politically effective. Pressures for a resumption of negotiations exerted by European leaders, in general, and the Federal Republic, in particular, opened the door for Gorbachev's initiatives. The result was the promulgation of the 1987 INF Treaty and the initiation of fundamental disarmament processes in Europe, providing for a more positive approach to *security* all around.

The Spectre of *Anti-Americanism*, 1979–1985

Anti-Americanism among Germans is often the product of overly active journalistic imaginations. In 1987, for example, *Stern* reporter Sebastien Knauer cited a disproportionate number of newspaper and journal articles on the topic as "proof" that anti-Americanism far outweighed anti-Sovietism in the FRG.[26] Yet the fact that more is written about anti-U.S. sentiment merely suggests that it is easily sensationalized (which sells papers), and/or that Germans are quite sensitive to this issue—not necessarily more anti-American per se.

Whatever antagonisms do exist stem from a variety of sources, one of the more important ones being generational change. The Economic Miracle Generation recalls the days of the United States as a liberating force (and Care-package provider) which brought peace and stability to war-torn Europe. The "heroization" of the USA ceased with the assassinations of John F. Kennedy, Robert Kennedy and Martin Luther King, Jr., although New Leftists and social-movement activists continued to borrow tactics and philosophies from manifold American grassroots campaigns. The Long March Generation witnessed a United States impeding the national liberation struggles of many peoples abroad, while engaging in racism and "consumer-terrorism" at home. Many LM-activists construed their elders' blind love for America as an ersatz-identity for a generation that denied its culpability for the Third Reich. The Turn-Around Generation seems to have found a happy medium regarding its feelings towards the United States, having accepted Coca-Cola, fast-foods, grassroots movements, rock music, high-tech and even problems of racism as part of the German way of life. Though recognizing their security-dependence, they prefer to limit German reliance on the U.S. "nuclear umbrella" because of its inherent risks for themselves and the environment.

For more than three decades West Germans had consistently named the United States as the FRG's "best friend." Despite frequent testamonials to their "special relationship," each country nonetheless came to harbor subliminal fears vis-à-vis the other by the 1980s. In some U.S. quarters, Germany's unshakable resolve to continue along the path of *Ostpolitik* induced recollections of Rapallo, while President Reagan's pursuit of war-fighting capabilities evoked fears of Armageddon within the FRG. The cause of German-American friendship was not particularly well-served by the ghettoization of U.S. soldiers in the once-occupied state (many away from home for first time, with easy access to alcohol); nor was it strengthened by repeated threats that the U.S. might pack up its troops and go home. As Zoll observed, postwar Germans are "constantly ambivalent" about their relation to the United States and its military presence: they "can't live with them, and can't live without them."[27]

A representative survey executed by SINUS pollsters in August/September of 1983 testified to a two-fold shift in West German attitudes towards "America," precipitated by the Double Track Decision.[28] First, the public evinced a declining faith in U.S. leadership capabilities in relation to, but not restricted to matters of military security. What the authors characterized as "a feeling of increasing dependence" upon the United States—from 70% in 1980, to 81% in 1983—might be more accurately interpreted as a growing dissatisfaction with the Federal Republic's already-existent dependency. In fact, 59% favored greater foreign policy autonomy; nearly 60% affirmed the need to cultivate good relations with the United States *and* the Soviet Union. The segment supporting an intensification of inter-German relations had increased from 72% in 1981 to 86% in 1983, in spite of—or more likely, because of—mounting tensions between the superpowers.[29]

The key issue was not a demand for complete military disengagement from NATO, although the proportion favoring West German neutrality had risen from 18% in 1981 to 29% in 1983. More importantly, 60% rejected the American penchant for pursuing major foreign policy shifts impinging on European security without prior consultation among the Alliance partners. Nor was NATO membership per se a reason for growing German unease towards the United States: 78% characterized the FRG's membership in NATO as "good" in 1983, a figure including 40% of the so-called "anti-NATO Greens," as well as 53% of the self-labeled peace movement activists.[30]

A second shift centered on the loss of faith in the protective powers of nuclear deterrence itself, in recognition of the physical threat this doctrine posed to the West German citizens. Reagan's on- and off-the-record remarks regarding a "winnable" nuclear war led 42% to think it "probable" that the United States would engage the Soviets in a military conflict limited to European territory.[31] The contingent perceiving an increased risk of nuclear war on German soil grew from 45% to 54% between 1981 and 1983, commensurate with a decline in the belief that new deployments would enhance the prospects for peace, from 30% to 17%. The 1983 Korean Airline crisis merely enhanced respect for the peace movement, as "sympathy" rose from 59% to 65%.[32] Some 77% approved the "idealistic" motives of the protestors, and 58% rejected the proposition that their activities were detrimental to the FRG's special friendship with the U.S.; only 18% suspected the peace movement of serving Soviet interests.[33]

West German citizens once again seemed to outpace NATO elites in turning to new security models, e.g., rejecting the "balance of terror strategy" in favor of intensified détente. Among the SINUS respondents, 87% saw détente as the best vehicle for securing peace in Europe; 83% were ready to back a renunciation-of-force treaty between the NATO and Warsaw Pact Alliances. A majority considered détente both desirable and divisible, even in the worst of times—in stark contrast to Americans' adherence to linkage (U.S. reactions to European developments were based on Soviet policies around the globe).

While two-fifths conceded that the presence of atomic weapons in Europe deserved most of the credit for the non-occurrence of war since 1949, an equivalent number maintained that nuclear deterrence would not secure Germany against Soviet attack in the future. Most opposed a strategy centered on nuclear weapons: 61% of the CDU/CSU voters, 68% of the FDP supporters, 83% of the SPD followers, and 95% of the Green sympathizers rejected a nuclear "defense" of German territory, for a total of 72%.[34] Yet 55% believed that the United States would not accept a non-nuclear defense strategy for Europe; three-fourths of those who knew about the American SDI proposal (Star Wars) also opposed its development. Three-fourths preferred a continuation of negotiations, as well as a moratorium on deployments if the superpowers failed to reach an agreement by late fall; 22% were willing to continue negotiations and proceed with deployments.[35] The seeds of protest disseminated by the peace movement were falling on fallow ground.

Curiously, it was a majority of CDU/CSU and FDP voters who foresaw the danger of mounting anti-Americanism, although only 31% attributed it to the peace movement. A second SINUS study publicized in December 1986 noted several non-military factors contributing to antipathy between Americans and Germans.[36] Included were the impact of U.S. interest rates on the global oil prices and efforts to prevent construction of the Yamal pipeline, disapproval of Reagan's interventions in Latin America and the Middle East, and U.S.-imposed bans on high-tech exports through CO-COM, inter alia. The SINUS-analysts concluded that Germans with direct ties to the peace movement were actually "more positively disposed towards many manifestations of cultural America . . . for example, [in] their judgment of jeans, jogging, American musicals, jazz, Elvis Presley and American pop music." Sharp criticisms of the USA voiced by peace activists were "not directed against the Americans in general but clearly against the central elements of contemporary American foreign policy."[37] The United States was geographically distant, they observed, yet undeniably present in the day-to-day lives of average West Germans, rendering it a convenient scapegoat for periodic ventings their own feelings of insecurity.

U.S.-FRG conflicts of interest are a function of the degree to which co-horts acquiring political consciousness during the 1970s and 1980s have re-defined the concept of security itself. In positing new sources of danger—such as links between nuclear waste and nuclear weapons—peace movement sympathizers compelled a reconsideration of acceptable means-ends rela-tionships. It does not make sense that one should "have to be destroyed in order to be defended," a possibility always implicit in nuclear deterrence. Charges of anti-Americanism have another source much closer to home, however. While the U.S. has sporadically threatened to withdraw its troops (through successive Mansfield resolutions and the Jackson-Nunn Amend-ment) as a lever for advancing its own NATO-interests, it has long feared that if Bonn succumbed to public demands for their departure, the rest of Europe would follow. This attitude conditioned U.S. responses to the Ger-man peace movement(s) prior to 1987.

From Many, One:
Consensus-Building in the Peace Movement

American media portrayals often misrepresented the composition of the West German peace movement through the crucial period of 1979 to 1984. It was either depicted as a collection of well-meaning, albeit weak-kneed cit-izens being duped and exploited by Moscow, or as a small but vociferous group of aging Sixties-freaks who had infiltrated the establishment under the "anti-NATO party" guise of the Greens.[38] In fact, neither the Greens nor groups directly affiliated with the Communist Party ever exercised pre-eminent influence in the peace movement's recognized decision-making body, the ad hoc Coordinating Committee [*Koordinierungsausschuss*] be-tween 1981 and 1984.[39]

Comprising the movement's grassroots "base" was a kaleidoscopic assort-ment of environmentalists, feminists, Christians, conscientious objectors, human rights activists, Old and New Leftists, punks and professionals. A surprising number of these groups opted to align themselves with one of six political spectra (see Appendix A) which emerged with the formation of the national Coordinating Committee (CC) in 1981. The thirty member-orga-nizations comprising the CC were broadly representative of the estimated 4,000 citizen groups active at the local and regional levels through the mid-1980s.

The first Citizen Initiatives (*BIs*), founded in the late 1960s, were viewed as political action committees intent on advancing the environmental policy ef-forts of the SPD. By the mid-1970s, the *BIs* had evolved into an autonomous political force, portraying themselves as a "reincarnated extra-parliamentary opposition" in their dealings with the established parties. The turn of the decade brought a rapid increase in their number; an estimated 38,000 action-

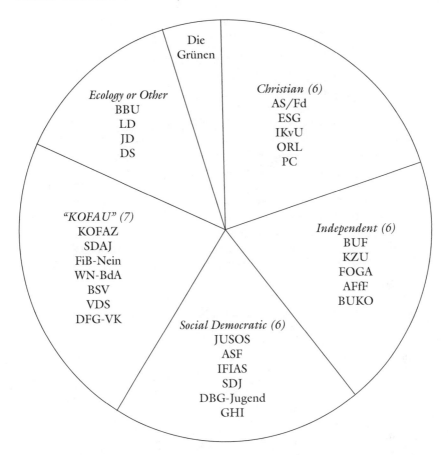

FIGURE 5.1   CC-Member Organizations According to Political Orientation*

*Loosely-defined; does not preclude other coalition possibilities.
Source: Adapted from Thomas Leif, *Die professionelle Bewegung: Friedensbewegung von innen* (Bonn: Forum Europa Verlag, 1985), pp. 24–30.

groups boasted some two to three million participants, outstripping the card-carrying memberships of the system parties.[40] Initiative-members were, for the most part, highly educated, critically informed and visibly self-confident with respect to their own political-organizational skills. No longer willing to settle for the *subject culture* label applied by Almond and Verba some two decades earlier, these citizens laid the foundation for a grassroots-democratic culture intent on pursuing a "post-materialist" agenda.

Post-materialism embodied a political-philosophical shift from the "paradigm of distribution" to the "paradigm of lifestyle."[41] The sudden fusion of the anti-nuclear energy and anti-atomic weapons movements rested on the

TABLE 5.2 Youth/Adult Support for the Peace Movement, Correlated with Sympathy for New Social Issues, 1982

Question: "Below are listed some of the social/political events and currents of the last few years, some of which have evoked political conflict. How do you feel about them personally?"

NOSYM = No sympathy   SYM = sympathizes with peace movement   Y = Youth   A = Adult

Event/Issue	Age Group	NOSYM	SYM	"New Left"a	"Old Left"a	"Old Right"a
1. Organized efforts to prevent the construction of new nuclear power plant	Y	21.9	81.3	83.8	41.1	25.9
	A	23.3	70.8	*	37.6	25.1
2. Continuing examination of Bundeswehr conscientious objectors	Y	33.8	31.7	22.1	36.0	49.8
	A	44.7	60.7	*	49.0	51.7
3. House squatting as a protest against rent and real estate speculation	Y	22.4	78.9	88.2	44.8	24.8
	A	16.3	58.4	*	35.7	20.4
4. Strikes for better working conditions as well as for wage increases	Y	55.8	91.2	94.1	77.3	64.3
	A	46.3	86.5	*	73.9	57.8
5. Plans for the deployment of new atomic weapons in the FRGI	Y	26.9	3.4	2.2	11.8	22.9
	A	22.0	6.7	*	12.1	19.7
6. Efforts of citizen groups to influence decisions made on issues, such as the expansion of highways, airports, etc.	Y	23.8	84.5	84.8	52.6	35.3
	A	18.7	65.2	*	39.5	23.1
7. Demands for a reduction in the number of foreign (guest) workers in the FRG	Y	63.7	44.0	27.9	62.8	75.5
	A	70.5	69.3	*	71.8	80.7
8. Demonstrations by the peace movement against rearmament	Y	34.2	91.9	97.1	64.0	45.1
	A	31.7	83.1	*	63.1	46.3
9. Entry of environmentalists and "alternative" candidates in city and state parliaments	Y	24.3	76.0	92.6	36.5	23.7
	A	11.4	55.1	*	37.6	17.0
10. Increasing criticism of US policy	Y	21.2	63.1	77.2	34.8	19.3
	A	21.1	44.9	*	35.0	19.2

11. Demands for restrictions/limitations on the right to demonstrate, as well as for harder measures against demonstrations	Y	45.8	12.3	5.1	36.0	57.7
	A	55.3	40.9	*	46.8	61.9
Number of cases	Y	117	409	136	337	270
	A	89	256	5	157	147

* due to small n of cases, computation of percentages was not possible.

a Of those sympathizing and self-identifying political affiliation.

Source: Courtesy of Kohr/Räder, Sozialwissenschaftliches Institut der Bundeswehr. Data base draws on representative random samples, n = 1,202 (ages 16–25) and n = 463 (ages 40–50) polled in December 1981.

belief that nuclear technology was "extremely counter-ecology" in its essence.[42] The result was an accelerated transfer of protest strategies, experiences and sympathies from one Initiative to another, from one cause to the next. Expressions of sympathy with the peace movement were strongly correlated with support for many "new social issues" around which the *BIs* mobilized. Different levels of support between youth and adults reflected individual perceptions of "issue-relevance" according to personal life-cycle dynamics. Younger citizens turned to the *BIs* as a way of expressing vexation with the establishment parties in general.[43]

It was the formalization of national coordinating roles among thirty major protest groups which led to the effective integration of otherwise internally competitive and ideologically incompatible social movement organizations (SMOs) during critical mobilization phases. Status and power differentials among the constituent organizations of the Coordinating Committee were apparent from the start. Neither internal homogeneity nor numerical strength determined the power-position of each member-organization but rather the public image and the degree of self-discipline displayed by its individual Coordinators. The combination of past protest experience, procedural savvy and public recognition accrued by specific personalities acting as spokespersons reinforced the internal balance of power and gave the CC unprecedented influence over the movement as a whole from 1981 through late 1984.

The mobilizational effectiveness of national Coordinators was not merely a function of personal charisma and good public relations management. Equally critical to the movement's growth and its success in redirecting public opinion were three developmental processes not commonly associated with fundamental-opposition campaigns: namely, professionalization, inter-organizational integration and movement institutionalization.[44] Professionalization is used here to signify a shift towards functional differentiation and specialization of personnel, reflected in the creation of separate executive, coordinating, decision-making and action-generating bodies. A division of labor and delegation of authority along national, regional and local lines promoted the creation of formal, regularly accessible communication structures. During the peak mobilization phase of 1983–84, the CC had at its disposal 16 advisory work groups and 25–30 staff members. Meeting every two weeks in Bonn, it distributed 10,000 copies of a 16–20 page newsletter on a more or less monthly basis. Formal organization and professionalization processes at the national level compelled grassroots initiatives to adopt comparable structures and procedures which sustained and strengthened the movement as a whole.

Integration can be understood as a process based on inter-organizational efforts to create recognized communication and input channels for the purpose of shared decision-making. These "shared" structures were neither intended nor permitted to induce the standardization or harmonization of member-organizations' internal goals and procedures, however; nor did integration, as practiced throughout the 1980s, imply the assimilation or absorption of one organization by another. Indeed, it was the emphasis on each member-organization's right to maintain its own "identity" that precipitated a rapid resegmentation of the movement after 1984.

Institutionalization pertains to the movement's need to formalize communication and decision-making structures in such a way as to render them recognizable as an "organization" (however temporary) to outsiders as well as to insiders. The Coordinating Committee's attempt to establish an image of internal *and* external legitimacy signaled an internalization of prevailing formal-democratic norms. Its selective embrace of structural-procedural requirements prevailing in the political system at large (e.g., the practice of conducting frequent press conferences, negotiating directly with the police over crowd-control, and ensuring the proportional representation of less well organized groups) had no parallels in the mobilizational campaigns of the late 1960s.

Hallmark of an earlier cycle of protest, the Easter Marches were reinstituted in 1982, attracting 150,000 participants across the land. Despite a growing number of protest activities, Berlin's Interior Minister reported in early June that the demonstrations themselves were extraordinarily peaceful in nature; there the number of citizens taken into police custody between September 1981 and April 1982 stood at 445.[45] Tensions began to mount, however, with the announcement that Ronald Reagan planned to visit Berlin after participating in a NATO summit meeting in Bonn during the week of June 10th.

Activists scheduled a major peace demonstration to coincide with the President's stay in Bonn under the primary sponsorship of the Evangelical Student Union. The June 10, 1982 rally attracted 420,000–460,000 participants, transported by over 6,000 buses to the capital city, where they were awaited by 17,000 imported police and border-guards; a parallel demonstration in Berlin drew an additional 70,000, many with small children in tow. Both events ran their course marked by only marginal acts of rowdiness.[46]

Berlin's Alternative List (Green) Party called for an anti-Reagan demonstration to overlap with his four-hour visit the next day but was denied a permit by the city's Administrative Court until after the President's mid-afternoon departure. Between 3,000 and 5,000 "Autonomous Ones" nonetheless assembled at Nollendorfplatz at 10 am on June 11th; other militant elements occupied Winterfeldplatz, where they were encircled by barbed-wire for nearly five hours in a violent clash with police. The protracted barrage of molotov cocktails, stones and teargas resulted in 87 police injuries, 271 arrests, multiple car-burnings and the demolition of a large furniture store.[47] The violence produced shock-waves within the peace movement as a whole. Holding seats in the Berlin Assembly, the Alternative List was compelled to renounce formally any call to violent protest. The next few months witnessed many movement-internal debates on the relation between peaceful ends and non-violent means. A strict non-violence position was eventually adopted by all organizations and initiatives affiliated with the national CC.[48]

Hopes stirred by the "walk in the woods" proposal for a Soviet-U.S. compromise in July 1982 were quickly dashed when Reagan rejected the offer without qualification. A multitude of opinion polls conducted over the next few months indicated that there was lots of public confusion or, more likely, a lot of inconsistent measuring of mass attitudes in regard to the Double Track Decision. An Allensbach poll found one-third of its respondents classifying themselves as peace-movement adherents at the same time Forschungsgruppe Wahlen registered opposition to deployments at levels of 66–75%. The "gap" between the two surveys had more to do with question wording than with voter ambivalence. Individuals were usually asked to take a position "for" or "against" the Double Decision but had no chance to express their views on each of its two parts: (1) further negotiations, and (2) proceeding with deployments. The formulations employed by pollsters were often highly suggestive, reflecting the political interest of parties commissioning the survey.[49] Studies executed by the Konrad Adenauer Foundation (CDU), for example, foregrounded questions with the threat posed by Soviet deployments and stressed the public's increasing fervor for "securing the peace" without ever specifying the means involved.[50] Others began their questions with references to weapons already deployed on FRG soil.

The perils inherent in the stationing of additional theater nuclear forces were not sufficiently "imminent" to affect the outcome of the March 6, 1983 elections. The electorate accorded higher priority to economic stability and unemployment than to "saying no to NATO." Concern for the environment garnered more voter attention than in previous elections, but the pull of traditional party loyalties was stronger. The SPD did not exploit the deployment question, largely because its own position was in a state of flux; Social Democratic conversion to a formal anti-missile posture would not occur until six months after the election.[51] While the CDU/CSU was positively associated with the deployments, "non-thematization" of the issue allowed voters to accord it no more than marginal importance.

Within weeks after the FRG election, Ronald Reagan proposed a space-based defense system, having already approved the procurement of additional B-1 bombers, deployment of one hundred MX-ICBMs (renamed "Peace-Keeper" missiles), and acceleration of the Trident II SLBM development.[52] The Strategic Defense Initiative, commonly known as Star Wars, was to "shield" the U.S. against Soviet intercontinental ballistic attacks; Reagan believed such a system would eventually eliminate the need for nuclear weapons—even if it would render Europe more vulnerable to tactical assault. Finding nothing of benefit to themselves in the USA's late-summer proposals, the Soviets withdrew from the INF negotiations in the fall of 1983.[53]

The imminence of deployments, scheduled to commence in November, brought an intensification of protests as well as an expansion of the movement's base. In May 1983, 89% of an FGW sample had characterized NATO as "necessary for peace in Europe"; only 46.7% saw a need for the peace movement, and little more than one-fifth expressed a willingness to participate. By June, the group rejecting the missiles had grown to 78.6%; three-fifths were ready to join the protests if stationing began in their own region (53.6% among men, 65.2% among women; 73% between the ages 18–24, and 52.1% of those 60 and older). By July 75.5% favored a continuation of negotiations with no deployments, and 71.7% openly supported a public referendum on the issue.[54]

The movement's expressly non-violent orientation, along with its extraordinary array of creative protest "happenings," made it easy for heretofore non-active citizens to find a personal niche within the movement while enjoying solidarity with the whole.[55] The high-point of mobilization was the "Action Week" of October 16–22, culminating in the Bonn-*Hofgarten* [university courtyard] demonstration with half a million participants on October 22, 1983. Other outstanding events of the day included a "human star" stretching between the eight embassies of countries known to possess nuclear weapons, parallel demonstrations in Berlin, Hamburg and Stuttgart and, last but not least, the formation of a "human chain" covering 108 kilometers along *Bundesstrasse 10* (labeled a configuration of "armies directed from Moscow" by CSU-leader Franz Josef Strauss). The highway they occupied, extending from deployment sites near Stuttgart to bases in Neu-Ulm, had been designated a main transit route in the event of NATO mobilization. All told, an estimated two to three million Federal Republicans joined the protest ranks on October 22. Sympathy demonstrations took place more or less simultaneously in Rome (500,000), London (250,000), across Belgium (400,000), in Vienna (100,000), Stockholm (35,000), and Paris (20,000).[56]

The SPD staged an Extraordinary Congress November 17–18, where it voted to oppose the Double Track imperative. Literally surrounded by thousands of protestors (whom police tried to keep from government buildings with high-powered water-hoses), Members of the Bundestag approved the deployments on November 21. Missile-site occupations continued through the spring.[57] The movement's last mass action was the staging of a "consultative referendum" on June 17, 1984 in conjunction with elections to the European Parliament; 58% (five million) of the citizens who turned out for the Euro-elections at 18,000 locales cast a second vote as well, 87%

TABLE 5.3   Acceptance of Military Defense on West German Territory, 1977–1986

The Federal Republic should be defended against Eastern aggression			
	Yes	*No*	*Don't know/no answer*
Agree in principle			
1977	58 (73)[a]	22 (27)	21
1979	57 (74)	20 (26)	23
1980	64 (77)	19 (23)	17
1984	66 (80)	17 (20)	17
1986	53 (75)	18 (25)	29
Mean 1977–86	60 (76)	19 (24)	21

If fighting would mainly occur on West German territory			
1977	57 (59)	39 (41)	5
1979	50 (63)	29 (37)	21
1980	53 (63)	31 (37)	16
1984	54 (66)	28 (34)	18
1986	43 (62)	26 (38)	31
Mean 1977–86	51 (63)	31 (37)	18

If nuclear weapons had to be used on West German territory			
1977	19 (24)	61 (76)	20
1979	15 (19)	66 (81)	20
1980	15 (17)	71 (83)	14
1984	16 (19)	67 (81)	17
1986	14 (18)	62 (82)	20
Mean 1977–86	16 (19)	65 (81)	18

[a] Percentages excluding "Don't know/no answer" responses appear in parentheses.

Source: Adopted from Hans Rattinger, "The Bundeswehr and Public Opinion," in Stephen F. Szabo, ed., *The Bundeswehr and Western Security,* New York: St. Martin's, 1990, p. 102.

of whom called for an immediate freeze on the deployments, according to its organizers.

The unique degree of consensus attained by a panoply of peace-organizations during peak mobilization phases conveyed the false impression that theirs was a single-issue movement. Many groups had already moved beyond a simple anti-Pershing position prior to their November 1983 "defeat" (the day the Bundestag voted to deploy). The movement did not die the day the first Pershing IIs arrived, as some external critics have argued.[58] At a minimum, the 1983–84 mobilizations opened a host of new debates about the long-term perspectives of "social" or alternative defense, civil disobedience, and possible lifting of constitutional limitations on future plebiscites.[59] Their longer-term impact on FRG security-thinking would first become evident in conjunction with the Gulf War of 1991.

West Germany's twenty-year acceptance of Flexible Response, introduced in the early 1960s, was fractured by the introduction of qualitatively different weapons. The Pershing II was not perceived as an upgraded Pershing Ia but as a first strike "use them or lose them" missile. The American stress on a war-fighting capability contravened the FRG's tolerance of deterrence as a war-preventing mechanism. The realization that P-II missiles could reach Moscow within six to eight minutes after launch would leave the Soviets virtually no time for reasoned deliberation over the need for a counter-attack; they would simply "go for broke." U.S. defense strategists also underestimated the psychological significance of the specified deployment sites. Germany was the only country selected to harbor first-strike/nuclear P-IIs, while other NATO states were to be blessed with dual-capable GLCMs. In effect, the most offensive weaponry was to be deployed on the soil of that country known to have inflicted the most pain and suffering upon the Soviet Union in the twentieth century. The Federal Republic would face the prospect of mass annihilation in the name of its own "defense," at the same time America's rhetorical emphasis on "limited nuclear war" implied that U.S. officials would not sacrifice Chicago for Hamburg. For the two Germanys, Flexible Response translated into Mutually Assured Destruction. Nor would the threat of extermination disappear with the removal of intermediate-range missiles, since that would leave behind those with a range of less than 160 kilometers (100 miles). As many critics noted, "the shorter the range, the deader the Germans."

As these strategic facts of life worked their way into public consciousness, many citizens grew more averse to the idea of waging war on their home turf. Their reluctance to undertake an active defense of the homeland is even greater if it is expected to entail the use of "nukes." Flynn and Rattinger determined that "military defense is endorsed by public opinion much more easily as an abstract principle than its burdensome practice"; once the ugly label of nuclear utilization was affixed in the early 1980s, it stood no chance "up against the more 'civilized' concepts such as negotiation and détente." Roughly 45% of the people sampled between 1977 and 1986 changed their minds regarding an active FRG-defense once the nuclear variable was introduced (Table 5.3).[60] Kohr and Rader likewise found that even non-PM sympathizers abandonded their pro-defense orientations once nuclear weapons were added to the equation.

Even more revealing of a declining tolerance for prevailing NATO strategies were the reponses of volunteer and conscripted members of the Bundeswehr itself. An extensive self-study conducted in 1982 focused on a serious erosion of "defense motivation" among new recruits. A significant number entered military service with an ostensibly limited commitment to "giving their all" and took their leave of the armed forces in the same frame of mind. Roughly three-fourths of all respondents found no justification for a war employing weapons of mass annihilation, irrespective of formal rank. Asked to imagine their reactions to an outbreak of hostilities, two-thirds of the soldiers held that no war could be justified as a matter of general principle.[61]

Younger cohorts displayed the strongest propensity for rejecting nuclear defense altogether before and after deployments. A Defense Ministry survey found that a majority of young men facing military conscription in 1985 personally approved of the peace movement as a stimulus to disarmament, despite the fact that it had become conspicuously inactive after 1984. In short, PM-support might easily be rekindled, should international developments once again move the nuclear issue up from the back burner.[62]

Once the "crisis" was perceived to have passed—and relations between the two Germanys improved, instead of eroding as feared—peace activists found it hard to sustain the public's interest in their cause. The movement had evolved from a state of extra-parliamentary opposition [APO] into an institutionalized political opposition [IPO] force. Finding many sympathizers inside the Bundestag, this grand coalition of Citizen Initiatives saw its demands for military "restructuring" gradually incorporated into mainstream-party platforms, beginning with von Bülow's plan for a Non-offensive Defense and climaxing with Genscher's 1989 espousal of a New European Peace Order. On the other hand, the movement lost its momentum according to a broader law which often comes to dominate major protest campaigns: "The more negative the consequences to be expected, the greater the displeasure and the willingness for engagement. The more the expected negative consequences fail to materialize, the less pronounced the motivation to protest and the greater the crisis facing the movement."[63] Activism per se, however, is a poor measure of the long-term impact and dispersion of attitudinal change among the public at large: the degree of sympathy potential exhibited towards the movement determines the recruitment potential among citizens with respect to future campaigns. Thus "skepticism regarding the meaning and use of [one round of] deployments is the prerequisite" for a cultivating a reconvenable coalition against future deployment cycles.[64]

The peace movement did succeed in its efforts to instill a rejection of nuclear weapons, in general, and war-fighting strategies, in particular, even if it failed to prevent the actual deployments. Survey data moreover show that PM-sympathizers were more broadly distributed in their party identifications than could have occurred, had the movement lived up to the "Communist dupe" or "eco-extremist" images projected by some politicians. It is the number of citizens resolutely *opposed* to peace movement activities

TABLE 5.4 Attitudes Toward Defense of the FRG Among Members of the Bundeswehr

| | I Agree | | Partially Agree | | Disagree | | The Very Thought is Senseless | | Basic Training[a] | Fully Trained[b] | Officers | Non-Com. Officers | Recruits | | Non-com. Officers | |
| | % | (n) | % | (n) | % | (n) | % | (n) | | | | | 1977/78 | 1982 | 1977/78 | 1982 |
Total n=									n=363	n=1,250	n=150	n=736	n=1,642	n=1,560	n=1,205	n=735
"If we are attacked, we must defend ourselves. We are not a nation of cowards."	36.1	(580)	38.2	(613)	7.4	(119)	18.3	(293)	39.7%	35.1%	39.5%	46.9%	42.9%	36.1%	50.1%	46.9%
"The prospect of dying in a war does not terrify me."	12.1	(195)	16.7	(269)	45.1	(727)	26.2	(422)	8.3%	13.2%	9.3%	15.2%	13.0%	12.1%	16.3%	15.2%
"Nothing can justify a war in which weapons of mass annihilation are used."	73.4	(1,180)	10.1	(162)	10.1	(146)	7.4	(119)	74.9%	73.0%	35.8%	62.9%	67.9%	73.4%	58.0%	62.9%
"In case of emergency our democracy will have to be defended with our lives."	29.7	(478)	44.5	(717)	18.7	(301)	7.2	(1196)	27.6%	30.3%	83.3%	62.6%	32.5%	29.7%	62.2%	62.6%
"I would rather die in battle than live in a communist country."	19.8	(318)	25.0	(401)	30.4	(488)	24.7	(396)	18.7%	20.2%	25.0%	27.9%	15.9%	19.8%	17.0%	27.9%

(continues)

TABLE 5.4 (continued)

Total n=	I Agree %	(n)	Partially Agree %	(n)	Disagree %	(n)	The Very Thought is Senseless %	(n)	Basic Training[a] n=363	Fully Trained[b] n=1,250	Officers n=150	Non-Com. Officers n=736	Recruits 1977/78 n=1,642	Recruits 1982 n=1,560	Non-com. Officers 1977/78 n=1,205	Non-com. Officers 1982 n=735
"It is inconceivable to me how people can think about another war after the last one."	58.6	(942)	20.1	(333)	13.2	(213)	7.5	(120)	58.5%	58.6%	12.4%	35.8%	54.6%	58.6%	34.4%	35.8%
"If I am really honest, I would be very glad to take part in a war."	3.1	(49)	5.1	(82)	30.8	(493)	61.0	(976)	2.8%	3.2%	0.7%	5.2%	3.1%	3.1%	4.4%	5.2%
"If the only way we can defend our freedom is though a war, then I would naturally participate."	31.8	(511)	42.2	(678)	18.8	(301)	7.2	(115)	29.0%	32.7%	76.5%	59.5%	37.6%	31.8%	58.7%	59.5%
"When I think about the endless suffering that is brought about by war, then I cannot imagine how anyone can justify if."	61.6	(981)	25.1	(402)	9.8	(157)	3.8	(61)	64.3%	60.4%	31.5%	46.9%	61.3%	61.5%	43.1%	46.9%
"Our democracy is not worth the many sacrifices/victims that a war would bring."	24.6	(391)	34.8	(553)	28.5	(453)	12.0	(191)	26.9%	24.0%	3.4%	11.0%	26.7%	24.6%	9.5%	11.0%

Statement												
"It would be better to fight a war against the communist states if necessary than to have to live in a communist country."	19.3	(305)	33.1	(524)	27.9	(442)	19.7	(312)	20.9%	18.8%	33.8%	29.9%	22.2%	19.3%	29.7%	29.9%
"Personally I would never reach for a weapon, but now I am obligated to do so."	31.4	(505)	33.5	(539)	26.3	(423)	8.7	(140)	33.0%	31.0%	5.5%	13.4%	36.1%	31.4%	16.8%	13.4%
"The Federal Republic must be defended even if it requires using nuclear weapons on its own territory."	19.1	(304)	28.0	(447)	35.3	(563)	17.6	(281)	17.2%	19.6%	47.7%	33.0%	—c	19.1%	—c	33.0%

[a] During first and second months in training.
[b] After ten months of training.

TABLE 5.5   Attitudes Toward the Peace Movement Among Young Men Approaching Military Conscription Age, 1985

Orientation	1983	1984	1985
"We need a broad-based peace movement to counter the arms races between East and West."	63%	62%	55%
"The peace movement can help the Federal Republic to push the East and West to engage in serious disarmament negotiations."	58%	55%	49%
"After the new missiles are developed here the peace movement will lose its significance."	—	25%	27%
"The peace movement endangers for us our necessary friendship with the Americans."	24%	20%	21%
"The peace movement is a danger for our security in the Federal Republic and Western Europe, because it weakens our defense preparedness vis-à-vis the East."	18%	18%	17%
"The Communists ultimately determine the direction taken by the peace movement."	16%	15%	16%

n = 1,505
Source: SINUS, "Jugendliche und Bundeswehr." op. cit., p. 18.

which consistently declined between 1981 and 1984; a glass once nearly empty is now at least "half full."

Resegmentation of the Peace Movement, 1983–1987

Many insiders attribute the PM's capacity for unified action between 1981 and 1983 to a so-called minimal consensus forged by leaders of its member-organizations. The participating SMOs unanimously agreed that prevention of the Pershing II and Cruise Missile deployments constituted the most pressing item on their collective protest agenda; many conflicts were quickly resolved on the basis of the "action-urgency" factor. "Minimal" agreement did not boil down to a single-issue focus, however, nor was movement-consensus defined in strictly negative terms, as a mutual exhortation to citizens to "just say no" to the missiles. One of the key operational principles adopted by the Coordinators rested with the motto, "Common goals must always take precedence over that which divides." Each manifesto developed by the CC prior to major protest actions contained up to six common points which all members were bound to uphold.[65] Once deployments commenced, the urgency argument could no longer be used to make radicalized groups toe the national-CC line; tactical questions were superseded by conflicts of principle, and unanimity was lost.

A very different rationale prevails when we attempt to assess the campaign's impact on national election campaigns. Individuals whose intense concern with a specific issue drives them to engage in unconventional, perhaps even illegal forms of protest may have already lost faith in the system's capability for processing their demands through established channels. Were elected officials perceived as responsive from the start, there would be little grounds for SMO members to engage in fundamental opposition. Furthermore, the intensity with which protesters pursue a certain issue usually stems from the "imminence of the threat" during a period of ostensible social crisis. Elections, by contrast, are intended to regulate and coordinate a broad spectrum of non-crisis conditions (to the extent that mass unemployment and nuclear proliferation can be considered "normal" developments in advanced industrial states); most voters focus on a few valence issues and generally ignore the rest. Social movements evince their own cyclical dynamic along comparable lines. Having "lost" the Pershing II battle, participant SMO's turned to other causes benignly neglected during the urgent-action phase; within months, a new wave of crises washed across the land reminding them of their specific "reasons-for-being." Six developments, in particular, led to a resegmentation of the movement, accounting for its "failure" to emerge as a cohesive electoral bloc by the time of the 1987 Bundestag elections.

The years 1984–1986 witnessed the revitalization of the ecology movement in the Federal Republic. Forests plagued by acid rain, a cyanide poisoning of the Saar River, and two catastrophic Rhine River spills soon reabsorbed the energies of countless local Initiatives whose "peace role" had been defined by the BBU or by the Greens throughout the mass mobilization phase.[66] The BBU's former charismatic albeit controversial spokesperson, Jo Leinen (SPD), quit his executive post to become the Saarland's Environmental Minister in 1985, leaving him little time to pursue further peace causes.[67] The Greens, meanwhile, were forced to place their substantive peace questions on hold, pending resolution of a vehement strategic debate staged by the party's *Fundi* (Eco-Fundamentalist) and *Realo* (Political-Realist) factions. At no time during its short history was the Greens' split personality—half-movement, half-party—more apparent than during this debate over whether "to coalesce or not to coalesce" with Social Democrats at the federal level. Rendered moot by the 1987 election results, the coalition question yielded to a re-emphasis on environmental policy amidst intra-party skirmishes over the federal budget.

The Rhine River fell victim to two major chemical spills during the fall of 1986, precipitated by the Swiss firms of Sandoz, Ciba-Geigy and BASF, which completely reversed a decade of conservation efforts. As the popularly coined code-name *Chernobasel* (or French: *Chernobâle*) indicates, concurrent ecological crises became inextricably intertwined in public consciousness, along with a mounting awareness of their economic costs, thus setting the stage for a return of the anti-nuclear energy protests. By the mid-

1980s scientists were confronted with the spread of bacterial strains which seemed to thrive on the higher water-temperatures generated by seven atomic power plants along the banks of the Rhine; some even speculated that forest damage might be linked to power plant radiation.[68] This triggered new protests against "start-up" at the French Cattenom Power Plant and construction of a nuclear-waste reprocessing plant at Wackersdorf (Bavaria). Regional mobilizations in both areas overshadowed anti–Cruise Missile protesters who reassembled at Hunsrück in October 1986 (under direction of the Independent spectrum). Yet the concerns with national security, health and environmental risks articulated at these sites paled against the backdrop of the century's worst nuclear accident to date, Chernobyl. The April 1986 explosion in the Ukraine shattered the bovine complacency of Bavaria—home state of the FRG's first Atomic Minister and ardent Wackersdorf proponent, Franz Josef Strauss—where iodine and cesium concentrations exceeded ten times the normal levels.[69] Already vexed by proposed cuts in EC agricultural subsidies, German farmers faced extensive crop and herd losses, rendered unsellable by EC-imposed becquerel limits. The Green/ecology spectra put their peace concerns on the back burner, while the Social Democratic peace-wing took off to do battle with the SPD mainstream, proposing a total withdrawal from nuclear energy production.

Chernobyl also refocused the attentions of another peace-movement segment largely taken for granted, namely, the feminists. Intense concerns over the lack of safe milk, over sandbox and playground contamination, and possible fetal damage among those pregnant—all defined as women's issues— were to be assuaged or at least bandaged by the creation of a separate Federal Ministry of the Environment in Bonn. Increasingly conscious of an electoral "gender gap," conservatives paid homage to women's concerns by adding responsibility for Women to Cabinet-member Rita Sussmüth's already complex duties as Minister for Youth, Health and Family.[70] The move to appoint numerous Commissioners for Women's Affairs and to establish a multitude of Equal Opportunity Offices at the state and municipal levels rendered feminist issues increasingly "public." The Greens' proposal for an Anti–Sex Discrimination Law, the SPD's adoption of a 40% quota "for both genders," and a victorious all-female Green slate in the 1986 Hamburg elections rendered their agenda ripe-for-parliamentary-action as well. Efforts to introduce affirmative action principles at academic institutions drew support from the Independent spectrum, e.g., the KfGD, which also remobilized in response to the Chernobyl accident.

Not well-known for their "light touch" in reaction to leftist protest and terrorism, federal and Länder officials unwittingly triggered a renewed campaign against restrictions on civil liberties. The assassination of State Secretary von Braunmühl, the shooting-death of Berlin's Police Director for Foreigners, the Berlin-disco tragedy (*La Belle*) and various RAF bombings polarized the conservative-liberal coalition in connection with the draft "Crown Witness" Law. Opposition to the criminalization of protesters at Wackersdorf, the 14-hour police-"encirclement" of 800 peaceful demonstrators (including their children) in Hamburg, and plans for a non-anonymous national census reabsorbed the energies of civil libertarians from the Social Democratic and Independent spectra.

Incidents of resurgent racism and creeping right-wing radicalism collided with an emotional debate over the asylum issue, which was again taken up by many groups from the Christian, Third-World-Solidarity and Independent camps. When the number of asylum applications peaked at over 100,000 in 1986, Berlin Interior Minister Lummer and Federal Interior Minister Zimmermann solicited GDR agreements to "seal up the Wall" in places where large numbers of Sri Lankans, Iranians, and other Third World nationals found easy transit to the West.[71] Heated reactions to West German engagement in South Africa and U.S. policy in Central America re-rallied the anti-militarists and anti-imperialists of the Independent and KOFAZ factions in 1986.

Last but not least, the Pershing II and Cruise Missile deployments were soon overshadowed by plans for a Strategic Defense Initiative, expected to militarize space but to leave Europe unshielded. SDI itself was quickly superseded by new hopes awakened at Reykjavik and Geneva based on Gorbachev's initiatives, however. The resumed superpower dialogue had a tranquilizing effect on less intensely committed PM-sympathizers, as well as on the public at large.

The peace movement did succeed in breaking the taboo on public participation in the national security debate by the time of the 1987 campaign. Heretofore untouched segments of the West German electorate found their consciousness raised as never before regarding questions of first-strike, nuclear-decoupling and forward-defense. Yet the very effectiveness of its campaign backfired for the peace movement. As more citizens opened themselves to the movements's message, their *Angst*-levels rose, rhetoric intensified, millions took to the streets, expecting the worst—and suddenly the missiles were in place with no "harmful" effects. Instead of disrupting inter-German relations, the deployments actually led to a flurry of new FRG-GDR meetings, credits and exchanges. Just as abruptly, the superpowers abandoned their collision course in favor of summit diplomacy and a resumption of arms-control talks.

Besides refusing to grant concessions over SDI, Reagan had displayed no qualms about reversing thirteen years of arms control through his unilateral reinterpretation of the Anti-Ballistic Missile (ABM) Treaty in 1985. In 1986 he announced the U.S. would no longer be bound by its tacit agreement to uphold SALT II (despite Congress' refusal to ratify the accord in 1979), hardly an auspicious setting for resumed negotiations. While the first Reagan-Gorbachev summit at Geneva in 1985 is largely remembered as a photo opportunity, the November 1986 encounter at Reykjavik left both alliance-blocs breathless in anticipation of a major arms control agreement: all the more reason for the FRG-electorate to return to "business as usual" in casting its ballots on January 25, 1987. Yet neither the winners, the losers, nor the peace-movers involved in that election were untouched by the unconventional experiences of the early 1980s.

The Greens emerged from the mobilizations much less ambivalent about their "half-party" identity, as *Fundis* and *Realos* began to outline the conditions under which they would consider red-green coalitions, based on the Hessian experience. Better organized than before 1983, grassroots groups became a more effective back-up system for the party-Greens, but they also grew capable of leveling more demands. Greens in the Bundestag were compelled to expand their issue agenda as caucus responsiblities multiplied, and their reliance on social movement activity as a tool for member recruitment found them competing directly with the system-parties which had begun to absorb their issues. Virtually all of the Länder added an Environmental Ministry to their respective cabinets, as well as a Minister with portfolio responsible for women's issues. Chancellor Kohl announced his intention to amend the Basic Law by adding an environmental protection clause to the catalogue of inalienable rights, a promise vaguely realized in 1993.

Admittedly, it was not the apocalyptic visions projected by radical eco-pacifists alone which spread the creed of anti-nuclearism in the FRG but rather the crash course in radioactive contamination after Chernobyl that turned most voters into environmentalists by the end of the decade. The success of the new social movements during the 1980s rested upon their ability to forge a consensus around a restricted set of issues. But as the record shows, moves to expand the protest agenda too rapidly or in several directions simultaneously tend to result in resegmentation. Party identification, which remains the primary vehicle for successful electoral mobilization, permits no such single-issue or issue-set concentration. Though noteworthy, the electoral successes scored by the Greens through the late 1980s portended neither a major partisan realignment nor a shift away from economic issues as the voters' first concern.[72]

It was, curiously, the excruciatingly boring nature of the elections that was most celebrated by politicians, pollsters and other takers of the national pulse in 1987, even though the crises outlined above should have engendered a livelier campaign.[73] The Federal Republic was perceived to be so stable that many otherwise duty-bound Germans decided to sit out the elections, resulting in the lowest turnout since 1949: 84.4%. As anti-climactic as the finale seemed, it is no small blessing that the FRG could accommodate both the cyclical intensity of widespread protest mobilizations and the ennui of business-as-usual election campaigns: proof that the country is, in fact, rather normal. A peace movement thus resegmented into professionalized component-organizations can also be quickly remobilized, however, should the need arise.

Disarmament and Its Identity Implications, 1985–1990

By the mid-1980s the tenets of security, sovereignty and identity had become intricately intertwined, rendering FRG citizens more intent on defining their own national interests.[74] A 1987 poll found 72.6% open to reunification under conditions of neutrality, should both German states withdraw from their respective blocs.[75] This openness to new modes of "reassociation" with the other Germany led citizen-patriots to espouse the need for a new approach to FRG security policy. The balance between deterrence and détente was seen to lie between maximal coupling and minimum provocation; the best strategy was one which ensured "as much cooperation as possible, as much competition as necessary," embedded in a New European Peace Order.

For the record, the idea of a New European Peace Order—later advocated by Hans-Dietrich Genscher—had its roots in the strategic thinking of the West German peace movement. Well before the protests abated, the national Coordinating Committee had approved a five-step plan, extending proposals for a Peace-Order set forth by the Palme Commission in 1982 and later promoted under the heading of security partnership.[76] It called for: (1) an immediate *Stopp!* or "freeze" on the further development and deployment of all nuclear weapons; (2) the rapid establishment of a nuclear-free zone along the East-West fault line, a 150-kilometer stretch encompassing both Germanys; (3) the introduction of a ban on all chemical/biological weapons, in light of their devasting effects on the environment; (4) the gradual creation of "tank-free" or conventional weapons–free zones, in view of the increasingly destructive nature of "normal" bombs and the perils of misperception linked to dual-capability systems; and (5) institutionalization of the Helsinki Process, emphasizing conflict-prevention and the direct participation of all affected European states in continuous disarmament negotiations.[77]

The most amazing aspect of this proposal, hammered out in late 1983, was that its prerequisites have largely been met as originally conceived, and at breathtaking speed, since the 1985 ascension of Gorbachev and the 1989 collapse of the East German regime. Under the influence of Gorbachev's New Thinking and Europe's positive response to the politics of *perestroika*, the three-pronged arms-control negotiations reinstituted by Reagan in 1985 developed a life of their own.[78] Concurrent negotiations produced three separate agreements, covering intermediate-range nuclear weapons (INF), strategic-arms reductions (START), and space-based systems (NST). The results of a new race to control arms can only be summarized here.

Clearly the most important outcomes for Germany lie in the area of theater nuclear forces, which saw a resumption of negotiations in March 1985. On January 15, 1986, Gorbachev introduced his sensational three-stage plan for a ban on all nuclear weapons by the year 2000; to prove his sincerity, he initiated a unilateral moratorium on all nuclear testing from August 1985 to February 1987 (a gesture ignored by the USA). The Reagan-Gorbachev summit at Reykjavik in October 1986 saw both sides agreeing to global ceilings of 100 INF warheads, none of which would remain in Europe. The Soviet decision to tolerate intrusive, on-site verification led to a major break-through, followed by Kohl's August 1987 declaration that the FRG was willing to scrap "its" 72 Pershing IA missiles without replacement. Gorbachev and Reagan met in Washington, D.C. on December 8, 1987, where they signed the path-breaking Treaty Between the United States of America and the Union of the Soviet Socialist Republics on the Elimination of their Intermediate-Range and Shorter Range Missiles.

Within a span of five years, arms controllers had shifted from the Zero Option (no new deployments), to the Double-Zero Option (reducing medium and longer-range capabilities), to partial adoption of the Triple-Zero Option (the elimination of short-range nuclear weapons). The INF Treaty was the first postwar accord to eliminate a whole class of weapons, in contrast to the usual pattern of making room for the development of new, technologically advanced systems. It included a detailed framework for mutual verification procedures and the novelty of a joint nuclear-crisis prevention center (regulated in a separate protocol). No one took particular note of the appointment of Manfred Wörner—Kohl's Defense Minister throughout the 1983 deployment crisis—to the post of NATO General Secretary in 1988, the first German to occupy this position. The individual responsible for overseeing the implementation of the INF accords was none other than the hard-line official who had helped to bring about the P-II deployments in the Federal Republic. The last Pershing II missiles were destroyed in the presence of U.S.-Soviet verification teams in early June of 1991.

Convened in Vienna on October 30, 1973, the Mutual Balanced Force Reduction Talks sought to impose ceilings on the NATO and WPO troops in Europe, but little progress had been made by 1988.[79] Prior to 1990, the number of troops (foreign and domestic) stationed in both parts of Germany stood at 1.5 million, yielding a ratio of one soldier per fifty-three "regular" inhabitants.[80] Rendered moot by the April 1991 dissolution of the Warsaw Pact, the MBFR designs were overtaken by the Conventional Forces in Europe (CFE) deliberations. Twenty-one states reached their first agreement on the reduction of non-nuclear forces, signed at the CSCE summit in November 1990. Under the new agreements, the Bundeswehr's maximum strength may not exceed a "self-imposed" ceiling of 370,000 soldiers; this amounts to a 40% reduction in the combined strength (670,000) of the standing armies formerly based in the GDR (now 50,000) and the FRG (now 320,000).[81]

The superpowers agreed to a major build-down of their strategic nuclear weapons stock on July 17, 1991, after nine years of negotiation.[82] Originally intended to halve the size of their arsenals, the Strategic Arms Reduction Treaty (START) produced a net reduction of 25–30% (7,132 warheads, leaving the U.S. with 10,000 and the Soviets with 8,000 warheads). Besides setting limits on nuclear delivery vehicles, ballistic-missile reentry vehicles and ICBM warheads, the treaty instituted confidence-building measures, including advance notification of major strategic exercises, detailed verification procedures, and restrictions on strategic-arms transfers to other countries. The number of long-range nuclear weapons retained by each side was roughly equivalent to the total possessed by each at the outset of negotiations in 1982, testifying to the formidable build-up of the Reagan years. Just as importantly, the disarmament advances of the late 1980s confirmed the anti-nuclearists' position that peace is attainable through means other than military deterrence.

The paradigm shift of 1989–90 brought the restoration of German sovereignty at the same time it secured the FRG's continuing membership in NATO. The terms were spelled out in the Treaty on Final Settlement with Respect to Germany ("Two-plus-Four"), signed on September 12, 1990.[83] It moreover offered a blessing in disguise for FRG defense planners. Experts had already predicted that widespread use of "the Pill" (as of the 1960s) would produce a short-fall of 100,000 males of draftable age by 1994; had NATO required the FRG to maintain its troop strength at 1980s-levels through the 1990s, it would have faced a "manpower" deficit of 200,000 (women are constitutionally barred from combat service).[84] Then-Defense Minister Wörner had hoped to expand the Bundeswehr's peace-time ranks to 495,000 by 1995, ostensibly overlooking a rapid rise in "CO" applications stimulated by the peace campaign.[85] Table 5.6 provides an official count of men who had sought to avoid the draft as conscientious objectors during the decade preceding unification. These figures cover only individuals who applied for CO standing or alternative service after they had been been called up for duty. The number of conscription-age males who refused to enroll in military service topped 75,000 in 1990.[86]

Defense planners originally expected the fusion of both Germanys to generate a fresh pool of young recruits (500,000 in 1991), equitably distributed among various social strata. But youth may not prove as malleable as anticipated, owing to the complex linkages that exist between the identity and security orientations of average citizens, on the one hand, and between domestic and foreign security needs, on the other. In addition to ignoring the resentment new forms of regimentation might engender among former GDR males (recently released from the bonds of a militarized state), officials

TABLE 5.6　Applications for Conscientious Objector Status in the Federal Republic, 1970–1990

Year Conscribed 1	Year of Birth 2	Number of Eligible Conscripts[a] 3	Number of Eligible Called Up[a] 4	Number of Recruits Obliged to Serve[a] 5	Co-applications Including Deckarations[a] 6	Proportion of Col 6 to Col 3[a] 7
1970	1951	375,902	241,752	16,896	2,216	0.6
1971	1952	380,634	253,588	22,466	2,678	0.7
1972	1953	376,780	259,779	30,190	3,635	1
1973	1954	386,424	290,470	70,543	5,365	1.4
1974	1955	389,644	288,763	76,085	7,686	2.0
1975	1956	408,043	312,963	88,852	11,976	2.9
1976	1957	426,068	325,886	94,896	19,088	4.5
1977	1958	434,093	330,751	98,033	37,322	8.6
1978	1959	457,574	348,356	101,214	51,212	11.2
1979	1960	646,297	350,088	102,246	52,169	11.2
1980	1961	483,954	370,045	101,515	56,770	11.7
1981	1962	486,920	374,408	100,117	56,815	11.7
1982	1963	502,640	391,587	96,873	58,897	11.7
1983	1964	506,363	402,737	88,695	58,989	11.6
1984	1965	491,364	398,021	79,038	58,961	12.0
1985	1966	492,352	400,297	75,418	60,183	12.2
1986	1967	478,576	396,157	65,586	63,037	13.2
1987	1968	461,550	377,872	67,400	61,360	13.3
1988	1969	425,480	346,402	60,750	57,028	13.4
1989	1970	374,837	292,482	48,306	47,078	12.6
1990	1971	351,771	185,827	29,466	74,569	21.1

[a] Stand: January 1991.
Source: My sincere thanks to Peter Conradi, Member of the Bundestag, for procur-
ing these figures through the Federal Ministry of Defense.

tended to downplay the importance of a "clash of cultures" between Eastern and Western soldiers, among seasoned officers as well as among new recruits.[87] Another identity question arising in this context is whether or not
members of the first Post-Wall Generation will continue to embrace the
anti-militaristic attitudes of the cohorts preceding them. It is not yet clear
what response the military conscription requirement will generate among
males in reunited Berlin, long the cradle of protest for draft- and war-resis-
tors; nor are we able to assess the nature and scope of anti-militarism among
typical Eastern Germans as of this writing. It is also difficult to predict what
the response to military service will be in those parts of the country plagued
by mass unemployment. It is doubtful that the Germans' sense of internal
security will be enhanced by providing militant teenage Skinheads and far-

right sympathizers with systematic training in the use of lethal weapons and the martial arts.[88]

Anti-militarist sentiment among post-Wall cohorts is but one stumbling block to a future reconfiguration of the Bundeswehr; the extraordinary costs of unification are another.[89] The 1991 claim that post-unity tax increases were needed primarily to finance Germany's contribution to the Gulf War handed the CDU its first electoral defeat in the Chancellor's home state of Rhineland-Palatinate in 44 years. The recognition that Germans might have to pay more for later wars, even if they are not obliged to fight them personally, could strengthen anti-militarist tendencies in both parts of Germany. The question for the 1990s is whether the New Germans will see fit to entangle themselves in a likely spiral of "out-of-area" conflicts in the name of collective security.

The Fourth Cycle of Protest: Lessons from the Gulf War

In many respects, the 1991 Gulf War confronted the newly united Germans with a premature "global" identity crisis, well before they had a chance to sort out the complexities of their reconstituted national identity. While some observers quickly set out to depict the Germans as the New Hegemons, others implied that once they "got what they wanted"—the restoration of national sovereignty—the Germans would no longer be willing to bear their share of the international security burden.[90]

The Iraqi invasion and the deployment of Allied troops to the Persian Gulf followed directly on the heels of Eastern Europe's miraculously peaceful revolutions of 1989–90. Those events reinforced a belief among the weapons-skeptical cohorts, at least temporarily, that even the most fundamental struggles for freedom should be subject to non-military forms of resolution. The feeling of *Betroffenheit* [affectedness] was rekindled by the Germans' ability to witness the war (and its ecological aftermath) in their own living rooms as it happened. *Angst* over the Gulf conflict pervaded both parts of Germany, as registered by FGW pollsters in February 1991: 56.5% in the West and 74.1% in the East expressed "personal fear." Old and new residents were not necessarily motivated by the same concerns, however; Easterners may have been more concerned about FRG involvement due to the diversion of federal funds essential to their own reconstruction. While it may be too early to assess the "staying power" of East-West differences, an analysis of German reactions to the Gulf War can at least help us to ascertain whether or not the torch of anti-militarism has been passed on to the next generation.

A majority of FRG citizens supported the Allied aim of liberating Kuwait, but they were far from sanguine about the means for achieving it, as mirrored in responses to questions over support for the war, and the FRG's proper contribution to the military effort (Table 5.7). Military actions

TABLE 5.7 Perceptions of the "Correct" German Role in the Gulf War

Responses (in percent)	Total	M	F	18–24	25–29	30–39	40–49	50–59	60+
						Age Groups			
Whether Western foreign criticisms of insufficient German support for the war is justified:									
Justified	27.4	33.6	22.0	31.2	36.8	30.4	31.3	23.7	20.3
Not justified	69.3	64.1	73.9	68.8	60.7	67.9	67.3	73.9	72.1
Don't know	3.3	1.2	4.1	—	2.5	1.7	1.4	2.4	7.6
Reaction to Germany's decision to increase its payments for the cost of war:									
Approve	50.0	58.7	42.4	44.4	49.3	49.4	54.8	54.6	47.9
Disapprove	48.4	40.0	55.7	55.0	50.7	49.8	43.3	42.5	50.0
Don't know	1.6	1.3	1.9	0.6	—	0.8	1.9	2.9	2.1
Reaction to the decision to raise taxes to cover the war costs:									
Approve	37.2	45.5	29.0	27.0	30.1	36.8	41.4	37.3	42.0
Disapprove	61.7	53.3	69.0	73.0	69.4	62.8	58.0	61.7	55.3
Don't know	1.1	1.2	1.1	—	0.5	0.4	0.6	1.0	2.7
Whether German troops should be deployed in Turkey if the War spreads to that territory:									
Deploy	51.4	61.8	42.2	58.9	61.1	61.2	58.9	43.2	38.4
Do not deploy	44.4	35.0	52.6	36.9	36.7	36.9	37.4	52.8	54.7
Don't know	4.2	3.2	5.2	4.2	2.2	1.9	3.7	4.0	6.9
Whether the Basic Law should be amended to permit use of Bundeswehr troops in out-of-(NATO)-area regions:									
Make utilization possible	28.2	37.8	19.8	34.5	35.4	29.2	29.6	29.1	20.6
Do not change	67.8	60.6	74.2	65.5	62.4	69.2	68.1	69.4	69.1
Don't know	4.0	1.6	6.0	—	2.2	1.6	2.3	1.5	10.3

Reaction to the FRG's decision to deploy additional
Bundeswehr troops to strengthen Turkey against an
Iraqi air assault:

Find it good	56.0	66.2	47.0	57.7	62.1	59.5	59.8	57.6	47.8
Find it bad	41.3	32.5	49.1	41.2	35.1	38.2	39.2	40.3	47.2
Don't know	2.7	1.3	3.9	1.1	2.8	2.3	1.0	2.1	5.0

Response to government's decision to send defensive
missiles and other weapons to Israel:

Agree with	55.8	62.9	49.6	66.2	67.4	60.0	53.3	59.7	43.9
Disagree with	40.3	34.9	45.0	33.0	32.6	37.9	43.4	36.9	47.6
Don't know	3.9	2.2	5.4	0.8	—	2.1	3.3	3.4	8.5

Source: Forschungsgruppe Wahlen, February 1991 Survey—West, op. cit. Questions in order of appearance, #32, #2526, #2324, #2729.

found less favor and were accompanied by a greater emphasis on the "special German responsibility" for peace among women than among men. Draft resisters could count on sympathy among women, as well as among persons most likely to be called up in case of national mobilization; indeed, 22,197 new CO applications were filed in January 1991 alone.[91]

Though they clearly supported the general war-effort, the Germans-united viewed concrete proposals for operationalizing that support (e.g., raising taxes) much more negatively. The best educated segments were most willing (61.3%) to increase the FRG's financial contribution and to send additional soldiers to Turkey, despite the anti-militarist image ascribed to intellectuals and university types. A majority was prepared to tolerate a temporary deployment of troops to Turkey (a first-wave contingent of 270 air-squadron members) and to furnish Israel with defensive weapons. Yet more than two-thirds of those surveyed rejected a change in the Basic Law that would permit future acts of out-of-NATO-area assistance with little qualification. Resistance to change was fairly evenly distributed across all age groups.

The presumedly U.S.-critical cohorts under the age of 40 tended to fault Saddam Hussein for the outbreak of war, instead of pointing to "the usual suspect" across the Atlantic. Their conviction that the United States was most likely to emerge victorious suggested that not all faith in the American way has been lost on younger cohorts; indeed, persons under 40 were more critical of their own country. One demonstration speaker went so far as to proclaim, "Anti-Americanism is when weapons produced in Germany and sold for extra profits to the Iraqis kill American soldiers."[92] Younger citizens associated German "guilt" with chemical weapons sales and help in bunker-construction supplied to Iraq by West German companies. Nearly 73% wanted to prohibit weapons sales to countries outside the NATO alliance, a figure that did not substantially decline (70.8%) when the likelihood of German unemployment was introduced as a control variable.[93]

Surveys commissioned by *Der Spiegel* through the critical weeks of the war registered similar levels of abstract support, as well as a reluctance to permit active German involvement: 68% considered military intervention "necessary," and 57% felt that the U.S. and its allies could not wait any longer to respond.[94] Core questions yielded little sign of a generational divide. While 90% favored humanitarian aid, and 69% accepted the need to participate in financing the military effort, 67% rejected the idea of Bundeswehr soldiers fighting alongside British, French and Italian units. Correspondingly, 58% agreed with the initial decision to deploy fighter-jets to Turkey, yet 51% opposed the use of German aircraft already stationed there.[95] Nearly three-fifths opposed sending further military aircraft to Turkey, not because—as Premier Turgut Oezal insisted—"Germany has become so rich that it has lost its will to fight," but in response to Turkey's record of human rights violations.[96]

TABLE 5.8   Attitudes Toward Parties Involved in the Gulf War, 1991

| | | | | Age Groups | | | | | | | | | | |
Responses (in percent)	Total	M	F	18–24	25–29	30–39	40–49	50–59	60+	CDU-CSU	SPD	FDP	Greens	Others
Military intervention of allied forces under American leadership:														
Agree with action	63.8	72.7	56.1	66.5	66.8	72.9	66.1	60.9	56.6	75.6	56.1	76.1	39.4	57.3
Disagree with action	32.9	25.9	39.0	33.5	31.8	25.1	31.6	65.7	36.6	20.0	41.6	20.8	59.0	39.1
Don't know	3.3	1.4	4.9	—	1.4	2.0	2.3	3.4	6.8	4.4	2.3	3.1	1.6	3.6
Key figure to blame is:														
Iraq Hussein	82.7	84.9	80.8	87.6	85.4	87.6	82.3	77.3	79.8	88.7	78.9	88.6	69.7	79.3
USA/Bush	4.9	3.1	6.5	1.3	3.9	3.4	3.4	9.6	6.1	1.3	7.9	2.7	8.4	6.1
The West	0.8	1.4	0.3	0.5	—	0.7	1.2	2.2	0.4	1.6	0.7	—	1.4	—
Others	5.8	7.5	4.3	6.1	7.4	5.4	6.7	4.9	5.2	4.8	6.7	5.3	9.2	5.1
Don't know	5.8	3.1	8.1	4.5	3.3	2.9	6.4	6.0	8.5	3.6	5.8	3.4	11.3	9.5
Who will win the war:														
The Americans	78.5	82.9	74.7	85.1	80.2	79.7	77.4	75.1	76.9	85.7	77.4	85.0	63.6	68.1
The Iraqis	1.3	0.7	1.9	0.3	0.6	1.5	2.6	1.6	1.0	0.3	1.3	2.6	0.9	2.5
No one	12.0	12.7	11.3	10.3	15.1	12.1	13.4	14.3	9.4	6.0	13.3	7.3	30.6	18.0
Don't know	8.2	3.7	12.1	4.3	4.1	6.7	6.6	9.0	12.7	8.0	8.0	5.1	4.9	11.1
Whether Germans are also "guilty" in view of FRG firms who aided in arming Iraq:														
Yes	58.0	52.1	63.1	63.3	70.0	64.1	48.4	55.7	54.8	51.1	62.8	55.5	64.1	61.0
No	39.0	45.1	33.6	34.0	30.0	34.9	47.6	37.0	42.7	45.6	35.0	43.4	32.9	33.8
Don't know	3.0	2.8	3.3	2.7	—	1.0	4.0	7.3	2.5	3.3	2.2	1.1	3.0	5.2

Source: Forschungsgruppe Wahlen, February 1991 Survey—West, op. cit. (Questions #1819, #20).

Germany's material contribution to the war was far from negligible. Gen-scher personally delivered a pledge of DM 250 million in humanitarian aid to Israel, supplemented after the first "Scud" attack by a battery of Patriot Missiles, 100,000 "ABC" protective-suits, and one million gas-mask filters. The Cabinet resolved to send 530 more soldiers to accompany an additional 18 Alpha jets to Turkey, and allowed 17 ships to patrol the Mediterranean as replacements for Allied vessels moved into Gulf waters. Its agreement to pay $3 million per month towards the war costs resulted in a final sum of DM 11 billion, excluding the DM 800 million paid directly to Britain. Allied troops were armed and deployed from Ramstein and Frankfurt, as were trainloads of munitions. The FRG supplied spare parts to Italy and Britain for their "joint-venture" Tornado Bomber, and delivered 60 special chemi-cal weapons–detecting Fox tanks. It provided special assistance to Turkey in the form of 80 Leopard 1 tanks, 350 defensive M113 tanks, added to 3,700 anti-tank missiles and further "ABC" protection devices for total value of DM 700 million.[97] These quasi-military assistance measures were grounded in a growing consensus that the New Germany should play a more active role in global affairs, historical constraints notwithstanding.

The Allies' *Blitzkrieg* response to the Iraqi invasion was bound to re-fuel anti-war orientations; what is striking about the post-unity reactions is that they did not mirror the usual Left-Right divide. The days preceding the air attacks against Iraq did bring a fourth wave of peace protest to the streets of the Federal Republic. Activities ranged from the usual demonstrations, to the "occupation" of schools and marches by pupils in major cities (10,000 in Kassel, 15,000 in Stuttgart, and 20,000 in Berlin).[98] Their slogans re-flected a mix of eco-historical consciousness: "No Blood for Oil" and "No Germans to the Front." Among the more provocative reasons offered for German engagement in the Gulf region was the comparison of Hussein with Hitler, raising the negative spectre of appeasement.[99]

The immediate remobilization of the peace movement was not an exer-cise in protest-as-usual for three reasons. First, this conflict saw the direct in-volvement of school-aged youth, although some of their protests were more spontaneous than others.[100] Whether led into town by elementary school teachers or class activists, youngsters' willingness to take action was the log-ical outgrowth of fifteen years of anti-militarist education (many of their teachers had been participant-observers of the '68 era). Added to this is their extensive exposure to unconventional forms of participation via the media, e.g., the marches, rallies, and site-occupations of the 1980s, not to mention the GDR turn-around of 1989 ("the radical is the routine"). They have discovered at a tender age that protest establishes a more direct link and provokes a more immediate response from power-holders than the bal-lot box can ever provide.

Secondly, hostilities in the Gulf region evoked a special crisis of identity among Long March cohorts, especially among the leftists. The Gulf War turned two heretofore unchallengable value-premises of postwar German culture into irreconcilable precepts: first, that the citizens of the new Republic would never again voluntarily engage in barbaric acts of war, and secondly, that Germans must bear a special responsibility for preventing genocidal attacks against Jews world-wide. Prominent pacifists such as Petra Kelly and Wolfgang Biermann joined the ranks of the war's supporters, *die Bellizisten*, while other protest veterans such as Alice Schwarzer, Vera Wollenberger and Günter Grass assumed more traditional stances.[101] Green Minister Joschka Fischer expressed sympathy for the targets of Scud-missile assaults in Tel Aviv, while Green parliamentarian Hans Christian Ströbele offended many with his observation (while in Israel!) that such attacks were "the logical, almost imperative consequence of Israeli policy."[102]

Particulars of the 1991 identity crisis witnessed among the Left trace back to the 1967 Arab-Israeli War, which had given birth to New Left ambivalence towards the state of Israel as a result of the older generation's failure to admit its complicity under the Nazis.[103] By thoroughly identifying with the FRG's official support of the Israeli state, NL proponents argued, their elders could relinquish personal responsibility for the politics of the "Final Solution." The Left's unquestioning support for the Palestinians, symbolized by the ever-present tassled red/white/black scarves at each demonstration, fit neatly into their scheme of revolutionary third-world, national-liberation causes. Exonerated from personal guilt by way of the blessing of having been born late, Student Movement activists had also faulted "the system"—the very system they now serve as public officials and as primary agents of socialization. In short, with the passing of the founding fathers and mothers, the mantle of national guilt and moral responsibility now falls directly on the shoulders of the Long March Generation. The children of the Sixty-Eighters may be anti-militarist at heart, but in many respects they are oblivious to the historical roots of German anti-interventionism. The protests of younger cohorts, children of the *Betroffenheitskultur*, stem instead from fears that Germany could itself be attacked and from concerns over the ecological consequences of war.

Thirdly, reactions to the Gulf War, especially the hair-raising responses of fundamentalists like Stroebele, cannot be divorced from the process of unification itself. Now in its forties and fifties, the aging Left is not only losing its ability to blame members of the founding generation for its failure to "process" the Hitler legacy. The other half of the equation is that the very country many protest-professionals loved to malign has ceased to exist as they knew it. The allegedly anti-fascist, socialist alternative next door (about which, in reality, they knew very little) has been exposed as a sham. The GDR leadership undertook few efforts to expunge the root-causes of anti-

Semitism; fascism was officially excoriated as the product of monopoly capitalism but never diagnosed and treated as a socio-cultural phenomenon. The dissolution of the other Germany has unleashed new forces of right-extremism: now nothing stands between the West Germans and the Old Reich, extending at least as far as the Oder-Neisse border.

Like it or not, members of the Long-March Generation must become the transmitters of the whole of German history, and they must assume personal responsibility in order to pass an effective measure of historical remembrance and moral responsibility on to their children. The "system" argument will not suffice to keep the memory alive. The Long-Marchers' inability to "close the book" on German history, or to eschew the mantel of personal responsibility, is reflected in their equally troubled reactions to civil war in the former Yugoslavia.

Peace-Keeping Versus the Just-War Theory: Yugoslavia and Beyond

Exponential increases in the number of young men unwilling to serve the German Fatherland since the Gulf War—150,700 in 1991, nearly 111,000 in 1992, and a record 160,600 in 1995—call to mind a wistful slogan typifying the anti-Vietnam protests of my generation: "What if they gave a war and nobody came?" While the anti-militarist orientations witnessed at the individual level are most welcome against the backdrop of WWII, they are increasingly problematic with respect to the post-unity thrust of German foreign policy. Though I can offer no more than a preliminary assessment as of this writing, I contend that the Gulf conflict and the outbreak of civil war in Yugoslavia portend another paradigm-shift in collective attitudes towards questions of direct military engagement on the part of the Federal Republic.

The initial FRG response to mounting violence in the Yugoslav Republics as of 1991 seemed grounded in the words of one of my round-table discussants in Stuttgart: "No war, no way, no where, no time, and especially no Germans." The passionately negative reactions of my friends, expressed as late as 1993, has been coupled with a paradoxical silence on the part of peace activists; their response to the Balkan crisis has thus far been one of "non-action, blindness and one-sidedness."[104] It is hard to judge whether this "blindness" mirrors a degree of sympathy with Yugoslav guestworkers in the FRG (a majority of whom are Croatian), or whether peace-activists have been stymied by the combatants' alleged goal of self-determination. Some activists have pleaded a measure of "exhaustion" after the Gulf War mobilization. The Balkan conflict, they explain, has not evoked the kind of personal *Betroffenheit* that moved Gulf War protestors, since more citizens (allegedly) saw a greater risk of actual Bundeswehr deployments in 1991—an odd proposition given Yugoslavia's geographical proximity. One pastor in Leipzig admitted that the inability to blame a favorite scapegoat, the USA, affords orthodox leftists less of an incentive to protest.

The timing of various non-military measures may have had a braking effect as well. The United Nations imposed a weapons embargo in September 1991, followed by a European Union ban on trade with Serbia as of November—neither of which was very effectively enforced. The Kohl Cabinet decided to recognize Slovenia, Croatia and Macedonia on December 11, after thirteen negotiated cease-fires produced no break in the fighting; the UN then sent two contingents of "blue helmets" (peace-keepers) in April and November 1992, respectively. Each effort to quell the conflict from without seemed to intensify desires for a fight-to-the-finish within the former Republic; thus, local organizers found it difficult to imagine other forms of non-military action that could be used to rally peace crusaders.

As the focus rapidly shifted from the independence drive in Slovenia, to the Serbian occupation of Croatia, to the slaughter of civilians in Bosnia (and many counter-massacres thereafter), the Balkan crisis was increasingly perceived as "a convoluted, purposeless and irrational conflict of nationalities."[105] Veteran campaigners have been "surprised and irritated" by the nationalistic character of the Yugoslav anti-war groups per se.[106] A silent march sponsored by the DGB in Baden-Württemburg on September 13, 1991 drew only 150 participants; its organizers were appalled when Croatian participants rolled out their national flag and anti-Serb banners. The Mother's Movement, a further example, staged protests in Bonn and Brussels, expecting its participants to declare that they would not allow their sons to join the aggressor forces. During one of their events, however, 1,000 women (whose trips had been financed by their government) lit candles in a call for the recognition of Croatia, not for an immediate cease-fire. A February 1992 demonstration, drawing 10,000 participants to Frankfurt, featured speakers from Croatia, Slovenia, and Kosovo; while some groups called for a UN peace-keeping mission, others rejected any military intervention in the name of peace-keeping. An estimated 25,000 joined various Easter Marches in 1992, increasing to 70,000 in 1993.

Other mobilizational efforts were more symbolic than pro-active in nature. "Round tables" were established in Stuttgart, Hannover and Munich, in the hopes of developing frameworks for dialogue among the antagonists; Munich activists created a Croatian-Serbian-German Peace Circle in November 1991. Several local groups pursued Sister-City relationships with Croatian towns between December 1991 and February 1992. The Committee for Basic Rights and Democracy [*KGD*] financed media ads and solicited contributions for victims, delivering DM 1.9 million in aid. Organizations like Pax Christi, Living without Weapons [*ORL*] and the War Resisters' Union [DFG-VK] issued newsletters and provided direct support to asylum-seekers and draft-evaders. The Network of Peace Cooperatives published an anti-war bulletin [*Zagreb ARKzin*], while the Association for Social Defense [BSV] undertook its own "fact-finding" mission during the summer of 1991.

In late September 40 FRG citizens joined 360 peace activists from other EU-states in a six-day march through the former Yugoslav federation. Sponsored by the Helsinki Citizens' Assembly, their "peace caravan" was far from effective; residents of the war-torn areas viewed their action as "peace-tourism" and themselves as the endangered species safari-participants had come to film. In addition to offering courses in non-violence at "anti-war centers" in Zagreb and Belgrade, subsequent visitors tried unsuccessfully to "de-militarize" the island of Vis off the Dalmation coast of Croatia. Back in the FRG, coordinators witnessed a rapidly declining response to diverse appeals for financial support by Christmas.[107]

A female delegation traveled to Zagreb for a display of "international women's solidarity" in February 1993, and the German Association of Women Doctors helped to open a therapy center for rape-victims in Zenica (Bosnia). Western feminists' ties to their anti-war counterparts in Croatia led military forces there to issue a call for the assassination of five indigenous female journalists.[108] While not all of the war's 1.2 million refugees headed for Germany, domestic human rights groups were suddenly confronted with a wave of brutal attacks against foreigners, coupled with a sea-change in public attitudes toward asylum-rights (Chapter 7).

The peace movement's failure to mobilize around a concrete set of objectives paralleled the non-action of NATO and UN decision-makers through the first three years of the conflict.[109] Still smarting from criticisms that it had failed to play a front-line role in the Gulf War, the Kohl Government "felt compelled to show the kind of leadership which, as everybody was impressing upon Bonn, came with unification."[110] "Arm-twisting" by Genscher impelled the EU to follow Germany in recognizing the new states. FRG officials had hoped to use recognition, one step not proscribed by the Basic Law's out-of-area restrictions, to internationalize the conflict, that is, to open the door to other options by eliminating charges of illegitimate meddling in Yugoslavia's "internal affairs." The wisdom of hindsight has led many to criticize this move, causing FRG leaders, in turn, to defend their decision in rather self-righteous terms. A 1993 position paper held that "critics of recognition should have the intellectual decency to admit that they regard Yugoslavia as a mere expanded Serbian nation-state anyway . . . and that they would have preferred to leave the small Yugoslav peoples and republics at the mercy of Serbian nationalism."[111] Intermittent, half-hearted UN-ultimata unfortunately served to fuel the nationalist fires; but one can also argue that Kohl's foreign policy team underestimated both the nationalistic aims of the Croatian forces and Serbian aversion to the prospect of a separate Bosnian state.

The debate over use of the Bundeswehr for "humanitarian purposes" was no less controversial in official circles than among peace activists through 1993.[112] Due to Croatia's complicity with the Third Reich and bitter memories of the Nazi occupation, almost any German presence on Yugoslav soil could lend credence to Serbian claims that this conflagration entails the same struggle for survival by means of other wars. Kohl insisted in 1993 that FRG soldiers would not participate directly in military interventions, though he did dispatch a destroyer and three spotter-aircraft to monitor the UN embargo against Serbia in the Adriatic. That position was reversed in June 1995, when the Bundestag approved the deployment of German troops and Tornado fighter-planes in response to attacks on UN peace-keeping forces. The debate was passionate and vehement, but few interview partners that week shared my perception that the FRG had crossed another historical threshold; Theo Sommer was one exception.[113]

The FRG's self-assertive recognition of Croatia and Slovenia on December 23, 1991 (three weeks ahead of the European Union) was a reaction born of unification. After forty years of involuntary division, Germany-united felt a special obligation to uphold the ideal of national self-determination, but this principle cannot be divorced from its moral corollary, protection of minority rights. Postwar democracy posits self-determination as a vehicle for securing individuals against the collective power of the state, not as a means for securing the nation at any price. Leicht blames "the West," in general, "for focusing on self-determination in the form of secession rather than in the context of human rights" at the outset of the Balkan crisis.[114] Yet its own historical experiences should have led the Kohl Government to distinguish between the precept of self-determination [defined as a search for *Lebensraum*] and the prerequisites of democratization, before it pursued the recognition course.[115] The first does automatically give rise to the second.

According to a February 1993 survey, 53% of the Germans opposed Bundeswehr participation in either UN "blue-helmet" operations or combat missions outside of NATO territory; 21% favored their inclusion in global peacekeeping activities under UN command, but only 12% agreed in principle that Germans ought to serve in out-of-area combat missions.[116] Nearly a month after the 15th UN-sponsored cease-fire had been signed and violated, 47% of the persons polled opposed any UN military intervention in the Yugoslav conflict, while 42% favored such action. The orientations of conscription-age males, 18–25, ran in the other direction, however. Dortmund researchers reported that 62% of this group supported and 32% opposed UN involvement in Yugoslavia; of those favoring international action, 44% were positively disposed towards direct participation by the Bundeswehr.[117]

Differences of opinion between residents of the old and new Länder were striking. Among Westerners, 45% favored and 44% opposed UN military action; only 30% of the Easterners supported UN involvement, 63% rejected it.

Some 31% of the West-sample maintained that the Bundeswehr ought to participate in a UN military response to the Yugoslav crisis, in contrast to only 16% of the Eastern pool. One also finds divisions among peace-activists on either side; long troubled by Western protestors' refusal to accord human rights as much importance as world peace, former GDR-dissidents turned *Bündnis '90* parliamentarians addressed an open letter to old-FRG peace organizations in August 1992, insisting that pacifist principles cannot be reduced to "ritualized professions" of self-righteousness. For East Germans, the Balkan crisis stands as one of many problems of psychological adjustment to a world turned upside-down by unification. As one East-Berlin academic observed:

> I just don't know whom or what to believe any more: we used to be able to watch *Heute*, then the Eastern news, followed by the *Tagesschau*, and by the end of the day, we managed to locate "truth" somewhere in the middle. Now I have to figure, especially after what has been revealed about the actual Gulf War conditions, that they are all lying. The problem may well be that there is no binding truth—no discernible force of good combatting evil—behind the current crisis in the Balkans, now that the respective "truths" of capitalism and communism are no longer pitted against each other.

Half of Allensbach's respondents agreed in 1993 that Germans should do more than contribute financially to (unspecified) UN military operations. Attitudinal differences between the citizens of West (53%) and East (42%) were more pronounced than those tied to party affiliation: 59% among CDU/CSU voters, 50% among Greens/Bündnis '90.[118] Up from 18% in 1992, 26% approved of Bundeswehr participation in UN military interventions world-wide, evenly matched by 26% who wanted to restrict the use of German soldiers to NATO territory. Only 13% directly favored the use of Bundeswehr troops to quell the Yugoslav war; 28% objected to their utilization in UN military operations, but 46% were open to their involvement in peace-keeping actions. There was widespread consensus that eventual participation in these operations should be largely a matter of conscience; 65% wanted to rely on career officers, 58% preferred the use of "volunteers"; only 8% favored troops comprised of mandatory conscripts.[119]

East/West differences were still evident in 1995, when residents were asked about their views on Bundeswehr participation in NATO-directed operations, based on peace agreements hammered out in Dayton, Ohio. Gender differences were just as substantial, however, as were variations among age groups. It is noteworthy that persons younger than 34, female and male, were most inclined to find FRG involvement in monitoring activities "right," whether they hailed from the old or new Länder—implying that these post-Wall citizens perceive their country as normal, and hence subject to same duties and rights one would ascribe to any regional power (see Table 5.9).

TABLE 5.9 Attitudes Toward Bundeswehr Participation in Monitoring the Yugoslav Cease Fire, 1995

The Bundestag has voted to have Germany send 4,000 Bundeswehr soldiers to participate in monitoring of the cease-fire in former Yugoslavia. Do you find this right, or not right?

November 1995

Bundeswehr-Participation	West							East						
		Women			Men				Women			Men		
	Total	under 34	35–59	60+	under 34	35–59	60+	Total	under 34	35–59	60+	under 34	35–59	60+
Find it right	62.8	64.4	61.3	41.4	72.0	71.2	68.5	46.3	45.2	36.0	29.4	67.0	52.2	55.8
Do not find it right	33.3	32.4	35.4	49.0	26.4	25.9	29.5	49.5	53.2	59.2	62.5	31.7	42.0	43.3
Don't know	3.9	3.2	3.3	9.6	1.6	2.9	2.0	4.2	1.6	4.8	8.1	1.3	5.8	0.9
n =	1,000	153	203	173	149	212	109	996	141	220	166	149	219	99

Source: Forschungsgruppe Wahlen (Mannheim). Representative Surveys for Politbarometer (Ost + West), November and December 1995.

December 1995

Bundeswehr-Participation	West							East						
		Women			Men				Women			Men		
	Total	under 34	35–59	60+	under 34	35–59	60+	Total	under 34	35–59	60+	under 34	35–59	60+
Find it right	65.7	61.6	53.8	54.1	76.2	77.0	75.6	52.6	53.2	40.9	42.8	65.3	59.5	61.1
Do not find it right	31.8	34.5	40.6	43.9	22.9	22.1	23.5	43.2	42.4	53.6	46.0	33.3	39.2	38.9
Don't know	2.5	3.9	5.6	2.0	0.9	0.9	0.9	4.2	4.4	5.5	11.2	1.4	1.3	—
n =	1,034	157	211	179	148	225	113	1,035	138	238	173	157	226	103

Source: Forschungsgruppe Wahlen (Mannheim). Representative Surveys for Politbarometer (Ost + West), November and December 1995.

Politicians and peace-activists alike offer Germany's historical legacy as grounds for their reluctance to play a more active role in the Balkans.[120] This makes it all the more ironic that the D-Mark, that proudly embraced symbol of a peaceful, post-national identification in the FRG, now functions as the coin of the realm in Sarajevo.[121] While the negative lesson of "appeasement" divided peace crusaders over the Gulf War, it has united them again, albeit in a state of paralysis, vis-à-vis the warring Yugoslav factions. The hardest question stemming from Germany's past, centering on the need for "resistance," has yet to be answered.

West Berlin author Peter Schneider summarizes the dilemma of his generation and, with that, the *Gretchenfrage* of Germany's post-Wall foreign policy thus:

> Only in the land of the aggressor can one share in the widespread inclination to lump aggression and the armed struggle against aggression in a simple catch-all rejection of war. . . . Is this really the lesson to be learned from Nazi fascism, that since we are responsible for the worst war crimes in history, we have the moral duty (and privilege) to restrict ourselves for all eternity to taking care of business, leaving other people to offer their lives for human rights? . . . If Auschwitz is our standard of measurement, there is no point intervening anywhere in the world, because none of the crimes currently being committed against human rights attains the scale of Auschwitz.[122]

The key factor behind the Germans' reluctance to "get involved," in Schneider's assessment, is that postwar generations have derived their negative lessons about war from the former aggressors (i.e., the founding generation), rather than from the Third Reich's victims. The barbarous conflict in Yugoslavia, he stresses, "does not permit a clear distinction between good and evil, but it does allow us to distinguish between criminal aggressors and victims who also commit crimes." The issue for all should not be that of choosing between Serbs, Croatians and Muslims but of rushing to the defense of civilians on all sides.

My own thesis regarding German reactions to the Yugoslav war follows a different albeit parallel track: aside from the overarching problem of being unable to distinguish the "good guys" from the "bad guys," average FRG-citizens are immobilized in part because they do not really understand nationalism any more, at least not the kind of nationalism that is being played out in the killing fields of Bosnia-Herzegovina. Against the backdrop of eventual European Union, nationality is seen not an absolute but as one of many cross-cutting identities; to some, it is merely "an administrative-technical necessity." The Federal Republic regained its sovereign statehood, its right to define and pursue its self-defined collective interests, by permanently foreswearing nationalism of the all-or-nothing, genocidal [alias "ethnic cleansing"] variety. Yet it is the formula, nationalism = racial/ethnic/religious superiority, that is being used to justify competing claims for sovereign-state status in the now-fractured Balkan federation.

It appears that scores of protest-veterans from the 1960s and 1970s find it hard to grasp that the very "isms" which had presented themselves as utopian alternatives to the barbarity of the Third Reich—socialism and communism—could metamorphose overnight into the ultra-nationalist nightmare of their elders. This now places me, a self-avowed pacifist, in the anomolous position of having to argue that not only peace-movement sympathizers but also countless members of the silent majority take anti-militarism so seriously that FRG-leaders may now have to seek ways to re-instill the concept of a "just war" in public consciousness. Helmut Lippelt, defense expert for the Greens, insists that it is time for the party of non-violence to "abandon pacifism" with respect to the carnage in the Balkans. Anti-Pershing activist Erhard Eppler (SPD) admits further that "in view of the mass rapes, the Sermon on the Mount is not the correct answer. What is needed now is not fundamental pacifism but rather an international monopoly of force."[123] Given her stance on the Gulf War, it is conceivable that even Petra Kelly, were she still alive, would prefer "an end with misery" over "misery without an end" for the war's countless victims.

Efforts to untie the Gordian knot of Balkan nationalism (dubbed "Mission UNpossible") show that theoretical distinctions between peace-keeping missions and combat missions can no longer survive the empirical test.[124] Germany's recent experiences in Somalia testify further to the slippery-slope character of peace-keeping operations (the details of which, regrettably, can not be examined here).[125] What nonetheless emerges from these scenarios is a realization that the Germans-united cannot confine themselves to questions of moral responsibility, once perceived as the hardest part of defining their postwar national identity. They must now address the intractible trade-offs inherent in concrete UN and NATO interventions and establish priorities among competing national and global interests, as summarized by Bertram:

> How politically comfortable foreign policy used to be in Germany before [Bosnia and Somalia]. It has become more complicated, riskier—and yet more necessary at the same time. Therefore nothing remains but to learn what we hardly needed to know in the orderly, predetermined world of yesterday: We must ask soberly from case to case what German interests respectively require. Should this recognition really be so difficult?[126]

At issue is not the Germans' commitment to internationally accepted ends but their "national" stake in specific means of intervention. The only national lesson clear to all participants in this debate is that the Yugoslav war cannot be used as a binding test case for a redefinition of united Germany's global security role.

In the minds of many who suffered through the Nazi reign of terror, Germany has changed very little; its people will be forever perceived as aggressively xenophobic, economically overbearing, and intent on reasserting their dominance over the whole of Europe. For others, such as hardliners in the United States, Britain or France, the Germans may have changed too much: they are viewed as unreliably pacifistic, economically-tight-fisted, and morally self-righteous. As far as German self-perceptions go, the truth lies somewhere in between. In the final analysis, the degree of political cultural change witnessed in Germany since 1949 far outweighs the measure of continuity. Hitler's attempt to carve out a power-political role for the German nation after 1933 was unilateral in nature; foreign policy in united Germany will remain predominantly multilateral in character, given its roots in Genscherism.

The real foreign-policy challenge for the bigger if not automatically better Federal Republic will be to prevent a re-nationalization of security policy on the part of its other Alliance partners. At least one school of international relations experts bemoans the loss of a clear-cut, Cold-War formula for security, when the primary aim of NATO policy was to keep the Americans in, the Russians out, and the Germans down.[127] In the old days, "security maintained borders and borders maintained security"; since 1990, however, the potential for military conflict has become something that is "limitless and transcends borders."[128] New conflagrations seem all the more intractable because they are occurring within recognized national borders, e.g., combat in Chechnya. Germany must find new ways to shield its post-national orientation from centrifugal tendencies without, as well as from ethno-national cleavages within.

Between 1949 and 1989, the NATO alliance spent trillions of dollars, engaged in "light-years" of technological research, and developed "generations" of mass-destruction weapons, only to discover that what it really needs are more effective crisis-prevention, conflict-mediation and confidence-building processes. The London Declaration of 1990 heralded an extensive search for new roles, missions and strategies among the Alliance members. Reform will take place within the forty-year framework, but new functions will be grafted on to pre-existing structures, as exemplified by the confidence-building role of the North Atlantic Cooperation Council. The 1992 Maastricht Treaty is another step towards multilateralism, although many years will pass before common defense strategies become facts of European Union life.

The moralizing component of FRG foreign policy did not arise solely in the context of anti-U.S. protests against Vietnam or the Pershing IIs. Nor is it a feature of public opinion which only surfaces as a vehicle for protecting German trade relations and resources, if not German lives. The moral dimension of German foreign policy has been cultivated by intellectual and religious groups across a span of four decades. Notwithstanding the biological replacement of individual members, this community as a whole consistently takes issue with the FRG's occasional reluctance or failure to honor post-Holocaust norms in its dealings with other states.[129] Its unbroken record since 1949 not only attests to the significance of organized anti-militarism for postwar German identity; it also ensures that citizens who reject war-fighting policies now have professionalized channels for articulating their protests. The latter will persist in their democratic demand that FRG foreign policy be legitimized through regular, meaningful public debates.

The Germans united must now find ways of coming to terms not with one but with two pasts. The questions of who was "really to blame" and who has "already atoned" for Third Reich atrocities, who precipitated the tensions and who paid the highest price for the Cold War, are viewed through very different lenses in the East and West. The processes of generational change already underway in the long-separated states may evince certain parallels, but they will not intersect for citizens over 30 years of age. Their mutually exclusive socialization experiences may well complicate Germany's understanding of its historical responsibility vis-à-vis the New World Order. East Germans quick to accept their new status as NATO members may be less inclined to shift their sympathies with regard to ex-adversaries or allies in Third World regions, for instance.

Another factor critical to the future determination of German identity and security needs is the long-existent overlap between domestic and foreign policy interests, one the one hand, and between national and international security concerns, on the other. Their day-to-day experiences with "interdependence," especially those of the last two decades, will keep the Germans in the driver's seat of European integration, irrespective of the financial burdens of unity. Post-Wall Germans will continue to perceive security as a relational concept, having accepted the need to recognize the defense concerns of their adversaries as valid ones. Post-1989 developments have brought home the lesson that security policy can no longer be limited to questions of territorial integrity or freedom from interference in one's "national" affairs. Domestic policy management, once subject to Occupational and Cold War influences, will now be increasingly shaped by the forces of regional conflict, in response to the flow of countless Eastern and Third World refugees.

Despite recent waves of violence on the domestic front, the New Germans still favor a concept of national security rooted in the ideal of a "positive" peace—reaching beyond the mere absence of war—and that is good news indeed. These fundamental changes in German security-thinking might not have come about, however, had the search for alternative paradigms remained solely the province of FRG men. Let us now consider the women of the Republic and their specific contributions to the transformation of postwar political culture.

Notes

1. Berthold Meyer, *Der Bürger und seine Sicherheit. Zum Verhältnis von Sicherheitsstreben und Sicherheitspolitik* (Frankfurt/M: Campus, 1983), p. 30.

2. *Emnid-Informationen*, 29. Jg., Nr. 7, 1977.

3. Joyce Marie Mushaben, "Cycles of Peace Protest in West Germany: Experiences from Three Decades," *West European Politics*, Vol. 8, No. 1, January 1985, pp. 24–40.

4. Forschungsgruppe Wahlen (FGW), representative survey conducted for *ZDF-Politbarometer*, August 1981, Question #12.

5. The survey was conducted July 22–August 7, 1981, as reported in *Emnid Aktueller Politischer Dienst*, August 1981.

6. Emnid-Institut (Bielefeld), *Aufrüstung und Pazifismus*, Tabellenband 1–4, October 1981; here Bd. 3, Table #58.

7. "Pazifismus '81: 'Selig sind die Friedfertigen,'" *Der Spiegel*, Nr. 24, June 8, 1981; Jürgen Leinemann, "Die halten uns alle für Nicht-Menschen," *Der Spiegel*, Nr. 26, June 22, 1981; and Horst Eberhard Richter, "Der Aufstand der Gefühle—Wer nicht kämpft, gibt sich auch innerlich auf," *Die Zeit*, Nr. 27, June 26, 1981.

8. Theo Sommer, "Bürgerinitiativen—Bürgerkrieg. Nach den Frankfurter Krawallen: Zeit zum Umdenken," *Die Zeit*, Nr. 48, November 27, 1981.

9. Karl-Heinz Janssen, Josef Joffe and Gerhard Spörl, "Deutschland im Herbst: Die neue Terrorwelle," *Die Zeit*, Nr. 40, October 2, 1981.

10. Joyce Marie Mushaben, "New Dimensions of Youth Protest in Western Europe," *Journal of Political and Military Sociology*, Vol. 11, Spring 1983, pp. 123–144.

11. Klaus Pokatzky and Gerhard Spörl, "Besuch in einer besetzten Stadt," *Die Zeit*, No. 39, September 25, 1981.

12. Karl-Heinz Janssen, "Friedenskongreß in Berlin: 'Es muß Unruhe herrschen im Lande,'" *Die Zeit*, No. 45, November 6, 1981.

13. Wolfgang Faigle, "Mit Kampfgas gegen Demonstranten: Wer nicht atmet, kann nicht fliehen," *Die Zeit*, Nr. 29, July 10, 1981.

14. Richard von Löwenthal, "Identität und Zukunft der Sozialdemokratie—Lassen sich die 'Aussteiger' integrieren?" and Willy Brandt, "Wir brauchen die Öffnung," both in *Die Zeit*, Nr. 51, December 18, 1981; further, Gunter Hofmann, "Alle stehen in der Gratsche. Nach der Friedensdemonstration: Die Integration belastet die Parteien," *Die Zeit*, Nr. 44, October 30, 1981.

15. The U.S. President misinterpreted two authors who seemed to think-the-unthinkable in a 1980 article, viz., Colin S. Gray and Keith Payne, "Under the Nuclear Gun (I)—Victory is Possible," *Foreign Policy*, Nr. 39, Summer 1980, pp. 14–27.

16. Nigel Young, "The Contemporary European Anti-Nuclear Movement: Experiments in the Mobilization of Public Power," *Peace and Change*, Vol. IX, No. 1, Spring 1983, pp. 1–16.

17. During the week of October 19–23, 1981 I participated in the U.S. State Department's annual *Scholar-Diplomat Seminar on European Affairs*, which included attendance at a closed meeting of White House security advisors who were debating the parameters of a major address Ronald Reagan was to deliver in mid-November. In deference to the massive turn-outs at European demonstrations earlier that month, those present decided to incorporate a new buzz-word, *Zero Option*, into the close of the President's speech: I wrote in my diary that evening that "the Presi-

dent's men" were primarily interested in the public-relations points they expected to score in suggesting a US willingness to delay deployments.

18. "Abrüstung: Die Zeit schrumpft," *Der Spiegel*, Nr. 48, November 23, 1981.

19. Strobe Talbott, cited by Karl W. Ryavec in *United States—Soviet Relations* (New York/London: Longman, 1989), p. 148.

20. Emnid, *Aufrüstung und Pazifismus*, op. cit., Tabellenband 1, Tables 7 and 9.

21. Ibid., Table 8; also, Jochen Lange, "Kriegsdienstverweigerer in der BRD—Der harte Kern der Friedensbewegung" in Hans Pestalozzi, Hg., *Frieden in Deutschland—Die Friedensbewegung, was sie ist, was sie werden kann* (München: Wilhelm Goldmann Verlag, 1982), pp. 126–131.

22. *Aufrüstung und Pazifismus*, op. cit., Bd. 2, Table 30.

23. Theo Sommer, "Wollen Sie auf einem Vulkan leben? Die Sowjets und die Nachrüstung—Eindrücke aus Gesprächen in Moskau," *Die Zeit*, Nr. 12, March 25, 1983.

24. Erich Weede, Dietmar Schlösser and Matthias Jung, "West German Elite Views on National Security Issues. Evidence from a 1980/81 Survey of Experts," *Journal of Strategic Studies*, 6 (1), 1983, pp. 82–95.

25. Ibid., p. 86–87.

26. Knauer presented his "data" at a 1987 conference sponsored by the Goethe Institute in Los Angeles.

27. Rolf Zoll, "Militär und Gesellschaft in der Bundesrepublik–Zum Problem der Legitimität von Streitkräften," in Zoll, Hg., *Wie integriert ist die Bundeswehr? Zum Verhältnis von Militär und Gesellschaft in der Bundesrepublik* (München: Piper, 1979), p. 49.

28. Commissioned by the Friedrich Ebert Stiftung, the study relied on questionnaires, interviews and group discussions among 1,600 eligible voters. See *Sicherheitspolitik, Bündnispolitik, Friedensbewegung. Eine Untersuchung zur aktuellen politischen Stimmungslage im Spätherbst 1983* (Munich: Sozialwissenschaftliches Institut Nowak und Sörgel GmbH), 1983.

29. Ibid., p. 28, pp. 31–32: 52% believed that the FRG had *more* to gain through the continuation of *Ostpolitik* than did the GDR (2%), 36% thought both states benefitted.

30. Ibid., p. 41, p. 86.

31. Ibid., p. 18. One highly publicized incident was a 1983 U.S. presidential radio broadcast during which Reagan declared, in jest, that "the bombing would begin in five minutes" against the Soviet Union—not realizing that the microphone had been turned on. West Germans did not find the joke amusing.

32. Ibid., pp. 47–51.

33. Ibid., p. 59.

34. Ibid., p. 36. Only one-fifth claimed familiarity with an SPD proposal for a "non-offensive defense" system under the title, "*New Strategies—War Prevention in an Atomic Age.*"

35. Ibid., p. 34, p. 39, p. 22. Only 36% considered both superpowers seriously interested in achieving a negotiated settlement; ibid., p. 47.

36. Commissioned by the Friedrich Ebert Foundation and *Stern Magazine*, the study of *Amerika und die Deutschen* sampled 1,800 voters in September/October 1986. Comparative data used in the analysis derived from the 1983 study, *Sicherheit-*

spolitik, Bündnispolitik, Friedensbewegung, op. cit. and *Die Bundesrepublik und die USA—Deutsche und Amerikaner* (1985).

37. Ibid., p. 85.

38. J.A. Emerson Vermaat, "Moscow Fronts and the European Peace Movement," *Problems of Communism,* November/December 1982, pp. 43–56.

39. Both did have formal membership status in the CC. Jürgen Fuchs, "Die DKP—das ist nicht die Friedensbewegung," *Die Zeit,* No. 43, October 29, 1982. For details on CC structures and procedures, see Joyce Marie Mushaben, "The Struggle Within: Conflict, Consensus and Decisionmaking among National Coordinators and Grassroots Organizers in the West German Peace Movement," in Bert Klandermans, ed., *Organizing for Change: Social Movement Organizations Across Cultures* (Greenwich, Conn.: JAI Press, 1987), pp. 267–298.

40. Marianne Gronemeyer, "Aufgewacht aus dem Tiefschlaf. Von der Unzufriedenheit zum Protest," in *Kursbuch 50: Bürgerinitiativen/Bürgerprotest—eine neue Vierte Gewalt?* (Berlin: Rotbuch Verlag, 1977), pp. 85 ff. Further, Bernd Guggenberger, *Bürgerinitiativen in der Parteiendemokratie* (Stuttgart: Kohlhammer, 1980).

41. Joachim Raschke, "Politik und Wertewandel in den westlichen Demokratien," *Aus Politik und Zeitgeschichte,* B 36/1980, p. 12.

42. Heinz-Ulrich Kohr and Hans-Georg Räder, eds., *New Social Movements and the Perception of Military Threat in Western Democracies,* Bd. 3 (München: Sozialwissenschaftliches Institut der Bundeswehr, 1983) p. 13. Also, Detlef Witt and Verena Lorenz-Meyer, Hg., *Atomkraft—Atombombe. Technische, wirtschaftliche und personelle Verknüpfung der Atommafia* (Berlin: Verlag Freunde der Erde, 1983).

43. Karl-Heinz Reuband, "Politisches Selbstverständnis und Wertorientierungen von Anhängern und Gegnern der Friedensbewegung, *Zeitschrift für Parlamentsfragen,* Nr. 1, March 1985, pp. 25–45.

44. Thomas Leif, *Die professionelle Bewegung: Friedensbewegung von innen* (Bonn: Forum Verlag, 1985). For a treatment of all three processes, see Mushaben, "The Struggle Within," op. cit.

45. "Senat sieht positive Auswirkungen der Auflagen bei Demonstrationen," *Der Tagesspiegel* (Berlin), June 9, 1982.

46. Police and organizer estimates vary considerably. See Bernd Weidmann and Herbert Meyer, Hg., *500 000 gegen Reagan & NATO* (Göttingen: Verlag die Werkstatt, 1982); Volkmar Deile, Ulrich Frey et al., *Bonn 10. 10. 1981. Friedensdemonstration für Abrüstung und Entspannung in Europa* (Bornheim: Lamuv Verlag, 1981); and Koordinierungsausschuß der Friedensorganisationen, *Aufstehn! Für den Frieden* (Bornheim-Merten: 1982).

47. "Schwere Krawalle am Nollendorfplatz," *Der Tagesspiegel,* June 12, 1981; and "Massengefangenenlager am Nollendorfplatz: 'Hier ist die Hölle los,'" *die tageszeitung,* June 14, 1982.

48. The Federal Ministry of Justice reported a total of 9,237 demonstrations in 1983, of which less than 2% entailed some violence; by contrast, 26% of the demonstrations in 1968 and 36% in 1969 had been classified as "unpeaceful." See Karl-Heinz Reuband, "An den Frieden gewöhnt. Gewalt ist nicht die Regel bei öffentlichem Protest," *Die Zeit,* Nr. 18, April 27, 1984.

49. Karl-Heinz Reuband, "Demoskopische Verwirrungen in der Nachrüstungsfrage: Was halten die Bundesbürger vom Nachrüstungsbeschluß?" *Vorgänge,* Nr. 66, 1983, pp. 64–80.

50. Helmut Vogt, Hg., *Friedenssicherung und westliches Bündnis in der Einschätzung der Bevölkerung* (Sankt Augustin: Konrad Adenauer Stiftung, 1986); further, "Question Wording Makes a Difference: German Public Attitudes Toward Deployment," *Public Opinion*, December/January 1984, pp. 38–39.

51. Karl-Heinz Reuband, "Mehrheitsmeinungen und Wahlentscheidungen. Paradoxien und Dilemmata 'rationalen' Wählens," *Gegenwartskunde*, Nr. 3, 1985, p. 304 ff.

52. Had the US followed through on these initiatives, "the number of deliverable warheads [would have increased] from about 9,000 when Mr. Reagan took office to 14,000 by 1990, in the process doubling and eventually tripling the hard-target kill capability," as argued in "The U.S. Adaptation to the Post-War World," in Joseph I. Coffey and Klaus von Schubert, eds., *Defense and Détente: U.S. and West German Perspectives on Defense Policy* (Boulder, CO: Westview Press, 1989), p. 58.

53. For a summary of key negotiation phases, see Gale A. Mattox, "Détente and Security," in Coffey and von Schubert, ibid., pp. 226–268.

54. Figures stem from FGW polls executed for *ZDF-Politbarometer*, May-July 1983.

55. For more on the action-options, see Joyce Marie Mushaben, "Grassroots and *Gewaltfreie Aktionen*: A Study of Mass Mobilization Strategies in the West German Peace Movement," *Journal of Peace Research*, Vol. 23, No. 2, 1986, pp. 141–154.

56. Ulrich Völklein, "Bricht die Friedensbewegung auseinander?" *Stern*, Heft 44, 27. October 1983, p. 26ff. As chagrined CC members told this author, French activists opposed the Pershing II and GLCM deployments but did not want to negotiate their own *force de frappe* out of existence. President Mitterrand supported the NATO decision yet refused to include French nuclear weapons in ceilings proposed by the Soviet Union. Claude Bourdet and Alfred Mechtersheimer, Hg., *Europäisierung Europas: Zwischen französischem Nuklearnationalism und deutschem Nuklearpazifismus* (Berlin: Verlag Europäische Perspektiven, 1984).

57. Horst Schreitter-Schwarzenfeld and Dirk Cornelsen, "Viele Wasserwerfer und 27 Fragen. Die Nachrüstungsdebatte des Bundestages und die Proteste an der Bannmeile," *Frankfurter Rundschau*, November 22, 1983; Peter Henkel, "Frieden vor den Friedensfreunden. In Mutlangen staut sich Unmut über Demonstranten vor dem Pershing-Lager," *Frankfurter Rundschau*, January 10, 1984; also, "Raketen-Gegner: Die Wacht am Nein," *Der Spiegel*, February 6, 1984.

58. One US negotiator spoke of the movement's "collapse," while an FRG-analyst outlined three future scenarios, only one of which echoed the demise of the 1968 APO campaign. See Jonathan Dean, "Alternative Defence—Answer to the Bundeswehr's Post-INF Problems?" in Stephen F. Szabo, *The Bundeswehr and Western Security* (New York: St. Martin's, 1990); and Theo Sommer, "Und nun kommen die Raketen," *Die Zeit*, October 28, 1983. Further, Gerhard Spörl "Wie, wenn die Apokalyse ausbleibt?" in *Die Zeit*, December 2, 1983; and Konrad Adam, "Der Spaß am Widerstand: Minoritätenkult, Mehrheitsentscheid und Widerstandstourismus," *Frankfurter Allgemeine Zeitung*, December 23, 1983. For movement-internal perspectives, see Johannes Nitschmann, "Wir müssen jetzt einfach durch dieses Loch durch," *Hamburger Rundschau*, February 16, 1984; "Friedenspolitisches Engagement langfristig stabilisieren," *Frankfurter Rundschau*, November 17, 1983; and Herbert Riehl-Heyse, "Die Friedensbewegung zwischen Resignation und Hoffnung—Den Schwung über den Herbst retten," *Süddeutsche Zeitung*, November 25, 1983.

59. "In Lebensfragen der Nation muß das Volk auch direkt entscheiden können!" *Die Zeit*, December 30, 1983; Martin Kriele, "Ziviler Ungehorsam als moralisches Problem," *Frankfurter Allgemeine Zeitung*, March 10, 1983; Rudolf Wassermann, "Gibt es ein Recht auf zivilen Ungehorsam?" *Kriminalistik*, October 1983.

60. Gregory Flynn and Hans Rattinger, *The Public and Atlantic Defense* (Totowa, NJ: Rowman & Allanheld, 1985), p. 127.

61. Although some of my interview partners were aware of this study, the data were not made public; the tables reproduced here were provided to this author by a Member of the Bundestag.

62. Bundesministerium für Verteidigung, Hg., *Jugendliche und Bundeswehr 1985. Eine Repräsentativbefragung bei jungen Männern der Jahrgänge 1967–1969* (München: SINUS, October 1985). Asked to name the positive aspects of armed service, 52% cited "comradeship"; also listed were the chance to learn about modern weapons (46%), educational opportunities for civilian use (31%), and the chance to travel abroad (24%); 26% gave no answer. On the negative side, prospective recruits mentioned the need to kow-tow to superiors (38%), limits on their personality (36%), alcohol abuse (27%) and "wasting time on duty" (19%); half lamented separation from their girlfriends. None of these findings suggest a definitive commitment to the real purpose of the armed services among the 1,505 young men surveyed.

63. Karl-Heinz Reuband, "Die Friedensbewegung nach Stationierungsbeginn: Soziale Unterstützung in der Bevölkerung als Handlungspotential," *Vierteljahresschrift für Sicherheit und Frieden*, No. 3, 1985, pp. 148.

64. Ibid., p. 150.

65. For details, see Mushaben, "The Struggle Within," op. cit.

66. John Tagliabue, "The Rhine struggles to Survive," *New York Times*, February 15, 1987.

67. Irene Mayer-List, "Große Worte, wenig Mittel—Umweltminister Jo Leinen: Ein Skandal deckt die Schwächen seines Amtes auf," *Die Zeit*, Nr. 33, August 8, 1986.

68. Herman Graf Hatzfeld, "Waldschäden durch Radioaktivität?" *Die Zeit*, Nr. 40, October 4, 1985.

69. "Bedrohliche Fracht—Nur weg aus Bayern," *Der Stern*, February 1987; John Tagliabue, "Bonn Plans to Destroy Radioactive Powdered Milk," *New York Times*, February 5, 1987.

70. Süßmuth's "quadruple burden" stands in stark contrast to the role of the new Environmental Minister, Walter Wallmann, who was appointed to take over half of Interior Minister Zimmermann's environmental and disaster-relief chores.

71. Bonn insisted it was "just a coincidence" that credits for inter-German trade rose from DM 650 million to DM 800 million once the GDR complied, in time for the 25th anniversary of the Berlin Wall. Joachim Nawrocki, "Peinliche Kumpanei an der Spree," *Die Zeit*, Nr. 35, August 30, 1986; "Der Druck muß sich erst noch erhöhen. Wie die CDU und CSU mit dem Thema Asylanten die Wahlen im Bund und in Bayern gewinnen wollen," pp. 76–79; and "Die Spreu vom Weizen trennen," pp. 80–89, both in *Der Spiegel*, Nr. 35, August 25, 1986.

72. The 1987 elections in Hesse showed that nuclear issues can make or break a government, without becoming a priority for the electorate at large. Rolf Zundel, "Immerzu wählen—Wann kann eigentlich in Bonn regiert werden?" *Die Zeit*, April 1987; also, M. Berger, W. Gibowski and D. Roth, "Verlüste auf allen Seiten," *Die Zeit*, Nr. 16, April 17, 1987.

73. The Greens nearly doubled the size of their Bundestag *Fraktion* from 27 to 40 delegates but did not win enough seats to throw their rivals into chaos over a possible red-green coalition. To unify the protest vote, a *party of the new type* would have to advance a platform on the "economics of ecology," reconciling alleged "trade-offs" between economic efficiency and environmental protection; the costs of unification have put this theme on hold, though ecological *and* economic problems afflicting the Five New Länder will compel future moves in this direction.

74. Harro Honolka, *Kollektive Identität und Friedenspolitik. Zu den Möglichkeiten und Gefahren einer Stärkung des friedenspolitischen Patriotismus in der Bundesrepublik* (Starnberg: Forschungsinstitut für Friedenspolitik e. V., March 1986).

75. FGW, representative survey for *ZDF-Politbarometer*, May 1987, Question #1718.

76. Chaired by Swedish Prime-Minister Olaf Palme, the Independent Commission on Disarmament and Security Issues included high-profile representatives from sixteen countries. Its major proposals were published as the *Report on (sic) the Independent Commission on Disarmament and Security Issues: Common Security—A Programm for Disarmament* (New York: Simon and Schuster, 1982). As an SPD-member, Leinen was acquainted with the Bahr and von Bülow designs, but the NEPO did not derive from those frameworks.

77. In April 1984, the Visiting International Scholars' Program at the University of Missouri-St. Louis financed a lecture tour for "peace-professional" Jo Leinen who spoke at several mid-western universities on the topic, "Towards the Creation of a New European Peace Order—The View from inside the West German Movement." This section builds directly upon his insights.

78. Mikhail Gorbachev, *Perestroika: New Thinking for Our Country and the World* (New York: Harper & Row, 1987).

79. Serious differences between the two sides arose over the veracity of "the data" as well as over the issue of residual forces. See Gale A. Mattox, "Détente and Security," in Coffey and Schubert, *Defense and Détente*, op. cit., pp. 226–268.

80. Figures derive from Dieter S. Lutz, *Brauchen wir noch deutsche Streitkräfte? Plädoyer des August-Bebel-Kreises für ein System kollektiver Sicherheit in und für Europa*, resolved on February 18, 1990 in Stuttgart. Further, "Wenn es die Führung will," *Der Spiegel*, Nr. 13, March 25, 1991, pp. 82–93.

81. Egon Bahr stressed that any figure above 250,000 would exceed the number of all troops stationed by the FRG's East European neighbors (based on CFE limits), at a Friedrich Ebert seminar held at the American Institute for Contemporary German Studies, Washington, D.C., October 17, 1990. On post-1990 restructuring, see Catherine McArdle Kelleher, "The New Germany: An Overview," pp. 11–54, and Harald Müller, "German Foreign Policy after Unification," pp. 126–173, both in Paul B. Stares, ed., *The New Germany in the New Europe* (Washington, D.C.: Brookings, 1992).

82. David Hoffman and John E. Yang, "U.S., Soviets Reach Pact Reducing Nuclear Arms;" and R. Jeffrey Smith, "Comprehensive Arms Pact May Be Last of Its Kind," both in *The Washington Post*, July 18, 1991.

83. The "Treaty on the Final Settlement" drew on the Ottawa Declaration of February 13, 1990, as well as upon agreements reached by the relevant Foreign Affairs Ministers at meetings in Bonn (May 5, 1990), Berlin (June 22, 1990), and Paris (July 17, 1990). Article 7 formally terminates Four-Power "rights and responsibilities relating to Berlin and Germany as a whole," dissolves all pre-existing quadripartite

agreements, decisions, and institutions, and accords Germany "full sovereignty in its internal and external affairs."

84. Dean, op. cit., p. 191.

85. For early projections of the Bundeswehr's size following unification, see "Abrüstung: Ein bißchen wursteln," *Der Spiegel*, Nr. 36, September 3, 1990, pp. 25ff. Also, Gerd Schmückle, "Neue Lösungen müssen her—Wie die Bundeswehr der Zukunft organisiert werden soll," *Der Spiegel*, Nr. 52, December 24, 1990, pp. 31–32.

86. Birgit Ziegenhage, "Anwalt: Verweigerer werden schikaniert," *die tageszeitung*, February 6, 1991; *Der Spiegel* cited a figure of 77,000.

87. The GDR introduced paramilitary training into the elementary school curricula in the late 1970s, intensified during the 1980s. I collected first-hand reports of the cultural clash when I was invited to address a travelling contingent of some 250 "blues" and "grays"—the uniforms of Eastern and Western *Jungoffiziere*—in St. Louis on November 12, 1991. Subsequent exchanges with some of those officers indicated that the military's problems of mutual adjustment had yet to be resolved by 1993.

88. Vera Gaserow, "Ausbildung in Stiefeln," *Die Zeit*, Nr. 31, 6. August 1993.

89. Averaging about DM 9,000 per East-inhabitant, domestic outlays will total about $100 billion per annum for the next ten years. Michael Kreile, "The Political Economy of the New Germany," pp. 55–92, and Andras Inotai, "Economic Implications of German Unification for Central and Eastern Europe," pp. 279–304, both in Stares, *The New Germany*, op. cit.

90. Andrei S. Markovits and Simon Reich, "Should Europe Fear the Germans?" in *German Politics and Society*, Summer 1991, Issue 23, pp. 1–20.

91. FGW, representative survey commissioned by *ZDF-Politbarometer*, February 1991, Question #2729. Regarding the rapid rise in CO-applications, see "Bundeswehr—Aufgabe fürs Leben," *Der Spiegel*, No. 6, February 4, 1991, pp. 98–99; "Wehrpflichtige und Zeitsoldaten sagen nein," *die tageszeitung*, February 4, 1991; and "Den Ernstfall nicht gewagt," *Der Spiegel*, Nr. 7, February 11, 1991, pp. 18ff.

92. DGB-Chief Heinz Werner Meyer, cited by Mirko Weber, "Friedensdemonstration bis zu den Knöcheln im Schlamm—'Ist doch super, wie auf einmal alle zusammenhalten,'" *Süddeutsche Zeitung*, January 28, 1991.

93. Data provided by Dieter Roth (FGW). Also, "Kontrollen werden verschärft. Industrie: Regierung fördert noch vor kurzem Projekte im Irak," *Süddeutsche Zeitung*, January 17, 1991; "Mein Vetter in Bagdad," *Der Spiegel*, Nr. 5, January 28, 1991, pp. 24–27; "Irak-Geschäfte–Nerven bloßgelegt," *Der Spiegel*, Nr. 6, February 4, 1991, pp. 33–35; Bruno Schrep, "Ein Prosit der Gemütlichkeit—über die Herkunftsstätte von Saddam Husseins Giftgas-Laboratorien," pp. 112–114, and "Rüstungsexporte: Knacker für Kaschmir," pp. 114–115, both in *Der Spiegel*, Nr. 8, February 18, 1991.

94. Newspaper articles forwarded by friends in Berlin and Stuttgart included one by Christiane Pauli-Magnus, "Krieg hat der Menschheit noch nie weitergeholfen," *Frankfurter Allgemeine Zeitung*, January 4, 1991. One sender wrote: "This article more or less brings together all of the sentiments I have heard from all of *my* friends and acquaintances throughout the Federal Republic. *No one* has judged the war good. For this reason I simply do not comprehend the *Spiegel*-statistics, that 2/3 of the Federal citizens are *for* the war."

95. "Furcht vor Öl in Flammen," *Der Spiegel*, No. 5, January 28, 1991, pp. 32–38; Erich Wiedemann, "Ihr holt uns den Krieg ins Haus," *Der Spiegel*, No. 3, January 14, 1991, pp. 122–123; and "Zwietracht im einig Vaterland," *Der Spiegel*, No. 6, February 4, 1991, p. 43.

96. Cited from an ARD interview in "Das wird ein schwieriges Jahr," *Der Spiegel*, Nr. 5, January 28, 1991, p. 16.

97. "Deutsche Bomben auf Bagdad. Die alliierten Truppen werden aus Deutschland aufgerüstet," *Der Spiegel*, Nr. 5, January 28, 1991, pp. 22–23; "Die Deutschen an die Front," op. cit.

98. "50.000 gegen, 3.000 für Golfkrieg," *die tageszeitung*, January 28, 1991; "Anti-Kriegsdemonstrationen gehen weiter. Weltweit Gebete, Mahnwachen und Menschenkette," *Süddeutsche Zeitung*, January 17, 1991; and "Friedensbewegung: Alle Tage Sabotage," *Der Spiegel*, Nr. 8, February 18, 1991, pp. 116–117.

99. Hans Magnus Enzensberger, "Hitlers Wiedergänger—über Saddam Hussein im Spiegel der deutschen Geschichte," pp. 26–28; Cf. "Die Deutschen an die Front," pp. 18–22, both appearing in *Der Spiegel*, Nr. 6, February 4, 1991. Also, Jörg Friedrich, "Appease now! Das Menetekel der Geschichte," *die tageszeitung*, February 2, 1991; Hermann Scheer, "Schlagwort statt Realismus. Der Appeasement-Vorwurf—ein Bumerang," *die tageszeitung*, February 6, 1991; and Günther Nenning, "Der Ajatollah des Westens. Hans Magnus Enzensbergers Wende zum Satanismus," *Die Zeit*, Nr. 8, February 15, 1991.

100. "Friedensbewegung: Mittel der Ohnmacht," *Der Spiegel*, Nr. 4, January 21, 1991, p. 33. "Dann wird alles anders—Was eine neue Protest-Generation auf die Straße treibt," *Der Spiegel*, Nr. 5, January 28, 1991, pp. 30–31.

101. For *pacifist* and *bellicist* arguments, see "An der deutschen Heimatfront," *Der Spiegel*, Nr. 10, March 4, 1991. pp. 238–245; further, Wolf Biermann, "Kriegshetze, Friedenshetze. Damit wir uns richtig mißverstehn: Ich bin für diesen Krieg am Golf," *Die Zeit*, Nr. 6, February 1, 1991; Max Thomas Mehr, "Diese Regierung muß zurücktreten. Interview mit Günter Grass über den Golfkrieg und die Bundesrepublik," *die tageszeitung*, February 16, 1991; Heide Platen, "Den Krieg in den Köpfen vermeiden," *die tageszeitung*, February 2, 1991. Also, Jürgen Habermas, "Wider die Logik des Krieges. Ein Plädoyer für Zurückhaltung, aber nicht gegenüber Israel," *Die Zeit*, Nr. 8, February 15, 1991; and Michael Walzer, "Irak ist nicht Vietnam," *die tageszeitung*, February 16, 1991.

102. There were some equally harsh reactions to the Germans; see "Unser Kampf. Henryk M. Broder über die Ressentiments der deutschen Friedensbewegung," *Der Spiegel*, Nr. 18, April 29, 1991, p. 261.

103. For a heated debate unleashed by Markovits' 1991 critique of the Left, see Jürgen Hoffmann and Andrei S. Markovits, "Ein amerikanischer Jude und eine deutsche Friedensrede," *Frankfurter Rundschau*, Nr. 40, February 16, 1991; Markovits, "Eine ernüchternde Erfahrung. Die Friedensbewegung aus der Sicht eines amerikanischen Juden," *Die Zeit*, Nr. 8, February 22, 1991; and "Die Linke gibt es nicht—und es gibt sie doch. Eine Antwort auf Reaktionen im Streit über den Krieg am Golf," *Frankfurter Rundschau*, February 23/24, 1991. For more opposing viewpoints, see Rainer Erd, "Deutsche Linke an die Front? Ein Plädoyer für den öffentlichen Zweifel und eine Antwort auf Andrei S. Markovits," *Frankfurter Rundschau*, Nr. 43, February 20, 1991.

104. Uli Jäger and Klaus Vack, "Untätig? Die Friedensbewegung und der Krieg im ehemaligen Jugoslawien," in *Jahrbuch Frieden 1993. Konflikte, Abrüstung, Friedensarbeit* (München: Verlag C.H. Beck, 1992), p. 195.

105. Zeljko Karajica and Marcia Maibach, "Vom Interessenkonflikt zum Nationalitätenkampf: Der jugoslawische Krieg," in *Jahrbuch Frieden 1993*, ibid., p. 41.

106. Jaeger and Vack, op. cit., p. 204.

107. Ibid., p. 202.

108. Dubravka Ugresic, "Alles, nur nicht den Tod," *Die Zeit*, Nr. 4, January 29, 1993.

109. Ulrich Schiller and Klaus-Peter Schmid, "Noch keine Befehle," *Die Zeit*, Nr. 33, August 20, 1993; Peter Glotz, "Wer kämpfen will, soll vortreten, *Die Zeit*, Nr. 3, January 22, 1993.

110. Müller, op. cit., p. 154.

111. "Recognition of the Yugoslav Successor States," position paper issued by the German Foreign Ministry in Bonn, March 10, 1993, p. 6.

112. See Karl-Heinz Janßen "Blei in der Luft"; Christoph Bertram, "Notfalls Gewalt," and Robert Leicht, "Kämpfen nur mit klaren Zielen," all in *Die Zeit*, Nr. 15, April 16, 1993. Also, Robert Leicht, "Vergeltung ist kein Kriegsziel," and Matthias Naß, "Gegen Barbarei hilft nur Gewalt," in *Die Zeit*, Nr. 7, February 18, 1994.

113. Theo Sommer, "Schritt über die Schwelle," *Die Zeit*, Nr. 27, June 30, 1995.

114. Robert Leicht, "Der Kampf zwischen Mächten und Rechten," *Die Zeit*, Nr. 9, March 5, 1993.

115. See Norbert Mappes-Niediek, "Kroatien, unsere Schöne," *Die Zeit*, Nr. 26, July 2, 1993.

116. Commissioned by *Die Woche*, this study of 1,008 respondents was executed by FORSA (Dortmund). Figures were supplied by the German Information Center; individuals classified as members of the *Turn-Around Generation* were between 24 and 32 by this point in time.

117. Data commissioned by the *Frankfurter Allgemeine* and the *SAT I* cable-network, published on February 10, 1993, were also provided by the German Information Center.

118. Renate Köcher, "Breite Mehrheit für Blauhelm-Einsätze deutscher Soldaten," *Frankfurter Allgemeine Zeitung*, Nr. 35, February 11, 1993; the term "broad majority" seems to be overstating the case, based on the statistics offered.

119. Alain Finkielkraut, "Hitlers später Sieg," *Die Zeit*, Nr. 34, August 27, 1993.

120. One local official claimed, "For the Deutschmark . . . one can get almost anything in Sarajevo even now. Wine, Schnapps, cigarettes in any case, but also fresh meat, fish from the Adriatic, vegetables, yes even champagne and French camembert." Dietrich Willier, "Der Deal kennt keine Grenzen," *Die Zeit* Nr. 9, March 5, 1993.

121. Peter Schneider, "Standing Aside in Self-Deluding Virtue," *International Herald Tribune*, June 1, 1993.

122. Cited by Dirk Kurbjuweit, "Frieden mit aller Gewalt," *Die Zeit*, February 12, 1993.

123. Kuno Kruse and Dietrich Willier, "Mission UN-möglich," *Die Zeit*, Nr. 16, April 23, 1994.

124. Robert Leicht, "Wenn es knallt—Krieg in Somalia: Was haben Deutsche da verloren?" *Die Zeit*, June 18, 1993; "UN-Truppen zerstören Adids Hauptquartier, *Frankfurter Rundschau*, June 18, 1993; Christoph Bertram, "Entschlossen ins Ungewisse," *Die Zeit*, Nr. 53, January 1, 1993; and Robert Leicht, "Weder Draufgänger noch Drückeberger, *Die Zeit*, Nr. 53 January 1, 1993.

125. On April 21, 1993, the Bundestag voted by a margin of 341 to 206 to send armed forces to Somalia; comprised of engineers, medical personnel, telecommunications experts and military police, the first 250 soldiers (out of a contingent of 1,700) departed for Africa in July. The action enjoyed broad public support; 68% (Allensbach) backed FRG involvement (71% West, 57% East), rising to 77% when Somalian deployments were depicted as "humanitarian aid." The humanitarian mission (cost: DM 184 million in 1993) soon became another UN operation embroiled in ethnic warfare, shifting public attitudes dramatically. The Kohl Government withdrew its forces in January 1994; its primary accomplishments, according to TV-reports, were self-maintenance and the construction of a well for use by seven UN-soldiers from India. See Michael Schwelien, "Frieden schaffen, möglichst ohne Waffen," *Die Zeit* Nr. 26, July 2, 1993; Bartholomäus Grill, "Wildwest in Mogadischu," Nr. 30, July 30, 1993; and Dirk Kurbjuweit, "Lacky zieht in den Krieg, Nr. 36, September 10, 1993, respectively. The Bundeswehr also sent 142 medical volunteers to Cambodia; its first soldier was killed there in July 1993.

126. Christoph Bertram, "Viele Prinzipien, keine Politik," *Die Zeit*, Nr. 26, July 1993.

127. One such lamenter is John J. Mearsheimer, "Back to the Future: Instability in Europe after the Cold War," *International Security*, Vol. 15, Summer 1990, pp. 5–56; also "The Case for a Ukranian Nuclear Deterrent," *Foreign Affairs*, Nr. 3, Summer 1993.

128. Dieter Dettke, "Multilateralism and Re-Nationalization: European Security in Transition," in Paul Michael Lützeler, ed., *Europe after Maastricht. American and European Perspectives* (Providence/Oxford: Berghahn Books, 1994), p. 179, p. 183.

129. Greens' objections to FRG exports of dual-use chemicals and nuclear hardware, voiced over a period of ten years, overlapped with complaints by the Bush Administration over Bonn's role in the Iraqi weapons build-up through the late 1980s.

6

Generational Differences and the Gender Gap: Identity and Security Consciousness Among West German Women

In war men kill men whom they don't know
under orders from men who know each other
and would not kill each other.

—Source unknown,
cited by Petra Kelly, 1981

Before me lies an informal montage of photographs, collected throughout the most dramatic period of postwar German history, between November 1989 and December 1990. The pictures show a triumphant-looking Chancellor Helmut Kohl, sharing the podium with interim GDR Premier Hans Modrow on December 19, 1989 in Dresden (*Der Spiegel*); Berlin Mayor Walter Momper, Chancellor Kohl, Foreign Minister Hans-Dietrich Genscher, former CDU-Mayor Eberhard Diepgen, and FDP-executive Graf Otto Lambsdorff, en route with spanned umbrellas to the opening of the Brandenburg Gate on December 22, 1989 (*Der Spiegel*); former Chancellor Willy Brandt, accompanied by four dark-suited "election assistants," campaigning in Magdeburg in January 1990 (*Der Spiegel*); and my own photo of Minister Genscher and the all-male slate of Liberal candidates, taken during a March 1990 election rally in Leipzig. Also depicted are FRG Interior Minister Wolfgang Schäuble and GDR State Secretary Günther Krause, affixing their signatures to the Unity Treaty on August 31, 1990 (*German Tribune*); then-Soviet President Gorbachev, joined by Foreign Ministers Dumas (France), Shevardnadze (USSR), Genscher (FRG), Hurd (Britain) and Premier de Maizière (GDR), having just signed an accord terminating Four-Power rights over Germany on September 12, 1990 (*The Washington Post*); and again, Baker, Genscher, Dumas and Schewardnadze observing the dismantling of the infamous "Checkpoint Charlie" border-post (*Der*

Spiegel). Last but not least, there is a profile of Berlin Mayor Momper, President Richard von Weizsäcker and Chancellor Kohl assembled before the Reichstag on unification night, October 3, 1990 (*Die Zeit*).

These photos remind me of an exercise often found in workbooks for children: amidst a dense assemblage of look-alike images, one tests youngsters' perceptual skills with the simple question: "What's wrong with this picture?" The answer here is obvious: not a single woman is featured in the photos documenting key unification processes and events. It is nonetheless the "life-choices" of women which have been most directly affected by the merger of two diametrically opposed socio-economic systems; they account for 52% of the West and 53% of the East populations.

Women's political orientations derive from the cumulative influence of changes in the broader socio-political landscape, as well as from conditions or constraints unique to their gender. The effects of two world wars and sustained Cold War tensions on American women pale in comparison to the impact these developments have had on German women. Three generations of mothers, daughters and workers have witnessed an extraordinary series of national rises and falls, from Kaiserreich to Republic, from Nazi-Reich to rubble heap, from rump-state to regional power. Gendered divisions of labor have afforded these cohorts very different political opportunity structures than those generally encountered by their male counterparts. Their contrasting experiences with the state make it possible to argue that variations in the political beliefs espoused by women and men—measured in terms of their responses to mass surveys—are likely to be not only "percentual" or quantitative but also perceptual and qualitative in nature. For this reason I have chosen *not* to subsume an analysis of female attitudes towards the German Question under the usual heading of "domestic" politics but to treat FRG-women as significant contributors to national change in their own right. Their search for new approaches to national identity and national security since 1990 has been complicated by the fact that women's struggle for equality in both parts of Germany derived from very different historical-legal foundations between 1949 and 1989. In this sense, women's search for a new, post-Wall identity lies at the very heart of a clash between the recently "unified" cultures of East and West.

Based on my original research design, this chapter focuses largely on the political status and security orientations of West-German women through 1995.[1] It begins with an overview of women's roles through the years of Occupation and democratic consolidation, followed by a look at the politics of feminist mobilization through the 1970s. It then considers their participation in formal-democratic institutions, along with the emergence of national security as a "woman's issue" in the 1980s. I aim to show that what moved women to take a Great Leap Forward with regard to direct engagement in politics during the 1980s was not their interest in traditional "gender issues" but rather their focus on nuclear energy and national defense, topics erroneously classified as "men's issues."

I then develop profiles of eight women interviewed in 1985–1986, compensating for the not-so-benign neglect accorded their views on the national question by most experts prior to 1989.[2] Besides proving that women do not all "think alike" as regards the defense-needs of the homeland, these profiles highlight generational differences across a broad spectrum of partisan orientations, based on each woman's specific experiences with war, peace and nationalism. Finally, we consider the immediate impact of unification on the national consciousness of German women. In addition to underscoring pre-existing differences in women's identity on both sides of the former border, unity has raised many new questions over the meaning of citizenship, not only as it pertains to the future of women's rights in Germany but also as it affects their ties to the nation's traumatic past.

Reconstructing the Patriarchal Order, 1949–1959

The road to meaningful political participation as voters, candidates and office-holders has been a very rocky one for German women. Promulgated in 1850, the Prussian Law on Association barred "female persons, the mentally ill, school children and apprentices" from membership in any political organization or assembly, a ban not rescinded until 1908.[3] Supported by the Left, women acquired the right to vote under the Weimar Constitution in 1918, but many responded by casting their ballots for center and right-wing parties. Even more moved to support the emerging NSDAP in 1932/33, leading to a stab-in-the-back legend that women had brought Hitler to power.[4]

Extreme economic insecurity, added to the pervasiveness of traditional religious beliefs regarding proper female roles, rendered women susceptible to the National-Socialist cause. Average female voters favored Hitler's promise to glorify motherhood (linking it to a "higher purpose") over feminists' arguments against a repressive division of labor defining their existence in the industrial age. Neither their political inexperience nor their unquestioning embrace of role-obligations dictated from above would shelter women from the reign of terror that ensued, however.[5]

The early years of Occupation following Nazi capitulation were no kinder and gentler towards women than the war itself. Their lot worsened considerably in the short run, due to sexual assaults by victorious soldiers, forced quartering, the captivity of their provider-mates, and the collapse of the rationing system.[6] Between 1945 and 1949 women were less concerned with the theoretical distribution of political power than with the practical distribution of scarce food resources in the four postwar zones; most were compelled to "hamster" their way through black market networks to secure adequate nutrition for themselves and their dependents.[7] Millions of

Trümmerfrauen [rubble-women] were mobilized and conscripted, paid according to the principle "she who works, must also eat." For three years they labored, nourishing their dependents with the increased rations they received for digging the former Reich out of its own ruins.

The personal survival strategies pursued by women were not without political content; the Occupational Powers deliberately relied on female-nurturing activity in their calculations for resource distribution and recovery.[8] The provisional Economic Council, officially charged with "scarcity management," was expanded in February 1948; only five of its 104 members were women, though they outnumbered men by seven million residents. Not a single woman served on the Committee for the Equalization of Burdens. Within days after the initiation of the June 1948 currency reform, residents in the Western zones saw a wide range of goods "miraculously" reappear on the market, albeit only for those who could afford to pay; prices rose 14% by December.[9]

To counteract the power vacuum emerging after surrender, women created their own local anti-fascism committees, over 6,000 in the eastern zone alone. Activists in the western zones quickly reestablished relations with British and American women's organizations, convened an assembly of 5,000 participants to address prisoner-of-war questions, and mobilized regular cooking classes to compensate for missing ingredients. Another 2,000 founded the Union of German Democratic Women [*Demokratischer Frauenbund Deutschlands*] in 1947. Cooperation transcended party lines until 1948, when the reconstituted CDU, SPD and FDP banned collaboration between party members and female Communists, many of whom had been incarcerated by the Nazis. The work of women's committees, focusing mainly on life-preserving functions, was reclassified as "low politics" as soon as economic conditions stabilized.

Promulgation of the Basic Law institutionalized a return to business and politics as usual after May 1949. Only four Founding Mothers were seated among the sixty-one Founding Fathers comprising the Parliamentary Council. Weimar-veteran Elizabeth Rohde Selbert (SPD) waged a protracted battle to ensure that the sexual-equality mandate found in Article 3 (*1. All persons shall be equal before the law; 2. Men and women shall have equal rights*) would not be anchored to a special protection clause for women. Anne Haag secured the inclusion of Article 4, Abs. 3 (the right to conscientious objection against service with a weapon) in the final draft.

Among the women of "the first hour" entering the Bundestag in 1949 were a number who had served as delegates to the National Assembly and the Reichstag prior to 1933, as well as those who moved into politics by way of their social-welfare careers. The first to preside over the Bundestag, Annemarie Renger (1972–1976), entered parliament in 1953.[10] *Frauenpolitik*—both women's politics and policies for women—centered on issues ranging from economic security for widows, dependents and the disabled, to the allocation of scarce housing. Article 3 GG notwithstanding, the 1957 Equalization of Rights Law specified the importance of a man's responsibilities as "preserver and provider," complemented by a woman's duties as "the female heart of the family" (20% of the female MdBs had children, 60% were single in the late 1950s).[11] The legal requirement that women adhere primarily to *Kinder, Küche und Kirche* roles remained intact until 1977.

The return to a life confined to the home by the mid-1950s was viewed by many women as a well-deserved respite from the multiple burdens of family maintenance during the war and its aftermath. But the return to "normalcy" was also essential for the consolidation of a capitalized industrial labor force.[12] Apathy towards politics was not confined to women: nearly three-fourths of all citizens surveyed in March 1949 expressed "little or no interest" in the constitution; an overwhelming majority knew nothing of its basic contents after ratification.[13] As late as 1965, 69% of the men and 86% of the women polled saw any form of political engagement as "nothing for me"; only 15% and 8%, respectively, indicated they would "gladly participate."[14]

The number of women sworn in as members of the Bundestag rose from 28 to 38 (9%) between 1949 and 1953, and from 45 to 52 (10%) during the second term, 1953–1957. Less than 5% of those seats owed to direct election; most entered parliament via the party-lists drawn up for the second, proportional vote cast. Having adopted a proportionality rule analogous to a "quota" at its 1908 Nuremberg Party Congress, the SPD declared it "no longer necessary" after 1949. The list-vote also helped to seat more women by the end of each legislative period; such replacement delegates [*Nachrückerinnen*] should not be confused with the widows of members who had died or resigned during the four-year term, labeled "coffin-hoppers" by male MdBs.[15]

Women's first decade under the new constitution was a relatively quiet one. The traditional division of labor rooted in gendered private and public spheres met with little opposition, as women became the trickle-down beneficiaries of an Economic Miracle in the making. Heightened Cold War tensions led women to stay the course with Adenauer through the elections of 1957 and 1961. The dialectic of international relations soon imposed a new set of harsh political realities upon women and men, however, suddenly cut off from family and friends by the Berlin Wall. By the end of the 1960s, many a daughter would turn against the role-identification of her mother (despite the latter's war-time display of self-reliance), just as many a son would turn against the political identity of his father (with its implicit respect for the patriarchal-authoritarian state). Both rejections emerged out of the heavy silence encountered by members of the '68 Generation, once they began to ask what daddy had done during the war and, to a lesser extent, why mama refused to talk about it.

Politicized Feminism and the 1960s

At another time, in another place, parental interrogations of the New Left sort might have gone the way of other classical generational conflicts, that is, fading away as a consequence of life-cycle effects. When coupled with SPD demands for "more democracy" and mounting opposition to the Vietnam War, however, young Germans' rejection of parental mores acquired a political significance extending well beyond campus boundaries. Brandt's reform exhortations legitimized pressures for change which had been gathering momentum from below. The 1967 death of FU-student Benno Ohnesorge and the 1968 assassination attempt against "Rudi the Red" Dutschke led to a fusion of disparate groups, increasing their potential for sustained mass protest. The gap between one's constitutional rights to equality and opportunity, on the one hand, and the real-life distribution of postwar wealth and unpaid labor, on the other, would become less tenable in theory and practice, especially for women of the next generation.

The Student Movement brought to light many "discrepancies" undercutting women's search for a more democratic FRG-identity. Comprising one-third of the student body, women attempted to carve out a niche for themselves inside the larger movement, beginning with the so-called children-problem. In January 1968, seven women from the West Berlin SDS created an Action Council for the Liberation of Women, having realized that married female students usually stayed home with the children while their radical men marched out the door to pursue higher causes, like demonstrating and master-minding the revolution.[16] Rather than resign themselves to surrogate modes of participation, women brought their offspring to the February 1968 Congress on Vietnam. They rotated responsibility for some 40 children sent out to play in the lobby of the Technical University, initiating the Berlin Child-Care Cooperative [*Kinderladen*] Movement which quickly spread throughout the city. Organizers coalesced to create local Citizen Initiatives, a hallmark of the New Social Movements over the next decade.[17] Parental activists issued the call for "anti-authoritarian education," a battle-cry that soon worked its way through the schools and into a university system still embracing an academic mission imposed by Humboldt in 1807.

Women took their cause to the 23rd SDS Delegate Conference in Frankfurt (September 1968), demanding an end to exploitation in the "private" as well as in the "public" sphere. Male leaders saw no contradiction between their goal of liberating the world and their expectations that the women at their sides would continue to make their coffee, engage in free (heterosexual) love, and tend children in their communal apartments. When the all-male panel dismissed the women's demands for "lack of a theoretical basis," one appellant responded with a few well-targeted tomatoes from her lunch bag. The move was quickly "seconded" by other female delegates, and within weeks independent women's groups took shape in all major cities.

Second-Wave feminists (as opposed to the First-Wave suffragette movement) were isolated from mainstream wives and mothers by virtue of their elitist university affiliations. Their New-Left ideals also clashed with strong "anti-communist" sentiments, especially in Berlin where the Wall served as a concrete reminder of conditions in the "so-called GDR." Anti-authoritarian activists were hostile to coalitions with elements of "the Establishment." Many women's groups were formed, disbanded and recreated, unable to agree on the best "consciousness-raising" strategy; their divisions gave rise to three distinctive factions (separatist, socialist, moderate).

Academic feminists absorbed the thinking of Betty Friedan, Simone de Beauvoir, and Kate Millett through literature imported from abroad; Alice Schwarzer's book, *The "Little Difference" and Its Major Consequences*, first appeared in 1975.[18] The socialist wing rediscovered the proto-feminist theories of Rosa Luxemburg, Clara Zetkin and August Bebel, but too many in this camp had been prematurely politicized by their association with various university factions (Spartakists, Maoists and other "K-groups"). Radicals refused to consider reforms which did not challenge the patriarchal/capitalist order per se. Polarization intensified to the point of total rupture, leaving behind a political landscape strewn with "wounded" participants. Previous New-Left involvement moreover closed the door on all graduates seeking public-sector employment during the *Berufsverbot* [career blacklisting] period that followed.

The Grand Coalition was an optimistic era for the moderate wing. Organized moderates did join NL-feminists in protests against the Emergency Powers legislation, the anti-Springer campaign and the Vietnam War, but cooperation was short-lived. The 1969 elections drew an unprecedented number of women with varying levels of protest experience into the SPD-fold. Helga Wex (CDU), Hildegard Hamm-Brücher (FDP), and Käte Strobel (SPD) assumed prominent posts in party and government. Women's share of Bundestag mandates nevertheless declined, from 9.4% through the 1961–65 term, to 7.9% between 1965 and 1969 (see Table 6.1). Paradoxically, their share dropped to a postwar low of 6.2% during the first three years of the SPD-FDP coalition–despite its promise to "dare more democracy."

Reform campaigns undertaken by second-wave parliamentarians had a major impact on the social and legal status of mainstream FRG-women, despite their unsuccessful efforts to decriminalize abortion in the early 1970s. Among those who entered the Bundestag between 1969 and 1976 were Marie Schlei (State-Secretary to Chancellor Schmidt, and later Minister for Economic Cooperation); Katharina Focke (SPD Minister for Youth, Family and Health); Antje Huber (Focke's successor after 1976); legal specialist Herta Däubler-Gmelin, consumer advocate Anke Martiny, and FDP-Presid-

TABLE 6.1   Women in the Bundestag, 1949–1990

Parliamentary Seats Held by Women[a]

Election Period	Beginning of Term		End of Term		Directly Elected Single-member Constituency		Ratio of Directly Elected to List-election Members
	Total	%	Total	%	Total	%	
1949–1953	28	6.8	38	9.0	12	5.0	1:01.3
1953–1957	45	8.8	52	10.0	9	3.7	1:04.0
1957–1961	48	9.2	49	9.4	9	3.6	1:04.3
1961–1965	43	8.3	49	9.4	7	2.8	1:05.1
1965–1969	36	6.9	41	7.9	8	3.2	1:03.5
1969–1972	34	6.6	32	6.2	6	2.4	1:04.7
1972–1976	30	5.8	36	6.9	4	2.0	1:06.5
1976–1980	38	7.3	41	7.9	7	2.8	1:04.4
1980–1983	44	8.5	45	8.7	11	4.4	1:03.0
1983–1987	51	9.8	—	—[b]	10	4.0	1:04.1
1987–1990	75	15.4	83	16.0[c]	17	6.8	1:04.4

[a] As a percentage of all directly and proportional elected seats.
[b] Not available
[c] As of June 1988

Source: Adapted from Peter Schindler, Datenbuch zur Geschichte des Deutschen Bundestages, 1949 bis 1982 (Baden-Baden: Nomos, 1984) and Datenbuch zur Geschichte des Deutschen Bundestages 1980–1984 (Baden-Baden: Nomos, 1986); 1987 data were graciously provided by the Informationsdienst des Landtags Baden-Württemberg.

ium member Liselotte Funcke. Efforts to formalize women's nonpartisan or
inter-party cooperation were modest at best. Their actions nonetheless led
to critical statutory reforms, gradually aligning FRG social policy with the
equal-rights imperative of the Basic Law.[19] By 1975 only 29% (Emnid sample) characterized the ideal woman as a "good housewife."[20]

Autonomous Feminism and the 1970s

The 1970s brought a new emphasis on *self-identity*, set in motion by the
proliferation of autonomous groups. Countless Initiatives were born
(*Women against Rape, Housework for Pay, Women in Technical Professions,
Aid for Turkish Women*), matched by the creation of feminist publishing
houses, journals (*Courage, Emma*), cafes, bars and art galleries. Though the
stress on *project-activism* solidified divisions between system-oriented reformists and radical separatists, involvement in feminist projects helped
many women to acquire key organizational skills, familiarity with state-administrative procedures, as well as a sensitivity to public relations and re-
source-mobilization processes.[21]

University campuses witnessed a rapid profusion of "Sponti" groups
[Spontaneous Ones], heralding the arrival of a new anti-ideological, issue-
oriented protest generation. The second Student Movement was quite wary
of the highly organized, overtly cerebral, and ultimately "no-fun" character
of the (old) New Left movement. The "Spontis'" affinity for small-is-beautiful thinking led them to prefer loose coalitions with neighborhood BIs
over mass meetings prior to the 1980 birth of the Greens. These groups,
concentrating on environmental protection, opened their membership to
anyone willing to work for the common cause.

Still dependent upon backdoor, list-system access to power, women
would close out the decade with only 7.9% of the Bundestag seats. By 1980,
67% of the men and 40% of the women polled were open to the idea of a female Federal-Chancellor; 30% and 45%, respectively, felt that gender should
not matter.[22] A body of parliamentary veterans evincing "distinctly ministerial qualities," in MdB Peter Conradi's words, began to move into governmental, party-executive, and state-administrative offices. No longer willing
to confine themselves to the role of homemakers or consciousness-raisers,
the women of the 1980s would commence their own "long march through
the institutions." Moved by issues far from the kitchen, they would mobilize
their children and their churches, carving out new identities for themselves
as national policymakers in the process.

Pragmatic Feminism and the 1980s

The Federal Republic offers no exception to the Law of Increasing Dispro-
portions: the higher the rung on the political ladder, the smaller the number
of women found in office, irrespective of their formal qualifications. Their

university enrollments rose from 26.7% in 1969 to 38.8% by 1979; by 1983, four-fifths of the female MdBs possessed higher educational degrees, in contrast to two-thirds of the men.[23] While amendments to the 1976 Framework for Higher Education Law barred discrimination in the hiring and promotion of female academics, lawmakers refused to block a lowering of state-exam grade requirements for would-be judges, once women began to overtake male applicants. Nor would they alter the cut-off rule at age—32 for civil service entry, ignoring the realities of female "life-cycles."[24] The subset of female judges and administrators grew from 13.3% (1969), to 18.9% (1975) and 20.5% (1983); women's share of part-time positions in federal civil-service increased from 82.3% to 92.2%, to 93.1% over the same periods.[25]

The Kohl Government first discovered an FRG gender gap in the wake of the very election that brought conservatives back to power after thirteen years. Female turn-out rates once again equaled those of men as of 1972, but by 1983 women exceeded men in absolute numbers, comprising 53.8% of all eligible voters. What distinguished the CDU/CSU's New Partnership between Man and Woman from earlier platforms was its embrace of women's participation in the paid labor market (52% of the adult females). Conservatives were quick to stress that such workforce activity should remain "flexible" (part-time), and that women desiring a life of *Kinder* and *Küche* had to be guaranteed "freedom of choice." Rita Süssmuth (CDU) became immensely popular, first as the Minister for Youth, Family, Health and Women (1985–1988), and then as President of the Bundestag.

The FDP has proved least effective in attracting the women's vote, although it evinced a higher percentage of female MdBs than the CDU/CSU by 1987. The low profile of Liberal women derives in part from the waning of the party as a whole, its electoral fortunes having been sorely tested by another party willing to coalesce with the SPD, the Greens. Like their Union peers, FDP women associate their own prospects for electoral success with "personal effort," while SPD and Green women attribute limited opportunities to "a male-dominated party culture."[26]

Beyond their support for *Frauenförderung* [affirmative action] in the educational and economic sectors, Social Democratic women pushed for female advances within the party. The Working Group of Socialist Women (ASF) successfully lobbied for a quota of "at least 40%" vis-à-vis all party offices by 1994, and all parliamentary seats by 1998. The pros and cons of intra-party quotas were hotly debated between older and younger parliamentarians. Vehement opposition voiced by one member of the Economic-Miracle Generation, Annemarie Renger, contrasted sharply with the qualified-to-enthusiastic support exhibited by women who had entered the Bundestag between 1969 and 1980. Quotas and "positive discrimination" were unanimously accepted among those whose mandates began with the 1983 and 1987 elections (based on this author's observations at key meetings).

The Greens have been the most successful in opening party offices to women, as well as in placing a wide range of feminist issues on the electoral agenda. Both the modified rotation principle (no more than one term in office) and the zipper principle (the alternation of female-male candidates on the "list" ballot) catapulted Long-Marchers like Petra Kelly, Antje Vollmer, Waltraud Schoppe, Eva Quistorp and Jutta Ditfurth into positions of prominence at state and national levels. Women demonstrated their political competence by way of the 1984 all-female Bundestag executive committee [*das Feminat*] and the all-female slate in Hamburg [called *die frechen Frauen*], which garnered a record 10% of the vote—though both were perceived by male Greens as "a totally crazy experiment."[27]

Long-March legislators have not only proved more self-assertive than their predecessors; they also display an "understanding of politics" often transcending class and party lines. Lacking the powerful class-action suit mechanism found in the USA, they developed their own network of legal advocates through the creation of over 230 municipal, state and academic Commissioners for Women's Affairs or Equal Opportunity Offices. They generated their own databases through Women's Studies projects, professional conferences and Bundestag inquiries. Pragmatic feminists of the Turn-Around Generation, emerging by the mid-1980s, are even less susceptible to all-or-nothing perceptions of power which had afflicted the feminists of earlier eras (perceived by the actors themselves as typically German). Their affiliation with diverse NSM organizations have provided a wealth of experiences with respect to both conventional and unconventional forms of participation.

The two decades preceding unity saw a steady increase in the number of women campaigning for the Bundestag. Accounting for 8.9% (207) of all candidates in 1949, 9.5% (249) in 1969, and 20.1% (592) in 1980, their numbers reached a high of 25.4% (685) by early 1987; the bloc of seats occupied by female MdBs grew from 9.8% to 15.4%.[28] By 1989 women held over 300 mandates in the national and state-level assemblies, 64% of whom had attained elected office after the onset of the 1983 quota-debate.[29] Yet even with a 3.5 million voter surplus, had women continued to gain political offices at the same rate that had characterized their progress since 1949, they could not have expected to achieve full parity before the year 2107![30]

In addition to modifying that calculation significantly, the anti-Pershing protests of 1983/84, followed by the national paradigm shift of 1989/90 would eventually give new meaning to the term "women's issues." Millions of West German women came to internalize post-materialist values irrespective of their party-affiliation, namely, a commitment to ecological preservation, social justice, grassroots democracy, and non-violence. No longer limited to hearth and playground, they would add to their list of "special interests" the problems of radiation exposure, toxic pollution, the perils of local nuclear "theaters" and structural unemployment. Persuaded that all citizens have a right to participate in determinations of the national interest, women would move towards a concept of security no longer defined in military terms. Let us now consider the national security needs voiced by FRG women prior to unification.

National Security as a Women's Issue: Saying No to NATO?

Any treatment of women as political actors needs to distinguish between the largely apolitical mainstream and those counting themselves among the well-informed, activist core. Women's anti-militarist orientations preceded the NATO Double Track decision, as evidenced by their involvement in the protest campaigns of the 1950s and 1960s. They did not function as an independent peace force until the 1970s, however. Increased access to higher education reduced gender differences with respect to "interest in politics," causing women to emerge as salient critics of West German national security policy.[31]

One outstanding example from the Economic Miracle Generation is theologian and Third-World activist, Dorothee Sölle (born in 1929). Following the "typical zigzag" of female biographies, Sölle completed university studies and bore three children during the Stop Atomic Death era of the 1950s, became an outspoken opponent of the Vietnam war in the 1960s, and emerged as a national spokesperson against INF deployments in the 1980s—punctuated by stints as a visiting professor at the Union Theological Seminary in New York.[32] She resumed her anti-war activism in reaction to the 1991 Gulf War and in response to violence in the former Yugoslav Republic.

Mainstream women and men of the 1960s and 1970s derived their perceptions of *Angst* from different sources. From the male vantage point (as far as survey data allow us to judge these things), the primary danger was seen to lie with ideological factors and Western military inferiority. From the female perspective, the key threat was seen to lie in the nature of the military itself.[33] A decade later men would remain fearful of potential Eastern military superiority over the West, while women believed that the best chance for preserving European peace lay in the elimination of nuclear weapons per se (60% among women versus 49% among men).[34] This is not to argue that women are "natural" peace-makers, however. During the same era a second albeit much smaller group of woman surfaced, posing a self-styled threat to domestic security under the banner of left-terrorism.

In addition to fostering an articulate coterie of unconventional yet democratic protesters like Petra Kelly, Eva Quistorp and Antje Vollmer, the Long March Generation produced a special class of radical-militant activists. Women made up a significant segment of the terrorist scene in both its first and second-wave manifestations, the *Baader-Meinhof* Gang and the Red Army Faction/2nd of June Movement. The best known BMG-leader was

SDS member-journalist-mother Ulrike Meinhof (born in 1934), whose descent into terrorism followed in the wake of the anti-Emergency Laws campaign of 1968. Another member of the BMG's hard-core was Gudrun Ensslin (born in 1940), a pastor's daughter, mother and student of German literature. Though both commited suicide in the Stammheim prison in 1979, they were quickly replaced by other women willing to engage in violent protest.[35] Marginal in terms of their numbers, female terrorists did elicit sympathetic support among better educated leftists, inciting an intense debate among activists over the relation between violent means and peaceful ends.

Added to the Basic Law in 1956 (tied to the creation of the Bundeswehr), Article 12a/3 GG explicitly barred women from military service involving weapons or combat forces. It left open the possibility of their voluntary service, resulting in the employment of some 80,000 women by 1960, as clerical, medical and kitchen personnel. The debate over the 1968 Emergency Laws raised the question as to whether women could exempt themselves from "service" in the event of a national crisis. Article 80a GG mandated that women could not only be compelled to render service as civilian laborers (as medical workers or food suppliers) in a "case of defense" but also during the prior stage of "heightened tensions." Because Article 12a/4 GG excluded women from service with a weapon, they were denied the right to conscientious-objector status afforded by Article 4/3 GG.

A majority of the public opposed women's incorporation into the military during times of peace but tended to support their training in the use of arms in the event of war. Polled at the time "universal" conscription was introduced, 38% of a 1963 Allensbach sample favored peace-time training for women without weapons; 52% supported such instruction in times of war. Only 3% accepted the idea that women's training should involve weapons, whether or not peace prevailed; the sexes were equally divided over the question.[36] Few seemed to consider the possibility that women receiving peace-time instruction in the use of weapons would probably defend themselves and the homeland more effectively than those just learning once they were under attack. In 1975 the Bundestag approved a law enabling women to pursue the military's medical career-track; it also declared them eligible for officer's status but otherwise left their obligations intact.

Mounting concerns over the FRG's ability to meet its "manpower" obligation to NATO soon triggered a new debate concerning the recruitment of women by the armed forces. A 1978 cover-story in *Der Spiegel* highlighted the military implications of the *Pillenknick*, i.e., the rapid decrease in births due to widespread use of "the anti-Baby Pill."[37] The pool of male recruits was expected to shrink to 259,000 by 1990 and 177,000 by 1994, making it impossible for the Bundeswehr to meet its quota of 495,000 active-duty conscripts. Defense-Minister Hans Apel began a search for ways to overcome the shortfall, bolstered by the German Bundeswehr Association's proposal for a universal, one-year "national-community service" obligation.

The year 1979 was characterized by two distinctive reactions: "the military look" dominated the fashion scene (implying the compatibility of women and army-life), and feminists undertook their own recruitment drive for a new initiative, "Women in the Bundeswehr—We say No!" According to one IfD survey, 16% of the public (9% of the women, hereafter F, 23% of the men, henceforth M) favored a service obligation for women including their use of weapons, while 76% objected (83% F, 68% M). The alternative, conscription for women specifically excluding weapons-duties, was accepted by 43% (37% F, 50% M) and rejected by 50% (55% F, 43% M). Older respondents voiced stronger opposition to both options.[38]

Arguments for and against female recruitment fell along four axes. The first position, upholding the legitimacy and necessity of the Bundeswehr's existence, stressed that women's ability to participate in this power-exercising institution be ensured on a voluntary basis (the view of second-generation SPD and CDU women). The second accepted the Bundeswehr as essential to national security but rejected an extension of women's roles beyond existing opportunities in the medical and clerical sectors (the view of first-generation figures like Liselotte Funcke and Annemarie Renger). The third and fourth positions testified to a split within the feminist movement itself. Alice Schwarzer cast the Bundeswehr as an institution which deliberately sought to exclude women from the ultimate exercise of power, at the same time it promoted an ideological "macho-mentality" as a prerequisite for participation in power. Demanding equal access to these springboards in principle, Schwarzer claimed that she would file for conscientious-objector status if conscripted in practice. The final posture was articulated by the pacifist wing, represented by Mechthild Jansen, Petra Kelly and Sibylle Plogstedt, which saw the recruitment of women as a further step in the militarization of civil society. This camp emphasized the need for disarmament, along with an end to the private-sphere manifestations of "structural violence" (rape, harassment and discrimination) against women in general.[39]

Thus the foundation had already been laid for an independent female response to questions of defense and disarmament prior to the implementation of the 1979 NATO decision. By the 1980s women had begun to cultivate alternative definitions of security focusing on the larger issue of structural violence. Their proposals derived from self-organized congresses, local anti-nuclear initiatives, or from knowledge acquired through other environmental action groups.[40] The anti-Pershing campaign brought a wave of publications addressing the historical dimensions as well as the theoretical parameters of feminist pacifism.[41] The idea of a "defense duty" for women still met with broad rejection as late as 1987, with some 60% against, according to Emnid figures. By then, however, the public's reason for opposing such service was no longer vested in the traditional image of women as mothers and home-makers; it was rooted instead in the growing support for détente and disarmament processes, coupled with a desire to "demilitarize" national security policy as a whole.

Profiles of the "Economic Miracle Generation"

My own interviews with prominent political women took place between the height of the peace movement in 1983 and the promulgation of the 1987 Intermediate Nuclear Forces Treaty. At a minimum, these discussions revealed that there is no such thing as "the" women's position regarding questions of national security and identity. While the broader distinctions of gender + generation have been treated in earlier chapters, it is important to consider the "contextual" aspects of national security-thinking among women, that is, the differential effects of socialization under the Reconstruction, Cold War, and détente eras. My characterizations, based on eight individual profiles and one group portrait, are divided into four parts, addressing personal background, national-identity perceptions, each person's ties to the GDR, and specific military-security themes.

Dr. Mzrion Gräfin Dönhoff: Identity Perceptions

Let us begin with Dr. Marion Gräfin Dönhoff, born December 2, 1909 in Friedrichstein/East-Prussia (interviewed on December 18, 1986 at the *Pressehaus* in Hamburg). Having traveled though the USA, Europe and Eastern Africa, Countess Dönhoff undertook studies in Frankfurt and Basel, completing her doctorate in 1935. She began managing the family estate of Friedrichstein (East of Königsberg, now Polish territory) in 1939 but was forced to flee on horseback in January 1945 to avoid the advancing Soviet Army. Having worked with the Resistance, she enjoyed a "clear record," and was thus deemed qualified to join the staff of what would become the FRG's premier weekly, *Die Zeit*, in 1946. Dönhoff became an editor-in-chief as of 1969, advancing to the position of publisher in 1972, a post she still holds as of this writing. She has authored several books dealing with topics as wide-ranging as the Prussian legacy, German-American relations, and the struggle against apartheid in South Africa; characterized by others as a strong pro-Atlanticist, she expressed no party affiliation.

According to Dr. Dönhoff, the renewed fixation with German identity in the early 1980s emerged, in part, out of the ennui which eventually overtakes many artists, intellectuals and even historians, causing them to resurrect old, provocative questions anew. In her assessment, the German Question [GQ] and its inevitable side-kick, reunification, was viewed more realistically abroad than at home. Efforts to define the GQ testified to major dissensus between the United States and the Federal Republic over operational issues, with the latter putting primary emphasis on tension-reduction, arms control and the normalization of East-West relations. The fueling of emotions stemming from the INF deployments, coupled with a mounting desire for disarmament, did mean that the interest in *deutsche Identität* was no longer restricted to intellectuals. The "new national-patriots," in her judgment, combined two disparate themes: thinkers on the Right found their roots in older traditions of nationalism, while the Left upheld the vision of the *Internationale*, that is, "a stronger orientation towards an independent Europe."

As one who had experienced Germany both whole and divided, Marion Dönhoff felt no need for a national consciousness, observing that most Germans had had this feeling "driven out of them" by the Nazi experience. She held that "more international thinking" had become the norm among postwar Germans, and that the proximity of neighbors, as well as the recollection of their frequent wars against each other, reinforced a proclivity for "caution." Citing Poland as a counter-example, she warned that national consciousness was often "strongly cultivated from above," and also manipulated; the "solidarity" witnessed among younger people (especially those involved in social movements) seemed a bit more "normal."

Dr. Dönhoff found it hard to judge why individuals would need a German identity, claiming she would be just as satisfied living in England. She recognized though that constitutional patriotism might not adequately replace a need for emotional ties, since few citizens are intensely familiar with the Basic Law; most appeared to have regional attachments, somehow held together through history and language. As to her own identity, the Countess described herself as a "German at home in Europe" who views the FRG "as the best state we ever had." She did not "feel" like a Federal Republican per se, as happy as she was that the new state had proved such a success. She praised von Weizsäcker's commemorative address of 1985 as a significant contribution to historical rectification, "the best speech held in Germany since the end of the war." The address made no attempt to cover-up the nation's ignominious history, thereby presenting a balanced self-picture to the world.

This highly respected publicist had "good friends" in the GDR, whose citizens she perceived to "have borne the entire burden of division." Although her own irregular visits had been confined mostly to East Berlin, she did not feel a "need to catch up" concerning the specifics of GDR-life, a condition typical of the general public. Her interest in Eastern developments had been relatively constant, but she saw a sharp increase in school-class visits as indicative of new interest among younger citizens. Though labeling the system itself "absurd," she was impressed by a GDR-specific sense of solidarity enabling most people to "get by" despite chronic shortages. She did not believe in either the possibility or the inevitability of reunification, emphasizing as more important the goal of transforming the GDR into a pluralist-democratic society. Her prognosis for the future embraced

280 Generational Differences and the Gender Gap

two German states in a European framework; she harbored "no personal ambitions to be surrounded by 80 million Germans" which she suspected would only engender international complications. Still, Dr. Dönhoff saw little prospect for eliminating the Preamble to the Basic Law, observing that anyone who attempted to delete it would likely be stamped a "traitor"; at best, one could "leave it be but not talk about it. . . . Nobody knows what can happen in history over the next twenty years." The idea of consummating a peace treaty four decades after the war struck her as impossible and "utopian."

Reaction to the USA and Nato Doctrines

Marion Dönhoff attributed the growing perception that Europeans ought to stick closer together not only to their common history but also to mounting political criticism vis-à-vis the United States (e.g., over Reagan's bombing of Libya). European cooperation had to be recognized as a significant variable in its own right, a position also espoused by her friend, Henry Kissinger. Though somewhat irritated by constant US pressures to sway German foreign policy, she rejected characterizations of the FRG as "an occupied state" as outrageous [unverschämt]. She would not, however, "scream out loud" against a 50% reduction of troops, consonant with her belief that a "tripwire" would suffice to keep the United States involved in German defense. Having "many good friends" there, she visited the USA at least twice a year; but she was disturbed by a degree of "American cultural imperialism"—especially the negative influences transmitted through violent TV programs, harmful to children.

As one routinely preoccupied with security themes, this veteran journalist believed that concepts like a community of responsibility, common security and security-partnership all "made sense," envisioning the two German states as separated but seeking community. In her view, these ideas had been intentionally misinterpreted by then-President Reagan and Defense-Secretary Weinberger, who failed to reflect on the prerequisites for their attainment. At the time of the interview, Dr. Dönhoff could have easily imagined a nuclear weapons–free Germany, expanding geographically over the years. Asserting that one would have to start somewhere, she thought that this first step would find great acceptance in both the East and West, contrasted with "the insane amounts of money [spent] for arms, and no feels one iota more secure." She rejected unilateral disarmament but favored a gradual push towards a nuclear-free Europe, recognizing that such decisions could only be taken at the highest collective level. The acceptance of a neutral Germany would depend on broader processes of demilitarization; she could envision the two German states undergoing a mutual withdrawal from their respective alliances "one of these days," albeit in conjunction with a dissolution of the military blocs. She urged leaders to recognize the "historical moment" afforded by pragmatically-oriented Gorbachev, who had already undertaken tremendous risks and "would not think for a moment" of rekindling war in Europe.

Dr. Dönhoff characterized the proposed SDI system as absolute *Quatsch* [nonsense], and accepted nuclear deterrence only if coupled with a no-first-use policy. She supported the idea of greater independence from the US by way of a European Defense Union, rejecting American charges of German "equidistance"—noting that no one in the FRG would want to give up the Western way of life. As to the West Germans' perceptions of their own normalcy, national self-acceptance would continue to depend on their geo-strategic position. In the Gräfin's final assessment, it would take at least two more generations before Germans would be deemed absolutely "normal" by other states and peoples, a process likewise embedded in geo-strategic considerations.

Dr. Ursula Besser: Identity Perceptions

My second profile focuses on Dr. Ursula Roggenbuck Besser, born January 5, 1917 in Berlin; we spoke together for five hours at her home in West Berlin on October 29, 1986. Like the previous interviewee, Ursula Besser experienced World War II first hand, having been bombed out of her apartment twice as a student. She married in 1937, becoming a widow with two children by 1942; she was also forced to flee Mecklenburg as the "Red Army" advanced westward but returned to Berlin at war's end. Though admitted to the Humboldt University, she fled a second time, from East to West Berlin in 1951. In contrast to the without-me orientations embraced by most of her peers, Dr. Besser became a hard-line Christian Democrat early on, drawn to the party "because [she] thought internationally." She held a seat for many years in the Berlin state-assembly, where I had first encountered her in 1977 as the CDU's higher educational expert.

Though instigated by intellectuals, the reemergence of the German Question, in Dr. Besser's view, reflected a pressing need on the part of younger cohorts, anxious to return to normalcy after forty years of nationhood-denied. She had observed a renewed student interest in the study of history as of 1978, which she construed as an antidote to their psychologically unsatisfying status as "timeless Germans." This politician defined *die deutsche Frage* in terms of closer cooperation with Europe, not as a return to the conditions of 1937 (which she nonetheless related to a right of self-determination). The real GQ had to orient itself to a common future for all Germans, even if no one knew how this was to be achieved; she mentioned "joint ventures" as a possible starting point. Anything less amounted to a never-ending interim solution, perpetuating a vacuum in national feeling which carried its own security perils. With an oblique reference to times past, Dr. Besser held that "courage [*Tapferkeit*] had unfortunately acquired a negative reputation," yet she believed division could be overcome "without the use of gunpowder." A feeling of self-worth is a prerequisite for one's own defense, she noted, hence the positive turn back to history.

Regaining identity and rejecting international utopias was important for the Atlantic Alliance since the Germans had to understand their own place within that community. The search for identity was not a topic that moved everyone, nor did it constitute a "personal emergency" for the majority; it was driven instead by minorities. Ideas generated by thinkers in Berlin were not "typical" because even workers there were likely to have some contacts in East; the city itself had become something of a myth, owing to its abnormal status.

In Besser's judgment, differences between Right- and Left-wing patriots were age-related, reflecting their varying degrees of historical knowledge and diverse life experiences; what the neo-nationalists nonetheless shared was a "yearning for a way of housing their identities." Their thinking was not always democratic; some evinced hierarchical, absolutist inclinations: While Peter Brandt hoped for international socialism, Wolfgang Venohr had no such ideological affinity; both overlooked the dangers of a "neutrality-dream," in her view.

As to national consciousness, Besser insisted that "there is no people on the face of the earth without one [even in] real-existing socialist states like Poland and Hungary." It would fly against nature to expect the Germans alone to do without. German identity should enable individuals to find their place in a specific state-community, foster discipline, the ability to obey and sacrifice, and ensure a capacity to act in a traditional sense; it provides substance for the functionality of the state, personal affirmation and engagement. Her own feelings of national identity had not been altered by developments of the last four decades: she perceived herself then and now as a German, as one stemming from the region of Pommern, who knew "the Memmel" of which the (banned) verses of the national anthem sang. Dr. Besser did not perceive herself as a Federal Republican: "For me Germany as a whole still lives," despite its special phase in history as divided nation. Both of her daughters had been born "over there" [in the East] and had therefore been sensitized to an over-arching German consciousness.

At the time of the interview, Ursula Besser no longer had living relatives in the East, nor was she allowed to visit the graves of those who had died. As an acting politician, she claimed she had "no time" to make use of her 30-day visiting rights as a Berliner. Her interest in the GDR was nonetheless as constant as her "hardline reaction against the Russians." She professed a fundamental belief in reunification, that "one day" common feeling would overcome the division; she found the term *Wiedervereinigung* more honest than talk of a confederation. The Preamble was to be valued internationally for its contribution to maintaining balance between the two parts, in the face of the Cold War.

Curiously, Dr. Besser was highly critical of fellow CDU-member Richard von Weizsäcker, both in terms of that family's history and its widely-touted religious engagement which, in her view, had not resulted in a strong stand against the Nazis [author's note: the now retired FRG-President established his reputation by serving as his father's defense lawyer at the Nuremburg Trials]. She dismissed "the Speech" as the latter's attempt to work through his own guilt as well as that of the whole, as "fishing for compliments" by meeting the expectations of international community. Being German could not be defined merely on the basis of fifteen years of historical travesty. Dr. Besser favored a reorientation in the presentation of German history, which would treat the imperatives of the times and ensure minorities their proper place, while also allowing Germans a chance to reestablish their sense of self-worth, grounded in cultural achievements, for example. This would assist in creating positive role models for the next generation.

Reaction to the USA and NATO Doctrines

Ursula Besser characterized the problem of US-cultural imperialism as "too much of a good thing" but explained the pervasive foreign influences on FRG language and music as reflective of the Germans' own insecurity; in the long run German culture would need to rediscover its own "national" identity. Her travels to the USA were irregular ("no time"), though she did attempt to cultivate professional and academic contacts. This Berliner did perceive her homeland as an "occupied state," based on the Reserved Rights of the Four Powers which had rendered it a land of limited sovereignty since 1949. While the withdrawal of US troops was "unthinkable" under existing international conditions, she favored an extension of Bundeswehr capabilities, claiming it would foster the discovery of national identity "since every country must be able to defend itself." A peace treaty, she insisted, was "indispensable," the failure to conclude such an accord having been "one of the major mistakes" of the postwar period. The lack of a final settlement had contributed to the rise of two new identities and had raised precarious questions as a great source of insecurity by 1985 because of a (then-tense) international situation.

Representative Besser found the idea of a nuclear weapons-free Germany of limited use "since Germans possess none"; atomic weapons were necessary to pose a credible threat, should politics fail, but not sufficient as a direct security mechanism. As "the wife of a soldier" she had never favored nuclear arms because they afforded no effective means of personal self-defense; she opposed the incorporation of women into the military, on the argument that they would be needed to care for the elderly, the sick, and the wounded. Her ability to envision a neutral Germany depended on the overarching distribution of power between East and West; neutrality was inconceivable in 1986.

Although the Kohl Government did not always avoid its use, this CDU-official labeled the term *Verantwortungsgemeinschaft* an "absolute slang-word." It presented a contradiction in terms, since each state was ultimately responsible for itself in the international concert of nations; the idea of a security partnership likewise obfuscated irreconcilable bloc-differences. Besser credited nuclear deterrence with having maintained the peace since 1949 and dismissed any desire to increase the FRG's independence vis-à-vis the United States as "unrealistic." She rejected proposed troop reductions as well as atomic-veto rights; a European Defense Union intentionally excluding the United States could not function, she claimed. A nuclear-free Europe would only be conceivable if SDI "worked;" she insisted that unilateral disarmament was nonsense, concluding that "suicide would achieve same effect faster."

Ursula Besser's predictions regarding an eventual return to normalcy hinged in part on generational factors. "How long" and "how quickly" this process might ensue depended on the framework conditions, that is, on the speed used in cultivating greater community and consciousness in Europe. Her best guess set the interval at ten to fifteen years, with the footnote that "as soon as Germans perceive themselves as normal they will immediately alter their behavior accordingly."

Renate Finchk: Identity Perceptions

My third profile centers on Renate Finchk, born in 1926 in Ulm, a representative of the silent but not indifferent majority. The interview (supplemented by comments from her husband) took place at her home outside of Stuttgart on November 27, 1986. In contrast to the consistently anti-fascist orientations of Dönhoff and Besser, Renate Finchk admitted to a strong affinity for National-Socialism during her youth. Her personal complicity with the regime involved active membership in the *Bund Deutscher Mädel*, the female division of the Hitler Youth. Having spent the war years in Southern Germany, her family was not affected by the bombing until 1942; hardship was sooner a question of food supplies. She experienced a virtual loss of identity with the collapse of the Hitler regime, shocked by the nature and extent of the atrocities she had unknowingly supported.

Although few comprehended themselves as Nazis after 1947, in her assessment, the emotional strains afflicting an entire generation socialized during this era remained. Three decades later, as wife and mother of eight children, Finchk had authored two books based on her own experiences in the BDM and the loss of identity conditioned by a shattered family life. "The more we tried to recount our experiences, the less our own children understood"—her own motivation for putting those experiences to paper. By the 1980s she had found a new identification, through the peace movement, since she resided just outside the Pershing II deployment area of Neu-Ulm.

This former Nazi-enthusiast speculated that the identity issue had been raised anew by the TV-airing of "Holocaust" in the late 1970s. It was hard to define the German Question in terms of reunification, a goal Adenauer himself had rejected, she pointed out. She was personally ambivalent as to a need for national consciousness, a concept "too tainted by the past." Yet she was quite disturbed by her children's reprimand "that [they] don't know what it means to be German." She linked the idea to a need for belonging, under the roof of a common language, history and destiny, which evokes a sense of responsibility and personal engagement. Having once embraced an intense if tragic German identity, she later sympathized with certain segments of the Student Movement, realizing that the price paid to establish a democratic Federal Republic had been too high to be thrown overboard for the kind of emotional identification she had known. Based on her childhood, she felt like a German but preferred to classify herself as a human, as a Christian, as a European. Von Weizsäcker's efforts to evaluate the past had "spoken out of her own heart," turning away from the customary vent of "anti-communism" and redressing the burden of proof. A processing of the rest of the German past, still necessary for successor generations, could only be achieved "milimeter by milimeter." She was uncertain as to how her children might characterize their own identities, as Germans or as Federal Republicans.

Finckh's personal contacts with distant relatives in East Berlin had been cultivated by her mother through years of package-sending and letter-writing. It was not until 1977 that she first took advantage of an opportunity to visit, traveling with two of her children to Stralsund and the Baltic Sea; a few of her offspring visited later of their own accord. All of them seemed interested in the other Germany, "but their interest has become more normal," meaning that they viewed Easterners as partners, "not as those who need to be provided for."

As the proverbial "average citizen," Finchk no longer believed in reunification, beyond an increasing measure of Europeanization. She had not given much thought to the Preamble but, once questioned, felt it was best to strike the problematic passage, to enable both states to exercise an important "fruitful influence" upon each other. Signaling her own ambivalence, she then noted that "in spite of everything . . . the GDR remained a piece of our own country—*ein Stuck Inland*."

Reactions to the USA and NATO Doctrines

Frau Finckh was as "mad as a boar" [*Sauwut*] when it came to American cultural domination, e.g., the expropriation of FRG-television; but she also saw the overarching identification with the US as an ersatz-identity of sorts.

She had visited Wisconsin once, and one daughter attended college in the States; some of her other children were "not so friendly towards America," however. Finckh had the impression of living in an "occupied state"—locally deployed troops and missiles (Pershing IIs) served as empirical evidence. While outright opposed to the nukes, she thought troop withdrawals would only make sense if coupled with fundamental economic reforms vis-à-vis the Third World and with the establishment of a world peace order. She wanted no strengthening of the Bundeswehr, the prospect of which awakened memories of the former military "state within a state."

As to a final peace treaty, Citizen Finchk was sure "that train had departed long ago," since not even the superpowers could directly eliminate the existing blocs. She lauded the idea of a nuclear-free Germany, projecting that one could be achieved fairly quickly, once the SPD returned to power. She commended the peace movement for stressing a need for "reform from below," through peace education. A neutralized Germany, by contrast, would only be desirable on the basis of a radically reformed economic order. She considered SDI "rubbish," as the liquidator of much needed capital, and described nuclear deterrence as a self-inflicted danger. She favored the idea of greater independence from the USA, the formation of a European Defense Community, troop reductions, as well as a German veto over the use of nuclear weapons. She welcomed a denuclearization of Europe, and advocated unilateral disarmament as a risky but critical step—as one "who would rather be occupied by the Russians than the victim of an atomic bomb."

The question of normalization would be complicated by declining German birthrates and new issues like the integration of foreign workers. Renate Finchk concluded that her country would only be viewed as "normal" by other states once the latter felt they could become "lazy" about monitoring Germany's actions, inside and out.

Dr. Hildegard Hamm-Brücher: Identity Perceptions

The final profile from the Economic Miracle Generation is that of Dr. Hildegard Hamm-Brücher, born on May 11, 1921 in Essen; the interview took place at her Bundestag office in Bonn on December 16, 1986. Her parents already deceased, Hildegard Hamm-Brücher was in her early twenties during the war; separated from her three brothers, she was bombed out of her living quarters several times in Munich. Hard times notwithstanding, she completed a Ph.D. in Chemistry in 1945, but her first job was that of a free-lance reporter. Dr. Hamm-Brücher assumed her initial political post in 1948, as an FDP delegate to the Munich City Council, interrupted by the chance to spend 1949/50 as an exchange student at Harvard University. Her professional record includes over twenty years of service as an elected delegate to the Bavarian State Assembly, three years as a State-Secretary for

Education and Science, and six years as State-Minister in the Ministry of Foreign Affairs under Genscher, after which she returned to her seat in the Bundestag. In 1975 she became a member of the Presidium of the German Evangelical (Lutheran) Church. Married with two children, this veteran parliamentarian managed to travel extensively, in addition to authoring ten books and numerous essays.

Dr. Hamm-Brücher interpreted the resurgence of the German Question in the early 1980s as a negative replay of the 1950s, that is, as an effort on the part of Conservatives to "relativize" the question of guilt. She did not attribute its rebirth to the peace movement, which she claimed "no longer existed" by 1986. This politician defined the GQ in terms of division, emphasizing the ongoing need to render its effects more bearable while accepting the "provisional" Federal Republic as a permanent Fatherland in its own right. The "middle generation" seemed particularly susceptible to the new arguments, although she welcomed renewed public debate as advantageous for the strengthening of postwar democracy. The identity issue did not really seem to be of major interest to average citizens, regrettable as that was.

National consciousness—based on language, history, culture—served as a vehicle for holding together diverse social elements, when used to greatest advantage; its potential for misuse would lie in its quality as an ersatz-religion. At the personal level, she had sensed "no more national feeling" since Hitler. Although she believed neither in the possibility of reunification, nor in the prospect of a peace treaty, she was prepared to retain the Preamble rather than abandon all aspects of its vision at once.

This left open the question as to why one might need a German identity, in particular. The democratic institutions were not yet so entrenched in personal consciousness, Hamm-Brücher lamented, because the Germans themselves had not struggled to establish them. Younger citizens were much cooler towards both, leading her to stress the need for more education. The interim phase of building a constitutional consensus concentrated largely on rights and duties, not identity. The FDP stateswoman identified herself as a European democrat in a German-speaking domain. As one who had suffered too much disappointment over other forms of nationalism, her own sense of political loyalty was grounded in the free-democratic order.

Though she hailed from a different party, Hamm-Brücher knew von Weizsäcker's speech "practically by heart" (based on the Evangelical-Lutheran position), and embraced it in its totality. Beyond offering guidelines for the conduct of practical politics, its most positive feature was the theme of "personal responsibility," rooted in the works of Niebuhr and Niemöller. "Working through the past" was a task that had never been directly undertaken by the political leadership; instead it was an assignment left to individuals and the media. "Reconciliation has recollection as its prerequisite," she observed.

Dr. Hamm-Brücher had spent part of her youth in Dresden but by 1986 had no more relatives in the East, though she continued to cultivate relations with school comrades and contacts linked to her church involvement. She had traveled to the GDR/East Berlin a few times in an official capacity but had not undertaken any private visits. Her interest in the real-existing socialist system was professional in character, linked to writings about the GDR school system.

Reactions to the USA and NATO Doctrines

This veteran parliamentarian visited the United States (where she has limited family ties) about twice a year. She did not agree that the FRG was an "occupied state," dominated by "US cultural imperialism"; on the contrary, she saw herself as a successful product of American-directed reeducation efforts. She recognized her generation as one that had experienced America as the Great Liberator, compared to the next generation whose breaking point had come with the Vietnam war.

Echoing her party's response to events of the early 1980s, Hamm-Brücher labeled the proposal for a nuclear-free Germany "an egotistical notion," stating that the preference should lie with a nuclear-free Europe. She could not imagine a neutralized Germany, at least as long as the blocs themselves persisted; the first step would be the unification of Western Europe itself. The terms community of responsibility and security partnership evoked little more than shrug of the shoulders, while the notion of a German confederation was rejected as "unrealistic." The former Foreign Ministry official was "strictly opposed" to SDI, yet accepted nuclear deterrence "as a political form of authority albeit not as a usable weapon." She favored neither greater independence from the USA nor the withdrawal of troops but would have supported an FRG veto-right tied to the utilization of nuclear weapons. Hamm-Brücher placed no value on a European Defense Union (potentially anti-NATO) nor on common security cum neutrality for the two German states; though open to unilateral moratoria on deployments, she opposed unilateral disarmament.

Hildegard Hamm-Brücher concluded that most Germans already considered themselves "normal," despite the persistence of certain scruples abroad. She was therefore reluctant to characterize the process of normalization as "a question of generations."

Profiles from the Long March Generation

Marlies Menge: Identity Perceptions
The next set of profiles begins with Marlies Menge, born in 1934 in Berlin, interviewed at her son's apartment in Köln on December 12, 1986. Al-

though technically a member of the first generation, Marlies Menge was only 11 years old at war's end. Her key political socialization experiences, rooted in the Reconstruction era, led her to identify with the second generation; she recalled "trading grenade splinters at school" after the war, the way kids now trade baseball cards or movie magazines. Her parents were "neither party members nor resistance fighters," though she learned later that they had supported the family of a childhood friend whose father was an active Communist (later imprisoned by the SED). The family was evacuated from Berlin to the East and then to Zelle. Though spared duty on the front owing to his job with the Esso Oil conglomerate, her father did time as a prisoner of war in England, after which all discussion of the war was "repressed." Ms. Menge sought training as a foreign correspondent, landing at the newly created Free University of Berlin. She was accredited in 1977 as a resident foreign journalist for *Die Zeit*, based in the GDR. Married with three children, she has authored several books dealing with regional cultures and daily life in the East.

Feeling touched by the debate, Menge held that the resurrection of the German Question was not confined to intellectuals but also indicative of tendencies among the Left (with which she appeared to sympathize). At the same time she was personally shocked by the "German-national tones" emitted by mainstream elites so reminiscent of the 1950s. The debate reawakened questions about National-Socialism among average citizens, while politicians all too willingly used it to play upon a *Wir sind wieder wer* [We're somebodies again] mood in the population at large. Menge objected to efforts to relativize history, observing that "the sins of Stalin should be processed by the Russians; the Germans have enough of their own sins to work through."

For Menge *die deutsche Frage* was primarily a question of FRG-GDR relations. Her years of service in the East underscored her belief that the two had "experienced so much of their own reality that there could be no doubt" that they had become separate states; there were still many lessons for reconciliation to be derived from their history, however. She did not see the Pershing II deployments as a proximate cause for the renewed debate, except among youth. It was good that "the people" were allowed to discuss the subject, but politicians had a special obligation to articulate a clear moral posture, in order to persuade youth that it also carried a certain responsibility. For average citizens, as she saw it, the GQ was grounded in the belief "that others should stop cursing at the Germans."

A new interest in the GDR among younger Germans was precipitated by the realization that they were as "dependent" on the Americans as their Eastern counterparts were subordinate to the Soviets; this had awakened a sense of parallelism, of solidarity. Young cohorts viewed their GDR counterparts as partners rather than as inferiors, a stance found among older Germans she knew. The new national-patriots of Left and Right embodied different traditions: the younger Brandt adhered to a holistic-communist notion of "the people," while Conservative Windelen (then Minister for Inner-German Relations) was less emotional about his faith in "Folk and Fatherland." Both sides, she observed, advocated a peace treaty but parted ways over its eventual content, as evidenced by the Right's desire to alter the borders drawn in 1945.

Menge was continually struck by "how little [national consciousness] the Germans had," juxtaposed against a child's "prayer for America" she had seen aired on American Forces Network-TV at the close of the broadcasting day. Nationalism's correlate, German identity, called to mind the image of Heinrich Mann's *Untertan* [the ludicrously subservient citizen who pursues ambition by embracing the authoritarian state to the point of self-destruction]. Menge had found it extremely difficult to answer Janssen-Jurreit's question, *"Lieben Sie Deutschland?"* She wrote not about Germany but about "homeland," grounded in particular landscapes, in her favorite Christmas oratorium, and in the poems of Heinrich Heine. She could easily live without nationalism, looking to other bases for political engagement and loyalty. Yet she felt "very touched and affected" by von Weizsäcker's 1985 speech, relieved that someone from the CDU had, at last, openly assumed the voice of morality.

Marlies Menge's national self-perception was "very torn" at best: recognizing herself as having come from both German states, she was ever reluctant to apply the designation "pan-German." She felt like a German in a painful way, not at all proud of the label, attributing her Germanness to her sense of "being responsible for both." Having been socialized "in the school of détente," the Berlin journalist perceived herself secondarily as a European. She surmised that her three children related to the GDR as a "foreign country," at the same time they identified with the larger German culture, e.g., classical music.

Ms. Menge's ties to the other Germany extended well beyond the professional domain; she visited relatives and old friends from her school days, cultivated formal contacts, and routinely traveled around the GDR. She denied any belief in reunification, explicitly rejecting the idea that one could return to the conditions of 1937. She nonetheless hoped that her children might one day enjoy a more intense "association" with the second German state, possibly under some other form of unity. As a resident of the divided city, Menge found the idea of a peace-treaty useful but not compelling, concurring with Peter Brandt that it could serve to "clarify conditions." She was glad that the Left had finally taken up the issue, pushing the idea as one to be discussed "in all due friendship with the Allies."

Reactions to the USA and NATO Doctrines

Marlies Menge admitted that her own orientation was "not so friendly towards America," a reaction against her father's strong affinity via Esso. She viewed the FRG as an "occupied land" in juridical but not in practical terms; she did not feel plagued by "US cultural imperialism," since there were ways of shielding oneself against such influences. She had only been to the United States twice, but her sons were eager to visit.

From her perspective, the community of responsibility formula addressed the special historical duty of both German states to preserve the peace. While the GDR had officially exonerated itself from the pursuit of fascism, it could not completely renounce a shared historical legacy, since three members of the reigning Politbüro had themselves been incarcerated by the Nazis. Menge strongly supported notions of common security and security partnership; as a first step, both German states needed to influence partners within their own blocs, as a precondition for intensifying the dialogue between themselves. Although she saw no prospects for the initiation of a German confederation in 1985, "it would be wonderful if it could come about," she mused.

Despite her sympathy for the peace movement, she was prepared to accept a withdrawal of NATO troops only on the condition that the Soviet Union likewise remove its forces from the GDR. An "incorrigible pacifist," Menge objected to any strengthening of the Bundeswehr's capabilities, except for outfitting it with a veto-right against the use of nuclear weapons. She rejected the doctrine of nuclear deterrence, yet placed little faith in a European Defense Union or unilateral disarmament, preferring the idea of a nuclear-free Germany in a nuclear-free Europe. She found it difficult to foretell when a state of self-perceived normalcy might come about among the Germans, many of whom already comprised a third generation. Marlies Menge predicted that the process would require a time-span of at least two more generations for outsiders.

Dr. Herta Däubler-Gmelin: Identity Perceptions

My next discussion partner, Dr. jur. Herta Däubler-Gmelin, born on August 12, 1943 in Pressburg/Slovakia, is a veritable personification of the Long March Generation; our discussion took place in her Bundestag office in Bonn on November 25, 1986. Herta Daübler-Gmelin recounted that her father had spent four years as a prisoner of war and two of her uncles had been killed, although she had no direct memories from the period. The daughter of a local politician, she studied law and economics in Tübingen and Berlin, where she actively participated in the Student Movement of the 1960s. While practicing law in Stuttgart she began mobilizing on behalf of the federal public service union (*ÖTV*), the Friends of Nature, the Evangelical Church and the Association of Social-Democratic Women. Joining the SPD in 1965, she had advanced to the position of local executive and state-party officer in Baden-Württemburg by 1971. Däubler-Gmelin, then 29, entered the Bundestag as its youngest member in 1972; she was elected into the party's national presidium and came to chair the Bundestag's Legal Committee by 1980. After 1983, she became acting director of the SPD's Parliamentary Caucus. Married with two children, she has co-edited and authored numerous texts on feminist political concerns, ranging from quotas and equal pay to affirmative action strategies.

As a member of the first truly postwar generation, this parliamentarian characterized the 1980s' resurgence of the German Question as "a highly interesting academic confrontation," aiming to pass on history without imposing personal feelings of guilt. Dr Däubler-Gmelin saw the INF deployments as having played a role in its resurgence but noted that a simultaneous "nostalgia wave among historians" arose out their sense of a "missing history." In her opinion, the primary GQ revolved around the existence of two curiously related states. Although younger people were developing an interest in an historical identity based on traditions "more important than the three verses of the German anthem," many older citizens found the idea disturbing.

Dr. Däubler-Gmelin saw no need for a national consciousness as "the earth under one's feet," yet realized (contradicting her personal feelings) that any attempt to configure or shape the future collectively would be unthinkable without such a framework. Reliance upon a "constitutional identity" alone left certain needs unfulfilled. A German identity, as she saw it, should convey to postwar citizens a sense of where they are coming from, enabling them to maintain ties to history even in the face of identity-lost; one had to grasp her country's traditions, whether or not one accepted or rejected them. Accepting herself as a "German" in a broader historical-cultural context, this Bundestag Member characterized her contemporary identity as a citizen of the Federal Republic, the first of my discussion partners born prior to 1952 to do so.

Däubler-Gmelin's interest in the other Germany had been triggered by her student experiences in Berlin and reinforced by her church involvement. Both she and her children regularly corresponded with Eastern relatives and friends, although she had only visited the GDR on three occasions. She expressed no belief in reunification, denoting the postwar borders and existence of adversarial blocs as "unassailable." As a self-avowed Federal Republican, she accepted the Preamble as a testimonial to pre-existing conditions but stressed the need for a formal recognition of GDR-citizenship. She noted that the younger generation viewed the GDR as "separate" from the FRG, just as they would Austria, and that the peace movement appealed more strongly to women and youth. Conceding that a peace treaty might help all parties to move beyond the status quo, she saw little chance of such an accord ever coming about.

Reactions to the USA and NATO Doctrines

Typical of her generation, Däubler-Gmelin admitted that she had been very critical of the US and its policies as a university student. She nonetheless emerged from the '68 Movement with an affinity for Pete Seeger and other imported protest-musicians, and her later involvement with an exchange program led her to appreciate the Americans' "pragmatic approach." Though vigorously opposed to the Pershing deployments, she did not ascribe "occupied" status to the FRG; she even confessed to watching occasional segments of *Denver* and *Dallas* "with pleasure." More disturbing was the ostensible arbitrariness of American political-economic and foreign policies. Däubler-Gmelin visits the United States frequently, and her children have attended schools across the Atlantic.

This politician's positive reaction to terms like security partnership and common security are not surprising, since these ideas were initially set forth by prominent SPD thinkers. In her view, these concepts "naturally make sense and have roots, although one needs to discuss further as to their substantive components." Dr. Däubler-Gmelin opposed SDI and dismissed nuclear deterrence as *Quatsch*. Rather than seeking greater independence from the USA, she advocated real co-determination among NATO partners, along with closer European defense cooperation. Favoring a reduction of foreign troops on German soil within the context of European withdrawals, she envisioned a nuclear-free Germany and Europe as the final product of a process to be set in motion via the Palme Commission framework. The neutralization of both Germanys and their eventual withdrawal from the existing security pacts could not occur in isolation; NATO's "25–30% overkill capabilities" would allow for a measure of unilateral disarmament "that couldn't hurt."

Herta Däubler-Gmelin diagnosed the question of German normalization as a subjective process, embodied in a course of action which the SPD had sought to pursue for the last two decades. External perceptions that the Germans once again merited treatment as normal members in the community of nations would follow suit.

Eva Quistorp: Identity Perceptions

The next profile covers another protest-activist turned politician, Eva Quistorp, born on August 27, 1945 in Detmold; this three-hour interview took place in two parts, at the Green Party headquarters on December 8, 1986, and a few days later at the *Bundeshochhaus* in Bonn. Eva Quistorp retained the

memory of her mother in an air-raid shelter and of later running through the
burning town of Essen; neither her mother nor her brother survived the war.
After Germany's defeat, her father worked as a pastor in the Confessing
Church; educated in a Judeo-Christian milieu, she heard countless sermons
attacking fascism as a child. She majored in German literature and theology
during the 1960s, trained as a comprehensive-school teacher. Ms. Quistorp
became an environmental activist in the early 1970s and helped to create the
Greens in 1979/80. She also co-founded a variety of feminist initiatives
against militarism, e.g., the border-transcending *Frauen für den Frieden*, and
served as a voting member of the peace-movement's Coordinating Committee. At the time of the interview, Quistorp was commuting between Bonn and
Berlin as a member of the party's national executive board; between 1989 and
1994 she served as a Green Member of the European Parliament.

In Ms. Quistorp's assessment, renewed debate over the German Question
was confined to select segments of the population, struggling for the right
"to define the past" as a way of processing "pressing feelings of guilt"—
hence, the simultaneous controversy over plans for a new Museum of German History in Berlin. Average citizens did not really want to be German
but neither did they enjoy being isolated individualists; for the most part,
they understood themselves as a "cosmopolitan, vaguely European, small
people"—cut adrift by mounting unemployment and many unresolved psychological problems. Out of this dilemma, they were quick to associate Bitburg with "reconciliation" and "legitimation."

A resident of the divided city, Quistorp felt Berliners were less diffident
but not automatically engaged in the revived GQ debate. She welcomed the
impulses generated by Peter Brandt but wanted the peace movement to
conduct its own intense debate over anti-Semitism among the Left and repression in the GDR. She had spent "many years thinking about" national
consciousness as well as German identity, concluding that there was no explicit need for either; working with European peace committees since 1983
had confronted her with certain "realities," however. Many arguments presented in progressive circles were *not* bloc-transcending, in her experience,
but rather spiced with national and East/West divisions at the expense of
global problems, e.g., environmental protection and women's rights. Italians were usually afraid of being overwhelmed by the "better organized
Germans," Germans had to confront the self-righteous "arrogance" of their
Dutch and English counterparts, and French activists insisted on keeping
their own *force de frappe*. Too little effort was made to engage in a Europeanized processing of the fascist past. This was not to deny the importance
of *Heimatgefühl*, rooted in language and culture; but the search for identity
had to be pursued in dialogue with other countries in order to draw the
Germans out of their own "narrowness." The main danger in resuscitating
the topic lay in leaving the contents of identity up to the Right.

Ms. Quistorp's national self-perception had been paradoxically altered by her involvement in the transnational peace movement: by 1985 she came to identify herself first as a German and secondarily as a European. She found it difficult to discuss identity with younger women, who were reluctant to recognize the possibility of a positive "German contribution" to history—a belief she had acquired, ironically, through contacts with the US-based Australian pacifist, Helen Caldicott.

Though personally moved by the 40th anniversary speech, this eco-peace activist criticized von Weizsäcker for failing to pressure hardliners within his own party into eliminating structural violence, the source of contemporary "helpless anti-fascism." More troubling than their historical "inability to mourn" was the politicians' "inability to take action" and their refusal to hold themselves, and scientists, responsible for arms proliferation.

This Long Marcher's interest in developments *drüben*—rare among Leftists of this generation—derived only partially from the fact that her father's family was based in the East; by the mid-1980s, all of her GDR relatives were deceased. Quistorp had visited East Berlin as a student in the 1960s but "ignored" the other state for a long time thereafter; interest was rekindled through her 1974 initiation into the anti-nuclear energy movement, which included sending balloon-messages across the border to raise eco-consciousness "over there." Her subsequent and sustained contacts with East-dissidents like Bärbel Bohley earned her the dubious distinction of being one of the last FRG-political figures to be denied GDR-entry after the opening of the Berlin Wall. More typical of her LMG-counterparts, Ms. Quistorp did not believe in unification, indeed she outright opposed the idea. She favored deletion of the constitutional Preamble as a symbolic gesture which might foster dialogue with the GDR. Well informed as to the specifics of NATO operations on German soil, she saw no prospects for concluding a peace treaty without the acquiescence of the superpowers; more important, in her judgment, was the need to discuss openly why this would not come about.

Reactions to the USA and NATO Doctrines

Eva Quistorp's experiences at deployment sites in Waldheide and Hunsrück, coupled with her arrests and apartment searches at the hands of English and West German police after 1979, reinforced her perception of living in an "occupied country." She resented the American presence because, she noted wryly, "they have so much room in their own country," though she realized that a down-sizing of forces would require a long-term program applying to all foreign troops. Far from an ostentatious consumer, she disliked Coca-Cola but praised songs by Joan Baez, California's art and sun, American jazz, its black and advant guarde cultures, and displays of personal generosity. Her first visit to the United States in 1972 took place en route to Latin America (to protest multinational imperialism); since 1981 she has traveled to the US once a year at her own expense to meet with peace and environmental activists.

Activist Quistorp opposed SDI and nuclear deterrence in principle as well as in practice. She advocated greater independence from the US along with troop withdrawals, albeit only in the context of mutual disarmament; she saw no pressing need to replace the existing Alliance with a Europe-centered defense structure but hoped for the gradual withdrawal of both German states from their respective Pacts. She favored unilateral disarmament measures to the extent that they contributed to multi-national accords. She harbored no reservations regarding the advent of a nuclear-free Germany and a nuclear-free Europe: "That would be wonderful . . . we marched for it!" Drawing on her multiple international contacts, she did not construe Germany's return to normalcy as a generational question. She insisted that her country's problematic status was a testimony to the longevity of clichés, as well as the product of specific world-political and economic interests, whose purposes could be served by manipulations of that history.

Profiles from the "Turn-Around" Generation

Mechthild Jansen: Identity Perceptions

Most of my discussions with younger citizens involved group settings. One exception was Mechthild Jansen, born October 2, 1952 in Cologne, who spoke with me about post-postwar identity at her Köln apartment on November 17, 1986. Due to "the blessing of late birth," Ms. Jansen had no direct experience with WWII, knew of no deaths in the family, and recalled few stories being relayed about the war at home. A class trip to Israel some three decades later afforded a first opportunity to confront and sort out her own images of that period. Jansen studied sociology and psychology at the Universities of Tübingen and Bremen, joining the second-wave of the Student Movement (the *Sponti* era) as an officer of the Socialist University League (SHB). An engaged member of the union *IG Druck und Papier*, this peace activist also co-founded diverse feminist "initiatives" and was a voting-member of the national Coordinating Committee. Deriving her livelihood as an independent writer, she has produced several books focusing on women's rights and anti-militarist themes.

Jansen maintained that the born-again debate over the German Question and national identity in the 1980s was confined to a small group, in particular, to independent peace activists. She spoke of the latent dangers inherent in this debate, citing societal efforts to exclude minorities or actions provoking anxieties among neighboring states. Reflecting on national consciousness, she observed that humans are not ahistorical subjects and therefore "need to know where they come from, where they live," especially in times of crisis or major social change. Attachment to the homeland, while essentially positive, also requires a measure of international consciousness.

Less palatable was the proposition that one might need a German identity in particular. Jansen found it impossible to "internalize" this notion; a reconceptualization of this more focused identity would have to include an end to public animosity towards foreigners and realization of the need for permanent disarmament. She showed no hesitation in characterizing her own identity as that of a Federal Republican, although she conceded that her parents and even her siblings continued to think of themselves as Germans. She was "not overwhelmed" by von Weizsäcker's much-lauded address but agreed with the need to recognize and compensate all victims who had been overlooked. She stressed the necessity of developing "deeper educational processes," extending beyond formal history lessons to include well-prepared concentration-camp visits, city-partnerships with neighboring states once victimized, and public responses to contemporary acts of hostility toward foreigners.

Ms. Jansen had neither relatives nor personal friendships among the citizens of the other Germany. Her contacts with "real-existing socialists" had been limited to conference delegations; she made some effort to sustain those contacts for political reasons but, in her words, "the people were strangers to me." She believed in the possibility of reunification only under a fundamental transformation of international conditions, unforeseeable in 1986. She favored deletion of the Preamble from the Basic Law, viewing it as an impediment to normalization, yet found the idea of a peace treaty superfluous, highlighting the need for many substantive treaties instead.

Reactions to the USA and NATO Doctrines

In contrast to other peace-coordinators interviewed by this author, Jansen had no direct contacts with the USA, since she "couldn't afford to travel there." She did not see herself as a resident of an "occupied state," a designation she characterized as "a fashion trend" among peace-movement factions. Like many other eco-peace proponents, she was "disturbed" by the pre-dominance of American films and fashions but did not fault the provider-country.

Even for this confirmed anti-militarist, the core issue was not a question of "NATO membership—yes or no?" but rather a deep-seated problem of "accentuation," the failure to seek symbiosis in place of emnity due to the bloc-system. She favored NATO withdrawal, albeit in the course of a broader process of East-West demilitarization. While she could personally envision a nuclear weapons–free Germany within "the space of 10–20 years," Jansen saw neutrality as "music for the future," requiring a major overhaul of the international framework. She welcomed all steps leading to disarmament, including unilateral ones. As an eventual beneficiary of "the blessings of normalcy," Mechthild Jansen predicted that it would be another 50 years before Germans could again perceive themselves as just like any other nation—provided that they engaged in no more heinous activities.

The group-setting preferred by members of the Turn-Around Generation makes it difficult to discern individual profiles, since their voices often overlapped on tape. What follows is a broad summary of the responses offered by four young women, all university students, who agreed to assemble one evening around a kitchen table in West-Berlin. I spoke with Annette, born in 1960 in Cologne; Katrin, born in 1963 in Göttingen; Marion, born in 1964 in Munich; and Andrea, born in 1961 in Munich, on October 30, 1986. Once an exchange student at Indiana University, Andrea (as of this writing) is a US correspondent for *die tageszeitung*. One of the most striking aspects of this round-table discussion was the general disdain with which the participants reacted to the subject of German identity; one participant left early, claiming to have "more important things to do." The German Question was viewed as an historical artifact, calling to mind the extermination of Jews, as well as "too much" or "too little" processing of the fascist past during their own years in school. These women felt that the Bitburg incident had been treated "too normally" in official circles, yet all were tired of being asked about the Nazis whenever they traveled abroad.

Although all four studied in the city where many debates over Germany's national status had arisen, they knew nothing about a "meeting of the minds" among Right/Left patriots. They dismissed national consciousness as "something sick," or as embodying "a need for subordination." German identity was useful only to the extent that it conveyed a sense of "from whence one came." Their personal identities depended on whether they were at home or abroad, couched in vague terms as "European." Their reactions to the GDR hardly suggested a fervent commitment to reunification, a notion characterized as "unthinkable," and "a non-topic." There was no sense of "connection," reinforced by the bureaucratic complications and high costs (i.e., per diem exchange requirements) of visiting life on the other side of the Wall. Retaining the Preamble was "hypocrisy"; a peace treaty would have a symbolic function at best.

Given the unique Four-Power status of Berlin, it was not surprising that these respondents saw themselves as residents of an "occupied state," but none favored the alternative of expanded Bundeswehr capabilities. Three had travelled to the USA and Canada, evoking a blend of positive and negative reactions. They agreed on the desirability of a nuclear weapons–free Germany but were divided over the benefits of neutrality (Switzerland and Austria were mentioned as models). The students unanimously rejected nuclear deterrence as well as the replacement of NATO by a European Defense Union; they concurred on the need for greater independence from the US, on troop withdrawals, bloc-disengagement for both German states, the establishment of a nuclear-free Europe and unilateral disarmament. Ironically, they did not posit a German return to normalcy as a positive state of affairs, especially "if it meant forgetfulness and repression of the past." It was better that the Germans and their neighbors all remain conscious of the events which had led to the country's peculiar standing in the court of nations, these women concluded.

Clearly this limited set of profiles cannot begin to define the full spectrum of identities embodied by each generation; there was much less consensus to be found among my mixed-gender sampling of students in Bonn and Mainz, for instance. The primary aim of this chapter is to show that German national consciousness, as posited by my "concentric" model of identity, acquires a very different shape and significance for individuals as a function of personal experience (or lack thereof) with its systemic ramifications. As represented here, the three generations do evince differences in the strength of their emotional ties to a larger German nation, as well as in their degree of "connectedness" to the Eastern state prior to the dramatic events of 1989–90. While they seemed to share the lesser-of-two-evils convictions of their male peers regarding existing security structures, my female interview partners were less satisfied with the status quo and more openly opposed to the specific features of NATO strategy. Nearly all embraced relative concepts of German identity, the focus of which was more self-defining and affective than principled or power-political in orientation.

The Morning After: German Women and the New World Order

The 1989 collapse of the GDR, the 1990 dissolution of the Warsaw Pact, and the virtual self-destruction of the Soviet Union in 1991 have effected a dramatic paradigm shift in the realm of German security policy, even if the much-hailed New World Order remains embryonic at best. The first challenge to that new order emerged less than one year after the East-West frontline had ceased to exist. As Chapter 5 argued, German reactions to the Gulf War were a logical consequence of a twenty-year re-orientation towards issues of war, peace, détente and disarmament in the FRG. Women too young to recall WW II voiced stronger opposition to the Mid-east intervention (up to 82.7% among those under 49) than women socialized under Reconstruction (59.7% among those 60 and older). Newly enfranchised Eastern women registered higher *Angst* levels than all other groups: 69.7% F versus 41.4% M in the West, compared to 87.9% F against 58.3% M in the East.[42]

The military response to Iraq nonetheless divided women into the same kind of pacifist and bellicist camps seen among the German Left as a whole.

While Vera Wollenberger (*Bündnis* '90-East) and Heidemarie Wieczorek-Zeul (SPD-West) thundered against the war during the Bundestag debate of January 14, 1991, Petra Kelly (Greens) joined the pro-intervention ranks of Wolf Biermann and Hans Magnus Enzensberger. An otherwise unshakeable Atlanticist, Marion Gräfin Dönhoff took a strong stance against her own editorial board at *Die Zeit*, decrying the all too brief application of sanctions against Iraq.[43] From her post in the European Parliament, Eva Quistorp helped to establish the Women's Action Group Scheherazade, calling for an immediate UN-sponsored cease-fire, as well as for a global referendum on the war itself.

Women were less supportive of the US-led invasion, voiced stronger reservations over constitutional changes permitting out-of-NATO-area engagements and were more willing to recognize "German guilt" based on illicit FRG weapons sales to Iraq. The latter orientation was perhaps best summarized by Third-World activist, Claudia von Braunmühl:

> Hussein is described as Hitler's successor, out of whose hands the weapons must be struck. If they had never been placed in his hands in the first place, by the same industries which also profited from National Socialism, then we could have spared ourselves this entire bombing-until-*kaputt*. . . . I am no Near-East specialist, but regarding everything I understand about Hussein's weapons base, it was delivered primarily from the outside, in contrast to National Socialism. And therein lies the key to stopping Hussein, with ourselves, in the industrial states.[44]

The New World Order, which millions had hoped would impel nations to jettison the arms-proliferation strategies of the Cold War era, has yet to transcend the principle of "business as usual." The Gulf War was no less gendered, in strategy or substance, than all of its twentieth century predecessors.[45]

The Re-Construction of National Identity Among New German Women

There are no "hard data" showing that Eastern women were any more national at heart, or any more disposed to believe in the prospect of unification prior to 1989. Indeed, national identity remained a taboo topic in the GDR until its collapse. There is evidence, however, that Eastern women were considerably less enthusiastic than their countrymen about the sudden push for national unity. Researchers in Leipzig determined that women accounted for one-third of the regular participants in candle-lit, silent marches, October through December of 1989; about one-half of all first-wave protesters were under the age of 35. Their banners called for reform, not revolution, focusing on free elections, the right to travel, and economic reconstruction under the rubric of "socialism with a human face."

The period January through March of 1990 witnessed a shift in the demands and composition of the protests; demonstrators resorted to rowdier calls for a Germany united Fatherland, accompanied by much flag-waving. During this phase the proportion of female marchers dropped below one-fourth; the rest were largely working class males, mixed with salaried employees. By April, 92% of the men expressed some support for unity, in contrast to 80% of the women surveyed; juxtaposed against 41% of the female respondents strongly in favor of unity were 20% who openly opposed the idea (figures for men were 58% and 8%, respectively). As to possible time-frames for the merger, 38% of the women and 43% of the men preferred the end of 1990; 21% of the former wanted to delay the process until after 1992, compared to 12% among the latter.[46]

There are at least three explanations as to why Eastern women seemed more reluctant to cross the Rubicon of rapid unification. First, their hesitation may have been more directly conditioned by the negative historical associations (e.g., war and fascism) inherent in the idea of a Greater Germany; bear in mind that there were more surviving WWII widows and pensioners than male veterans by 1989. Secondly, it is conceivable that the "ethic of relationships" associated with female socialization rendered women more sympathetic to the collectivist/equality aspects of socialism, at least as an ideal.[47] They may have been more inclined to reject many forms of exploitation attributed to capitalism (which is not to argue that their own system was any less exploitative). Last but not least, women were more sensitive to the prospect of mass unemployment and new forms of social insecurity (higher prices, rising crime, violence, right-extremism)—with the understanding that they would probably become the first victims of a major social dislocation.[48] The one development that neither they nor their Western counterparts could anticipate was being drawn into a variety of globalized wars so quickly after they had completed their peaceful national revolution.

Post-unity exchanges with a number of women interviewed during the 1980s reveal that most are now positively disposed towards unification, albeit for many different reasons. Yet they are also sensitive to the extraordinary costs that have ensued as a function of the haste with which negotiations and accession were completed. Marion Gräfin Dönhoff is one figure who has repeatedly criticized "the directionless Bonn leadership" for failing to develop strategies for active reconciliation and change from within since 1989.[49] Unification has fundamentally redefined the socio-economic status of Eastern women, a process I have documented extensively elsewhere. Focal concerns over security once directed against "the enemy without" (the repressive powers of the Soviet Union, as well as the threat of annihilation posed by NATO) have been overtaken by the reality of security-lost from within. Few anticipated the sweeping roll-back of "equal opportunity" that would follow directly on the heels of unification, either in representational or in social-policy terms.

Occupying 32% of the GDR *Volkskammer* seats in 1988 (up from 25% in 1960), women accounted for only one-fifth of the delegates to the first democratically elected People's Chamber as of March 18, 1990. Clearly the old parliament had been little more than a rubber stamp for the designs of the communist party; the point here is that when the *Volkskammer* did become a body with real decision-making powers, women were largely excluded as a result of deliberate party-political strategies. The first all-German Bundestag, convened on December 20, 1990, contained the highest proportion of female membership ever witnessed in the FRG, 20.5%. The incorporation of the Five New Länder increased the size of the assembly, from 522 to 662 members.[50] The new Kohl Government likewise boasted of the largest number of ministerial posts occupied by women in postwar German history, a feat achieved by chopping up the former of Ministry of Youth, Family, Women and Health into three new units: the Ministry of Health (Gerda Hasselfeldt), the Ministry of Family and Elderly (Hannelore Rönsch), and the Ministry of Women and Youth (Angela Merkel). Of the Ministries accorded to the FDP, Regional Planning, Construction and Urban Development went to Irmgard Schwaetzer, and the Ministry of Justice fell to Sabine Leutheusser-Schnarrenberger. Professor Rita Süssmuth began her second term as Bundestag-President, while Birgit Breuel (CDU) became Director of the *Treuhand* in April 1991, the "holding company" responsible for the privatization of former GDR-state properties. Hildegard Hamm-Brücher was nominated (but defeated) for the Federal Presidency in 1993, and Jutta Limbach (SPD) assumed the office of President of the Constitutional Court in 1994. Claudia Nolte (CDU), a vehemently anti-choice Catholic from Thuringia, was named Minister of Women and the Elderly after the 1994 elections, and Merkel moved on to head the Environmental Ministry.

Eastern women's pre-unity concerns over likely increases in crime, rightwing violence, and their own joblessness proved to be well founded. Prior to 1989, 90% of all GDR women aged 15–60 were engaged in paid labor, only 27% part-time; this contrasts with 54% in the old Länder, of whom only 48% were employed full-time.[51] Women comprised 58.8% of the newly unemployed by August 1991; many were forced out the market by the elimination of child-care facilities (roughly one-third of all children born in the 1980s had single mothers).[52] By 1995, nine out of ten new jobs would go to men.[53] The new Länder have registered a 50% drop in the birthrate, and a 400% increase in the number of sterilizations since 1991. The dramatic decline in fertility rates is not only linked to a loss of economic security among Eastern women but also to a fundamental revision of their reproductive rights since 1993.

Legal and free upon demand in the GDR as of 1972, the prospect of a restrictive abortion code along FRG lines proved so controversial that it was deliberately excluded from the Unity Treaty. Both laws remained in force until the all-German parliament approved a tri-partisan Group Resolution (357 to 284) in June 1992, securing a woman's right to decide, subsequent to mandatory counseling.[54] The High Court overtuned the law in May 1993, declaring abortion illegal but unpunishable for all German women and subject to many new restrictions, enshrined in a revised "compromise" law of June 1995.[55]

For Eastern women, the verdict was a bitter pill, providing a negative lesson on the workings of "democracy." Overturning a substantial, freely-elected majority, the Court itself was perceived as a "grotesque misrepresentation" of *das Volk*: the judges were 100% Western, 87.5% male and 50% Catholic, averaging 57.6 years of age.[56] The Court eliminated the "social hardship" indicator (grounds for over 80% of the Western abortions prior to 1993); yet lawmakers postponed funding for a major benefits-package to assist pregnant women in need until 1999.[57] The abortion outcome reinforced many Easterners' feelings of second-class citizenship: the democratic *Rechtsstaat* appeared to be even more patriarchal than the socialist *Unrechtsstaat*, allowing for more "state" and fewer "rights" in relation to the nation's women. A constitutional reform commission, consisting of 11 women and 53 men, proposed a reformulation of Article 3 which might, in another twenty years, lead a new generation of all-German judges to reconsider abortion rights.[58]

The ideal of citizenship and its correlate, political identity, cannot be restricted to one's formal membership in a national community. Identity is intricately connected with social standing which, in turn, lays the foundation not only for theoretical rights to participation but for actual, meaningful opportunities to influence national policy. As Shklar argues, the "struggle for citizenship . . . [is] overwhelmingly a demand for inclusion in the polity, an effort to break down excluding barriers to recognition."[59] Inclusion by way of unification is a necessary though hardly sufficient condition for meaningful political participation among East German women; women in the new states have nonetheless begun to mobilize in hopes of redirecting the course of FRG politics.[60] The key to their eventual success, the search for common ground among all German women, cannot be divorced from the larger questions of national identity per se.

The Return of the Repressed:
Women, Nationalism, and Identity

Women's political gains of the last two decades owe much to the relentless engagement of activists from the Long March Generation, most of whom proudly label themselves feminists. While postwar feminists never sought to deny or downplay atrocities committed in the name of the German *Volk* under the Third Reich, they have, until recently, neglected to confront their own relationship to national history with the same degree of theoretical profundity or *Gründlichkeit* with which they have excoriated patriarchy's role in those developments. It is therefore somewhat ironic that the process of rendering Germany whole again has precipitated a paradigm shift among FRG-feminists intent on analyzing issues of sexism, nationalism and racism. Many have begun to re-assess their own relationship to national history, moved, in part, by a wave of rightwing violence among unified German youth (examined in Chapter 7).

The mutually exclusive courses pursued by the two Germanys after 1949 regarding questions of collective guilt and responsibility left a distinctive imprint on the respective "national" identities of Eastern and Western women. Given the overwhelming significance of the Nazi era for German historical consciousness, protestors from the Long March Generation, as well as their GDR equivalents, often failed to distinguish between two modes of nationalism highlighted by Christian Joppke: namely, between ethnic nationalism and civic nationalism.[61] For most postwar activists, the meaning of nation was permanently inscribed on ruins of former Nazi concentration camps after 1945, with the result that the precepts of nation and democracy were construed as antithetical—although they need not be. There are several factors tied to the existence of two separate German states which precluded feminist scholars, in particular, from engaging in a no-holds-barred confrontation with the national past prior to 1990 (recall that no women participated directly in the *Historikerstreit* of the late 1980s).

First, the links between the Western women's movement and the New Left of the 1960s promoted a focus on global liberation from patriarchy, inter alia; patriarchy was often perceived to have its roots in monopoly capitalism. In retrospect, one can argue that "the '68 Generation, and that also applies to feminists, wanted to bring about radical change in the world, for which their own rearing during the reactionary '40s, '50s and '60s had not prepared them internally. The fixation of "the elders" with organs of authority, with 'Führer' and State, was related to the position of the '68ers to ideologies and Marx, Engels, Lenin, Mao, Che through and through." [62]

Feminists of the '68 Generation interviewed by this author during the 1980s were among those who responded most negatively when asked if they "felt like a German." Few appeared to recognize the contradiction inherent in their own "distance" from the Nation: having openly faulted the older generation throughout the protest era for its refusal to accept full personal qua moral responsibility for the crimes of fascism, many have felt few qualms about personally disassociating themselves from their own country—viewed as a systemic re-embodiment of the past. Their reluctance to assume, and thus to transmit, a sense of personal accountability vis-à-vis the new nation is partly to blame for the rise of ultranational sentiment among members of the first Post-Wall Generation.[63]

Second-Wave feminism's roots in the New Left Movement also rendered it vulnerable to a desire to attack any and all semblances of nationalism, too quickly equated with resurgent fascism. This linkage not only undercut activists' ability to identify positively with a democratized Federal Republic in lieu of the once-totalitarian nation; it also led to a new historical paradox: "that simply out of the permanent pressure to learn from history . . . that one slipped past the entire phenonmenon of Stalinism with vague language, because one was always afraid that one had to guard the Bundesrepublik against neo-fascism, that this so-to-speak was the main task."[64]

The orthodox-Stalinist Left in the GDR, meanwhile, targeted monopoly capitalism as the root-cause of fascism but ignored its own manifestations of patriarchy by insisting that socialism had achieved the full emancipation of women. There was no extensive communication between the women of East and West which might have fostered an understanding of linkages between the forces of industrial production (whether capitalist or socialist), the power of patriarchy, and the socio-cultural roots of fascism. The fact that GDR women were unable to seek active discussion partners beyond their own borders suggests that the main burden of initiating such a dialogue should have rested with west-feminists.

Secondly, special ties to the New Social Movements of the 1970s enabled FRG-feminists to "think globally, act locally"—blessed as they were with time, money and the rights to travel and protest. GDR-women were increasingly overwhelmed with the deterioration of the socialist economy; what time and energy remained was used to cultivate their own eco-peace movements, at the expense of building an autonomous feminist movement (with minor exceptions). Preventing the occurrence of future wars on German soil took precedence over a common processing of wars past. Thus, feminism's NSM linkages provided both groups with legitimate reasons for obscuring and/or avoiding the troublesome national question altogether prior to 1989.

Last but certainly not least, it is also clear that the feminist rule, the personal is the political, sets a very difficult standard for any scholar seeking to explore the contours of German national identity, plagued as she may be by a laming guilt-consciousness. Guilt, Koppert observes, "means at least theoretically that one's self or the others could have behaved differently."[65] Most feminists gravitated towards historical explanantions portraying women as the victims of patriarchal oppression (albeit to different degrees) in a nation gone berserk; they circumvented the argument that women are "naturally" subordinate by recounting the heroic deeds of a few self-sacrificing resistance fighters and tenacious *Trümmerfrauen*. A focus on gender obviated the need to address one's Germanness, by tying women's Third Reich experiences to universal forms of oppression; questions of female anti-Semitism were rarely raised.[66] What emerges from this retrospective is the realization that German women intent on analyzing the past after 1949 often cultivated their own "repressed-memory strategies" regarding their ties to the nation. They did overlap with their countrymen in one critical respect, however: in their tendency to deem nationalism as an all-or-nothing proposition.

The task of re-identifying with the nation-united may prove twice as hard for East German women, although most harbored no more love for the old *Vater-Staat* than did their Western peers. According to an ISDA survey, women in the new states still feel less "German" than men: 30–40% of the females versus 40–60% of the male respondents perceived themselves as *deutsch*, first and foremost.[67] As one new citizen reflected,

> It is usually men, the ones who are in power, who express themselves regarding the state of the nation. . . . I, a woman, without power—and on top of that, one from the East—would sooner have to intone a lamentation. One expects me to be happy about belonging to the bigger Germany, so experienced in democracy and the market economy. But I feel alien in this nation, in this Fatherland. [68]

National pride plays a subordinate role even among female adolescents drawn to far-right movements. One such teen, asked about her feelings towards the Fatherland, responded, "Proud, I don't know, well yeah, I am kinda proud, or let's say, I'm lucky: Germany is a rich country."[69] Researchers find that young women often develop anti-foreigner sentiments in reaction to perceptions of gender inequality and personal anxiety, rather than out of a principled concern for the nation.

East-women have been on the defensive since 1990, fending off West-criticisms over their earlier "failure" to develop an autonomous movement, and also coping with their loss of real-existing social rights (abortion, daycare) by way of "democratization." GDR women had fewer grounds to mobilize around feminist themes than their FRG-peers prior to 1989, given the many forms of state assistance that enabled them to combine career and family (though the SED's aims were more pro-natalist than emancipatory in nature). They also had fewer grounds to challenge their relation to the national question, having "paid" for fascism in ways that West-feminists often failed to count, i.e., their deprivation of fundamental political freedoms in exhange for collective exculpation. The upsurge of democratic opposition in the GDR was in no way based on a presumed "moral superiority" of the FRG-historical paradigm. Unity was embraced not as an end per se but as a means to attain other intensely desired ends. In short, "The female FRG-citizens neither made the revolution happen, nor did they even want one."[70]

Women's adverse reactions to rapid unification "sprang from a rational perception that the civic and the national dimensions of the East German revolution did not coincide."[71] West German feminists who believed that their own political and economic institutions were patriarchal to the core could not have welcomed their imposition on East women. Yet this did not stop them from hoping that once the merger occurred, the GDR experience might provide certain institutional correctives (legalized abortion), since most were not particularly well-informed as to the real nature of equality-made-in-the-GDR prior to the Wall's collapse.

Women on both sides of the former border are now absorbed with the disadvantages each group has itself encountered as a result of unification. A general polarization of identities in the old and new Länder [*the Wall in my head*], added to specific tensions afflicting the mind-sets of Eastern and Western women [codeword: *step-sisters*], confirm my initial hypothesis that *die deutsche Nation* had indeed become little more than an "imagined community" by 1990.[72] Perceived differences in the identities of East and West women testify to the spurious nature of blood-based notions of citizenship as a foundation for collective identity. Atrocities committed not only *in the name of* but also with the ostensible acquiescence of the German people is the one dimension of national-consciousness that FRG and GDR women have shared over a span of four decades. Their "common reference point" will remain a negative one, as long as they continued to divorce their sense of nationalism from the precept of democratic self-determination.

My point here is not that women are especially to blame for each Germany's failure to process the past in ways that might shield the nation's youth from an ultranationalist resurgence. Indeed, as interview responses presented in Chapter 3 indicate, women were generally unwilling to "close the book" on a processing of the Third Reich. I argue instead that alternative explanatory frameworks linking women to National Socialism—e.g., as self-interested collaborators [*Mittäterinnen*, to borrow from Thürmer-Rohr]—would have retained their marginal character throughout the 1990s had division persisted.[73] As Birgit Rommelspacher observes,

> unification has, to the same extent for the Germans of East and West, shattered their self-perceptions as Germans. Ground-in self-constructions are being put to question, for the ugly German can no longer be made out on the other side of the Wall. If the Westerners, for example, saw the tradition of German militarism and the authoritarian state living on in the East, the Easterners saw in the West a society that continued after Nationalism without a single break, without distancing itself. Now that is not so simple any more. The projections have to be taken back, and the question of being-German has to be raised anew.[74]

Though the forces of generational change might have triggered new interpretations by the end of the 1990s even under division, it seems clear that the need to reinfuse German history with a common "meaning" for citizens suddenly (re)united has pushed the issue of self-responsibility back to center-stage, for women and men. Still, the return of the repressed can be put to positive use: the last five years have given rise to numerous articles exploring gender-specific forms of complicity with the Nazi regime, as well as postwar manifestations of racism within the women's movements themselves.[75]

Women in the new Länder are likely to experience qualitatively different feelings of "guilt" and responsibility towards German history, confronted now by the need to work through two authoritarian eras. But a processing of the GDR past cannot be confined to Eastern women, insofar as FRG-feminists, committed to a leftist utopia far removed from daily GDR-life, did little to combat the state-oppression faced by their "sisters" next door prior to 1989. It has never been the West Germans' collective incapacity to mourn but rather their personal unwillingness to identify directly with the negative or positive components of the national past (made easy by division) which has undercut even feminists' ability to empathize with women in the East or with women of other cultures living in their midst.

The lesson emerging from this chapter is that equality-activists from the Long March Generation, in particular, will have to accept their identity as German women—and the historical continuity that implies—in order to secure the full benefits of citizenship. It is no coincidence that many investigations-in-progress on women of the New Right are being conducted by members of the first Post-Wall Generation.[76] Nor is it accidental that most of that research is taking place under the direction of self-avowed feminist professors of the Long March Generation. The former may not feel particularly blessed by virtue of their having been born either "late" or female, but they do evince a quality characterized in Chapter 1 as the "New Unencumberedness." Among the latter, "the defense mechanisms against guilt still function. . . . The past continues to permeate one's individual and collective subconsciousness."[77]

Empowerment is a cumulative process. For the last two decades, German women have been increasingly moved to participate in politics by questions of science and technology once said to comprise "a man's world"—by problems of acid rain, toxic waste disposal, the hazards of genetic research, as well as by the deployment of nuclear weapons in their own backyards. Their long march through the institutions may not have been a sufficient condition for securing democracy in the postwar state but it was certainly a necessary one. The chance to advance their own rights will not come easily, given the current competition for resources in unified Germany. Too often the victims of the politics of exclusion, women will need to promote the substantive dimensions of citizenship, and they will have to lobby hard for a more inclusive concept of national identity devoid of ethnic determinants. The New German women must develop an active line of defense against the would-be ultranationalist forces in their midst, the subject to which we now turn.

Notes

1. Parts of this chapter stem from my essay, "Feminism in Four Acts: The Changing Political Identity of Women in the Federal Republic of Germany," in Peter Merkl, ed., *The Federal Republic of Germany at 40* (New York: New York University Press, 1989). For more on East women, see Joyce Marie Mushaben, "Second-Class Citizenship and Its Discontents: Women in United Germany," in Peter Merkl, ed., *The Federal Republic of Germany at Forty-Five* (New York: New York University Press, 1995), pp. 79–98; and "Germany and Gender," *German Politics and Society,* Issue 24–25, Winter 1991–1992.

2. Werner Weidenfeld's edited volume, *Die Deutsche Identität* (München: Carl Hanser, 1983) had one female among fifteen authors; his *Nachdenken über Deutschland* (Köln: Verlag Wissenschaft und Politik, 1985) offered two chapters by women, out of twelve. Two further works pertaining to identity relied on 19 female contributors, out of 136, and 3 women among 66 respondents: see Werner Filmer and Heribert Schwan, Hg., *Was heißt für mich Frieden?* (Oldenburg: Stalling "forum," 1982); also, Rudolf Birkl and Günter Olzog, Hg., *Erwartungen. Kritische Rückblicke der Kriegsgeneration* (München/Wien: Günter Olzog Verlag, 1980). Neither the New National-Patriots—Wolfgang Venohr, Hg., *Ohne Deutschland geht es nicht* (Krefeld: Sinus Verlag, 1985)—nor those ruminating over post-unity security needs—Dieter Wellershoff, Hg., *Frieden ohne Macht? Sicherheitspolitik und Streitkräfte im Wandel* (Bonn: Bouvier, 1991)—consider the views of the demographic majority.

3. Electoral data are taken from Joachim Hofmann-Göttig, *Emanzipation mit dem Stimmzettel. 70 Jahre Frauenwahlrecht in Deutschland* (Bonn: Verlag Neue Gesellschaft, 1986). My survey of the reconstruction years derives from Annette Kuhn, Hg., *Frauen in der deutschen Nachkriegszeit*, Vols. 1 and 2 (Düsseldorf: Schwann, 1986); also, Anne-Elisabeth Freier and Annette Kuhn, Hg., *Frauen in der Geschichte* (Düsseldorf: Schwann, 1984).

4. Annemarie Tröger, "Die Dolchstoßlegende der Linken: 'Frauen haben Hitler an die Macht gebracht,'" *Frauen und Wissenschaft* (Berliner Sommeruniversität, July 1976), pp. 324–355.

5. Renate Bridenthal, Atina Grossmann and Marion Kaplan, *When Biology became Destiny. Women in Weimar and Nazi Germany* (New York: Monthly Review Press, 1984); Gerda Szepansky, *Blitzmädel, Heldenmütter, Kriegerwitwe—Frauenleben im Zweiten Weltkrieg* (Frankfurt/M: Fischer, 1986); and Hanna Elling, *Frauen im deutschen Widerstand 1933–1945* (Frankfurt/M: Röderberg Verlag, 1981).

6. Helke Sander's documentary film, *BeFreier und Befreite*, reports that some two million women aged 14–74 experienced violent, sexual degradation; one women was raped 128 times. See Viola Roggenkamp, "Warum haben die Frauen geschwiegen?" *Die Zeit*, Nr. 40, October 2, 1992. "Several tens of thousands" of rapes by Red Army soldiers were registered in Berlin between April 24 and May 3, 1945; 1,198 were attributed to French troops in Stuttgart, and 971 US soldiers were convicted by military courts. See Ingrid Schmidt-Harzbach, "Eine Woche im April. Berlin 1945—Vergewaltigung als Massenschicksal," *Feministische Studien*, Nr. 2, November 1984, pp. 51–65.

7. Daily consumption fell from a per capita average of 2000 calories during the last months of the war, to official "lows" of 775–794 calories in the American and French Occupation Zones through 1947. Kuhn, op. cit., Vol. 2, p. 41 ff.

8. Freier, op. cit., p. 52.

9. Kuhn, op. cit., Vol. 2, p. 81.

10. For more on the Founding Mothers, see Mushaben, "Feminism in Four Acts. . . ." For details on their successors, try Johanna Holzhauer and Agnes Steinbauer, Hg., *Frauen an der Macht. Profile prominenter Politikerinnen* (Frankfurt/M: Eichborn, 1994).

11. Eva Kolinsky, *Women in Contemporary Germany. Life, Work and Politics* (Providence/Oxford: Berg, 1993 ed.), p. 223.

12. Hanna Schissler, "A Social Contract for the Fifties: 'Normality,' Anti-Communism, and the Social Production of Unconsciousness in Gender Relations in West Germany," presented at the 19th Annual German Studies Association Meeting, Chicago, Illinois, September 21–24, 1995. Employment rates among married women fell to 25% in 1950, while the rate for single women stood at 82.4%; 20% of the women-workers (1.6 million) had children under 15; another 1.4 million ran households consisting of at least one other person.

13. Elisabeth Noelle and Erich Peter Neumann, eds., *Jahrbuch der Öffentlichen Meinung, 1947–1955* (Allensbach: 1956), p. 159, p. 94.

14. *Allensbacher Berichte*, No. 15, 1965, Table 2, Table 4.

15. Beate Hoecker, *Frauen in der Politik. Eine soziologische Studie* (Opladen: Leske + Budrich, 1987), p. 72.

16. Lottemi Doormann, Hg., *Keiner schiebt uns Weg. Zwischenbilanz der Frauenbewegung in der Bundesrepublik* (Weinheim/Basel: Beltz, 1979), p. 23ff.

17. Male researchers ignore the conceptual and strategic innovations rooted in this campaign which were later adopted by NSM groups. See Silvia Kontos, "Modernisierung der Subsumtionspolitik? Die Frauenbewegung in den Theorien neuer sozialer Bewegungen," *Feministische Studien*, Nr. 2 (1986), pp. 34–49.

18. Alice Schwarzer, *Der "kleine Unterschied" und seine grosse Folgen, Frauen über sich, Beginn einer Befreiung* (Frankfurt/M: Fischer Verlag, 1975).

19. Notable exceptions were the "Monday Club" (some 400 members strong after two decades of existence) and bills sponsored by the women of all parties to strengthen testing requirements for food products in the mid-1970s. See Mushaben, "Feminism in Four Acts," op.cit.

20. *Emnid-Informationen*, 27. Jg., Nr. 5, 1975, Tables 8 and 9.

21. The conflict between Autonomists and charitable/religious organizations over the creation of battered women's shelters offers a case in point. See Kathrin Kramer and Claudia Pai, "Frauen auf der Flucht," *Die Zeit*, Januar 17, 1986.

22. *Emnid-Informationen*, Nr. 2/3, 1980, Table 14.

23. While 82% of the male legislators were married with children, 43.1% of the female MdBs were single, divorced or widowed, yet nearly half were mothers. Hoecker, op. cit., p. 87.

24. For "positive discrimination" with regard to men, see Heide Pfarr, "Quotierung und Rechtswissenschaft," pp. 86–97, in Herta Däubler-Gmelin, Heide M. Pfarr and Marianne Weg, Hg., *"Mehr als nur gleicher Lohn." Handbuch zur beruflichen Förderung von Frauen* (Hamburg: VSA Verlag 1985). The European Court of Justice overturned a cut-off age of 27 in Britain (*Price v. Civil Service Commission*), rendering the German restriction invalid.

25. Statistisches Bundesamt, Hg., *Personalstandsstatistik*, Fachserie 14, Reihe 6 (Wiesbaden: 1985).

26. Eva Kolinsky, "Political Participation and Parliamentary Careers: Women's Quotas in West Germany," in *West European Politics*, Vol. 14, No. 1 (January 1991), p. 56; and Mechthild Jansen, Hg., *Halbe-Halbe, Der Streit um die Quotierung* (Berlin: Elefanten Press Verlag, 1986).

27. Heide Simonis, "Macht Macht Frauen männlich?" in Otto Kallscheuer, Hg., *Die Grünen—Letzte Wahl? Vorgaben in Sachen Zukunftsbewältigung* (Berlin: Rotbuch Verlag, 1986), p. 89.

28. Hoecker, op. cit., p. 75.

29. Kolinsky, "Political Participation," op. cit., p. 63.

30. This figure was repeatedly cited by SPD women interviewed by this author.

31. While Allensbach surveys stressed a persistent "interest gap" through 1977, Berthold Meyer saw a measurable decline in women's "don't know," "undecided" and "no opinion responses" across three decades. Dieter Roth claims that age and education levels remain the chief determinants of "political interest" but concedes the persistent influence of socialization differences in "Charakteristische Einstellungsunterschiede zwischen Männern und Frauen," unpublished paper (March 16, 1989).

32. Background derives from an interview with this author, conducted at Sölle's home in Hamburg in October 1983.

33. B. Meyer, op. cit., p. 59.

34. Roth, op. cit., p. 2.

35. As to their motives, see Ulrike Meinhof, *Die Würde des Menschen ist antasbar, Aufsätze und Polemiken* (Berlin: Verlag Klaus Wagenbach, 1986); also, Jillian Becker, *Hitler's Children. The Story of the Baader-Meinhof Terrorist Gang* (Philadelphia/New York: Lippincott, 1977).

36. IfD Allensbach, *Jahrbuch der öffentlichen Meinung 1965–67*, and *Allensbacher Berichte*, 1964/24, Tables 1 and 2.

37. Ariane Barth, "Etwas anders als Sex," *Der Spiegel*, Nr. 46, 13. December 1978.

38. *Allensbacher Berichte*, No. 18, Summer 1979, Tables 1 and 2.

39. See the report of a Friedrich Naumann Foundation congress, *Frauen und Bundeswehr—Eine Allgemeine Bürgerpflicht für Männer und Frauen?* held in Gummersbach, July 3–5, 1981 (Sankt Augustin: Liberal Verlag, 1983). Also, Ekkehard Lippert and Tjarck Rössler, "Weibliche Soldaten für die Bundeswehr?" *Aus Politik und Zeitgeschichte*, B8/81, February 21, 1981; Margrit Gerste, Karin Hempel-Soos and Viola Roggenkamp, "Ende der Schonzeit," *Die Zeit*, Nr. 23, June 3, 1983. Further, Astrid Albrecht-Heide and Utemaria Bujewski, *Militärdienst für Frauen?* (Frankfurt/M: Campus Verlag, 1982).

40. See *Frauenwiderstand im Hunsrück, Frauengeschichte(n) 1983–85* (Frankfurt/M: Selbstverlag Frauenwiderstand, 1985); further, Die Grünen, *Materialsammlung zum Kongress Frauen und Ökologie*, 3–5 Oktober 1986 in Köln-Holweide (Bonn: 1986).

41. See the special editions of *Beiträge zur feministischen Theorie und Praxis*, "Gegen welchen Krieg—für welchen Frieden," Nr. 8, 1983; *Feministische Studien* under the title "Krieg und Unfrieden," Nr. 2, November 1984. Further, Christa Randzio-Plath, Hg., *Was geht uns Frauen der Krieg an?* (Reinbek: Rowohlt, 1982); and Harrad Schenk, *Frauen kommen ohne Waffen. Feminismus und Pazifismus*

(München: C. H. Beck, 1983). Margarete Mitscherlich offers a psychological assessment in *Die friedfertige Frau. Eine psychoanalytische Untersuchung zur Aggression der Geschlechter* (Frankfurt/M: Fischer, 1985).

42. FGW, representative sample for *Politbarometer West*, February 1991; also see data in Chapter 5.

43. Marion Gräfin Dönhoff, "Ein dubioser Sieg: Lieber Drückeberger als Mittäter," *Die Zeit*, No. 12, March 15, 1991.

44. Interview with Claudia von Braunmühl, "Der Schüssel, Saddam zu stoppen, liegt bei uns selbst," *die tageszeitung*, February 20, 1991.

45. Cynthia Enloe, *The Morning After. Sexual Politics at the End of the Cold War* (Berkeley: University of California Press, 1993). For a German reprint of Garry Trudeau's "checklist" of the Old/New World Order features, see "Alles über die Weltordnung (neu und alt)—Wie die Guten und die Schlechten zu unterscheiden sind," *Die Zeit*, Nr. 13, March 22, 1991.

46. Peter Förster and Günter Roski, *DDR zwischen Wende und Wahl. Meinungsforscher analysieren den Umbruch* (Berlin: LinksDruck Verlag, 1990), p. 161 ff. Until 1989, the Central Institute for Youth Research (ZIJ), established in 1966, was subordinate to the Office for Youth Questions under the Council of Ministers. Margot Honecker attempted several times to dissolve the Institute after 1981, but Western officials closed it down [*abgewickelt*] in 1990 as too "regime-friendly"; its archives were absorbed by the Deutsches Jugendinstitut in Munich.

47. Carol Gilligan, *In a Different Voice. Psychological Theory and Women's Development* (Cambridge, MA: Harvard University Press, 1982).

48. For data, see Mushaben, "Second-Class Citizenship," op. cit.

49. Marion Gräfin Dönhoff, *Weil das Land Versöhnung braucht*, and *Weil das Land sich ändern muß;* both were published by Rowohlt, the first in 1993, the second one cited in 1992. See also *Die Zeit* of September 17, 1993.

50. Women's gains cannot be solely ascribed to the new seats, in view of the losses suffered by the two parties employing quotas: the SPD, whose share fell by 4%, and the Greens, who dropped from 44 seats to none.

51. One of the best statistical overviews of women's lives in the GDR is provided by Gunnar Winkler, Hg., *Frauenreport '90* (Berlin: Verlag Die Wirtschaft, 1990).

52. FRG day-care costs range from DM 250 to DM 1,500 per month, but the main problem is scarce supply. Less than 12% of all Western children under the age of three were in day-care, compared to 85% in the GDR; the figures for children 3 to 5 years old were 60% versus 90%, respectively. The Berlin Senate eliminated 18,000 day care places in the Eastern sector after 1990, although 20,000 children were on western waiting lists at the time.

53. Interview with Angelika Barbe (SPD-East), November 19, 1995.

54. The untenable consequences of the dual-approach became evident in the case of "Kathrin K." A 22-year old married mother of two was arrested on suspicion of abortion while crossing the border between Holland and the FRG in 1992; she was subjected to a forced vaginal exam in a state hospital, becoming a cause célèbre when it was revealed that she had fled to the West from Jena in 1988—where the procedure was still legal. Reported in "Abtreibung. Zwangsuntersuchung an der Grenze," *Der Spiegel*, Nr. 10, March 4, 1991. For details on earlier abortion campaigns see

Mushaben, "Feminism in Four Acts," op.cit; and Herta Däubler-Gmelin and Renate Faerber-Husemann, *§218—Der tägliche Kampf um die Reform* (Bonn: Verlag Neue Gesellschaft, 1987).

55. "Das Bundesverfassungsgericht erläßt eine Übergangsregelung," *Frankfurter Allgemeine Zeitung*, Nr. 123, May 29, 1993; "Abtreibung nur nach Beratung straffrei," *Der Tagesspiegel*, June 30, 1995. For reactions, see Gisela Dachs, "Gute Christen, schlechte Christen," *Die Zeit*, Nr. 24, June 12, 1992; "Auf Kosten der Frauen," *Die Zeit*, February 12, 1993; Karin Flothman, "Der Neue §218 ist völlig paradox," *die tageszeitung*, June 7, 1993; Bert Holterdorf, "Es herrscht eine ziemliche Leere," *Leipziger Volkszeitung*, June 8, 1993; "Die Suche nach Hintertürchen," *Frankfurter Rundschau*, June 17, 1993; and Eva Maleck-Lewy, *Und Wenn Ich Nun Schwanger Bin? Frauen zwischen Selbstbestimmung und Bevormundung* (Berlin: Aufbau, 1994).

56. Judge Ernst-Wolfgang Böckenförde was an active member of the Lawyers' Association for the Right to Life until 1990; Klaus Richter had openly declared his refusal to consider the trimester approach, and Hugo Klein had filed the conservative case against the 1974 reform. Hanno Kühnert, "Wenig Hoffnung auf Karlsruhe," *Die Zeit*, Nr. 50, December 11, 1992. Some three-fourths of the East residents are atheists or agnostics.

57. "Recht auf Kindergartenplatz erst von 1999 an geplant," *Der Tagesspiegel*, June 17, 1993; and Susanne Mayer, "Wo, bitte, bleiben die Kinder?" *Die Zeit*, Nr. 17, April 30, 1993.

58. "Gleicht Vorteil B den Nachteil A aus?" *Süddeutsche Zeitung*, May 29–31, 1993; "Gleichberechtigung—unverbindlich," *die tageszeitung*, May 29, 1993; and Margrit Gerste, "Endlich gleich!" *Die Zeit*, Nr. 12, March 28, 1993.

59. Judith N. Shklar, *American Citizenship. The Quest for Inclusion* (Cambridge: Harvard University Press, 1991), p. 3.

60. Helga Welsh reports a higher percentage of women campaigning for and gaining offices in the new states, due to more open nomination procedures in "Political Elites in Transition: The Case of Eastern Germany," presented at the American Political Science Association Meeting, New York City, September 1–4, 1994.

61. Christian Joppke, "Intellectuals, Nationalism, and the Exit from Communism: The Case of East Germany," *Comparative Studies in Society and History* 37, No. 2 (April 1995), p. 217.

62. Claudia Koppert, "Schuld und Schuldgefühle im westlichen Nachkriegsdeutschland: Zu Wirksamkeit des Vergangenen im Gegenwärtigen?" *Beiträge zur feministischen Theorie und Praxis* 30/31 (1991), p. 225.

63. Joyce Marie Mushaben, "The Rise of Femi-Nazis? Women's Participation in Extremist Movements in United Germany," *German Politics*, Vol. 5, No. 2 (August 1996).

64. Claudia Wolff, cited in Koppert, p. 226.

65. Ibid., p. 219.

66. Gisela Bock neglects to address anti-Semitism in her 600+ page text on *Zwangssterilisation im Nationalsozialismus: Studien zur Rassenpolitik und Frauenpolitik* (Opladen: Westdeutscher Verlag, 1986). For more examples, see Joyce Marie Mushaben, "Coming to Terms with *Mittäterschaft*: Feminism, Nationalism and Identity Politics in Unified Germany," forthcoming.

67. Ursula Schröter, "Ostdeutsche Frauen im Transformationsprozeß. Eine soziologische Analyse zur sozialen Situation ostdeutscher Frauen (1990–1994)," *Aus Politik und Zeitgeschichte*, B 20 (12. Mai 1995), p. 37.

68. Ibid., p. 38.

69. Hilde Utzmann-Krombholz, "Rechextremismus und Gewalt: Affinitäten und Resistenzen von Mädchen und junge Frauen," *Zeitschrift für Frauenforschung*, Heft 1/2 (1994), p. 30.

70. Schröter, p. 35.

71. Joppke, p. 230.

72. Katrin Rohnstock, Hg., *Stiefschwestern. Was Ost-Frauen und West-Frauen voneinander denken* (Frankfurt/M: Fischer, 1994). For a study taking "the glass half full" approach, see the Institut für Demoskopie Allensbach, Hg., *Frauen in Deutschland—Lebensverhältnisse, Lebensstile und Zukunftserwartungen* (Köln: Bund-Verlag, 1994).

73. Christine Thürmer-Rohr, "Aus der Täuschung in die Ent-Täuschung. Zur Mittäterschaft von Frauen" (1983), reprinted in Thürmer-Rohr, Hg., *Vagabundinnen. Feministische Essays* (Berlin: Orlanda Verlag, 1987).

74. Birgit Rommelspacher, "Rassismus im Interesse von Frauen?" *Zeitschrift für Frauenforschung*, Heft 1/2 (1994), p. 36.

75. For further analysis, see Sara Lennox, "Divided Feminism: Women, Racism and German National Identity," *German Studies Review* XVIII, No. 3 (October 1995), pp. 481–502; Mushaben, "Coming to Terms with *Mittäterschaft*," op. cit.

76. Examples include Fransiska Tenner, *Ehre, Blut und Mutterschutz. Getarnt unter Nazi-Frauen heute* (Berlin: Aufbau Verlag, 1994); Ursula Birsl, "Frauen und Rechtsextremismus," *Aus Politik und Zeitgeschichte*, B3–4 (January 10, 1992), pp. 22–30; and Britta Ruth Büchner, *Rechte Frauen, Frauenrechte und Klischees der Normalität. Gespräche mit Republikanerinnen* (Pfaffenweiler: Centaurus, 1995).

77. Koppert, p. 217.

7

What It Means to Be *Non-German*: After Unity, the Deluge

Hier stehtst du schweigend.
Wenn du dich wendest, schweige nicht.
—Memorial Plaque at the Jewish Cemetery, Prenzlauer Berg

It is hard to assume a strictly "scientific" posture when speaking or writing about the violent acts that have taken place on FRG territory since 1989. At the time this book was conceived, the West Germans gave every indication of having become much more tolerant of foreigners in their midst. Younger generations, especially, displayed a strong sympathy for the desparate plight of Third World citizens. Indeed, many New Leftists found it easier to rally on behalf of persecuted tribes in Central America or torture-victims from Iran than to display solidarity with the victims of state oppression next door. For this reason, my interviews with public figures during the 1980s did not directly incorporate questions about right-extremism or animosity toward foreigners.

Unification has nonetheless opened a Pandora's box of unresolved issues tied to a German concept of citizenship grounded in ethnicity. The nation-united now faces a double burden of history rooted in the genocidal practices of the Third Reich era and forty years of authoritarianism under the German Democratic Republic. Adding to the chaos of societal restructuring is a young, troublesome breed of street-fighters in both the old and new states which deliberately seeks to expose the raw nerve of a shared German history. These cohorts can no longer be counted as members of the Turn-Around Generation described and analyzed in earlier chapters. Born after 1972 and socialized under the Western conservative *Wende* or, alternatively, under the revolutionary *Wende* in the East, these youths (aged 13 to 21 by 1993) constitute a small but vociferous segment of the first Post-Wall Generation.

This chapter focuses on the violent turn taken by an appalling number of young Germans in an effort to "reclaim" their national identity since unification; it also looks to the shocking support they seem to garner among older cohorts and its significance for German identity in the larger context. The argument pursued here is three-fold in nature. With regard to post-unity policy developments, I contend that while socio-cultural barriers seem to outweigh legal and economic impediments to the integration and naturalization of foreigners in Germany, these barriers have been instrumentalized and reinforced by politicians in order to justify such impediments. Secondly, I argue that it is necessary to differentiate between an ostensible rise in anti-foreigner sentiment among adults, on the one hand, and diverse manifestations of xenophobic intolerance on the part of youth, on the other. The problem among the former is that too many continue to accept an arcane concept of citizenship, relying upon ethnic descendancy or "blood" (*jus sangunis*), increasingly at odds with the needs of a democratic polity. The crisis involving the latter (viz., youth's attraction to violent, ultranationalist causes) stems from a broader "crisis of values" afflicting post-industrial society. Though one is easily tempted to draw quick historical parallels, neither case can be directly attributed to a "typically German" commitment to fascist ideology.

This chapter begins with a review of the complex legal distinctions used by FRG-officials to determine who is German and who is not-German, concentrating on those who might best be understood as immigrants. It then considers the status of an especially controversial group of foreigners, asylum-seekers, whose conditions for entry were radically redefined through a revision of the Basic Law in 1993. Next I evaluate shifts in public attitudes towards foreigners before and after unification. I then describe select acts of rightwing violence that have taken place on FRG soil since 1990, coupled a "psychogram" of unified German youth. The concluding section explores old and new linkages between the concepts of citizenship, identity and security in the nation-united. Though filled with lots of "facts," this chapter contains several moral admonitions which supersede the data. The history of the Germans does not permit otherwise.

The Conundrum of Immigration:
Legal and Policy Dimensions

Prior to 1990, the West German Basic Law contained two separate articles addressing the contours of citizenship. Both Article 16 and Article 116 of the Basic Law were broadly accepted as a response to unconscionable deprivations of citizenship that had denied all forms of legal protection to countless Third Reich victims. Article 16 posited an unqualified right to political asylum in 1949, recognizing the many Germans who had been forced to seek refuge in other countries or who had perished because they lacked such refuge after 1933. Article 116 offered more than symbolic compensation by reinstating the rights of those forced to abandon or renounce their citizenship during the Nazi era. It continued to define as German any persons displaced by virtue of forced resettlement or by a redrawing of the national borders after unconditional surrender.

Article 116 applied a further set of delineations to those who desired to return to the Federal Republic after 1949, holding different political and financial aid consequences for each group. An individual might be classified as a refugee [*Flüchtling, Vertriebener*], as a resettler [*Umsiedler/Übersiedler, Aussiedler*] or as an asylum-seeker [*Asyl-Bewerber*].[1] Three categories dominated the headlines from 1984 to 1989: *die ÜbersiedlerInnen*—those who "settled over" directly from East Germany as legal migrants, usually after waiting-periods of two to six years; *die AussiedlerInnen*—German-blooded ethnics who "settled out" of territories tied to the Reich prior to December 1937 (portions of postwar Poland, Hungary, Czechoslovakia, Romania); and *die Asyl-BewerberInnen*—asylum-seekers and refugees stemming predominantly from the Third World, many of whom arrived via the Eastern bloc. In this section we consider statutes defining the status of German "resettlers" and non-German migrants known as guestworkers, reserving the discussion of asylum-seekers for later.

Prior to unification, East Germans who relocated to the West, legally or illegally, experienced no change in their "citizenship" status under the Basic Law; they were immediately granted new passports, along with all other rights of membership in the polity. The influx of 343,854 *ÜbersiedlerInnen* prior to November 9, 1989 included 100,000 legal emigrés, as well as those who decided to "vote with their feet," without exit papers, by crossing the Czech or Hungarian "green border" in late summer.

Officially designated a "transitional" passage, Article 116 had become a legal anomaly by the 1980s with regard to the status of *AussiedlerInnen*. Equating "nationality" with ethnicity in relation to the former Eastern territories, it warrants that even the second and third-generation offspring of expellees can claim the protected status of citizen-refugee. This "law of return" means that the children of Eastward-driven, ethnic-stock parents who have never lived outside the Volga region (and actually possess limited command of the mother-tongue) need only reactivate their citizenship—they are German by definition. By contrast, the returning offspring of a German mother forced into US exile to escape the Nazis must still run the gamut of naturalization requirements after several years of FRG-residency, even if married to a German.[2] As absurd as it seems, by 1989 there were four million more World War II "refugees" at home in the FRG than in 1949, owing to the inheritable nature of this status![3]

This group enjoyed critical electoral influence through the 1950s, due to its numerical strength (23.9% of the population in 1960) and its lobbying abilities, channeled through the All-German Bloc of Expellees and Victims of Injustice [*Heimatvertriebenen*]. The flow of *AussiedlerInnen* fluctuated in response to international political events over the next two decades, rising for a time as a result of behind-the-scenes negotiations initiated under SPD diplomats in the 1970s.[4] The number of newcomers fell from 58,062 in

TABLE 7.1   Migrant Population in the Federal Republic, 1980–1992

Year	Asylum-Applicants	Resettlers [AussiedlerInnen]	Total Foreign Population	Naturalized Citizens*
1980	107,818	52,065	4,453,308	14,969
1981	49,391	69,455	4,629,729	13,643
1982	37,423	48,170	4,666,917	13,266
1983	19,737	37,925	4,534,863	14,334
1984	35,278	36,450	4,363,648	14,695
1985	73,832	38,968	4,378,942	13,894
1986	99,650	42,788	4,512,679	14,030
1987	57,379	86,000	4,240,532	14,209
1988	103,076	202,673	4,489,105	16,660
1989	121,318	377,055	4,845,882	17,742
1990	193,063	397,073	5,342,532	20,237
1991	256,112	221,995	5,882,267	27,295
1992	438,191	230,565	6,495,792	37,042

* Excludes the repatriated *AussiedlerInnen*.

Source: Compiled from statistics provided by the German Information Center (New York) and the Federal Ministry of the Interior.

1978 to a low of 36,387 in 1984, but rose to a new high of 372,000 in 1989.

The crumbling of the Wall brought a "tidal wave" of new arrivals, some more German than others but all compelling the state to overextend its social services budget. In 1989 a total of 343,854 GDR citizens took to heart a popular FRG cigarette advertisement—"Let's go West"—as did 372,342 German-stock migrants, added to 121,318 asylum-seekers from predominantly Third World countries.[5] Hundreds of thousands more from Poland and Czechoslovakia crossed the border in search of a better life, followed by migrants from Romania and the Soviet Union. In contrast to earlier years, the new *AussiedlerInnen* were perceived as competitors by the "real Germans" entering from the GDR (still numbering 10,000 per month by January 1991). Sometimes labelled the "Bible Germans," the ethnic-descendants tended to be older, less well-educated and more rigidly/religiously conservative than their GDR counterparts; many were not even fluent in German.[6] Over 2.5 million aliens entered the FRG between January 1989 and 1992; percolating ethnic strife in the dissolving Soviet Union induced a further sense of national panic in anticipation of the multitudes yet to come (see Table 7.1).

The striking thing about the categories routinely used by FRG-officials was that the list never included the term immigrant [*Einwanderer/In*]. Basic Law provisions were supplemented in 1965 by a detailed set of Alien Laws, revised in July 1990; these statutes pertain to the rights and duties of foreigners once they are inside the country. There is no "law of entry" providing for the systematic admission of non-EC aliens into the FRG on a long-term basis, accounting for much of the "abuse" associated with the asylum guarantee.

The onset of the Economic Miracle, coupled with the "missing generation" problem besetting Germany after the war, precipitated a serious shortage of skilled labor by the mid-1950s. The Italians were the first to respond, providing workers for the agricultural and construction sectors as of 1956. The Berlin Wall ended the flow of prospective workers from the East in 1961, leading Bonn to negotiate employment contracts with the governments of Greece, Spain, Turkey, Portugal and Yugoslavia. In 1964 Armando Rodrigues from Portugal was officially welcomed as the one-millionth guestworker to arrive, receiving a Moped as a gift from the FRG government. The influx peaked at 2,595,000 in 1973, with Turkish laborers comprising the largest segment.[7]

"Guests" who had lived in Germany for five years or more were entitled to various "unlimited" residence permits, provided their presence did "not prejudice the important interests" of the host state.[8] Acquiring FRG-citizenship, a status enjoyed by less than 3% during the 1980s, was viewed as the exception to the rule, even among workers who had started families and businesses. Low rates of naturalization were commonly attributed to the foreigners' dreams of eventually returning to the homeland with a substantial D-Mark nestegg, but the criteria for attaining citizenship were quite daunting in and of themselves. An applicant had to live on German soil for at least ten years (five years if married to an FRG native), enjoy full legal standing (which excluded minors), possess an "unblemished character," occupy her/his own dwelling, and demonstrate an ability to support her/himself and all eventual dependents. It was up to the bureaucrat processing the case to determine whether the naturalization of each individual was desirable "from a general political, economic, and cultural viewpoint."[9]

Created in 1978, the Federal Commissioner for Foreigners [*Ausländerbeauftragte*] bears chief responsibility for informing aliens of their rights and coordinating integration or repatriation processes. By the onset of unity ten-year veteran Liselotte Funcke (FDP) relied on eight co-workers and an annual budget of DM 100,000 ($56,000), intended to service the needs of 6.5 million people (out of a total population of 80 million). She resigned one year later in protest against the Government's failure to foster active integration and to counteract post-unity hostility towards foreigners. Her successor, Cornelia Schmalz-Jacobson, reported in 1991 that nearly one-fourth had resided in the FRG for more than two decades, 55% for more than ten years. Some 2.5 million are under the age of 25, 1.5 million under 18, suggesting that most foreign youth have been born and/or educated in the host-country.[10] The revised Alien Laws of July 9, 1990 now allow minors aged 16–23 to acquire citizenship on their own, provided they have resided in the FRG at least eight years and attended schools there for six years; they must also renounce their original citizenship and possess no criminal record (§85). Instead of ten years of consecutive residence for adults, the law now specifies fifteen years (§86) and raises the application fee from DM 50 to DM 100 (§90) for each family member. A purported "easing" of restrictions lies in the fact that applicants will now have an automatic right to citizenship once they have met these conditions; the decision no longer falls to the bureaucrat processing the case. A key deterrent for Turkish residents is not their "dream" of going home but rather the need to renounce their original citizenship, which often means giving up all rights to inheritance in the old country. A further problem for males is the "home state's" refusal to release them from citizenship prior to fulfillment of a two-year military obligation. One way to circumvent this dilemma would be to permit dual-citizenship, an option steadfastly rejected by the Kohl Government.

The state's failure to promote positive integration over the last two decades has played a major role in fostering the public's reluctance to accept their country as a land of immigration. By treating these workers as an industrial reserve army, to be recruited and dismissed according to the needs of capital, politicians have pre-ordained their second-class status as non-citizens. Officials banned the import of new foreign labor after the oil shock of 1973 but paid scant attention to the adjustment problems confronting those who remained.[11] The economic crises of the 1980s saw a further deterioration of public sympathy, as well as the rise of an intellectual right-wing campaign against their presence (the Heidelberg Manifesto of 1982).[12] Bonn's campaign to repatriate Turkish workers in exchange for one-time cash payments through the 1980s was recognized as a flop.

"The number of foreign co-citizens [*Mitbürger*] must be reduced," Chancellor Kohl announced in 1983.[13] The term *Mitbürger* suggests that foreigners enjoy similar rights and incur the same obligations as regular citizens, but the reality is rather lopsided. Though subject to all of the same taxes, foreigners routinely face discrimination in the housing market and the higher educational arena. As of 1990, 62% of the *Wessis* and 43% of the *Ossis* opposed the extension of communal election rights to foreign residents.[14] Schleswig-Holstein's effort to extend the rights of legal aliens by allowing their participation in local elections was overturned by the Constitutional Court in October 1991.

Although integration has been declared "a prime objective of the German government's policy on aliens," its pronouncements on the subject sound more like a demand for full assimilation than an appeal for mutual tolerance and respect. The 1990 Alien Laws reflect the state's desire to

> encourage [foreigners] to become German citizens and *integrate themselves* not only into Germany's economic life, but also into the social, cultural and political texture of their adopted country. In doing so the government *does not propagate a multi-cultural society*. Instead it expects those foreigners, irrespective of their cultural traditions and private religious beliefs, to accept the basic ethical, legal and cultural principles that govern public life in Germany [my emphases].[15]

It is one thing to expect persons living within the FRG's borders to accept overarching constitutional principles (gender equality, religious freedom), and to abide by civil/criminal statutes (e.g., by renouncing murder as a means of "protecting" the family honor). It is another thing altogether to presume that one must embrace an entire spectrum of "German" cultural values, behavioral standards, eating habits, and child-rearing practices to ensure national law and order.[16] Integration is not a one-way street.

Article 16 GG: The Theory and Practice of Asylum Rights

The touchiest non-German designation of all involves asylum-seekers, most of whom arrived from strife-torn areas in Sri Lanka, the Middle East and Africa prior to the outbreak of the Yugoslav war. Both the FRG's liberal asylum provisions and its image as a land of economic miracles have exuded a tremendous magnetic force. Legally classified as *AsylbewerberInnen* [asylum-applicants], recent migrants are often labeled *Asylanten* (which has a negative sound in German, like *Querulanten*), or worse, "pseudo-asylants"— even in official circles. Stemming from different religious and cultural milieus, "economic refugees" have unwittingly unleashed older feelings of xenophobic intolerance, especially among Germans occupying the lower-income brackets. The number of persons filing for FRG-asylum more than tripled between 1989 and 1992, from 121,000 to 438,000 (300,000 out of Yugoslavia); they accounted for 60% of all persons seeking refuge within the European Community during that period.

As Table 7.2 indicates, 1985 marked the beginning of a significant bureaucratic log-jam. The number of refugees whose cases were officially decided fell significantly behind the number of new applicants; a 1987 decline provided a temporary breathing space for case-workers, only to find them overwhelmed the following year. In 1989 the FRG established "quotas" for Southeast Asians, Chileans, Cubans, Argentinians and Kurdish refugees. While the number of asylum applications rose dramatically from 57,605 in 1989, to 256,112 in 1991 and 438,191 in 1992, 68.3% arrived not from the Third World but from Eastern and Southeastern Europe.[17] Many Soviet soldiers facing a return to the not-so-prosperous homeland, for example, deserted their units in hopes of securing asylum.[18] The number of claims filed bears little relation to the proportion of individuals granted legal status, suggesting that the guarantee of political asylum was never as generous in practice as it seemed in constitutional theory. A mere 4.4% were accorded official asylum status in 1990, rising to 7.5% in 1991. Few are immediately deported once their claims have been denied, fueling public resentment over the ongoing support costs.

As of 1990, the FRG paid out DM 5 billion in annual assistance to applicants in waiting and to 490,000 persons denied asylum status but not de-

TABLE 7.2   Political Asylum Seekers, 1980–1992

Year	Number of Applications	Cases Decided	Cases Approved	Approved Cases in Percent
1980	107,818	106,757	12,783	11.97
1981	49,391	110,717	8,531	7.71
1982	37,423	90,853	6,209	6.83
1983	19,737	36,702	5,032	13.71
1984	35,278	24,724	6,566	26.56
1985	73,832	38,504	11,224	29.15
1986	99,650	55,555	8,853	15.94
1987	57,379	87,539	8,231	9.40
1988	103,076	88,530	7,621	8.61
1989	121,318	120,610	5,991	4.97
1990	193,063	148,842	6,518	4.38
1991	256,112	168,023	11,597	6.90
1992	430,191	216,356	9,189	4.25
Total	1,592,268	1,293,712	108,345	8.37%

Source: The Week in Germany, January 15, 1993 (New York: German Information Center), p. 2.

ported (for reasons stated in the Geneva Convention on Refugees); the average monthly stipend was DM 468. Prior to 1991, asylum-seekers were legally barred from paid employment for two years, meaning that most costs for their housing and security fell to state and local governments. This led Western governors to insist that incoming waves of migrants be distributed among the old and new Länder according to a "burden-sharing" formula which took effect in 1990. The smallest city-state of Bremen was required to absorb only 1%, while the largest state of Northrhine-Westphalia was allocated 22.4% of the new arrivals at the time the quartering-quotas were introduced. A 15% increase in the number of applicants brought the five new states into the process in late 1990, reducing wealthy Bavaria's quota by 3,000 and the indigent Saarland's by 375—a policy move which assuaged irrate voters in the prosperous West at the same time it fueled resentment among the economically depressed Easterners. A majority (58%) in the old Länder initially felt that refugees ought to be dispersed equally across united Germany, a stance shared by 68% in the new Länder. But 30% of the East Germans wanted newcomers spread mainly across the old FRG; 27% of the West Germans preferred to see them sheltered mostly in the new states. Ostensible public support for attacks on hostels in Hoyerswerda and Rostock led 60% of the new arrivals to refuse relocation to the East in 1992, with many going underground.[19]

The Union of Romas and Sintis estimates that 1.5 million East European "Gypsies" are currently on the run as a consequence of civil unrest in their home-countries. The war in Bosnia, ethnic violence in Chechnya, the slaughter of innocents in Rwanda—such events suggest that the "German problem" with respect to refugees and asylum-seekers cannot be divorced from broader questions of international responsibility. The first meeting to address the immigration dilemma at the European level took place in Luxemburg in June 1985, when the FRG, France and the Benelux states agreed to coordinate their asylum policies by way of the Schengen Agreement. Initially aiming to secure the gradual elimination of borders in line with the Single European Act, the accord was amended in June 1990, obliging the signatories to respect the existing asylum laws and procedures of neighboring states. Expecting a mass influx of migrants after the collapse of the Berlin Wall, the Member-States unanimously resolved at their June 1990 meeting in Dublin to define asylum and immigration regulations as a matter of "common interest" but to respect national provisions. The 1991 Maastricht Treaty took European cooperation one step further, though not necessarily in the right direction. Intent on enhancing the free movement of labor, capital, goods and services within the Single Market, Article 8 expands the participatory rights and civil liberties of EU citizens, irrespective of where they reside in the region. It distinguishes between EU-nationals and non-EU citizens, however, leaving the freedoms accorded second and third-generation resident aliens to the discretion of the Member-States.

With refugees pouring across the FRG border at the rate of 1,000 per day in 1991 (due largely to war in Yugoslavia), federal officials began to invoke the Schengen Agreement as a justification for tightening existing asylum provisions.[20] On December 6, 1991 Social-Democrats agreed to join Kohl's conservative coalition in tightening the asylum guarantee found in Article 16 of the Basic Law: "Persons persecuted on political grounds shall enjoy the right to asylum." Affording an unconditional right in constitutional-legal terms, Article 16 had given birth to an extraordinarily complicated web of juridical-administrative procedures. The Bundestag declared in January 1992 that it would expedite decision processes, in addition to placing restrictions on eligiblity. The announcement was perceived as an act of political capitulation vis-à-vis the right, especially among those who had engaged in brutal assaults against foreigners.[21]

The Government's interest in limiting the asylum guarantee was grounded in electoral dynamics. Since 1987, the CDU/CSU had seen its share of the vote undercut by new parties to the far-right, notably, the *Republikaner* (*Reps*, founded in 1983) and the German People's Union (*DVU*, founded in 1987). The former jumped the "5% hurdle" in 1989, allowing them to assume parliamentary seats in Bavaria and Baden-Württemburg, as well as in the once left-liberal bastions of Berlin and Bremen. The SPD's reasons for an about-face on the proposed amendment were less apparent. Countless Social Democrats had been forced into exile, were interned or even executed, first under the Nazis, and later under the Stalinists in the GDR—actions of state which had impelled the FRG's founders to enshrine an unqualified right to asylum in the Basic Law of 1949. Willy Brandt—the mayor who rallied Berliners in 1961, and later the Chancellor who fell on his knees in repentance at Auschwitz—had been forced to seek asylum in Norway as an anti-Nazi resistance fighter. His party-comrades would approve the restrictive amendment seven months after his death, having already been punished by voters for a reluctance to embrace hasty unity in 1990.

In August 1992, Interior Minister Rudolf Seiters reiterated the official line that "the Federal Republic is and remains a land friendly to foreigners." On September 24 he signed a controversial pact with his Romanian counterpart, Victor Babuic, allowing both sides to return illegal residents, whether or not they were in possession of valid identity papers for the home-state. Neither Minister was oblivious to the one-sided intention of the treaty which took effect in November: more than 57,446 Romanian asylum-seekers had entered the FRG between January and August 1992; only about 0.2% of this nationality acquire legal status each year, in contrast to 4% for all ethnic groups. The FRG insisted the accord was similar to agreements with Poland, Belgium, France, Luxemburg, and the Netherlands.

Formal deliberations on the proposal to amend Article 16 commenced in the spring of 1993. The ten thousand demonstrators who attempted to block Members' entrance to the Bundestag on May 26th were confronted by 4,000 police; 521 voted for, 132 against a change in the Basic Law. In a separate vote, 497 delegates (out of 654) approved rule changes for processing asylum applications; 540 agreed to a reduction in social assistance benefits for such applicants.[22] The new Article 16a defines the "political grounds" according to which a multitude of displaced persons from Eastern Europe, Africa and the Mid-East are able to qualify as "truly persecuted." Many Bosnian refugees had already discovered under the old Article 16 that not even war provides an iron-clad guarantee for asylum.[23] By specifying a list of countries judged to be in "a state of war" and shifting the burden-of-proof to individual refugees, officials aim to prevent the "undeserving" from entering Germany in the first place. One highly contested provision under the new rules now denies asylum rights to persons who arrive in Germany by way of "safe third countries," for example, on trains passing through such states; they will no longer be guaranteed a right to legal appeal. The CDU/SPD compromise included an effort to limit the influx of German-blooded "resettlers" by imposing a cap (roughly 200,000) on the number who may enter via the open EU-frontier as of January 1993.

Constitutional-legal measures aimed at foreigners will not, in and of themselves, put a brake on assaults against resident aliens or other disadvantaged citizens. The changes which became operational on July 1, 1993 have stemmed the flow of refugees, but the real problems have hardly been

solved. The number of new asylum applications fell from 31,705 in May of
that year, to 14,521 in August; the first quarter of 1994 registered a 69.7%
decline over the same period in 1993. Untold numbers of would-be legal
applicants now resort to illegal modes of entry instead.[24] The new Article
16a has done nothing to eliminate the sources of anti-foreigner feeling, nor
does it offer a remedy for juridical bottlenecks stemming from the lack of a
bona fide Immigration Law. Distinctions inherent in the new amendment
will no doubt foster the careers of a new generation of lawyers in united
Germany, but they are useless in weeding out the racism that mobilizes a
small yet violent segment of the country's youth. The self-proclaimed neo-
Nazis who fire-bombed the home of Turkish residents in Mölln did not in-
quire as to their residency status before precipitating their deaths in late November. Copies of the revised Article 16, adopted on May 26th, had not yet
rolled off the official presses before the next blow to national consciousness
was struck with the five deaths in Solingen on May 29, 1993. "Only" 1,500
rightwing crimes were registered in 1995—after the number of new asylum
applicants had been more than halved.

Public Attitudes Toward Foreigners Before and After Unity

Despite the successful integration of nearly twelve million Eastern refugees
through the 1950s and the effective accommodation of four million "guestworkers" during the 1960s and 1970s, many Western Germans have persisted in their belief that "we are not a land of immigration."[25] This is one instance where postwar German perceptions have failed to keep pace with the
realities of everyday FRG life. One contributing factor is the negative media
coverage accorded foreigners, which gravitates towards stereotypes emphasizing "irreconcilable" cultural differences over shared societal concerns.[26]

As defined earlier, the legal standing of 6.5 million non-German residents is
defined with as much *Gründlichkeit* as that of German-blooded migrants, yet
many citizens tend to cast all four groups (ethnic-migrants, guestworkers,
bona fide asylum-seekers, and illegal but undeportable aliens) into a single
non-melting pot. Resentment against all groups, whether they have lived in
Germany for twenty years or two months, remains tied to persistent housing
shortages and unemployment. Anti-foreigner feeling runs stronger in small
towns and rural areas where migrants are less common and hence more "visible" than in major cities, where apartments and higher-skilled jobs are actually
in greatest demand. Westerners tend to fear a decline in their own living standards, a phenomenon referred to as "the chauvinism of affluence." East Germans exhibit a greater willingness to sympathize with a few nationalities, owing to their extended personal experience with an authoritarian regime.

The importation of foreign labor was initially viewed with skepticism: a
1965 Emnid poll found 27% of the citizens "rather in favor of" but 51%

"rather against" this trend. Only 22% believed guestworkers ought to be allowed to remain in the FRG "as long as they wanted," given a need for their services; 15% favored five-year contracts, while 15% preferred only two-year stays. By 1978, 58% held that only those who had already lived in the FRG "for a long time" ought to be allowed to remain; respondents under 30 were more likely to support integrated neighborhoods. As late as 1979, 60% claimed to have had no personal contact with guestworkers, numbering over three and a half million by then.[27]

Despite the many strictures on the naturalization of foreigners, a strong majority of West Germans (75% of those younger than 19) felt by 1981 that the children of long-term guestworkers ought to enjoy "equal employment opportunities."[28] Generational distinctions were even more apparent in Berlin, where foreigners made up 12% of the population: 32.8% of those under 24, 51.3% of the 25–29 year olds, and 30.1% between the ages of 30–39 perceived their presence as an "enrichment," versus 19.3% among 40–49 year olds, 9.6% for persons aged 50–59, and 9.8% among those 60 or older.[29] Residents with less education and lower socio-economic status tended to view them as a "burden" for the city.

The presence of foreign workers has not only influenced the culinary tastes of most Germans (pizza and döner kebab) since the 1960s; there is also a growing recognition in elite circles that the country's fiscal well-being relies heavily upon their continuing economic contributions. Extremist attacks after 1990 induced government and industry to begin publicizing foreigners' contributions to Germany, though neither was exactly driven by an overnight conversion to universal human rights. Comprising 8.5% of the paid labor force at the time of unity, foreign-workers have become a self-sustaining segment of the economy. The number of self-employed rose from 51,000 in 1970 to 200,000 by 1990, while some 33,000 Turkish-owned businesses generated more than 700,000 jobs in 1991—refuting the claim that migrants take away jobs which rightfully "belong to the Germans." Registering DM 25 billion ($ 15.4 billion) in taxable sales, these entrepreneurs invested over DM 6 billion in the local economies, adding 9% to the Gross Domestic Product. The self-employed moreover contributed DM 12.8 billion to the national pension insurance fund, only DM 3.7 billion of which was paid out to foreign retirees. The remaining two million guestworkers poured DM 16 million into the general tax fund, coupled with DM 8 billion in value-added taxes for daily consumption. The purchasing power of 1.7 million Turkish consumers alone amounts to DM 50 billion ($30.8 billion), based on average monthly earnings of DM 3,650 ($2,253 netto).[30]

A 1991 study by the Federation of German Industries concluded that "some areas of public life, such as garbage collection, janitorial services, and gastronomy would collapse" without foreign laborers.[31] The low-status nature of these jobs—in Wallraf's terms, *ganz unten*—shrouds the importance

TABLE 7.3   Preferred Treatment of Future Migrants, 1991

Types of Migrants	West Germans	East Germans
Ethnic-Germans (*Aussiedler*)		
*Take them in	15%	13%
**Starkly reduce their number	38%	30%
Political refugees		
*Take them in	25%	30%
**Starkly reduce	39%	18%
Family members of guestworkers		
*Take them	21%	17%
**Starkly reduce	39%	35%
Economic refugees (*Armutsflüchtlingen*)		
*Take them	3%	2%
**Strongly reduce	76%	62%

Source: Schubarth, "Fremde als Sündenbocke," op. cit.

of foreign laborers (14% or more) in nine of the country's fifty-two key industrial sectors, including mining, construction and automobile production.[32] Economists estimate that declining birthrates in Germany will neces-
sitate the hiring of one million more guestworkers to sustain its social
security network by the year 2000.[33] The Institute of German Business pre-
dicts that the "demographic gap" will impel the FRG to recruit an additional 12.5 million migrant workers (400,000 per annum) by the year 2020,
due to the expanding Single European Market. Employers reported a shortage of 230,000 apprentices in 1992; like their same-age counterparts, foreign youth educated in the FRG are increasingly drawn to white-collar occupations, up from 11.9% in 1970 to 18.9% in 1990. In stark contrast to
German industrial orientations of the 1930s, major corporations like Daimler-Benz have recognized that their interests and market shares "are much
too internationalized and Europeanized, in order to engage in a right-radi-
cal direction."[34] Lufthansa Airlines sought to assuage its non-German cus-
tomers with an advertisement—"We are foreigners every day. Feeling
global"—after the extremist attacks in Rostock and Mölln.

The public's willingness to embrace immigrants evincing varying degrees
of Germanness has fluctuated with each wave of newcomers (see Table 7.3).
The percentage of citizens supporting the assimilation of new GDR-reset-
tlers rose from 28% in March of 1989, to 44% in August, then 63% in October, falling to 59% in November (Wall-opening) and 33% by January 1990.
Based on the November sample, 81% of the West-Germans feared that the
influx of thousands of East Germans would create economic bottlenecks;
57% anticipated long-term problems for the labor market.[35] Their initial
sense of moral obligation towards persons legally defined as "real Germans"
overrode their macro-economic concerns during a period of relative fiscal

stability. The subsequent collapse of other East European regimes shifted the paradigm considerably.

The mass influx of refugees in 1991 precipitated a sea-change in attitudes regarding Germany's historical obligation to provide unlimited political asylum. Surveys from this period found as many as 96% rejecting economic motives as grounds for permitting refugees to enter the expanded FRG, 76% advocating restrictions on the Basic Law's guarantee of asylum, and 69% favoring absolute curtailment of that right.[36] Prior to the deaths in Mölln (see below), 43% of the Federal Republicans reportedly rejected the slogan *Ausländer 'raus!*; 69% denounced the slogan after the tragedy. The number embracing a belief that "the right to asylum is a human right" rose from 39% to 61%.[37]

For all their other differences, the newly united Germans overlap considerably in their prejudices towards specific groups of foreigners. Based on a 1990 comparison, East and West residents differed only slightly in their affinities for the French, US-Americans, and Russians; in a 1968 ZIJ-Leipzig survey, by contrast, 85% of the East Germans had classified the Soviets as peace-loving, but only 17% saw US citizens in this way. Old and new Federal Republicans are also closely matched in their animosities towards Roma and Sinti "Gypsies," Polish and Turkish migrants.[37] Prejudicial attitudes towards the latter have probably been absorbed via the Western media, since there were no Turkish workers in the East prior to 1989. Before the Wall opened, fewer than 190,000 foreigners worked among more than 16 million GDR natives, most of whom were recruited from Vietnam, Mozambique and Cuba; 90,000 were deported following the initiation of the Social and Monetary Union.[39] Thereafter, roughly 48% on both sides felt that officials displayed "too little" tolerance towards foreigners, while 17% held they showed "too much" sympathy.[40]

Admittedly, there are limits to the number of refugees any city or state might be expected to absorb peacefully. A favorite stopping place for new entrants, Berlin already carries a population density of 3,800 people per square kilometer, in contrast to 90 residents per square-kilometer in Brandenburg. The resentment felt is by no means proportionate to the number of foreigners, legal and illegal, seeking a better life in *Modell Deutschland*. In Hoyerswerda, a site of major violence, foreigners made up less than half a percent of the population; they accounted for 12% of the residents in Bremen, where Mayor Klaus Wedemeier (SPD) ordered the deportation of illegal Roma and Sinti refugees housed within city limits prior to September 1991. His assertion that Bremen was "unable to support" additional foreigners coincided with his decision to restore a "luxury public pissoire" at the cost of DM 900,000.[41] The right-extremist German People's Union (DVU) later secured 6.2% of the vote, despite the mayor's concessions to anti-foreigner feeling; it garnered 10.2% in Bremerhaven.

Average citizens often fail to distinguish between truly needy foreigners and other outlaw elements. The behavior of many so-called Gypsies has hardly been stellar. In July 1992, Pastor Reinhard Enders in Leipzig told me about his experiences at the Nikolai Church (cradle of the 1989 "peaceful revolution"). He and other parishioners invested time and money in an effort to feed and clothe recently arrived Romanians, who then dumped the food in the garbage can—before they robbed the church. Adult-beggars often drug their children to invoke the sympathy of passers-by with their listless, hungry appearance. Such behavior does not automatically exonerate Western politicians who have failed to respond adequately to economic collapse in Eastern Europe.

While morally reprehensible, neither economic discrimination nor electoral backlash aimed at "outsiders" can be equated with support for physical attacks against such persons. Prior to unity, 86% of the Germans (IPOS poll) opposed violence against foreigners; 81% of the West-citizens cited right-extremism as "the greatest danger" to democracy, compared to 90% in the East.[42] Then how do we account for various public displays of "understanding" and "sympathy" for youth attacks on foreigners subsequent to unification?

A Turn for the Worse: Post-Unity Violence

"Behind the smoke screen of the calumous debate over asylum," Jürgen Habermas wrote in late 1992, "the old Federal Republic has changed in a more deeply reaching subconscious fashion and more quickly over the last three months than over the preceding one and a half decades."[43] It is easier to quibble with Habermas' time-frame than with his basic proposition. The turning-point for the Federal Republic with regard to open displays of anti-foreigner sentiment was not 1992 but 1991, the year during which the number of attacks against foreigners increased ten-fold on German soil.

Statistics involving extremist acts began to rise dramatically following the July 1990 creation of a Social and Monetary Union.[44] Incidents have ranged from gang-attacks on individuals in subways and shopping areas to fire-bombings of their temporary quarters (tents, container ships and community centers). The first year of unity saw a dramatic escalation in the number of physical attacks, up to 1,483 cases. Nearly 500 assaults occurred between September and October 1991; three-fourths of the arson attacks took place in the old Länder. The Federal Interior Ministry reported 2,368 incidents of a xenophobic nature that year. A ZDF poll executed in September found that 44% accepted the presence of foreigners, a figure which rose to 60% in October. An Emnid survey simultaneously determined that 38% of the West Germans, compared to 21% of their allegedly more radical Eastern compatriots, expressed "understanding" for rightwing tendencies.[45] In 1992, the Office of Constitutional Protection registered a 54% increase over the preceding year, 2,584 physical attacks (out of 7,121 rightwing acts) resulting in seventeen deaths—nine in the West, eight in the East. In 1993, it recorded 8,109 rightwing crimes (e.g., dissemination of hate-materials, threats) but "only" 1,814 acts of violence against foreigners, Jews and other "political opponents," adding eight more fatalities. The number of arson cases dropped from 708 to 302.[46]

Of the 11,515 individuals indicted for rightwing offenses to date, 60% have been minors. Attacks have occurred in German towns stretching from Aalen (Westphalia) to Zwickau (Saxony). Assaults in the new states often receive sensational coverage, but major incidents there have triggered parallel foreigner-bashings in Western cities; Hoyerswerda, for example, led to "actions" in Bochum, Brandenburg, Freiburg, Hagen, Saarlouis, Neumünster and Hünxe. Radical gangs have ascribed a "signal" character to such deeds; according to former ring-leader Ingo Hasselbach, Hoyerswerda "was a fresh start. . . . [We] were glad that a little steam came into the rightwing scene."[47] Hearing about attacks elsewhere, local gangs set out to prove that they are no more "lame-assed," in their words, than the rest.

One of the more dramatic incidents was the molotov-cocktail bombardment of a dormitory occupied by 70 Yugoslavs, Mozambiquans and Turkish workers on September 17, 1991. Instigated by 150 young male radicals who battled with the police for several hours, the onslaught in Hoyerswerda (Saxony) drew international press coverage as a result of the applause proffered by 150 bystanders as windows were shattered by steel balls and cobblestones. Described as a town of 70,000 "with no disco, no cinema, and bars that close at 10 pm," Hoyerswerda lost 5,000 jobs in late 1991, due to a shut-down of its major industry, the *Schwarze Pumpe* coal mines.

The eastern coastal city of Rostock is another area which has seen its key industry, ship-building, collapse as a consequence of unification. A February 1992 survey of 200 residents showed that anti-foreigner feelings were not confined to fringe groups; 34.7% wanted tough restrictions or an absolute halt to the admission of asylum-seekers. The reasons they gave included high unemployment (73.6%), housing shortages (69.9%) and the nature of the asylum debate among politicians (43.5%); only 42% cited the behavior of the asylum-seekers themselves.[48] The desire for a foreigner-free Germany draws on the idea that taxpayers' money should be used to shelter and supply work for the indigenous population. At the time, the city's official unemployment rate was 17%; the number of de facto jobless stood closer to 40%, according to local authorities.

Rostock became the site of a new wave of xenophobic attacks less than one year after the Hoyerswerda outbursts. The siege commenced with a week of nightly rioting during the summer of 1992. On August 26th, neighborhood-dwellers in Lichtenhagen cheered on neo-Nazi youths as they stormed and fire-bombed a ten-story hostel housing over 200 Romanians and 115 Vietnamese. Citizen-enthusiasm grew more subdued a few nights later when 500 Skinheads took on 1,000 police, resulting in 195 arrests and 65 injured officers. Organized radio networks, the use of mobile phones and walkie-talkies, as well as the "scheduled" nature of many assaults (occurring immediately after police withdrawals from specific neighborhoods) testified to the provocative leadership role played by "traveling" rowdies: many males arrested hailed from Hamburg, Kiel and Berlin. Reports of the Rostock "happening" unleashed attacks against asylum-hostels stretching from Prenzlau, Cottbus, Lübbenau and Greifswald, to Wismar, Eberswalde, Erfurt, Leipzig, Eisenhüttenstadt, Quedlinburg and Darmstadt. Within days, two hundred Romanians were permanently evacuated from Rostock.

The next event attracting international media attention took place in the bucolic state of Schleswig-Holstein. A Turkish grandmother and two children perished on November 22, 1992 as the result of a late-night arson attack on their home in Mölln; nine other people sustained injuries. Aged 51, Bahide Arslan had lived in Germany for more than a decade; her granddaughter Yeliz Arslan (10) had been born in Mölln, and her niece, Ayse Yilmaz (14), was visiting for the first time. Five days later some 10,000 residents participated in a memorial service, before the three were flown back to Turkey for burial.[49] Labor unions held a twenty-minute work stoppage in solidarity, accompanied by demonstrations in more than twelve cities; one rally involving 12,000 people in Mölln was marred by physical clashes between rival Turkish groups. That same month 27-year-old Silvio Meier was stabbed to death in Berlin, and 53-year old Karl Heinz Rohn was severely beaten in Wuppertal, set on fire and dumped across the Dutch border after a bartender told Skinheads he was Jewish. He was not.

During a state-visit to Turkey in May 1993, Chancellor Kohl extended a verbal "guarantee" that the Mölln tragedy would never be repeated. Less than two weeks later, the town of Solingen in prosperous Northrhine-Westphalia was rocked by similar arson-related deaths. On May 29th, four youths set fire at 1:38 am to a three-story house owned by the Genc family; fire engines appeared at the scene nine minutes later. Trapped on the second floor, Kamil Genc's two sisters Hatice and Gürsun, his niece Gülüstan, his daughters Hülya (9) and Saime (4) perished in the blaze; nine others were injured, including a six-month old infant and a boy with second- and third-degree burns. Older members of the family had arrived in Germany in 1970; they had purchased their wooden house in 1981.

Neighbors held a silent watch in front of the ruins on Pentecost Sunday, culminating in a peaceful demonstration of 3,500 several days later. Some federal officials rushed to visit the injured, while politicians of all persuasions called for the introduction of dual-citizenship—with the notable exception of Chancellor Kohl. Two days of turbulence ensued when 3,000 Turkish radicals descended on the arson-site, battering police cars or windows and hurling molotov-cocktails; 62 were arrested. State Interior Minister Herbert Schnoor deployed 1,400 police from the Federal G-9 Anti-terrorist Unit, threatening immediate deportation of all who engaged in violence.[50] Another 500 police were used to quell a display of force in Hamburg. President Richard von Weizsäcker gave the keynote address at a memorial service attracting 6,000 participants in Köln on June 4, 1993.

A town of 166,000 with 20,000 foreigners, Solingen is administered by an SPD government which had established its own German-Turkish communications center several years earlier. It maintains an active sister-city relationship with Israel, and has allowed a school to "adopt" its Jewish cemetery. Yet resident aliens complained that two mosques had been attacked in April, inflicting DM 20,000 in damages, with no effective investigation. Police were aware of the right-extremist affiliations of local youth prior to the arson-deaths in Solingen and Mölln. In both cases, the search for murder suspects entailed many legal irregularities, raising doubts about the admissibility of their confessions. Fatalities might not have occurred, had Father-State committed as many of its "anti-terrorist" resources to tracking earlier reports of extremist groups as it did to quelling foreigners's unrest after the fact.

The question of "who is to blame" was rendered all the more compelling by another incident which took place in Magdeburg (Sachsen-Anhalt) on May 12, 1994. On Ascension Day [the German Father's Day], some 40 to 60 alcoholized members of the extremist scene chased several Africans through the downtown pedestrian zone, yelling "Germany for the Germans or Foreigners out!" smashing store windows along the way; witnesses made repeated calls to police but none intervened. Law enforcement officials claimed their initial restraint owed to the fact that they were unable to distinguish between perpetrators and victims—a curious argument in view of police-report references to Black-Africans and (visibly shaven) Skinheads. The Africans sought refuge in two restaurants operated by Turkish residents, soon stormed by the rowdies. Destroying the facilities, the invaders also attacked the staff, who then defended themselves with knives; three were wounded on each side. Police entered the Marietta Bar but were only temporarily successful in separating the two groups. Violence flared up again after one hour, by which point the number of antagonists had increased to 100; the battle for control turned against the police two hours later.

Of the 49 combatants taken into custody (including 14 foreigners), 46 were released; a man from Mali was charged with weapons violation, and one Skin was detained, based on a previous warrant for his arrest; two were rearrested in July for subsequent assaults of the same nature. One officer cited in *Der Spiegel* noted that "most of [the extremists] have been well-known to us for years," yet the Chief of Police insisted the case did not really entail hostility to foreigners: in his words, "the role played by sun and alcohol was much greater." The Chancellor's Office issued a statement declaring that the federal government could not judge the work of the Magdeburger police, though records indicated that the State Office for Constitutional Protection had told local authorities on May 11th to deploy more officers, knowing that gang activities were planned for the 12th.[51] By 1995, 34 persons had been indicted, but only 10 guilty-verdicts ensued; sentences ranged from twelve months on probation to three and a half years in juvenile detention. The court refused to try the rest, claiming it was "overloaded" with cases.

Home to 17,000 Germans and 700 non-citizens, Mölln has no *Ausländerbeauftragte* of its own; the officer responsible for the needs of resident foreigners is located in the county seat of Ratzeburg. Two independent multi-cultural initiatives (*Verein Miteinander Leben* and *Förderverein Multikulturelle Begegnung*) were formed to restore the Arslan house as a memorial site, but the DM 3 million in promised funding had not materialized by 1993. The house in which the Turkish grandmother and two girls died stands in a narrow, cobbled street, *die Mühlenstrasse*, the kind that echoes every sound, especially at night; neighboring buildings were separated only by a walkway leading to one of Mölln's many "cure" parks. This was not a "foreigners' ghetto" like Berlin-Kreuzberg or Stuttgart-Sindelfingen; the house stood within a few blocks of the main market-place. A second building set on fire that night stood atop a hill on a busy thoroughfare. It was hard to imagine how the fire could have wiped out an entire story without anyone noticing (since many Germans sleep with their windows open). It was the arsonists themselves who notified the police and fire departments, ending their anonymous calls with "*Heil*, Hitler."

It is even harder to grasp what might lead the townspeople of Mölln or Solingen to feel that they have more in common with unknown residents of Jena or Cottbus—not to mention those in Königsberg or the Sudetenland—than with Turkish families who have lived next door to them for more than a decade.[52] Ethnicity is neither a necessary nor a sufficient condition for creating a sense of political community. The rudimentary protections denied foreigners in Hoyerswerda, Magdeburg and Mölln should not depend on formal delineations of citizenship: they ought to constitute the foundation of any civilized society. A Government which deliberately pushed for rapid unification can hardly declare it bears no responsibility for extremist developments in the new Länder, any more than it can exonerate itself from violent trends in the old ones.

Socio-Psychological Dimensions of Youth Extremism

My own efforts to study European youth movements, violent as well as peaceful ones, date back to 1981. Having followed the phenomenon for more than twelve years, I do not believe one can explain post-Wall trends in Germany without examining the "big picture" of changes in post-industrial society, though the catalyst for resurgent extremism lies in the disruptive processes of unification itself. The New Intolerance towards outsiders—reflected in the (re-)emergence of far-right parties as well as in the proliferation of violence-prone gang members—seems to stem from feelings of social displacement and economic insecurity, rather than from explicit ultra-nationalistic designs. Still, xenophobic tendencies have deep roots, suggesting that many of the indicators were in place well before the Unity Treaty was signed.

Prior to unity, few FRG-politicians knew much about the existence of GDR Skinheads, Punks, Heavy-Metal Fans and Nazi-Rocker groups, which emerged during the 1980s in opposition to the sclerotic Honecker regime. According to the GDR Constitution (Article 6), the new socialist state "true to the interest of the people" had "eradicated German militarism and Nazism within her territory" as of 1949. Research conducted by Wolfgang Brück in Leipzig nonetheless confirmed the existence of several groups located at the far-right end of the GDR-youth spectrum.[53] Skinheads comprised the alleged "monster faction," prone to random outbursts of violence; their most sensational attack against "leftist" Punks and ecology activists took place at the *Zionskirche* in East Berlin during October 1987. These *Glatzköpfe* [Bald-heads] fell between the ages of 18 and 25; largely male, they were usually slated for low-skilled occupations. They had already begun to recruit their own successor generation, Baby Skins aged 13–15, prior to 1989.

Ultra-right tendencies were likewise evident among Western youth well before unification. A 1987 study conducted by Bielefeld sociologist Wilhelm Heitmeyer estimated the proportion of 16–17 year olds with radical-right proclivities at roughly 16% among the less well educated, 7–8% among college-bound students.[54] Attributing youth's aggressive orientations towards foreigners to latent persecution complexes and rigid value-hierarchies, Castner and Castner held that their use of Nazi symbols, intended to shock the adult world, did not equal a return to Hitlerian ideology.[55] One West Berlin rock-concert promoter observed during the 1980s that the Skins "look like Hitler youth, they sound like Hitler youth, but they don't know who Hitler was."

There is an observable generation gap between the organized conservative far-right (whose ranks contain a number of WWII hold-overs), and the active street-fighters who evoked public applause in Hoyerswerda and Rostock. While Chancellor Kohl may be reluctant to sever ties with older, hardline voters insisting on a return of "lost" Eastern territories (despite the 1990 Settlement Treaty), such demands are construed as legalistic and "boring" among members of the action-oriented successor generations. Petty struggles for power among party-professionals such as Czaja, Schönhuber and Frey spark no long-term interest among the-young-and-the-restless cohorts. The latter are more intent on defending the homeland (their term) against the hordes of "culturally alien" job-competitors who might yet pour into the Land of Economic Miracles.

The movement has also exhibited a clear-cut gender gap, at least prior to 1993, to the extent that 95.5% of the persons convicted for acts of rightwing violence were male.[56] Instead of attracting women with promises of a glorified motherhood role, a position skillfully manipulated by Hitler, the new extremists have alienated many potential female accomplices with distinctively macho-mysoginist behavior and speech. Neo-Nazi aversion to feminism, rooted in male fears of increasing competition for limited job opportunities, as well as a penchant for physical violence is usually viewed as a detriment to female participation in such groups.

Like all other rules, the one inferring that female socialization patterns render women more immune to violent behavior has its exceptions. As I have documented elsewhere, the spectrum of female participants in far-right groups ranges from Neo-National Sympathizers and Fascho-Brides, to Extra-Parliamentary Organizers (the New APOS), militant Streetfighters or Reenies, and established Rep-Party Women.[57] A survey of 300 apprentices in Lower Saxony found that a majority of the female respondents displayed xenophobic rather than nationalistic, tendencies. Researchers speculated that their belief in the biologically determined nature of women's inferior social position leads them to vent frustrations over inequality by way of intolerance towards foreigners.[58] Females differ from male radicals in their aversion to sexual harassment, in their desire to transcend subordinate political roles, as well as in their general support for a woman's right to choose abortion.[59]

These are not the only traits distinguishing post-Wall neo-Nazis from Hitler-era fascists. In contrast to the highly organized bands of the 1930s, leadership among contemporary extremists is highly diffuse and fraught with personality conflicts. Most groups are "headless," notwithstanding the efforts of certain figures to construct their own cults of personality, such as Schönhuber (*Reps*). Many key figures appealing to youth have already died (Michael Kühnen of Hamburg, Rainer Sonntag of Dresden), dropped out (Ingo Hasselbach), or recanted (the heavy metal band, *Böhse Onkelz*).[60]

Estimates relating to membership in extremist organizations are hazy at best. *Verfassungsschutz* figures range from 4,200 Skinheads to 42,000 far-right party members, but organizations tend to splinter and regroup, making it difficult to control for drop-outs or overlapping memberships. The Nationalist Front, formed in 1985, was outlawed in November 1992, for example; many of its supporters turned to the Free German Workers' Party [*FAP*], subsequently outlawed in October 1993. A Rhineland-Palatinate study based on 1,300 police files found that many persons indicted for crimes of violence were tied to groups or cliques lacking any specific ideological or political motives. Nearly 70%, between the ages of 15 and 20, experienced an authoritarian upbringing.[61]

The societal context facing younger cohorts in search of their own identity—through rebellion against the older generation—is fraught with perils quite different from those experienced by "the '68ers." Youth's rejection of The Establishment since 1989 underscores a negation of their own individual prospects, as reflected in the motto, "Live intensely, love ambitiously, die young." There seem to be few positive, heroic figures for youth to emulate these days. The Long March Generation was treated to a sense optimism and idealism, in a world not yet permeated by images of Chernobyl, school-yard violence and neighborhood drug-dealers. It borrowed many idols and role-models from abroad, including John F. Kennedy, Robert Kennedy, Gloria Steinem, Martin Luther King, Jr., Angela Davis and even the Beatles; these figures persuaded them—along with millions of US Baby-Boomers like myself—that all we needed was "love," and they urged us all "to give peace a chance." As Wolfgang Stürzbecher noted in a 1995 discussion with me, "the kids" don't recall Sylvester Stalone as the hard-working prize-fighter, Rocky. They only know anti-heroes like Rambo, The Terminator (I, II and III), and self-avenging Mutant Ninja Turtles. Attempts to put a leash on collective acts of violence cannot be decoupled from a need to limit media glorification of militarized aggression and all-or-nothing macho personalities.

Eager to supply a highly simplified message of salvation, far-right mobilizers urge young extremists to see themselves as the victims of an historical responsibility that will not go away, implying that "Germany was once full of war-invalids, now it is full of postwar-invalids."[62] Still missing from "the school of the nation" is a form of political re-education which promotes empathy with the victims of aggression. Scores of media reports focused on ultra-right fanatics after the outbursts in Hoyerswerda and Rostock; the victims and their relatives were rarely featured, until some Turkish activists became violent offenders themselves.

One citizen of Rostock-Lichtenhagen insisted after the summer riots, "Those are no Nazis. Those are our children," suggesting that the real problem lies with journalists who use the terms neo-Nazi, right-radicals, Skinheads and fascists interchangeably, if inaccurately. Adolescents schooled in the GDR were exposed at tender ages to the atrocities of German history by way of obligatory field-trips to concentration camps and then left to cope with traumatic reactions on their own.[63] Obligatory classroom treatments rarely cover questions of local complicity, as Schneider's experience in Celle shows, with the result that youth see little connection between the dynamics of the Holocaust and their own desire to "get the foreigners out."[64] Heiner Geissler (CDU) insists that "information and knowledge are the enemies of radicalism, and therefore the best weapons against it," yet his party-colleagues are loathe to incorporate the personal testimony of the surviving witnesses to history, as well as tales of neighborhood collaboration into the required curricula, especially in Bavaria.[65] If the young thugs engaging in violent assaults are merely politically alienated, economically anxious, or emotionally troubled teens at heart, then the question of parental responsibility looms even larger. Though it contradicts much of their own experience, post-Wall parents must teach their children that it is possible "to just say no." Ironically, it has taken another American film, Spielberg's Oscar-winning *Schindler's List*, to turn "resistance" into a renewed topic for public debate.[66]

Extremist orientations of the 1990s are sooner rooted in "the anti-politics of post-modernism" than in a deep-seated willingness to sacrifice for the nation.[67] One East Berlin squatter named Thomas, then 18, advised me in June 1990, "these youth, the Skinhead elements are not really pro-fascist but anti-anti-fascist" after years of state propaganda; his characterization made a lot of sense at the time. But the proliferation of youth violence in both parts of Germany suggests that many other causes are at work; GDR-experience adds an extra layer to the resentment and uncertainty afflicting potential aggressors. Both sets of radicals are anti-party, anti-internationalist, anti-intellectual, as well as anti-communist and anti-capitalist. Theirs is a paradox of "negations": they attempt to solidify their own national identity by excluding non-Germans, and this negative demarcation, as they perceive it, opens up their personal prospects for positive social change.

In certain respects, the first post-Wall cohorts have more in common with the pre-materialists of the Depression years than they do with the post-materialists immediately preceding them. As the quality of their hang-outs and dwelling-places suggests, younger radicals are less interested in ostentatious consumption. Certain groups seem to shirk regular forms of paid employment—a moot point among East-youth, given the high unemployment affecting all ages in the new states. But jobless youth also move towards greater alcohol-consumption and physical abuse; this is reflected in the motto of one Skin-Club located in Apolda-Nord, outside Berlin: "Who Germany loves and unity too, occasionally likes to quaff a few."[68] The official drinking age in the FRG is 16, yet the price of beer is lower than that of cola or juice at many neighborhood "watering holes."

The more one drinks, the lower the threshold for violence. Excessive group-consumption, vandalism and violence are especially prevalent on holidays like Father's Day. Curiously, judges have accepted drunkenness as grounds for meliorating the sentences of violent defendants but not of reckless drivers. Officials interviewed for this work were loathe to discuss the possibility of raising the drinking age, since "the industry" would never accept such a change. Drugs were not a problem prior to 1989, since the presence of many police controlling the borders prevented their entry into the country; substances which did make it through were too expensive for general consumption. Crack-cocaine has now entered the region; it goes by the local name of *Mauerstaub* or "Wall-Dust."

Violence has also increased due to the sudden availability of weapons from a variety of sources. Three weapons stores opened in the Mehringdamm/Kreuzberg neighborhood within a year of the Wall's opening, though gun-ownership is still regulated. Departing Warsaw Pact soldiers have added to the supply by selling off their military equipment on a cash-and-carry basis, though the "weapon of choice" among street-Nazis is often an American baseball bat. Attempts to apply the "iron fist" of the state does not provide an immediate remedy; during many outbursts of 1991, rioters were often better armed than the uniformed officials sent to quell their disturbances.[69] Many of the veteran East-police were fired due to *Stasi*-ties, and those who remained had neither the training nor the equipment necessary to ensure effective crowd-control. Police responses, or lack thereof, (e.g., in Magdeburg) make it clear that formal law enforcement is only the first step towards social peace.

Young citizens have been influenced by years of TV-exposure to fictionalized violence (on average, 28 hours per week for 8–12 year-olds), as well as to "unconventional modes of participation" ranging from strikes and riots, to missile-site occupations and Velvet Revolutions. Indeed, the greatest political victory ever scored by downtrodden Easterners, deposing the SED regime, was achieved by taking to the streets. Raised in a system where all forms of *societal* activism were more or less banned, rowdies are still apt to define their situation in terms of the political: If "red is dead," then the ideological alternative must lie in a shift to the far-right. Sensationalized media coverage renders young streetfighters the center of national attention; though a poor substitute for treatment of their ills, the "oxygen of publicity" enhances their desire to "shock" observers with the adoption of Nazi-slogans and attire.[70] "Rock against the Right" concerts and neighborhood initiatives opposing xenophobic intolerance are less well publicized.

While the perpetrators of violence are by no means "typical" of the first Post-Wall Generation, one needs to recognize that the events of 1989–90 had a dramatic psychological impact on all Eastern youth. In contrast to West-adolescents, whose socialization processes remained intact, the GDR "kids" were compelled to restructure their identities in a legal-moral vacuum which persisted for over a year. I was utterly shocked, one June day in 1990 around 10 am, to find myself in the midst of several beer-bottle-throwing teenage males on the S-Bahn en route to the southside of East Berlin. Sitting across from me was a Soviet military officer, reading a book; no other authority figure was in sight. It was clear that the old rules no longer applied, and that the new ones had not yet taken effect.

The one policy which the GDR pursued with great consistency was that of recruiting youngsters and adolescents into mass organizations in hopes of binding them to the socialist Fatherland. With the rise of underground peace and ecology movements, even the Communist Youth League [FDJ] had to vie for members by way of rock concerts, discos and other recreational activities. In addition to wiping out an extensive network of after-

TABLE 7.4 "Understanding of Democracy" Among Youth, 1990: Features That Are Absolutely Essential in a Society, in Order to Label It a "Democracy"

Feature	Total (in percent)	FRG-Youth	GDR-Youth
Equal Rights for Women	83.4	82.1	84.9
Freedom of Expression	94.7	93.7	95.8
Protection of the Environment	74.2	71.2	77.7
Freedom to Travel	73.4	77.5	68.5
Equal Educational Opportunity	81.5	76.8	87.0
Right to a Workplace	80.1	74.4	86.7
Equal Protection before the Law	86.8	84.7	88.6
Free Elections	94.5	92.7	96.6
State guarantee of basic medical care	76.0	79.4	73.1
Free economic order, free enterprise	59.0	58.4	59.5
Protection of foreign religious or political Minorities	57.4	63.0	50.8

Source: Compiled from Dennhardt et al., *Deutsche Schüler im Sommer 1990,* op. cit., Part II, pp. 23–28.

school programs and youth clubs, the collapse of the SED regime put an end to guaranteed apprenticeships, permanent jobs and accustomed mechanisms of social security, without providing the skills needed for competition under a free market. Most adults, facing extraordinary circumstances, will try to conduct their business as usual; for those who can buy beer at age 16 and have no place else to go, the sky is the limit.

The last three years have seen many new opinion polls involving questions of anti-foreigner violence and rightwing extremism. Most suggest that serious problems lie ahead with regard to the political (re)integration of youth, though mood swings are quite common among adolescents. I will summarize four studies of the "representative" sort, in an effort to show the direction in which the German identity of Post-Wall youth seems to be heading.

In 1990, the Central Institute for Youth Research in Leipzig combined forces with the Munich-based German Youth Institute (DJI) to compare the "democratic" orientations of 1,231 Western and 1,049 Eastern adolescents. Conducted prior to unity, this survey focused on secondary school pupils aged 14–18. Its primary aim was to determine the degree to which youth socialized under diametrically opposed systems now overlap or disagree with respect to their understanding of democracy.

While the influences of divergent political socialization processes cannot be overlooked entirely (e.g., greater support for legal protection among youth born into a "state of law," a stronger commitment to job-rights among the offspring of "the socialist workers' state"), their mutual acceptance of certain components is clear, as indicated by Table 7.4. Most expect democracy to provide freedom of speech and expression (94.7%), free elections (94.5%), equality before the law (86.8%), equal rights for women (83.4%), equal educational opportunities (81.5%), and a right to paid employment (80.1%). Both sides are less sanguine about the beneficial impact of a free-market system (59.0%).[71]

Whether they believe that Germany united is capable of delivering the goods is another matter entirely. Asked about their faith in public institutions, 40% of the West-youth had "little or absolutely no trust" in major corporations and the military. Less than one-third (32%) voiced confidence in the Bundestag, and only 27% had faith in the government as a whole; 40% of the East-youth openly distrusted the latter. Only 22.7 % of the West-youth strongly favored unification, in contrast to 47.3% of the GDR-Germans, though 38.6% (W) and 57.6% (E) claimed to feel "strongly attached" to *Deutschland*. One can easily understand why only 27.9% of the Easterners might feel strong ties to their own defunct state; it is less clear why only 36.7% of the Westerners felt closely connected to the old FRG.[72]

Prior to the sustained wave of attacks against foreigners, over 60% of the *Westjugend* and nearly 68% of the *Ostjugend* were strongly or very strongly "troubled" by right-extremism. More than half of the young women, Eastern and Western, feared a repeat of National Socialism, a concern shared by only two-fifths of the young men. Roughly 64% in the FRG and 52% in the GDR voiced anxiety over mounting hostility towards foreigners.[73] By contrast, 19% of the female pupils and 32% of the males in the old Länder said they were "disturbed" by foreigners already in their land; figures for the new Länder were 35% and 48%, respectively. One-tenth of the sample accepted the proposition that Germany once again needed an iron-handed *Führer* to ensure the well-being of all; the idea found favor among 21% of the GDR males and 11% of their FRG peers but only 10% (E) and 3% (W) among young women.[74]

A second study, initiated in 1991, focused on the political orientations of 1,644 Brandenburg youth between the ages of 14 and 18.[75] Here the fear that neo-Nazism would spread was shared by 70.3% of the young women, versus 57% of the young men. Influenced, perhaps, by their own exposure to an authoritarian state, 23.1% of the females and 31% of the males agreed that Germany required a *Führer* or "strong man" to guarantee "the well-being of *all*" (my emphasis). Yet 35.4% of the girls and 47.6% of the boys echoed the sentiment, "Foreigners, get out!" Consonant with stereotypical adult views, 31.3% of the female and 45.2% of the male pupils blame foreigners for unemployment in Germany; 21.3% (F) and 36.3% (M) held that one should "hunt them down and throw them out," a strategy nonetheless rejected by 50.6% and 40.4% of the remaining respondents.[76] This is not to suggest that Germans have already begun to "grow together," as exhorted by the late Willy Brandt. East-adolescents' desire to identify with Western

Germans had declined considerably by 1991: 57.6% of the females, along with 59% of the males, agreed with the provocative statement, "Westerners screw [literally, *bescheißen*] Easterners wherever they can." Only 12.5% of the girls and 16% of the boys expressly disagreed.[77]

When questioned as to whether they perceived democracy as "the best possible form of government," only 23.7% of the girls answered positively, compared to 40.2% of the boys; 68.6% of the former and 47% of the latter had no opinion on the subject, suggesting mass alienation after a mere two years of exposure to the "free-democratic order." The good news is that Brandenburg youth displayed a stronger inclination to reject subcultural groups prone to violent behavior: 41.3% oppose the Punks, 52.7% reject rightwing Skinheads, 55.1% are against leftwing Skinheads, and 53% actively disapprove of Hooligans.[78]

A third, equally disturbing DJI survey conducted during the autumn of 1992 solicted the opinions of 16–29 year olds, 2,564 from the old FRG, 4,526 from the GDR.[79] At least one caveat is in order with respect to this sample: individuals in their twenties are already adults whose increasing commitments to work and family are likely to reduce their tendency toward violent behavior (the average child-bearing age in the GDR fell between 19 and 23). Both the "revolutionary break with the past" and the extended normative vacuum encountered by these cohorts makes it hard to judge whether younger groups will be as quickly subdued by "life cycle" effects, however. Many members of the extreme-right scene over the age of twenty have characterized the "successor generation" of Baby-Skins as much more militant and brutal than their own.

Asked to describe their political orientations, 4.3% of the East-youth and 3.8% of the West-youth placed themselves on the right end of the spectrum; another 15.5% (W) and 16.5% (E) labeled themselves "sooner to the right." Compared to the Brandenburg sample, these respondents displayed much greater "sympathy" for violence-prone groups, 72% for Right-Skinheads versus 19.4% in the former study (Table 7.6). While neither Left-Skins nor Autonomists are hostile towards foreigners per se, they are classified as violent owing to their penchant for street-fights with the "fascists," e.g., in Berlin's *Pfarrerstrasse*. Differences in the results of these two studies do not owe solely to regional factors or age categories. Recall that 1992 was a year marked by an extraordinary escalation of violence, sensationalized media coverage, and few state efforts to combat such activities in ways immediately apparent to youth.

The correlation between right-affinities and an acceptance of violence is indisputable. Although three-fourths of the DJI sample rejected the notion that "some conflicts can only be resolved through force in every society," 65.1% of the self-avowed Western rightists openly supported this idea, as did 47.3% of their Eastern peers.[80] The rightist perception that the use of force is

TABLE 7.5   Orientations Toward Democracy in Brandenburg, 1992

Figures (in percent) indicate reactions to the statement, "Democracy is the best form of government *[Staatsform]*."

Social Groupings	Agree	Disagree	No Opinion
Urban residents	34.2	10.8	55.0
Rural residents	30.6	9.9	59.5
Gynasium	39.6	9.1	51.3
Comprehensive Schools	29.6	9.7	60.7
Regular secondary	32.3	12.5	55.1
8th Grade	26.6	10.4	63.0
9th Grade	30.5	8.8	60.8
10th Grade	39.2	9.4	51.4
Vocational *(Azubis)*	32.3	12.5	55.1
Females	23.7	7.7	68.6
Males	40.2	12.8	47.0

Source: Brandenburgische Landeszentrale für politische Bildung, Hg., *Die Situation von Jugendlichen in Brandenburg* (Potsdam, 1993), p. 29.

endemic to human nature quickly translates in to a personal willingness to engage in such behavior, especially on the part of males (Table 7.7).

As analyses of youth violence and hate-crimes in the United States make clear, it is not a unique aspect of an older national character that has found new life in unified Germany but rather a particular configuration of socio-economic circumstances which "legitimizes" certain aggressive modes of behavior.[81] The designation "Right" among youth has, in fact, lost much of its political content with regard to systemic variables (e.g., the free market, limited government). It now stands for an individualized set of self-survival strategies against a world based on Social-Darwinism, the very conditions the postwar welfare state was expected to transcend.

The final study considered here was sponsored by the Kohl Government itself; encompassing 1,015 Western and 1,190 Eastern "youth" between the ages of 14 and 27, it was executed by IPOS/Mannheim during February and March of 1993.[82] The age-ranges involved may again lead one to under-estimate the problems of political integration lying ahead. Nearly 70% of the Easterners (82% of the women) aged 25–27 already had children, in con-trast to 23% of their Western counterparts (29% among women). Thus some 28% of those polled are likely to have already distanced themselves from the radical scenes; a dramatic decline in Eastern birth-rates since 1990 implies that subsequent cohorts may not settle down to "real life" as quickly or as complacently.[83]

Minister Angela Merkel reported optimistically that "youth in Germany see their future as predominantly positive—and this in the face of a realistic

TABLE 7.6   Sympathy for Groups Inclined Toward Violence

Sympathize with (in percent)	Eastern Youth	Western Youth
Skinheads	72.0	48.2
Faschos/Neo-Nazis	75.6	48.2
Ultra-nationalist Groups	63.4	49.6
Leftist Groups (Autonomists)	34.7	41.5

Source: Deutsches Jugendinstitut, Hg., *Gewalt gegen Fremde. Rechtsradikale, Skinheads und Mitläufer* (München: Verlag Deutsches Jugendinstitut, 1993).

TABLE 7.7   Willingness to Engage in Violence, 1992

Social Groupings (in percent)	Willingness to Engage in Violence [Gewaltbereitschaft]		Previous Engagement in Violent Behavior [Gewalthandeln]	
	East	West	East	West
Age				
16–17 years	26.4	12.2	6.9	2.3
18–20 years	18.6	11.9	6.0	2.3
21–24 years	15.8	11.2	3.0	1.2
25–29 years	9.5	8.6	2.0	1.6
Gender				
Male	21.8	13.7	5.8	2.4
Female	9.7	6.8	1.9	1.0

Source: Deutsches Jugendinstitut, Hg., *Gewalt gegen Fremde. Rechtsradikale, Skinheads und Mitläufer,* op. cit.

assessment of the current problems . . . 95% of the West German youth and 83% in the East are satisfied with their lives."[84] They may be happy with their own lives, but they are substantially less satisfied with the way their country is governed. In a Republic ostensibly based on *Volksparteien*, 21% of the West-youth and 30% of the East-youth feel that *no* political party represents their future interests.

While 13% in the old Länder and 15% in the new states held that there are conflicts in every democratic society which need to be resolved with force, 28% in the West and 34% in the East believe that there are particular reasons justifying the use of force among youth themselves, not only in self-defense (22% West, 65% East) but also in times of "frustration" (nearly 25% of both).[85] The sense that they are on-their-own leads to a troubling internalization of violence as an effective strategy for personal conflict resolution. Providing no age break-downs, the analysts insist there is "clearly more understanding" for anti-foreigner violence among the younger cohorts, as well as among males (22% versus 14% for females). By contrast, 66% of the Western adolescents (70% F) and 58% of the Eastern youth (62% F) felt personally shamed by fel-

low citizens who took part in assaults.[86] Some 68% said they would call the police if they witnessed an attack (70% West, 67% East), a surprising figure in
view of the limited trust placed in police, according to other surveys. Only
34% said they would aid the victim themselves (49% West, 21% East), suggesting that most expect Father-State to solve the problem.[87]

Although a clear majority condemned such acts, an even larger number
wanted leaders to admit fewer foreigners into the country, 58% in the old,
75% in the new states. The desire to prohibit future immigration was
strongest among West-youth (100%) who could not imagine becoming
friends with a foreigner; nearly two-thirds did claim to have foreigners
among their friends, compared to less than one-fifth in the East. No data
were provided on the ethnic backgrounds of these friends, however—a weak
point insofar as *Wessis* are more likely to participate in exchange programs
with other European (as opposed to Turkish or African) youth. The interest
the two sides display in establishing friendships with each other is quite imbalanced: 55% of the West-youth had never visited the new states, compared
to 6% in the East who had yet to see the old Länder. While 50% of the East-
women and 56% of the East-men saw their broad expectations regarding
unification as having been fulfilled, only 32% (34% M, 29% F) felt they were
better off with respect to occupational opportunities; only one-fifth enjoyed
greater social security.[88]

My purpose in presenting these studies is not to write off "the" German
youth as a horde of xenophobic, violence-prone anti-democrats; the overwhelming majority are quite normal, that is, more interested in music, sports
and friends than in the national cause (despite an increased tendency to accept
violence as a "normal" part of society). My core argument here is that often
times the wrong means have been used to convey critical lessons about German history to post-Wall youth whose socialization needs differ significantly
from the generations preceding them. The foundation for a truly multicultural society consists of many different stones, several of which have yet to be
laid in the expanded Federal Republic. The key to change rests in a qualitatively different display of political will "from above" and the widespread cultivation of greater personal responsibility "from below." The slogan *Germany,
Awaken!* acquires a new historical significance in this context.

Conclusion: Identity, Security,
and Democratic Citizenship

One might have expected a German leader claiming to have "mastered the
lessons of history" to set a moral standard for the nation. Instead, a rather disconcerting division of labor seems to have emerged since 1989: certain conservative politicians continue their business-as-usual appeals to radical-right
voters, while a select few extend the hand of reconciliation to frightened for-

eigners. The rhetoric employed by some of Kohl's own advisors after unification had an ominous, inflammatory ring, for example, Edmund Stoiber's declaration that a "flashflood" of immigrants would produce a "multinational society on German soil, *durchmischt und durchrasst*" [of mixed, and by implication, inferior races].[89] Another metaphor common among politicians, "the boat is full," infers that only persons already on board are worthy of saving. President Richard von Weizsäcker, by contrast, visited numerous scenes-of-the-crime and uttered moving words of moral atonement at funerals of the most recently murdered, until his 1995 retirement.

The so-called Unity-Chancellor has proclaimed on many occasions that "Germany is a land friendly to foreigners and it will remain so." Shortly after the Rostock riots, Kohl declared in a TV-interview that "xenophobia is a disgrace for our country." The arson-related deaths in Mölln were likewise described as "a disgrace to our country" and as "a particularly depressing example of the increase in crime in Germany," with no reference to the rightwing nature of the attack.[90] On the second anniversary of unification, the Chancellor spoke out against the forces "of Right *and* Left-extremism" (my emphasis) which he claimed had caused much suffering to the Germans. He moreover berated disruptive elements who had demonstrated *against* xenophobic violence in Berlin; the demonstrators' willingness to besmirch Germany's peaceful and prosperous image in the eyes of the world was, for Kohl, "the real crime."[91]

The statistics prove that day-to-day assaults on foreigners and weaker elements of society are clearly the work of the Right. For 1993, the count stood at 2,232 acts of violence attributed to right-extremists, added to 8,329 crimes with related motives; left-extremists reportedly engaged in 1,357 crimes, of which 1,085 were defined as violent.[92] Whatever their violations of human rights—ranging from merciless shootings along the Wall, to forced adoptions, imprisonment and murderous kidnappings—neither the former communist leaders of the GDR nor the Red Army Faction terrorists ever engaged in a systematic extermination campaign targeting millions of "racially inferior" or disabled persons; the Holocaust remains the legacy of the extreme Right.[93] The Chancellor would have sent a stronger moral message to younger citizens, had he joined in the counter-demonstrations coordinated by leftists after August 1992, instead of impugning the motives of those who did. Refusing to participate in another memorial ceremony following the Solingen deaths, Kohl declared that he had no intention of becoming a "Chancellor of Funerals."

The best way for united Germany to come to terms with its complex dual-past is to prepare its youth for a morally responsible and economically productive future. Providing DM 2.1 billion ($1.4 bil) in assistance to Yugoslav war victims, the Kohl Government spent only DM 100 million ($67 mil) on youth programs during the first year of unity, despite early signs of trouble.[94]

In 1991 the Ministry for Women and Youth initiated an Action Program against Aggression and Violence (AgAG), offering DM 20 million per annum for three years. As of 1993, its 155 federally financed personnel were distributed across thirty regional "burning points," assisted by 268 privately or communally funded co-workers. Most are limited to two or three year work-contracts [*ABM-Stellen*], hardly time to establish the kind of long-term trust that might channel violent offenders into more productive activities.[95]

The main thrust of the state's response to youth-on-the-rampage has been retributional rather than rehabilitative in character, however. In 1992 five Skinheads aged 19–21 were convicted in Frankfurt/Oder for the November 1990 beating death of a 28-year old Angolan; they received prison terms of two to five years. Reacting to the escalation of violence, the courts handed down maximum sentences in December 1992 with respect to the Mölln defendants. The 20- and 27-year olds responsible for the beating/burning death in Wuppertal were sentenced to eight and fourteen years, respectively. They were exempted from the maximum term, life imprisonment, because of their alcoholism; the bartender will spend ten years behind bars. The trials for suspects involved in the Solingen deaths—Christian Reher, Felix Köhnen, Christian Buchholz and Markus Gartmann—resulted in 10-year sentences for the first three and a 15-year prison term for the last. The point is not that long-term imprisonment is needed to deter youth from crimes of violence, for that is exactly what many "hooligans" and "rowdies" have already experienced under the Honecker regime. Former NA-leader Hasselbach argues that the qualities necessary for getting by in prison "are absolutely ideal for one's subsequent life in the neo-Nazi scene."[96] More important is the realization that the proffered ounce of cure lacks a pound of prevention.

Juridical or symbolic responses are more likely to trigger spiteful resistance than to redirect youth orientations, e.g., the High Court ruling of April 1994 that *Auschwitz Lies* do not enjoy the protection of "free speech." Some ten far-right organizations have been banned thus far. Officials now plan to expand the powers of federal intelligence agencies, to extend permissible periods for temporary police detention, and to broaden the framework for police surveillance of private homes. None of these tactics treats the root causes of extremism. One program in Lower Saxony, the only one of its kind in Europe, offers violent youth offenders constructive, rehabilitative alternatives.[97]

Younger citizens largely perceive government officials as political opportunists, manipulating divisive socio-psychological currents for electoral purposes. Such feelings have been reinforced by an aura of self-serving scandal which surrounded the Kohl Government between 1989 and 1993. The *Treuhand*, a federally subsidized "holding company" responsible for the privatization of 10,000 formerly state-owned industries, reported in 1991 that

it had been bilked for DM 1.2 billion (roughly $700 million) by unscrupu-
lous Western "buyers," funds that should have gone for investment and
modernization.[98] A lack of trust in most public office-holders may explain
why 18.9% of the male and 9.1% of the female voters aged 18–23 cast their
ballots for the West Berlin *Reps* in January 1989, as a protest vote.[99] It may
also explain why less than 50% of all eligible Eastern residents between 18
and 25 chose *not to vote* in the first all-German elections to the Bundestag in
December 1990.

The "political re-education" of Post-Wall youth can only lead to democratic outcomes to the extent that older citizens are willing to renew *and*
demonstrate their own commitment to tolerance and diversity. It was not
until late 1991 that attacks against defenseless foreign men, women and
children began to unleash a counter-wave of solidarity displays among the
silent majority. One such rally attracted 10,000 demonstrators to Cologne,
some with placards imploring, "Dear foreigners, please don't leave us alone
with these Germans." The Network of Peace Cooperatives held a nation-
wide Action Day against Xenophopbia on November 9, 1991, marking the
second anniversary of the Wall's opening, fifty-three years after the anti-Jewish *Kristallnacht* attacks. A Berlin demonstration of 300,000 on November
8, 1992 was described as a "promenade by democrats," even though it was
disrupted by "left radicals."[100] In addition to rallies in Mölln and Solingen,
December brought a number of candle-lit demonstrations attended by over
400,000 residents in Munich and Hamburg, leading one pundit to observe,
"The country now seems to consist of pyromaniacs. Some throw torches,
others hold candles."[101] A number of conservative politicians openly disparaged these events as little more than "Olympic Good Will Games."
"Demos" and processions are exercises in symbolic politics, to be sure, but
they have re-directed public opinion: the *Forschungsgruppe Wahlen* found
that identification with ultra-nationalist ideas among persons younger than
25 fell by half between June and December 1992; "understanding" for violent assaults against asylum-applicants fell from 17% in the East and 12% in
the West in October 1992 to 8% and 5%, respectively, by January 1993.[102]

Participant-observation in countless anti-nuclear and peace demonstrations in the Federal Republic during the 1980s taught me that all it takes to
mobilize police, intelligence, and financial resources for the purpose of "defending democracy" is sufficient political will among the leadership. Germany's history necessitates a clear demonstration by all FRG authorities that
acts of xenophobic aggression will meet with swift and direct punishment—a
practice which all parties but the Greens have been quick to adopt vis-à-vis
leftist terrorists (most recently in Bad Kleinen), "squatters" in Hamburg and
Berlin, and anti-nuclear demonstrators in Wackersdorf. Long "blind in the
right eye," the federal government should work to remove nationalistic ideologues ensconced in public service jobs with the same amount of energy it

sought to oust leftists deemed "too internally cool" towards the nation to enjoy the blessings of *Beamtentum*. The democratic state—*die wehrhafte Demokratie*—has the right and the duty to protect itself against manifestations of right-extremism in the 1990s with as much conviction and vigor as it did against the anarcho-left terrorism of the 1970s and 1980s.

One concerned citizen, writing to the editors of *Die Zeit* in 1991, recommended that 70,000 border-soldiers in search of a new mission be sent to the rescue of foreigners under attack. The idea that troops intended to secure the citizenry against an external, nuclear-powered enemy be deployed to protect thousands of unarmed refugees housed in former barracks and community halls struck me as rather naive at first reading. Upon further reflection, however, this simple proposal reveals the crux of the post-Wall German security dilemma: The quest for security *without* has been superseded by the search for security *within*. The link between generationally divergent perceptions of national-identity and national security is no less critical to an understanding of the Germans-united than it was to an understanding of the Germans-divided. If anything, that linkage has become much more explicit.

The Cold War had the effect of rendering East and West Germans more sensitive to the global condition, that is, to the domestic consequences of international affairs, than most of their European counterparts. The higher the level of global tensions, the less Germans on either side were forced to look inwards, that is, to examine the extent to which a particular concept of national identity in the past had turned them into security-hostages in the nuclear age. The easing of tensions between the FRG and the GDR in the early 1970s brought to the fore a new generation that rejected but did not replace the pre-war identity paradigm; the process of forging a new national consciousness would have also required a disconcerting "turning inward" during a period of general material comfort and many new opportunities to "see the world." As long as Germany remained divided, the search for a positive national identity seemed superfluous to most citizens; the pursuit of national security, on the other hand, became a matter of paramount importance. The paradigm shift of 1989/90 means that there is now more of *Deutschland* but less of everything else—jobs, living-space, neighborhood security, even fewer parking places—to go around. National security relative to the outside world no longer guarantees security within Germany's borders, leading certain vulnerable groups to seek an escape from freedom (to borrow from Erich Fromm) through a one-dimensional, ethnicized search for national identity.

In his first address to the United Nations on September 23, 1992, Foreign Minister Klaus Kinkel voiced regret over "the return of barbarity to the European House," referring not to violent acts intended to rid Germany of foreigners but to so-called ethnic cleansing in the Balkans. The opening of the Wall, added to the dissolution of the Soviet Union, has allowed the by-products of international conflict to wash across the German borders in ways that have affected even the most politically disinterested citizens. The more victims of oppression who enter their territory, the more Federal Republicans are forced to turn inwards again, particularly if their suffering is analogous to that once inflicted by Germans themselves, e.g., concentration-camp survivors from Bosnia. They must determine what it is, for better or worse, that distinguishes them from other peoples. Eastern and Western Germans have had to confront many old and new questions concerning their personal and collective identities since 1989. They have discovered that the few ties which still bind them—yet simultanously separate them from others with whom they have shared their homelands for many years—are largely historical and negative in character.

The wisdom of Pogo haunts the Germans no less than it ought to pique other peoples in the community of nations: "We have met the enemy and it is us." Though the spectre of right-extremism has also befallen Britain and France, it continues to cast a special veil of "shame over Germany."[103] The cry of "Germany for the Germans" is no more insidious than that of "France for the French" or "Britain for the Brits" vis-à-vis the multitudes who have tried to flee destitution and death since the fall of the Wall, whether they stem from Europe's heartland, Sri Lanka or Rwanda. Politicians across Europe have failed to act upon one of the most fundamental lessons conveyed by two world wars: when they are based on "blood" rather than birthplace, the concepts of nationality and citizenship are by definition exclusionary and divisive rather than integrative and democratic. The FRG's preferred strategy for defining citizenship, underscored by the Maastricht Treaty, remains one of demarcation: national as well as Euro-national identity is being defined primarily in terms of *what it is not.*

It is easy for other powers to cast Germany in the role of the eternal bad-guy, despite the end of the "postwar" era. A British Superior Court made the headlines in 1991 for granting asylum to a Sudanese refugee who feared physical assault if re-deported to Germany. Yet Britain had tightened its own immigration laws four times, in 1965, 1968, 1971 and 1981; the strictest conditions, applauded by the far-right National Front, helped to secure Prime Minister Thatcher's re-election.[104] Historically speaking, the Germans can and must be measured by very different standards when addressing questions of racial intolerance. With respect to post-1989 developments, the same standard, rooted in the universality of human rights, should obtain all around. According to UN reports, there were over 18 million refugees worldwide as of 1994, not counting a further 24 million displaced by wars within their own borders. The best way to avoid the "tidal-wave" of refugees projected by far-right forces is to ensure human rights and economic opportunity in each and every homeland.

Though it has made great strides since the 1950s, the Federal Republic might further demonstrate a permanent commitment to democracy by abandoning its arcane reliance on the principle of blood over birthplace as a pre-condition for citizenship. The first step would be to refute the myth that "Germany is not a land of immigration" by adopting a pro-active legal framework—a real *Einwanderungsgesetz*—enabling specified numbers of persons not subject to persecution to acquire admission and residency rights. The next step would be to embrace more effective integration policies by further liberalizing naturalization requirements for two million "guestworkers" and their descendents. The third step, tied to the second, would be to accept the principle of dual citizenship, at least as a transitional mechanism, analogous to the recognition of dual-citizenship and the right-of-return inherent in Article 116 GG. Last but not least, state authorities need to mount more effective, day-to-day educational campaigns stressing the "national" benefits inherent in a multicultural society.

Recent developments in Lübeck may set a standard for the nation, where a January 1996 arson attack on a hostel occupied by some 50 foreigners resulted in 10 deaths. Initially relieved to learn that three German youths arrested near the scene were not to blame (though the case has yet to be solved), local residents did not return to business as usual, following a memorial rally at the arson site. Instead, they have begun to turn inward, critically examining their own indifference towards the persons who lived there and even violating new federal regulations in an effort to extend benefits and job opportunities to that group.[105]

The alternative to demarcation and, ultimately, intolerance is a *positive*, self-reflective, though not self-contained concept of Federal Republican identity. I have long wondered how one could expect Turkish guestworkers to "assimilate or get out," given the reluctance of many postwar citizens (especially those of my own generation) to specify the positive contours of their own Germanness. The beneficiaries of "late birth" are discovering that it is easier to focus on traits which entitle them to certain privileges than to address features which historically oblige them to sacrifice for the benefit of others. Membership has its privileges, one could argue; yet ten of the seventeen deaths registered in 1992 involved native-born Germans, six of whom were homeless. Thus citizenship reduced to a question of ethnic origin affords no real protections; rather, the value of citizenship in a democracy derives from "its capacity to confer a minimum of social dignity."[106]

Article 1 of the Basic Law posits: "The dignity of man [and woman] shall be inviolable. To respect and protect it shall be the duty of all state authority." The guarantee of inviolability specified by Article 1 does not differentiate between "the deserving" and "the undeserving," between Germans and other human beings. Lemke has argued that the so-called culture of ethnicity "was reinforced by German unification not only because the German nation state was now reconstituted, but because the East German heritage was likewise monocultural."[107] The socialist state did try repeatedly to legitimize its power-monopoly through a return to the all-German heritage and tradition, especially after the 1970s, but this does not mean that all segments of GDR society identified with the same periods of German history for the same reasons. For many Easterners, reinvoking an older German legacy (the Luther era, for example) offered a chance to escape the SED's polemicized, self-glorifying treatment of twentieth century history. For younger GDR citizens, an interest in pre-Weimar history provided a basis of identification with the better life afforded by the Western state—but not necessarily because it was German per se.

While I recognize that all is not well in the FRG, I still have faith in the basic pillars of postwar German democracy, encouraged by the countless average citizens who have displayed both constitutional patriotism and moral responsibility in their protests against the violence. But since unification I have also come to share the cynicism of many German youth vis-à-vis the current generation of national leaders; politicians' expressions of "grave concern" over a growing acceptance of violence among Post-Wall cohorts, in particular, has not been matched by a will to use the resources at their disposal to root-out sources of xenophobia and intolerance. (The same might be said of federal politicians in the United States who seem to view violent inner-city gangs as the responsibility of mayors and local police authorities.)

Still, my own experiences as a foreigner in Germany—albeit as a white, middle-class professional hailing from the FRG's "best friend," the USA—make it difficult for me to subscribe to the fear that "the womb is still fruitful, out of which fascism crawled," to echo Berthold Brecht. The generation of German mothers which provided the soldiers and guards for Hitler's army and death camps is certainly no longer capable of giving birth, despite astounding developments in the area of fertility medicine. The wombs of subsequent generations belong to a genre of predominantly self-emancipated women, unlikely to place their reproductive organs in the service of "the nation," as the heated debates over abortion reveal. Many have raised their daughters—and sons—to oppose all forms of military mobilization as well.

Legal impediments to immigration and naturalization are but the formal manifestation of persistent socio-cultural barriers to integration. The events of 1989–90 offered all Germans an extraordinary opportunity to define their national consciousness anew. In addition to deepening their own sense of positive identity, the Germans-united could promote a greater sense of security among millions of neighbors inside and outside their borders by adopting a concept of citizenship—*Staatsangehörigkeit*—which stresses a commitment to democratic values over demographic accidents of birth. What is really at stake is not the future of ethnic identity but rather the life-chances of the new underclasses who have taken a beating in the battle for jobs and market-shares since unification. The Federal Republic needs to replace its arcane constitutional emphasis on ethno-nationalism with the modern construct of civic nationalism, and it needs to instill an understanding of national "belonging" thus defined in ways more comprehensible to all German youth.

Notes

1.Hartmut Koschyk, "Deutsche zweiter Klasse? Mangelnden Information schafft Vorurteile"; Wolfgang G. Beitz, "Deutsche ohne Muttersprache"; Ludwig König, "Aussiedler und Übersiedler—Ihre Rechtsstellung"; also, Stefanie Wahl, "Wer sind die Neuankömmlinge?"; all in *Das Parlament*, Nr. 35, August 25, 1989.

2. Friedrich Christian Delius, "Dachdecker und Dachdenker, Blut und Licht," in Bahman Nirumand, Hg., *Deutsche Zustände. Dialog über ein gefährdetes Land* (Reinbek: Rowohlt, 1993).

3. Peter Ködderitzsch and Leo A. Müller, *Rechtsextremismus in der DDR* (Göttingen: Lamuv, 1990), p. 103. Until the early 1980s, the "bloodline" requirement nonetheless foresaw a different legal status for foreign men and women who married native Germans.

4. Details were conveyed to me in a December 1986 interview with Brandt's personal assistant, Klaus-Henning Rosen, in Bonn.

5. "Aussiedler: Schwebendes Volkstum," *Der Spiegel*, Nr. 3, January 15, 1990, p. 77.

6. Often subject to minority persecution in the East, many new arrivals had no German-language sources beyond their family Bibles, with all the linguistic anachronisms this source implies.

7. Douglas B. Klusmeyer, "Aliens, Immigrants, and Citizens: The Politics of Inclusion in the Federal Republic of Germany," *Daedalus*, Vol. 122, No. 3, Summer 1993, p. 88. Further, Ray Rist, *Guestworkers in Germany: The Prospects for Pluralism* (New York: Praeger Publishers, 1978); and John Bendix, *Importing Foreign Workers: A Comparison of German and American Policy* (New York: P. Lang Publishers, 1990).

8. Werner Kanein, *Ausländergesetz* (Munich: C. H. Beck, 1974), p. 3. The 1990 Alien Laws specify four types of *Aufenthaltsgenehmigungen*: an *Aufenthaltserlaubnis*, not tied to a particular activity or time-frame; an *Aufenthaltsberechtigung*, granted after eight years or sixty months of contributions to the state pension program; an *Aufenthaltsbewilligung*, acquired for a special purpose and pre-determined length of time under two years; or an *Aufenthaltsbefugnis*, based on humanitarian grounds.

9. Kay Hailbronner, cited by Klusmeyer, op. cit., p. 89. Further, Christian Wernicke, "Langer Weg zum deutschen Paß," *Die Zeit*, Nr. 13, March 31, 1989.

10. Discounting new refugees from Yugoslavia, the share of ten-years-plus residents rises to 60%. Cornelia Schmalz-Jacobsen, *Daten und Fakten zur Ausländersituation* (Bonn: 1992); and Barbara John (the first urban *Ausländerbeauftragte*), *Zur Lage der jungen Ausländergeneration*, (Berlin: Verwaltungsdrückerei, 1989).

11. Joyce M. Mushaben, "A Crisis of Culture: Isolation and Integration among Turkish Guestworkers in the German Federal Republic," Ilhan Basgöz and Norman Furniss, eds., *Turkish Workers in Europe* (Bloomington: Indiana University Press, 1985), pp. 125–150.

12. Hanno Kühnert, "Rassistische Klänge: Was sich deutsche Professoren bei der Unterschrift unter das 'Heidelberger Manifest' dachten," *Die Zeit*, Nr. 6, February 12, 1982.

13. Cited by Klusmeyer, op. cit., p. 92.

14. Schubarth, op. cit., p. 48–49.

15. *Foreigners in Germany. Guest Workers, Asylum-Seekers, Refugees, and Ethnic Germans*, published by the German Information Center (New York: November 1991), pp. 2–3.

16. In 1995 Hannelore Kohl published a cookbook of the Chancellor's favorite, fat-laden recipes, insisting that the Germans' taste for foreign food undermines their sense of national community.

17. *Foreigners in Germany*, op. cit., p. 5.

18. "Asylrecht: Oskar quält sich," *Der Spiegel*, Nr. 32, August 6, 1990, p. 32 ff.

19. "Lieber sterben als nach Sachsen," *Der Spiegel*, Nr. 40, September 30, 1991.

20. Klaus-Henning Rosen, Hg., *Die zweite Vertreibung. Fremde in Deutschland* (Bonn: Dietz, 1992).

21. Robert Leicht, "Eine Kapitulation, kein Kompromiß," *Die Zeit*, Nr. 51, December 18, 1992.

22. "521 gegen 132 Stimmen für neues Asylrecht," *General Anzeiger*, May 27, 1993; "Tatsächlich Verfolgte erhalten auch in Zukunft Asyl," *Das Parlament*, May 28–June 4, 1993.

23. Günther Renner, "Asylrecht in Deutschland nach der Grundgesetzänderung," *Neue Justiz*, Nr. 6, 1994, pp. 241–245; and Kuno Kruse, Stefan Scheytt and Michael Schwelien, "Krieg is kein Asylgrund," *Die Zeit*, Nr. 28, July 10, 1992.

24. See Karl-Friedrich Kassel, "Konjunktur-programm Asyl," *Die Zeit*, Nr. 3, January 22, 1993; and "Schöne Zeiten für Schlepper," *Der Spiegel*, Nr. 27, July 5, 1993.

25. The west-zones had absorbed 8 million refugees by 1950, adding another 1.7 million by 1960 and 3.6 million who fled the Soviet-occupied zone between 1950 and 1962. See Rainer Roth, *Was ist typisch deutsch? Die Deutschen—Image und Selbstverständnis* (Freiburg/Würzburg: Ploetz, 1979), p. 53.

26. For a media critique, see Beate Winkler, Hg., *Was heißt denn hier fremd?* (Augsburg: Humboldt-Taschenbuchverlag, 1994).

27. *Emnid-Informationen*, 17. Jg., Nr. 49, December 6, 1965; ibid., 25. Jg., Nr. 10, 1973; ibid., 30. Jg., Nr. 8, 1978; ibid., 31. Jg., Nr. 7, 1979; ibid., 33. Jg., Nr.2/3, 1981.

28. Ibid., 1981.

29. Forschungsgruppe Wahlen, *"Berlin vor der 750 Jahresfeier." Repräsentative Bevölkerungsumfrage in Dezember 1986*, Question #11, and Question #26, respectively.

30. German Information Center, *Right-Wing Radicalism in Germany*, (New York: February 1993), p. 6; and Dietmar Lamparter, "Die edle Art der Diskriminierung," *Die Zeit*, Nr. 45, November 6, 1992.

31. *Foreigners in Germany*, op. cit., p. 4.

32. Free-lance journalist Gunter Wallraf went undercover as a Turkish mineworker for his best-seller report, *Ganz unten* (Köln: Kiepenheuer & Witsch, 1988). On conditions in the auto industry, see Juliane Wetzel, "Integration im Großbetrieb—das Beispiel BMW," in Wolfgang Benz, Hg., *Integration ist machbar. Ausländer in Deutschland* (München: C.H. Beck, 1993), pp. 93–108.

33. *Unemployment in Germany*, issued by the German Information Center (New York: March 1994).

34. Delius, op. cit., p. 20.

35. Cited in Klusmeyer, op. cit., p. 102.

36. Figures cited in Klusmeyer, op. cit., p. 102

37. Emnid survey, reported in "Nach Mölln ein Volk im Schock," *Der Spiegel*, Nr. 50, December 7, 1992.

38. Wilfried Schubarth, "Fremde als Sündenbocke," in *Das Profil der Deutschen. Was sie vereint, was sie trennt* (Hamburg: Spiegel Verlag, 1991), p. 47.

39. The treatment of conscripted laborers in the GDR sorely contradicted official notions of "international solidarity" among the proletariat. See Irene Runge, *Ausland DDR—Fremdenhaß* (Berlin: Dietz Verlag, 1990).

40. Peter Meroth, "Deutschland 2000—Der Staat, den wir uns wünschen," *Süddeutsche Zeitung*, January 4, 1991, p. 9.

41. Heiner Geissler, "Wir brauchen die Ausländer," *Die Zeit*, Nr. 42, October 18, 1991; also see Wolfgang Gehrmann, Kuno Kruse, Reiner Scholz and Eberhard Seidel-Pielen, "Dossier: Vereint im Fremdenhaß" in the same edition.

42. IPOS figures were provided by Dieter Roth.

43. Jürgen Habermas, "Die zweite Lebenslüge der Bundesrepublik: Wir sind wieder 'normal' geworden," *Die Zeit*, Nr. 51, December 18, 1992.

44. From July 4 to September 9, 1990, there were 22 documented cases of group violence against foreign residents in East Berlin alone, as reported by Dr. Nguyen van Huong during a June 1990 interview. See Magistratsverwaltung für Gleichstellung—Ausländerbeauftragte, Hg., *Bericht über die Sicherheit für das Leben ausländischer BürgerInnen in Berlin (Ost) in den letzten Monaten* (Berlin: September 11, 1990).

45. Cited by Rosen, op. cit., pp. 96–97.

46. Figures vary, depending on the reporting agency; some include all forms of rightwing extremist activity, others refer to violent acts involving human injuries. The Federal Criminal Police recorded 2,200 acts of violence during the first eight months of 1992, compared to 2,450 for 1991. See "1991 mehr als 300 Brandschläge gegen Asylbewerber und Ausländer," *Frankfurter Allgemeine Zeitung*, January 18, 1992; also, *The Week in Germany*, January 21, 1994, p. 2.

47. "Mölln war für mich der Knackpunkt," *die tageszeitung*, June 18, 1993.

48. Karl-Otto Richter and Bernhard Schmidtbauer, "Zur Akzeptanz von Asylbewerbern in Rostock-Stadt. Empirische Ergebnisse aus dem Frühjahr 1992," *Aus Politik und Zeitgeschichte*, B2–3/93, January 8, 1993, p. 47, p. 51.

49. On the complex question of final resting places for long-term residents, see Rainer Finne, "Wohin mit toten Gastarbeitern," *Die Zeit*, Nr. 10, March 12, 1993. For detailed accounts of "the murders of Mölln," see *Die Zeit*, Nr. 49, December 4, 1992.

50. "Krawalle und Blockaden in vielen Städten. Politiker drohen mit harten Maßnahmen," *Süddeutsche Zeitung*, June 2, 1993.

51. "Mit den Schlachtruf 'Hooligan' durch den Breiten Weg," *Frankfurter Allgemeine Zeitung*, May 19, 1994; "Nach Magdeburg sind sich Bonner Parteien einig in ihrem Entsetzen und ihrer Ratlosigkeit," also in *FAZ*, May 19, 1994.

52. The same front page reporting the Solingen deaths bore an article on the annual Sudentenland-Refugees meeting, demanding "homeland rights" for German-ethnics still within Czech borders; "Stoiber fordert Heimatrecht für Sudetendeutsche," *Süddeutsche Zeitung*, June 1, 1993; and Michael Kumpfmüller, "Königsberg und andere Kleinigkeiten," *Die Zeit*, Nr. 14, April 8, 1994.

53. GDR researchers were barred from conducting projects on extremist groups just as they began to make their physical presence felt in metropolitan areas. Wolfgang Brück's work on this topic led to problems with the Stasi; see *Skinheads im Meinungsbild Jugendlicher* (Leipzig: ZIJ, November 1988); "Rechtsextremismus und Jugendliche," pp. 76–90, in Rosen op. cit. Further, M. Stock and P. Mühlberg, *Die Szene von Innen. Skinheads, Grufties, Heavy Metals, Punks* (Berlin: Linksdruck, 1990); and Walter Süß, "Was wußte die Stasi über Neonazis in der DDR?" *Die Zeit*, Nr. 18, May 7, 1993. On music and politics, see Max Annas and Ralph Christoph, *Neue Soundtracks für den Volksempfänger. Nazirock, Jugendkultur & Rechter Mainstream* (Berlin/Amsterdam: Edition ID-Archiv, 1993); and Andre Schäfer, "Der gesungene Haß," *Die Zeit*, Nr. 50, December 11, 1992.

54. Wilhelm Heitmeyer, *Rechtsextremistische Orientierungen bei Jugendlichen. Empirische Ergebnisse und Erklärungsmuster einer Untersuchung zur politischen Sozialisation* (Weinheim/München: Juventa, 1988), p. 184.

55. Hartmut Castner and Thilo Castner, "Rechtsextremismus und Jugend," *Aus Politik und Zeitgeschichte*, B 41–42, October 6, 1989, pp. 32–39.

56. Gender biases inherent in many well-publicized studies have led to misinterpretations of female interest in these movements. See Hilde Utzmann-Krombholz, *Rechtsextremismus und Gewalt: Affinitäten und Resistenzen von Mädchen und junge Frauen* (Düsseldorf: Ministerium für die Gleichstellung von Frau und Mann in Nordrhein-Westfalen, January 1994); Ursula Birsl, "Frauen und Rechtsextremismus," *Aus Politik und Zeitgeschichte*, B 3–4, 1992, pp. 22–30; Christine Holzkamp and Birgit Rommelspacher, "Frauen und Rassismus—Wie sind Mädchen und Frauen verstrickt?" *Päd Extra & Demokratische Erziehung*, January 1991, pp. 33–39; and Joachim Hofmann-Göttig, "Die Neue Rechte: Die Männerpartei," B41–42, 1989, pp. 21–31.

57. Joyce Marie Mushaben, "The Rise of *Femi-Nazis?* Female Participation in Extremist Movements in United Germany," *German Politics*, Vol. 5, No. 2 (August 1996).

58. "Gender and Ideology," TWIG, December 10, 1993.

59. Sonja Balbach, *"Wir sind auch die kämpfende Front."* *Frauen in der rechten Szene* (Hamburg: Konkret Literatur Verlag, 1994): Britta Ruth Büchner, *Rechte Frauen, Frauenrechte und Klischees der Normalität* (Pffaffenweiler: Centaurus, 1995).

60. Kühnen died of AIDS in April 1991; Sonntag, involved in organized crime, died of a gunshot-wound in June 1991. Hasselbach, co-founder of the National Alternative, broke with the movement as a consequence of indiscriminate violence against women and children. See "Mölln war für mich der Knackpunkt," op. cit. Far-right groups receive much of their contraband propaganda from Gary Lauck, a Nazi/Aryan Nation leader based in Nebraska; see Till Bastien, "Der 'Leuchter-Report,'" *Die Zeit*, Nr. 40, October 2, 1992; and George Hermann Hodos, "Tom Metzger und die US-Arier, *Die Zeit*, Nr. 49, December 4, 1992.

61. "Study Shows That Most Xenophobic Violence Is Perpetrated by Informal Groups," *TWIG*, July 16, 1993.

62. Bodo Morshäuser, "Die guten Menschen von Deutschland," *Die Zeit*, Nr. 34, August 27, 1993; also, Peter Schneider, "Erziehung nach Mölln," *Kursbuch 113* (Berlin: Rotbuch Verlag, 1993), p. 132. For contrasting viewpoints, see Claus Leggewie, "Pläydoyer eines Antiautoritären für Autorität, *Die Zeit*, Nr. 10, March

12, 1993; Klaus Hurrelmann, "Mitdenken, mitfühlen, mitziehen, *Die Zeit*, Nr. 13, April 2, 1993; and Robin Detje, "Kleine Fluchten, große Gesten," *Die Zeit*, Nr. 16, April 23, 1993.

63. Wilfried Schubarth, "Wirkungen eines Gedenkstätten-Besuches bei Jugendlichen: Ergebnisse einer Wirkungsanalyse von Besuchen in der Nationalen Mahne- und Gedenkstätte Buchenwald" (Leipzig: ZIJ, May 1990).

64. Peter Schneider, "The Sins of the Grandfathers. How German Teenagers Confront the Holocaust and How They Don't," *New York Times Magazine*, December 3, 1995, pp. 74–80.

65. Geissler, "Wir brauchen die Ausländer," op. cit. Bavarian officials have repeatedly used the courts to prevent Passau's so-called "Nasty Girl," Anna Rosmus, from publicizing materials on local Nazi collaborators.

66. As was true of the TV-series *Holocaust,* Spielberg's film split the Germans into two camps: one portraying it as a trivializing melodrama, rooted in "scattered historical inaccuracies" (*Die Welt*), the other as an accessible moral-documentary (*Frankfurter Allgemeine Zeitung*). See Andreas Kilb, "Warten, bis Spielberg kommt," Nr. 4, January 28, 1994 and "Des Teufels Saboteur," Nr. 10, March 11, 1994, both in *Die Zeit*; Helga Hirsch, "Wohltäter aus Angst," *Die Zeit*, Nr. 11, March 18, 1994; Thomas Kleine-Brockhoff and Dirk Kurbjuweit, "Die anderen Schindlers," *Die Zeit*, Nr. 14, April 8, 1994; and Janusz Tycner, "Bei Schindlers Polen, *Die Zeit*, Nr. 11, March 18, 1994. Provoking controversy of another sort (over the limits of free speech) is the German-made film, *Berufsnazi*; produced by Winfried Bonengel (who aided Hasselbach in leaving the "scene"), this documentary has been banned for commercial use.

67. Hans Georg Betz, "The New Politics of Resentment. Radical Right-Wing Populist Parties in Western Europe," *Comparative Politics*, Vol. 25, Nr. 4, July 1993, pp. 413–427.

68. Cited in Ködderitzsch and Müller, op. cit., p. 23.

69. Police in the old Bundesländer confiscated over 400 deadly "Ninja Stars" between 1989 and 1991, ranging from a mere DM 3.90 to DM 40 in price. One investigation found that 145 out of 150 schools in Frankfurt/M. were experiencing increasing incidents of violence among students; one-fifth of the students sampled admitted they carried weapons (gas-pistols, mace, handguns); see *Der Spiegel*, editions of January through March 1991. There is a mind-boggling move afoot to "liberalize" current restrictions on gun ownership. See Arthur Kreuzer, "Wie du mir, so ich dir," *Die Zeit*, Nr. 18, May 7, 1993; Jürgen Dahl, "Können Sie schießen? Treffen Sie Freunde," *Die Zeit*, Nr. 8, February 25, 1994.

70. Richard Thurlow, "The State and the Radical Right in Italy, France and Britain—A Historical Perspective," presented at the Conference on the Radical Right in Western Europe, University of Minnesota, November 7–9, 1991, p. 25.

71. The sample included 262 Western and 8 Eastern-based foreigners. Rudolf Dennhardt, et al., *Deutsche Schüler im Sommer 1990: Skeptische Demokraten auf dem Weg in ein vereintes Deutschland*, München: DJI, 1990), pp. 33–48.

72. Ibid., Part II, Table 17.2 and Table 17.3.

73. Ibid., Part II, Table 14.6, Table 14.2.

74. Ibid., Part I, Table 2 and Part II, Table 23.3.

75. Brandenburgische Landeszentrale für politische Bildung, Hg., *Die Situation von Jugendlichen in Brandenburg* (Potsdam, 1993). Prior to 1994, Brandenburg was the only new state governed by a left-coalition of Social Democrats, Greens/Alliance '90 and PDS delegates, headed by GDR-born Manfred Stolpe. Then Education Minister Marianne Birthler (*Bündnis '90*, a former GDR dissident) introduced "life-structuring ethics" into the classroom, but later resigned in protest over Stolpe's refusal to admit to ties with the *Stasi*; Joachim Nawrocki, "Mit Stolpe siegen," *Die Zeit*, Nr. 14, April 8, 1994.

76. *Die Situation von Jugendlichen*, op. cit., pp. 30–37.

77. Ibid., p. 34.

78. Ibid., p. 23.

79. Deutsches Jugendinstitut, Hg., *Gewalt gegen Fremde. Rechtsradikale, Skinheads und Mitläufer* (München: Verlag Deutsches Jugendinstitut, 1993).

80. Ibid. These figures stem from an executive summary provided by the Ministry of the Interior, devoid of page numbers.

81. A 1993 study by the US Office of Juvenile Justice and Delinquency Detention revealed a 68% increase in the number of "serious crimes" committed by minors bewteen 1988 and 1992, 80% in cases of aggravated assault; 81% of the crimes involved males.

82. Bundesministerium für Frauen und Jugend, Hg., *Zur Lage der Jugend in Ost- und Westdeutschland* (Bonn: June 1993), p. 32.

83. The DJI study offered no figures on parenthood. Though the authors justified their use of telephone interviews in the West, and face-to-face interviews in the East at great length, they failed to mention that their mode of "household" selection neglected youth living in "occupied" buildings or transitional quarters; "Streetworkers" cite the lack of affordable housing as one of the three major problems confronting their clients.

84. Ibid., p. 1. *Frauenministerin* Merkel neglected to mention that 59% of the *Ossis* and 52% of the *Wessis* thought too little has been done to ensure equal rights for women and men, p. 32.

85. Ibid., p. 81, p. 83.

86. Ibid., pp. 86–87.

87. Ibid., pp. 91–93.

88. *Die Zeit* reported that the Government ignored its own study in favor of more optimistic prognoses offered by the 1992 German Shell survey. Jugendwerk der Deutschen Shell, Hg., *Jugend '92. Lebenslagen, Orientierungen und Entwicklungsperspektiven im vereinigten Deutschland* (Opladen: Leske + Budrick, 1992).

89. Cited in Klaus-Henning Rosen, op. cit., p. 98. Also, Claus Leggewie, *Druck von Rechts. Wohin treibt die Bundesrepublik?* (München: C.H. Beck, 1993).

90. As cited in *TWIG*, November 27, 1992.

91. Cited by Habermas in "Die zweite Lebenslüge," op. cit.

92. It is unclear why the Verfassungsschutz characterizes "resistance," robberies and disruption of public transportation as *violent-acts* with regard to leftists but not in relation to rightwing thugs, since the latter often attack foreigners riding the Berlin S-Bahn. *Verfassungsschutzbericht 1993* (Bonn: 1993), Part I, p. 5, Part II, p. 6. The number of left-wing attacks *against right-extremists* grew from 132 in 1991 to 389 in 1992, versus 2,283 right-assaults *on foreigners* during the same period.

93. For more on efforts to equate Right with Left extremism, see Peter Marcuse, "Feindbild Stasi sichert dem Westen den Status quo. Die Art der Debatte über die DDR Vergangenheit," *Frankfurter Rundschau*, May 14,1992; and Herbert Obenaus, "Stasi kommt—Nazi geht?" *Die Zeit*, Nr. 32, August 7 1992. Cf. Helmut Rannacher, "Eine neue Dimension der Gewalt? Das Aufschaukeln von Rechts- und Links-extremisten," *Recht und Politik*, Heft 3, September 1993; and Eckhard Jesse, "Linksextremismus in der Bundesrepublik Deutschland. Von den Anfängen bis zur Gegenwart," *Aus Politik und Zeitgeschichte*, B3–4, 1992, pp. 31–39.

94. Gisela Ulrich, "Zur Situation der Jugendhilfe in Leipzig," *Aus Politik und Zeitgeschichte*, B 38, September 11, 1992, pp. 29–35.

95. Irina Bohn, Dieter Kreft and Hans-Georg Weigel, Hrsg., *Zwei Jahre AGAG: Erfahrungen aus der praktischen Arbeit mit gewaltbereiten Jugendlichen* (Frankfurt/M.: Institut für Sozialarbeit und Sozialpädagogik e.V., 1994).

96. Michael Peters, then 26, will spend life in prison, having been convicted on three counts of murder, thirty-nine attempted-murder counts and one arson charge. His parents divorced, his father an abusive alcoholic who died in 1990, Peters claimed at his trial that he had joined the NPD because it often provided free beer; when that stopped, he lost interest. Lars Christiansen was found guilty of the same crimes but the maximum punishment for minors is ten years. Ingo Hasselbach, with Winfried Bonengel, *Die Abrechnung. Ein Neonazi steigt aus* (Berlin: Aufbau Verlag, 1994), p. 33.

97. Established in 1987, the "Anti-Aggression Training Program" has thus far treated 71 males aged 17–25, as reported in *TWIG*, April 23, 1994.

98. Three Cabinet members had to resign after using their offices for personal gain, Stoltenberg (Defense), Mölleman (Economics) and Krause (Transportation); Seiters (Interior) left his post after a hunt for two **left** terrorists ended in a bloodbath at a small Mecklenburg train station; Wolfgang Gehrmann and Wolfgang Sischke, "Zehn Tage Innere Unsicherheit," *Die Zeit*, Nr. 28, July 16, 1993. On unity-related corruption, see Heinz Blüthmann, "Boom für Betrüger," *Die Zeit*, Nr. 42, October 16, 1992; Peter Christ and Ralf Neubauer, *Kolonie im eigenen Land. Die Treuhand, Bonn und die Wirtschaftskatastrophe der fünf neuen Länder* (Berlin: Rowohlt, 1991).

99. Dieter Roth, "Sind die Republikaner die Fünfte Partei? Sozial- und Meinungsstruktur der Wähler der Republikaner," *Aus Politk und Zeitgeschichte*, October 5, 1989, pp. 10–20.

100. The Autonomous Ones precipitating the violence were not Marxists but anarchists. Klaus Hartung, "Ein Spaziergang der Demokraten," *Die Zeit*, Nr. 47, November 20, 1992.

101. Moreshäuser, op. cit, p. In January 1994, 10,000 Halle residents marched in solidarity with a woman confined to a wheelchair, alleging a swastika had been carved into her cheek by three skinheads; the wound turned out to be self-inflicted.

102. Norbert Kostede, "Erleuchtung für die Politik," *Die Zeit*, Nr. 5, February 1993.

103. Theo Sommer, "Das Schandmal des Fremdenhasses," *Die Zeit*, Nr. 42, October 18, 1991.

104. French Communist Party leader George Marchais and Conservative Jacques Chirac have also exploited anti-foreigner sentiment, albeit less successfully than Le Pen's National Front. One French farmer told an NPR reporter he voted against the

1992 Maastricht Treaty "because then all of those foreigners and refugees in Germany will come over here."

105. "Zehn Tote—Warum nur immer wieder Lübeck?" *Stuttgarter Zeitung*, January 19, 1996; "Trauer, Hilfsbereitschaft und politische Forderungen," *Stuttgarter Zeitung*, January 20, 1996.

106. Judith Shklar, *American Citizenship. The Quest for Inclusion* (Cambridge, MA: Harvard University Press, 1991), p. 2.

107. Christiane Lemke, "Crossing Borders and Building Barriers. Citizenship and the Process of European Integration," presented at the German Studies Association Conference, Washington, D.C., October 5–10, 1993. p. 10.

8

Conclusion:
From Two States in One Nation
to One Volk in Two Cultures

So rissen wir uns ringsumher
Von fremden Banden los
Nun sind wir Deutsche wiederum,
Nun sind wir wieder groß. . . .
Und Fürst und Volk und Furst
Sind alle frisch und neu!
Wie Du Dich nun empfinden wirst
nach eigenem Sinne frei!

—Johann Wolfgang von Goethe,
Epimenides

After the party comes the hangover,
and the hangover usually lasts longer.

—Peter Schneider,
St. Louis, October 9, 1991

One day after the Berlin Wall opened, the honorable Willy Brandt eloquently summarized the hopes of millions of postwar European citizens:
"Now that which belongs together can grow together." I believe it will take
the coming-of-age of a new Post-Wall generation to realize that dream. In
order to devise strategies for recreating a spirit of national community between the Germans of East and West, one must first comprehend how far
the peoples of the two states have grown apart over a period of four
decades. The search for German identity has not ended with unification; on
the contrary, that process has unleashed a new search for identity.

The questions this study originally sought to answer concerning the
changing West German attitudes towards the national question and the
North Atlantic Alliance not only persist; they have actually acquired new significance in light of unity. Four decades of division have lent themselves to
the formation of separate East and West German identities, although certain
bonds of "common consciousness" persist. The ties that bind are rooted
largely in historical memory, but even that memory proves to be highly selec-

tive, since the two states viewed the past through mutually exclusive political lenses over a forty year period. It is no longer history per se but historical memory fractured by the prism of generational change which has given shape to manifold national identity and security needs among postwar Germans.

Invoking a wide variety of quantitative and qualitative "data" centering on West Germans, I have tried to persuade the reader that there is a strong link between the national identity paradigms of three postwar generations and their distinctive national security orientations. This work has traced the diverse historical and political socialization experiences of the Economic Miracle Generation, the Long March Generation and the Turn-Around Generation, respectively. It has focused on four factors—postwar demographics, the Federal Republic's unique geo-strategic location, the accelerated pace of political-economic change, as well as the absence of a shared sense of "German" identity—in an attempt to explain certain conflicts inherent in the internal and external security needs projected by each generation. It argued that in addition to having played a key role in the mobilization of the West German peace movement of the 1980s, generational change has impelled a systematic re-evaluation of Germany's role in the development of a broader security partnership between the West European allies of old and the newly liberated the states of Eastern Europe. Of all the modern powers, Germany-united is the one in which the constructs of citizen consciousness, external security and history are most intricately intertwined; though Japan runs a close second, it has not faced the cross-cutting forces of a divided citizenry across four decades.

It is no easy task to trace the specific influences of an extraordinary range of historical, political, economic and environmental variables in defining the needs, interests and ideals of a given generation, as the theoretical treatment in Chapter One suggested. I attempted to render the complex interplay of those variables more comprehensible by focusing on a limited number of identity-building processes which appear to incorporate both the internal and external dimensions of German national consciousness. Included were the processes of generational self-socialization, domestic self-definition and other-identification, international self-definition and image-projection, as well as the processes of internal and external community identification. These processual labels derived from my interdisciplinary overview of the multiple meanings and functions attributed to "identity."

I tried to simplify the complex, interactive web of human, environmental and systemic relations still further by presenting a concentric model of identity, which reminds us that national identity is a composite of the many overlapping and sometimes contradictory needs of "real people" aligning themselves with a particular state; it rarely assumes the exact shape or significance projected by ruling elites. Identity begins with a socio-psychological core, reflective of democracy's emphasis on the rights and interests of the individual; it then unfolds and expands in accordance with a more or less universal need for a sense of belonging. An ever more focused search for "the good of the community" eventually gives rise to various forms of collective identity, some cross-cutting (party membership), some mutually exclusive in nature (gender or race). A set of overlapping collective identities first makes "national" identity possible; indeed, the rise of the nation-state is a fairly recent phenomenon in historical terms. Reliance on a particular state as the framework for national-consciousness building does not preclude the simultaneous existence of competing or conflicting types of identification among individuals, especially within the context of a pluralist democracy.

I then developed five question-complexes in the ensuing chapters, each addressing a particular "ring" of identity. Treating both individual and mass levels of analysis, I sought answers to the questions:

- What does it mean to be an FRG-German, from the vantage point of "average" citizens?
- What was the relationship between Federal Republicans and their "brothers and sisters" in the GDR prior to unification?
- What was the Federal Republic's relationship to NATO, and how was it perceived by average citizens?
- What were the attitudes of West Germans with regard to specific foreign policy and international security strategies?
- How have the Germans-united reacted to increasing numbers of non-Germans living in their midst?

Let us review the answers to these questions, based on the evidence presented in the preceding chapters.

Domestic Dimensions of German National Identity

Centering on the process of internal self-definition, Chapter Two explored the extent to which old myths about German national character have lost their meaning for the postwar generations. I assessed the importance of the national question at a variety of levels, discovering that the socially cohesive (some would say, organic) ultra-nationalism of old has given way to much more fragmented, individualized and often contradictory notions of what it means to be a (West) German. In-depth interviews were used to analyze individual perceptions regarding "the need for" and "the functions of" German identity, queries which seemed to produce little inter-generational consensus. I then examined generational perspectives concerning the "positive" and "negative" features of that postwar identity, including but not limited to their respective attitudes towards existing institutions, constitutional values and new modes of political participation. Despite the limits imposed by a "blood-based" concept of citizenship, all three postwar generations appeared to embrace an identity of many layers, one that is fundamentally democratic and "open to the world."

As regards their historical consciousness, there is substantial evidence that West Germans underwent a fundamental change of heart with regard to past personalities and events between 1949 and 1989. Many elites nonetheless stressed a need for additional information, or at least for more effective ways of conveying knowledge about the Nazi period to the country's youth, even before the resurgence of rightwing violence. They were less likely to agree on *which* lessons ought to be derived from the past and transmitted to future generations. The lesson receiving the least amount of attention at the time is the one most desparately needed in the wake of post-Wall developments: At issue is not the nation's past and future right to engage in "power politics" world-wide but rather its ongoing duty to inculcate its citizens with a strong enough sense of personal responsibility to resist the politics of intolerance in their own backyards. More important than the "ability to mourn" victims of the past is the ability to emphathize with the victims of the present—without attempting to re-classify one's self as the victim.

As we further discovered in Chapters Two and Five, state, administration and society are no longer perceived to comprise an organic whole among the citizens in the West-Länder. The principle of the *Rechtsstaat* [state of law] has been reinterpreted since 1949; West Germans now emphasize the importance of citizen rights and individual self-actualization, over the reification of state interests. The "old" Federal Republic evinced a high degree of consensus as to the fundamental characteristics of a secure, effective democracy. Citizens accord highest priority to freedom, followed by popular sovereignty, justice and tolerance of political opposition. Protest demonstrations and Citizen Initiatives have often taken precedence over ballot-box politics, in part because many contemporary activists were exposed to unconventional forms of participation years before they became eligible to vote. A vast array of "alternative cultures" flourished throughout the 1980s; in addition to absorbing many would-be rowdies or dropouts, these movements enhanced a tolerance for diversity among younger cohorts. The civic culture which took root in the FRG has embraced the notion of "do-it yourself politics," exhibiting high levels of self-worth and citizen efficacy.

Impelled by the sentimentally-rooted national identities of their neighbors, as well as by the anomolous existence of a second German state until 1989, Federal Republicans have increasingly accepted the need for some form of collective identity, especially since 1979. They continue to stress individual freedom, however, defining a personal identification with "their" state as loosely as possible. West Germans are quick to mobilize when they feel their own interests are affected, but they are harder to rally when there is no personal loss at stake—unless, of course, circumstances call for a critical position vis-à-vis the United States. The successor generations have substantially broadened the institutional foundations of democracy, and they seem quite sincere in their efforts to define what it does not mean to be a German. Yet many remain reluctant to deepen their "understanding of democracy" by extending fundamental protections and rights to the non-Germans living within their borders.

While preferred modes of identity are clearly not a function of age or birthdate alone, they are definitively influenced by one's proximity to or distance from key historical and political events. Chapter Two established different degrees of emphasis regarding individual and collective, personal and historical "implication" or guilt, occasionally resulting in direct clashes between the generations. These differences can best be characterized in terms of *Befangenheit*, *Betroffenheit* and *die neue Unbefangenheit*. The Economic Miracle Generation found it nearly impossible to escape the surly bonds of *Befangenheit*, a kind of caught-in-the-act complicity, stemming from the 1930s and 1940s. It is generally an older, more conservative camp that views the German travesty of 1933–1945 as a matter of political destiny. Select members of these cohorts have tried to "normalize" Germany's standing in the international community by situating the Third Reich experience in a broader context of world-historical violence.

The first generation was eventually challenged by its antithesis, the Long March Generation, caught up in the passion of *Betroffenheit*. The successors shared a perception of being directly affected by the negative consequences of escalating global tension, environmental destruction and unfettered technological change. Paradoxically, the very cohorts who recognized the importance of "doing their own thing" were the ones to discover a new "tragedy of the commons" (leaving FRG-security up to NATO), of which they themselves could become victims. As to the past, liberal elements among these cohorts stressed the historical role of political will (or lack thereof, e.g., the collective failure to organize a national resistance movement).

Members of the third generation were free to embrace *die neue Unbefangenheit*, a synthesis phase not yet completed, linking historical cognition to personalized political experience and "feeling." The New Unencumberedness personified by the Turn-Around Generation is most easily understood as a form of self-exoneration, as a release from responsibility relative to past events. Coupled with their psychological liberation from "the eternal yester-year" is a casual identification with the new brand of do-it-yourself politics; even the would-be ultranationalists among them call on perceptions of personal insecurity, or *Betroffenheit*, to justify their self-mobilized street campaigns.

Numerous polls canvassing attitudes towards Hitler, anti-Semitism, national symbols, and democratic institutions support the argument that diverse segments of the FRG citizenry had cast off "an extraordinary amount of historical ballast" prior to the onset of German unity. This is not to say that gen-

erational succession alone accounts for major societal change. Clearly the ignomy of defeat, political re-education under the Occupiers, the consolidation
of democratic institutions at home, and membership in value-reinforcing organizations abroad (NATO, the European Union) also played important roles
in the re-structuring of German national consciousness. The impact of structural variables on the political consciousness of individual citizens is nonetheless impossible to establish. While the collective identities of the pre- and postwar German states may be intricately connected, the individual identities to
which various age or status groups aspire often divorce themselves from the
"ballast of the past" by way of selective memory. The dilemma of German
identity rests with the need, in Schonbaum's words, "to be *and* not to be."

Comprising two-thirds of the West German population, the cohorts born
since 1945 have distanced themselves from the very character traits for
which Germans have been known and feared historically. Most younger citizens (counterparts of the American Me-Generation) reject a simplistic attachment to duty, diligence, law and order; self-proclaimed neo-Nazis constitute an obvious exception to this rule. Whatever negative trade-offs might
be inherent in their focus on immediate gratification and individual satisfaction, youth's New Unencumberedness has helped to foster a climate of mo-
bility plus diversity within the postwar political culture, despite an indisputable increase in anti-foreigner feeling since unification.

Between 1949 and 1989 the leaders of the Federal Republic paid abstract
homage to the persistence of an all-German consciousness (reflected in their
rhetorical appeals to the Preamble), while their day-to-day policies centered
on the cultivation of an identification with the political-economic successes
of the Western state per se. Those achievements were impressive ones, far
outweighing occasional lapses in the direction of the overbearing state
(*Berufsverbot*) or extremist activities among select segments of the population (Baader-Meinhof or the Defensive Sport-Group Hoffmann). Inevitable
contradictions between the two levels of West German identity—namely,
between the official projections of collective culture and the ever more indi-
vidualistic aspects of peer culture—came to head during the generational
conflict of the late 1960s, finding a workable if not entirely harmonious synthesis in the new "subject culture" of the 1970s and 1980s.

Like its Western nemesis, the GDR's forty-year history embodied a complex interplay of continuity, change and contradiction. While official policies
focused on the development of a separate national identity, the day-to-day
operations (and provocations) of the regime invoked a perpetual comparison with conditions west of the Wall which, dialectically speaking, reinforced a sense of connectedness with the other Germany. Subordination to
the new state in 1949, under leaders who had proven their commitment to
an "anti-fascist, democratic" alternative (by way of imprisonment under the
Nazis) allowed many otherwise implicated East Germans to circumvent

their own painful need to "master the past." A potential clash of the first
and second generations was narrowly averted with the rapid termination of
the so-called Prague Spring (1968); a more serious struggle between the
generations surfaced in the mid-1980s when the GDR's political-economic
failures began to outstrip its successes, especially in the eyes of younger cohorts who had not experienced the bitterness and scarcity of earlier years.[1]

Official policies aside, what kinds of bonds persisted among the people-
divided, and how strong was each generation's ability to identify with the
other Germany prior to unification? The process of other-identification
treated in Chapter Three challenges most conventional assumptions regarding the postwar "dream" of German unification. As admitted at the outset
of this book, I had already concluded by the early 1980s (along with millions of Germans) that the restoration of a united *Staatsnation* would not
come to pass during my lifetime; my goal was to determine whether the
German *Kulturnation* still existed, and if so, in what form it might survive
the millennium. The evidence presented throughout this book suggests that
the development so many deemed impossible, the reestablishment of the
nation-state, may prove to have been the easier task after all; its chief requirements are territorial unity, political sovereignty and a common set of
governing institutions. The cultural-nation, by contrast, emerges out of the
interplay of ethnicity, common language, religion and customs, out of
shared systems of values, social communication and economic interchange,
a common pride in achievements coupled with common regret over failures,
all of which are ensconced in a framework of shared interpretation of history. With the exception of language and ethnicity, few of these other elements were in place at the time of unification, depriving the expanded Federal Republic of an immediate sense of national community. Irrespective of
their other ideological errors, I believe that GDR historians Kosing and
Schmidt were correct in distinguishing between the objective and subjective
components of national identity; it is also true that the bonding-potential
inherent in the latter may persist well beyond a generation.[2]

An eclectic methodology once again allows us to highlight many sources
of cultural difference between the Germans of East and West. By the mid-
1980s, an overwhelming majority of FRG citizens had come to accept national division as a more or less normal state of affairs; not even sensational
escape stories or deaths along the Wall could evoke the sustained public outrage typical of the 1960s. The unity mandate enshrined in the "provisional"
constitution was construed by ever more citizens as a profession of abstract-
legal faith, devoid of a need for direct political action. Though most welcomed the "liberation" of East Germany in 1989, few West Germans were
ready, willing or able to assume the burdens of national unity placed upon
them by way of elite-driven "power politics."

We reviewed diverse sources of information about "life in the GDR"
available to average Western citizens, allowing us to determine that the in-

fluences of Father-Time have been far more effective in diminishing their interest in the other Germans than were Father-State's efforts to sustain the myth of a single national identity. Individual as well as mass perceptions of the Germans "over there" revealed a certain reluctance on the part of both groups to intensify their contacts with people East of the Wall. I highlighted differences in the "mentalities" of FRG and GDR Germans by considering problems of adjustment experienced by Easterners who had fled to the West prior to November 1989.

Abandoning the dream of a unified nation-state after 1961, West Germans of all ages more or less accepted the idea that "provisional" division had become permanent. By the 1980s an overwhelming majority no longer believed that unification was particularly desirable, few thought it was likely to occur during their lifetime, and almost no one expected to pay a great deal in order to make the nation whole again. The deprivation of liberty suffered by GDR citizens was sooner perceived as a question of humanitarian rather than national concern. Thus, it was relatively easy for FRG-citizens of all persuasions to join in the euphoric celebrations marking the collapse of the Wall in November 1989. They found it extremely difficult to digest the course of events that followed, however.

Unification may be a necessary condition for restoring familiarity between the citizens of the two postwar states, but developments of the past five years have proven that it is certainly not a sufficient condition. Born of an interdependent world, East and West German youth are more attuned to the robber-barons featured on video and the World Wide Web than in the eighteenth century prototypes made famous by Schiller and Kleist. Even the ultra-nationalists among them (most of whom seem to lack a proficiency in *Hochdeutsch*) have acquired their musical tastes by way of imports from Britain (*Oi*) and the Caribbean (*Ska*); there is little comfort to be found in their potentially shared interest in the historical anti-culture of Nazi Terminators.

The "clash of cultures" between the Germans of East and West was not long in coming, but it does evince a number of unusual contours from rather unexpected quarters. In an effort to come full circle, I return briefly to the group whose seeming indifference to the National Question served as an inspiration for this book, members of the Long March Generation. Pivotal in the sense that these numerically-strong cohorts will assume the leadership of Germany's most powerful institutions well into the next century, I sample a number of their individual reactions to unification in order to speculate about prospects for a rapid growing-together of a people which now officially belongs together.

Eulogies to the Nation Divided: Identities Lost and Found

Unlike many of his New Left peers, Peter Schneider (born in 1940) has reflected regularly on the processes of other and community identification vis-à-vis the now-defunct German Democratic Republic. A resident of Berlin-West since 1961, Schneider assumed a preeminent role among members of the "post-postwar" literary scene with his 1982 publication of *The Wall-Jumper*, presenting tales of "life in the Siamese city."³ His portrayal of the Wall's place in everyday life echoed the perceptions of my resident-friends prior to 1989. Frequently asked as to "whether it is not peculiar to live in a city surrounded by cement and barbed wire," Schneider responded, "one doesn't live any differently here than in any other city. Actually I don't see the Wall any more: this, despite the fact that next to the Chinese version it may be the only piece of construction on earth which one can recognize with the naked eye from the moon."⁴ Westerners' interest in life beyond the Wall waxed and waned in response to current events. The Wall itself "became a mirror for the Germans in the West, which told them day by day, who was the fairest in the land. Whether there was life on the other side of the death-strip is something that soon interested only pigeons and cats."⁵

Despite the constitutional exhortation to see themselves as "one people"—divided only by ideological forces and occupying armies—the citizens of both states were regularly subjected to inimical images of "the other" [*Feindbilder*], as well as to projections of themselves as "the better Germans." It was Schneider who unwittingly prophesied in the early 1980s, "To tear down the Wall in the head will take longer than any undertaking required to tear down the visible Wall . . . we cannot talk with each other, without having the state [from which we try to distance ourselves] speak out of us."⁶ In contrast to pro-unity politicians, he had even fantasized about "How would it be if the Wall fell?" in a June 1989 *New York Times Magazine* article. But the night of its veritable collapse found Schneider in Hanover, New Hampshire, as shocked as all the rest: "I can't believe it, that cannot be, not so fast and not so easily! . . . Apparently we had so accustomed ourselves to this crazy condition that we now perceived the normalization as crazy."⁷

His first post-Wall book focuses on the dilemmas of Germans who now find themselves at the "extreme center." One possible explanation for differences between the two postwar cultures, he muses, lies with the so-called "deep-freeze" theory: one can argue that communism had served as a kind of freezer into which the historical characteristics and passions of the East Germans were placed for storage. Given sufficient time to "thaw out," they might be expected to take up where they had left off as "normal" Germans forty-five years earlier; as the theory goes, all of the socialist "virtues and achievements" with which they had been enveloped will eventually "fall from them like old snow."⁸ Juxtaposed against this national-character approach is the milieu theory, insisting that one is but the product of a specific "nurturing" system, determining everything from patterns of childhood education to proper relations between the sexes.

While it is now apparent that state-campaigns to instill a separate GDR-identity failed to take root, both "theories" lose some of their power of explanation owing to a number of inherently faulty assumptions. The deep-freeze framework implies, first, that East Germans have not been transformed in any unpredictable manner through their years of TV-exposure to the "western way of life." It moreover presumes that even though West Germans were not frozen in time, they did preserve or cultivate multiple virtues of yore which can now be easily re-internalized, now that the other side has thawed out. As any *Hausfrau* can attest, foods kept frozen for many years lose much of their original taste and texture, and are best served up to the family dog. Humans, by contrast, are dynamic life-forms, capable of adapting themselves to a wide array of environmental conditions. But the milieu theory also has its weaknesses. The East Germans initially displayed an extraordinary desire to divorce themselves from products and institutional processes made-in-the-GDR, until they realized that clothes, cars and cigarette brands were not at the heart of their own identities. Socialization experiences cannot be easily displaced, no matter how tempting the new milieu may be, as even the first Post-Wall cohorts have found. Whatever their origin, differences between the two cultures are real.

Beginning with that which divides, another Long-March era veteran confronts the processes of generational self-socialization and self-definition. On a visit to Paris at the time, Patrick Süskind reacted quite positively to early reports that the Wall was open: "Very good! . . . Finally something is happening. Finally these people are getting the elementary right to freedom of movement." By the end of the evening, however, he found himself catapulted into the throes of an age-specific malaise, perceived in terms of "Germany-as-midlife-crisis."[9]

"Forty and two-thirds years old" in 1989, this West German playwright searched in vain for a cognitive "stage" that might enable him to join in the dramatic refrains of his generational predecessors. The options ranged from Mayor Walter Momper's November 9th proclamation ("Tonight the German people are the happiest people in the world!"), to the November 10th declaration of his youth-idol, Willy Brandt ("Now that will grow together which belongs together"), to the celebratory toast uttered later by an air-born Chancellor Kohl in February 1990 ("Well then: To Germany!"), after a meeting with Gorbachev which cleared the path to unity. Süskind could imagine nothing less capable of weaving itself back together than the two German states:

Different societies, different governments, different economic systems, different educational systems, different standards of living, different bloc-memberships, different histories, different levels of alcohol permitted for drivers—nothing at all will grow together there, because nothing at all belongs together.[10]

Experiencing future-shock, Süskind comes to the self-defining realization that his own socialization simply "forbade me from using certain words and figures of speech, whether right or wrong." Another outcome of that process was his "complete indifference," long internalized, as to whether the Germans made their homes in two, four or twelve states, as "regrettable" as it was that the ones behind the Wall had paid a much heavier price for World War II atrocities. The one politician who spoke a language Süskind could still comprehend was Oskar Lafontaine (born in 1943), who talked about "real problems" and about major asymmetries between the residents of Paris or Frankfurt, and the citizens of East Berlin, Dresden or Leipzig. Yet the first SPD Chancellor-candidate of Long March vintage was wounded in a crazy assassination attempt (another German political "first") shortly after the Wall crumbled. The world, Süskind observed, was no longer "in order."

For that world, the only one ever experienced by the revolutionary '68 Generation, rapidly approaching middle-age, was no longer a provisorium. As they had matured and mellowed, so had their relationship to the Federal Republic, which "at first [was] reserved, skeptical, later ornery, then pragmatic, and finally, perhaps, even imprinted with a distanced sympathy. This state had proved itself well, completely unprovisionally, it was free, democratic, based on justice, practical—and it was exactly as old or as young as we were, and in a certain sense, our state."[11] The overnight transformation of the postwar order evoked a mid-life crisis of major proportions at the worst conceivable moment, that is, coincident with the realization that the personal biographies of his own generation have been half completed:

> we find ourselves in that interval of life where a human being is inclined to call for a time-out, to look inwards, to reflect back, to draw a balance and gradually to orient oneself towards the second half of one's life. . . . Just as we believed that we had gained control of our own existence and comprehended the world, and at least had a general idea "which way the rabbit runs" and where he will keep on running . . . now suddenly we are rolled over by this midlife-crisis in the form of German unity! We might have been prepared to deal with impotence problems, with prostate disease, false teeth, menopause and a second Chernobyl, with cancer and death and the devil—but never with *Deutsch-land-ei-nig-Va-ter-land* [Germany-united-fatherland]!.. . . *Angst?* No anxiety is not the right word. Whoever stands in a state of shock feels no anxiety.[12]

For the Economic Miracle Generation, the (re)establishment of a unified, sovereign German state marks a "return" of sorts. To be sure, the landscape has changed with time; the buildings are much shabbier than one remembers, one's former friends and relatives have grown older, but conceivably wiser, as has the observer. The surroundings are different but familiar, and one has certainly mastered the art of adapting. The Turn-Around Generation, by comparison, has yet to concretize its own system of historical-political coordinates. Mobile, flexible, open to the world and always ready for action, it will, sooner or later, assimilate the new borders and social relations into its own life-paradigm.

For self-reflective members of the Long March Generation, however, the end of the Federal Republic as they knew it evokes a surprising sense of loss—the very citizens who thought they might best be served by little or no "national identity" at all. As nostalgically summarized by Süskind, "Yes, . . . I am a little sad to think that this dull, small, unloved, pragmatic state of the *Bundesrepublik* in which I grew up will no longer exist from now on."[13] Paradoxically, the very cohorts who always insisted they had nothing to gain from a fusion of the postwar states are also the ones who will be forced to shoulder most of its political-financial costs.

The recognition of cultural differences, expressed in terms of physiological processes, is not confined to citizens west of the former border. A long-time dissident pastor and co-founder of the former GDR opposition group, Democratic Awakening, Friedrich Schorlemmer (born in 1944) observed:

> Wonderful that there was such a thing as the Basic Law. The West Germans had to take us. And we gladly allowed ourselves majority-wise to be swallowed whole. Now we lie rather heavily in the stomach of the well-nourished and groomed Federal Republic—with our heavy metals, asbestos-palaces, rotted landscapes, kaputt cities, Stasi-snares that reach all the way to Bonn, with broken-down, unsellable factories. Now it's a question of digestion. Cramps are unavoidable. For many it is a gall-bladder attack.[14]

For Schorlemmer, the cure will eventually follow the disease. Gregor Gysi, by contrast, expects the illness to be a long and painful one. From the start, Gysi (born in 1948) was much less enthusiastic about the dissolution of the GDR, a state his father, Klaus Gysi, had helped to found and govern as the former Minister for Culture and liaison-official for State-Church Relations. Serving until January 1993 as head of the Party of Democratic Socialists (the PDS, which rose out of the ashes of the former Socialist Unity Party), the younger Gysi has also characterized the unification process in visceral terms, albeit in fewer words: "The snake that swallows the porcupine is likely to experience serious digestion problems."[15]

The digestion metaphor also dominated the thinking of one Israeli writer (born in 1937) whose extended family had perished under the Nazi regime. Reacting to renewed rightwing violence subsequent to unification, Asher Reich warned the European public, one has to pay twice as much attention to a topic so rooted in destiny. "A people which has soured its own stomach so much in the past like the Germans, one that has fouled Germany and almost the entire continent with its vomit, is obliged to have itself immunized right after the first stomach pains. Caution, friends! The heavy cramps of the German stomach have been all too easy to hear during the last year."[16]

Though much more graphic in his comparison, Reich implies that the new German malaise is not destined to become another epidemic, provided one attends to the first symptoms. Recuperation, in any case, is expected to be a lengthy affair. Just how long it will take to render the patient whole-some is reflected in another comparison often invoked by Eastern Germans: they point to the long-persistent tensions between the North and the South subsequent to the American Civil War.[17]

One begins to wonder which metaphor might have prevailed had unity been attained under §146, instead of §23 of the Basic Law; the "European House" comes to mind, in which the Germans might have eventually shared the master bedroom with a substantial prenuptial agreement. It is striking, in any case, that few women have offered sweeping assessments regarding the digestive capacities of the nation. Prominent female members of the Long March Generation have either focused on particular developments, or they have disappeared (at least media-wise) from the public arena. Outspo-ken unity-opponent Jutta Ditfurth lost her footing in an identity struggle among the Greens; Petra Kelly met with an untimely death in 1992, and Bärbel Bohley moved on to a crusade against former Stasi workers (includ-ing Gysi).

As Chapter Three revealed, women tended to be more ambivalent than men regarding the need for national consciousness. Ambivalence among women of the second generation was aptly summarized by Antje Vollmer, who sees the now "united Fatherland" as the fulfillment of "the dream of old men." She admits that men ranging from Rudolf Augstein and (his nemesis) Franz Josef Strauß, to Chancellors Brandt and Kohl made their own sacrifices in an effort to create a "better" Germany for the next generation:

> These men meant well. They have already done a lot for us. They built a free and democratic Republic. They built a free and critical press. They built a polit-ical opposition capable of governing. Now they want to do one last thing for us. They want to return Germany to us forty-five years after the war's end, and not even a nationalistic one. No, simply a civilized one. For the happiest people in the world from the happiest politicians in the world.[18]

But they missed one very important step, in Vollmer's assessment:

> It certainly counts as one of the major acts of negligence of German politics over the years, that [the old men] never made this feeling [of eventually en-countering] the sensational historical happy-event the core of a new, more modest and more satisfied German identity . . . the political Right thought that we are only getting out of this happy-event what was ours all along. The politi-cal Left . . . to which I belong . . . construed as a case of bad luck that which, without a doubt, is really good luck for many people. Both sides have missed the chance for forming a positive identity.[19]

The failure of both sides to move from a concept of *what German identity is not* to a model of what German identity can and should become was, until 1990, tied to a belief imposed by history that nationalism and democracy are antithetical values. The paradigm shift effected by unification lends itself to a new synthesis with regard to these two concepts.

BRDDR: One Volk in Two Cultures

The events of 1989/90 imply that the Western state, with its stable free-de-mocratic order and its booming social market economy, ultimately "won" the battle for the hearts and minds of the post-postwar Germans. Yet those quick to characterize the dissolution of the German Democratic Republic as the triumph of "capitalism" over "communism" overlook the fact that an identity does not die as a consequence of new borders and a new currency alone. Were this the case, one would have found no socio-cultural founda-tion for the reestablishment of German national unity after forty years of di-vision, since less than one-third of the current FRG residents have ever ex-perienced anything more than their own "rump-state."

But there is also validity to Schneider's proposition that the Berlin Wall "created the illusion that only the Wall separated the Germans."[20] What might have been inconsequential differences in the identity-orientations of Germans living apart take on a new significance, now that their union has received the blessing of the international community. Outsiders should not expect a common national consciousness to emerge spontaneously. As Egon Bahr asserted more than twenty years ago, "reunification is not a single act that can be put into practice on the basis of an historical resolution on an historical day at an historical conference but is rather a process with many steps and many stations."[21]

The initial image of King-Kohl-to-the-rescue has given way to major disil-lusionment as to the effectiveness of free elections in bringing about a rapid economic transformation of the East.[22] Some chroniclers of the GDR's col-lapse glorify the Chancellor's role in bringing about unity within a year of the Wall's opening, under terms extremely favorable for German sover-eignty.[23] The real blessing befalling the CDU Chancellor during the months of feverish negotiation was not the fate of "late birth" per se, but his pres-ence "at the right place at the right time." Without the daring concessions of Mikhail Gorbachev, without the courageous protests of East German op-position groups and the internal collapse of the SED, without the support-ive acquiescence of the Atlantic Alliance partners, unity would have re-mained an impossibility for years to come. It is also clear, as Brigitte Young has recently shown, that the decision-making processes used to bring about unity contravened the conventional (neo-corporatist) rules of policy-making in the FRG. Not only did the mechanisms employed systematically exclude women from participation in the reconfiguring of Germany; they also helped to consolidate a creeping centralization of state power.[24]

Since the two states officially became one on October 3, 1990, researchers have conducted countless surveys in an effort to determine whether the unified Germans are "different" or "alike." Self-assessments by citizens in the new Länder disclose a pervasive lack of self-confidence, the very trait which could move them beyond the confines of "second-class" culture. Coupled with four decades of authoritarian education, rising crime rates and mass unemployment reinforce a desire for greater internal security and more state-centeredness among Eastern citizens. The newly enfranchised are more "emancipated" than their Western peers, however, given their overwhelming support for career opportunities for women, state subsidies for child-care provision, and liberal abortion regulations. As of 1993, three-fourths of the *NeufünfländerInnen* expected to retain their status as second-class Germans for several years to come.[25] A certain inability to empathize with foreigners is a national trait "typical" of both populations.

De jure unity has not resolved the Germans' mutual dilemma of finding an appropriate name for each other, devoid of slanderous connotations. Behind the eliptical post-Wall delineation of *Ossis* and *Wessis* lies the insinuation of the *Jammerossi* [whining Easterner] and the *Besserwessi* [know-it-all Westerner], stereotypes which have been reinforced by a proliferation of acerbic *Ossi* and *Wessi* "jokes" since 1990.[26] The elimination of the Iron Curtain has forced the Germans of East and West to recognize the existence of multiple latent tensions between the two cultures, now described as the Wall in their heads. As Schorlemmer observes: "Now we recognize, how little we knew each other. . . . The Wall that we could see has been torn down almost everywhere. The Wall that we could not see at first seems to be getting higher. Our communication has been deeply disturbed, filled with prejudices and resentments on both sides. We talk more about each other than with each other."[27] Forty years of political, economic and social "difference" can not be overcome with the stroke of a pen, nor with the imposition of a single set of state and national institutions.

Initially preoccupied with the enormous legal and financial burdens of Eastern reconstruction, federal officials devoted little energy to the equally formidable task of reforging a sense of national identity from within, beyond a reinvocation of national symbols. United Germany's health as a nation will depend upon the extent to which its predominantly Western leadership succeeds not in "Kohlonizing" but in grafting Eastern political culture on to its own. The Germans united must now come to terms with not one but two authoritarian pasts, from which each side is likely to derive different lessons. "The old Federal Republic," it seems, "intends to defend and continue its successful history, with as little disturbance as possible from the history of the

German Democratic Republic," a tactic quite counterproductive to the form-
ing of a shared national consciousness; for "were the West to try and divest itself of the GDR's legacy it would be refusing to share the country's historical
burden and to permit a true understanding of the course of that history. Neither side has the option to declare itself 'not affected' by the other's fate."[28]

The campaign to "work through the history and consequences of the
SED-dictatorship in Germany" is a process laden with party-political strife.[29]
Consider, for example, the absurd exchanges coloring the Bundestag debates of mid-March 1992: The father of *Ostpolitik*, Willy Brandt, accused
Chancellor Kohl of abetting the authoritarian regime by having invited
GDR premier Erich Honecker to visit in September 1987—an invitation
first extended by SPD Chancellor Helmut Schmidt in 1979. Kohl argued in
self-defense that *his* official contacts had fostered the liberalization of travel
rules which, in turn, resulted in the mass exodus and non-violent "turn-
around" of 1989—claims that should have been made by the SPD, based on
its support of the 1975 Helsinki process and its 1987 "Common Paper"
with the SED, both of which afforded GDR dissidents a quasi-legal framework for critiquing their state from within.

Having claimed for many years that they "did not know about" all of
Hitler's atrocities at the time, it is striking how quickly many West Germans
have turned to admonish former GDR-citizens for their complicity with the
old SED regime.[30] Von Weizsäcker rightly argues that it is essential "for the
western Germans to recognize that under the conditions of communism,
they would probably have behaved no differently."[31] The number of GDR
professionals displaced by institution-wide purges since 1990 already exceeds the number of regime-loyal state officials, civil servants, judges and
teachers who were expelled from their positions after 1945. A resistance
fighter in his own right, Schorlemmer has stressed that "the mountain of
files in the *Normannenstraße* [former Stasi headquarters in Berlin] are terri-
ble, but it is not the mountain of corpses from Auschwitz." Equating the
two dictatorships "diminishes the crimes of Nazism."[32]

In fighting to secure citizen access to personal *Stasi* files (to foster rehabilitation and reconciliation from within), East officials have had to compete with
Bonn-based intelligence organs, interested in securing detailed records for
their own purposes, e.g., prosecuting former East-bloc spies and covering up
the illicit entanglements of select Western politicians. Former Rostock Pastor
Joachim Gauck has directed the arduous work of classifying, assessing and re-
leasing over "100 miles of files" confiscated from the East German *Stasi*. A
self-critical analysis of the GDR past is made all the more difficult by the fact
that many of the "little people" were, in Gauck's words, "victims and perpetrators at the same time."[33] The acceptance of a mutual responsibility for history is but the first step towards finding a common definition of that history.
Though I often disagree with the partisan pronouncements of Michael

Stürmer, I must concede one important point regarding the "re-processing" of history already underway: S/he who "fills the memory, forms the concepts and interprets the German past[s] shall win the future in a land deprived of history."[34]

Westerners should take no particular pleasure in hearing their Eastern counterparts denounce (publically, if not privately) the so-called "social achievements" of their former country, policies that included reproductive rights, after-school youth programs, and anti-lockout provisions vis-à-vis employers. On the contrary, one should be somewhat suspicious of persons who evince no feelings of displacement or loss towards a country in which they had spent most of their lives. *Ein Volk* with no feeling for its own past is a people open to future mass manipulation. As of 1993, a reported 82% of the Eastern residents were deeply troubled that West-officials "haven't left us any of things that we could also be proud of" as citizens of the GDR.[35] Attempts to disparage all goods and services once "made in the GDR" have led to backlash under the motto "we buy East," a phenomenon also known as *Ostalgie* [East-nostalgia].

One can admittedly "fast-forward to the start" of a shared consciousness by way of new constitutions and the transfer of administrative-organizational designs, but democracy-building is a normative as well as an institutional process.[36] As evidence from the FRG's own Reconstruction shows, it can take a population 10 to 20 years to internalize the value-paradigm essential to a new system's survival. Still other conditions must be met in order for a collectivity of largely self-interested and self-determining human beings to become an engaged community. In order to acquire a sense of mutual commitment, as well as a shared attachment to specific political institutions, citizens need to develop "networks of organized reciprocity and civic solidarity," identified first by de Tocqueville and later by Putnam as the cornerstones of *civic culture*.[37] Solidarity networks require a degree of generational and geographic closure.

The main problem with the process of growing together is that the networks which had evolved on both sides of the border over a period of three generations are fundamentally different and in many respects irreconcilable ones. Many newly enfranchised Easterners resent the orientation that West German political culture comprises the mainstream, reducing their own public and private norms to a marginal force slated for extinction. Their "re-discovery" of GDR-identity since 1991 is an effort to reposition themselves as a mainstream group, if only within a smaller territory. If Eastern Germans appear devoid of initiative, it is because they have been deprived of their "cultural template," inherent in the notion of social capital; indeed, they used to be known as masters of improvisation. Besides providing a collective, organizational memory essential for community discourse and problem-solving, social capital strengthens an individual's sense of self-worth by linking it to a more encompassing sense of belonging. Without this corresponding "we" feeling, Eastern Germans will find it hard to shift from the individual/*Heimat* level to national feelings of identity.

Nearly two-thirds of the East German citizenry have been born "too late" to perceive unity as a return to nationhood but "too early" to benefit from a New Beginning. Having accommodated themselves to the old rules of the game, most East-residents over the age of 35 have little hope of undertaking the long march through the institutions for which they were originally destined; by contrast, their offspring, *die Wendejugend* once devoid of optimism and "future prospects" under the GDR regime, now face a world of expanding (if not unlimited) opportunity. Generational change, added to the effects of mutually exclusive East-West socialization processes, means that the Germans united will not only continue to embrace competing and conflicting interpretations of their "shared" history. Their combined influences will also continue the 1980s trend of generating not one but rather a multitude of Post-Wall German identities over the next decade.

External Dimensions of Identity and Security

Subject to many agents and environmental influences, national identity formation takes place at many levels simultaneously, as my concentric model posited. Thus identity may be fraught with logical inconsistencies (rooted in selective memory), and more subject to change over time than is generally apparent to outsiders. We therefore need to examine not only how Germans have sought to transform their relations with states abroad but also how other countries have responded to their new "national image." It is clear that the Western cohorts born between 1949 and 1972 would have preferred to maintain the divided status quo between the two German states. But how did the concepts of "national sovereignty" and "neutralism" figure into their search for security prior to 1989? To what extent have the FRG's postwar generations differed in their perceptions of the Atlantic Alliance as the most effective "keeper of the peace" in Central Europe? What implications might their evolving attitudes towards NATO now hold for a "security partnership" between the states of East and West? These questions lie at the heart of the process of external community identification, considered in Chapters Four and Five.

In addition to rejecting a wide assortment of self-subordinating "German virtues" once judged essential to their personal development, postwar citizens have jettisoned the imperialistic underpinnings of Prussian military tradition and Bismarckian diplomacy. I demonstrated that the Federal Republic's commitment to a foreign policy course of regional integration and East-West cooperation offered postwar Germans a new source of positive identification with their own state, especially after 1969. Born of a unique set of security needs, *Ostpolitik* successfully linked national interests at the macro-political level with a positive notion of "what it meant to be German" at the individual level. It did so by servicing both sets of needs simultaneously: by expanding trade, extending visitation rights, encouraging disarmament, and opening the door to public debate over formerly taboo security questions. The perceived effectiveness of the Eastern Treaties and the Helsinki Accords contributed to the internalization of a new security formula at both the elite and mass levels: SECURITY = DEFENSE + DÉTENTE.

Invited to address Werner Weidenfeld's class at the University of Mainz on the "paradoxes of German identity" in 1986, I suddenly recalled a simple toy from my own childhood, acquired at a local summer carnival, known then as "Chinese hand-cuffs." It was a small tube, woven out of bamboo, about four inches long; the weaving was such that once I inserted my two index fingers and tried to pull them out again, the tube would stretch, becoming longer but tighter. The harder one tried to pull the two fingers apart, the more difficult it became to release them from the tube. The only way to free my digitals was to push them further into the tube, counter-intuitively; moving the fingertips closer together loosened the bamboo casing, making it possible to liberate them. In many respects, this toy seems like an apt metaphor for the dialectics of FRG foreign policy since 1949.

Painful though it may have been (admittedly to different degrees for FRG and GDR citizens), forty years of division seem to have been a necessary though not sufficient condition for the *peaceful* unification of the two German states. The bamboo tube represents the binding elements of their ideologically polarized Occupation and the subsequent entrappings of Cold War alliances. The policies of "non-recognition" (FRG) and "demarcation" (GDR) predominating throughout the 1950s and 1960s meant that the harder the two states attempted to pull away from each other, the more tightly they were bound into a superpower security system whose primary interests were often at odds with their own.

Having substituted pride in their respective reconstruction miracles for outright feelings of nationalism by 1969, the two systems pursued step-by-step improvements in their relationship, set in motion by the Brandt Government. Moves towards the easing of inter-German tensions were hesitant and even counter-intuitive at first, but German leaders accelerated their pace once the superpowers signaled their consent (if not active support) within the broader framework of détente. Egon Bahr's prescription of "change through growing closer" [*Wandel durch Annäherung*] unintentionally gave way to a process of "growing closer through change" [*Annäherung durch Wandel*]: FRG rapprochement gestures expected to induce a liberalization of the GDR regime intensified as a consequence of the changes taking hold in *both* systems. The latter was manifested in the CDU's eventual acceptance of the "politics of negotiation" and its quasi-recognition of the other German state after 1982.

One can argue, in retrospect, that the Germans of East and West had to struggle through forty years of division and that the two states had to move farther away from each other, in order to comprehend how their slow but steady *Annäherung* might help to loosen the binds of the Cold War system itself. The "space" afforded by one Western successor generation would not have sufficed to ensure the internalization of a new, positive conception of Germany-as-democracy. Left to its own devices, the reconstruction generation would have found it difficult to redirect its long-standing animosity towards the Soviet Union. Mounting opposition to nuclear proliferation and a pervasive lack of German "identity" among the second and third generations allowed the seeds of "Gorbi-mania" to fall on fertile ground. The fact that Federal Republicans did *not* actively or aggressively pursue the restoration of national unity but opted instead for a wide range of multilateral confidence-building policies (which most never expected to produce unity during their lifetimes) affords a potent guarantee that German unification shall not be abused for hegemonic ends. The lessons of generational politics are best summarized by the observations of a prominent father and his son. Reflecting on the dynamics of *Ostpolitik*, Brandt the elder once posited, "one must accept the status quo in order to change it." Brandt the younger countered ten years later, "more important than a common heritage . . . is the will to a common future."[38]

The question of German neutralism was effectively laid to rest with the Final Settlement of 1990, which not only secured the old Federal Republic's ongoing membership in NATO but also immediately incorporated the East German states, with promises of later membership for other former Warsaw Pact countries. Ironically, the countries which experienced the greatest suffering at the hands of Nazi invaders are the ones most actively seeking new forms of economic and military cooperation now, namely, Russia, Poland and France. Not all historical spectres have been laid to rest, of course, but there is strong evidence that Germany's postwar democratic image has gained credibility among former allies and adversaries alike. The *Bundesrepublik* has given every indication that it wants to avoid a "go it alone strategy." German involvement in the Balkan and Somalian crises has focused heavily on humanitarian forms of aid, the ostensible impatience of Defense Minister Volker Rühe notwithstanding. While the High Court ruling of July 1994 ordains new avenues for the exercise of national sovereignty (permitting Bundeswehr participation in "out-of-area" conflicts), any commitment of German troops remains tied to organs of collective security (NATO, the WEU and the UN)—and subject to a majority vote by a democratically elected Bundestag.

The centrality of *Ostpolitik* in postwar German security thinking not only laid the foundation for a process of peaceful unification but also for a creeping "democratization" of foreign policymaking within the FRG. Chapter Five focused on efforts by the post-postwar cohorts to forge a direct link between their "domestic identity" as Germans, that is, as constitutional patriots living under a Western-style democracy, and the identity attributed to Germany well beyond its borders. The emergence of a critical opposition rooted in church and labor during the 1950s gave rise to university based "counter-experts" in the 1970s. Ensconced in their own research institutes, anti-militarists have transcended the knowledge-gap that used to render national security policy the exclusive province of federal officials. Members of the informed public no longer view domestic affairs and foreign policy as worlds apart, one subject to public review, the other reserved for governmental elites.

The process began with a successful campaign to break the taboo on public debate over rearmament and nuclear deployment, limits initially imposed by the Victorious Powers but often instrumentalized by FRG-leaders to preclude challenges to existing policies. The activists of the 1970s and 1980s sought a greater measure of foreign policy autonomy for their own government as a member of NATO; their emphasis on "unconventional" forms of participation, developed in conjunction with the New Social Movements at home, led to a revaluation of the violent means used to secure peaceful ends abroad. Public support for the peace movement impelled the Kohl Government to become an ardent supporter of the INF Treaty and to urge recalcitrant Alliance partners to respond positively to Gorbachev's New Thinking.

The Gulf War of 1991 raised new identity questions among peace movement activists, linked to the process of unification itself. Biology has begun to take its course vis-à-vis the Republic's founding fathers and mothers, causing the mantle of national moral responsibility to fall directly on the shoulders of the next generation. Long March veterans have not only lost the ability to blame the older generation for its failure to "process" the Hitler legacy; they have moreover lost the very country they loved to protest against, as well as the allegedly anti-fascist, socialist alternative next door. Now nothing stands between the West Germans and the Old Reich (up to the Oder-Neisse border). Subscribing to "the blessing of having been born late," many middle-aged Marchers continue to fault "the system" for an inability to process the past, the very system in which they themselves now serve as prominent agents of socialization. Having been effectively taught to abhor the potential ecological consequences of war, children of the Sixty-Eighters have lost sight of the historical roots of German anti-interventionism.

The second generation's inability to "close the book" on German history is reflected in its ambivalent reactions to the Balkan war. Having regained their own sovereignty as a state and as a people by permanently foreswearing nationalism of the "ethnic cleansing" sort, average Germans are confounded by the idealized, militarized nationalism that has led to the self-destruction of Yugoslavia. But the process of selective qua collective memory is still at work in Germany, which as Markovits and Reich point out, "has much more to do with" present-day efforts to accrue power than it does with power manifestations of the past.[39] The past can be instrumentalized by politicians and protestors alike, to legitimize German involvement in some wars (the negative lesson of "appeasement," for example, which led many of the latter to accept military action, albeit by other countries, against Saddam Hussein), as well as to preclude German engagement in others (in Yugoslavia prior to 1995, for instance).

In many respects, it is the international community which has yet to digest and appreciate a number of significant postwar changes that Germany has come to embody. For forty years, the Federal Republic constituted the most peaceful, prosperous and stable Germany Europe has ever known, exceeding the life-span of Weimar and the Third Reich combined. More than two-thirds of all citizens now at home in "greater Germany" were born after World War II; the post-postwar generations are not Germans who have become different—they are truly different Germans. They are to be credited for having mobilized the biggest, most influential peace movement ever witnessed in Western Europe. The "utopian" vision of a New European Peace Order, first espoused by members of the *Friedensbewegung* in 1983, has now become an operational concept at the NATO headquarters in Brussels. It must further be recognized that the now-extinct German Democratic Republic gave rise to the largest underground eco-peace movement in all of Eastern Europe, whose coordinators and sympathizers in turn provided the launch-pad for the peaceful "revolution" of 1989. While youth's ostensible sympathy for extremist qua neo-Nazi movements seems to contradict a dramatic rise in conscientious-objector applications, post-Wall cohorts also overwhelmingly favor Bundeswehr transports carring food and equipment over weapons and body-bags. Last but certainly not least, one must note that over 52% of the Germans-united are *women*; rarely war's active proponents, always its defenseless victims, they have become the most ardent supporters of peace by other means.

A second challenge facing the Federal Republic with regard to security matters is the need to secure the continuation of its externally projected, post-national identity against centrifugal tendencies from without. One feature consistently distinguishing the two Germanys from their respective alliance partners between 1949 and 1989 was the never-ending overlap of their "domestic" and "foreign" security concerns. First-hand experiences with positive and negative interdependence, accumulated over a period of four decades, will keep the Germans in the driver's seat of European integration. Those lessons in interdependence will assume new importance over the next decade, for the social-policy management capabilities of most West European states will be sorely tested by the ongoing flight of political-economic refugees from less developed countries.

Germany's postwar generations construe security as a relational concept, recognizing that one will only be as "safe" as one's adversary feels. They have played a critical role in persuading NATO officials to shift their security focus from worst-case-scenarios and crisis-management strategies to the processes of conflict-prevention and confidence-building. It is increasingly obvious that the framework for global security can not be limited to questions of territorial integrity or freedom from interference in one's "national" affairs; it must simultaneously encompass the right to self-determination for minorities inside and outside one's own borders. Despite disturbing ultranationalist displays at home, most New Germans still favor a concept of security rooted in the cultivation of a "positive" peace.

Identity and the Politics of Inclusion

In Chapters Six and Seven I attempted to trace old and new linkages between citizens' conceptions of identity and their perceptions of security in light of post-1989 developments. Historically "overlooked" in the search for peace and security, FRG women have assumed a new political identity ensuring their participation in future searches along these lines. While the citizeness is subject to the same systemic rules as her male counterpart, political decisions often produce very different consequences for women's daily lives; this forces us to consider qualitative as well as quantitative differences in female/male identity and security needs. Chapter Six advanced the argument that neither women's national identity nor their national security orientations can be subsumed under the heading of "mainstream" qua malestream politics.

What moved women to take a great leap forward with regard to direct involvement in government and politics after 1968 was not their interest in traditional "women's issues" but rather their concern over Third World developments, nuclear energy and NATO deployments. We drew upon eight profiles of politically active FRG-women, highlighting the "contextual" aspects of their attitudes towards nationalism, NATO and the other Germany. The fact that no definitive model of national consciousness emerges from these profiles testifies to the concentric nature of identity: personal experience leads an individual to accord different weights to the familial, generational, historical, ideological, territorial or international dimensions of her own identity.

Unification has had a significant impact on the political and socio-economic identities of German women, in the old as well as in the new Länder. Against the backdrop of "societal achievements" they once took for granted, East German women may push to restructure the social-rights agenda of the nation-united. There is already evidence that they have started to carve out their own political "space" throughout the new Länder, in communal and state governments—perhaps because many other avenues of employment once open to them have been cut off since unification.[40] Noticeably absent on either side of the former border is a transformation in the self-consciousness of men with regard to the division of societal labor. A new "long march through the institutions" may not be a sufficient condition for the realization of equal rights for German women, but it is certainly a necessary one. Feminists' inability to pursue a positive German identity of their own stemmed from a reluctance to address questions of personal-as-political responsibility vis-à-vis the generation of their mothers. Since 1990, a new sympathy for ultra-right movements displayed by women young enough to be their daughters has impelled them to pose such questions anew. All too familiar with the politics of exclusion, New German women can promote their own cause by advancing a more inclusive concept of "national" identity.

Chapter Seven revisits the process of internal self-definition, exploring one brand of "new German nationalism" not anticipated at the outset of my research. Select members of the Post-Wall Generation are intent on propagating an assertive national identity of their own making, if necessary, by violent means. The themes stressed by these self-designated agents of the new nationalism are sooner grounded in personal feelings of deprivation and insecurity than in questions of ideology and military might per se, setting them apart from hardline nationalists of the first generation. But they also seem far removed from the anti-state, multicultural leanings of the generation immediately preceding them. The parents of one youth convicted of the arson deaths in Solingen were both engaged participants in the new social movements—his father a member of "Doctors for Peace," his mother a local Green activist.

The vague, "half-strong" and partly-tabooed nature of national consciousness prior to 1989 has rendered the first post-unity generation vulnerable to older conceptualizations of German identity, in a world where other countries are adamantly defending their "national" interests—sometimes thousands of miles away (Kuwait), sometimes not too far from their own borders (Yugoslavia). Official responses to rightwing violence have done little to provide them with positive sources of identification with the nation united. The FRG's continuing reliance on a blood-based concept of citizenship [*jus sanguinis*] has resulted in misdirected efforts among disaffected citizens intent on "reclaiming" their national identity. The state's restriction of the once unqualified guarantee of asylum [Article 16a GG] has reinforced the "anti-" orientations of youth who engage in extremist acts; many problems of the nation united suddenly become the fault of those who are *not-German*. Instead of targeting groups less privileged than themselves, the Germans of East and West must learn to empathize with foreigners in a way that does not automatically elevate *their own status* to that of the ultimate victim.

The extraordinarily rapid resurrection of the German *Staatsnation*—proposed, negotiated and delivered within the space of ten months—rested on a number of faulty premises regarding its links to the German *Kulturnation*. Prior to World War II, the ability to determine the ideals and values of the cultural nation remained largely the province of elites. The combined forces of democratization, mass communication and globalized consumption, primary achievements of the postwar era, have replaced the cultural nation of old with the phenomenon of mass culture, complemented by do-it-yourself "alternative cultures." The *Kulturnation* projected by elites holds little direct relevance for the average citizens of united Germany, especially now that symphonies, theaters and the arts are no longer heavily subsidized and hence too expensive for Eastern residents to enjoy. By shifting to the model of the *Volksnation*, federal officials hoped to bridge a substantial gap between these two concepts.

De jure unification, for better or worse, was based on an erroneous conflation of *Volk*—Nation—Citizenship—Identity. Of these four variables, only the first is relatively static in nature, tied to concrete referents of descendency and language. A modern nation, by contrast, is best understood "as a construct, whose meaning is never stable but shifts with the changing balance of social forces."[41] Citizenship and identity are likewise socially constructed (as Women's History proves), bound to individuals sharing a configuration of "particulars" at various points in historical time. There is no universal law warranting that the emotional and material needs of a people must be either logically consistent or symmetrical. National identity is anything but rational; the passage of time nonetheless leads people to merge mentally certain asymmetries perceived as normality. Time is therefore one of the most critical resources vis-à-vis the process of identity formation, and time was in markedly short supply with regard to the non-legal aspects of unification.

Given the overwhelming significance of the Third Reich for German historical consciousness, many postwar citizens failed to distinguish between two quintessentially different modes of nationalism: ethnic nationalism and civic nationalism. Just as appeals for reform on behalf of "the German nation" were considered taboo among GDR-dissidents prior to 1989, the precepts of nation and democracy were construed as antithetical in the West, although they need not be. The German emphasis on ethno-nationalism has always had an unquestionably anti-democratic touch, yet both principles, paradoxically, have been enshrined in the Basic Law since 1949. *Ethnos* can not be equated with *demos*, but ethnic-derivation remains a primary requirement for attaining the full benefits of citizenship. This has precipitated a new German identity paradox: How does one justify the existence of a monocultural society within the framework of a pluralist democracy, a system created to protect competing interests, as well as the unique needs of individuals?

Germans on both sides were compelled to make a radical break with the heinous ethnic nationalism of the past, in order to promote their own moral renewal and political rehabilitation after 1949. Without a sense of fundamental national continuity, however, "no mastery of the past was possible because the subject of guilt and remembrance [would have] vanished," a process tantamount to self-exculpation.[42] Millions of Germans, but especially the Long-March activists, neglected to realize that nationalism can also serve as "the memory that [withstands] the force of organized forgetting."[43] They assumed that the meaning of nation was permanently inscribed on the memorial plaques of former Nazi concentration camps after 1945, when, in fact, democracy is supposed to establish the paramenters within which "the struggle over the meaning of nation" takes place. The aim of civic nationalism, stressing plurality, diversity and tolerance within a defined territorial space, is to transcend the (largely imagined) unity of identities imposed under ethnic nationalism [*Volksgemeinschaft*].[44] In order to forge a more perfect, non-sexist, anti-rascist democratic union, old and new FRG residents need to ally themselves with the principle of civic-nationalism. Unlike its ethnic counterpart, civic nationalism is not antithetical to constitutional patriotism; the nation is the legal collectivity in which democratically professed freedoms are made real.

Genuine democracy is rooted in the principle of government of, by and for *the people*. Its emphasis on popular sovereignty does not dictate that all people must be the same—with regard to race, religion, or gender, for example—in order to enjoy equal rights and equal protection before the law; unfortunately, the German word *gleich* carries both meanings. I concur with Reinhard Merkel that the concept "Nation" in democratic states—if it still means anything at all—cannot exist as a demarcation of an ethnic specialness vis-à-vis the outside; rather, it must stand as "the symbol of an internal-societal plebiscite, conducted every day to ensure democratic participation in [a country's] political self-organization."[45] The democratic version of a pre-existing *Staatsnation* is not the *Volksnation*, but rather the Citizen-Nation or *Staatsbürgernation* (one presumably according full rights to its *Bürgerinnen* as well).

The hundreds of thousands of GDR citizens who joined in silent marches through the summer and fall of 1989 did not do so for the purpose of restoring Germany as a "national state." The explicit aim of the peaceful revolution was to secure democratic freedoms and economic opportunities for a people long denied the right to individual self-determination. The call for rapid unification was viewed primarily as a means to that end (a few of my Eastern friends jested, they wouldn't have minded annexation to Sweden, "but the latter had no Article 23"). GDR-Germans did not expect their overthrow of an authoritarian regime to result in the complete expropriation of their historical, cultural and social capital.

Bloodlines do not in and of themselves give rise to shared national consciousness: 62% of the East-citizens polled in February 1996 held that the Germans have grown farther apart since unity (as opposed to 48% in September 1995); the figures for Westerners were 30% in 1995 and 41% in 1996. Nearly 40% who maintained ties with West-relatives or friends prior to 1989 say those relationships have deteriorated or ended since the Wall's opening; only 20% have intensified those contacts. One-third claim to have gained new friends, suggesting that voluntary associations, not "imagined communities" are the key to a new post-Wall political culture.[46] As many West Germans quickly point out, they were not allowed to register a formal vote on the subject until December 1990, two months after unification had become an established constitutional-legal fact. These trends, added to Western resentment over unity-taxes, offer further proof that a single German identity has not been preserved by way of the "deep-freeze" effect. Only the healing influences of generational change will alleviate a mutual lack of trust between the Germans of East and West, in view of the latter's perceived penchant for "know-it-all-ism" [*Besserwisserei*].

The oft-cited argument against dual-citizenship, that "one cannot have two fatherlands—just as one cannot have two mothers," flies in the face of many modern relationships.[47] The real world consists of many children who love, and are loved by, step-parents in the context of second-marriages: I happen to have two step-children who fit the mold. The contention that one cannot serve two masters with regard to military conscription is just as irrelevant: a majority of those who would benefit from dual-citizenship are not even eligible for the draft, namely, women, children, and men over the age of 26. Democracy is moreover supposed to protect individuals against scenarios in which a German-born Turkish youth might be forced to demonstrate his absolute loyalty to one ethnic community over another (neither Bosnia nor Rwanda are "democratic" models). The assumption that one will only risk one's life for freedom and family under national military commanders (a belief shared by U.S. Republicans) is further undermined by Europe's increasing reliance on multi-national forces such as NATO (of which both Germany and Turkey are members), the UN peacekeeping units, and the German-French brigade.

Legal and fiscal impediments to immigration are formal manifestations of persistent socio-cultural barriers to integration—barriers that have proved more self-destructive than self-serving in the past. Not only has Germany become a de facto land of immigration; it is a land whose quality of life has been significantly enriched as a consequence of multicultural influences. As the Chancellor's wife complains, Germans consume more foreign cuisine than *Saumagen* (stuffed pig-belly, Kohl's favorite). Most persons comprising my in-depth sample would rather spend their vacations in Italy, Greece, or even the United States than in Idar-Oberstein or the Bavarian Alps.

The New Germans: Thesis—Antithesis—Synthesis?

This has not been an easy book to write, and it has probably been a difficult one to read, given the detailed nature of the evidence presented herein. The fault does not lie entirely with the author, however; as Federal Republicans freely admit, "German politics per se is very hard to sell, because despite the fact that we are present throughout the world, we have an unusually complicated thinking process that also reveals itself through unusually complicated political processes which others cannot see through."[48]

National identity formation and the pursuit of national security are but two of the "unusually complicated processes" that have affected the evolution of West German political culture since 1949. The fledgling Republic relied on new mechanisms in its efforts to resolve a unique set of internal and external security dilemmas throughout the first two decades of its existence. Problems of internal security were resolved by way of the social-market economy: economic stabilization and growth strategies were to safeguard the republic against the hyperinflation and mass unemployment that had rendered the Germans susceptible to National Socialism. Having twice catapulted the masses along a trajectory of aggression, the problem of postwar identity was deemed secondary to that of socio-economic security. West Germans offered their commitment to constitutional values, democratic institutions and, later, grassroots movements as proof that the earlier national-identity paradigm had been rejected and buried.

The identity issue was likewise subsumed with respect to questions of external security. Its exclusive reliance on the trans-Atlantic partnership allowed the Federal Republic to transcend its negative past, even if it was forced to recall painful aspects of its history on certain occasions (at Bitburg and select World War II anniversary events, for example). Its new relationship with the other Germany after 1969 afforded a unique opportunity to disavow further its old national identity and to present itself as a country in search of security by consistently peaceful means. As a consequence of *Ostpolitik*, however, the separate searches for national identity and national security took a curious turn—they began to merge. By the mid-1980s those searches had become mutually reinforcing; policy decisions intended to address one had an observable impact on the other. A "good German" at home was one intent on preserving the peace through non-violent means abroad.

Prior to 1989, I would have concluded this book by predicting the consolidation of separate West and East German identities by the year 2000, cushioned by shared security concerns. German unity has become a fact-of-life, provoking substantial turbulence with respect to both sets of orientations; the merger of the two postwar states has not resulted in a de-coupling of those orientations, however. If anything, unification has forged even closer links between the identity and security perceptions of the New Germans, internal as well as external.

As hypothesized at the outset of this study, it ultimately "does not follow . . . that there is some peculiar and unique way in which Germans can define their identity by not having one."[49] As the so-called Turn-Around of 1989 attests, a fundamental lack of personal identification with one's country holds tremendous consequences for its survival: for it is precisely a measure of internalized, sentimental attachment that ensures a reservoir of legitimacy, and hence stability, during those periods when the state finds itself incapable of meeting the citizenry's instrumental or material expectations, specifically, in times of major societal crisis.

Has the generational approach employed by this author withstood the "test" of national transformation? Chapters Three, Five, Six and Seven offer strong testimony with regard to the explanatory powers inherent in this particular approach—which is not to discount the validity of other methodological frameworks. As to the heuristic value of a concentric model of identity, the in-depth interviews conducted by this author confirm the existence of competing German national-identity types, assigning different weights to individual, collective, historical and systemic factors, before and after the paradigm-shift of 1989/90. "That nothing will change is not possible"—as diverse as these identities already seem to be, and despite the fact that two-thirds of the Westerners polled in 1993 believed most residents of the "old" FRG would prefer to live as if unity had never come to pass.[50]

Physically distant from the day-to-day anxieties and crises of Eastern residents, the Kohl Government has yet to internalize an all-German mentality of its own. The manner in which it pursued rapid unification was based on recycled precepts from the 1950s—"negotiation through strength" and "no experiments." Now that formal unity has been achieved, the CDU has returned its leitmotif of the 1980s: "Carry on as is, Germany."[51] But the slogan *Weiter so, Deutschland* pays homage to a Federal Republic that no longer exists, as Peter Glotz (SPD, born in 1939) contends:

> We are not organizing the "reunification" of a people that has lived together for hundreds of years or even thousands of years, rather we are shoving together two societies that have now lived apart for forty years, previously witnessed 75 years of common history and prior to that lived for centuries in prettily separated states. . . . We are not going back to the house of our father that has always stood on the same spot since mythical times and that has always served the same family as the center of life and home. It is more prosaic: We are expanding, on the same site where a number of us have already lived before.[52]

Politicians in Bonn have thus far viewed unification as a one-way street, when in fact it has become become a multi-lane highway with countless new drivers, plagued by traffic jams and collisions. This orientation is bound to change once federal officials take up full-time residence in Berlin, where they will encounter the conflicts of unity on a day-to-day basis. Virtually all of the strategies and mechanisms utilized by the *Bundesregierung* to date have been grounded in the expectation that East Germans can and must adapt to all aspects of Western German life—the same position it has long espoused with respect to the integration of foreigners. For unification to succeed at the level of citizen-consciousness, one needs an agenda which actively incorporates the self-articulated needs of East Germans. Kurt Biedenkopf, the West-CDU politician who governs the East-state of Saxony, charges that the Unity Treaty itself codified a number of systemic errors which have hindered the unification process. The most striking examples are the principle of "restitution over compensation" with regard to the privatization of property in the new states, and the Union's continuing emphasis on the "criminal" nature of abortion.[53] His criticism echoes the sense of resignation expressed by one of my Eastern friends: "We *were* the people."

What has distinguished the Bonn Republic, at least in part, from the failed experiment of Weimar was its return to an older foundation of federalism. Despite the cross-cutting jurisdictions imposed by advanced industrial society, the division of powers (Bund/Länder) remains one of the most important pillars of FRG democracy; what held true for the eleven Länder of the old Federal Republic must also hold true for a Germany made "greater" by the addition of five new states. This is not to argue that state lines within the FRG are as irreversible as the Oder-Neisse border. A reconfiguration of the smaller entities might challenge their respective identities but also ensure their economic viability; citizens and elites may accord very different priority to these two variables, however, as the 1995 rejection of a Berlin-Brandenburg merger illlustrates. Thuringen's Minister-President, Bernhard Vogel (CDU-West), is persuaded that new borders transcending the demarcation lines of the old Iron Curtain would contribute to rapid integration and foster "self-consciousness" among the new states.[54]

The Länder offer an important framework for reprocessing and promoting a sense of national (re)identification among former GDR citizens in these turbulent times. By reasserting their identity as Saxonians or Mecklenburgers, Eastern Germans separate themselves from an officially suspect *DDR-Identität*, and simultaneously distance themselves from what is perceived to be a cold and selfishly competitive *West-Identität*.[55] Old and new Länder affinities will constitute an important component of concentric identity among Eastern Germans for years to come.

What new dimensions of German identity are likely to surface as a function of political cultural merger? Although the Federal Republic seems quite intent on pursuing free-market strategies, it is possible that unification, in the long run, will bring about a redefinition of the social market economy, conditioned by a gradual infusion of East German "socialist idealism."[56] Many pundits have concluded that the demise of the East European regimes, indeed the disintegration of the Soviet Union itself, has discredited the idea of a leftist-collectivist utopia for several generations to come. Gräfin Dönhoff notes, however, that the chronic deficiencies of a rigidly planned economy do not in and of themselves "prove" the moral superiority of a profit-driven market system:

> Certainly as an economic system socialism has failed. . . . as the sum of age-old ideals of humanity: social justice, solidarity, freedom for the oppressed, help for the weak, it is everlasting. . . . Unemployment, alcohol and drug abuse, prostitution, cuts in social programs, tax reductions and the budget deficits. Is this really supposed to be the perfect society which has triumphed for all time over socialism?[57]

The electoral "comebacks" achieved by the PDS, especially in 1994–95 (crossing the 20% threshold in a number of district and communal elections) should not be dismissed as mere protest votes, nor as an exercise in *Ostalgie* [Eastern nostalgia].[58] Easterners may be a lot more leftist at heart than they realize: Peter Hacks claims "there are fewer communists than one says but more than one thinks."[59] They still display a widespread preference for state-guaranteed forms of social security. It is conceivable that a socialist "counter-culture East" will eventually re-emerge, capable of finding new allies in the already well-entrenched "alternative-culture West." As the 1989 proliferation of opposition groups (New Forum, Democracy Now, Democratic Awakening, Independent Women's Association) indicates, there is a tremendous reservoir of *reform-fervor* waiting to be mobilized from within.

Gegenwartsbewältigung or "coming to terms with the present" means seeking remedy for a lack of civil courage common to both populations during the darkest hours of their respective histories (not discounting the valiant struggles of self-sacrificing individuals during the Nazi and Stalinist eras). A capacity for collective resistance in times of oppression depends on citizens' willingness to emphathize with the victims, on the one hand, and on feelings of personal responsibility for the fate of their country, on the other. Westerners too young to have learned directly from the Nazi era can be taught via the GDR experience "that in most cases, the weaknesses and guilt of people in society are banal in character. They involve not so much unperformed heroic deeds, but a rash, fearful willingness to conform . . . the most important experiences, on the other hand, are cases in which individuals have recognized and courageously used their scope for action."[60] People who engaged in brave albeit isolated acts of protest against systemic injustice in the former GDR, even the so-called Skinheads, faced greater risks than citizens who routinely took to the streets or occupied nuclear missile-sites in the Western state. I agree with one female politician in Berlin who insists that

> Eastern Germans must learn from the Western Germans how to do things: ranging from the private use of a bank account, to complying with tax legislation, to [grasping] parliamentary practices. But Western Germans . . . have to

learn something about the whys and for-what-purposes. Anyone who has 40 years of experience with dictatorship behind her can explain to the other what democracy is really worth.[61]

The collapse of the Weimar Republic has often been attributed to the fact that it was supported by "too few democrats"; I contend that the problem nowadays is that the old Federal Republic may be weakened by too many democrats who have come to take their own constitutional values for granted. The period since unification has witnessed a dramatic decrease (by German standards) in the level of electoral participation, a drop of nearly 15%. Popular indifference toward politics is, in part, a response to the arrogance of the major parties, a phenomemon openly criticized by former President Richard von Weizsäcker. But a people who rallied so effectively to halt the proliferation of nuclear weapons in Europe ought to be quite capable of mobilizing for the expansion of substantive participatory rights from within, e.g., to the benefit of permanent foreign residents.

A free-democratic order necessitates a mutual willingness to give and take, a *Mut zur Mischung* [courage to mix], including an openness to constitutional revision. East German accession under Article 23 of the Basic Law has not, in and of itself, eliminated the need for "a new constitution adopted by a free decision of the German people" as mandated by Article 146. The evidence regarding Westerners' "courage to mix" has not been very encouraging to date. While it is true that constitutional changes can only come about as the product of "compromise and consensus, not as compensation for political failure," revisions approved by the Bundestag in 1994 substitute vague promises for an expanded catalogue of material rights.[62] Environmental protection has been incorporated into Article 20, albeit as a symbolic appeal to the state to protect "the natural foundations of life." Instead of accepting grassroots proposals as a basis for constitutional reform, law-makers opted for party-politics-as-usual:

> Recognition of non-marital partnerships? Rejected. Respect for the identity of minorities? Rejected. Protection against the data processing bureaucracy? Rejected. Animal protection? Rejected. The right to shelter, the right to work? Rejected. A check on the parties' surfeit power? Also rejected. The long list of rejections is a victory for the CDU and CSU. . . . The political parties were not content with the task, assigned to them by the Basic Law, of working with the political will of the people. Instead they strove for complete control over the commonwealth. . . . The [Christian Democratic] Union has given its motto— *Weiter so, Deutschland*—constitutional force.[63]

Sorely missing in the New Germany are politicians-of-the-new-type, ready to recognize that "compromise" is not a dirty word, and that Round-Table democracy does not augur the return of communism.

As it now stands, I believe that the New Germans will reject a concept of national identity based upon ideology, in favor of one centered on institutional loyalties. Citizens in the former Federal Republic have internalized the Western values inherent in democratic institutions, known as constitutional patriotism. The newly enfranchised Eastern citizens have had more than their fill of absolutist ideology and its consequences. I moreover expect the New Germans to cultivate a national consciousness that is more instrumental than sentimental in nature, at least for the span of another generation. Younger citizens will accept as legitimate that state which best secures their rights *and* delivers the goods. The Post-Wall cohorts, along with the postwar generations preceding them, have earned the right to feel good— not superior or *überheblich*, just good—about being German. As a "born-again" Federal Republican, Richard Schröder describes the New German identity in the following terms: "What do we mean when we, the Germans East and the Germans West now say 'We are Germans'? I answer: Nothing special but something particular."[64]

These elements of change and continuity notwithstanding, I do believe it is time for the New Germans to adopt a national anthem which more appropriately reflects the positive elements of their dialectical identity. This "new note" of patriotism should not prove too disruptive to pre-existing national consciousness, given the fact that 30% of the Westerners and 57% of the Easterners are unable to recite the first-line of the current anthem correctly anyway.[65]

Through years of exposure to German literature and culture, I have come across many suitable substitutes, but my favorite remains the offering below. Its contents may seem less profound than the current anthem's avowal of "Unity and Justice and Freedom" (in the third verse); but the sentiments it expresses will be much less troubling to all who hear them than those contained in the (unsung) first and second verses of *Deutschland, Deutschland über alles*. Its author, Bertolt Brecht, personifies German identity won and lost, rediscovered and betrayed again, as a consequence of the same historical events that have rendered his successors' search for identity so difficult. Born in the Bavarian city of Augsburg in 1898, Brecht was educated in Munich and forced to emigrate during the Third Reich; his period in exile included stays in Prague, Vienna, Switzerland, France, Denmark, Sweden, Finland and Moscow. He acquired international renown as a poet and playwright following his voluntary return to East Berlin in 1948, where he had hoped to participate in the construction of a truly anti-fascist, democratic Germany. Brecht's unrelenting denunciation of capitalism (a system he experienced first-hand during a year in the United States) was a bane to FRG officials; his sympathetic defense of the "little people" in the face of Stalinist orthodoxy rendered him a thorn in the side of GDR leaders as well. Brecht died in 1956, a subject of the Cold War system. His grave in Prenzlauer Berg has been vandalized since unification, spray-painted with anti-Semitic slogans, although he was not Jewish (his wife, Helene Weigel, was). Like so many foreigners who have sought refuge on FRG soil since 1989, Brecht has become a "man without a country."

The anthem I propose underscores the importance of New German youth, and the role they might be expected to play in the formation of a Wall-transcending national consciousness. Evoking a pride in country that is neither too self-effacing nor too overpowering, the text combines a sense of historical responsibility with a belief in a brighter future. Titled *The Children's Hymn*, this composition incorporates my own vision of a peaceful and prosperous Germany, one that I am hoping—with all my heart—the Post-Wall generations will succeed in realizing beyond the year 2000:

> *Grace spare not and spare no labor*
> *Passion nor intelligence*
> *That a decent German nation*
> *Flourish as do other lands.*
> *That the people give up flinching*
> *At the crimes which we evoke*
> *And hold out their hand in friendship*
> *As they do to other folk.*
> *Neither over nor yet under*
> *Other peoples will we be*
> *From the Oder to the Rhineland*
> *From the Alps to the North Sea.*
> *And because we'll make it better*
> *Let us guard and love our home*
> *Love it as our dearest country*
> *As the others love their own.*

Notes

1. For more on GDR identity, see Joyce Marie Mushaben, *Identity without a Hinterland? Continuity and Change in National Consciousness in the German Democratic Republic, 1949–1989* (Washington, D.C.: American Institute for Contemporary German Studies, 1992).

2. Alfred Kosing, *Nation in Geschichte und Gegenwart* (Berlin: Dietz Verlag, 1976).

3. Peter Schneider, *Der Mauerspringer—Erzählung* (Darmstadt und Neuwied: Luchterhand, 1982).

4. Ibid., pp. 8–9.

5. Ibid., p. 13.

6. Ibid., p. 117.

7. Peter Schneider, *Extreme Mittlelage. Eine Reise durch das deutsche Nationalgefühl* (Reinbek: Rowohlt, 1990), p. 9, p. 29.

8. Ibid., p. 126.

9. Patrick Süskind, "Deutschland, eine Midlife-crisis," *Der Spiegel*, Nr. 38, September 17, 1990.

10. Ibid., p. 119.

11. Ibid., p. 123.

12. Ibid., pp. 123, p. 125.

13. Ibid., p. 125.

14. Friedrich Schorlemmer, "Graben statt Mauer: Wir brauchen euch—ihr braucht uns nicht," *Die Zeit*, Nr. 27, July 5, 1991.

15. Gysi made this statement during a luncheon meeting I attended in East Berlin on March 16, 1990, arranged by the German Marshall Fund. He repeated this line many times during his campaign appearances.

16. Asher Reich, "Der Nazismus ist nicht tot—er schläft nur," in Bahrman Nirumand, Hg., *Deutsche Zustände. Dialog über ein gefährdetes Land* (Reinbek: Rowolht, 1993), p. 56.

17. See Norbert Finzsch and Jurgen Martschukat, eds., *Different Restorations. Reconstruction and "Wiederaufbau" in the United States and Germany: 1865, 1945 and 1990* (Providence: Berghahn, 1996).

18. Antje Vollmer, *Die schöne Macht der Vernunft* (Berlin: Verlag der Nation, 1991), pp. 45–6.

19. Antje Vollmer, "Die Deutschen kennen ihre Grenzen nicht," in Bahman Nirumand, op. cit., p. 123.

20. Schneider, guest lecture at Washington University, St. Louis Missouri, October 9, 1991.

21. Bahr is cited by Helga Haftendorn in "Wurzeln der Ost- und Entspannungspolitik der Sozial-Liberalen Koalition," in a volume edited by Horst Ehmke, Karlheinz Koppe and Herbert Wehner, *Zwanzig Jahre Ostpolitik. Bilanz und Perspektiven* (Bonn: Verlag Neue Gesellschaft, 1986), p. 19.

22. The term "King Kohl" appeared in *Bild Zeitung* headline the day after the March 18, 1990 elections.

23. Wolfgang Schäuble, *Der Vertrag. Wie ich über die deutsche Einheit verhandelte* (Stuttgart: Deutsche Verlags-Anstalt, 1991); and Horst Teltschick, *329 Tage* (Berlin: Siedler Verlag, 1991).

24. Brigitte Young, *Triumph of the Fatherland: German Unification, the State and Women* (forthcoming, University of Michigan Press).

25. Richard Hilmer and Rita Müller-Hilmer, "Es wächst zusammen," *Die Zeit*, Nr. 40, October 8, 1993; the authors take a glass-half-full approach, but the multiple complaints raised by Easterners imply that the glass is more than half-empty as far as a cultural merger is concerned. Also, "Erst vereint, nun entzweit," *Der Spiegel*, Nr. 3, January 18, 1993, p. 56.

26. See Ingolf Serwuschok and Christine Dölle, *Der Besser Wessi* (Leipzig: Forum Verlag, 1992); and Christine Dölle, *Mach's besser Ossi! Aber locker* (Leipzig: Forum Verlag, 1992).

27. Schorlemmer, "Wir brauchen euch . . ." op.cit.

28. Richard von Weizsäcker, address on receiving the 1991 Heine Prize, delivered in Düsseldorf on December 13, 1991, p. 1; translation provided by the German Information Center of New York.

29. See the *Bericht der Enquette-Kommission "Aufarbeitung von Geschichte und Folgen der SED-Diktatur in Deutschland,"* Deutscher Bundestag, Drucksachen 12/2330, 12/2597 of May 31, 1994.

30. In 1991 a number of West German journalists from the *Frankfurter Allgemeine* and *Die Zeit*, inter alia, launched an ad hominem attack against writer Christa Wolf, alleging her to have been the regime's "most prominent apologist," oblivious to the fact that many East Germans had seen her as the "conscience of the nation," despite her privileged status. The Western publicists leading the charge against Wolf's "opportunistic" publication of her own encounters with the Stasi [titled, *Was bleibt*] had not supported GDR opposition forces themselves, in contrast to Günter Grass and others who have come to Wolf's defense. See "Nötige Kritik oder Hinrichtung? Spiegel-Gespräch mit Günter Grass über die Debatte um Christa Wolf und die DDR Literatur," *Der Spiegel*, Nr. 29, July 16, 1990; also, "Thomas Anz, Hg., *Es geht um mehr als Christa Wolf. Der Literaturstreit im vereinten Deutschland* (Frankfurt/M: Fischer, 1995).

31. Von Weizsäcker, Heine address, p. 3.

32. Friedrich Schorlemmer, "Eigentlich möchte das Volk schnelles Vergessen," *Berliner Zeitung*, September 7, 1991.

33. Personal interview, conducted in East Berlin on May 22, 1990.

34. Michael Stürmer, "Geschichte in geschichtslosem Land," in *Historikerstreit. Die Dokumentation der Kontroverse um die Einzigartigkeit der nationalsozialistischen Judenvernichtung* (Munich/Zurich: Serie Piper, 1987), p. 36.

35. Hilmer and Müller-Hilmer, op, cit. p. 6.

36. Martin Heisler, "Normative and Institutional (Re)Constructions of German Identity in Comparative and Historical Perspective," paper presented at the American Political Science Association Meeting, Chicago IL, 31 Aug.–3 Sept. 1995.

37. Robert D. Putnam, "Bowling Alone: America's Declining Social Capital," *Journal of Democracy*, Vol. 6, (January 1995), p. 66.

38. Peter Brandt and Herbert Ammon, Hg., *Die Linke und die nationale Frage. Dokumente zur deutschen Einheit seit 1945* (Reinbek: Rowohlt, 1981), p. 21.

39. Andrei S. Markovits and Simon Reich, "The Contemporary Power of Memory: The Dilemmas for German Foreign Policy," presented at the American Political Science Association Meeting, Chicago, IL, August 31–September 3, 1995, p. 4.

40. See Helga Welsh's post-Wall study "Parliamentary Elites in Times of Political Transition: The Case of East Germany," *West European Politics*, Vol. 19, No. 3 (July 1996), pp. 507–524.

41. Katherine Verdery, "Whither 'Nation' and 'Nationalism,'" *Daedalus*, Vol. 122, No. 3, p. 41.

42. Christian Joppke, "Intellectuals, Nationalism, and the Exit from Communism: The Case of East Germany," *Comparative Studies in Society and History* 37, Nr. 2 (April 1995), p. 221.

43. Ibid., p. 215.

44. Ibid., pp. 218–19.

45. Reinhard Merkel, "Wahnbild Nation," *Die Zeit*, Nr. 10, March 9, 1990, also cited by Jürgen Habermas in "Der DM-Nationalismus," *Die Zeit*, Nr. 14, April 6, 1990. Contrast the view of Foreign Minister Klaus Kinkel, who insists "it is necessary that we . . . find a *natural* national consciousness" [my emphasis]. Cited in *The Week in Germany*, January 8, 1993, p. 1.

46. "Umfrage: Daumen runter," *Der Spiegel*, No. 9, February 26, 1996, p. 49; Hilmer and Müller-Hilmer, op. cit., p. 9.

47. Ingo von Münch, "Gegen 'Blut' und 'Boden,'" *Die Zeit*, Nr. 2, January 10, 1992.

48. Henning Wegener, cited by Elisabeth Wehrmann, "Deutschland," *Die Zeit*, Nr. 41, October 9, 1992. Officials at the Foreign Ministry are working to project a less complex albeit uniform "cultural image" abroad, stripped of controversial features; plans include a modernization of the German Pavillion at Disney World (Florida) and diverse "folklorish and artistic" multi-media shows intended for US shopping malls.

49. Ralf Dahrendorf, cited in Pollack, *German Identity—Forty Years after Zero*, published by the Friedrich Naumann Stiftung (Sankt Augustin: COMDOK, 1985), p. 47.

50. Interview with Richard von Weizsäcker, "Daß sich nichts ändert, ist nicht möglich," *Süddeutsche Zeitung Magazin*, Nr. 1, January 4, 1991, p. 16 ff. Further, "Erst vereint, nun entzweit," *op. cit.*, p. 56.

51. Gunter Hofmann, "In der Einbahnstraße des alten Denkens," *Die Zeit*, Nr. 2, January 10, 1992.

52. Peter Glotz, "Über die Identität des grösseren Deutschland. Der Weg nach vorn in eine europäische Struktur," *General Anzeiger* (Bonn), October 3, 1990.

53. Kurt Biedenkopf, "Die geeinte Nation im Stimmungstief," *Die Zeit*, Nr. 41, October 9, 1992. The Bundestag did not pass a "compensation" law until mid-1994, with the result that most persons filing claims demanded restitution of "their" property. More than two million claims were submitted; thousands of Eastern Germans have already been driven out of their homes or apartments in the East by way of psycho-terror tactics (including attempted murder) on the part of speculators and "inheritance communities," i.e., grandchildren, in-laws and distant cousins who file joint claims, hoping to profit from a speedy sale of whatever property is returned. See Daniela Dahn, *Wir bleiben hier oder Wem gehört der Osten?* (Reinberk: Rowohlt, 1994).

54. Cited by Peter Glotz, "Wenn Mecklenburg und Schleswig-Holstein zusammengehen," *Frankfurter Rundschau*, June 21, 1990.

55. Joyce Marie Mushaben, "Can You Ever Go Home Again? The (Re)Discovery of *Heimatgefühl* in the Five New Länder," presented at the GDR-Studies Association Meeting, Washington, D.C., October 1992.

56. More than one discussion partner believes that unification is being used as an excuse to dismantle the "welfare state," with little thought as to what might take its place.

57. Marion Gräfin Dönhoff, "Am Ende aller Geschichte?" *Die Zeit*, September 29, 1989, p. 1.

58. See Sabine Rückert, Wolfgang Gehrmann, Kuno Kruse and Dirk Kurbjuweit, "Die Einheiz-Partei," as well as Klaus Hartung's essay, "Sozis im Dilemma," both appearing in the July 1, 1984 edition of *Die Zeit*, Nr. 26.

59. Cited in Clement de Wroblewsky, Hg., *Wo wir sind ist vorn. Der politische Witz in der DDR* (Hamburg: Rasch und Röhring, 1990), p. 139.

60. Von Weizsäcker, Heine address, op cit., p. 5.

61. This unnamed official was cited by Peter Bender in "Was kann bleiben? Was soll bleiben? Was wird bleiben?" *Frankfurter Rundschau*, December 28, 1990, p. 14.

62. Robert Leicht, "Viel Rauch und wenig Feuer. Vom Sinn und Unsinn der deutschen Verfassungsdebatte," *Die Zeit*, Nr. 14, April 3, 1992.

63. Cited in TWIG on July 8, 1994; the original quote stems from a July 2, 1994 article in the *Süddeutsche Zeitung*. In early 1990 East German Round-Table members proposed a new GDR constitution, completely ignored by the Kohl Government in the rush to negotiate the "Unity Treaty." See Arbeitsgruppe "Neue Verfassung der DDR" des Runden Tisches, Hg., *Verfassung der Deutschen Demokratischen Republik* (Berlin: BasisDruck, 1990). Following election to the Bundestag, former Round-Table participants like Wolfgang Ulmann helped to draft a reformed all-German constitution, which included many of the rights listed here.

64. Richard Schröder, "Ich bin Deutscher. Was heißt das?" *Die Zeit*, Nr. 4, January 29, 1993.

65. *Das Profil der Deutschen*, op. cit., p.14.

Appendix A

Interview Questionnaire: FRG-German Identity

(All interviews were conducted by the author in German.)

Date of Interview:
Discussion Partner:
Profession: Place/Date of Birth:

I. Background

Just for starters, could you please give me a brief description of your own associations with World War II? Are there any personal or family experiences that you would regard as "special?" Or do you count yourself among those who have experienced "the blessing of having been born late?"

II. Significance of German Question, Peace Movement and Détente

1. It is my impression that the beginning of the 1980s brought with it the "renaissance" of the GERMAN QUESTION. In your opinion, does this reemergence amount to just a fashionable intellectual endeavor, "much ado about nothing," or is this an expression of the "manifest latency" of a not-yet-resolved chapter in the history of the two German States?" Has the question of the [Pershing II/Cruise Missile] deployments provided the new impetus for this development?
How would you personally define "the German Question?"
2. Do you consider the new or re-emergent interest in the German Question good, bad, or without significance? What positive effects might you imagine resulting from a broader public discussion of this topic? What possible dangers might you see in this debate?
3. How representative do you think this increased interest in "German identity" is

   - Among the average citizens of the FRG?
   - Among peace movement sympathizers and activists?
   - I've noticed that the debate seems to have derived from works by Peter Bender, Peter Brandt and Herbert Ammon, all residents of Berlin. Do you think that Berliners do or should think more intensely about this topic, given their special situation?

4. If you are familiar with the current literature on this topic, e.g., Brandt and Ammon's book [*The Left and the National Question*], or Venohr's edited

volume [*German Unity will certainly come!*], in what points do you see an
overlap between the "national patriots/new nationalists" of the Left and
those on the Right these days?
In what points are there marked differences?
5. a) Why might one need some kind of "national consciousness" in general?
   b) Why might one need or be served by a sense of "German identity" in
   particular?
   c) What kind of new substance, definitive values and national security
   orientations or perspectives might be contained in this new identity?
6. In your opinion, are pacifism-neutralism-FRG nationalism synonymous
   terms?
7. a) Can you imagine a nuclear-[weapons]free Germany?
   - In what conceivable time frame?
   - Would you find this a desirable state of affairs?
8. b) Can you imagine a neutralized Germany?
   - In what possible time frame?
   - Would you wish for this to come about?

III. Perceptions, Connections in Reaction to the GDR

9. Where do you stand with respect to **your own** national consciousness or
   "German" or Federal Republican identity? Do you feel like a citizen of the
   FRG? Like a German? Like a European? Can you "rank-order" these
   feelings? [*Wie fühlen Sie sich in erster Linie?*]
10. How would you assess your relationship to the GDR?
    - Do you have acquaintances or relatives currently living in the GDR?
    - Have you already traveled around in the GDR or visited people there?
      [Do you have children? Have they traveled there?]
    - Has this contact strengthened or put a damper on your interest in the
      GDR?
11. Do you believe in [the possibility of] "reunification" [*Wiedervereinigung*]?
    If so, in what form?
    Do you think that the clause referring to unity in the Preamble to the Basic
    Law ought to be deleted? Why/why not? For what reason(s)?
12. What do the following terms or concepts mean to you?
    - "community of responsibility" [*Verantwortungsgemeinschaft*]
    - "security partnership" [*Sicherheitspartnerschaft*]
    - "common security" [*Gemeinsame Sicherheit*]
    - "German Confederation" [*Deutsche Konfederation*]
13. Based on your personal experiences (as a politician, as a professor, and as a
    mother or father . . .), what kinds of differences have you observed among
    the generations (older vs. younger), or are their attitudes basically the same,
    with regard to:
    - the peace movement?
    - membership in NATO?
    - attitudes or perceptions of the United States?

- relationship to the GDR?

IV. Processing the Past

14. Would you characterize the land in which you live as an "occupied country" [*ein besetztes Land*]?

    - Would you favor or oppose the withdrawal of NATO or US-American troops from the Federal Republic at some future date? For what reason(s)?
    - Are you irritated (*Stört es Sie*) or do you feel that you sometimes suffer under the presence of "American cultural imperialism" here in your own country?
    - Have you ever been to the United States? Do you have close American friends or relatives over there?

15. Are you familiar with the speech given by Federal-President Richard von Weizsäcker on the 8th of May 1985?

    - Did you feel personally addressed or moved by this speech?
    - What did you find to be the especially positive or negative elements of this speech?

16. Do you think it is still necessary for both German states to undertake steps to "conquer the past?" Do you think it is time for a "rediscovery of German history?"
    In your judgment, what concrete measures would you consider well-suited to this task? What about in relation to the younger generations?

V. National Security Orientations

17. Which of the following (alternative) security-political doctrine(s) or concepts do you profess or accept?

    - Nuclear deterrence
    - Greater independence vis-à-vis the USA
    - Foreign troop withdrawal
    - Veto right over the use of nuclear weapons on FRG soil
    - European Defense Union
    - Security partnership with the GDR
    - Disengagement or freedom from the NATO/WPO alliances for both German states?
    - Nuclear weapons-free Europe
    - Unilateral disarmament
    - SDI

VI. Return to Normalcy

1. What "typically German" character traits do you consider to be especially positive? Especially negative? Or are there no such traits? Have the Germans really changed or become different since the war's end?

2. How long will it take, in your personal evaluation, before "the Germans" perceive themselves as "normal" in world political terms? Is it really a question of generations?
3. How long do you think it will take for other countries and populations world-wide to see and to treat them as such, that is, as normal citizens in normal states?

Thank you for your time, insights, and patience!

Appendix B

Participants in Structured Interviews

I. Peace Movement Activists (1983–1984, 1986)

Interviewee	Organizational Affiliation	Place/Date of Interview
Deile, Dr. Volkmar	Action Reconciliation	West Berlin: December 7, 1983
Eberhardt, Thomas	Die Falken,	Heilbronn:November 13, 1986
Ebert, Prof. Dr. Theodor	Gewaltfreie Aktion Otto Suhr Institute/FUB West	Berlin: December 5, 1986
Gollwitzer, Helmut	Theologist, Free University of Berlin	West Berlin: December 7, 1983
Howald, Cordeliz	Jusos, SPD	Stuttgart: November 16, 1983
Leinen, Josef M.	KA, BBU, SPD	Bonn: October 18, 1983; St. Louis: April 14–16, 1984
Menz, Gunther	DFG-KK	Heilbronn: November 14, 1983
Randzio-Plath, Claudia	Frauen für den Frieden Hamburg	Hamburg: October 30, 1983
Schorr, Manfred	ORL/Greens	Heilbronn: November 13, 1983
Sölle, Dr. Dorothee	Theologist	Hamburg: October 29, 1983
Vogt, Dr. Roland	KA/Greens	Bonn: October 18, 1983
Zumach, Andreas	Action Reconciliation, SPD	West Berlin: December 7, 1983; St. Louis: 1984

II. Formal "Identity Interviews" (1985–1986)

Interviewee	Year of Birth	Organizational Affiliation	Place/Date of Interview
Bahr, Egon	1922	MdB, SDP, and Director, Ifs	Bonn: June 13, 1986
Batzer, Klaus	LM-Generation	DFU-HFF	Hamburg: November 30, 1986
Beckmann, Else	1908	Hamburg and Stuttgart Landtage	Stuttgart: December 1, 1986
Bender, Peter	1923	journalist, publicist	West Berlin: May20,
Besser, Dr.Ursula	1917	Berlin Abgeordneten Haus,	West Berlin: October 29, 1986

Borgmann, Annemarie	1942	MdB/Grünen	Bonn: December 9, 1986
Brandt, Dr. Peter	1948	AL/Historian	Bonn: October 1985; West Berlin: May 20, 1986
Brandt, Willy	1913	SPD/former Berlin mayer, Bundeskanzler	written response: December 1985
Bruns, Dr. Wilhelm	1943	Forschungsabteilun-DDR Friedrich Ebert Stiftung	Bonn: November 3, 1986
Buro, Prof. Dr. Andreas	EM-Generation	KGD, University of Frankfurt	Frankfurt: February 21, 1986
Conradi, Peter	1932	MdB, SPD	Stuttgart: July 15, 1986
Czaja, Dr. Herbert	1900	Vertriebenenverband MdB, CDU	Bonn: October 16, 1986
Daubler-Gmelin, Dr. Herta	1943	MdB/SPD	Bonn: November 25, 1986
Diner, Dr. Dan	1946	Historian	Frankfurt: February 24, 1986
Dönhoff, Dr. Marion Grafin	1909	Editor, *Die Zeit*	Hamburg: December 18, 1986
Druwe, Dr. Ulrich	1955	political scientist, University of Stuttgart	Stuttgart: August 29, 1986
Eppler, Dr. Erhard	1926	MdB, SPD, and Grundwerte Kommission	Schwenningen: November 26, 1986
Finchk, Renate	1926	Former group-leader, Bund Deutscher Mädel	Esslingen: November 27, 1986
Fuchs, Katrin	1938	MdB, SPD	Bonn: November 12, 1986
Gaus, Gunter	1929	First Permanent Mission GDR; WDR journalist	Hamburg: December 22, 1986
Grunenberg, Nina	1936	*Die Zeit*	Hamburg: December 18, 1986
Haftendorn, Prof. Dr. Helga	EM-Generation	Otto Suhr Institut/FUB	West Berlin: May 21, 1986
Hamm-Brücher, Hildegard	1921	MdB, FDP	Bonn: December 16, 1986
Hupka, Herbert	1915	MdB, CDU Vertriebenenverband	Bonn: October 21, 1986
Jacobsen, Prof. Dr.	1925	political scientist, University of Bonn	Bonn: December 16, 1986
Jansen, Mechthild	1952	KA, FiB-WSN, journalist	Köln: November 17, 1986
Koppe, Karlheinz	1929	DFGK peace researcher	Bonn: October 20, 1986
Lange, Torsten	1945	MdB, Greens	Bonn: October 21, 1986
Langguth, Dr. Gerd	1946	Staatssekretär, CDU Berlin-Landesvertretung	Bonn: November 13, 1986
Maier, Jurgen	1963	Landesvorstand, Greens Baden-Württemberg	Stuttgart: July 15, 1986

Martiny, Dr. Anke	1939	MdB, SPD	Bonn: November 25, 1986
Menge, Marlies	1934	journalist, *Die Zeit*	Köln: December 12, 1986
Meyer, Dr. Berthold	LM-Generation	Hessiche Stiftung Friedens-u. Konfliktforschung	Frankfurt: February 24, 1986
Quistorp, Eva	1945	Frauen für den Frieden; MdB, Greens	Bonn: December 8, 1986
Rommel, Manfred	1928	Oberburgermeister, Stuttgart, CDU	Stuttgart: August 20, 1986
Rupprecht, Dr. Wilfried	1934	Referent, FDP (MdB Schäffer)	Bonn: December 3, 1986
Schierholz, Henning	1949	MdB, Grünen	Bonn: October 14, 1986
Schmude,	1936	MdB-SPD Evangelical Synod	Bonn: December 3, 1986
Schneider, Dirk	1939	MdB/Berlin Alternative Liste	Bonn: October 12, 1986
Schöffmann, Dieter	post-1960	BUF	Saarbrucken: March 2, 1986
Sommer, Dr. Theo	1930	publisher, *Die Zeit*	Hamburg: December 18, 1986
Sontheimer, Prof. Dr. Kurt	1928	political scientist, University of München	München: July 1985
Steinweg, Dr. Rainer	1939	Hessische Stiftung	Frankfurt: February 26, 1986
Sternstein, Wolfgang	LM-Generation	Gewaltfreie Aktion	Stuttgart: January 30, 1986
Thaesen, Alfred	1959	Parliamentary aide (MdB Hupka)	Bonn: November 3, 1986
Veen, Dr. Hans-Joachim	1944	Konrad Adenauer Stiftung	Bonn/Sankt Augustin: November 17, 1986
Voigt, Karsten	1941	MdB, SPD	Bonn: December 10, 1986
Vollmer, Dr. Antje	1943	MdB, Greens	Bonn: December 2, 1986
Wensierski, Peter	1954	journalist	West Berlin: May 12, 1986

1. Student Group—Bonn: interviewed in Bad Godesberg, December 1986

Franke, Andreas	Universität Bonn
Kroschel, Heike	Universität Bonn
Lorz, Stephan	Universität Bonn
Unger, Harmut	Universität Bonn

2. Student Group—Berlin: interviewed in West Berlin, October 30, 1986

"Annette"	Free University of Berlin
"Katrin"	Free University of Berlin
"Marion"	Free University of Berlin
Böhm, Andrea	Free University of Berlin

3. Student Group—Bonn: interviewed in Bad Godesberg, December 8, 1986

Farthmann, Rainer	1963	Universität Bonn
Neuenfeld-Zvolskey, Daniele	1962	Universität Bonn
Schleicher, Ruth	1961	Universität Bonn

III. Semi-structured Interviews, Institutional Perspectives

Interviewee	Organizational Affiliation	Place/Date of Interview
Harper, Edward	US Mission	West Berlin: January 3, 1986
Hans-Rautenberg, Oberst Ltn.	Defense Ministry (BWV)	Bonn-Hardthöhe: December 15, 1986
Mahnke, Prof. Dr. Dieter	Bundespräsidialamt (now BMV)	Bonn: 1986 (multiple discussions)
Czempiel, Prof. Dr. Ernst	HSFK and Universität, Frankfurt	Frankfurt: Fall 1986
Janse, Dr. Marlies	Ministry for Inter-German Relations (BMIB)	Bonn: April 1986
Klar, Olaf	BMIB	Bonn: April 1986
Weidenfeld, Prof. Dr. Werner	Universität Mainz	Bonn: October 1986
Holzle, Dr. Peter	editor, *Evangelische Kommentare*, SPD	Stuttgart: 1985 (multiple discussions)
Janning, Dr. Josef	Universität Mainz	Mainz: October 1986
Reuband, Dr. Karlheinz	Zentralinstitut für empir. Sozialforschung	Köln: 1985–1986 (multiple discussions)
Wulf, Dr. Herbert	Inst. Friedens/Sicherheitsforschung	Hamburg: April 10, 1986
Gonsior, Prof. Dr. Bernhard	physics department, Universität Bochum	Bochum: 1985 (multiple discussions)
Hegel, Dr. Hannelore	Wissenschaftssenat	Berlin: multiple discussions
Presler, Eckard	journalist, *Stern*	Hamburg: multiple discussions
Dobiey, Dr. Burkhard	BMIB	Bonn: 1986
Michael, Robert	Formerly Consul-General	Stuttgart: August 1985
Hubner-Funk, Dr. Sybille	Deutsches Jugendinstitut	Munich: November 30, 1983
von Baudissin, Graf	director, IFS/University of Hamburg	Hamburg: December 1, 1983
Wasmuht, Dr. Ulrike	IFS/Hamburg Politische Bildungs-Zentrale Bonn	Hamburg: December 1, 1983; April 1986
Roth, Dr. Dieter	Forschungsgruppe Wahlen	Mannheim: multiple discussions

Appendix C

CC-Member Organizations According to Primary Constituency, Activity Field, or Task Domain

Political Parties or Party-Affiliates (10)

Die Grünen	The Greens
Liberale Demokraten (LD)	Liberal Democrats
Demokratische Sozialisten (DS)	Democratic Socialists
Arbeitsgemeinschaft Sozialdemokratische Frauen (ASF)	Task Force Social Democratic Women
Jungsozialisten (Jusos)	Young Socialists
Sozialistische Jugend Deutschlands-Die Falken	Socialist Youth of Germany-The Falcons
Sozialistische Deutsche Arbeiterjugend (ISDAJ)	Social German Worker Youth
Initiative für Frieden, internationalen Ausgleich, und Sicherheit (IFIAS)	Initiative for Peace, International Balance, and Security
Komitee für Frieden, Abrüstung, und Zusammenarbeit (KOFAZ)	Committee for Peace, Disarmament, and Cooperation

Christian and Religious Groups (6)

Aktion Sühnezeichen/Friedensdienste (AS/Fd)	Action Reconciliation/ Peace Services
Aktionsgemeinschaft Dienst für den Frieden (AGDF)	Action Community Service for Peace
Evangelische Studentengemeinschaft (ESG)	Evangelical (Lutheran) Students Association
Initiative Kirche von Unten (IK)	Initiative Church from Below
Aktion "Ohne Rüstung Leben" (ORL)	Action "Live Without Weapons"
Pax Christi (PC)	Pax Christi

Youth Associations (3)

Deutscher Gewerkschaftsbund-Jugend (DGB-J)	German Trade Union Federation-Youth Group

Bundesschülervertretung
(BSV)

Federation of School
Representatives

Vereinigte Deutsche Studentenschaften
(VDS)

Association of German Student
Governments

Coordinating, Confederated, or Clearing-House Groups (3)

Koordinationsstelle Ziviler Ungehorsam
(KZU)

Coordination Office for
Civil Disobedience

Bundeskonferenz unabhängiger
Friedensgruppen (BUF), formerly BAF

Federal Conference of
Independent Peace Groups

Föderation Gewaltfreier Aktionsgruppen
(FOGA)

Federation of Nonviolent
Action Groups

Feminist Groups (2)

Anstiftung Frauen für den Frieden (AFfF)

Activating Women for Peace

Frauen in die Bundeswehr—
Wir sagen Nein! (FiB-Nein)

Women in the Military—
We Say NO!

Personal Membership Groups (2)

Gustav Heinemann Initiative (GHI)

Gustav Heinemann Initiative

Komitee für Grundrechte und Demokratie
(KfGD)

Committee for Basic Rights
and Democracy

Ecology Movement (1)

Bundesverband Bürgerinitiativen
Umweltschutz (BBU)

Federation of Citizen Initiatives
for Environmental Protection

Conscientious Objectors (1)

Deutsche Friedensgesellschaft—Vereinigte
Kriegsdienstverweigerer (DFG-VK)

German Peace Society—
United War Service Resisters

Antifascists (1)

Vereinigung der Verfolgten des Nazi-Regims—
Bund der Antifaschisten (VVN-BdA)

Association of Victims of the Nazi
Regime—Organization of
Antifascists

Third World Solidarity (1)

Bundeskongress entwicklungspolitscher
Aktionsgruppen (BUKO)

Federal Conference of Political
Development Actions Groups

Appendix D

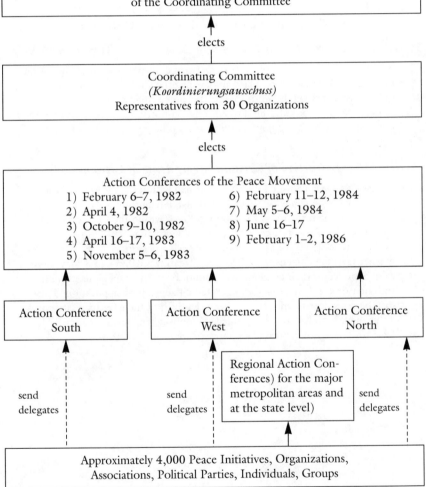

FIGURE C.1   Structure of Representation and Decision Making in the West German Peace Movement.

Source: Adapted from Leif (1985, p. 254).

Appendix E

The Constitutional Bases of German Citizenship

Article 16 ("Deprivation of Citizenship, Extradition, Right of Asylum")

1. No one may be deprived of his (sic) German citizenship. Loss of citizenship may arise only pursuant to a law, and against the will of the person affected only if such a person does not thereby become stateless.
2. No German may be extradited to a foreign country. Persons persecuted on political grounds shall enjoy the right of asylum.

Article 116 ("Definition of German, Regranting of Citizenship")

1. Unless otherwise provided by law, a German within the meaning of the Basic Law is a person who possesses German citizenship or who has been admitted to the territory of the German Reich within the frontiers of 31 December 1937 as a refugee or expellee of German stock [Volkszugehörigkeit] or as the spouse of such a person.
2. Former German citizens who, between 30 January 1933 and 8 May 1945, were deprived of their citizenship on political, racial or religious grounds, and their descendants, shall be regranted citizenship on application. They shall be considered as not having been deprived of their German citizenship if they have established their domicile [Wohnsitz] in Germany after 8 May 1945 and have not expressed a contrary intention.

Index